THE

TEACHING

OF

ANTHROPOLOGY

THE
TEACHING
OF
ANTHROPOLOGY

EDITED BY

David G. *oodman* Mandelbaum

Gabriel W. Lasker

Ethel M. Albert

1963

Berkeley and Los Angeles

UNIVERSITY OF CALIFORNIA PRESS

University of California Press
Berkeley and Los Angeles, California

Cambridge University Press
London, England

Preface

THIS WORK IS the outcome of the Educational Resources in Anthropology (ERA) project of the Department of Anthropology, University of California, Berkeley. The project was presented to the Executive Board of the American Anthropological Association and has been supported by grants from the Course Content Improvement Section of the National Science Foundation. Much of the preliminary work was done for a series of ten symposia on the teaching of anthropology, held between April, 1960, and March, 1961; the list of participants in the symposia follows this preface.

All the papers in this volume and three in the companion volume *Resources for the Teaching of Anthropology* were first presented at the symposia, discussed there, and then revised by the authors in light of the discussion and subsequent correspondence. Of the ten symposia arranged under the auspices of the ERA project, eight were held at meetings of specialized or regional anthropological societies; the authors and principal discussants were selected by officers and program committees of those societies. Two general symposia were held, one under the sponsorship of the Wenner-Gren Foundation at its European Headquarters at Burg Wartenstein, the other and final one of the series at Berkeley.

Each author received a series of communications from the project staff, outlining the over-all plan, indicating where his prospective contribution fitted into the plan, and suggesting topics which might be considered. Most contributors exchanged correspondence on their papers with members of the project staff and with other colleagues before completing a final version. While the flow of memoranda and correspondence was useful, in the end each author wrote on the subject he wanted to cover, in his own style, and expressing his own views. The over-all plan of the project provides the frame of this work, but each paper is the product of its author's own viewpoint and is not in any way an expression of consensus at a symposium.

Each editor, in addition to the papers and introductory notes he wrote for this work, took responsibility for one phase of the project, Ethel M. Albert for the editing of the publication, Gabriel W. Lasker for the bibliography and surveys, David G. Mandelbaum for the general plan.

We thank the two officers of the National Science Foundation, Richard E. Paulson and Charles A. Whitmer, who have fostered the ERA project. Professor Leslie White gave it encouragement as our liaison with the Executive Board of the American Anthropological Association. As is generally true for such projects, the aid of those anthropologists who participated in the work as graduate students was very valuable. They are Theron A. Nunez, Jr., Kenneth A. R. Kennedy, Lewis L. Klein, Paul Hockings, and Zenon S. Pohorecky. Our colleagues in the Department of Anthropology at Berkeley have been most helpful in their suggestions and support.

The Wenner-Gren Foundation not only made possible the International Symposium, but its President, Dr. Paul Fejos, and Mrs. Fejos contributed wonderfully to its spirit. They command our warm appreciation.

Our reliance on our secretaries was great as are our debt and thanks to them. Miss Dorothy Szorc was editorial secretary; Mrs. Alice Davis as project secretary was with the project from its beginnings and helped us through every stage of its work.

DAVID G. MANDELBAUM
GABRIEL W. LASKER
ETHEL M. ALBERT

Contents

PART I

THE UNDERGRADUATE

CURRICULUM

IN ANTHROPOLOGY

PART IV
ANTHROPOLOGY COURSES
ON REGIONS AND
CIVILIZATIONS

PART V
THE TEACHING
OF ARCHAEOLOGICAL
ANTHROPOLOGY

PART VI
THE TEACHING
OF LINGUISTICS
IN ANTHROPOLOGY

PART VII
THE TEACHING
OF APPLIED
ANTHROPOLOGY

Contributors

Richard N. Adams, Professor of Sociology and Anthropology at Michigan State University, has carried on social and applied anthropological studies and teaching under the auspices of the Smithsonian Institution, the World Health Organization, the University of California, Berkeley, and his home university. His professional work kept him in Latin America from 1949 until 1956, and he has returned annually since to continue research and consultation. Publications relating to this work include various articles, *A Community in the Andes* (1959), *Cultural Surveys of Panama–Nicaragua–Guatemala–El Salvador–Honduras* (1957), *United States University Cooperation in Latin America* (co-author, 1960), and *Human Organization Research* (co-editor, 1960).

Ethel M. Albert, Assistant Director for Ethnology of the Educational Resources in Anthropology Project, is Associate Professor of Speech at the University of California, Berkeley. She has previously taught at Brooklyn College, the University of Wisconsin, and Syracuse University. Her major interest is comparative ethnophilosophy, especially values. She participated in the Harvard Values Study, did field work in Ruanda-Urundi, and was a Fellow at the Center for Advanced Study in the Behavioral Sciences, 1957-58. She is the author of various articles and reviews and co-author of *Great Traditions in Ethics* and *A Selected Bibliography on Values, Ethics and Esthetics.*

Conrad M. Arensberg is Professor of Anthropology and Social Psychology at Columbia University. He has also taught at Harvard University, Massachusetts Institute of Technology, and Brooklyn College, lecturing in both sociology and anthropology. He has done field work in Europe, Syria, and Japan; written extensively about community study methods, applied anthropology, and ethnography, including the culture of the United States; and has done research and written on the use of social science in industrial relations and in institutional analysis. His interest in an anthropological comparison of the social institutions of mankind is reflected in his teaching—currently, primitive and comparative political organization, economic anthropology, and social anthropology of modern complex societies, in courses open to sociologists and social psychologists as well as to graduate students of anthropology.

DAVID A. BAERREIS, Professor of Anthropology at the University of Wisconsin, Madison, has taught various anthropological courses at that institution since 1947. In addition to conventional academic courses in the archaeology of the Old World and the Americas, his teaching experience includes summer field training courses in archaeology. His archaeological field work includes investigations in Oklahoma, New Mexico, South Dakota, and Wisconsin, and in Brazil.

HOMER G. BARNETT, Professor of Anthropology, has taught at the University of Oregon since 1939. He has also taught at the University of New Mexico, and has held summer session appointments at Harvard, Columbia, and at the Universities of British Columbia and Hawaii. He was an instructor in the Army Specialized Training Program at the University of California. He has served as Staff Anthropologist for the Trust Territory of the Pacific Islands, and is currently the president of the Society for Applied Anthropology. His books include *Innovation, Anthropology in Administration, Being a Palauan,* and *Indian Shakers.*

RALPH L. BEALS is Professor of Anthropology and Sociology at the University of California, Los Angeles. In 1936 he was the first anthropologist appointed to the faculty of the University of California, Los Angeles, when the institution was little more than a four-year college. Since then he has participated both in the development of a department with a large graduate program and in the great expansion of the teaching of anthropology in other institutions of southern California. His research has been mainly in Latin America. He is co-author of a general text, *An Introduction to Anthropology.*

JOHN H. M. BEATTIE, Senior Lecturer in Social Anthropology at Oxford University, has taught graduate anthropology there since 1953. He carried out field work in Bunyoro, Uganda, and has published a short monograph and various articles on Nyoro culture as well as papers on general and comparative topics in social anthropology. His main research interests are in anthropological theory and method and in East African ethnography.

REXFORD S. BECKHAM is Assistant Director of Libraries for Science and Technology and an Assistant Professor at the University of Nebraska, where he also teaches book selection for libraries. A graduate of the University of California, Berkeley, and of the University's School of Librarianship, he was employed by the University of California Library from 1949 to 1960, holding the position of Art-Anthropology Librarian from 1956 to 1960.

JOHN W. BENNETT, Professor of Anthropology and Sociology at Washington University at St. Louis, is a cultural anthropologist with special interests in the fields of socio-economic development and comparative education. His principal geographical specialization is Japan, and he is senior author of two books on that country: *In Search of Identity: The Japanese Scholar in America and Japan* and *Paternalistic Organizations in the Japanese Economy*. He is at present engaged in comparative research on social organization and economy in American and Canadian society. He has taught anthropology at the Ohio State University, the University of Oregon, and the University of Puerto Rico. He has been President of the Society for Applied Anthropology and the Central States Anthropological Society.

RAY L. BIRDWHISTELL, Senior Research Scientist at Eastern Pennsylvania Psychiatric Institute, is Professor of Research in Anthropology in the Department of Psychiatry, Temple University. At present engaged in longitudinal research on communication development in humans, he is primarily concerned with descriptive kinesics, the structural analysis of the communicative aspects of body motion. He has taught anthropology at the Universities of Toronto, Louisville, and Buffalo.

ROBERT J. BRAIDWOOD, Oriental Institute Professor of Old World Prehistory and Professor in the Department of Anthropology, University of Chicago, is field director of the Oriental Institute's prehistoric projects. He has taught Old World prehistory at Chicago since 1941 and has been involved in Oriental Institute field work in Southwestern Asia since 1933. He is the author of various field reports and general articles, and of *Prehistoric Men* and *Archeologists and What They Do* at a more elementary level.

EDWARD M. BRUNER, Associate Professor of Anthropology at the University of Illinois, has also taught at Ohio State University, University of Chicago, and Yale University. In 1960-61 he was a Fellow at the Center for Advanced Study in the Behavioral Sciences. He has done field work with American Indians, and is currently engaged in studies of social change in Sumatra. The author of various articles, he contributed to *Perspectives in American Indian Culture Change*.

CORA DU BOIS, Zemurray Professor, is affiliated with the Departments of Anthropology and Social Relations at Harvard. She has taught at various colleges and universities, and has served as a research director in the Department of State, as social science consultant to the World Health Organization, and as Director of Research for the Institute of International Education. Her field work began with the Indians of California. Subsequently her area interests centered on South and Southeast Asia. She has written *The People of Alor, Social Forces in Southeast Asia, Foreign Students and Higher Education in the United States,* as well as various monographs and professional articles.

JOSEPH B. CASAGRANDE is Professor of Anthropology and Head of the Department of Anthropology at the University of Illinois, Urbana. He has also taught anthropology at Queens College, the University of Rochester, and The American University. For the period 1950-1960 he was a member of the staff of the Social Science Research Council in New York City. He is the author of linguistic and ethnographic studies based on field work among the Comanche, Ojibwa, and Navaho Indians, and has recently edited a book, *In the Company of Man: Twenty Portraits by Anthropologists*. He currently serves as a member of the Executive Board of the American Anthropological Association.

FRED EGGAN, Professor of Anthropology and Director, Philippine Studies Program, University of Chicago, has been at the University of Chicago since 1935, and has carried out field research on the American Indians and in the Philippines. He has been particularly concerned with the graduate program at the University of Chicago. He is the author of *Social Organization of the Western Pueblos* and editor of *Social Anthropology of North American Tribes*.

ROBERT W. EHRICH is Associate Professor in the Department of Sociology and Anthropology at Brooklyn College, where he has taught anthropology since 1947. He also taught for one year as Visiting Associate Professor at the University of Pennsylvania. His first paper on the place of anthropology in liberal arts education appeared in 1947. His major interests are in archaeology and physical anthropology. He has done fieldwork in Czechoslovakia, Yugoslavia, Turkey, and Iraq. He is COWA area editor for the Balkans and co-editor for Central Europe. He is the author of various articles and reviews, and has edited *Relative Chronologies in Old World Archaeology*.

RAYMOND FIRTH is Professor of Anthropology in the University of London, attached to the London School of Economics and Political Science, where he has been since 1933. He is a social anthropologist, among his major interests being economic anthropology and religion. He has done field work in Tikopia, British Solomon Islands Protectorate in 1928-29 and again in 1952, and in Malaya 1939-40 and 1947. He has also made short surveys in New Guinea and in West Africa. He is the author of *Elements of Social Organization* and various other works.

MEYER FORTES, William Wyse Professor of Social Anthropology at Cambridge University, was a pupil of Malinowski and Seligman before undertaking field work in West Africa. His first teaching experience, at the London School of Economics (under Firth, 1939-40) and at Oxford (under Radcliffe-Brown and Evans-Pritchard, 1946-1950), was almost wholly concerned with postgraduate students. His current duties include both undergraduate courses and the supervision of postgraduate field research and thesis work.

DAVID H. FRENCH is Professor of Anthropology at Reed College, and has taught at Columbia, Harvard, and the University of Washington. He has also trained undergraduate and graduate students in the field. His first field research was among Pueblo Indians, and he was a Community Analyst in a Japanese-American Relocation Center. More recently, his field work has been among various Pacific Northwest Indian groups. In addition to research and writing on social organization, ethnoscience, conceptual systems, and ethnolinguistics, he is the author of *Factionalism in Isleta Pueblo* and the Wasco-Wishram section in *Perspectives in American Indian Culture Change*.

GUTORM GJESSING, Director of University Museum of Ethnography (Oslo), is Professor of Ethnography (Cultural and Social Anthropology) at the University of Oslo. He has taught prehistoric archaeology and ethnography since 1942, and has published textbooks on the methods of prehistoric archaelogy, the relationship between ethnography and human geography, and on general ethnography. He has lectured on archaeological and ethnographical subjects at universities in several European countries and in the United States, and was Visiting Professor on the Scheme of Northern Studies at the London School of Economics and Political Science. One of his current interests is the relationship between prehistoric archaeology and social anthropology.

GORDON W. HEWES, Associate Professor of Anthropology at the University of Colorado, started teaching at North Dakota in 1946, and has taught also at the University of Southern California. He has done field work in North American archaeology and ethnology, and recently has been studying cross-cultural aspects of postural habits. In 1955-56 he was a Fulbright lecturer in Tokyo, mainly at Keiō University, and in 1960 taught at San Marcos University in Lima, Peru, and in 1961 at the Summer Institute in Anthropology for College Teachers at Boulder, Colorado, sponsored by the National Science Foundation. He has written various papers and reviews.

E. ADAMSON HOEBEL is Professor of Anthropology at the University of Minnesota, where in 1959 he was cited for outstanding contribution to undergraduate teaching. He has previously taught at New York University and the University of Utah, where he was Dean of the University College, and at Chicago, Harvard, Oxford, Washington, Wisconsin, Utah State, and Claremont. He is the author of the basic text book, *Man in the Primitive World,* and *The Law of Primitive Man*. His field work has been centered on law among the Comanche, Cheyenne, Shoshone, and Pueblo Indians, and in West Pakistan. His current research is in Islamic law and legal reform in Pakistan.

FREDERICK S. HULSE is Professor of Anthropology at the University of Arizona. He began teaching at the University of Washington in 1936, and has introduced several thousand students to anthropology there and at other institutions where he has served on occasion. He has engaged in field work in Cuba, Hawaii, Japan, Mexico, Spain, Switzerland, and the United States. His major interest has been the effect of culture upon human biology, and he has published a number of papers upon this topic and others.

DELL H. HYMES is Associate Professor of Anthropology and Linguistics at the University of California, Berkeley. He has taught previously at Harvard University (1955-1960) and the Linguistic Institute (University of Michigan, summer 1959). His major interests in teaching and research have been language and culture and the American Indian, with a bias toward history, theory, and method. His chief field work has been with Chinookan speakers in Oregon.

JESSE D. JENNINGS, director of the Glen Canyon Archeological Salvage Project, is Professor of Anthropology at the University of Utah. He began full time archaeological field work in the Chickamauga Basin in 1936, and supervised excavation of an Early Mayan archaeological site near Guatemala City in 1937 for Carnegie Institution of Washington. He worked for the National Park Service from 1938 until 1948 (with interruption for military service from 1942 to 1945) in such places as Montezuma Castle National Monument, Arizona; Ocmulgee National Monument, Georgia; Natchez Trace Parkway, Mississippi; and Region Two, Omaha, Nebraska. He began teaching anthropology—introductory, North American prehistory, primitive law and scientific method—at the University of Utah in 1948, and was awarded the Viking Medal in Archaeology in 1958.

ALFRED KIDDER II, Associate Director of the University Museum, University of Pennsylvania, has been teaching North and South American archaeology and ethnography at Harvard and the University of Pennsylvania for over twenty-five years. His particular interest is in the archaeology of the Central Andean highlands. He has also worked in Venezuela, Honduras, and Guatemala, but is now principally concerned with museum administration. He has been active in the affairs of the American Anthropological Association and the Society for American Archaeology, of which he is treasurer, and is chairman of the Committee on International Anthropology of the National Research Council.

SOLON T. KIMBALL is Professor of Anthropology and Education at Teachers College, Columbia University. His teaching career began in 1945 at Michigan State University following nine years of service in the federal government. Subsequently, he was head of the Department of Sociology and Anthropology at the University of Alabama, coming to New York in 1953. He has done field work in Ireland, with Navaho Indians, and in American communities. He is a past president of the Society for Applied Anthropology.

GABRIEL W. LASKER, Associate Professor of Anatomy at Wayne State University, served as Assistant Director of the Educational Resources in Anthropology Project. He has taught human anatomy since 1946, but has also taught anthropology on occasion at Wayne State University, University of Chicago, University of Wisconsin, and Northwestern University. He has engaged in research in physical anthropology in Mexico, Peru, and elsewhere. He edits the quarterly journal *Human Biology*, has held various offices in the American Association of Physical Anthropologists and is the author of a new textbook, *The Evolution of Man: A Brief Introduction to Physical Anthropology*.

WILLIAM S. LAUGHLIN, Professor of Anthropology and Chairman of the Department of Anthropology, University of Wisconsin, has taught anthropology at the University of Oregon from 1949 to 1955 and at the University of Wisconsin from 1955. He has done field research on the blood group genetics of Basques and Caddoan Indians, and blood groups, morphology, population composition, and prehistory of genetic isolates among the Aleuts and Eskimos of Alaska, Canada, and Greenland. He is currently Editor of the *American Journal of Physical Anthropology*.

CHARLES LESLIE is Assistant Professor of Anthropology at Pomona College, Claremont, California. He has taught at the University of Minnesota, the University College of the University of Chicago, and Southern Methodist University. His major interest is in the study of style traditions and world views. His field research has been in the United States and Mexico, and he has recently begun field work in India. He is the author of *Now We Are Civilized* and the editor of *Anthropology of Folk Religion*.

KENNETH LITTLE is Head of the Department of Social Anthropology, University of Edinburgh. He taught previously at Cambridge University and the London School of Economics, and has held temporary appointments at California, Fisk, Northwestern, and Khartoum. His field work has been conducted mainly among Negroes in Cardiff, Wales, and the Mende of Sierra Leone, about whom he has published *Negroes in Britain* and *The Mende of Sierra Leone*, as well as articles about West African social change and race relations. His main interests are in these subjects, and he is currently directing an interdisciplinary study of urbanization in Sierra Leone.

FRANK B. LIVINGSTONE, Assistant Professor at the University of Michigan, has taught there since 1959. He has taught courses on race, population genetics, Africa, and human evolution. As a postdoctoral fellow of the National Science Foundation, he conducted research in Liberia on the distribution of the blood groups and abnormal hemoglobin in West Africa. He is the author of numerous publications on this research, one of which has been republished in S. N. Garn, ed., *Readings on Race*.

FLOYD G. LOUNSBURY is professor of linguistics at Yale University.

DAVID G. MANDELBAUM, Director of the Educational Resources in Anthropology Project, is Professor of Anthropology at the University of California,

Berkeley. He began teaching at the University of Minnesota; his first paper on teaching anthropology appeared in 1940. Since 1946 he has been at Berkeley; in recent years he has taught the introductory course in cultural anthropology. His field work has been with American Indians and in India. His current research is in social organization in India.

McKim Marriott is Associate Professor of the Social Sciences in the College of the University of Chicago and Associate Professor of Anthropology. Since 1957, he has taught general education courses to undergraduates in the social sciences as well as teaching graduate courses in social anthropology. He has done rural and urban field studies in India, and served for two years on the research staff of the University of California, Berkeley. He edited *Village India*, co-edited *Pilot Project, India,* and has written extensively on caste, applied anthropology, and communications.

Margaret Mead is Associate Curator of Ethnology, American Museum of Natural History; Adjunct Professor of Anthropology, Columbia University; Visiting Professor of Anthropology, University of Cincinnati College of Medicine and Menninger School of Psychiatry. She has combined a series of field trips between 1925 and 1958 to the South Pacific with writing, from *Coming of Age in Samoa* (1928) to her forthcoming *Continuities in Cultural Evolution,* and with lecturing and teaching at Columbia University and other universities, and has given short courses and special lectures in many other institutions. She has been President of the Society for Applied Anthropology and the American Anthropological Association.

Harold Nelson is an anthropology instructor at Santa Monica City College, Santa Monica, California, where he has taught introductory courses in physical and cultural anthropology since 1955. He has also taught the introductory course in physical anthropology for University of California Extension in the Far East and at Sacramento City College. He has engaged in research in several California communities, with special emphasis on culture change among Armenians.

David L. Olmsted is Professor of Anthropology and Chairman of the Department of Anthropology and Geography at the University of California, Davis. At various times he has taught anthropology, linguistics, Russian, psychology, geography, and sociology in such institutions as Cornell, Northwestern, the University of Chicago, and Yale. He has done field work in Korea, Cuba, Mexico, the Southwestern United States, and California, and is currently engaged in a long-term study of the culture history and comparative linguistics of the Hokan peoples.

Benjamin D. Paul, Associate Professor of Anthropology and director of the Social Science Program at the Harvard School of Public Health, also holds a faculty appointment in the Harvard Department of Social Relations where he has been teaching anthropology since 1946. He has done field work among the Maya Indians of highland Guatemala. He has published material on ethnographic, methodological, psychocultural, and public health topics, and has edited a book of teaching materials entitled *Health, Culture, and Community: Case Studies of Public Reactions to Health Programs.*

KENNETH L. PIKE has been Professor of Linguistics in the Departments of English and Anthropology at the University of Michigan since 1948. He is President and Director of Courses, Summer Institute of Linguistics (with summer sessions at the Universities of Oklahoma, North Dakota, and Washington, as well as in England and Australia), and has taught at this Institute since 1936. He has taken field trips to Mexico, South America, and New Guinea. In 1961, he was President of the Linguistic Society of America. His books on linguistics include: *Phonetics, Phonemics, Tone Languages, Intonation of American English,* and *Language in Relation to a Unified Theory of the Structure of Human Behavior* (3 volumes).

ROBERT N. RAPOPORT, Lecturer on Social Anthropology at Harvard University, is Executive Officer of the Harvard Training Program for Social Scientists in Medicine. Aside from offering a seminar on the applications of social science in the fields of medicine, he teaches applied anthropology and, with other members of the Department of Social Relations, a general graduate interdisciplinary survey course. His field work has been among the Navaho Indians, in a Canadian maritime province, in a British psychiatric hospital, and has involved experimenting with the "therapeutic community" approach. He is author of many professional articles and reviews and the Peabody Museum Monograph *Changing Navaho Religious Values, Community as Doctor,* and co-author of *People of Cove and Woodlot.*

VERNE F. RAY is Professor of Anthropology at the University of Washington, where he has been a member of the faculty since 1933 and Associate Dean of the Graduate School from 1947 to 1951. During the latter period he participated in the planning and development of programs in general education at several universities. As Visiting Professor of Anthropology and Education at Yale University, 1952-1954, he taught in the graduate general education program. He served as Research Director for the Human Relations Area Files from 1951 to 1954, was President of the American Ethnological Society from 1953 to 1955, and editor from 1955 to 1960. His major books and papers reflect researches with the Indians of Northwestern America and he has conducted research programs with the Eskimos and in Mesoamerica.

ROBERT ROSSOW is a Foreign Service Officer, who was, in 1960-61, a Fellow at the Center for Advanced Study in the Behavioral Sciences. His principal assignments have been in Canada, Panama, Bulgaria, Iran, India, Nepal, and Afghanistan. He is South Asia specialist and a graduate of the Na-

tional War College. From 1954 to 1957 he was Head of the Department of
Mid-Career Training and Chairman of the Mid-Career Course on Foreign
Affairs at the Foreign Service Institute of the Department of State.

JOHN HOWLAND ROWE is Professor of Anthropology at the University of California, Berkeley, where he has taught since 1948. Before coming to Berkeley he taught general anthropology at the National University of Cuzco,
Peru and the University of the Cauca, Popayán, Colombia. He acquired his
interest in library problems as an undergraduate at Brown University,
where he worked for four years in the Circulation Department of the University Library. He has organized anthropology libraries at all the universities in which he has taught.

GEORGE D. SPINDLER is Professor of Anthropology and Education at Stanford University. He began teaching in the high schools of Wisconsin in 1940.
His first article on the teaching of anthropology in secondary schools appeared in 1946, and he has continued an interest in the application of anthropology to education since that time. He came to Stanford in 1950, where
he teaches the introductory course in cultural anthropology, cultural dynamics, and personality and culture. He has done field work with American
Indians, in California communities, and in rural Germany. His current research is on psychological adaptation in culture change.

J. N. SPUHLER is Professor of Anthropology, Chairman of the Department
of Anthropology, and Professor of Human Genetics at the University of
Michigan. He teaches an introductory course in physical anthropology for
freshmen and sophomores, a course in biology, culture, and society for juniors and seniors, and upper-level courses in population genetics. He has engaged in research in human biology in the American Southwest, Ann Arbor,
and Japan. He edited *Natural Selection in Man* and *The Evolution
of Man's Capacity for Culture.*

LAURA THOMPSON, Professor of Anthropology at San Francisco State College,
has engaged in applied anthropology projects in Fiji, Iceland, Guam, Hawaii, Mexico, and among the Indians of the United States. She is a charter
member of the Society of Applied Anthropology, and has taught anthropology at the City College of New York, the University of North Carolina,
North Carolina State College, Pennsylvania State University, and Utah
State University. She is the author of *Fijian Frontier, Guam and Its People,
The Hopi Way* (with Alice Joseph), *Culture in Crisis, Personality and Government,* as well as over sixty articles and monographs. Her most recent book,
Toward a Science of Mankind, presents a unified theory of man which may
serve as a basis for field projects in applied anthropology. She has in prepara-
tion a textbook on clinical anthropology.

EVON Z. VOGT is Professor of Anthropology at Harvard University and Curator of Middle American Ethnology in the Peabody Museum. He has

taught at Harvard since 1948, and has done field work in the Southwest and in Mexico. His current research is in the processes of cultural change in the Maya Indian area of Mexico and Guatemala. He is author of various articles and reviews and of *Navaho Veterans, Modern Homesteaders,* and co-editor of *Reader in Comparative Religion.*

CHARLES WAGLEY is Professor of Anthropology and Chairman of the Department of Anthropology at Columbia University, where he has taught both undergraduate and graduate anthropology since 1946. He has been concerned with the development of foreign area studies in the university curriculum for many years. His field work has been mainly in Guatemala and in Brazil.

SHERWOOD L. WASHBURN, Professor of Anthropology at the University of California, Berkeley, has taught human anatomy at the medical school of Columbia University and anthropology at the University of Chicago. He was elected President of the American Anthropological Association for 1961. His research is on baboons and human evolution.

RICHARD B. WOODBURY, University of Arizona, is currently investigating prehistoric agriculture as part of an interdisciplinary study of arid lands. Previously, he was Associate Professor of Anthropology at Columbia University, and began his teaching at the University of Kentucky. His major research and writing have been in New World archaeology. He has edited the journal *American Antiquity,* and was the assistant editor of *Societies around the World,* a two-volume social science reader published in 1953.

Participants
in Symposia
on
Teaching

THE TEACHING OF SOCIAL AND CULTURAL ANTHROPOLOGY. April 23, 1960. Held as part of the meetings of the American Ethnological Society at Palo Alto, California.

> *Organizing Chairman:* Bernard Siegel. Papers by V. F. Ray, G. D. Spindler, G. W. Hewes, David French.
> *Principal Discussants:* Harry Hoijer, A. H. Whiteford, C. C. Lantz, Conrad Arensberg, W. D. Hohenthal, Valene Smith, J. B. Watson, John Gillin.

THE TEACHING OF AREA COURSES. April 22, 1960. Held as part of the Central States Anthropological Society meetings at Bloomington, Indiana.

> *Organizing Chairman:* Milton Singer. Papers by J. W. Bennett and McKim Marriott.

THE TEACHING OF ARCHAEOLOGY. May 5, 1960. Held as part of the meetings of the Society of American Archaeology at New Haven, Connecticut.

> *Organizing Chairman:* J. D. Jennings. Papers by R. B. Woodbury, A. V. Kidder II, D. A. Baerreis.

THE TEACHING OF LINGUISTICS IN ANTHROPOLOGY. April 23, 1960. Held as part of the Central States Anthropological Society meetings at Bloomington, Indiana.

> *Organizing Chairman:* C. F. Voegelin. Papers by D. H. Hymes, K. L. Pike, Mary Haas.

THE TEACHING OF PHYSICAL ANTHROPOLOGY. May 13, 1960. Held as part of the American Association of Physical Anthropologists meetings at Washington, D.C.

Organizing Chairman: S. M. Garn. Papers by F. P. Thieme, E. E. Hunt, Jr., F. S. Hulse.

THE TEACHING OF APPLIED ANTHROPOLOGY. May 30, 1960. Held as part of the Society for Applied Anthropology meetings at Pittsburgh, Pennsylvania.

Organizing Chairman: R. N. Adams. Papers by Laura Thompson, R. N. Rapoport, H. G. Barnett.

THE TEACHING OF ANTHROPOLOGY IN PROFESSIONAL SCHOOLS, LIBERAL ARTS COLLEGES, AND SECONDARY SCHOOLS. May 7, 1960. Held at the New York Academy of Sciences.

Organizing Chairman: S. T. Kimball. Papers by R. W. Ehrich, Anthony Leeds, S. T. Kimball.

THE TEACHING OF ANTHROPOLOGY IN SMALL DEPARTMENTS AND IN JUNIOR COLLEGES. April 9, 1960. Held as part of the Southwestern Anthropological Association meetings at Claremont, California.

Organizing Chairman: J. F. Goins. Papers by D. L. Olmsted, Harold Nelson.
Main Discussants: J. E. Weckler, Ruth Landes.

THE TEACHING OF ANTHROPOLOGY. AN INTERNATIONAL SYMPOSIUM. August 9-16, 1960. Held at Burg Wartenstein, Austria, sponsored by the Wenner-Gren Foundation for Anthropological Research.

Organizing Chairman: D. G. Mandelbaum. Co-Chairman: K. L. Little. Rapporteurs: Ethel M. Albert and G. W. Lasker.
Papers by D. G. Mandelbaum, Margaret Mead, Raymond Firth, Gutorm Gjessing, F. G. Lounsbury, W. S. Laughlin, R. L. Birdwhistell, Meyer Fortes, J. H. M. Beattie, K. L. Little.
Main Discussants: Daryll Forde, S. C. Dube, V. L. Grottanelli, R. F. Heizer, Monica H. Wilson, J. J. Maquet.

GENERAL CONFERENCE ON THE TEACHING OF ANTHROPOLOGY. March 2-4, 1961. Held at Berkeley, California, under a special grant from the National Science Foundation.

Papers by S. L. Washburn, Cora Du Bois, D. G. Mandelbaum, G. W. Lasker, G. D. Spindler, E. M. Bruner, R. J. Braidwood, C. M. Arensberg, E. Z. Vogt, Fred Eggan, Lauriston Sharp, F. B. Livingstone, J. B. Casagrande, C. M. Leslie, B. D. Paul, E. A. Hoebel, Robert Rossow, R. L. Beals, J. H. Rowe, Charles Wagley.
Principal Discussants: T. D. McCown, J. H. Steward, Ethel M. Albert, F. M. Keesing.
Rapporteurs: R. T. Anderson and Gallatin Anderson.

DAVID G. MANDELBAUM

The Transmission
of Anthropological
Culture

WHEN, in the late summer of every year, anthropologists begin thinking seriously about their courses in the new term soon to start, more than a few find themselves caught up in a zestful anticipation of teaching that seems quite dissociated from their professional training and pursuits. Anthropologists are trained to be research workers, not teachers. Anthropological meetings are given over to discussion of problems of anthropology, rarely of teaching. Anthropological journals offer articles on teaching only infrequently.

This is quite understandable. Members of a discipline must develop it through research. In anthropology as in most other disciplines, those who develop anthropological culture also have the task of transmitting it, else the culture will not be perpetuated. So they have a natural interest in the dissemination of what they have helped develop. But as important as any other motivation for their devotion to teaching is the anthropologist's firm conviction that anthropology has something especially important to give to a student. To be sure, members of every academic department tend to be zealous champions of the importance of their own subject. But, as the papers which follow show, anthropologists find that their concepts are particularly vital, not only for undergraduate education, but for the whole outlook for man at the present juncture of history.

How these concepts may best be transmitted to the larger society by

1

the relatively few anthropologists is of concern to the profession. Internal, technical communication within the profession is no less essential than before. Dissemination of anthropological ideas through books, journals, public lectures and mass media, has had marked influence and must be continued. But the main sphere for the transmission of anthropological culture is the college classroom, where day by day many thousands of students come to know what anthropology has to teach about human life, and thus about themselves.

American anthropologists began to write about their teaching quite early in the formation of the discipline; one bibliography begins with two papers of 1892 (de Laguna 1960:912-915). Two useful sets of papers on the subject have been published more recently (Roberts and Weiner 1958, Whiteford 1960). But such contributions appeared only sporadically; they were scattered in diverse sources and were not periodically reviewed or revised to provide a useful fund of information. Each writer began afresh without much benefit from the experience and observations of his colleagues. In the earlier years there was little experience to draw on. But in recent decades, the teaching of anthropology in the United States has greatly increased and with its growth has come an increased need for a systematic examination of anthropological teaching.

This work presents the results of such an inquiry. It is intended to provide a general appraisal of the teaching of anthropology, together with information useful for the planning of courses. It should provide a base for continuing discussions toward the improvement of our teaching. It is not a code of approved procedures or a do-it-yourself manual in course construction. Diverging views on some matters are to be found and opposing statements on basic questions may appear among the papers of a single section. The symposia at which the papers were first presented were intended to bring out those issues on which there were differences and which might be clarified through a discussion. The discussions did serve that purpose; they also revealed a considerable basis of agreement about objectives in teaching anthropology.

The anthropological teaching which is here considered is mainly that of undergraduates in the United States. There are three papers specifically on graduate training and frequent mention of graduate work in the other essays. Teaching in other countries is particularly noted in the five papers written by authors from outside America, four British and one Norwegian, but the main focus is on teaching in the United States.

The principal problems of that teaching rise from the success of anthropology in recent decades. There has been a vast increase in anthropological publications, a rapid outpouring of ideas and data, an intense development of special fields. Hence the teacher of undergraduate courses, who may keep abreast of recent developments in one or two special fields, faces the problem of the selection of concepts and readings for broad teaching purposes.

This is a common enough situation in most disciplines; in anthropology it is coupled with the problems of an unusually high rate of increase in enrollments, of the relatively small size of the profession, and of the frequent requests for anthropologists to assist with projects other than their own teaching and research.

Enrollments in anthropology courses have climbed sharply. In one year, between 1959 and 1960, there was a 20 per cent increase in anthropology enrollments in California schools; sizable increases have occurred in other parts of the country. One main reason is simply a greater interest in the whole subject. Another is the greatly increased awareness of peoples studied by anthropologists in Asia, Africa, and other parts of the world.

The magnitude of anthropology enrollments is indicated in Lasker and Nelson's survey of California colleges and universities. They count 27,969 course-enrollments in anthropology in 1960 in California, 68 per cent of that total (19,060) being in introductory courses. While California is a main locale for the teaching of anthropology, there are large institutions elsewhere in which a considerable proportion of all undergraduates include anthropology in their study programs. At the University of Minnesota, for example, E. A. Hoebel estimated that 18 per cent of all students enrolled in 1957-58 were taking a course in anthropology (1958: 636). There has also been a large increment in the number of anthropology courses and teachers. Lasker's survey of catalog listings shows that 82 per cent more anthropology courses were listed in 1960 than in 1950 in 60 institutions. The anthropology faculties in 59 of these institutions increased by 77 per cent in the same decade.

This increase means that the instructor must plan his teaching carefully, coordinate it with that of his now more numerous colleagues in a department, revise his courses frequently to keep them scientifically alive, and adjust his teaching procedures to meet new conditions of academic demography. He must do so not only to fulfill his teaching responsibilities but also to be able to retain sufficient time and energy for his research. Such planning, revision, and adjustment requires access to a fund of relevant ideas and information. This work is a first attempt to provide it.

Ideas about teaching are the main focus of the essays of this volume. Factual information for teaching and planning is given in the companion volume, *Resources for the Teaching of Anthropology*. The present volume begins with a section on the undergraduate curriculum as a whole and continues with sections on the teaching of physical anthropology, of cultural and social anthropology, of regional and civilization courses (treated in a separate section because of the special problems and new developments in them), of archaeological anthropology, of linguistic anthropology (both more awkward designations than the more common "archaeology" and "linguistics" but also more apt), of applied anthropology (in which the teaching has become both important and controversial) and on graduate training. External considerations are treated in three sections, on the relation to other curricula, on the general academic environment, and on anthropology in liberal education and its contribution, through the students, to the future condition of culture and society.

Many of the authors have formulated their views of the fundamentals of anthropological thought and some have recommended a pattern of priorities in communicating anthropological ideas and data. Hence these essays deal with anthropology as well as with the teaching of it; they provide one kind of conspectus of the current state of the discipline.

FUNDAMENTALS

What then, does anthropology in its current state have to transmit to undergraduates? The success of that transmission is a test of the vitality of the subject. Professionals in any discipline can communicate with each other in their special technical dialect, they can usually find personal reward in playing out the scientific and scholarly procedures appropriate to their field. Without such internal, professional interchange there can be no real discipline. But without effective communication of the results of that interchange to the non-professional society, the profession can become quite irrelevant to its own culture and eventually inert in itself. It is true that anthropology, like any other discipline, cannot develop scientifically if anthropologists rush to do what seems to be in the current popular interest. They must follow the discipline's own logic and unfolding, working on ideas and problems for which there may be no popular interest whatsoever but which are significant in the eyes of at least some anthropologists. Yet, as these essays indicate, many anthropologists know well that the imparting of ideas which students will find illuminating is a main achievement of a discipline and a sure mark of its viability.

The ideas which are repeatedly emphasized in these papers have to do with the whole of human behavior, as viewed in the context of reality, and as studied in the manner of science. The holistic theme lays down that anthropological studies relate to as many phases of life as does the particular reality which is being studied. This is in contrast with other ways of studying man, in which disciplinary boundaries are more narrowly defined and problems outside the defined limits are not seriously examined. Anthropology takes into consideration both present behavior and past, familiar cultures and remote, the commonplace in life and the extraordinary, the lowly in society and the élite, the rational in behavior and the irrational, the cultural and the biological founts of action. This holistic ideal, as is pointed out in several papers, may be more honored in the breach than in the observance, but it is a principle which encourages the pursuit of ideas in whatever way a problem requires.

It is the practice of field research, of collecting data and testing concepts in the context of real behavior, that makes the holistic ideal a heuristic guide. The field anthropologist who sets out to study a group's economic activities need not feel constrained from studying mythology or child rearing if he finds that the economy is crucially involved with such other aspects of culture. Anthropological training, as Mead, Fortes, and other authors in this work note, should invest the student with an expectant awareness of a wide range of possibilities in behavior, so that he may be able to follow clues to understanding whenever and however they may turn up. Even the student who takes only an introductory anthropology course should take over from his teachers, as David French and others advocate, this model of a field worker, alert to multiple potentialities in culture and behavior, ready to see and seize diverse explanatory factors.

The student, like all the rest of us, must move in an alien culture from time to time, even if it is only the unfamiliar environment of a new job or neighborhood. His movement will be facilitated and his understanding deepened if he can learn to use the approach of the field anthropologist, looking closely, clearly, and dispassionately at what people actually are doing, as well as listening to what they say they are doing and learning what others say about them; gathering his information at first hand, rather than relying exclusively on documents and statistics; taking his leads from what is important to them, the observed, rather than what may be important to the observer; testing his ideas about them within a frame of ideas which has been developed out of a broad spectrum of knowledge about mankind, rather than one which pertains to a few cultural settings or a single civilization.

This approach can be taught in every special field of anthropology. The student of archaeological anthropology learns to uncover the evidence and to examine carefully artifacts, bones, settlement patterns, ecology, and anything else that may contribute to his knowledge of the

life that then was lived. The student of physical anthropology learns
to collect evidence pertinent to human evolution by observing primates as they actually live, rather than only in the artificial environment of zoo, laboratory, or dissecting table. The student of linguistic
anthropology learns about the beautifully articulated universe of language by piecing together the evidence he gets from the lips of speakers.

Science is both molar and molecular, but scientists tend to specialize in either the microscopic view or the macroscopic. Anthropologists
often try to combine the two. An ethnologist can relate his minutely
detailed study of a ceremony to generalizations at successively higher
levels of abstraction: in the first instance to the structure of ceremonies
in that culture, then perhaps to economic and social activities within
the society, and finally to the use of ceremonies in a large range of cultures and societies. Thus the undergraduate student of anthropology
is introduced to the work of those who analyze a text as meticulously
as any exegete, of those who are astronomers of the social sciences, and
of those who combine both kinds of analysis.

He can also learn that the method of science does not pivot on any
one technique. Those who think of the locus of science as quintessen-
tially in controlled experiment hold that anthropology is not a science
at all. Those who equate social science either with theoretical models
as used in economics, or statistical compilations of the kind done in
social psychology and sociology, exempt anthropology from the social
sciences. Yet in all branches of anthropology there is exemplified the
careful, systematic collection of evidence, the construction of concepts,
the continuous testing of theory which are the bases of scientific
method. Anthropological method, as Kimball and other authors note,
has been that of natural science. And this method is fruitful whether
used in studying the few relics of fossil man or the superabundant evidence on a great and going civilization.

The student also learns from anthropology that the humanities are
not contra-science, to be placed in another room of the mind, walled
away from the sciences of man. The essays by Leslie, Kidder, Bennett,
and Marriott show how useful an interchange between anthropology
and the humanities can be. The anthropological approach is different
from that generally used in the humanities, as is well attested in the
same essays, especially in the accounts of joint teaching with scholars
from the humanities. But humanities scholars find themselves in close
accord with the ethnologist's attempts to understand and translate a
people's own view of their lives, with the archaeological anthropologist's long sight in culture, with the linguistic anthropologist's portrayal of language as structure, as tool, as art form, and with the physical
anthropologist's conception of the unity and continuity of man's career.

If the undergraduate discovers in his anthropology courses a new eclecticism in ways of understanding people, he is also confronted with certain firm postulates on which anthropological inquiry is based. He is taught that all men are of one species, all have the same general attributes of biology and of learning culture. All men have ways of life which are worthy of serious study, and in the lives of all there is, and has been, an interplay of biological and cultural forces. Every element of culture, whether it be an axe or an economic development plan, must be observed in its cultural setting. Each cultural form can be understood only when its meaning is also considered; the text of a myth must be read in the context of the religion of which it is a part, just as the text of a law must be viewed in the context of the legal and political system within which it appears.

What is the upshot of teaching from these postulates, through the holistic approach, using the field work model, following scientific method? It should give students a wider acquaintance with other peoples, a better understanding of diversity and similarity among cultures, and of cultural stability and change. It should open the way to a deeper appreciation of their own culture, and should provide incentive and intellectual equipment with which they will continue to develop their knowledge after they leave the classroom. It should do so, and as several authors in this work mention, it does do so for a gratifying number of students; though we must heed Firth's warning that it does not *necessarily* have such effect.

Wider acquaintance with peoples comes simply from the factual information given about them in anthropology courses. Great reaches of humanity, not only tribal peoples and ancient cultures, but those of the contemporary nations of Africa, Asia, and the Americas, may come within an undergraduate's ken only in his anthropology courses. More importantly, once a student learns to ask the anthropologist's questions, new avenues of understanding can open before him. He may discover, perhaps for the first time, that cultural differences are not necessarily dangerous, that alien cultures can be studied with an attitude of compassionate neutrality, that he can learn something from any person, and that he can be more securely engaged with his own values and causes when he sees them in some contrastive perspective.

While it is not impossible to give a dull course on anthropology, the subject has an intrinsic interest for many students. The juxtaposition of the unfamiliar with the very familiar captures their interest. Kinship or growth patterns may be explained with reference to Eskimos or Bushmen, but each student can contrast his kin and his growth with those traced in the examples. Rites of passage, phonemes, blood types, can all be quickly recognized close to home, even when the instructor analyzes them among the Navaho. While following a discussion of the criteria of social status among an African people, a student may see in a flash that the same kind of analysis is appropriate in the campus milieu. It is intellectually exciting to discover in anthropology a "mirror for man," to see self in not-self. Further, the calm anthropological inquiry into puberty customs, race differences, intragroup hostility can induce the student to make calm appraisals of his own environment. For some undergraduates the tone of anthropological discourse is especially appealing; it appraises but does not immediately condemn or extol and, as Ethel Albert's paper shows, its ethical implications are strong, but they are built in and not tacked on.

The central problems of American higher education, according to one extensive study, are not those of talent, expansion, or money. "Rather the central problems are student boredom, their indifference and hostility to learning, and the irrelevance of their associations and relationships with other students to their education" (Clark and Trow 1961). If so, the teaching of anthropology has some innate advantages in meeting these problems; boredom can readily be checked by our very case materials; indifference can be countered by the direct applicability of anthropological ideas to the students' problems and interests; their actual associations can be used to illustrate and test the validity of anthropological concepts.

Each special field within anthropology has its special lessons to give. In linguistic anthropology students find striking demonstration of underlying patterns in a culture, of order, neatness, predictability. The intricacy of that order can be revealed in the language one has been speaking all one's life without knowing how refined an instrument it is. And if such order can be discerned anywhere in culture, something like it can exist everywhere. A course in linguistics, as Pike's paper shows, can bring together for a student much of what he has previously learned about language in disparate segments. Hymes and Lounsbury tell how linguistic anthropology enhances the study of language by considering the cultural environment and social use of language forms.

In archaeological anthropology, students learn about the common cultural roots of all mankind, as well as about the branching of separate traditions and the continual change which is organic in culture. Jennings' essay notes that some students have a special affinity for archaeology. It is partly their interest in working with material objects, of discovering treasure from the earth, of recreating the otherwise lost record of human endeavor. And studying the archaeology of their locality or of their forebears meets the perennially fascinating questions: "Who was here before us?" and "Who gave rise to us?" It is a field whose basic data are limited to the objects which have been preserved, but this very limitation has the advantage of showing general features of human life which can be traced over long spans of time. If the archaeologist needs a strong back in his field work, he must have a sharp mind to use the products of his excavation. Gjessing shows the significant relation between archaeology and politics in some countries. No set of papers in this volume places greater emphasis on the conceptual problems of a field than do the essays on archaeological anthropology.

In physical anthropology, the student discovers the biological underpinnings of culture and society. He learns that man has been constantly remaking himself, biologically as well as culturally, and so it is important to study both ancient evolution and contemporary differentiation. The papers on the teaching of physical anthropology indicate how the broad stream of biological science can be channeled into an understanding of man and, conversely, how students of biology can be shown the cultural dimensions in human biology.

The great majority of courses are in cultural and social anthropology; some of the salient lessons have already been mentioned, others are discussed in Arensberg's essay. Three developments in the teaching of this field may be particularly noted: the inclusion of civilized as well as tribal peoples, the use of applied studies to illuminate basic theory, the relation between cultural and social anthropology.

The study of civilization and civilized societies was part of the birthright of anthropology and has never been relinquished. For reasons both internal and external to the discipline, anthropologists concentrated on non-literate cultures and tribal peoples. In recent years, the impetus of anthropological research in such areas as Japan and India, and on problems of civilization and complex societies, has brought a freshet of new data and concepts into teaching.[1] The works on primitives remain integral to most courses, though it is increasingly realized that primitive cultures are not usually as simple as they may be made out to be (cf. Lévi-Strauss 1954:97, Opler 1947). The use of data from complex societies introduces new complexities into anthropological teaching and some believe that it is not suitable fare for beginning students. But the whole of anthropological teaching is enhanced by including discussion of the languages and literature, the archaeological and historical evidences, the complex social and cultural patterns of civilized peoples.

Work in applied anthropology has increased and is increasingly utilized for teaching purposes. While the authors in the section on applied anthropology present differing views—with Thompson, Barnett, and Rapoport giving several models for undergraduate courses in this field, Little emphasizing the context of social anthropology, and Adams advocating separate courses on the subject at the graduate level only—all agree that studies in applied anthropology can strategically be used to show how theoretical concepts are deployed empirically and how the empirical data feed back into the development of theory.

The question of distinguishing cultural anthropology from the more narrowly focused field of social anthropology is not an issue which the authors of these essays found necessary to expound. Beattie mentions that social (or cultural) anthropology is regarded as a social science in its own right in England and has as close connections with other social sciences as with other branches of anthropology. There are indeed advantages in delineating a field of study like social anthropology rather than trying to cover the whole universe of man in one curriculum. The danger in the universalistic sweep has often been pointed out: the teaching may be spread so thinly over so many subjects that it becomes superficial and trivial; everything may be mentioned and nothing explained. The best countermeasure to this danger lies in designing a course so that selected concepts and case examples are explored in depth. To this principle of selection, it is well to add a constant regard for relevance—for the relevance of the artifact or the institution being examined to other aspects of the culture, of the concept being discussed to other elements of theory, of anthropological theory to the flow of intellectual history.

With such selection and concern for relevance, the advantages of teaching anthropology in its wider ambit can be maintained. One main advantage is that it reinforces the holistic approach. Over and over again in these essays the watchword is sounded that all anthropology is one. This theme tends to appear whenever American anthropologists discuss the state of the discipline. It is sounded even by those who point out, as Laughlin does in his paper, that in the practice of teaching and writing, unity is often neglected. But such neglect does not vitiate the importance of the theme, which is an insistence on non-fragmentation of inquiry, on freedom to carry on teaching and research over a very broad expanse, on potential—even when unused—communication with a broad array of specialists within a single professional group. Many of the essays stress the centrality of the concept of culture to all of anthropology. Hence it is wise to begin an introductory course or course sequence with a thorough discussion of culture, illustrating the aspects and dynamics of culture with examples from a few societies.

The concepts which an undergraduate discovers in anthropology can have a double impact; they throw fresh light on some of his old ideas, they open up new vistas of knowledge. Every student comes into a beginning anthropology course already equipped with some ideas about the subjects to be discussed. He may enter a trigonometry course without knowing that logarithms exist, but when he registers for introductory anthropology, he already has absorbed notions about racial and cultural differences, about the nature of culture and society—at least of his own. The course can induce him to reconsider some of his more provincial ideas, though the displacement of naive ethnocentrism in itself is not enough. Cora Du Bois appropriately comments that "detachment without attachment is at least vacuous, at most corrupting." It is important that the student also find in anthropology positive ideas and the prospect of continual exploration in extending his knowledge of man.

In *The University and World Affairs,* a study made by a committee of the Ford Foundation, there appears the recommendation that "During their undergraduate years, all students should get at least an introductory acquaintance with some culture other than their own" (J. L. Morrill *et al.* 1961:17). Such study becomes especially rewarding when the other culture is not seen as completely alien or quaintly exotic but is placed in a meaningful relation to our own and to all cultures. When Fred Eggan comments below that anthropology is destined to take over the role formerly occupied by the classics in a liberal education and Verne Ray writes that anthropology is to the behavioral sciences what philosophy formerly was for all of the sciences, they are reflecting the views of many anthropologists about the special importance of their teaching.

STUDENTS AND TEACHERS

The undergraduates who are now taking courses in anthropology are, in overwhelming majority, students whose major interests are in some other subject and who take only one or, at best, a few anthropology courses in their college careers. In the calendar year 1959 there were 23,309 course-enrollments in anthropology in California higher institutions. A total of 81 California students were graduated with a major in anthropology in the academic year 1958-59. The total of first degrees in anthropology in the United States in that academic year was 433. It is a fair guess that over 95 per cent of students in anthropology classes are nonmajors; in the California survey 68 per cent of all course-enrollments in 1960 were in the introductory courses.

There are several reasons for this imbalance. Many students have not heard of anthropology when they enter college and by the time they take an anthropology course they are already firmly committed to some other curriculum. In many institutions where anthropology is taught, a major in the subject is not offered. There are fewer trained teachers of anthropology than there are in most disciplines. As anthropology becomes more widely known, both to high school students and to the general public, and as more college freshmen study anthropology, the number of undergraduate majors will very likely rise rapidly. This has already occurred in universities and colleges with strong and long established anthropology faculties. But for some years to come major students will still form a small fraction of all students in our undergraduate classes. They should have the benefit of our closest planning and attention, because from their number will come many of our graduate students and through them we fulfill a main professional obligation, that of bringing up our successors.

All teaching, as Bruner and Spindler note, involves assumptions about the students. It is particularly appropriate for anthropologists to have some objective information about the character and culture of their students, if only to know what ideas about human beings they bring into the course and what ideas they can best absorb at different stages of their education. Certain it is that the range is wide and variation great among classes and schools, but on these matters there are as yet few data. While we have been referring to "the" student, that convenient fiction is no more (and no less) real than is "the" anthropologist. Still, some general questions may result in useful generalizations. One question, raised in Ehrich's paper, is whether anthropological teaching should be especially directed toward the talented student, with the others given only routine attention. While this involves the practical matter of the best allocation of teaching time, it also entails the question of whether there are many students who are not capable of gaining much from anthropology. Some would argue that such students, apathetic and intellectually uninterested as they may be, stand in special need of the stimulus of anthropological concepts; the gifted ones may acquire them on their own. Similarly, it has been asked whether college students, struggling to establish their own identity, can take the neutral posture of anthropological observation. One answer to this is that young men and women who are concerned about their personal conformity can achieve a steadier view of their own problems when they can see them in the perspective of similarities and differences among people in general.

Not all of anthropology is equally suitable to every stage of schooling, but some concepts are particularly suitable for certain stages. Anthropological subjects have long been taught from the early grades up through high school, but very rarely with any teaching materials prepared by anthropologists. A beginning of participation by anthropologists in planning secondary school curricula has been made; as that enterprise develops, the matching of anthropological ideas to stages of development among students should be more adequately understood than it now is.

At the college level, motivations for taking anthropology are important; Fred Eggan remarks that in the selection of graduate students motivation and interest are probably more important than previous grades. I asked the students in an introductory cultural anthropology class of some 300 to write a brief note on why they had enrolled in the course. Very few replied that they had done so on the recommendation of a faculty adviser; most indicated that they had heard something about the subject and wanted to learn more about it. Another kind of selection may operate in introductory physical anthropology when that course can be used to fulfill a biological science requirement and does not entail laboratory work. Some who enter this course to work off a requirement go on from it with interest kindled in the study of man.

One anthropologist who teaches in a university with highly selective admission standards reports that he no longer can give the same kind of introductory course that he gave a decade ago. Most of his students already know the beginning lessons and are ready for more advanced and sophisticated work. In contrast, we have Bennett's sketch of the freshmen in his classes, thoroughly unsophisticated in anthropology though eminently teachable. Some adjustment in the pitch and pace of teaching is obviously necessary for such different kinds of students,[2] though that adjustment must not lead to a dilution of content to the point of insipidity. Even in those junior colleges which have very few selective requirements, teachers of anthropology generally aim to give their courses at a level comparable to that in more selective institutions. And, as Nelson's paper reports, a considerable proportion of the students in such junior colleges go on to take a degree in a college or university.

There is a student sub-culture in most schools which anthropologists can examine, with the active help of their own students, to their advantage in teaching anthropology. Clark and Trow's study of college student sub-culture concludes that the organization of the college as community has profound effects on student life and learning. The organization differs in a small residential college from that in a large commuter university, but in both, by reason of the structural situation, most students are far more concerned with the development of their grade records or acquaintance network than with the cultivation of intellect. These authors recommend that teachers do more to encourage students who are intellectually motivated. "The main thing is to get such students together so that they can stimulate and support one another's often precarious commitments, and to provide direct and personal encouragements and rewards for such commitments by similarly committed faculty members" (1961:63).

David French indicates that the demands of student culture foster aims which are antithetical to those of the teacher. He urges that the anthropology teacher conduct himself in a manner that will induce students to act like anthropologists rather than grade seekers. In many schools the anthropologist must also avoid being drawn too tightly into the purely local concerns of some of his faculty peers; with them also he must insist on his role as anthropologist in addition to his role as member of the local academic community.

The role of teacher of anthropology, as Wagley and other authors assert, demands that the teacher be an active research anthropologist, and he therefore must have time and opportunity for field work. This raises the common issue in academic circles of the relation between teaching and research. The crucial nexus between them is important for our whole society, as is shown in a widely known report from a panel of the President's Science Advisory Committee. This report emphasizes that ". . . *basic research and scientific education* go together" (Seaborg *et al*. 1960:1807). They do, but we must also recognize that undergraduate teaching generally requires a different kind of effort than does research or the training of advanced students. This has been pointed out in a leading article by the editor of *Science,* in which he notes that a university faculty member typically teaches undergraduates, does research and supervises graduate students.

These tasks demand quite different talents. To arouse interest, to lay bare the bones of a subject without too much qualification, in short to make an art of teaching, are the requirements of one task; to carry on research, to teach by example, and to give general guidance to students already well immersed in the subject are the requirements of the other. (DuShane 1961).

Because it is not always feasible to carry on both tasks simultaneously, a teacher of anthropology should periodically be able to reserve an ample block of his time for the research experience which is not only in itself a vital enterprise but which will enliven his teaching.

Certainly some superb teachers, even in anthropology, are not research workers, and some eminent research men are not good teachers at all. But it is also certain that anthropological field research and writing usually give a quality of verve, of constantly renewed freshness, of cogency to an anthropologist's teaching as nothing else can do. Margaret Mead writes below that acceptable teaching can be done by one whose own teacher has been a field worker, but that good teaching cannot survive more than one generation without the renewal of vigor through field research. But every teacher of anthropology should have some cross-cultural training and experience. From Lasker and Nelson's paper we learn that of the 56 junior college teachers covered in their survey (who taught about one third of all students enrolled in anthropology courses), only ten had either a Ph.D. or M.A. in anthropology. A good many had been assigned to teach the subject, under the lamentable practice of treating teachers like interchangeable parts of a machine, with little or no previous study of the subject.

METHODS

All teaching, Raymond Firth remarks, is a mode of personal communication. In anthropology, the teacher's personal field experience is an important element of that communication, because through discussing it the teacher can trenchantly convey the essential features of an anthropologist's approach. (He can also convey utter boredom if tales of his favorite people saturate the course.) Because anthropologists often use their own field experience and research interests in their courses, there has been little stereotyped, textbook teaching of the kind which is a problem in some other fields. Yet there are certain choices of teaching method which a teacher must make, deliberately or unwittingly, in outlining a course. There are able teachers who use methods which are quite unsuitable for others; each anthropologist should make the choices which best fit his capacities and the purposes of a course. It is well to know what choices there are and why certain methods have been recommended above others.

One choice is between breadth and depth. It is not usually presented quite so starkly, but a teacher of a beginning course, for example, must decide whether to introduce the students to every major phase of anthropology, to give them a passing acquaintance with many topics, or to concentrate on more thorough discussion of a few. This issue is most specifically examined in the papers by Pike and by Lounsbury. My own views on the drawbacks of superficial, if broad, coverage have already been mentioned and in my paper on curriculum design I suggest that it is well to establish a general and coherent frame of ideas first, then to analyze selected case examples in some detail, and finally to return to an overview of the subject.[3]

One of the more elusive teaching virtues is to know what to omit and to omit it. Anthropology teachers have been known to stand amazed at students' ignorance of, say, geography, or statistics, or art. But if we cannot do justice to all of one field in a course or a curriculum, still less can we add coverage of other fields. It is more important that we teach about gene flow than where the Ganges flows, about stimulus diffusion rather than about standard deviation, about social structure than about the Sistine Chapel. One exception, if it is that, is that at every level we should try to make it possible for the students to write and to have their writing carefully read not only for anthropological content but also for clarity and cogency of expression. And while anthropologists should not try to teach elementary lessons in other fields, they should utilize the multiple relations of anthropology with other disciplines. Casagrande, Leslie, Livingstone and Spuhler show how significant these relations are both for our teaching and for that in the other disciplines. Benjamin Paul demonstrates the basic contribution which anthropologists can make in a public health curriculum, as Hoebel and Rossow do for law and foreign service training, and as Kimball does for professional training in education.[4]

As for the choice between emphasis on concepts or on facts, the prevailing preference in these essays is to build a course around concepts and to bring in those facts which are needed to demonstrate the concepts. Perhaps priority is given to the teaching of concepts because it is more difficult to do so effectively than it is to set forth a body of factual data. However, neither should be slighted. Thus in discussing graduate seminars Beattie comments, ". . . the point needs to be made that anthropological theory without any kind of real content is as barren—perhaps more barren than—bare ethnographic information devoid of any kind of systematic (i.e., theoretical) organization; evidently both must be combined." A model for such combination in regional courses is suggested by Vogt.

Ideas can be highlighted against the history of ideas; the case for teaching the history of anthropological concepts is given by Du Bois and Hymes. But Fortes points out that some creative anthropologists have known very little about the antecedents of their operational concepts, and Washburn remarks that the student should not spend his time on controversies and typologies which have no present reality. Perhaps the main point to be made here, as it is in the paper on curriculum design, is that the history of anthropology, at whatever length or level given, should be more than a catalogue of great men and an index of erroneous theories; it should relate the place and effect of anthropological ideas in the development of science and scholarship.

Another question of teaching method raised in several of the essays is this. Should the anthropology teacher steer his course within what is well known and generally agreed upon or should he also venture in directions where lie the interesting unsolved problems and unknown dimensions? Those who raise the issue are unanimous in their choice. Woodbury recommends that anthropology be taught with awareness of gaps in our knowledge and of the excitement of new findings. Ehrich writes that we must point out controversy, unresolved questions, and the vast lacunae in our data and our thinking. Doing so, he adds, may mitigate some of the intellectual harm done by more cut and dried teaching practices.

As between lecturing and conducting discussions, the important choice is not whether to use the one or the other but when and how to utilize each in combination with the other. Each is suitable for certain purposes and circumstances: one can hardly carry on a protracted discussion in a class of several hundred, but some discussion can be useful even there. Conversely, it is bootless to address from the lectern three advanced students gathered in seminar, yet a formal exposition may occasionally be necessary before them also.

Since there is little prospect for a general decrease in size of classes, the lecture will necessarily be the major vehicle of undergraduate teaching. A lecture can be a powerful instrument; it can—as was said of a lecture by Sartre—plough up the minds of the listeners as a tractor ploughs up a field. But Sartre did not attempt to sustain that effect through the American semester pattern of three lectures a week for fifteen weeks. In such an assignment, even the most stirring lecturer must do a good bit of routine harrowing. One sociologist considers this long series of teacher lecturing and student listening to be one of the great sources of waste—together with the examination system and the departmental system—in American higher education (Glazer 1961: 147-148).

Fred Eggan mentions that an anthropologist's first teaching assignment is frequently a traumatic experience because he has had so little preparation for it. A very little preparation can help a good deal. There are a number of useful publications on college teaching (e.g., Buxton 1956; for a bibliography see Eckert 1959).

There is a booklet written mainly by an historian at Cambridge University which gives simple and useful directives in a simple and useful way. Thus, "It is a good thing to take your class into your confidence and tell them how you intend to arrange your course. Above all they want to know clearly what you are after." (Clark and Clark 1959: 14-15). Some quite elementary techniques of good lecturing may not be known to a teacher. I had been lecturing before large undergraduate classes for a good many years before I learned how very useful it is for the students to have a brief outline of the topics to be discussed written on the blackboard at the start of each lecture. A well known American writer told me that he had recently stumbled upon a good teaching device for large classes. He found that if he asked for questions two or three times during a lecture period, this gave a good change of pace and since many of the questions were about matters he was going to discuss anyway, it provided a better way of talking about them than did straight lecturing.

For large lecture classes, the use of audio-visual aids can be particularly helpful, but as Birdwhistell and Baerreis emphasize, this use must be carefully planned. Hewes writes that a technological revolution in teaching aids is in the offing: in anthropology there has as yet been little development of the technical means which are already available. Thus there are many movies with anthropological content, very few of which have been specifically designed for the teaching of undergraduates. Anthropology museums have long contributed to anthropological teaching, but only a small fraction of undergraduates taking courses in anthropology are able to benefit from museum facilities.

Still, we are not utterly without technical resources. Daryll Forde remarked in a symposium discussion that the book is the finest visual aid for teaching. Rowe's paper discusses the building of library collections. Further, an anthropologist has the advantage of being able to bring a material object into the classroom and discuss it as an example of congealed culture. Firth mentions using a Trobriand arm-shell or a Polynesian composite fish-hook to show the complex social relationships involved in its manufacture, use, and display.

Discussion sections, teaching assistants to lead them, and special sections for specially motivated students are noted in my paper on curriculum design. It takes skill and planning to lead a small group of students in a useful discussion. Graduate students need preparation and supervision if they are to make effective discussion leaders. A discussion section under the charge of a bumbling teaching assistant can be just as vapid and pointless as the dullest lecture.

A teaching procedure enthusiastically recommended in every field of anthropology is that of setting problems and exercises in which a student can organize his own observations and share in the excitement of scientific discovery. Lasker and Hulse suggest how this can be done in laboratory work in physical anthropology, as Jennings does for archaeological anthropology and Olmsted for linguistic anthropology. For students in introductory cultural anthropology, I discuss below the use of field assignments.

One main aspect of anthropological teaching remains a neglected and (to some) vexatious problem. It is the problem of examinations. Ehrich and Rapoport comment, and teachers in all disciplines agree, that an examination should be a learning experience and not a stimulus for regurgitation. By reason of the structure of academic institutions, a student cannot but focus his academic concerns on his grades, whether he is trying for a fellowship or for a gentleman's C. His grades depend largely on his success in examinations; what he must derive from the course is the ability to pass the examinations. For large parts of anthropology, the so-called "objective" examination cannot accurately reflect the purpose of the teaching, but when used it fixes the student's orientation to the course. Multiple-choice and true-false questions, if carefully constructed, can test some phases of the teaching, but much is beyond the capacity of such examining formulae.

The obvious solution is to base the final grade more on written work, done in response to essay questions, to laboratory problems and field assignments. Term papers, as conventionally conceived, are too often done in so listless a manner as to have little worth. The obvious difficulty is that of securing competent readers to help the teacher. I suggest in the paper on curriculum design that this difficulty can be mastered in most schools, and when students do more writing in anthropology courses and have their work carefully reviewed, the lasting effectiveness of the teaching will be greatly enhanced. This is no new suggestion either for anthropology or for any of the other social sciences and humanities. It may be that anthropologists, invigorated by the record and promise of their discipline, well regarded and encouraged in various quarters, can be among the leaders in setting new standards for higher education in the United States.

PROSPECTS

The contribution which anthropology will make to higher education depends considerably on the kind of recruitment and training done by graduate departments. On the subject of graduate training, as symposium discussions showed, anthropologists generally believe that there is much need for improvement. The shortcomings which Bernard Berelson found in his survey of graduate education in the United States pertain also to anthropology, and his recommendations are relevant (1960:233-260). Establishment of a firm four-year doctoral program, tightening the program, shortening the dissertation, are the first three of his nineteen recommendations. All are applicable and feasible for anthropology. Adopting them should help toward increased recruitment of able students for graduate work in anthropology. Ralph Beals' paper indicates the nature of the recruitment problem. It is part of the general problem of recruitment within the social sciences and humanities: the need for talented people is greatest in these areas, but the talent tends to be drawn into the other academic and professional fields.

Yet students have not in the past and will not in the future decide to become anthropologists mainly on the basis of the cost and conditions of graduate training. The powerful attaction is in the image of a worthy career, and that image is usually projected through undergraduate teaching. And while these essays point out many parts of that teaching which need better development, they also show that future development will be built on the firm foundation that anthropology now possesses.

NOTES

[1] Cf. A. J. Toynbee in Vol. XII of *A Study of History*. "Anthropological method is indeed a key that promises to unlock doors when it is applied to the study of civilizations. . . . From now onwards I shall pick this tool up and try it myself. 'Better late than never'" (1961, 601-602).

[2] For discussion of student differences in the United States by type of school see McConnell 1959. At the Burg Wartenstein symposium (briefly reported in Mandelbaum 1961) several discussants referred to significant differences in student approaches to anthropology; V. L. Grottanelli told of the differences between teaching anthropology to seminarians and to university students in Italy; S. C. Dube sketched the expectations for anthropology in India; Monica Wilson told of teaching about race in South Africa.

[3] This suggestion is also made in Mandelbaum 1940 in relation to the radio broadcasting of an introductory course in anthropology.

[4] In the ERA project we have not attempted to deal with the contributions of anthropological studies to the understanding of educational processes. On this subject see Spindler 1955, Rosensteil 1954, Brameld 1957, Brameld and Sullivan 1961, Ashley Montagu 1958.

REFERENCES CITED

BERELSON, BERNARD
    1960   Graduate education in the United States. New York, McGraw-Hill Book Company.

BUXTON, CLAUDE E.
    1956   College teaching, a psychologist's view. New York, Harcourt Brace and Company.

BRAMELD, THEODORE
    1957   Cultural foundations of education, an interdisciplinary exploration. New York, Harper and Brothers.

BRAMELD, THEODORE, AND E. B. SULLIVAN
    1961   Anthropology and education. Review of Educational Research. 31:70-79.

CLARK, B. R., AND MARTIN TROW
    1961   Determinants of college student subculture. Mimeographed. To apppear in The study of college peer groups. T. M. Newcomb and E. K. Wilson, editors. New York, Social Science Research Council.

CLARK, G. K., AND E. B. CLARK
    1959   The art of lecturing, some practical suggestions. Cambridge, W. Heffer and Sons.

DE LAGUNA, FREDERICA, EDITOR
    1960   Selected papers from the American Anthropologist 1888-1920. Evanston, Illinois, Row, Peterson and Company.

DUSHANE, GRAHAM
    1961   The system. Science 134:159.

ECKERT, RUTH E.
    1959   Study guide; effective college teaching. Minneapolis, Department of Education, University of Minnesota. Fourth Revised Edition.

GLAZER, NATHAN
    1961   The wasted classroom. Harper's Magazine 223:147-153.

HOEBEL E. A.
  1958   Anthropology, universities, and American society. American Anthropologist 60:633-639.
LAZARSFELD, P. F., AND W. THIELENS, JR.
  1958   The academic mind. Glencoe, Illinois, The Free Press.
LÉVI-STRAUSS, CLAUDE
  1954   The place of anthropology in the social sciences and the problems raised in teaching it. *In* The university teaching of social sciences, sociology, social psychology, and anthropology, pp. 96-124. Paris, UNESCO.
MCCONNELL, T. R.
  1959   A look at the total education scene. *In* The changing university. G. H. Daigneault, ed. Chicago, The Center for the Study of Liberal Education for Adults.
MANDELBAUM, D. G.
  1940   Basic concepts in anthropology. *In* Essays in anthropology presented to Rai Bahadur Sarat Chandra Roy. D. N. Majumdar and others, editors. Lucknow, Maxwell Company.
  1961   International symposium on the teaching of anthropology. Current Anthropology 2:508-509.
MONTAGU, ASHLEY
  1958   Education and human relations. New York, Grove Press.
MORRILL, J. L., AND OTHERS
  1961   The university and world affairs. New York, The Ford Foundation.
OPLER, M. E.
  1947   Cultural alternatives and educational theory. Harvard Educational Review 17:28-44.
ROBERTS, D. F., AND J. S. WEINER, EDITORS
  1958   The scope of physical anthropology and its place in academic studies. New York, The Wenner-Gren Foundation for Anthropological Research.
ROSENSTIEL, ANNETTE
  1954   Educational anthropology: a new approach to cultural analysis. Harvard Educational Review 24:28-36.
SEABORG, G. T., AND OTHERS
  1960   Scientific progress and the federal government. Science 132:1802-1815.
SPINDLER, G. D., EDITOR
  1954   Education and anthropology. Stanford, Stanford University Press.
TOYNBEE, A. J.
  1961   A study of history, Volume XII, Reconsiderations. London, Oxford University Press.
WHITEFORD, A. H., EDITOR
  1960   Teaching anthropology. Logan Museum Publications in Anthropology No. 8. Beloit, Wisconsin, Beloit College.

PART I

THE
UNDERGRADUATE
CURRICULUM
IN
ANTHROPOLOGY

Introduction

THE THREE PAPERS of this section look at the undergraduate curriculum as a whole. They were originally prepared for the general conference held in Berkeley and were there discussed as related approaches to the same basic problems. These problems, as Fred Eggan noted in opening the conference discussion, are: (1) to provide for the needs of students with different purposes in studying anthropology and (2) to have a curriculum which is maximally developmental and minimally repetitive. All three authors of the papers of this section on the undergraduate curriculum are more concerned with propounding objectives and themes than with reviewing current practice.

Cora Du Bois begins by sorting out the principal levels of a curriculum and then turns to the central issues which should be treated at all levels. Generic culture and specific cultures, comparisons and universals, lead the list. Presented next are a series of ideas and positions which come from viewing culture as an anthropologist does. One such idea is that of cultural relativism, taken in the sense of placing Western thought and culture within the whole of the human scene rather than above or apart from it. Another principal idea is that of understanding the work of anthropologists as "brokers of tradition," summarizing the past in the historical mode, opening the future in the scientific. Entailed in the anthropologist's perspective are certain attitudes and ethics which should be conveyed, we are reminded, throughout the teaching of anthropology, to every kind of student.

In Washburn's paper, the main concern is with the prime purpose and central theme of physical anthropology. Washburn is confident that once the newer concepts of evolution are integrated into physical anthropology as the core of the subject, increased collaboration between physical anthropologists and other anthropologists will be possible. This will apply both in teaching and research, and a more efficient curriculum in physical anthropology can then be developed.

The design for a curriculum which I have outlined can accommodate both Washburn's central concerns and Du Bois' central issues, although the possible interchange between the two main divisions of anthropology is given only passing mention in these papers. One comment made during the conference discussion was that the suggested curriculum design resembles some of the current graduate programs, and the question was raised as to whether it was suitable for undergraduates. The answer suggested in the paper is that we should now raise the general level of our undergraduate teaching. In so doing, we would enhance its value as liberal education, without inserting into the undergraduate curriculum that acquisition of technical skill and professional knowledge which properly comes at the graduate level. If anthropology is to make its full contribution to undergraduate education, teachers of anthropology must plan their courses and curricula so as to encourage students to extend themselves to their full intellectual reach.

                                                                    D.G.M.

CORA DU BOIS

The Curriculum
in Cultural
Anthropology

NOTHING SAID in this paper can be considered original or avant-garde. It is clearly not its function to debate possible break-throughs in anthropological theory but rather to propose the kinds of concepts that should appear in an integrated and balanced curriculum.

I have assumed that a university and a department of anthropology are adequately staffed for such purposes. Practical considerations of administration, pedagogy, and course designs are not at issue. Rather the primary considerations are the salient ideas and their interconnections in cultural and social anthropology, archaeology, and linguistics as well as their relationship to physical anthropology. All this is to be in the context of an ideal program for undergraduate majors.

LEVELS OF A CURRICULUM

There is a wide agreement that an undergraduate curriculum may be divided into three levels. Professor Mandelbaum's paper sketches such a curriculum in some detail. What follows is a somewhat different and more generalized formulation.

Introductory Level

An introduction to anthropology at the college level is usually in one of two contexts, either as a session of a few weeks in a general introductory course to the social sciences or as a full year's introduction to a major. Whether anthropology is introduced in one or the other context, two types of material seem essential, the historic and the ethnographic.

Whether three weeks or a year's work is involved, it seems fairly clear that human paleontology and prehistory are requisite to provide students with both a sense of human history and the concepts of human evolution and culture. Similarly, whether the schedule is three weeks' or a year's work, ethnographic descriptions are requisite to provide students with both a sense of relativism and comparison and with the concepts of holism, structure, and functionalism. Human history and human variation, in whatever depth and detail, are the *sine qua non* of an introduction to anthropology. Without necessarily shocking, ideas should be presented to challenge and enlarge the ethnocentric world that the undergraduate usually brings to an introduction to anthropology.

One may argue whether in the short or long introductory courses readings should be synoptic or monographic. My predilection is for a synoptic coverage of the historic and a monographic coverage of the ethnographic. However, each instructor obviously must select readings as he sees fit.

Intermediate Level

At the second or intermediate level continuity in curriculum building requires that the interest presumably raised in introductory courses should be broadened and deepened. For undergraduates the widest offering of courses will be clearly at this level. They would presumably be directed to incipient majors in anthropology and to students already committed to fields whose subject matter or central problems impinge on those of anthropology. Faculty resources will obviously determine specific offerings. If the faculty is inclined to give introductory topical courses in physical anthropology, language, archaeology, ethnographic regions, and social organization, then a course on the history of anthropology seems essential to provide balance and scope. If, on the other hand, the faculty tends to stress conceptual and problem areas, such as the comparative approach and relativism, personality and culture, value orientations, primitive religion and culture change, then majors should be required to balance such heady offerings with limited regional or area offerings, presented in terms of social, linguistic, ecologic, and historic components.

Advanced Level

At the third or advanced level, in which both advanced or gifted undergraduate majors as well as graduate students would participate, the course work—whether pursued as lecture courses, seminars, or individual and group reading courses—should range from narrowly regional training (including languages when relevant) to specific problems that preoccupy faculty specialists. At the third level, what seems to me of major importance is intensity, rather than broad coverage. It is at this stage only that technical questions need be stressed. I refer to such questions as the various rating techniques in archaeology, lexicography or glotto-chronology in linguistics, the intricacies of kinship analysis in social organization, or the administration and evaluation of projective tests in personality studies.

Rationale

In sum, just as I believe that the best anthropologists are those who are intensely interested in their work but who have oscillated in the course of their careers between preoccupations that are specializing and generalizing, so by analogy I would suggest a sequence in the undergraduate curriculum that runs from interest aroused (first level), to a balanced generalized survey of conceptual considerations (second level), to specific questions of exploration (third level). Nevertheless and ideally every course is presumed to be equally concerned with requiring a considerable body of data and with providing a framework of concepts, problems, or theories around which data can be meaningfully assembled.

It seems to me that the professional and pedagogic rationale for such an integration of the undergraduate major program needs little explanation. It moves from the general to the specific *as a curriculum,* but not necessarily in terms of specific course lectures and readings. It should provide those who wish to go on to professional anthropology with a background quite adequate for a reversal of direction at the fourth (graduate) level—namely, moving from a well-informed selection of special interests, once more toward a general comprehension of anthropology at the level of predoctoral examinations. The young professional then once more moves to the fifth and specialized level required in a Ph.D. thesis.

An undergraduate curriculum so structured should provide appropriate offerings for undergraduates who want only to sample as they run; for those who want to test the peripheries of their own major concentration; and, finally, for those who wish to waste as little time as possible in becoming productive professionals.

CENTRAL ISSUES

The following topics are not necessarily listed in terms of a pedagogical sequence but rather in terms of an order of salience.

The Concept of Culture

There is wide agreement among at least American anthropologists that culture is a core concept of our discipline. It is also a term that will come all too readily to the tongue of most young students. Yet, ever since Kroeber and Kluckhohn published their review of that concept, our profession must have been much chastened and also, hopefully, stimulated to re-examine the central idea. Leslie White's formulation of culturology as a separate field of anthropology bears on this issue and certainly should not be neglected in curriculum building at either the elementary or advanced levels.

Whatever our theoretical position, we should present fully and fairly the range of views that cluster around the term "culture." We should not sidestep all the ambiguities of that concept, whether we view it as a descriptive generalization, an analytic tool or a terminal definition. A semester's course at the intermediate or advanced level devoted exclusively to a scrutiny of this central concept of our discipline would seem appropriate.

If we are to help our students achieve any clarity we must very early in the introductory course distinguish for pedagogic purposes between generic culture (culture with a capital C) and specific cultures (cultures with a small c). Similarly early and for the sake of clarity, we should insist that there are analytic distinctions to be made between the psychic, the social and the symbolic usages inherent in the term "culture." These seem to be minimal and preliminary distinctions necessary as a basis for subsequent courses and as a rationale for our broadly ranging interests.

Generic Culture

Once we have established the simplest distinction between culture as generic and specific cultures we are prepared to put into proper perspective biologic and cultural evolution as well as historical ethnology. This may also be the appropriate place to distinguish between diachronic and synchronic approaches to problems and the kinds of answers each approach provides.

Speaking diachronically, no training in anthropology is profitably undertaken without an early and thorough introduction to human biological and cultural evolution. Here the human paleontologist, the prehistorian and the great philosophers of history cannot be ignored. How do the "models" of cultural evolution compare to those proposed by men like Spengler, Toynbee, or Kroeber—to name only a few proponents of non-evolutionary models of regularity in socio-cultural change at the generic level of cultural analysis?

Fortunately, ideas of this type that should be presented early in a curriculum are also vastly interesting to young minds.

Specific Cultures

In the discussion of specific cultures questions of holism, the comparative approach, relativism and the similarities and differences in human behavior become salient considerations.

In dealing with specific cultures we are in the domain of ethnography. Good ethnographies remain a basic resource of cultural anthropology, just as a good linguistic description remains the core of linguistics, or a good archaeological site report is fundamental to that specialty. Monographic reports are not only basic but markedly effective in communicating the intent of the discipline to undergraduate students. They are essential in giving them a grasp of the world and the range of human behavior. Ethnographies can be studied not only for their substantive content but also for changing fashions in what has been considered significant in successive generations of observers. We cannot drill our students too thoroughly or too early in the rich resources of basic field reports.

However rich such resources are, we are well aware of the issues involved in studying separate population aggregates. They raise questions we cannot dodge and with which students should be presented. Those questions should be integral to, and explicit in, any regional or topical course in cultural anthropology. Regional courses at the second level, taught with an eye to the basic assumptions underlying the nature of our descriptions and the problems raised by such entities, are ideal vehicles for presenting the issues involved here. Let me suggest a few of them.

What is the theoretic validity of describing a population aggregate as if it were an entity? Can studies be made of communities that represent part-cultures, or little traditions, in a wider context of high cultures or great traditions? What is the validity of our traditional ethnographic approach to tribes and communities? Why are we so concerned with integration and equilibrium models (whether static or oscillatory)?

What validity is there in the structural categories we commonly employ (e.g., family and kinship with its various sub-categories; religion; livelihood; socialization)? What does "function" mean? How far have we, as ethnographers, preoccupied with structural-functional and equilibrium models, faced clearly and explicitly the significance of the psychic and symbolic dimensions of the peoples we describe? Are we really attempting to understand, in specific ethnographic studies, human behavior in all of its intricacies? Or have we been content to describe, as best we could, a series of indigenous social institutions and symbolic formulations? Do we go beyond the description of the unique in an effort to extract concepts that permit comparisons between ethnographies, languages, or archaeological sites, in a search for human universals and for processes in culture change? Obviously, I have loaded this rhetorical question. It leads nicely to my next point, the comparative approach. But before going on to that issue, I wish to repeat that we cannot better teach undergraduate students than to present them with traditional field reports but to ask them at the same time to be alert to the often inexplicit assumptions underlying them.

Comparisons and Universals

Ethnographers, at their best, see the world from inside the persons being observed. Theirs are exercises in empathy and in translation. Ethnology moves from inside such worlds to the position of a presumably objective outsider. Ethnology searches for generalizations. Comparisons are its preeminent approach. When we compare phenomena it is either because we are searching for variations on a theme in order to describe historical affinities or processes of change; or because we are concerned with what is common as opposed to what is rare in human behavior; or because we are concerned with discovering underlying universals of human nature. Teachers concerned with human biology, with personality and culture, with language, with social structure or with symbolization—whether in religion, art, ethno-science or value-orientations— must face squarely the issue of comparisons. These are subjects that can profitably be presented to students in the context of the comparative approach, which may range from perceptive insights to rigorous methodologies.

An extremely useful course at the third level would systematically examine the ways we have approached the question of comparisons, beginning perhaps with Tylor's classic article on the patolli game, through the controlled comparisons of the social structuralist, in Africa and the Southwest, the trait analyses of Kroeber, Driver, *et al.,* the statistical approaches of Murdock and his colleagues associated with the Human Relations Area Files, and the experiments with the newer qualitative mathematics. A careful treatment of the comparative approach may either lead into, or follow on, specialized courses in which instructors may wish to underline not only human, social, and cultural generalities, but also the unique patternings and emphases of particular socio-cultural groups.

Relativism and Western Science

If we consider the implications of our ethnographic community studies, of holism and various equilibrium and integrational ideas on the one hand and of systematic cross-cultural comparisons on the other, we appear to be caught in a dilemma. That dilemma is usually subsumed under the term relativism. It is too complex to be analyzed here, and I shall attend only to one of its features.

The importance of understanding how different peoples perceive external reality or selectively value only portions of the total potentials of human behavior and perception is beyond dispute. One of the chief virtues of this study is that it throws into relief the character of our own tradition of scientific perceptions and analyses. It helps us to see, if not to resolve, the problems of our Western materialistic and rationalistic science, and it enables us to distinguish more sharply between those Western formulations which we call science and the formulations of the peoples we study.

Clearly, no undergraduate major in anthropology *must* include a course on the philosophy of science viewed comparatively. I doubt if there are many of us capable of giving such a course. However, many different courses can raise the question of the degree to which our Western scientific treatment of socio-cultural data is itself a patterned and partial phenomenon. In this context and in the context of values, of modal personality and in a host of other areas of human behavior, relativism points not only to the need for close studies of variations in order to establish the range of potential human behavior, it also stresses the need for refined comparative work and careful conceptualization. And in all this, the prime importance of relativism in the perspective of the undergraduate student is that it places Western thought within rather than above the rest of the human scene. Second and third level courses in human ecology, ethno-science, personality and culture, and comparative economics, for instance, can approach the questions raised by relativism at whatever level of sophistication the students (or instructors) are capable of meeting.

Anthropology: History or Science

Whether the distinction between history and science is a valid one has been repeatedly debated within our profession as well as within the context of other disciplines. In one sense we can consider anthropologists as brokers of tradition, scholars who are concerned both with chronology and theory. Our problem is to summarize the past and yet open up the future. Somewhere in an undergraduate curriculum this distinction between history and science, whether real or false, should be discussed. At an introductory level it may suffice simply to raise the issue and to point out that valuable work has been done from a purely historical viewpoint and that synchronic and diachronic studies are both acceptable and valid approaches to varying types of inquiry.

At the upper division level the whole question which leads into a philosophy of science and a theory of the nature of historiography, can and probably should be in the curriculum, not perhaps as a separate course offering but in conjunction with a number of course offerings. For example, is archaeology essentially devoted to historical reconstruction or does it give us necessary keys to cultural evolution? There are practitioners who profess with fervor each of these positions. Does calling cultural development "evolution" mean it is more scientific and therefore less historical? Does reluctance to generalize in archaeology make that field more scientific or more historical? Courses in New World or Old World archaeology, whose material seems to have much inherent fascination for most students, are excellent vehicles for raising such broad theoretical questions.

In linguistics, is historical linguistics less scientific than the descriptive branch? And to what extent can historical linguistics be considered valid if it is not based on descriptive linguistics? Are the elegantly patterned formulations of descriptive linguistics more scientific than quantified historical linguistics? It has always seemed to me that an introductory course in language should include questions of historical linguistics, of the lexico-statistical and of the psychological aspects of language. Otherwise, it fails to do justice to the rich resources of this most sophisticated branch of research in the field of human symbolizing.

Turning to social anthropology, is it one of the "social" sciences or does it belong to disciplines called "behavioral"? If we consider ourselves social scientists, have we given sufficient attention to demographic, ecologic, and economic factors? If ours is classified as a behavioral science, do we really treat human behavior as our raw data? And if so, are we stretching the point mightily when we include the world of cognitive content and values in our treatment of behavior?

Whether or not we profess to be social or behavioral scientists, should we reject or ignore the rich historical and conceptual heritage that we have from the diffusionists: for example, culture areas, complexes, cores, and climaxes; parallelism and independent invention; age-area and survivals; necessary and accidental adhesions, selective borrowing and patterning? I would hope not, for in such ideas lie many insights into the directional changes in man's history, into the processes of adaptation and change, and into man's psychic potential.

History of Anthropology

In the preceding sections the questions have been posed concerning relativism and comparisons, the nature of western science and anthropology as history or science. It is clear that we are not in a position to give definitive answers on these scores. Possibly one of the most effective ways of exploring such indeterminate questions is a working knowledge of the history of anthropology as a discipline. Were anthropology a simple and rigorous science in which a steady accumulation of theory and data proved or disproved earlier formulations, we could disregard the history of anthropology at the undergraduate level and forget anything published more than ten or fifteen years ago. Patently, this is not the case, though I have heard at least one promising young professional argue just this. In thirty years of observing our discipline, I have been puzzled by the way legitimate problems go out of fashion, not because they are resolved but simply because of what might be called the quest for generational autonomy. By the third professional generation, old questions are raised once more, but with no awareness that they had earlier and valuable formulations. One cannot escape the impression that we are producing a group of young professionals who are uneducated in the history of their discipline. One way of dealing with this problem is to see that both undergraduate major and graduate students are grounded in the history of anthropology.

ATTITUDES AND ETHICS

An examination of curriculum continuity does not of necessity involve discussion of attitudes to be fostered in students or of ethics to be maintained by instructors. Yet one of the most frequent and heartfelt expressions by fellow-professionals who appraise our discipline is that "anthropology is a way of life." It is clear that the inculcation of certain attitudes in students is an important professional preoccupation. Briefly summarized, the viewpoints that professional anthropologists hope for in their students are empathy, curiosity and objectivity. These are indubitably admirable virtues even though they are not the exclusive possession of our disipline. If only about one per cent of the students who enroll in undergraduate anthropology courses go on to major in the field, we had best see that efforts to cultivate these virtues are part and parcel of all introductory courses. I should like to suggest an additional quality as a *sine qua non* of our profession. I hestitate to label it a virtue. Some may not prize it. I refer to a tolerance for ambiguity. By this I mean a capacity to entertain uncertainty, to cope with paradox, to allow for the indeterminate. This is not a trait commonly found among the young, and as profesional training and aspirations develop, the tolerance for ambiguity may often diminish.

Empathy, curiosity, objectivity, and a tolerance for ambiguity are not always comfortable attitudes. Nor are they likely to be congenial to temperaments wedded to rigorous and elegant abstractions for whom rationalism, materialistic determinism and science are focal values. Rather, they are attitudes and virtues congenial to humanists. Nevertheless, we have professional colleagues whose aspirations are rigorously scientific. They often adorn the profession. They counteract the humanists' tendency to become somewhat untalented publicists.

I am less concerned here with the wholesome range of temperaments among colleagues than with what our undergraduate courses should communicate as a "way of life." Those who are adept in such matters should stress the human aspects of our profession, present our personal experiences of field work, or refer students to the all-too-scarce and sensitive published statements of cross-cultural experiences. Such material seem to me an essential part of the course on all of the three levels of the undergraduate curriculum. On the other hand, I have no conviction that *courses* on field methods are useful at any level of undergraduate training. This kind of learning is best experienced personally rather than read about. I am firmly convinced that undergraduates are often quite mature enough to begin field work in any branch of anthropology, given suitable supervision. I would wish to see such opportunities developed. Whether or not undergraduate majors go on into professional life, the experience of field work engenders better than any course the attitudes we profess, and it vivifies better than any amount of reading the importance of commanding data. For those who do not continue in anthropology, a summer or semester of field experience may ultimately be far more important than all the data, problems, concepts, theories, methods, or techniques we impart in classes. For those who may be uncertain about a professional future in anthropology, early field experience should be helpful in reaching a decision. For those who will go on to graduate work, undergraduate field experience should provide an accelerating factor in our much too long-drawn-out Ph.D. program.

In a discipline properly as wide-ranging as ours and properly still as unformulated, professionals will vary greatly in their specialties and theoretical convictions. Different instructors will make salient different kinds of problems. It is desirable that the students be presented with diverse views. But it seems to me highly improper for instructors in their contact with students to derogate the specialities and theoretical views of fellow anthropologists, unless they are prepared to consider in detail those specialties and views. To denigrate, without careful explanation, the work of colleagues, living or dead, is to set an example at variance with the attitudes that I am assuming we wish to cultivate in our students.

There is another and somewhat more general ethical principle that seems to me important in an instructional staff. It has to do with the handling of our own cultural materials in the context of cross-cultural materials. Certainly, no one can profess that we live in the best of all possible worlds. Objective appraisals of our culture should be freely expressed where they can be empathically perceived and objectively substantiated. For the young, detachment without attachment is at least vacuous, at most corrupting. On the other hand, to accept uncritically our own culture without the perspective afforded by sympathetic comprehension of other cultures is also short of professional standards. Attachment without detachment in the realm of ideas is at least stereotypic, at most authoritarian.

I raise these issues of classroom ethics because I believe they bear on the building and integration of a curriculum.

THETREACH OF ANTHROPOLOGY

ιy comments have been restricted to issues and ethics that can
dered central and traditional in American anthropology. They
minimal essentials of undergraduate training. But it is striking
ξree to which anthropologists have been receptive to the theories,
pts, methods, and techniques of other disciplines. On all these
ιores, eclecticism has been our weakness as well as our strength.

Aside from theoretical orientations already mentioned, such as cultural evolution and diffusionism, there are today many concepts useful, even essential, to analysis in anthropology, that are either deeply rooted in other disciplines or at least are shared by those disciplines. The undergraduate major should be made clearly aware of these areas of overlap. With no attempt to be exhaustive, but only in an effort to illustrate, several areas of overlap that might serve as adjunct courses for undergraduate majors are suggested below.

Sociology

Any undergraduate major has been poorly trained who does not command basic analytic or descriptive concepts that we, in conjunction with sociology, have developed. I refer to such ideas as: primary and secondary groups, institutions, status, and prestige; roles; authority and power, etc.

Personality Theories and Clinical Psychology

Socialization (enculturation) has for over three decades been a consistent concern in much of our descriptive as well as our theoretical work. Students who major in cultural anthropology might well be expected to have a preliminary grasp of the major theories of personality and learning on which our observations and hypotheses have been based. In this realm the instruments devised by clinical psychology should be given at least preliminary appraisal, e.g., projective tests, various kinds of questionnaires and interview grades, and systematic observation.

Languages

Language and linguistics are essential ingredients of course requirements for majors. But linguistics and the command of languages as working tools are quite different matters. One consistent difficulty in graduate departments has been with language requirements. There is a notable lack of tool languages among entering students. This question, of course, involves a wider curriculum consideration. For departments of anthropology, student acquisition of tool languages is chiefly a counsel-

ling question, since they must be learned elsewhere. The impo
of acquiring cross-cultural perspectives in the process of learning
languages is patent. Hence, within the university context, a departm
of anthropology has vested interests in this aspect of undergradua
training.

Undoubtedly such suggestions could be expanded considerably.
Courses in genetics, acquaintance with the experimental method, history of various world areas, comparative courses in the Great Religions
—these are just a few additional suggestions that the faculty of a department of anthropology may wish to consider as desirable adjunct
courses for majors in their field.

SHERWOOD L. WASHBURN

The Curriculum in Physical Anthropology

T HE PRINCIPAL PURPOSE of physical anthropology has been to give an understanding of human evolution. Originally, this purpose was expressed in the effort to determine "man's place in nature," but recently the emphasis has changed more and more from classification to the attempt to understand process. This changing emphasis and purpose is altering the nature of physical anthropology. Stressing process brings the constituent parts of anthropology together more closely than before. But attempts to understand the process of human evolution introduce techniques and vocabulary which are unfamiliar to most anthropologists. Theoretical progress is leading to a more functionally related general anthropology, but technical progress is leading to diversity of specialization. In considering the problems of teaching, this paper will attempt to show both the nature of the unity of anthropology which stems from evolutionary theory and the difficulties which arise from the multiplication of effective, important techniques. The first part will deal with evolutionary theory and the second part with technical advance.

EVOLUTION

The understanding of evolution is based on two quite different sorts of evidence, the *record* (fossils, comparative anatomy, and physiology) and *experiments* revealing the nature of the evolutionary process. In both zoology and anthropology emphasis was necessarily first on the record: to demonstrate that evolution had taken place and to discover the major stages in the history of life. In human evolution this emphasis is clearly shown in traditional books and courses. The topics covered were: the primates, fossil man, and race. The sort of questions asked were: Is man descended from an ape or from some more primitive form? How ancient is *Homo sapiens?* How should races be described? Obviously, these are important questions, and a consideration of the record will always be a part of the study of evolution. But the answers to the questions which naturally arise from a consideration of the record depend on theories of evolution as well as on fossils, anatomy, or blood groups. Progress comes both from the continuing discovery of the record and from theoretical advance. In anthropology the emphasis, in both teaching and research, has been on the record, and the difficulties have come from the theory. If students of the future are to avoid the errors of the past, they must start their physical anthropology with modern evolutionary theory.

My first recommendation is that the student of anthropology start his reading on human evolution with a book like *The Meaning of Evolution,* by G. G. Simpson (1949).[1] A whole book is essential, and I am convinced that a few pages or paragraphs here and there are totally inadequate to convey even a minimum understanding. In an elementary course, the student is far more likely to understand human evolution if *The Meaning of Evolution* is read as well as such books as *Mankind in the Making* (Howells 1959) or *The Evolution of Man* (Lasker 1961). The student of anthropology needs more descriptive information on man than can be found in the biology books but much more information on evolution than is contained in the anthropology texts. Many combinations of books are possible for different level courses. An elementary course might use those already mentioned or *The Theory of Evolution,* (Smith 1958) and *History of the Primates* (Clark 1959). A more advanced course might be built around *Introduction to Evolution* (Moody 1953) and *The Antecedents of Man* (Clark 1960). *The Major Features of Evolution* (Simpson 1953) and *An Introduction to Physical Anthropology* (Montagu 1960) offer an advanced pair. The teacher, or advanced student, will find *Primatologia* (Hofer, Schultz, and Stark 1956, Vol. I) and *Traité de Paléontologie* (Piveteau 1953, Vol. VII) invaluable on the record. In all these combinations, the basic principle is the same—the statement of the record of human evolution must be supplemented by a substantial, recent statement on biological evolution.

The reasons for stressing a balance between the description of the events of human evolution and an understanding of evolutionary theory will be made clear by some examples. But, before going to specific cases, a general statement on evolution is necessary. The theory of evolution took its modern form during the 1930's. The new formulations became available in *Evolution; the Modern Synthesis* (Huxley 1942) and *Genetics, Paleontology, and Evolution* (Jepsen, Mayr, and Simpson 1949). A whole series of important books and symposia have followed. To review them lies beyond the scope of this paper, but the contributions of Dobzhansky have been particularly influential in anthropology. The outcome of foment and controversy in the 1930's was a new statement of evolutionary principles. Since theory was based on paleontology, systematics, and genetics, it has been called the synthetic theory. Positively, the synthetic theory makes numerous statements about the nature of evolution, and, negatively, it shows that many evolutionary theories are wrong. Many of these now discarded notions have been of *major importance* in anthropological research. The last two decades have been a time when anthropologists needed to borrow conceptions and remove misunderstandings at a very rapid rate. Every major controversy about evolution in anthropology long antedates the synthetic theory, and, if teaching is not thoroughly revised, we may do no more than indoctrinate students with dead controversies and outmoded techniques.

The synthetic theory[2] states that evolution is caused by changes in the frequency of genes in populations. The unit of study is the Mendelian population. Survival is defined as reproductive success. Changes in gene frequencies are due to: mutation, migration, drift, and selection. The origin of variation is random (relative to use), and order and trend in the evolutionary process come from selection. Positively, this formulation stresses the history of adapting populations as the subject matter of evolution. Negatively, it removes vitalistic notions and the idea of inevitable trends and inheritance of acquired characteristics. Because these discarded notions have been major factors in anthropological theory, the majority of anthropological evolutionary controversies simply have no relation to evolution as interpreted by the synthetic theory. Some examples will be cited to show how pervasive these notions have been. The notion of inevitable trend, usually conceived as a trend from simple to complex, is deeply imbedded in physical anthropology and appears also in cultural anthropology. Such a notion finds no support in modern biology. Trends continue only so long as selection continues to favor one direction. At any moment in history when selection changes, the trend will change. The trend can only be understood in terms of the history of the group, and it is not something which inevitably moves a species along a predetermined course. Kroeber (1960) has remarked that evolution is history. The kind of monotypical evolution which Boas criticized many years ago on cultural grounds would find no support in the synthetic theory. The theory of evolution has really changed, and the interpretation of trends as due to continued selection, instead of orthogenesis, changes evolution from magic to history. Only a few years ago the belief was widespread that since trends were innate, even minor reversals in form were impossible. Practically every known primate was removed from the ancestry of man in this way. Just which groups are ancestral to man is debatable, but no longer can one simply appeal to the principle of irreversibility and remove practically every known fossil from consideration. The synthetic theory stresses selection and the adaptation resulting from selection. Again, only a few years ago attempts were made to understand evolution in terms of non-adaptative characters. This led to emphasizing minor traits, such as the details of the arrangement of bones, at the expense of trying to understand the animals and their way of life. Aside from the fact that most of the supposedly nonadaptative characters are adaptive, this whole trend of research distorted the facts of human evolution.

So far it has been stressed that synthetic theory is a great intellectual advance. It shows why a whole class of ideas (inevitable trend or orthogenesis, irreversibility, importance of nonadaptive characters) are wrong. But the synthetic theory does much more than remove mistaken notions. The statement that changes in gene frequencies in Mendelian populations are due to mutation, migration, drift, and selection sets evolutionary problems in a form in which culture is important. If tooth size, for example, were determined by an orthogenetic trend, then the evolution of teeth could be completely understood without reference to custom. But if custom, through the use of tools, changes the selection which controls tooth size, then the biological and cultural problems are connected, and one cannot be solved without the other. The rate of mutation is affected by radiation, which of late is culturally as well as cosmically determined. Genetic drift is the result of population size, which depends on cultural factors. Migration in man is determined almost entirely by culture. Selection is a single word covering the result of a vast number of biological and social problems, problems of economics, child care, social control, mating; of shelter, religion, and language. In human evolution the history of genetic systems is intimately linked to the history of social systems. This close linkage between the biological and the social in human evolution is essential, according to the synthetic theory. Human evolution cannot be understood without the reconstruction of both man and culture (see Spuhler *The Evolution of Man's Capacity for Culture* 1959).

The biology of race is a very simple matter. It is more complex in man than in other primates, because culture creates mobility and social complexity. But the elaborate classifications and principal complexities of race in the anthropological literature are the results of pregenetic typology. Race has always been of concern to anthropologists, and the synthetic theory brings simple ordering principles to this much-debated subject. The genes of individuals segregate and re-combine so that, over the generations, it is the frequencies of genes in a population which are characteristic, not the individual. Descriptions may apply to populations, groups of populations, or to the species composed of populations which exchange genes, but there is no way to divide an interbreeding population into types which represent ancestral strains. This point is made in *Genetics and the Races of Man* (Boyd 1950, 1958), and it cannot be stressed too strongly. The racial method by which individuals are sorted out of an interbreeding population according to a few criteria (long head, tall, blonde, etc.) is incompatible with genetic theory. Boyd is too mild in his criticism, for at least 75 per cent of the racial studies of the last sixty years were a complete waste of time. Hundreds of students were trained in complex procedures which are wrong. There is no place in the anthropological curriculum where correct biological information is more necessary than in the study of race.

In summary, the union of genetics, paleontology, and systematics has created a synthetic theory of evolution. The student of human evolution should understand this theory in its full implications first. Then he may see the evolution of man in proper perspective and avoid the errors and controversies of the past. There has been great progress both in the discovery of fossils and in the theory of evolution. The paired readings suggested earlier offer one way of bringing anthropology up to date and creating lively discussion.

Belief in orthogenesis, emphasis on non-adaptive characters, and the typological approach to race allowed the physical anthropologist to operate practically without regard to real history. The synthetic theory compels the student of evolution to consider adaptation, behavior, and the fossil record. In the case of man this means that his biological evolution cannot be understood without the aid of archaeology, ethnology, and linguistics.

PROBLEMS OF TECHNICAL PROGRESS

The first part of this paper has discussed the way modern evolutionary theory compels the student of human evolution to consider adaptation, that is, behavior and its structural base. This emphasis gives a unity to anthropology, because human adaptation is both biological and cultural. The interrelations of disease, culture, and a gene are illustrated by Livingstone (1958), and his paper may be taken as a model for much of the anthropology of the future. But at the moment when progress in theory and problem suggests a greater unity in parts of anthropology, technical progress is having the opposite effect. It used to be that the training of a physical anthropologist consisted in the acquisition of a few skills. These could easily be understood by other anthropologists, and many anthropologists received some technical training in biometry. But the interest in adaptation does not lend itself to technical limitation. Biometry is useful, but it must be supplemented by a large variety of biological techniques. The problems caused by the rapid advance of knowledge are common to many sciences, but they are especially severe in physical anthropology. Here is a specialty with very few practitioners which is involved in both biological and social science and the interrelations of the two. It used to be that physical anthropologists were characterized as a group both by an interest in human evolution and a common set of research skills. Now the central interest remains, but each year the skills become more and more diversified. I am convinced that the profession should welcome this development and should encourage every anthropologist to take substantial technical training in other fields, even at the undergraduate level. The aim should be to enrich the anthropological profession with diversified technical proficiency, not to train so broadly in anthropology that progress, technical efficiency, and interdisciplinary research are stifled.

The introductory course in physical anthropology might be a part of anyone's general education. It should outline the main problems and indicate the kinds of evidence and methods used in their solution. Technical difficulties are at a minimum here, but, as soon as the student progresses to the more advanced physical anthropology courses, the problems of specialization arise. As I see it, there is no longer one pattern of education for a physical anthropologist, but several more or less distinct models are open to the student whose interest has been aroused in the introductory course. These might be outlined as follows.

Introduction: Human evolution, primates, fossil man, race.
Advanced Courses: Continuation with emphasis on:

1. Evolution.
   Long-term evolution of the primates, paleontology, anatomy, zoology.
2. Primate behavior.
   Psychology, ecology, animal behavior.
3. Fossil man.
   Geology, archaeology.
4. Race.
   Genetics, statistics, biochemistry.

The four fields indicated are not courses but major areas of interest and technical speciality. A list of courses might be quite different, including more than one major topic or devoting several courses to a single topic. A topic such as growth might be treated as needed in each major area or put in a separate course. This is not an attempt to outline a department's courses, but to call attention to the fact that each of these areas has become intellectually and technically complex and has quite different relations with related sciences and other parts of anthropology. The four developments from the elementary course have merely been indicated, but the essential point is that each of these major anthropological interests is best pursued with the aid of substantial training in other fields. This is not a new idea, but I believe that the suggested amount is new. Also I think that it is new formally to recognize that physical anthropology has become so complicated that no one can master the whole field at a research level.

The question of the relation of physical anthropology with the rest of the field is often raised, and it may be thought that divisions and technical progress in physical anthropology might further complicate these relations. I believe that precisely the opposite is true and that technical progress will make the interrelations in the whole profession closer. The interrelations are not between physical anthropology and the rest of anthropology in any general sense, but, beyond the general relation made essential by the theory of evolution, there are a large number of specific problems of mutual interest. For example, the discovery of tools with the australopithecines (Leakey 1960) provided the information that all the difference between the brains of apes and men came after tool use and in response to culture (Washburn 1960). It appears that protoculture (Hallowell 1960) is as old as any physical feature which separates ape from man. In linguistics, glottochronology (Hymes 1960) offers an area of utility to physical anthropology, while increasing understanding of the *Speech and Brain-mechanisms* (Penfield and Roberts 1959) opens a field of importance to any who would understand human behavior. Anthropological studies of personality and culture have largely ignored biological factors, but the interplay of biological and social factors has long been recognized in psychiatry. Studies of stress have been put into an evolutionary perspective by Hamburg (1961 a,b). Population size, mating patterns, and basic adaptations are of importance in human genetics and social anthropology. Anyone who takes modern evolutionary theory seriously will find himself immersed in a mass of problems which cross the traditional bounds of the parts of anthropology and also link anthropology with other fields. The simplest way of stating the issue is that the more physical anthropology is concerned with problems of adaptation, the less it can be contained in its traditional boundaries.

Undergraduate training should open the student's eyes to the possibilities which the changing boundaries open. Technical progress has already opened the way to a vastly more significant physical anthropology, but our educational system lags far behind. No minor changes in the old courses will meet the challenge of today's opportunities. If anthropologists understand their own culture, this is the time to show it by forging educational patterns which take full advantage of an age of rapid technical advance.

SUMMARY

In the last twenty years a theory of evolution has emerged from a union of genetics, paleontology, and systematics. This intellectual synthesis clarifies and modifies evolutionary theory in important ways. The intellectual base of physical anthropology should be founded on this new evolutionary synthesis, and the student should not spend his time on controversies and typologies which have no present reality. Interest in behavior and adaptation and technical advance offer new possibilities, both for the understanding of human evolution and for the appraisal of the biological factors in human behavior.

It is important to evaluate our educational procedures at this time so that new models of education can be efficiently encouraged. But to provide training time for the new means the judicious elimination of the old. Anthropologists need to devise new intellectual institutions which, while preserving the core of the past, will encourage intellectual adaptation to the future.

NOTES

¹ There are comparable books which would adequately serve the same purposes. In this paper, references are mentioned only to make my meaning clear. This is not an attempt to make reading lists for other people's courses.

² No adequate description can be given in this brief space. Readers are referred to the books mentioned earlier.

REFERENCES CITED

BOYD, WILLIAM C.
    1958   Genetics and the races of man. Boston, D. C. Heath and Co.
CLARK, W. E. LE GROS
    1959   History of the primates. Chicago, University of Chicago Press.
    1960   The antecedents of man. Chicago, Quadrangle Books.
DOBZHANSKY, THEODOSIUS
    1962   Mankind evolving. New Haven, Yale University Press.
HALLOWELL, A. IRVING
    1960   Self, society, and culture in phylogenetic perspective. *In* The evolution of man, S. Tax, ed. Chicago, University of Chicago Press, Vol. II.

HAMBURG, DAVID A.
    1961a   Emotions in perspective of human evolution. (In press.)
    1961b   Relevance of recent evolutionary changes to human stress biology
             (In press.)
HOFER, H., A. H. SCHULTZ, AND D. STARK (EDS.)
    1956   Primatologia: Handbuch der Primatenkunde. Vol. I. Basel and New
             York, S. Karger.
HOWELLS, W. W.
    1959   Mankind in the making. Garden City, New York, Doubleday.
HUXLEY, J.
    1942   Evolution; the modern synthesis. London, Allen & Unwin.
HYMES, D. H.
    1960   Lexicostatistics so far. Current Anthropology 1:3-45.
JEPSEN, G. L., E. MAYR, AND G. G. SIMPSON
    1949   Genetics, paleontology, and evolution. Princeton, New Jersey, Prince-
             ton University Press.
KROEBER, A. L.
    1960   Evolution, history, and culture. In The evolution of man, S. Tax,
             ed. Chicago, University of Chicago Press, Vol. II.
LASKER, G. W.
    1961   The evolution of man. New York, Holt, Rinehart and Winston, Inc.
LEAKEY, L. S. B.
    1960   Finding the World's earliest man. National Geographic 118:420-436.
LIVINGSTONE, FRANK B.
    1958   Anthropological implications of sickle cell gene distribution in West
             Africa. American Anthropologist 60:533-562.
MONTAGU, M. F. ASHLEY
    1960   An introduction to physical anthropology. Third edition. Springfield,
             Illinois, Charles C Thomas.
MOODY, PAUL AMOS
    1953   Introduction to evolution. New York, Harper Brothers.
PENFIELD, W., AND LAMAR ROBERTS
    1959   Speech and brain-mechanisms. Princeton, New Jersey, Princeton Uni-
             versity Press.
PIVETEAU, JEAN
    1957   Traité de paléontologie, Vol. VII. Paris, Masson et Cie.
SIMPSON, GEORGE G.
    1949   The meaning of evolution. New Haven, Yale University Press.
    1953   The major features of evolution. New York, Columbia University
             Press.
SMITH, JOHN MAYNARD
    1958   The theory of evolution. Baltimore, Penguin Books, Inc.
SPUHLER, J. N., et al.
    1959   The evolution of man's capacity for culture. Detroit, Wayne State
             University Press.
WASHBURN, S. L.
    1960   Tools and human evolution. Scientific American 203:2-15.

David G. Mandelbaum

*A Design for
an Anthropology
Curriculum*

The anthropology curriculum has come to require more planning than formerly was necessary. When departments were generally small, major students few, and class enrollments modest, there was not much need for an extensively planned and neatly articulated curriculum design. A chairman could draw up, in fairly short order, a list of course offerings compatible with the interests of the teaching staff and with the requirements of the institution. But now that enrollments are much greater and faculties have grown larger, the list of courses is often more elaborate than it was; anthropologists in many institutions have had to give more thought to what courses should be offered and what relationships should obtain among the course offerings.

Some reasoned progression is obviously needed so that a student can build his anthropological knowledge systematically, and so that teachers are not handicapped by great diversity in anthropological background among the members of a class. All too often a student finds himself fruitlessly going over the same fundamentals in course after course and teachers find that in a single class they have some students who are innocent of any anthropological training and others who are fairly well along in it.

Yet it is not a simple matter to lay out an orderly, generally satisfactory curriculum. Apart from the particular and inevitable problems of departmental resources and institutional requirements, and apart from the generic difficulty of sorting our ideas and data into successive teaching stages, a main problem is that a curriculum design must meet

49

the needs of different kinds of students. It must provide for the large number who take only a beginning course, for those who are stimulated by their introductory plunge to take an advanced course or two, for upper-classmen who have strong reasons for taking a particular advanced course even though they have not had an introductory course, and for those who decide to major in anthropology. Should separate courses be offered for these separate purposes? If so, what kinds and at what levels?

Further, major students have diverse purposes. Some have firmly decided to become professional anthropologists; others are anthropology majors for purposes of a liberal education. Should there be a different kind of curriculum for preprofessional training and for liberal arts education?

The curriculum design suggested here attempts to meet these needs by setting up six categories of courses, arranged in three levels, as shown on the accompanying chart. The same introductory courses are given for all types of students. A student must take the introductory course sequence (or part of it) before he can take a course in the intermediate level categories on concepts and comparisons and on methods. Introductory courses are advisable though not mandatory preparation for two other categories, the regional and the special-interest courses. Upperclassmen who have not had introductory anthropology can thus take either regional courses or special-interest courses. The latter are specifically designed for such students or for those in a particular professional curriculum.

Major students should proceed from the introductory courses, to concepts, regional, and methods courses, to the integrative course at the senior level; those who qualify can study in the specialized and honors courses. The sequence is the same for majors who will go on to do graduate work in anthropology and those who will not, but presumably all of the preprofessional majors will take the specialized and honors courses.

In all large classes, say with an enrollment of more than fifty, provision should be made for a special section, meeting one or two hours a week in addition to the regular course meetings, in which students who want to do more intensive work can register for extra unit credit and in which they can do special reading, writing, and discussion.

The rationale and content for each of the six categories follows, but the design is to be understood as a model which can and should be modified to serve the special needs of a particular institution. No department, to my knowledge, uses precisely this classification and progression, although a number have similar course groupings. In adapting this curriculum design or in using some other, a faculty in anthropology is better advised to offer those courses in which the teachers have interest and competence than to attempt to fill in all the slots of some plan.

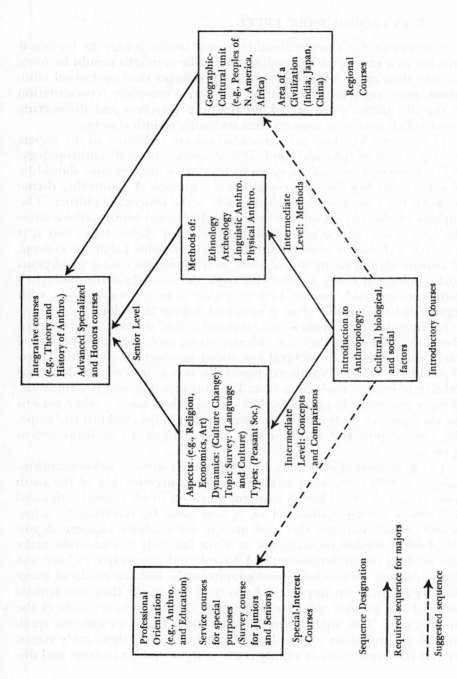

AN UNDERGRADUATE CURRICULUM IN ANTHROPOLOGY

Geographic-Cultural unit (e.g., Peoples of N. America, Africa)

Area of a Civilization (India, Japan, China)

Regional Courses

Methods of: Ethnology Archeology Linguistic Anthro. Physical Anthro.

Intermediate Level: Methods

Integrative courses (e.g., Theory and History of Anthro.)

Advanced Specialized and Honors courses

Senior Level

Introduction to Anthropology: Cultural, biological, and social factors

Introductory Courses

Aspects: (e.g., Religion, Economics, Art)
Dynamics: (Culture Change)
Topic Survey: (Language and Culture)
Types: (Peasant Soc.)

Intermediate Level: Concepts and Comparisons

Professional Orientation (e.g., Anthro. and Education)

Service courses for special purposes (Survey course for Juniors and Seniors)

Special-Interest Courses

Sequence Designation

Required sequence for majors

Suggested sequence

1. INTRODUCTORY LEVEL

These courses (or course) should present anthropology in its broad
purview as a way of understanding man. The emphasis should be more
on man than on anthropology, more on concepts than on factual tabulation, more on selected examples than on a complete representation
of the discipline, more on asking relevant questions and discovering
how to elicit pertinent answers than on listing technical terms.

The reasons for these recommendations are indicated in the papers
on introductory physical and introductory cultural anthropology.
When these two courses are given in separate semesters, they should be
planned to fit together as a coordinated sequence. A connecting theme
between the two, as well as within each, is the concept of culture. The
authors of the papers on the teaching of physical anthropology stress
the importance of the concept of culture. Fred Hulse writes that it is
a unifying theme of physical anthropology. It follows that the concept
of culture should be presented early in a beginning course in physical
anthropology in order to establish from the start the anthropologist's
main concern with *human* biology rather than general biology, with
human behavior rather than generalized animal behavior.

In introductory cultural anthropology, the student should learn
about the biological basis for culture, about race and other biological
variation as viewed in cultural and social perspective, about the interdependence, which Washburn especially notes, between biology and
culture in human evolution. Cora Du Bois says that an early introduction to evolution is necessary. We can add that, among other reasons
for doing so, an early discussion of evolution helps establish the scope,
the time depth, and the desirable objectivity of an anthropological
approach.

The discussion of evolution, in a beginning course in cultural anthropology, should come soon after the opening presentation of the main
concept of culture. Then it is useful to go on to view similarities and
differences among cultures. This is best done by referring to a few
peoples whose cultures the students can learn about in some depth.
Good ethnographic monographs, as Cora Du Bois recommends, make
fine reading for undergraduates. I have found it effective to have students read one or two brief monographs in the first few weeks of introductory cultural anthropology. Even in a few weeks they can acquire
some of the leading concepts which they can apply to the data in the
monographs. The analytic, problem-tackling, frontier-exploring qualities of anthropology can be brought in usefully in these early stages,
so that the student is not simply reading about quaint customs and dis-

covering that he too has customs and culture, but is also encouraged to set his mind to seeing some order, themes, and linkages within a culture.

Cultural differences and similarities can be examined in the principal aspects of culture, as in social organization, economics, technology, religion, art. Social organization is usually discussed more extensively than are other aspects, according to the findings in Bruner and Spindler's paper, and this discussion can well begin with the universal elements of kinship. One kinship system can be demonstrated in detail and compared with one or two other systems chosen for close study. The initial exposition, for the sake of clarity, should be on one kind of kin organization understood as a system, and then can follow the comparisons. Studies of our own kin patterns can usefully be brought in by way of indicating both contrasts and similarities. The emphasis in this presentation should not be on the general classification of kin systems nor on a full list of terms used in kinship analyses. Such classifications and terms are better taught at the intermediate level. The student should first absorb the main idea of kin organization, the use of kinship in societies of various kinds and places, and the nature and importance of kin bonds in the students' society.

Culture history and prehistory may fruitfully be taught at this level with similar concern for fundamental ideas. The beginning student must learn the main facts on which the ideas are based, but should not be put through rote memory drills on detailed professional vocabulary. For example, in studying cultural development through the paleolithic periods, the student should learn about the development of tool types so that he can understand what the artifacts indicate about culture. He should note the relationship between tool using and biological evolution and know the time scale involved in paleolithic development. All this entails learning certain technical terms, as hand-axe, Neanderthal, Pleistocene. But, as Braidwood notes, the beginning student need not memorize the detailed classification of flint artifacts. The better occasion for classification is in an advanced course, after the student has learned why the distinctions are significant.

In teaching about the rise of civilizations, the instructor is better advised to present the fundamentals of civilization and to compare how civilizations developed in several centers than to discuss the details of site excavation or pottery sequences. Similarly, in introductory physical anthropology, the student should be taught the nature of human evolution, as reflected in the fossil and living evidence, rather than be asked to memorize, right off, the bones of the human skeleton.

An instructor who is engrossed in his own research is inclined, not without reason, to teach the professional vocabulary which he uses in his research and to expect even beginning students to acquire the information, whether of bones or artifact types or kin types, which is essential for specialized research. There are several reasons why it is preferable to teach such things at a later stage. One is that many students in the introductory sequence will take no other anthropology course in which they could reinforce and use a more technical knowledge. Discrete lists of terms are quickly memorized and quickly forgotten. But basic concepts, demonstrated with different sets of data, verified in various ways, shown to be relevant to the student's own way of life, can have great and lasting significance in a student's education. Even for those few beginning students who will become professionals, it is probably better to outline the main intellectual framework of the discipline at first rather than to begin with intensive learning of one small corner of it.

As for teaching procedures, one has already been mentioned. Case examples are best taken from a few societies whose cultures the students can come to know quite well, well enough to appreciate each culture as a whole way of life. An instructor discussing the people among whom he himself has worked usually manages to convey a lively sense of social reality and of a whole culture.

Another useful procedure is to have the students do exercises in direct observation and analysis. That has been done in the two-semester introductory course in cultural anthropology at Berkeley. Each student observes several instances of a patterned event; the whole class observes the same kind of event, such as court trials, engagement or marriage ceremonies. The students are prepared for the assignment in lectures and in discussion sessions; they are required to use certain concepts and procedures. Each student writes a paper giving an analysis based on his own observations.

Similar exercises have been used in teaching all fields of anthropology, as is indicated in the papers by Lasker, Pike, Marriott, and Jennings. They help teach concepts and methods through direct participation, one of the best of teaching devices, and one especially suited for the teaching of anthropology. Such an assignment engages the active interest of many of the students, not only because it demonstrates that the methods and concepts can be used in real situations, but also because it provides students with the opportunity to exercise their own resourcefulness and stimulates them to use knowledge in a context other than that of the usual examination.

An assignment of this kind encourages students to do writing quite different from that done in the ordinary term paper. Since they are reporting their own observations, they are less likely to paraphase what has been written or to string together excerpts from authoritative statements. Moreover, it helps dispel a common blight of American higher education, the student whose only intellectual role is that of passive spectator, temporarily holding on to bits of information which may be useful in passing a coded examination.

These assignments can be quite simple exercises, such as reports on the student's own set of kin terms, and subsequent analysis of the reports of the whole class. Or the assignments may be longer, entailing repeated observations and a more comprehensive paper. In either case, the resultant improvement in student learning is well worth the additional time and effort which these assignments require. While Bruner and Spindler found that most of their respondents did not use such exercises, and some were quite averse to them, they also learned that there are a variety of ingenious and promising field exercises being tried in introductory courses.

It takes additional time to devise such an assignment and to read the papers, but not so much extra time as to make the assignment impractical. In a large class, the instructor must have teaching assistants or readers. The students should have a set of written instructions which suggest the concepts to be noted, procedures to be followed, and format to be used in the writing. These assignments must be planned as an integral part of the course if they are to be of full educational value. They can provide the same kind of learning experience which is provided by the best kind of laboratory work in other disciplines. And this laboratory practice in anthropology courses is likely to be very much less expensive than it is in the physical or biological sciences.

The exercises suggested for introductory cultural anthropology entail some study of our own society. Some anthropologists strongly believe that their undergraduate students, and certainly the beginning students, should study only about primitive peoples. While it is important to use the well-tested case materials from tribal peoples, there is much to be gained by using one's own culture and society as an example of possible human behavior in the roster of ethnological case examples. Doing so can impart a vivid sense of the relevance of anthropological concepts to the student's experience, and quashes any stereotype of cultural anthropology as dealing only with quaint customs of far-out savages.

The matter of class size figures importantly in teaching procedures. Every teaching procedure (and these are well set forth in Rapoport's paper on applied anthropology) is obviously affected by the number of students for which it must be used. My own view is that some lecturers can be very effective even with very large classes and that an anthropologist who can do well with a class of thirty is likely to hold a class of several hundred, though the larger class demands a much greater

expenditure of energy. When a class is large, certainly when there
are more than fifty students, an anthropology teacher must have readers to help with examinations and papers and teaching assistants to
lead small discussion groups, if the course is to make efficient use of the
time and efforts of both students and teacher. Yet simply providing
discussion sections, as Bruner and Spindler point out, does not guaran-
tee that they will be useful to students. Too often they are unsuccessful
because the teacher has little opportunity to plan and supervise them.
Properly organized, they can add greatly to the educational impact of
a course. And as noted above, it is desirable and economical to provide
a special section in a large class for specially motivated and able
students.

Recruitment of teaching assistants, even in a department with a
sizable roster of graduate students, presents problems. Under present conditions, many graduate students get fellowships and research
assistantships which preclude working as teaching assistants. Service
as a teaching assistant tends to protract the already overlong period
in the status of graduate student. Yet Bernard Berelson concludes his
comprehensive survey of graduate education in the United States
(1960:248-249) with recommendations that all doctoral candidates
have some teaching experience. A year's experience as a teaching assistant can be of great benefit to a graduate student, provided that he
can be guided by a senior faculty member.

It is generally more efficient for an experienced anthropologist to
lecture to a large class and have the students also meet in small groups
with a teaching assistant than to exhaust teaching verve by repeating
the same lecture in the same day to several smaller classes or to insist
that every staff member teach an introductory class. An introductory
course is one of the easiest courses to give badly. It should be the special
charge of an able teacher, who has time to prepare for it, to work constantly at improving it, to supervise readers and assistants, and to give
attention to individual students. In university departments there
should be rotation in giving the introductory courses. After giving
such a course for perhaps five years, a teacher does better if he turns to
other courses for a time and then comes back afresh to the fresh minds
of the beginning students.

In junior colleges and small colleges such rotation may not be feasible, and teaching assistants may be out of the question. Anthropologists
in these institutions have particular need for frequent leaves to do other
anthropological work and for the employment of readers to assist with
examinations and papers. Able readers are available in most metropolitan areas among women who have had training in anthropology
—women whose family responsibilities do not permit full-time employ-

ment but who will work as readers with genuine interest and to the great advantage of the students. The funds needed for readers are modest, especially in view of the greater opportunities they provide for students to write and to have their writings carefully and critically read. These comments on teaching procedures apply to all courses, but they are especially relevant to introductory courses because classes in them are larger and the effectiveness of the teacher is particularly important.

The introduction to anthropology cannot adequately be taught in less than an academic year: that is, two semesters or three quarters during which there are three meetings (not necessarily three lectures) a week. A three-semester sequence, the pattern in some California schools, offers considerable advantage. Students can get a more thorough grounding in the subject, the longer continuity of presentation is preferable to shorter, chopped-up courses; the three-semester sequence allows for a design in which the cultural aspects are emphasized in one semester, the biological in another, and the social aspects in a third semester. This sequence also affords a more satisfactory preparation for advanced courses than is possible in a shorter sequence. Non-majors may take only part of the sequence as a preparation for certain of the advanced courses, but a well-planned and well-taught sequence will induce capable students to complete the whole introductory presentation. While it is conventional to begin with the biological factors, there are advantages in beginning with the cultural part of the introductory sequence and then bringing in the biological factors. When the student grasps the nature of culture, the peculiar attribute of man, he then is better able to appreciate the biological components of man's physical structure and social behavior.

In sum, the introductory course is the main locus of anthropological teaching in point of numbers of students; it is a main forum for the dissemination of anthropological ideas; it is a principal recruiting agency for majors and graduate students; it prepares students for more advanced work in anthropology and in other disciplines as well. Above all, it should start a student thinking about culture and society in ways he had not previously discovered. It can add new, important, and lasting perpectives to his view of peoples and cultures.

2. INTERMEDIATE LEVEL: CONCEPTS AND COMPARISONS

This takes in all courses organized around the comparative presentation of a set of concepts. In these courses the principal concepts of a field of inquiry are presented, the nature of cultural variations is examined, processes of stability and change are studied, cultural uniformities as well as differences are formulated. Four kinds of courses can be distinguished in this grouping: culture aspects, dynamics, topic surveys, and social-cultural types.

Courses on aspects of culture, such as social organization, religion, technology, and art, are commonly offered. The course on social organization is often a required course for major students. Courses in dynamics include those on long-term change and on short-term process. It may be straining our classificatory scheme to group together a culturological course on evolution and one on applied anthropology, but this may be a reminder that both courses should deal with the same general processes of culture change, seen in different time perspective.

Topic surveys bring together ideas and data from two or more analytic methods. Examples are courses on culture and personality, archaeology and society, language and culture. Courses on social-cultural types have to do with such subjects as peasant societies, nomadic peoples, neolithic cultures.

In all these courses, students can learn how to bring concepts and data from different sources to bear on a set of general problems. They should see the main problems within the scope of each course and find out how anthropologists grapple with them. They should read in the relevant technical literature, learn the factual support for the concepts, come to know the principal taxonomic tools, and follow the ramifications of theoretical ideas. Since all students in these courses will have had an introductory course, the instructor can assume that they know the fundamentals of anthropology and can carry on discussion at a more advanced level.

Lest some anthropologist conclude that this procedure is an impractical counsel of perfection for the level of his students, we should note that it may be more difficult for an instructor to plan a closely coherent course of tough intellectual content than it is for his students to grasp it. Further, those students whose intellectual reach or motivation is not up to this standard should be shunted elsewhere. In many institutions, the recent improvements in high school teaching and the competition for college entrance have already brought to our classes students who are better equipped for intellectual efforts than their predecessors generally have been.

Each major student should take at least two courses in the concepts and comparisons category. A departmental curriculum should include some courses on aspects and some on dynamics, but there is no need to list a full roster of every kind of course in any category. A useful sequence is one in which a course of the concepts and comparisons category is linked with one on methods. Thus a language and culture course, essentially a survey course, can be followed by one on linguistic methods in which students learn how to do phonemic analysis, gather data for a study of dialect variation and its social concomitants, and work out problems in descriptive and historical linguistics. Such a sequence in ethnology could be the kind of "unitary course" in this field which Arensberg discusses.

3. INTERMEDIATE LEVEL: METHODS

In a course of this category, the student learns how to get the data, how to use them, how concepts are developed and hypotheses tested. The methods and techniques of a field of anthropology are taught through doing exercises on significant problems. The focus is on the problems, and in this respect these courses can be quite different from "methods and techniques" courses as they are sometimes given. Thus students learn to do ethnological interviewing by conducting interviews on a real problem. Similarly, in archaeological anthropology, students learn methods of excavation through working on a site and analyzing the findings. In physical anthropology, the classical anthropometric measurements should be learned in the context of the problems for which they provide data. In linguistic anthropology, students in a class on methods should do analyses of a spoken language.

A methods course can readily be given in linguistic anthropology; the laboratory materials, as noted in the papers on the teaching of linguistics, are easily available. For archaeology and physical anthropology, suitable sites and laboratory resources are often available. In ethnology, it is more difficult to have students learn methods through working with peoples of a going culture, and perhaps more library exercises are necessary here. Yet if our own culture and its subcultures are not ruled out, there can be field problems and materials in plenty on which members of a methods class in ethnology can work, certainly in metropolitan areas.

Each major student should take at least one methods course, to learn how data are obtained and how to use them once obtained, and also as preparation for work at the senior level. In this category as in others, there is no overriding necessity that a department offer a methods course in every field within the discipline. Only those methods courses should be offered which can be taught by instructors who will give a full measure of interest, time, and energy to teaching such a course.

4. REGIONAL COURSES

These deal with peoples and cultures within certain geographic bounds or within the sphere of a civilization. Students in these courses not only learn about a region, they also come to understand the holistic approach of anthropology. Cora Du Bois' paper suggests some of the basic questions which the students should learn to ask of the ethno-

logical materials and the kinds of answers toward which they can
be guided. Factors of various kinds can be examined—ecological, biological, cultural, social—and their effects on the peoples of the region
can be assessed. Culture history can be presented, and the relevance of
historical developments to the contemporary scene can be discussed.
The ways in which the various peoples of the region are alike can be
contrasted with the ways in which they differ one from another. The
cultural themes of a civilization can be singled out and traced over
time.

A regional course necessarily includes considerable factual information and so may tend to become an inventory of names, places, and
traits, garnished with a sprinkling of native terms. To avoid the orderly
presentation of chaotic and inconsequential information, particular attention should be given to the cultural themes common to the area and
to the theoretical concepts best illustrated in the study of it, so as to provide the theoretical framework needed. Thus a course on circumpolar
peoples can emphasize both the limitations imposed by natural environment and opportunities for cultural development which are possible
even within a closely pressing environment. A course on the peoples
of India can bring to the fore the power of a literate tradition and the
nature of a high degree of social stratification. The need for a theoretical
frame and other facets of regional courses are discussed in the papers of
Section IV.

Each major student should come to know something of the peoples
and the culture history of the main parts of the world. Some of this ethnographic reading will be done in courses of the senior sequence, as
suggested below. But more detailed knowledge should be acquired
through at least two of the courses in this category, one on a predominantly tribal region and another on a civilization area.

These courses should be open to all upperclassmen even if they have
not taken an introductory course. Since such a course is about the people within a geographic perimeter, it can begin with the nature of the
area and of the groups within it. Relevant anthropological concepts can
be brought into the descriptive account. Thus no great handicap is imposed on teacher or student if a class includes students who have no
anthropological background and those who do, because it is feasible
to assume that all are on the same level of knowledge with respect to the
cultures of the region.

With the mounting interest in Africa, Asia, and Latin America,
classes on these regions can be quite large and students who have special motivation to study one of these regions may go unnoticed by the instructor. It is useful to arrange for a special section as mentioned above.

It can meet one hour a week; entail extra reading, writing, and discussion; carry an additional hour credit; and be taken only by those who want to do additional work in the course.

It is not likely that a department will be able to offer good courses on all regions and civilizational areas. There is some inclination to try to cover the ethnographic world, but it is really far better for a department to offer a few regional courses that have been planned with care and are given by instructors who are interested than to try to provide world coverage and assign some hapless instructor to teach a regional course regardless of his interest in and prior knowledge of the region.

There have been some notably successful courses in world ethnography. But they have been successfully given by a few particularly gifted and experienced teachers. With the growth in ethnographic knowledge, it is increasingly difficult to do justice to a course of world-wide scope.

Given a course of more restricted compass, there still remains the previously-mentioned question of designing it so that it is more than a flat ethnographic inventory. A feasible procedure is to devote one part of the course to an over-all view of the region, giving the principal culture areas, the ecological picture, the main historical development, and the leading concepts which are relevant to the study of the peoples of the region. Another part of the course can concentrate on a few cultures, each from a different culture area, each presented holistically both in lectures and in readings. A final part of the course can be concerned with major problems in the study of the peoples of the region. While an instructor who has done work in the region, and who is interested in it, is far and away better suited to give a course in that region than one who has had no firsthand experience and has little interest, the experienced instructor must carefully resist the inclination to devote most of the course to a discussion of My Village or My Tribe.

It is desirable that courses on both tribal regions and civilizational areas be offered. A single course sequence can comprise both: a year course on the peoples of Middle America, for example, can present the archaeological record and the tribal cultures in one semester and in the second semester deal with contemporary national cultures and societies. Cooperation of an archaeologist and a social anthropologist in giving this course has much to recommend it. The joint teaching of any course presents difficulties but can also lead to increased teaching effectiveness in many ways.

One semester, the time generally allotted for a regional course, may not be enough for adequate presentation. A semester course on the peoples of India or of China can do little more than begin to acquaint the students with these historic cultures and vast societies. In a year course on India, for example, it is possible to devote one semester to culture history and to the main themes of Indian civilization and in the second semester to take up the social aspects and the contemporary developments.

Regional courses reverse the usual order of presentation followed in courses on concepts and comparisons. In the latter, the concepts are in the foreground of presentation and the descriptive data are adduced to illustrate and validate the concepts. In regional courses the descriptive material is in the foreground, presented according to some explicit or implicit theoretical order, but with the relevant concepts shown as being derived from the descriptive data.

5. SPECIAL-INTEREST COURSES

These are geared to some special purpose not met by the other course offerings. Such a course may be given for students in a particular professional curriculum, as education, public health, social work, or for students being trained for work overseas. It commonly begins with a general introduction to anthropology, followed by a presentation of anthropological concepts and data which have special bearing for the practice of the profession.

In a few professional schools a general introduction to anthropology is given without special emphasis on the students' professional training. This is comparable to service courses which are offered for students who want to take a general course in anthropology but cannot enroll in an introductory course, often because upperclassmen are not allowed to take a freshman-sophomore course for credit. Thus there is need for an upper-division introductory course, mainly on cultural anthropology, which is given in somewhat more accelerated manner than is the regular introductory course. Similar service courses have been offered by a few graduate departments whose members do not want to become much involved in undergraduate teaching.

In this category also are integrated social science courses and area courses given jointly by teachers from different disciplines. These courses can be useful for both students and teachers, as Casagrande, Bennett, and Marriott show in their papers, but anthropologists who participate in them must realize that if they are to be done well they take a great deal of time for planning and consultation, and that anthropologists must continue to take an active interest in the course through successive years if the students in it are to have a fair opportunity to learn something of the anthropological approach.

6. SENIOR LEVEL: INTEGRATIVE AND ADVANCED SPECIALIZED COURSES

In his senior year, each major student should take an integrative course on theory and on the history of anthropological ideas. The student should be assigned certain theoretical themes and examine them through extensive reading of monographs and articles. This reading should be selected both to illustrate different theoretical approaches and to widen the student's knowledge of ethnography. Thus if a student in this course has had no regional course on Asia, his reading here should include accounts of Asian peoples.

The history of anthropological ideas should be illustrated in the readings. In discussing this history, it is well to avoid extensive flogging of dead hypotheses or circling about in a long round of purely negative criticism. It is more difficult, but also far more useful, to consider the development of anthropological thought in the context of the intellectual history of the times and to assess the validity of concepts within the larger corpus of scientific knowledge as well as within the discipline.

Another part of the senior-level sequence should be reserved for honors students, those whose academic records warrant giving them special attention. These students can do independent study, under the direction of a faculty member, on a research problem. In this way they can apply their previous anthropological training to working out a genuine problem through the several stages of inquiry.

The two courses at the senior level are of a kind which could also be taken by first-year graduate students. In departments which give both undergraduate and graduate work, these courses could well be at the graduate level. It is far better to treat the best of the senior majors as beginning graduate students than to follow the reverse practice of putting graduate students in undergraduate courses. At the present juncture of the development of anthropology and of higher education in general, it is well to upgrade, beyond much of current teaching practice, all of the curriculum in anthropology. This does not mean that professional training should be given at the undergraduate level. It does mean that undergraduates should be expected to do more reading, observing, thinking, and writing on their own than has usually been required of them. The tendency in the United States is to lecture at students too much and to develop their thinking too little.

This curriculum is intended to take the student from the general survey in the introductory sequence through the more specific discussion at the intermediate level to specialized honors study at the senior level. The integrative course at the senior level is intended to help major students integrate their knowledge at a stage when they have some knowledge to be integrated. A student who takes only the introductory course should carry away a set of ideas about man which will illumine his understanding of his culture and himself. Those who major in anthropology should derive from their studies that view of mankind, that range of knowledge, that zest for new knowledge which are hallmarks of truly educated men and women.

REFERENCE CITED

BERELSON, BERNARD
    1960   Graduate education in the United States. New York, McGraw-Hill.

PART II

THE
TEACHING
OF
PHYSICAL
ANTHROPOLOGY

Introduction

ANTHROPOLOGISTS in America, when they consider the teaching of physical anthropology, come immediately to the dual question: which concepts of physical anthropology are relevant for study of other aspects of anthropology, and which concepts of cultural anthropology are relevant for the study of physical anthropology? Each of the physical anthropologists who has contributed to this section (Laughlin, Hulse, and Lasker) has had something to say about the second half of this question. Apparently many physical anthropologists are convinced that the scientific study of human biology requires some understanding of that which makes man human, his culture. Cultural elements, notably tool-using and speech, probably affected the direction of evolution of the genus Homo: certainly clothes, houses, the use of fire, food production, the control of diseases and many other cultural elements affect the selection pressures responsible for ongoing human evolution, human growth, body composition, and virtually every other process of concern to physical anthropology.

The relevance of physical anthropology for other fields of anthropology is discussed by Laughlin, whose paper was prepared for the international symposium at Burg Wartenstein. He believes that linguists, archaeologists, and ethnologists interested in the history of peoples need to apprise their students of the physical anthropological evidence. The same point is made elsewhere by Vogt in respect to regional courses taught with a "genetic" focus. Laughlin also points out that the study of social and biological kinship can best proceed together, since in fact they affect each other.

Hulse's paper was presented at a symposium on the teaching of physical anthropology held at the 1960 meetings of the American Association of Physical Anthropologists. In it Hulse forcefully states the relevance of concepts of culture for physical anthropology, as for other

67

branches of the discipline. Similar views were expressed by other participants in that symposium, and elsewhere on previous occasions, as in S. M. Garn's comments on cultural factors affecting the study of human biology (*Human Biology* 26:71-79, 1954), and in the papers prepared by Washburn and by Spuhler and Livingstone elsewhere in this volume.

My two papers were prepared for the general symposium at Berkeley. In opening the discussion on advanced courses at that symposium, T. D. McCown commented that, although the nature of an advanced course in physical anthropology will depend a great deal on what has been taught at the elementary level and on the interests of the staff, there will remain the question of whether the course is meant to be presented only for those students who concentrate in physical anthropology. McCown believes all anthropology students might well take advanced courses in physical anthropology which emphasize ideas, information, and concepts. He thinks that courses in methods and techniques using laboratory work (with or without lectures and examinations) are less necessary for cultural anthropologists, since the methodology is not specifically transferable to most problems which interest such students.

On the other hand, many physical anthropologists, themselves educated essentially as apprentices of a distinguished master, deplore large classes and regret that students often lack adequate opportunity to work out concrete problems under the personal guidance of their instructors. As McCown has said, in a discussion of the training of the professional physical anthropologist, "It is his anthropological teachers who must educate him not to lose his perspective, to show him that he is an anthropologist concerned with man, a mammal in a world context unlike that of any other mammal" (*American Anthropologist* 54: 313-317, 1952).

No great center of research and teaching of physical anthropology now exists on the scale of several devoted to the study of cultural anthropology. Perhaps we need more concentration on classroom methods for general education in physical anthropology at the introductory level to free the teachers for more intimate direction of those who seek advanced knowledge of the field.

G.W.L.

FREDERICK S. HULSE

Objectives and
Methods

O F ALL THE PRACTITIONERS of the anthropological art, I suppose that we physical anthropologists have been the most gadget conscious. Our laboratories and even our offices are likely to attract the wide-eyed stares of children, to evoke the pretended horror of teen-age girls, and sometimes to elicit the awe of adults as they observe the array of old bones, measuring instruments and centrifuges upon display. Even students of anthropology, if their previous experiences have been only with ethnologists or sociologists, are likely to be somewhat upset at the notion of drawing blood samples, dissecting defunct monkeys, and calculating chi-square. And all too often, students reach us only after having been introduced to anthropology, or even physical anthropology, by scholars whose understanding of our interests, aims and methods is, to say the least, minimal. Only a relatively small number of colleges and universities employ physical anthropologists, though a large number offer courses titled Physical Anthropology or Human Evolution.

An understanding of the biological origin of the human stock and of the biological substrate of behavior is, then, officially recognized as a necessity for sound anthropological training. But it may be questioned whether these two aspects of physical anthropology are the only ones of importance. We certainly have other valid interests, and in any discussion of techniques in teaching physical anthropology, some attention must be paid to what we are, in fact, trying to do. After inquiring from a number of my colleagues, I find that despite the distinctions made between the so-called Old and the so-called New physical anthropology, and despite a great variety of individual research

69

interests, there does seem to be a large area of agreement. Physical anthropology is recognized as including more than human biology, more than the study of evolution or genetics, more than designing equipment which will fit human beings, more than description and classification of human variety. There seems to be agreement that we have as a unifying theme the concept of culture—just as do the other aspects of anthropology. In the words of one of my colleagues: "Physical anthropology's one claim to a place in the sun is its ability to interpret biological variability in its cultural setting."

Culture, from the zoological point of view, may be thought of, I suppose, as the ecological plateau which humans occupy, exploit, and adapt to. The attempt to understand the implications of this fact—of how it came about, of what its causes were, of what its results are and will be—upon the human animal, is a vast, absorbing, and important task. Whatever techniques we use in teaching must be those which are designed to clarify this unifying theme, which justifies the existence of physical anthropology as a discipline. Techniques are, at the same time, bound to vary in accordance with our individual proclivities, with the type and number of students, and with the circumstances of the time and place. This does not seem to be a tragedy, or even an unfortunate necessity, but rather a circumstance which can be exploited to advantage. The study of evolution shows us that animals have found many ways in which to solve their problems, and the study of anthropology shows us that people have found many ways to solve theirs. Some methods, some techniques, are certainly less inefficient than others, but a rigid party line of any sort seems, in the end, to be the least efficient of all.

One must bear in mind, first of all, that at least three levels of teaching exist in institutions of higher learning. It is desirable to give some degree of enlightenment and anthropological sophistication to just as many students as can be reached. It is more than desirable to equip potential members of a variety of professions with a deeper comprehension of the concepts and methods of arriving at conclusions characteristic of physical anthropology. It is vitally necessary to train professionals to carry on further research in all the aspects of physical anthropology. These different purposes cannot all be fulfilled by using the same techniques. The characteristics of the students are too different, at these three levels, for such a program to be effective.

TECHNIQUES FOR THE ELEMENTARY LEVEL

At the elementary, introductory level, classes are likely to be large. In some cases many hundreds of freshmen and sophomores attend each lecture, of whom many have never heard of anthropology, physical or cultural, ever before in their lives. Many of these students are intelligent and alert, and all should at least be given the opportunity to find out what an exciting and significant discipline physical anthropology can be. At once we are faced with a problem. Work in the laboratory is essential to the practice of physical anthropology, and practice in the laboratory is therefore needed for a complete understanding of our subject. Yet, at this elementary level, is such practice possible? Would it be real? For some students, and at certain institutions, undoubtedly the answer is yes. For the vast majority, I am highly sceptical. Without trained and competent assistants in large numbers and adequate space and equipment, it is in any case impossible. Unfortunately, in only a very few cases can any of the requirements be met at the present time. It is to be hoped that in the future, circumstances will be different. Departments in any one of the natural sciences now include in their budgets, as a matter of course, funds for laboratory assistants and technicians. We anthropologists ought to be more insistent in demanding the same sort of help and more vigorous in training the proper personnel to fill the needed positions.

Until such time as this has been done, the methods and techniques of physical anthropology can best be taught, at this level, by class-room demonstrations and the extensive use of visual aids. Indeed, laboratory work should not neglect the use of either. Simple points concerning the relation between heredity and environment can be made by eliciting class participation, especially if the class is large. Students may be asked, for instance, whether they are taller than like-sexed parents, in order to bring home to them the fact of the secular increase in stature which is still in progress, for the greater number will certainly be taller than their parents. The stability of genetic traits in a population from generation to generation can then be demonstrated by asking the same students similar questions concerning their eye-color and that of their parents and siblings. In my experience the accuracy of the Hardy-Weinberg law has invariably been demonstrated by the students' answers. Some students can almost always be persuaded to let themselves be blood-typed or measured (attractive coeds are, naturally, the best subjects to select), and casts and anatomical specimens can be shown to illustrate various points. The University Museum of the University of Pennsylvania, among other institutions, can provide casts of the more important human fossils; most zoology departments have on hand a large number of animal bones for comparative purposes; and our archaeological colleagues are usually glad to supply us with human skeletons from their excavations. A blackboard and maps are always obtainable and are exceedingly useful. Genetic diagrams and phylogenetic trees, simple calculations and unfamiliar terms can be sketched in the former; geographical localities should always be pointed out on the latter.

When classes or sections are small enough to permit controlled and directed discussion, this is an invaluable teaching technique, but in most cases the number of students will be too great to make it practical. Moving pictures demonstrating various aspects of genetics are available and serve to clarify points which have been made in reading and lectures. Should there be a zoo in the area, a conducted tour of the primate house not only arouses the interest of the students but serves to demonstrate many points which reading, lectures, pictures. or even casual trips would have left obscure. Postures, methods of locomotion and manipulation, and aspects of social behavior of various species may be carefully watched and then related to the appropriate anatomical details by close observation or even palpation—if the subjects are not too vociferously reluctant. Such observation of how our arboreal cousins use their anatomy is both fascinating and convincing. If there is no zoo handy, it may be possible to obtain the loan of a few living specimens from a pet shop or a medical laboratory. A zoo is, of course, best. Establishing good relations with the officials and especially with the keepers pays dividends to any physical anthropologist.

Terminology is a real problem at the introductory level. There is no way to escape the use of a large number of words and phrases which are new, strange, and apparently sometimes rather terrifying to the student. Since there is often emotional resistance to the concepts of physical anthropology, and especially to the narrative of human evolution, the story told ought to be phrased as simply and convincingly as possible. Whenever an ordinary word can be used rather than a scientific one, it should be; the phrase "Reduction Division" is preferable to the word "Meiosis," and it is better to talk about Neanderthal Man than Homo Neanderthalensis. Nevertheless, as a testing technique, requiring the students to explain the significance and connotation of terms to which they have been introduced is very useful. Requiring them to distinguish between factual data, strong inferences and wild speculations, when they are given tests, also helps them to learn how anthropologists analyze their material and come to conclusions concerning its meaning. Examples of factual data include such statements, as, "The typical number of human chromosomes is 23 pairs" and "The pelvis of Australopithecus resembles that of modern man much more than it does that of any living ape." Examples of valid inferences include such statements as, "Genetic characteristics are transmitted by means of units of chromosomal material" and "Australopithecus was able to move about on his hind legs without difficulty." Examples of speculations include such statements as "Humans have 100,000 genes" and "Gestures were the chief means of communication used by Australopithecus." Locating items upon a map teaches the importance of geographical factors in ecology and phylogeny.

Although telling the students a story interesting enough to awaken their curiosity is very important at the introductory level, the use of a single text has dubious value. There are many unsolved problems in physical anthropology, and the students need to know that disagreements exist. We do not know either the extent or the functional utility of human body plasticity due to environmental changes; we do not know anything whatever about our Pliocene ancestors; we do not know the mode of inheritance of most human genetic characteristics. There is disagreement about the use of the word "race"; about the functional significance, if any, of most characteristics in which humans show diversity, either on an individual or a population basis; about proper Rh terminology; about the importance of constitutional studies; about just what (or who) Oreopithecus was. These lists could be extended more or less indefinitely. And students need to realize that the opinions of scholars have changed as new evidence and new methods of analyzing old evidence have become available. The use of laboratory techniques in disposing of the Piltdown hoax makes a fascinating story which is very appropriate to tell. Readings by various authorities, ought to be assigned when possible, even though a text be used as a major source of reference. No text, furthermore, can ever be up to date: new discoveries are constantly being made, and fresh insights and points of view are always available. It is one of the tasks of the instructor of an introductory course in physical anthropology to keep up to date and to be in a position to present important new material to the class. If only for this reason—although there are many other reasons, too—the most important technique in teaching such a course is to use a trained physical anthropologist to do the job.

TECHNIQUES FOR THE ADVANCED LEVEL

In view of the present numerical strength of our profession, it may be just as well that fewer students take the more advanced courses in physical anthropology than take the introductory course, for they need much more individual attention. We would be happy to have more of them, nonetheless. A survey of the course offerings in colleges and universities in the United States indicates that it is usually in this upper division of the undergraduate level of instruction that laboratory work in physical anthropology is first offered. In a majority of cases, only at this level will a course which is strictly and entirely in physical anthropology be offered at all. The students who take such a course are almost always majoring in anthropology, zoology, or premedical and predental fields. Some will be graduate students just beginning to study anthropology. Many of them will have had, and all of them should have had, some courses in biology, preferably comparative anatomy and introductory genetics. But their backgrounds and interests will differ.

At this level, the emphasis should be, and apparently usually is, upon preprofessional training rather than general enlightenment. The story of human evolution is no longer important, but many myths concerning human heredity may still need to be dispelled. Those students who have had little or no anthropology are likely to need the importance of culture emphasized and reëmphasized. Set lectures are less important, directed discussion more important than before. Much more reading can be and should be insisted upon, and from more varied sources, too —including the professional journals. One of the greatest and most widespread misfortunes of college libraries in this country is, apparently, the lack of adequate series of journals dealing with physical anthropology and even of a wide enough selection of books. It has been our good fortune, on the other hand, that the association between departments of anthropology and museums of natural history has long been close and intimate. Let us make sure that this never ceases, for access to the study collections of such museums is a priceless asset to teaching. The actual handling and prolonged, detailed observation of specimens by the students is a vital part of teaching physical anthropology from this level on.

Some knowledge of statistical methods will certainly be required of students at the advanced undergraduate level. It would be desirable for this to have been gained in a course on statistics. In fact, however, at least up to the pesent, this will rarely have been the case. The instructor must therefore devote some time to imparting such knowledge to the students, for whatever results they may obtain in the laboratory will have to be subjected to statistical manipulation before they become meaningful. Overcoming the revulsion to the use of numbers and the feigned inability to do simple arithmetic, which is so widespread among students, is often quite a problem. Most important, however, is leading them to realize which statistical techniques are most suitable for each occasion, what a sample is, and not to mix up different sorts of categories. When the student counts, he should know what he is counting.

The type of laboratory and the types of laboratory work suitable for advanced undergraduates who may or may not become professional physical anthropologists cannot be decided except by the teacher. In the past, laboratory work in physical anthropology used to mean little more than the identification and measurement of bones. We have now learned to do a great deal more, and every year sees further advances into new types of research. A student does not have to go through an embryological recapitulation of the phylogeny of physical anthropology in his training. He ought rather to be exposed to as many approaches and diverse techniques as possible. We are still vertebrates, and the characteristics of our bones are important. But so are growth processes, biochemical and hematological characteristics, and a multitude of other things. Perhaps the most important thing to start with, in any sort of laboratory work, is emphasis upon the necessity for precision and accuracy to the degree required by the project being undertaken. This is true whether we are operating upon mice, breeding fruit-flies, controlling the diet of monkeys, testing blood samples, or measuring bones.

In any case, actual practice in laboratory routine, starting with the simpler operations, is necessary, if only to show the practical as well as the theoretical difficulties involved. Probably only a minority of the students intend to become physical anthropologists: experience in the laboratory is likely to show whether they are capable of doing so. Laboratory manuals are of considerable assistance in offering helpful suggestions, maintaining orderly progress, and freeing the instructor and his assistants for other sorts of work. So too, of course, are record forms. Whether either of these aids to discipline should be standardized for the entire profession is open to question, however, because of the legitimately wide varieties of studies which are undertaken. More important, I think, from the material point of view is the provision of adequate work space and suitably designed instruments in quantity great enough to fit the needs of the class. All students, incidentally, must be taught, emphatically taught, to care properly for all the equipment made available for their use. Respect for one's tools is an absolute necessity for any honest workman.

The tools themselves will be bound to vary. At a minimum, however, anthropometers, a variety of calipers, an ample supply of bones, slides, and test tubes, an incubator or constant temperature water bath, a centrifuge, a good microscope, and some standard guage for measuring pigmentation are required. The bones should include not only those of individuals from a variety of racial stocks but also those of males and females, adults and children, and those of tetrapods for comparative purposes—especially, of course, those of apes and monkeys. With such materials available, it is possible to introduce students to several of the many lines of research engaged in by physical anthropologists, such as blood-typing, growth studies, comparative dental morphology, constitutional typology, anthropometry and others. In this way they may have, at the least, an intelligent understanding of what we are trying to do; while those whose future careers depend upon mastery of the techniques will be in a position to drill themselves more thoroughly, under the supervision of the instructor

—who is, after all, the most valuable piece of equipment in the laboratory.

As a teaching device, work with living people as well as dead bones and experimental animals should be and often is introduced at this level. The obvious subjects for work on serology and anthropometry are the members of the class themselves. Their frequencies and means may be compared to those of various natural populations in such a way as to demonstrate to the students the hazards of assuming that socially selected groups are representative samples. The instructor, whose blood types and measurements should previously have been established, can be used as a check on the accuracy of the students' work: he can also demonstrate, as they attempt to obtain his cooperation, the various forms of resistance which a physical anthropologist is likely to meet in trying to do research with living subjects. Anyone who has worked with voluntary subjects will recall at least some of their evasive techniques. Inability to be still, pretense of misunderstanding, a suddenly remembered appointment elsewhere, unanticipated violent sickness, modesty about removing one's coat or even one's hat are among the standard reactions. It is vital that students learn patience and respect for their potential subjects before attempting any field work.

Some students, at any rate, will wish to engage in studies of their own. Mature students should certainly be encouraged to do this. The actual experience of organizing and executing a research job which deals with subjects who can, and often do, refuse to cooperate teaches students a great deal about anthropology. Some physical anthropologists in the past, who never bothered to learn the techniques of persuasion, have had sad experiences. It was really unwise, for instance, to try to insist upon taking photographs in the nude of all female freshmen at one university. The necessity of treating one's subjects with consideration and of learning to pay attention to cultural factors which affect their biological characteristics and behavior must be taught. The more responsible among the students at this level can begin to learn these lessons by experience. But their activities do need to be under rather close supervision and should not be of a nature which might evoke hostility from the public. Nor should it be anticipated that such student projects will make any great contributions to science; they are primarily teaching devices. This is not to say that really significant work is not sometimes accomplished, for it has been. But the student will benefit, even should he simply confirm, by his own work and to his own intellectual satisfaction, something already known. One student of mine, for instance, said that college athletes had the reputation of being especially hirsute in association with their presumptive strong masculinity. He wanted to test this allegation, so I told him to go ahead, if the athletes didn't mind being put on the spot. He found out that, at least at one university, the athletes were not hairier than other male students of similar age and ethnic origin, and discovering this for himself gave him considerable satisfaction.

Of course, not all advanced undergraduate courses need to involve laboratory work. Courses in primatology, fossil man, the genetics of race, growth, and constitution are offered in various institutions at this level without laboratory work. Such courses are important in the training of physical anthropologists, and some of them are important to students of other aspects of anthropology. Demonstrations and discussion of problems are necessary, even if laboratory work is inappropriate or impossible. Visits from the zoo instead of to the zoo should be arranged in courses dealing with primates, so that the behavior and anatomy of these creatures may be studied at length and in more intimate detail. Independent work by the students should be insisted upon. In my opinion, term reports are better than set examinations for such courses, because they permit, if they do not indeed encourage, considered thought rather than snap judgments on the part of the student.

THE GRADUATE LEVEL

Graduate training is not preprofessional but professional, and the presence of students from other disciplines should as such be ignored. If any such individuals wish to take a graduate course in physical anthropology and are qualified to do so, splendid. But they should be expected to meet the requirements fully. Qualifications for entrance should include plenty of biology and some statistics as well as anthropology. Both laboratory and seminar courses are, as they should be, offered at the graduate level, and field research is necessary for the professional as well. There is a constant and no doubt inevitable hazard of overnarrow specialization at this level. Unless the student has already had a background in general anthropology which is both broad and deep, he finds it easy to forget the importance of culture. The exchange of communications in the *American Journal of Physical Anthropology* between Garn (1954) and Kaplan (1955) illustrates this point.

In my opinion, it cannot be expected that a physical anthropologist will be a virtuoso in every technique of research which is available to us. He will usually have colleagues with whom to take counsel, and, if his basic training has been adequate, he should be able to learn new techniques as they become useful for his own lines of research. What can be expected of him is that he should remain an anthropologist: a scholar who has the aim and the ability to study the problems of human diversity from the point of view of the natural sciences and who will automatically think in terms of culture. If he is to be a professional rather than a technician, he cannot afford to lose his breadth of viewpoint, and techniques of teaching should be used which will tend to encourage this.

Since his profession requires the use of laboratory techniques very extensively, however, further drilling along these lines is a necessity. It is probable that universities will continue to differ from one another in the facilities which they have available for graduate training in physical anthropology and I think we can view this situation with equanimity. A part of the training of a professional physical anthropologist probably ought to be in the laboratories and classes of allied disciplines in any case. Human anatomy, for instance, can best be studied in a medical school and biochemistry under a professional biochemist. Provision for the study of comparative primate anatomy, on the other hand, will in almost all cases have to be made by the teacher of physical anthropology. Statistical theory can best be studied under a professional statistician, but its application to the problems of human population genetics will usually have to be made clear by the physical anthropologist. If a research-minded blood bank is available, students should be referred to it for precise up-to-date training in serological techniques.

Much, if not most, of the laboratory work of the graduate student in physical anthropology will be of an individual nature, and this will become more and more true as his training advances. Formal examinations, therefore, become less and less important as a means of assessing his progress and abilities. Group research may, on occasion, be undertaken by a number of students under the supervision of the professor, but this is not, in my opinion, very profitable as an educational experience. All too often the less able students simply exploit the imagination and drive of a superior individual under the guise of such coöperation. At the graduate level of training, a student needs to be encouraged to strike out on his own, to take the responsibility for devising the best means of testing hypotheses, and then to test them himself. He will almost certainly need guidance: a typical mistake is to pick too broad or complex a problem, one which would take much more time, effort, and money than could be made available. To restrain, without discouraging, an enthusiastic graduate student is not an easy task, and I am in no position to propose a simple solution. After he has demonstrated to himself as well as to his mentor that he has the ability to accomplish a given task, he can more safely undertake joint research projects. Gaining self-confidence by the successful execution of one's own project is important to the professional in training, however, and he should not be denied this exhilarating experience. Extensive and intensive discussion between the teacher and the budding professional is probably just as important and as useful as independent research, however. There is no substitute for thinking. Competence in laboratory techniques, affability in relations with the subjects of one's research, excellence in statistical manipulation are all needed by the physical anthropologist, but if he is unable to draw meaningful and fruitful conclusions from his work, it will have been a waste of time and effort on his part and a disappointment to himself as well as to others. Continued extensive reading and participation in seminars are very useful for a student in graduate training. But frequent, honest discussion of professional interests, problems, and ideas between the teacher and the student are stimulating to the thoughts of both and provide the best possible guide and check to the thoughts of the student as he is in the process of becoming a real professional himself. The necessity for combining imagination and patience, a keen critical ability with an open mind, willingness to work hard and also to contemplate can scarcely be taught without a great deal of such individual contact. So for a third time, and now to conclude my paper, I must say that the most essential item in the teaching of physical anthropology is a physical anthropologist.

REFERENCES CITED

GARN, S. M.
   1954   On the education of the physical anthropologist. American Journal of Physical Anthropology n.s. 12:607-609.
KAPLAN, BERNICE A.
   1955   More on the education of the physical anthropologist (from the point of view of general anthropology). American Journal of Physical Anthropology n.s. 13:351-355.

WILLIAM S. LAUGHLIN

Concepts and
Problems

T HE ECOLOGICAL NICHE of the animal that runs on two legs, climbs trees, swims, hunts, makes tools, stores, recalls and communicates vast amounts of information, and breeds freely with similar animals of appropriate sex and age is the greater part of the world. In contrast, the academic niche devoted to teaching younger members of this agile species the facts and explanations concerning the origin and maintenance of human population variability and to suggesting ways in which they might contribute better explanations is considerably more limited. Yet, the academic niche available to physical anthropology is much greater than the area presently occupied. Expansion depends as much upon internal intellectual adaptation as upon external factors. Offerings in physical anthropology must reflect the scope, and the scope is undergoing constant reappraisal as progress is made in academically separate disciplines which in fact have important molar relations with it that are considerably more than metaphorical analogies. I assume two objectives of teaching physical anthropology: the edification of all students in evolution, human biology, and the relevance of human biology to human behavior; and the training of selected graduate students who will subsequently be superior to their teachers in their contributions to the field.

PHYSICAL ANTHROPOLOGY
IN THE UNDERGRADUATE PROGRAM

Basic to the observations offered here is the concern that the instructor must teach students, not subjects. Course content, structure, and scheduling necessarily vary over the years and between colleges, and the instructor must adapt to the particular students before him within a particular academic situation over which he may have little control. Further, the same objectives may be achieved equally well in more than one way. Any fond notions of didactic orthodoxy can be dispelled by consulting the vitae of distinguished anthropologists. An examination of the Huxley Memorial Lecturers or of the Wenner-Gren laureates suggests that the routes to competence and distinction are multifarious. Although there can be no prefabricated, universal course or curriculum which will fit all students in all times and places, an examination of what has been done and what ought to be done is in order. There is much value in some consensus and thus of academic offerings for physical anthropology as a subject in a liberal education which aims to edify the nominal as well as the phenomenal student.

There are two overriding considerations: first, the constitution of physical anthropology and teaching students accordingly; second, the relation of physical anthropology to archaeology, ethnology, and linguistics in the academic curriculum and in research.

The arguments for offering physical anthropology at an elementary level as an educational of liberal discipline, as well as at an advanced level as a specialized professional subject, have been presented in cogent form elsewhere in this volume and also in *The Scope of Physical Anthropology and its Place in Academic Studies* (Roberts and Weiner 1958), especially in the papers of Professor J. Z. Young and of Dr. J. S. Weiner. Two points to be emphasized here are (1) the need for early exposure to human biology in order that pertinent facts and concepts may become a working part of the conceptual structure of the advanced student in any of the sub-areas of anthropology, rather than a body of *disjecta membra* to be memorized for the purpose of passing examinations, and (2) the need for early exposure in order to acquaint students with the field before they are fully absorbed in pre-professional or major programs which leave them no time to study subjects offered in the department of anthropology. Aside from reaching a large number of students among whom specially interested students may be encouraged to continue, physical anthropology at the elementary level has a unique function to perform for the students and the university in acquainting students with man's place in nature, the variability of human populations, and their relevance to other aspects of man. There is an unresolved or at least fluctuating body of opinion and academic practice concerning the relations of physical and cultural anthropology. A common American view has been expressed by Clyde Kluckhohn: "One of the cherished axioms of American anthropology is the unity of the science of man," with the corollary belief that even the social anthropologist must familiarize himself with genetics and other aspects of human biology if he wishes to be, in the strict sense, an anthropologist (Kluckhohn and Griffith 1950:401). This point of view provides a charter for human biology instruction in the academic program of every kind of anthropologist. The specific social science ingredient of anthropology, as distinguished from cultural anthropology, ethnology, or ethnography, is recent, scarcely a generation old in the estimation of A. L. Kroeber (1954). It is relatively inexpensive to teach and easily accommodated to mass education, and it has therefore been offered, particularly in newer institutions or new departments, where physical anthropology, archaeology, and linguistics have been offered in limited form or not at all.

Another point of view, in effect the other point of view, has been expressed by Dr. A. E. Mourant in the course describing a "unified physical anthropology":

Such an anthropology will take into account all the anatomical and physiological characters of man, tracing, where possible, their development by the methods of palaeontology and embryology, and studying their relationship at the present time both to heredity and to environment. Above all, it will include an examination of the interplay between the last two factors, to the mutual enrichment of physical anthropology and of all the other biological sciences of man. (Mourant 1956: 13)

For evident, but not self-evident, reasons the axiom of American anthropology concerning the unity of the science of man has been abundantly cherished, especially in the prefatory remarks of introductory textbooks, but it is then demoted to an implicit postulate with little sign of intellectual affection farther along and an astonishing celibacy between units when the traditional invocation for integration is offered in the terminal chapter. Departmental constituency has often betrayed the same uncertainty of the unity of the science of man.

CONTEMPORARY COMPARTMENTALIZATION

Compartmentalization of the different areas of anthropology exists in serious and identifiable form. It results in failure to utilize pertinent information, thus partially vitiating various studies, and it misleads students. Anthropologists, of whatever persuasion, are necessarily obliged to employ diverse kinds of data. They are in the business of comparing apples and inkwells, of finding the relations between genes, phonemes, and shattered stones. Whether there has been retrogression in the profession since 1871 cannot be determined without a thorough survey. What is certain is the presence of excellent studies employing diverse data in the earlier literature and the presence of contemporary studies on a more parochial level. The need for "interdisciplinary" projects may in part reflect the interdiction of techniques, methods, and concepts which, from a more anthropological point of view, fall within the confines of only one or at most a few disciplines. Acceptance of the broader definitions of physical anthropology should permit us to focus on intradisciplinary aspects.

A case in point of the the legitimate and sophisticated use of diverse forms of data is provided by Lewis Henry Morgan (1871) in his chapter on "System of Relationship of the Eskimo." Concerned with the divergence of the Eskimo system from those of the American Indians, he used physical evidence quite skillfully, even casting up a table of cranial measurements and including morphological observations on the three Eskimos with whom he worked. He considered the question of the separation of the Eskimo from the remainder of the American aborigines of great importance in American ethnology and studied their system of consanguinity and affinity with special interest in the bearing it might have upon the solution of this problem. This chapter need not be reserved for a course in anthropological theory but can be used to advantage in introductory courses.

Morgan's utilization of physical and kinship data to bolster each other in treating the dichotomy between Eskimo and Indian is generalized by Edward Sapir (1916) in his discussion of inferential evidence for time perspective. In considering the evidence of physical anthropology, he indicates two kinds of uses of physical data for cultural purposes, one depending upon distinctiveness and the other upon population density. As to the former, he wrote: ". . . but the simple fact that the bearers of a distinctive culture are often marked off from the bearers of other cultures by a distinctive physical type enables us not infrequently to employ the racial evidence for cultural purposes." The second type is derived from a statistical side of physical anthropology: "With all due reservations, however, the value of density of population as an index of length of occupancy of a region cannot be gainsaid." (Sapir 1916)

A contemporary example of the employment of diverse kinds of data, including physical, is found in a study by Felix M. Keesing, of early migrations in the southwest Pacific area, (1950). Having collated various kinds of information which bear upon migrations, he notes:

Summarizing the general themes of this paper, it presents a wider frame of reference than is usually taken in anthropological discussions of early migrations in the southwest Pacific. The potentialities of greater inter-disciplinary cooperation in future research on migration routes are suggested; related ethnological and archaeological data are summarized; and the need is stressed for taking full account of genetic perspectives in interpreting the racial history of such a region. (Keesing 1950:114)

Anthropologists have neglected the wider frame of reference in several other respects. Current compartmentalization has not been limited to deficient employment of biological material but to linguistic as well. In supporting the thesis of an Alaskan origin for Eskimos, advanced in 1916 by Sapir, and speaking directly to the point of associating language with skeletons or artifacts, Professor L. L. Hammerich remarks:

It seems to be forgotten that the objects found have been made and used by human beings who have possessed a language. It seems to be taken for granted that the science of language, linguistics, can afford no assistance in determining the origin of these arctic cultures. . . . only if it could be *proved* that the Dorset people did *not* speak Eskimo, the linguistic facts of the Eskimo language could rightly be disregarded in determining the origin of the Dorset Eskimo language which mainly preceded, partly was contemporaneous with Thule. . . . On the contrary: even if it is perhaps equally impossible to prove strictly that the Dorset people did speak Eskimo, it is overwhelmingly probable. (Hammerich 1958:641-642)

Eloquent evidence of compartmentalization is finally rendered in his observation that:

I should not intrude upon the territory of the archaeologist and ethnographer, but I cannot refrain from confessing that since some years, in reading papers on the origin of the Eskimo culture, I have been silently wondering if the peculiar conditions of the SW territory of the Eskimos, where they are or have been neighbors of the Aleuts, have attained the consideration they deserve. I am thinking especially of the Iliamna district with the adjoining regions to the S, and W, and the NW. (*ibid.* 643)

The fact of the matter is that the compartmentalization inside anthropology has proceeded to the point that it has even been termed a phobia. This bears directly on the first exposure to anthropology in the most elementary course and, therefore, deserves close scrutiny.

Comparing blood groups of Goajiro and Paraujano Indians in Venezuela, noting that the genetic relationship paralleled the linguistic relationship especially for the Diego antigen, Dr. Layrisse provides an additional insight into a facet of contemporary anthropology:

In any case, however, we believe that the phenomenon as such appears to be anything but surprising, since the fact that two tribes speak demonstrably related languages, has always been accepted as the most indubitable evidence of past historical connections. The reason why we hesitate to think along these lines, must have been rooted in the phobia anthropologists habitually exhibit when cultural and genetic data are to be correlated. (Layrisse *et al.* 1960)

A recent work on peoples and cultures of South American Indians (Steward and Faron 1959) carries the current compartmentalization to an extreme. Not only is no use made of serological, genetic, or mor-

phological evidence of affinities between populations or of their movements, but when transoceanic influences are discussed, the chromosomes
of cotton are considered, but not those of humans. Artifacts are made by
humans, languages are spoken by humans and humans are at least as
pertinent to the study of anthropology of any area as cotton and pots.

More recently than Morgan or Sapir, and in similar vein, but clearly
in anticipation of a different kind of audience, an audience conditioned
to compartmentalization of race, language, culture, and archaeology,
there is a revealing rationalization of the use of physical anthropological materials, with the explicit statement that no apology is offered. In
his book on the peoples and culture history of Africa, Professor Murdock, after denying that race is relevant to culture, states the minimal
conditions for utilizing anthropometric and somatological criteria as
an aid in historical reconstruction. He notes that they show enough areal
uniformity, temporal stability, and persistence in mixtures to provide
the archaeologist and ethnologist with a highly welcome additional
tool for tracing culture-historical movements (Murdock 1959:7). His
concluding sentence illustrates the intellectually impoverished state
to which anthropologists have fallen heir, "We thus offer no apologies
for the fivefold division presented herewith." The idea that an apology might be in order was clearly not present in 1871. The idea that
various populations might be expected to be both physically and
culturally divergent appears quite a modest and well-documented
expectation, in view of the fact that boundary maintaining mechanisms which inhibit gene flow are cultural as well as geographical, and
cultural barriers (linguistic, economic, kinship, and mating regulations, etc.) are invariably present even in the absence of physiographic
barriers. If no progress has been made in the utilization of physical evidence since 1871, it cannot be attributed to lack of physical materials.
There is a splendid body of material on the peoples of Africa, including
many other genetically determined factors than simply the major blood
groups. In addition, there are specific studies of critical importance to
the origins of such people as the Malagasy, in which both morphological
and serological evidence has been used.

One example of a common practice, unfortunately preserved in
current textbooks, is the use of morphological comparisons between apes
Negroes, and Europeans to prove that Negroes are in fact not closer to
apes than Europeans. The thick everted lips of the Negro are contrasted with the thinner lips of anthropoid apes and Europeans, and
the hairiness of apes and Europeans is contrasted with the relatively
glabrous condition of the Negroes, etc. What this exercise does, as Professor Washburn (1944) pointed out some years ago, is keep alive the idea
of the validity of such comparisons. No matter how well-intentioned
the practice may be, it preserves the absurd notion that at this remove

of several millions of years, since the separation of the human stock from that of anthropoid apes, there might conceivably be some human groups perceptibly and significantly closer to the apes than other groups.

The point to be emphasized is that the utilization of diverse forms of evidence whether conceived as inter- or intra-disciplinary, should be represented in the first exposure to anthropology for all students of whatever current persuasion or eventual area of concentration. Immediately related to this is the desideratum that the facts, processes, and consequences of the variability of human populations, past and present, be presented in an orderly and dignified form. Contemporary focus on rebuttal and denial, the disavowal of any connection between race and culture so frequently emphasized in introductory books, suggests that physical anthropologists have labored since the time of Blumenbach with their greatest reward being the assurance that their labors can be disregarded. If there were no other relevance of human biology to culture, then the cherished axiom of the unity of the science of man should be discarded, with no apologies. If human biology is relevant to human behavior, then the areas of relevance should be delineated and presented in introductory courses.

MUTUAL RELEVANCE OF HUMAN BIOLOGY AND CULTURE

The existence of physical anthropology does not depend upon its utility to ethnology, and each of the subareas or independent disciplines of anthropology, archaeology, ethnology, and linguistics is quite capable of independent existence. The unity of the science of man is not well reflected in textbooks or in departmental organization. It is, however, found in various studies and in a few departments. A number of recent symposia reflect the return to more substantial considerations of man's place in nature. A few of these are: *The Evolution of Man's Capacity for Culture* (Spuhler, ed. 1959), *Behavior and Evolution* (Roe and Simpson, eds. 1958), *The Processes of Ongoing Evolution* (Lasker, ed. 1960), *Medical Biology and Etruscan Origins* (Wolstenholme and O'Connor 1959), *The Social Life of Early Man* (Washburn, ed. 1960), *The Nature and Transmission of the Genetic and Cultural Characteristics of Human Populations* (Milbank Memorial Fund 1957).

The numbers of studies in which anthropologists, ethnologists, archaeologists, and linguists have collaborated on the same people is remarkably limited. Nevertheless, it is possible to pick out those general areas that have repeatedly received attention as areas in which there is common interest or in which the object or process must be studied in more than one way. A minimum list would necessarily include at least the following:

1. *Human evolution,* beginning with the most likely antecedents.

If humans did not first evolve and then discover culture but rather evolved through the use of tools and language, then it is relevant to investigate the behavioral aspects of man which have participated in his evolution. There is probably a relationship between the use of tools and reduction of teeth, and between language, brain size and, especially, the rapid rate of early postnatal brain growth. Linguistic studies, such as Professor C. F. Hockett's *Logical Considerations in the Study of Animal Communication* (1959) are also important for understanding the origin of humans.

2. *The Biological Basis of Human Sociality,* to use the title of a study by Professor Earl W. Count (1958), embodies an area capable of infinite subdivision. If there is a morphology of the nervous system, there must, by analogy, be a morphology of behavior. The fact that there is no specific genetic basis for a particular language nor a special cranial nerve for specific cultural behavior does not disqualify the biological basis of human behavior from etiological and complex relations to its derivatives. The morphology and behavior of nonhuman primates and other animals throw much light upon their counterparts in humans.

3. *Genealogy:* As remarked by George W. Marshall in 1866, "Genealogy assists us to view man in his two great aspects, physical and intellectual" (Marshall 1866:69). Students rarely learn to equate the distinctions of a kinship system with coefficients of relationship. This reflects the tendency to describe systems without presenting quantitative evidence of conformance to the system. The use of genealogies for both cultural and genetic purposes can be presented in the first course of anthropology, physical or general.

4. *Population delimitation.* From the standpoint of morphological, physiological or genetic studies, the delimitation of groups may be placed under the rubric of sample description. Mating preferences are affected by a gamut of forces ranging from ideas of beauty and formal mating regulations to physiographic barriers. Determining who is a member of a local race, i.e., those who have given or received genes, is a necessary first step in the study of a group (Laughlin 1960). Adequate sample description is essentially an ethnological undertaking. Skeletal series obviously cannot employ genealogies and must therefore, focus on grave types, grave furniture or other associations to delimit groups for comparison.

5. *Population composition.* Not only demographic details may be placed under this rubric (the O.E.D. still places demography under physical anthropology), but more important, it includes the pathway coefficients between all individuals. Whole villages or isolate genealogies are seldom published, but their analysis at least is essential to ex-

tracting the different kinds of samples (Spuhler and Kluckhohn 1953, Spuhler 1959). Groups differ significantly in the degree to which their members are related to each other (Laughlin 1960), and estimates of gene frequency ratios can efficiently be based on samples of specified relationships (Gray and Laughlin 1960). The matrix of pathway coefficients of a population are fully as important as the morphological or serological manifestations of those pathways.

Sapir's second use of the evidence of physical anthropology is one of the several kinds of uses that can be found in this category, the value of density of population as an index of length of occupancy. An examination of population density may reveal interesting associations among longevity, ecology, technology, overlap between generations, sex ratio, continuity between populations cultural complexity, and genetic stability, as in the contrast between the sparse populations of the Central Arctic and those of Southwestern Alaska.

6. *Inter-population distance.* Since the demise of the old Coefficient of Racial Likeness, a number of sophisticated methods of comparing three or more populations have come into use (Penrose 1954, Roberts 1954, Spuhler 1954). These provide quantification for the earlier observation of Sapir and Morgan that bearers of a distinctive culture are often similarly distinguished by a distinctive physical type, and they permit comparisons at much lower levels of abstraction than could be made earlier. This is of great utility in archaeological studies.

7. *Racial physiology.* In addition to studying the metabolic activities of natives under laboratory conditions, enticing Australian aborigines to sleep in a refrigerated truck or Eskimos to run on a treadmill, there are also valuable studies of the natives engaged in their characteristic activities. Wainwright Eskimos have now been studied as they hunted on the ice. Exact knowledge of the daily and annual round of activities and some estimates of the number of generations in which they have been followed are clearly of value in assessing the evolutionary importance of physiological adaptation. Studies of human plasticity likewise require exact knowledge of the behavior of the humans under consideration. Growth and constitution may also be included here.

8. *Strain differences in behavior.* Certainly an area of relevance is the possible existence of family line or strain differences in behavioral traits. A general statement is found in a recent book review by Kluckhohn, in which he challenges only one "crucial postulate":

In the light of accumulating information as to significantly varying incidence of mapped genes among different peoples, it seems unwise to assume flatly that "man's innate capacity does not vary from one population to another." Conceivably, if there were a calculus whereby pluses and minuses could be totaled, the overall figure for all populations might come out approximately the same. But, on the premise that specific capacities are influenced by the properties of each gene pool, it seems very likely indeed that populations differ quantitatively in their potentialities for particular kinds of achievement. (Kluckhohn 1959:1098) (See also Gerard, Kluckhohn, and Rapoport 1956.)

In summary of the question of the relevance of human biology and human behavior, or race and culture, it would appear that this is the area which distinguishes humans from other animals and the study of man from other disciplines. This is not to say that any simple equations exist, that cord blood has anything to do with the disposition of the umbilical cord, nor that a genetic component in criminal behavior or in musical ability indicates a gene for crime or for musical virtuosity. Most forms of behavior have to be elicited after appropriate maturational development. At the simplest level, discussion of origins, affinities and migrations which omit the evidence provided by the humans themselves are clearly deficient. The nature of human populations is squarely in the center of anthropological competence and is eminently suitable for the first introduction to anthropology.

ON OBSERVING THINGS AS THEY ARE

Current pedagogical practice has tended to emphasize the role of lectures and reading but to minimize direct investigation. It is possible to lecture to the full capacity of any given room, the content of the lecture will be the same for those in the back row as for those in the front row, though not always as audible. It is not, however, possible to tutor to the full capacity of a room. Adequate training, at the professional or graduate level especially, requires a good deal of personal attention, of tutoring, demonstrations, and of laboratory work as well as comprehensive reading. Reading a book is not a substitute for learning the materials, just as "taking a course" is not the equivalent of studying a subject. Anatomy cannot be learned from looking at pictures, any more than phonemics can be painlessly acquired by reading. In an introductory remark "On Observing Things as They Are," Le Gros Clark (1949) has noted, "One of the advantages of practical dissection is the opportunity it provides for developing powers of observation. Bearing this in mind the student should avoid placing too much reliance on descriptions found in books, but should learn to observe and record things as they really are." (xv). Blood typing is not learned from lectures but by actual participation under the tutelage of an experienced teacher. It requires much repetition, the testing of large series of specimens with different techniques and the acquisition of many controls and checks, so that the student realizes what he is doing and why he is doing it and develops a measure of competence and confidence.

Aside from the use of a few casts, the study of fossil man is relatively inaccessible to American students. The study of the human skeleton, however, is possible, and the study of fossil forms can only follow after the acquisition of considerable familiarity with range and form of variation in contemporary or post-Mesolithic skeletons. Actual work in blood grouping is an indispensable prerequisite or accompaniment to blood groups genetics. So much of our current knowledge of human races and the agencies operating on them has come from blood group genetics that the student of physical anthropology who does not receive a grounding in this area is seriously handicapped. The data of blood groups should affect our ways of thinking about human evolution, not merely the content of our thought.

The same remarks can be made for statistics. Utilization of statistics as a research tool requires tutoring and practice, not simply lectures on the importance of statistics. Archaeology and ethnology have been realistic in coming to grips with the fact that "things" must be handled. It is an easily verified observation that most American universities do not have departments of anthropology or interdepartmental programs that are prepared to provide adequate training for physical anthropology. Most departments do not have laboratories, skeletal collections, anthropometric instruments, incubators, centrifuges, refrigerators, and glassware, to name only some of the obvious requirements. Departments of anatomy, dental schools, or growth research centers and museums are among the affiliated facilities to which the student may need access, if indeed physical anthropology is not offered by a department of anatomy as such. There are some institutions so far removed from academic tradition and the current of anthropological history that they do not have a physical anthropologist in the department that titles itself anthropology. Others appoint a physical anthropologist who must teach so many other subjects that he cannot develop a research program, though this is essential to the training of students. Another category of academic institution offers a course in physical anthropology that is taught by a social anthropologist or someone concerned with race relations. As a consequence of these deficiencies many departmental programs require the major portion of upper division and graduate work to be given in areal courses, topical courses and "theory" courses in cultural anthropology, lesser amounts in archaeology, a small amount in linguistics and a roughly comparable small amount in physical anthropology. Courses in the natural sciences are minimized, and anatomy, genetics, population genetics, statistics, immunology, geology, etc. tend to be treated as semiextra-curricular electives which may be nice to have but should not be permitted to interfere with a well-grounded and dynamic approach to the study of man and his works.

Training in physical anthropology is expensive and requires much laboratory work with many specimens. If these can not be provided inside a department of anthropology, a department should make such training and experience available to the student by judicious interdepartmental arrangements. Inter-institutional programs are occasionally necessary. The seminars in primate anatomy which have been offered by Dr. Erik Erikson of Harvard University and by Professor S. L. Washburn, formerly at the University of Chicago and then at the University of California, Berkeley, and the various seminars held at the Wenner-Gren headquarters in New York, with laboratory dissections at the Columbia College of Physicians and Surgeons, are examples of instruction which could not have been offered at only one institution. The procurement and preparation of several specimens of New and Old World primates for dissection requires an enormous amout of preparatory labor and is beyond the facilities of most single departments.

Perusal of the membership of the American Association of Physical Anthropologists indicates that there is a great variety of training and of interests, ranging from the drosophila geneticist to the odontologist. There seems to be a consensus that anatomy, statistics and genetics, broadly conceived, must be represented in any background preparation. This can be accomplished in a variety of ways. There are many models available; an especially attractive example is the suggested scheme of practical classes as part of a B.Sc. Hons. Anatomy Course, presented by Dr. Weiner (Roberts and Weiner 1958:50). The course, entitled "Methods of Studying Morphological and Constitutional Variation in Man," includes classes on Evolutionary Variation, Age and Sex Determination, Body Form and Composition, Integumentary Features, and Statistical Treatment of Biometric Data.

The category of laboratory courses might well be divided into intra- and extra-parietal, for most colleges in the New World have access to small communities that are eminently worthy of study and suitable for training graduate students. Whether they are aboriginal Indians or transplanted communities of Lapps, Basques, or Kalmucks, they are numerous and as much an educational resource as the museum.

CONTINUITY OF THE LIVING
AND THE DEAD

It seems probable that the present course structure, with its emphasis on morphology of the small numbers of fossil man, maximizes a dichotomy between the living and the dead. Primary emphasis on craniometry, with secondary attention to sex ratio, age at death, pathologies, discrete traits, anomalies, age changes and biochemical analyses, has no doubt contributed to this orientation. This is unfortunate, for anthropologists have a historical charter, generally considered incontestable, to study the human skeleton, and there is much information that can be secured only from skeletons. If population genetics provides an area of interest common to physical and cultural anthropologists, skeletal studies provide an equally basic area of common interest with archaeologists.

The archaeologist clearly has an interest in knowing to what extent a population dominated an area, to what extent it evolved or remained stable for the periods under examination, and to what extent there is evidence of population replacement, mixture, or the arrival of new people. When skeletal series have been composed of samples from different isolates, much intergroup variation has been ignored. Thus, both Jochelson and Hřdlicka treated all skeletons from the Aleutians as a single series, without regard to geographical variation over a distance of some one thousand miles, even though von Baer and Dall had already commented on differences between Eastern and Western Aleuts. Hřdlicka was the first to note the variation in historical sequence, an easily sensible difference between pre-Aleut and Aleut, but he partially vitiated this insight by largely ignoring stratigraphic considerations. Such examples can be multiplied many times over. Aside from discarding much valuable biological information, the practice of composing large aggregate series removed much data pertinent to archaeology. Preoccupation with the skull of adult males discouraged the study of infant and child skeletons. Archaeologists excavate more skeletons than physical anthropologists. It thus behooves the physical anthropologists to persuade them to a high regard for complete recovery of all skeletons. The number of archaeologists taking a laboratory course in the human skeleton is good evidence of better future recovery of skeletal materials.

Professor Schapera (1955:25) has remarked that the genealogical method has the advantage of providing a time perspective, since by its use one can ascertain the reproductive histories of dead women as well as of living, and of two or three past generations. There are many areas where the data of three past generations will carry into skeletal series and contribute to both the analysis of population composition and of direction of migration or direction of gene flow. The use of small, contiguous isolates and the computation of intergroup distance is making skeletal studies of greater value to archaeologists and ethnologists (Laughlin 1960).

Odontologists have probably been most active and successful in their use of living and dead populations. Their work illustrates the pertinence of skeletal studies to those of child growth. A formal laboratory course on the skeleton should, of course, supplement and stimulate interest in experimental studies and in problems of growth.

Lest these remarks create any undue optimism concerning the state of skeletal studies, the still pertinent remark of Professor Hooton is cited:

Companies of archaeologists and ethnologists, platoons of linguists, are pursuing researches in cultural anthropology in the New World. A corporal's guard of physical anthropologists cannot subjugate an area of equal extent, even by the Herculean labors of an Hřdlicka, the colossal industry of an Oetteking, and the occasional brilliant forays of a Boas. (Hooton 1933: 163)

PRACTICAL CONSIDERATIONS FOR THE STUDENT

Field work and actual laboratory experience are indispensable to the training of the physical anthropologist. A discussion of sequence and timing in academic training can be firmly grounded on three considerations: those courses which must precede others as prerequisites, those which should be taken early in order to form part of the active thinking or theoretical orientation, and those which need to be taken in order to qualify the student for an appointment as research assistant or member of an expedition.

It may be helpful to observe that students are, in certain respects, in competition with natives and are handicapped by the expense of travel, equipment and academic schedule. Many Aleuts and Eskimos not only can excavate but also can identify the artifacts and animal bones as they excavate them, provide genealogies, and crank and repair a centrifuge. Traditional lecture courses are only partial preparation for enabling the student to secure field experience.

It is sometimes the case that a major in any subject other than anthropology is the surest way of securing the opportunity of working in an anthropological laboratory and of securing research experience and field experience. A major in zoology or biology, genetics or geology, with some course work in anthropology, provides an excellent background for the student who plans to enter graduate studies in anthropology, particularly physical anthropology (Sturtevant 1959). Not only should the student avoid placing too much reliance on descriptions found in books, he should similarly avoid too great reliance upon catalog descriptions of programs. Ability to cook or fly an airplane, in addition to appropriate competence in physical anthropology, may be the determining factor in being included on a field expedition. Work in a blood bank or primate laboratory or a photographic laboratory may be as important as any formal course listed on his curriculum vitae.

An example of a neglected resource available to aggressive students is the collection of a few skeletons interred in departmental or museum collections. These were often recovered by an archaeologist or explorer. A trained student can analyze such a series and prepare a report, often in lavish detail, which demonstrates his ability to handle such materials, is a welcome aid to the archaeologist, and makes the information available to later synthesizers.

It should be noted that in the field the physical anthropologist often enjoys a distinct advantage over the ethnologist, in that his operations are objective and understandable to the people and thus elicit their cooperation. It is no mere accident that ethnography grew out of physical anthropology in Sweden (Linne 1957), for the study of the knowledge of primitive man requires advance information on the subject known to "primitive" man. The training in natural science that goes into the preparation of a human biologist is equally good background for the ethnologist who elects to include ethnozoology or primitive science in his studies.

SUMMARY

The first exposure of the college student to physical anthropology, preferably in a separate course and with laboratory instruction, is of crucial importance. The study of the origin, distribution, and maintenance of human variation is of value to all students as a part of their liberal education, and it is important as a stimulus to students who may later enter physical anthropology as their professional discipline. Graduate training will necessarily be more individual, with much emphasis on laboratory work, individual research, and seminars. The current shortage of physical anthropologists is traceable partly to inadequate introductory courses. All members of the human species deserve an explanation of their origins, their composition, and their affinities.

REFERENCES CITED

BOYD, W. C.
    1950   Genetics and the races of man. Heath, Boston.
CLARK, W. E. LE GROS
    1949   Practical anatomy. Edward Arnold and Co., London.
COUNT, EARL W.
    1958   The biological basis of human sociality. American Anthropologist 60:1049-1085.
GERALD, R. W., CLYDE KLUCKHOHN, AND ANATOL RAPOPORT
    1956   Biological and cultural evolution, some analogies and explanations. Behavioral Science 1:6-34.
GRAY, MARGERY P., AND W. S. LAUGHLIN
    1960   Blood groups of Caddoan Indians of Oklahoma, American Journal of Human Genetics 12:86-94.
HAMMERICH, L. I.
    1958   The origin of the Eskimo. Proceedings of the Thirty-Second International Congress of Americanists, 1956. Copenhagen; Munksgaard, 1958. pp. 640-644.

HOCKETT, CHARLES F.
  1959   Logical considerations in the study of animal communication. University of Indiana.
HOOTON, E. A.
  1933   Racial types of America and their relation to old world types. *In* The American Aborigines, Diamond Jenness, ed. University of Toronto Press. pp. 133-163.
HŘDLIČKA, ALEŠ
  1945   The Aleutian and Commander Islands and their inhabitants. The Wistar Institute of Anatomy and Biology, Philadelphia.
JOCHELSON, WALDEMAR
  1925   Archaeological Investigations in the Aleutian Islands. Carnegie Institution of Washington, 367.
KEESING, FELIX M.
  1950   Some notes on early migrations in the Southwest Pacific Area. Southwestern Journal of Anthropology 6:101-119.
KLUCKHOHN, CLYDE
  1959   Review. Man's Way: A Preface to the Understanding of Human Society. Walter Goldschmidt. New York, Henry Holt and Company Inc. American Anthropologist 61:1098-1099.
KLUCKHOHN, CLYDE, AND CHARLES GRIFFITH
  1950   Population genetics and social anthropology. Cold Spring Harbor Symposia 15:401-415.
KROEBER, A. L.
  1954   The place of anthropology in universities. American Anthropologist 56:764-767.
LASKER, GABRIEL W. (ED.)
  1960   The processes of ongoing human evolution. Human Biology 32.
LAUGHLIN, WILLIAM S.
  1960   Aspects of current physical anthropology: method and theory. Southwestern Journal of Anthropology 16:75-92.
  1962   Correspondences in human biology and culture. The Centennial Review of Arts and Science 6:98-119.
LAYRISSE, M., Z. LAYRISSE, AND J. WILBERT
  1960   The blood group Antigens in Goajiro Indians. (in press) American Journal of Physical Anthropology.
LINNE, S.
  1957   Technical Secrets of American Indians. Journal of the Royal Anthropological Institute 87:149-164.
MARSHALL, GEORGE W.
  1866   Remarks on genealogy in connexion with anthropology, Memoirs, Anthropological Society of London, 1865-1866. Vol. II, pp. 68-73.
MILBANK MEMORIAL FUND
  1957   The nature and transmission of the genetic and cultural characteristics of human populations. New York.
MORGAN, LEWIS H.
  1871   Systems of consanguinity and affinity of the human family. Smithsonian Contributions to Knowledge, Vol. XVII, Washington. pp. 267-277.
MOURANT, A. E.
  1956   Blood groups and human evolution. The Advancement of Science 50:1-13.

MURDOCK, GEORGE PETER
 1959   Africa, its peoples and their culture history. New York, McGraw-Hill
         Book Company. See especially page 7, Race.
PENROSE, L. S.
 1954   Distance, size and shape. Annals of Eugenics 18:337-343.
ROBERTS, D. F.
 1954   The Cretans: a geographical analysis of some aspects of their physical
         anthropology. Journal of the Royal Anthropological Institute, vol.
         84, parts I and II, pp. 145-157.
ROBERTS, D. F., AND J. S. WEINER (EDS.)
 1958   The scope of physical anthropology and its place in academic studies.
         A symposium held at the Ciba Foundation, November 6, 1957. New
         York, Wenner-Gren Foundation for Society for the Study of Human
         Biology.
ROE, ANNE, AND G. G. SIMPSON (EDS.)
 1958   Behavior and evolution. New Haven, Yale University Press.
SAPIR, E.
 1916   Selected writings of Edward Sapir, David G. Mandelbaum, ed. Uni-
         versity of California Press, 1949.
SCHAPERA, I.
 1955   An anthropologist's approach to population growth: studies in the
         Bechuanaland Protectorate. In The Numbers of Man and Animals,
         J. B. Cragg and N. W. Pirie, eds. London, Oliver and Boyd. pp. 23-29.
SPUHLER, J. N.
 1954   Some problems in the physical anthropology of the American South-
         west. American Anthropologist 56:604-626.
 1959   Physical anthropology and demography. In The Study of Population,
         Phillip M. Hauser and Otis Dudley Duncan, eds. University of Chi-
         cago Press. pp. 728-759.
SPUHLER, J. N. (ED.)
 1959   The evolution of man's capacity for culture. Detroit, Wayne State
         University Press.
SPUHLER, J. N., AND CLYDE KLUCKHOHN
 1953   Inbreeding coefficients of the Raham Navaho population. Human
         Biology 25:295-317.
STEWARD, JULAIN H., AND LOUIS C. FARON
 1959   Native peoples of South America. New York, McGraw-Hill Book
         Company.
STURTEVANT, WILLIAM C.
 1958   Anthropology as a career. Washington, Smithsonian Institution.
WASHBURN, S. L.
 1944   Thinking about race. Science Education 28:65-76.
WASHBURN, S. L. (ED.)
 n.d.   The social life of early man (An international symposium sponsored
         by the Wenner-Gren Foundation for Anthropological Research, to be
         published in 1960).
WOLSTENHOLME, G. E. W., AND CECILIA M. O'CONNOR (ED:)
 1959   Ciba foundation symposium on medical biology and Etruscan origins.
         London, J. and A. Churchill Ltd.

GABRIEL W. LASKER

The Introductory
Course

I N GENERAL, physical anthropologists probably underestimate the extent to which their subject is actually being taught and the opportunities that occur for wider and fuller dissemination of their subject. On the basis of a survey, we know that in California alone, 9,636 students in thirty-seven institutions took a course in physical anthropology in 1960. The totals for the country as a whole are not known but are surely considerable. Yet, few physical anthropologists teach physical anthropology. On the basis of the last membership list of the American Association of Physical Anthropologists, I note that, of three hundred and thirty odd members, not over sixty teach undergraduate classes of any kind. Only about thirty, that is 9 per cent of the members, have direct responsibility for an introductory course in physical anthropology. An appraisal of the extent and level of teaching in physical anthropology may provide a background for the discussion of what can be done to improve the teaching of the subject.

THE TEACHERS

In the great majority of colleges and universities, introductory physical anthropology is taught by teachers without training in this field of anthropology. Among twenty-eight teachers of full-semester, lower-division courses in introductory physical anthropology in junior colleges in California for whom I have data, at least ten have had no formal training in physical anthropology, and only eight have earned a degree in anthropology. In many of the four-year colleges and the universities in this state, the biological aspect is a significant segment of the anthropology taught, but few of the teachers have had much training in biology in general or in physical anthropology in particular.

99

THE STUDENTS

Surveys of enrollments in physical anthropology point to sharply increasing enrollments. In the whole country 58 colleges and universities offered a course in physical anthropology in 1940-41; the number had increased to 135 by 1948-1950 (Voegelin 1950). In colleges with degree programs in anthropology, the number of courses in physical anthropology increased another 86 per cent since then—from 92 to 171 (Lasker elsewhere in this work). Allan Smith, in a communication to the Educational Resources in Anthropology Project, indicates that, of thirty-eight selected colleges and universities from which he received answers to a questionnaire, twenty offered a course in physical anthropology which was open to freshmen and sophomores, and 2,868 students were enrolled in these courses. Eleven (55 per cent) of the institutions granted credit as a biological science to the course and these accounted for 89 per cent of the enrollments.

The growth of the teaching of physical anthropology is very marked in California. Enrollments in the introductory course in physical anthropology increased from 8,438 in 1959 to 9,211 in 1960 and in other courses in physical anthropology from 306 to 425 during the same period (Lasker and Nelson elsewhere in this work). Over one half of these enrollments are still in junior colleges. The expansion of the enrollments in physical anthropology during the year is limited to the four-year state colleges and the various campuses of the University of California, and the proportion of enrollments in physical anthropology that the junior colleges account for has gone from 57 to 51 per cent.

Although the situation in California may be unusual, an increasing number of students are entering introductory courses in physical anthropology throughout the country. Few of these students have any previous knowledge about the subject or any intention to continue. They choose it to fulfill a natural-science credit requirement or because of curiosity about human evolution. A small number of them will major in anthropology, and a miniscule proportion will become professional anthropologists. This proportion varies from college to college and from class to class. In numerical terms, at least, the chief contribution of the introductory course in physical anthropology is as part of a liberal education. Furthermore, the introductory course does not seem to be important in the training of professional physical anthropologists, for many graduate students in physical anthropology never take an elementary course and yet succeed in making up the ground by independent reading and advanced course work.

CLASS HOURS AND CLASS SIZE

The three-hours-per-week, semester-long course is the most common, but by no means universal, introduction to physical anthropology. Fif-

teen of the twenty colleges and universities for which Allan Smith provides this datum have about 48 hours per term of class sessions and five
have about 32 hours. Four courses include one hour a week of discussion,
quiz or demonstrations, and five others have from one-half hour to four
hours of laboratory work per week; in general, the larger classes are
divided for part of their work into groups averaging from fifteen to
thirty students, but four straight-lecture courses with attendance of
one hundred or more students are also reported.

The nature of the course depends to some extent on the type of institution. In junior colleges, the predominant pattern is that of a three-
hour lecture course. Since no assistance is available, discussion or laboratory sessions are usually lacking, and examinations and tests are often
of the short-answer "objective" variety for the same reason. In the universities, graduate-student help is available, and quiz sessions are often added to, or substituted for, one hour of lecture per week

Essentially the same elementary course in physical anthropology
with ample material of a distinctively anthropological and legitimately scientific nature can be taught in almost any institution which
has a competent teacher of the subject on its staff; but there remains
scope for differing content and for alternate approaches. The largest
classes usually include small discussion sessions, guided by a teaching
assistant, in which there may be demonstrations. Because of limited laboratory facilities, introductory courses with laboratory sessions are generally feasible only where the class enrollment is small.

PHYSICAL ANTHROPOLOGY IN A SHORT
INTRODUCTION TO ALL OF ANTHROPOLOGY

A semester introduction to all of anthropology with the first six weeks
(eighteen class periods) on physical anthropology is a common type
of course. Human evolution is also sometimes taught together with prehistory as a semester course. Several textbooks are written for a combined course in physical and cultural anthropology, but the section
dealing with physical anthropology in such textbooks tends to be meager.

In 1959 one large state university shifted from a year-long freshman
introductory sequence of three quarters (five hours per week) to a
one quarter survey of all anthropology for freshmen. This change was
accompanied by the shift of the year-long sequence to the sophomore
level. One result has been that the one quarter devoted to physical anthropology now has only about thirty students per quarter rather than
the well over one hundred per quarter it had when taught at the freshman level.

Where a single semester or quarter course in all of anthropology is
given, it is usually considered as a "feeder" for the more advanced of-

ferings of the department. Since such courses are usually taught by a
single teacher whose chief interest is in only one branch of the subject,
the treatment of other aspects may be deficient. S. M. Garn of Antioch
College says of such kinds of courses that he does not consider a couple
of weeks of aimless drifting over obsolete material by an untrained
instructor to constitute teaching of physical anthropology. I too have
considerable reservations about courses which try to tell what physical
anthropology is about in two or three weeks (four lectures at one college of which I know). There are disadvantages in introducing physical anthropology as a small part of a general course in anthropology.
In such a presentation it is likely that only past evolution will be mentioned and that the student will fail to come to realize that evolution
applies to himself also, connecting him with the future as well as with
the past. I prefer a full semester (or quarter) of introductory physical
anthropology combined with another semester or two of introductory
cultural and social anthropology. Where only a small part of a general
course can be devoted to physical anthropology, it is better to deal with
a single problem (such as that raised by the little volume, *The Evolution of Man's Capacity for Culture*, edited by Spuhler, 1959) than to
attempt a general survey.

THE ONE-SEMESTER INTRODUCTION TO
PHYSICAL ANTHROPOLOGY

The introductory course in physical anthropology should be the normal basis for the subsequent professional study of the subject. Even
more important, it should be the way in which the main ideas of the
field are conveyed to the general college-educated public. The course
should prepare those who take it for an understanding of new developments in physical anthropology as they occur. Discoveries and new interpretations would thus find wider audiences, both anthropologists and
others, prepared to understand, critically evaluate, and apply these ideas
to other areas of thought and action.

The course must have a focus and structure and not be an assortment
of unrelated information. It can focus on the sources of human biological variability. The last time I taught a semester course in physical
anthropology, I centered it on the theme of human evolution, with the
first half devoted to past evolution, using Clark (1955), *Fossil Evidence
for Human Evolution*, as a point of departure, and the second half on
present evolution, using Boyd (1950), *Genetics and the Races of
Man*. I took up the topics in the order I follow in *Evolution of Man: an
Introduction to Physical Anthropology* (Lasker 1961), giving about a
week to the topic of each chapter. The syllabus was arranged in this
order:

1st Week: What is anthropology? What is physical anthropology and how has it developed? Evolution as fact and theory.

2nd Week: Origin of life. Taxonomy of living things and the place of the primates.

3rd Week: The Primates. The preconditions for an animal with culture and the extent to which these occur in the structure and behavior of living primates.

4th Week: Geologic time and its measurement. The Pleistocene. The nature of fossils. Paleontological principles and evolutionary "laws."

5th Week: Pre-Pleistocene fossil primates.

6th Week: The Australopithecines.

7th Week: Pithecanthropines and some other fossil hominids.

8th Week: Neanderthaloids and the origin of Homo sapiens.

9th Week: Question of racial differences in Upper Paleolithic man. Peopling of America.

10th Week: Genetic basis of human diversity. Mendelian principles.

11th Week: Population genetics. Mutation, natural selection, random genetic drift, and gene flow.

12th Week: Population differences in blood groups, hemoglobins.

13th Week: Population differences and the biological history of groups. Genetics versus typology in racial classification.

14th Week: Race and capacity. Fallacies about racial differences in intelligence. The role of climate.

15th Week: Anthropometry, plasticity, and growth.

16th Week: Applications of physical anthropology. Problems for the future. Review.

Others might retain these topics but vary the amount of time devoted to each. Some instructors might prefer a different order, a reversal of the first and second halves or other changes. In fact, it seems to be the consensus of the most experienced teachers that revision of the syllabus every few years and use of new texts stimulates the teacher and produces a better course.

Whatever the nature or order of material or the pedagogical methods employed, the chief purpose of the introductory course in physical anthropology is to have the student learn the method of science and to see its applicability to the study of man. I do not consider the learning of facts or techniques or even concepts (in the narrow sense) an adequate goal for the beginning student of physical anthropology. All of these may be used to arouse interest and to exemplify the subject matter, but in addition one would wish the student to understand the process by which new knowledge is gained.

Facts are the necessary base in science, of course. Every beginning student should learn that facts are observed or observable aspects of events and be able to distinguish them from opinions. Human evolution is a fact. This aspect of evolution can be introduced by having students bring in pictures of their parents at college age and comparing them with recent photos of themselves in the same poses. A comparison of the pictures can be used to demonstrate inheritance but with change. The distinction between the fact of evolution (i.e., merely inheritance with change) and theories of evolution which explain the nature and causes of some such changes can then be meaningfully introduced.

Techniques should be considered as secondary in an elementary course, most of whose members will never "practice" anthropology. Anthropometric measurements can be demonstrated in the classroom, as can blood group or taste reaction tests, and observations of palatine and mandibular tori, cusp patterns, and skin color. Little class time is needed to enable the students to try these techniques, provided the necessary materials and instruments have been laid out in advance and the instructor has gone over the exercise in a "dry run." The purpose of showing a technique to beginning students is to demonstrate objective methods of accumulating the facts necessary for further tests of hypotheses and theories. Thus, a demonstration of blood grouping in an elementary physical anthropology course should be introduced in conjunction with the discussion of population genetics. Likewise, a few anthropometric measurements can be introduced in connection with the discussion of human variability. Where techniques of data collection are linked to the hypotheses which can be tested, concepts are seen by the student in the framework of their testability. Thus, a scientific understanding of race is most likely to come through a positive understanding of biological differences between populations and the dynamics by which such differences between populations develop and wane.

PHYSICAL ANTHROPOLOGY FOR NATURAL SCIENCE CREDIT

Physical anthropology has a certain advantage in introducing the freshman student to science, because it touches the student at least as intimately as any other science. The interest in the subjects of appearance and health can be carried over into having him see himself among the vast variety of humankind.

In respect to enrollments, one of the principal questions is whether the elementary course in physical anthropology carries credit toward fulfillment of a natural-science requirement. Those colleges which do not give such credit claim that for students to appreciate science and understand how it is advanced through scholarship, laboratory work (or, in the case of geology, field experience) is essential. It is of course true that direct participation in experiments can be a stimulating learning experience. But this is not the case when laboratory work becomes cut and dried, permitting no originality of approach or genuine discovery, as is all too often the case. More thinking can be sparked by an instructor who, gifted with a sense of discovery and the art of communicating his zeal, through lecture, demonstration, and discussion, introduces his students to the creative atmosphere of true scientific inquiry. He would not have time to go through this process with individual students in the laboratory; and nothing is less apt to inspire a student than the perfunctory reproduction of experiments in a manual. Classroom demonstrations and accounts of concrete scientific studies may be a meaningful introduction to science. In physical anthropology, as in any science, the student's discovery is the key to the development of his interest and insight. Whether in the laboratory or the classroom, the instructor should guide the student to draw his own conclusions from the evidence and to use pertinent evidence rather than authoritative dicta.

DEMONSTRATIONS AND LABORATORY

One example of classroom demonstration is that used by the late Professor Felix Keesing of Stanford University in discussing racial differences. He sorted the students according to one physical characterisitc, such as stature, and then according to another, such as hair color, so that each student could see that the physical characteristic in one trait does not determine how he will be classified in respect to another. Thus it is demonstrated that specific traits have genetic and environmental determinants independent of those of other traits. Among Americans of European extraction, "racial groups" can be seen to correspond to abstract conceptualizations based on a number of arbitrary criteria. Since different criteria give different groupings and increasing the number of criteria leads to a multiplication of possible types, the method has little value in the study of the process of racial differentiation. This learning is then applied to the evaluation of differences between white and non-white groups, in which the potential independence of differences in stature and hair color may not previously have been apparent to the student. The exercise also provides an opportunity to discuss the nature of sampling and the bias involved in using a classroom of students, since they do not represent a natural breeding population. Such simple demonstrations, which can be carried out in the lecture hall of an elementary course with the participation of all the students, can be as effective as a laboratory session.

Laboratory exercises, if they are effective, are a real contribution to an elementary course, but many teachers believe that laboratory work is not the *sine qua non,* and some contend that the objectives are in fact better met through lectures. In discussing this issue, Professor Joseph

B. Birdsell of UCLA emphasized that laboratory experience or lack of it is not the telling factor in determining whether physical anthropology introduces the student to the methods of natural science (and can appropriately be counted towards natural science requirements). The basic question, he contends, concerns the challenge and intellectual rigor of the course.

A visit to the zoo is a practical exercise. In the field of primatology, fine anatomical and physiological distinctions will be difficult for a beginning student to appreciate. On the other hand, the actual behavior of primates in the zoo and in such films as those of Carpenter and his associates (1960) on macaques and howler monkeys, or that of DeVore and Washburn (1960) on baboons, will allow the student to see a sample of nonhuman primate behavior. An exercise in timing with a watch and describing in detail a bit of social interaction between monkeys is excellent training in observation, objectivity, and avoidance of anthropocentrism. What is more, these exercises can be interesting and, since such behavior is repetitive (but with individual sex, age, species, and situational differences), the student may get for himself the sense of discovery of some general concepts.

In respect to exercises in human genetics, some equipment and skill are needed for simple ABO blood-group determination in a class. Tests of taste reaction to PTC by the serial dilution method, however, take little more than cups and spoons; those students who live at home can try it on members of their family. The theory behind threshold values and the checks on replicability give the student a glimpse of the methods of control in science. If genetic principles can be tested or, better yet, inferred anew from the data, the gain is greater.

Part of the exercise involves determination of the exact relationships between individuals and construction of genealogies. One of the difficulties of classroom genetic projects is that the population from which the subjects are drawn is heterogeneous, and students tend to make false assumptions about common or disparate origins on the basis of genetic similarities and differences. Any attempt to divide the class into subgroups by national origin, race, or religion must be accompanied by an analysis of the rate of interbreeding between such categories and the extent to which each of them is subdivided, from a genetic point of view, by breeding preferences based on proximity, economic status, and other factors. The purpose is not, or not only, to relate physical anthropology to cultural anthropology, but to show that genetic findings have meaning only when referred to the degrees of common descent.

In respect to growth, the end products as seen in cross-sectional growth studies do not usually lend themselves to dramatic laboratory lessons. I would defer most anthropometry to a specialized course for the same reason that I would defer all but a little simple anatomy:

both emphasize the static aspects and can best be learned as necessary tools when the student has had a glimpse of the dynamics, wants to specialize, and is ready to embark on his own investigations. But certain tissues such as hair and nails grow rapidly enough for self-study as part of an introductory exercise. If a fingernail is marked by a filed line at the level of the cuticle, the filed notch can be made visible by wiping a little ink over it. The distance between successive filed lines can be measured. So little is actually known of the effects on nail growth of sex, age, climate, diet, race, and health, that well-planned class exercises could be a genuine contribution to knowledge. It is also possible to shave a small area on the arm or leg and to follow and measure or weigh the growth of individual hairs. Introduction of the student to the use of cameras, microscopes, and balances is a secondary gain from careful studies of nail and hair growth and is perhaps helpful in relating physical anthropology to other sciences and their methods.

These are only a few samples of ways in which teaching of the major principles of physical anthropology can be reinforced by simple direct experiences in and outside of the classroom, without elaborate set-ups or great expenditure of time. The very fact that the instructor is willing to depart from a prescribed text to engage in such exercises with his students adds to his impact on his class.

MAPS, CHARTS, SLIDES, AND CASTS

Visual aids have an important place in the introductory course in physical anthropology. Professor E. A. Hooton of Harvard, who was one of the most successful teachers of such a course, made a great deal of use of such materials. According to Hunt (1960), "A large collection of lantern slides of human faces and physiques from all over the world was part of his secret. He performed brilliantly with a mounted skeleton or a tray full of bones."

Slides (especially of maps, outline drawings and semi-diagrammatic materials), can help the students through an analysis of quite complex relationships. Thus, to show gene flow a series of maps of gene frequencies can be used (such as those published by Mourant [1954] on blood groups and by Neel [1957] on sickle-cell trait and other abnormal hemoglobins).

For the study of fossil man, excellent sets of Kodachrome slides are available, one prepared by W. W. Howells for the Audiovisual Division, University of Wisconsin, Madison, Wisconsin, another by the Photography Department, American Museum of Natural History, New York. The Denoyer-Geppert Company sells a chart, prepared in Germany, which illustrates skulls of various forms of fossil man and man-like primates, including some of the more recently discovered specimens. It illustrates several specimens at each morphological level

and, therefore, permits a comparison of various Neanderthaloid specimens with each other, for instance, as well as a comparison of these
with Australopithecine, Pithecanthropine, or modern forms. Unfortunately, speculative reconstructions with soft parts and hair are also
illustrated on the chart. Charts in English with finer detail are needed.
The University Museum, University of Pennsylvania, Philadelphia 4,
Pennsylvania, sells a wide range of casts of fossil men, which are much
used in the classroom and laboratory for demonstrating morphological characteristics. For comparisons with modern man, well-preserved
human skeletons, which can be purchased through any medical supply
house, generally show more detail and are, therefore, preferable for use
in the elementary course to broken bones from archaeological collections. Anatomical wall charts are also available from the last-named
source.

TEXTBOOKS AND READINGS

Some teachers like to use a textbook, others a book of readings, and
still others a list of paperback books or library readings. A combination
of a textbook and supplementary readings is preferable, since the
textbook can give a comprehensive and consistent account, and the
readings will give an insight into continuing problems and differences of opinion. Use of readings alone may present special problems,
since the articles may have been written for a variety of types of audience. Key technical terms—especially taxonomic terms—are used in different ways by different authors, and unless a textbook or extended
syllabus is used, an undue proportion of class time may be lost in purely
semantic discussions.

EXAMINATIONS AND TERM PAPERS

Large classes often lead to the use of "objective" examinations. At the
University of California, Los Angeles, however, examination questions
of the essay type are successfully used in very large classes. Most teachers believe that since the course is intended as a part of a liberal education, the student should have practice in organizing his views and
writing them out. In large classes, essays pose the necessity for extra
readers and the risk that these will not have identical standards, but
this should not preclude their use. Sometimes it is possible to give some
essay questions in the final examination or to give a take-home essay
question as well as a short-answer final. Two teachers have mentioned
that it helps the good students if the short-answer examination
includes opportunities for amplified answers. Professor W. S. Laughlin
of the University of Wisconsin writes at the top of one mimeographed
test: "In any case of apparent ambiguity explain your answer by means
of marginal or inter-linear emendation. Evidence of erudition, such as

comparative or critical observations, citations of other sources, as well as correct answers, are invited." He might have added: "and will be graded as part of the answer." Students should be told in advance exactly how grades are determined.

If it is practicable to do so, the writing of a term paper should be assigned. Such assignments have maximum value if, instead of requesting merely reviews of books and articles, they call for some synthesis of the student's own experience in laboratory exercises with the literature on the subject. Papers can be retained and filed in the library for the edification of future students and, if this is explained when the task is set at the outset of the course, it may encourage the student to write for an appropriate audience. Likewise, if the teacher insists on journal style it will make the task simulate that of the professional more closely. Laughlin utilizes another device for the same purpose. He requires an abstract of not over 250 words to be submitted by a fixed date prior to the due date for the papers. The abstracts are then duplicated and distributed to all students so they can be discussed in class. For similar reasons S. M. Garn asks his students to prepare an application for a grant for a piece of research in physical anthropology. In any case, everything that gives the student the experience of acting like a professional—investigating, discussing, writing, editing, and abstracting—will prove valuable in presenting physical anthropology as science. I do not believe that this will be at the expense of acquisition of knowledge. Rather it should stimulate the mastery of the necessary grounding in fact.

THE INTERESTS OF THE TEACHER

Most of the teachers whom I have interviewed believe that the elementary course requires more skill and experience to teach than any other. Several have specified that it is the task for the most accomplished anthropologists on the faculty. But it is evident that these are often also the persons with the heaviest burden of research, editing, administration, advising, and teaching of specialized material. A system which lightens the burden by rotating this task, by placing some of the responsibilities on teaching assistants, and by prevention of undue duplication is likely to result in the greatest concentration of effort. At one large university some twenty separate sections of four different elementary courses were given each year until recently, and at another each teacher gives two elementary sections each semester. This may be necessary while a program is being founded; but unless the staff is extraordinarily devoted to the method, it is desirable soon to consolidate the elementary courses and to give the teachers a change of pace (and some block time for research).

What is lost by large lecture sections and the inexperience of teaching assistants may well be gained by the improved quality of the lectures. Time saved in the classroom in this way may more profitably be spent in more individual instruction. An adequately prepared teacher giving one or two classes can do a more effective job than an overworked one who is obliged to reuse the same course notes many times and even to rewarm the same jokes several times a week.

ACKNOWLEDGMENTS

Citations from S. M. Garn, E. E. Hunt, Jr., and Allan Smith are from mimeographed and manuscript materials. References to experiences of various teachers at numerous institutions are from interviews and duplicated materials. I wish to thank all those who have cooperated by being thus willing to share their teaching experiences with fellow teachers.

REFERENCES CITED

Boyd, W. C.
   1950   Genetics and the races of man. Boston, Little Brown.
Clark, W. E. LeGros
   1955   Fossil evidence for human evolution. Chicago, University of Chicago Press.
Hunt, E. E., Jr.
   1960   The teaching of physical anthropology (at Harvard). Typescript manuscript (9 pp.) of paper presented at annual meeting of the American Association of Physical Anthropologists, Washington, D.C., March 1960.
Lasker, G. W.
   1961   The evolution of man: a brief introduction to physical anthropology. New York, Holt, Rinehart and Winston.
Mourant, A. E.
   1954   The distribution of human blood groups. Oxford, Blackwell Scientific Publications.
Neel, J. V.
   1957   Human hemoglobin types, their epidemiologic significance. New England Journal of Medicine 256:161-171.
Spuhler, J. N.
   1959   The evolution of man's capacity for culture. Detroit, Wayne State University Press.
Voegelin, E. W.
   1950   Anthropology in American universities. American Anthropologist 52:350-391.

FILMS CITED

Carpenter, C. R.
   1960   Howler monkeys of Barro Colorado Island. 27 min., 16 mm., black and white, sound. The Pennsylvania State University.
DeVore, Irven, and S. L. Washburn
   1960   Baboon behavior. 31 min., 16 mm., color, sound. University of California Extension, Berkeley.

GABRIEL W. LASKER

Advanced Courses

MANY OF THE LEADING physical anthropologists in America never taught anthropology to undergraduates. Aleš Hrdlička, Franz Weidenreich, Raymond Pearl, T. Wingate Todd, and many of their successors were employed in a faculty of medicine or a research institute. Although they were trained in and still are identified with other disciplines, Th. Dobzhansky, W. E. Le Gros Clark, A. A. Dahlberg, Melvyn Moss, W. L. Straus, Jr., and G. G. Simpson, among others, contribute enormously to physical anthropology both through their writings and by associations with students of physical anthropology. Research in physical anthropology in departments of genetics and biology and in schools of medicine and dentistry is important in introducing into these disciplines and professions knowledge of human evolution, human variation, human genetics, human growth and the influence of culture on human biology. But it has a limited influence on the development of anthropology. If students majoring in anthropology are to learn about physical anthropology and to integrate its concepts into their approach to general anthropological problems, physical anthropology should be taught in the same department as cultural anthropology. Since the specifically cultural variables are usually relevant in human biology, it is up to trained anthropologists in anthropology departments to accept the principal responsibility for the teaching of the subject, and in this way its value in liberal education will be increased.

PHYSICAL ANTHROPOLOGY IN THE ANTHROPOLOGY DEPARTMENT

In the relatively few anthropology departments in which advanced courses in physical anthropology are offered, there is a wide variety in the number, subject matter, approach, and level of the courses. Although they are not necessarily either superior to others nor typical, the arrangement of the curricula in physical anthropology at Harvard and at two campuses of the University of California will be outlined to indicate some of the possibilities for teaching physical anthropology in conjunction with other branches of anthropology.

PHYSICAL ANTHROPOLOGY AT HARVARD

A large segment of advanced college work in physical anthropology derives from a single institution, Harvard University, and from the teaching elsewhere by Harvard graduates. Edward E. Hunt, Jr., in an unpublished paper delivered at a symposium on the teaching of physical anthropology held at the 1960 annual meeting of the American Association of Physical Anthropologists, told how the teaching of physical anthropology developed at Harvard. Hunt says: "If the initial curricular affiliation of somatology in America had been medical or zoological, I suspect that the cleavage between biological and cultural anthropology would have been early and absolute. . . . But the facts of history are that American somatology traces quite clearly to museums and exploration."

After listing the role of F. W. Putman, Frank Russell, and W. C. Farabee in uniting physical anthropology to ethnology and archaeology, Hunt describes the teaching of E. A. Hooton, who was on the faculty at Harvard from 1913 until his death in 1954. "Although the core of the curriculum was much as Russell taught it, Hooton's students were exposed to far more evidence on fossil man." Hooton was a brilliant teacher who trained most of the present generation of American physical anthropologists, stimulated some cultural anthropologists to a lifelong interest in the biology of man and interested thousands of physicians, dentists, and Harvard undergraduates in his beloved subject.

Hunt adds:

It is rather curious how he taught Mendelian genetics. His principal vehicle . . . was his course in race mixture. He taught the subject rather uncritically, with apparently an undue stress on hybrid vigor and the dominance of some physical characters whose heredity today is stated in far less conclusive terms. It is fair to say that not until J. B. Birdsell and William C. Boyd lectured sporadically at Harvard just after World War II, and James N. Spuhler gave a few small colloquia not long afterwards, was the subject of modern genetics brought into focus. Today a good curriculum in physical anthropology would probably dismiss the literature on race mixture with a nod to history and a summary of the recent studies of gene flow models.

Hooton sought to relate individual biological endowment to human behavior. At first he taught a course dealing mainly with the anthropometry of criminals, Hunt says, but after the Second World War Hooton became less sure that criminals were biologically inferior and saw, rather, an occupational specialization according to physique, whether in criminal, civilian, or military careers. He taught a course in constitutional anthropology to which Hunt contributed lectures on body composition. In the late 1940's Harvard added a course on body growth, and, from time to time, courses in primatology and population genetics. Statistical methods useful to physical anthropologists were also introduced into the courses.

According to Hunt, the heart of the curriculum in physical anthropology at Harvard under Hooton was a brilliant display of teaching virtuosity in the elementary course, followed by a catch-all, year-long lecture-plus-laboratory course half devoted to osteology, half to living man, into which every topic and technique of interest was introduced. In this course there was much emphasis on the methods and detailed facts of physical anthropology. Such a course continues to the present and is called: "physical anthropology: a. the skeleton, b. biometry and statistics." Special topics like primatology, growth, genetics, constitution, racial systematics, and applied physical anthropology are offered by the department's junior physical anthropologist or when a particularly capable graduate student or a visiting professor is available to teach them.

PHYSICAL ANTHROPOLOGY AT THE UNIVERSITY OF CALIFORNIA

A somewhat different development of the teaching of physical anthropology has taken place at the University of California. At Berkeley an advanced course in human evolution and a course on living races of man normally have an optional laboratory section which is primarily for those concentrating in physical anthropology. These laboratories carry two extra semester hours of credit. There is also a course on primate social behavior—a topic involving interests of social anthropologists as well as of physical anthropologists.

There is much to recommend an optional laboratory open to undergraduate anthropology majors, a device introduced at the University of California, Berkeley. The teachers say that it is especially effective to have in the laboratory only a small group of students who have voluntarily signed up for this extra work. They believe that the optional laboratory serves to recruit students for graduate study in physical anthropology. Many students in cultural anthropology or linguistics who take the advanced courses in physical anthropology merely to fulfill their degree requirements prefer not to take the laboratory work. Students at Berkeley who have taken the course in both class and laboratory state that they appreciate the personal attention of the instructor which they get in the small laboratory section and that they do not find the lectures, addressed to a larger group of non-laboratory students, too elementary for their needs.

At the University of California, Los Angeles, there are laboratory sessions in the advanced physical anthropology (human osteology) course, but none are listed for the course in the genetics of race. Instead a term paper based on research is required. Thus, the last time the course was given, most of the students worked on genetic studies of frontal hair patterns and occipital hair whorls. In addition, two mathematics majors collaborated in preparing a program for the 709 computer which will calculate Rh-chromosome frequencies by Fisher's maximum likelihood method, and an anthropology major attempted to create a model for the calculation of the number of loci involved in polygenic characters from hybridization of heterozygous populations.

THE COURSE IN HUMAN EVOLUTION

At many other universities and colleges the curriculum follows the pattern of the institutions mentioned above in that it offers an introductory course of one semester followed by two one-semester courses, one sometimes titled "Human Evolution," on the physical anthropology of people of the past, and one on the physical anthropology of the living.

Following the pattern of the two volumes of Martin's *Lehrbuch der Anthropologie* (1914), one course is often still given over primarily to osteology—the examination of skeletal remains. The hallmark of this course is the "bone quiz" in which the student is expected to identify human bones and fragments of bones. Such skills are anatomical, and courses of this kind are sometimes popular with premedical students anxious to get a head start in their study of human anatomy. The course itself deals with the application of anatomical skills to the problems of identification which face archaeologists.

I would replace this limited professional approach by a course with more intellectual content. Thus, I would emphasize the methods by which the human fossil record can be interpreted. The story of man's evolutionary past, if not adequately covered in the elementary course, can best be introduced in connection with the discussion of the methods by which it has been unfolded. The students should learn about such topics as the following:

1. Behavior of nonhuman primates and its significance for human behavior.

2. Anatomy of the primates in relation to function.

3. The skeletal characteristics of primates, in relation to skeletal structures of other animals.

4. The primate fossil record and its significance.

5. The principles of paleontological interpretation, including examples from non-primate evolutionary lines such as shellfish and ruminants.

6. Sex, age, and pathology as determined in human bones and teeth, and the paleodemography and paleobiology of man.

Throughout it is important for the student to learn how, using human and comparative anatomical methods, facts about the skeleton are related to those about function in living beings; students should attempt to construct and defend their own primate phylogenies.

Books which can be used in such a course will always have to be supplemented, I believe, by readings from original reports of research, laboratory work, and, where possible, the use of museum materials. Presently available textbooks, such as Ashley's Montagu's *Introduction to Physical Anthropology* (1960) and Le Gros Clark's *Fossil Evidence for Human Evolution* (1955), contain the kinds of material and point of view that can be used as sources of data and grounds for discussion. J. N. Spuhler's and S. L. Washburn's contributions to *The Evolution of Man's Capacity for Culture* (Spuhler ed. 1959) represent the challenging extension of thinking which is likely to escape the writers of textbooks and which is best presented to the students in the original.

PHYSICAL ANTHROPOLOGY OF THE LIVING

The course that treats the physical anthropology of the living sometimes has consisted of detailed instructions in anthropometry and in statistical methods for the analysis of such measurements. As research in physical anthropology turns more and more to other kinds of data, teachers have tried to adapt this course to present needs by teaching methods of genetic analysis, including blood-grouping techniques and population genetics. In fact, however, few of the teachers, themselves educated for the most part under such a system as that described by Hunt, have the requisite training and experience to teach the methods used in the analysis of living populations. Some examples of these analytic methods are examination of enzyme systems (sometimes by use of radioactive isotopes in tracer studies of living people), chromosome counts on cultures of human tissues, immunological tests, serological reactions, and electrophoresis of hemoglobins. On the other hand, biochemists and physicians who have learned one or two of these skills rarely comprehend the problems of analysis which face the anthropologist who tries to account for the variable effects of environment or who attempts to associate scientific observations with historic and prehistoric facts. The teacher of physical anthropology, therefore, still has an important role in interpreting the findings in studies by physicians, zoölogists, and others and in teaching students how to make such interpretations.

The dilemma posed by the increasing specialization has led to a shift in some schools from the emphasis on technique to an emphasis on theory. The former course in anthropometry has become a course in the process of intra-specific human evolution and the dynamics of race formation in man. This should be accompanied by enough concrete material to permit the student to design studies to test random genetic drift or heterosis, for example. I would also extend the coverage to include studies of body form and composition and growth and plasticity, and I would introduce just enough statistical method to permit the students to summarize and generalize from the results of the laboratory exercises (e.g., the t test for differences between means and the χ^2 test of association).

The methods for studying the physical anthropology of the living can be found in the standard textbooks, such as that of Montagu (1960), and the principles of human population genetics are well set forth in numerous books which have followed Boyd's classic *Genetics and the Races of Man* (1950). The material concerning differences between populations and their relevance for race is summarized in Garn's *Human Races* (1961), and this can be put in wider perspective by the use of original reports and symposia discussions, such as those reprinted in the work Garn edited, called *Readings on Race* (1960). Likewise, Dobzhansky's book, *Mankind Evolving* (1962), constitutes a stimulating attack on most of the problems of anthropology and genetics. It would set the stage for many lively classroom discussions. I believe that understanding of these kinds of material will be shallow unless it is backed up with first-hand laboratory experience with some of the methods. The need for the laboratory in connection with the study of growth and body composition seems equally pressing.

LABORATORY

Despite the fact that many traditional exercises in physical anthropology are obsolete and deal with techniques little used in current research, I do not view with equanimity a purely theoretical approach. Whether or not laboratory work is a requirement in the elementary course in physical anthropology, it should be mandatory in courses at the advanced level. In research in human biology, whether in reference to medicine, public health, demography, growth and development, or human ecology, physical anthropologists have been contributing more than one might expect from their small number and limited technical training. There is a method of integrating diverse types of observational data on man in a meaningful way, a method which physical anthropologists often are well equipped to manage. This method involves judgments based on analogies drawn from a wide range of knowledge, including much that is and much that is not within the reach of experiment. The method is apparent, for instance, in the handling of ecological and cultural variables in the studies of genetic differences between populations by Birdsell (1957) and Baker (1960). Students of physical anthropology, even at the undergraduate level, should be taught this method. To learn it they will need insight into the *nature* of data, which will come from lectures and reading. In the writing of term papers students should, therefore, be encouraged to combine any commentary about articles they have read with an analysis of their own data accumulated in the field or laboratory.

Since laboratory exercises provide data for subsequent analysis, exercises in measurement and observation are still useful. Measurements of body segments can be applied to a variety of problems about growth, variability, environmental effects, assortive mating, and indeed, race differences. The basic methods of analytical statistics, or morphological analyses, and of population genetics can be learned even from a study of the limited samples available to students.

The device of optional laboratory work is practicable even in an institution with limited facilities and staff; it might well be tried out pending possible appeal to the university or outside agencies for funds for laboratory facilities for all students in the course, if that seems preferable. In the meanwhile the instructor will gain experience in planning and conducting laboratory sessions.

In his contribution to a British symposium on the teaching of physical anthropology, Weiner (1958) gives a list of laboratory assignments (Table 1) for a course at Oxford University, where undergraduate physical anthropology is taught in the anatomy department. It may serve as a model in planning the laboratory sequence for the advanced courses in physical anthropology. If it were used in a full year sequence one could add more basic anatomy, especially of the skeleton, and include tests of the Rh system, of the salivary secretion of blood group substances, and of taste reaction to PTC, genealogy construction and analysis, and other exercises that relate to the research of the particular instructor.

The exercises proposed by Weiner relate to a series of problems which can be covered in concurrent lectures and reading. Class 1 applies comparative anatomical evidence to (a) evolution of the brain for specific functions, (b) locomotion and manipulation, (c) mastication, smell, sight, and hearing. Classes 2 and 3 apply to the order in which man acquired his characteristic diet, locomotion, and mentality. Classes 4 and 5 supply skills in sex and age determination which, since they can be practiced on material of known sex and age, provide the student with methods for testing reliability. Class 6 has relevance to prob-

TABLE 1

Methods of Studying Morphological and Constitutional Variation in Man

Evolutionary Variation

Class 1   Primary characters of man: identify and compare with the specimens provided (lemur, tarsius, monkey, ape, and man) the following: (a) in the brain—sensory and motor areas; (b) in the limbs—movements of hand and fingers, digital formula, nails and pads, limb ratios; (c) in the skull—face: neurocranial ratio, basicranial angle, orbital structure, ear structure.

Class 2   Pongid and Hominid: compare in *Australopithecus,* chimpanzee and modern man: (a) teeth and jaws; (b) pelvis; (c) skull.

Class 3   Human evolution: compare (including by measurement) features in *Pithecanthropus,* Neanderthal man, and H. sapiens: (a) skull; (b) jaws; (c) teeth.

Age and Sex Determination

Class 4   Methods of sex determination: (a) by sex chromatin in epithelial cells; (b) by features of skull, pelvis, scapula, and limb bones.

Class 5   Age determination: (a) from skeletal material; (b) from eruption of teeth; (c) from skeletal maturation as seen on X rays of wrist and knee.

Body Form and Composition

Class 6   Determine body composition (on volunteer from class)—fat, lean body mass, water and cell volumes from (a) body specific gravity by immersion methods; (b) dilution methods (e.g., urea by mouth).

Class 7   Determine (on a volunteer from class)—fat, muscularity, bone development, and physique by direct and indirect anthropometry—linear measurements, circumferences, subcutaneous thickness, and ergometry.

Integumentary Features

Class 8   Skin and hair colour determination by reflectance spectrophotometry; hair form.

Class 9   Finger and palm prints; enumeration of sweat glands; measurements of nail growth.

Genetic Variation

Class 10   Blood groups as genetic markers (ABO blood grouping to be practised).

Class 11   Haemoglobin types as genetic markers (paper electrophoresis demonstration).

Statistical Treatment of Biometric Data

Class 12   Population values (sampling, means, standard deviation, standard error, tests of difference) using anthropometric data.

Class 13   Growth curves (simple, velocity, allometric).

Class 14   Frequency data (using bloodgroup and haemoglobin data; tests of difference).

Class 15   Correlation methods (using twin analysis data).

Source: *The Scope of Physical Anthropology and Its Place in Academic Studies* (Weiner 1958).

lems of stability and change in body composition including such practical considerations as the relevant factors of physique for various types of ill health. Class 7 teaches simpler short-cut methods for approaching the kind of factors considered in Class 6. Classes 8 and 9 present objective methods of approaching other features in which men vary and, since their hair and nails grow rapidly, pigmentation alters, but fingerprints are stable, the problems of studying more or less age-related characteristics are brought to the fore. Classes 10 and 11 involve characteristics which are stable in the individual, and Class 12 deals with characteristics in populations where the change is represented in successive generations. Classes 13 through 15 then deal with the mathematical conceptualization of these processes, and, since data will have been collected in the prior exercises, some of it can be statistically analyzed. Taken as a whole such exercises are a selection of the kinds of research current in physical anthropology and lead the advanced student to an understanding of how to learn what is not now known in this field.

Graduate students who are likely to teach the elementary course in physical anthropology, whatever their field of specialization in anthropology, should have had some such advanced laboratory course. If they received no such opportunities as undergraduates they will need to make good the deficiency in graduate school, so that they will enter a career of teaching adequately equipped to introduce laboratory exercises or demonstrations into their own pedagogy.

To encourage anthropology students to take laboratory work in physical anthropology, all courses in physical anthropology should offer credit toward fulfilling the natural science requirement for graduation, and anthropology majors should not be required to fulfill their natural science requirement by a series of introductory courses in other departments. Instead, the student majoring in cultural anthropology should be allowed and encouraged to meet his biology requirements by taking the courses in physical anthropology. This departs from common practice today, since often only the elementary course in physical anthropology or no course in anthropology is listed as a "biological science" in announcements of degree requirements.

SUMMER INSTITUTES AND GRADUATE TRAINING IN PHYSICAL ANTHROPOLOGY

Summer institutes for teachers of physical anthropology would certainly attract those interested in adding to their offerings a modern laboratory program; their attendance should refresh them with new ideas and give them more mastery of laboratory techniques. The faculty of such institutes would no doubt attend each other's demonstrations and broaden their own teaching skills, too. Formerly the Viking Fund summer seminars in physical anthropology fulfilled this function to some extent, but they were primarily directed to the reorientation of physical anthropology rather than to teaching.

In respect to the training of professional physical anthropologists and human biologists, Garn (1954) emphasized the need for training in biological methods and techniques and the difficulty of acquiring these skills after graduation. Garn would not recommend that additional training should replace courses in other fields of anthropology—because of the danger of cutting off physical anthropology from the very background that makes it distinctive. He recommends, instead, expansion of the training period and the foundation of an institute of physical anthropology, or at least the development of summer interuniversity study seminars. Kaplan (1955) answered Garn, pointing out the difficulty of further extending the graduate course or of substituting training in such techniques as determination of 17-ketosteroids or human blood groups for thorough grounding in principles and a problem-oriented approach.

It seems to me that, at the graduate level, there is opportunity for wide diversity in patterns of training in respect to both theories and techniques—provided that the student as an undergraduate or in his first year of graduate work has had a full year of basic physical anthropology with laboratory exercises. One would hope that he would learn many of his other skills from physical anthropologists also, so that the basic concepts would be reinforced. But at this stage in his career the graduate student might also study special topics with teachers from other biological disciplines: anatomists, biochemists, radiologists, serologists, paleontologists, geneticists, and immunologists. If these specialists can be gathered at a summer anthropological institute, so much the better, for this will make it easier to focus their attention on anthropological considerations to which their specialties relate.

The planning of courses for future needs will have to reckon with the fact that too high a degree of specialization is as apt to lead to error as it is to lead to usable knowledge. In the face of increasing specialization in the study of human biology, it is largely up to anthropology to see that the student receives an adequate background of general scientific knowledge and the ability to use what other disciplines have to offer. At the graduate level the student must be prepared for an easy collaboration with researchers in other disciplines. As the era of progress by high specialization begins to make way for an era of synthesis and team work, the courses in physical anthropology should equip the gifted student in the cultivation of an imaginative approach to knowledge. These students should be ready for more than the accumulation of data so that, in collaborative work, they can contribute an independent intellectual assessment and not merely the work of their hands.

REFERENCES CITED

BAKER, PAUL T.
   1960   Climate, culture and evolution. Human Biology 32:3-16. Reprinted
             in The processes of ongoing human evolution, G. W. Lasker, ed.
             Detroit, Wayne State University Press, 1960.
BIRDSELL, J. B.
   1957   Some population problems involving Pleistocene man. Cold Spring
             Harbor Symposia on Quantitative Biology 22:47-69.
BOYD, W. C.
   1950   Genetics and the races of man. Boston, Little Brown.
CLARK, W. E. LE GROS
   1955   The fossil evidence for human evolution. Chicago, University of
             Chicago Press.
DOBZHANSKY, THEODOSIUS
   1962   Mankind evolving. New Haven and London, Yale University Press.
GARN, S. M.
   1954   On the education of the physical anthropologist. American Journal
             of Physical Anthropology, n.s., 12:607-609.
   1960   Readings on race. Springfield, Illinois, C. C. Thomas.
   1961   Human races. Springfield, Illinois, C. C. Thomas.
KAPLAN, BERNICE A.
   1955   More on the education of the physical anthropologist (from the
             point of view of general anthropology). American Journal of Physi-
             cal Anthropology, n.s., 13:351-355.
MARTIN, RUDOLF
   1914   Lehrbuch der Anthropologie. Jena, G. Fischer.
MONTAGU, ASHLEY
             Introduction to physical anthropology. 3d ed. Springfield, Illinois,
             C. C. Thomas.
SPUHLER, J. N. (ED.)
   1959   The evolution of man's capacity for culture. Detroit, Wayne State
             University Press.
WASHBURN, S. L.
   1959   Speculation on the interrelations of the history of tools and bio-
             logical evolution. Human Biology 31:21-31. Reprinted in The evo-
             lution of man's capacity for culture, J. N. Spuhler, ed. Detroit,
             Wayne State University Press, 1959.
WEINER, J. S.
   1958   Courses and training in physical anthropology and human biology.
             In The scope of physical anthropology and its place in academic
             studies, D. F. Roberts and J. S. Weiner, eds. New York, The Wenner-
             Gren Foundation for Anthropological Research.

PART III

THE
TEACHING
OF
CULTURAL
AND
SOCIAL
ANTHROPOLOGY

Introduction

WHILE THE AUTHORS of the papers in this section are of quite diverse backgrounds and teaching experience, the papers contain some common themes. One is that the teacher should incorporate his personal experience as a field anthropologist into his teaching. Thus Firth discusses anthropological teaching as personal communication. French emphasizes the importance of the teacher's role as professional anthropologist. Arensberg notes that the personal interest, experiences and expeditions of an anthropologist can well provide the basis for his courses. Bruner and Spindler recommend that the teacher not hesitate to bring his particular interests, field experiences, and special enthusiasms into the classroom.

These recommendations could scarcely be made if the authors felt that each course ought to be a standard vehicle loaded with uniform blocks of information which had to be transmitted to the students. The authors do not disclaim the necessity of imparting the basic information: they do assert that the implanting of ideas is essential. In like manner, the anthropologists who responded to the inquiries of Bruner and Spindler about introductory courses indicated that their main purpose is to communicate a point of view. Firth also stresses the importance of the exploration of ideas above the furnishing of facts or of "right" answers. French asserts that it is essential for anthropology students at all levels to comprehend *disciplined modes of inquiry,* rather than to acquire information only.

From this shared conception of the main purpose of studying cultural and social anthropology, the authors reach similar views about implementing that purpose. No sharp distinction between social and cultural anthropology is sought here. Raymond Firth's paper is specifically on social anthropology; he notes that he deliberately ignores the differing academic alignments of social and of cultural anthropology. The recommendations in his paper and in the others of the section apply as well to the one as to the other alignment and hold good for both.

One common recommendation is that students use and test anthropological ideas as they acquire them and that they be continually aware of the problems and concepts involved in the subjects they study. Teachers who rouse this awareness can remedy the condition to which Hewes refers when he writes that anthropologists have done a good job of threatening the naive ethnocentrism of the students but have perhaps done less well in challenging their minds. Such challenge can usefully be posed by following Firth's advice that the student's attention be drawn constantly to the significance of his study for the analysis of his own behavior in society.

Another matter on which these authors are in general accord is a lack of enthusiasm for textbooks, at least those which are now available. Bruner and Spindler state that 35 per cent of the respondents to their questionnaire use no textbooks in the introductory course. About three quarters of those who do regard them as unsatisfactory. Hewes and French both recommend that undergraduates read monographs and articles in anthropological journals. French finds that books of readings are better than textbooks, partly because they are not as uniformly and uninterestingly didactic as textbooks are wont to be. But he also notes that books of readings, journal articles and monographs do not provide needed continuity. Being written for diverse audiences, they often assume either too little or too much knowledge to be suitable for class use. From the statements in these papers, it appears that continuing effort is needed to provide books for the teaching of anthropology which will be intellectually challenging, which will give continuity to the various parts of a course, and whch will show the relevance of anthropological concepts to contemporary culture and society.

D.G.M.

RAYMOND FIRTH

Aims, Methods, and Concepts in the Teaching of Social Anthropology

THE PREPARATION of a paper on the teaching of social anthropology is a formidable task. Questions of complexity face one at every turn: the great range of institutions in which the subject is taught; the variation in mode of incorporation into the academic program; the rapid growth of teaching in the subject, which makes it difficult to keep abreast of modern developments. Add to these the differences in general approach and academic background of those who are taught and the variation in their theoretical and applied interests, and it will be seen how difficult it is to say anything which is both representative of the general position and stimulating on any particular issue.[1]

TEACHING AS PERSONAL COMMUNICATION

In writing about the teaching of any subject one should bear in mind the general point that teaching in the proper sense of the term is essentially a mode of personal communication between someone with knowledge to impart and someone wishing to acquire it. It is not, I think, too optimistic to assume that for a high proportion of the instances in our field these basic conditions are satisfied. For all of my university colleagues whom I know, teaching is regarded as a serious part of their profession, and many of them devote a lot of time to thinking out what knowledge is most important, and how best to implant it.[2] Similarly, I think it would be correct to say that, so far in the history of our subject, most of the students who present themselves do so from a genuine interest and not simply to make up an item in an academic program. Granted, however, seriousness of purpose on both sides, there are still so many factors in the intangible quality of the teaching relationship that one runs the risk of losing the real significance of what is happening by trying to set it out in a formal way. The two great figures in the earlier history of British social anthropology, Malinowski and Radcliffe-Brown, were both superb teachers, but they differed very much in their temperamental approach and in their methods. Broadly speaking the one was Socratic, the other Aristotelian. The one was probing and exploring, drawing on the student to examine the problem further and to clarify his self-expression; the other was didactic, clear, and ready with manifold stimulating answers. Like most other teachers of their period, while conscious of their methods they took the situation for granted and concentrated upon what they had to give.

THE AIMS OF TEACHING

To ask the question, "For what purpose do we teach?" opens up a very wide range of interests. I concern myself with only a few.

We teach because we assume as part of our basic values that knowledge in itself is a prime good. We think it important that, as regards social institutions, values, and modes of conduct, comparative knowledge is a necessary part of the total fabric of social understanding, essential to anyone who regards himself as a specialist in some aspects of the study of man. I think there is some variation in the degree to which members of our profession think there is a moral involvement in this. But it is certainly held by some of us that the comparative and structural approach to the study of human relationships can provide a useful addition, not only to the intellectual, but also to the moral equipment of educated people and that we, as teachers of social anthropology, have a duty to make such a contribution. A position which to some extent conflicts with this appears to be adopted by some of our colleagues in other disciplines. They regard the primary role of the professional scientist as making contributions fo knowledge directly by personal research, not indirectly by instructing others. In Great Britain, in the natural sciences especially, this attitude apparently has some generality, and as such it has become a matter of concern to some educationalists, notably to that august body, the University Grants Committee. But for social anthropology I would think that there are few of us who find great difficulty, except for limitations of time, in reconciling the roles of research worker and teacher. For most of us some pre-occupation with personal research is regarded as essential, if one is to fulfill adequately the obligation of giving one's best as a teacher to students.

One aspect of teaching social anthropology seems to me to be of very great importance—the emphasis upon the need for exploration of ideas rather than upon the furnishing of facts and the giving of "right" answers to theoretical questions. In my own personal view, this probably relates to a particular epistemological standpoint which takes account of human fallibility and the relatively imperfect grasp of relationships which it is possible for any one person to obtain. It is true that some degree of firmness and order must be given to the thinking of students, especially at the introductory stage. It is particularly necessary for this to be given by teachers personally in a subject such as ours, where the range of ethnographic material and consequently of variation of data is so great, and where few good textbooks exist to act as reliable guides. Nevertheless, while we may not be likely to discover whole ranges of new facts to overturn our present theories, changes in the climate of opinion and the development of more systematic enquiries into social relationships tend to give many of our basic postulates a temporary quality. To me, therefore, the development of the student's capacity to "think for himself," to pursue the implications of existing generalizations, to challenge accepted views (including those of his teachers), is one of our outstanding tasks.

We talk much of the aims of the teachers, but what are the aims of those who are being taught? Here we must distinguish clearly between those who hope to be professional anthropologists and those who do not, and by whom social anthropology is regarded as a cultural subject. These latter again are divided into those who take it as a general enlargement of their intellectual equipment and those who wish it to help them solve some practical problem, either personal or in connection with their work.

I doubt if we know as much as we should about the range and distribution of interests of even our senior students in these respects. With this in mind, some seven years ago I asked the members of my graduate seminar in a short questionnaire to give me their opinions on the values which they saw in the study of social anthropology and the reasons why they took up the subject. The answers were, of course, highly subjective, but were surprisingly varied. Simple classification of them proved difficult. But, out of a seminar of twenty people, only half-a-dozen said they had come to social anthropology through their past experience abroad or other practical interests. The remainder seemed to have been attracted to the subject by a wide range of elements of intellectual interest: what may be called aesthetic reasons—an interest in the formal framework of the study; the provision of a scientific background for earlier notions about human relations; giving a new perspective on society; allowing the testing of the hypotheses of Freud against a non-Western social background. All the replies admitted changes in outlook and habits of thought since taking up social anthropology, but there was much uncertainty as to how far the study of social anthropology alone was responsible for this. About a quarter of the replies gave the subject fairly full credit for such a change in outlook, a few denied that it was in any way responsible, most simply did not know. The general feeling seemed to be that social anthropology supported and systematized already partly formed ideas and directed to some extent the trend of their future developments, but that it did not create new ideas or values. A significant proportion thought that the training in social anthropology had tended to increase their tolerance and understanding of social differences of hitherto unfamiliar ways of behaving and to lessen ethnocentric beliefs. In personal morals, politics, religion, and the relations of marriage it seemed that for at least half the members of the seminar some greater objectively was associated with a training in social anthropology, though there was some specific denial that social anthropology was necessarily associated with a relativist outlook.

In 1960, for comparative purposes, I asked the members of my seminar the same set of questions—although if it had not been for the wish for comparison I would probably have rephrased some queries. In this seminar group of fifteen people the practical interest seemed rather stronger than earlier, and six of the group gave such interest as their major reason for undertaking the study. But the difference is probably due to a chance alteration in the composition of the seminar rather than to any change in general trend, and of those with a practical interest some linked this with an interest in the theory of social differences. The theoretical interests ranged from the ethnographic study of language to model building and the theory of social conflict. Most members of the seminar, however, showed a predilection for theoretical studies in the field of social change, and this was perhaps a more marked interest than seven years earlier. Again there was a strong tendency to regard a training in social anthropology as linked with a greater tolerance and objectivity about social differences. But again there was uncertainty as to the character of this linkage. About half the members of the seminar said positively that a knowledge of social anthropology had given them a wider range of ideas about social life and an improved ability to ask themselves relevant questions when making value judgments. Some intimated that their work in social anthropology had made them more interested than before in social differences and the interpretation of these rather than in the search for regularities in social behavior. A few were very strongly of the opinion that social anthropology had helped to give them more tolerance. On the other hand, the general feeling was that their values as such had not been basically altered. The possible connection of social anthropology with a relativistic view of morality was hardly raised.

I cite this material not with any idea of trying to pronounce upon the precise nature of students' interests but to show two things. First, even this very small and possibly unrepresentative sample of graduate students of social anthropology showed a wide variation in the way in which the students conceived their own interests in the subject. Secondly, I regard this as a warning against the easy type of formulation in which we sometimes engage—that social anthropology is *necessarily* a training in understanding and tolerance for other people's ways of life. While there did seem to be some support for this view among my students, some explicitly denied this proposition, and interpretation of the replies of others leaves it open whether it was social anthropology which had been responsible for broadening their minds, or whether it was those whose minds were already broadening who sought out social anthropology.

A possible implication of this from the teaching point of view is that we have to cast our bread upon the waters and see whether or not it returns to us again, rather than be sure in advance that, even with the best category of students, our subject will have the definite effect we wish. Again, the evidence of an apparent shift in the interest of graduate students over the period—or at least in their forms of expression— raises the important point of the need for flexibility in teaching our subject. We often have a tendency to think or speak as if social anthropology consisted of a known body of problems, data, and generalizations, and that it is our job to impart these known resources by the best means. But we must be careful lest, by the over-codification of "resources," we may set a pattern too fixedly. The character of our teaching must be prepared to change as the body of problems and knowledge is reformulated by generation after generation of *students,* as well as of writers and teachers. But a basic question to which there is no simple answer is—how does the teacher of social anthropology ascertain and measure these changing interests, needs, and patterns of thought of the students? The only way that I can see is by teachers maintaining a considerable degree of personal contact, including informal contact, with their students.

QUALITY OF STUDENTS

The aims of students in social anthropology are related in some ways to their quality. In the ordinary undergraduate field I would guess that, as far as the British universities are concerned at least, we have to deal with a student of only medium caliber—who intellectually on the average is a grade or two below the upper levels of those taken into the natural sciences, history, or economics. This is partly the result of the traditional structure of teaching in British schools and universities, and partly the result of the wider range of careers open to those taking such subjects. Social anthropology is not taught or even mentioned in the schools. I personally am not in favor of its being so taught, because I think it requires a kind of neutralist approach to questions of moral values which is to be found only in people of more mature years—or at least requires more experience of life than such young people have.[3] One implication from this is that the first-class people in the schools tend to be offered the plums of scholarships, and so on, in their own subjects at the universities, whereas subjects such as social anthropology, which are new at the university level, tend to get those who have not been so successful in the other subjects earlier. This is not necessarily a drawback, because we do get some people who mature intellectually rather late and who grow into our subject with great profit. We also get others of a rugged individualist type, highly intelligent, dissatisfied with the traditional disciplines and seeking something new to get their teeth into. These factors notwithstanding, I would think that my generalization probably has weight, and not only in the British universities.

On the other hand, one factor tends perhaps to keep up our quality a little, and that is the known relative scarcity of jobs in social anthropology. An ordinary middle-range student who takes history or geography is sure, if he is not completely worthless, of finding his level in school teaching. Social anthropology has no such backlog of posts in the schools. To that extent we are relieved from a crowd of pedestrian folk who only want a craft training. I think we tend to get a number of the more adventurous spirits who are willing to risk their job possibilities in favor of a more interesting subject. In the graduate field the situation is probably more diversified, but some of the same reasons may operate.

In teaching terms this means that we have an attractive subject, but one which needs also a fairly lively presentation to satisfy the diversity of interests and capabilities of the students. I think they demand, for the most part, something more than routine training. They expect to be interested, and are critical if they are not. Moreover, whereas one can absorb much dull material in the natural sciences or in economics, feeling that it ultimately relates to significant principles in the conduct of the world today, much of the detail in social anthropology seems rather obviously to be of no concern whatever to everyday life and to be justified only by its relevance to general theory. But what the teacher can do here is to draw the students' attention constantly to the significance of social anthropology for the analysis of their own behavior—leadership, gift-exchanges, family relationships, etc. All this means a constant awareness of ethnographic detail in relation to a systematic theoretical frame, which has always to be kept before the mind of the teacher in a way not necessarily so in a longer-established discipline. On the whole, I think that the tradition in social anthropology has been one of a sensitive awareness of the importance of this theoretical frame, though I sometimes wonder whether we do not tend to be over-whelmed by the mass of ethnography. The relevance of this point to the quality of the student is that the poor student may be satisfied with picturesque ethnographic detail. The good student will regard this as only so much clutter unless it is presented in a highly integrated form, and only the best student will provide his own frame to make it intelligible to himself.

CONCEPTS

This leads into questions of the content of teaching. The initial diffi-culty, that there is by no means complete agreement upon the definition of the scope of social anthropology, I do not mean to discuss. I assume from statements made by colleagues that there is a sufficient measure of agreement to allow teaching content and teaching standards to be comparable over the range of the universities where this subject ap-pears. I propose also to ignore the way in which social anthropology in some places is specifically singled out as a separate discipline, and in others is merged within the broader discipline of cultural anthro-pology or general anthropology—or sociology.

The first question I raise is one of whether the teaching of social an-thropology should include material from the "Western," "developed," "industrial" societies as well as from the primitive, preliterate or ex-otic societies. I think we have to examine this with care. As far as I know, the general practice throughout our profession is to use material from the "primitive" societies as the basic data for our generalizations. But I think that the practice is growing of bringing in a limited amount of material from other types of society. The intermediate field of peas-antry in the Oriental civilizations is already an established source, now that we have a significant number of studies from India, South-East Asia, and Latin America, for example, to provide us with material. There is also cautious use of material on kinship, social status and strati-fication, and religion from Western societies, although as yet such ma-terial specifically provided by the research of social anthropologists is essentially episodic. The arguments against any widespread use of such material are threefold. First, many of such data lie squarely in the recog-nized field of sociology, relations with which in themselves constitute a significant set of problems for many teachers of social anthropology. Second, much of the material does appear to be not only relatively com-plex as compared with the primitive material, but also more difficult to see as part of an integrated social system capable of analytical study by students. This is a traditional argument, but one which I think still has substance, although more sophistication in sociological studies has tended to reduce its force. Third, and in my own view probably the most important reason, is the lack still of good monographic studies of specific aspects or institutions of the Western type of society, comparable with what has been accumulated over a quarter of a century or more by social anthropologists in the more exotic field. Yet material from the more complex types of society does help to provide the general framework for our teaching, whether we use such material explicitly or not.

The next question concerns the general manner of approach to the data which provide the content of our teaching. It hardly needs saying that such an approach must be comparative, since this is inherent in the very existence of our discipline. But at what level should the comparison be undertaken? It seems to be generally agreed that even at an early stage of the student's training, he should not be furnished simply with a set of descriptive materials about human customs. The approach should be analytical, concerned with type and variation of behavior as classes of events to which a considerable degree of abstraction has been applied. Some teachers advocate "shock tactics," presenting to the student right from the start a problem involving such a concept as filiation or status relations and worked out in quasi-diagrammatic form. There are some who would argue that such treatment is not only intellectually stimulating but is also necessary in order to inculcate in the student a proper respect for the subject. While I fear that at times we tend to confuse complication of terminology with sophistication of argument, there is in my view some grounds for this. There are strong reasons for giving the student right at the start a notion that he is going to encounter disciplinary training, and not simply a set of interesting human variations. But our comparative treatment, certainly in the earlier stages of the subject, must be selective. Systematic comparison over any wide range is difficult if only because of the unevenness in the quality of our ethnographic data. It is better, in my view, to restrict the teaching period to a few instances which have good supporting documentation, and which can bring out variation in the elements of the relationship, rather than to attempt broad coverage with much weaker data.

Granted the need for an analytical approach, the question is, from what particular angle should it be made? In theory it should be possible to examine analytically the total structure of the major units which we call societies as part of our teaching program. In practice this is exceedingly difficult, if not impossible. The material we have at hand is still very imperfect. Pedagogically, the effort to master the complete structural complications of even one apparently simple society would be extreme. It seems general in our teaching then to adopt what is in effect an institutional approach, examining in turn local organization, the family, kinship, marriage, age grades and other associations, political organization, etc., in a rough, comparative way, with "key" illustrations.

In recent years, partly through the influence of Talcott Parsons, "frames of reference" have become popular in social anthropology. For teaching purposes one can argue whether a structural frame of reference, an actor/role frame, or a "model" frame is the most effective. Personally, I think that it is useful to employ each of these according to circumstances, especially in showing how a particular writer has used such a frame in the tackling of a particular problem.

For elementary students, for example, I have found that a good way of attracting their attention at the beginning and impressing upon them the conception of the interelatedness of institutional elements is to take a simple material object, say a Trobriand arm-shell or a Polynesian composite fishhook, and dissect out for them the complexity of social relationships, of an economic, political, and ritual order, involved in its manufacture, technical use, and display. Then to follow this up and impress upon them structural concepts, a comparative analysis of forms of kinship and marriage is very useful, say in the classic comparison between Kariera and Aranda. This can be made also to yield the contrast between structural and organizational (or operational) conditions by pointing out what takes place when, through lack of appropriate partners, "alternate" or "wrong" marriages occur. Every teacher has his own budget of favored examples for such demonstrations. How eclectic such a treatment should be will presumably continue to be a matter of argument. What I think we all agree upon is first the requirement that the teacher should have and present to the student a fairly clear-cut, intelligible theoretical framework within which the bits of ethnographic details which he learns can be fitted. We also want to give the student a clear conception of the outline of the nature of a structural problem so that, when questions come to him about social relationships, he looks on them in terms of their structural effects. We may differ as to what is the most important element in our teaching—some would contend that it consists in our study of jural relations—but the major outline presented by most university departments is very similar.

A more difficult problem exists in the boundaries which we set to our theoretical coverage. At various points in our teaching we deal, for example, with questions of economic anthropology and political anthropology. How far can we do so effectively without either supplying ourselves or demanding from the student the fruits of some systematic study in the classics of the parent discipline—economics or political theory? The more sophisticated the parent discipline, the more apparent is our weakness here. Our comparative teaching in primitive politics has been able to go some way because of the relatively under-developed character of political science in some of the concepts of government with which we have to deal. But our teaching of economic anthropology undoubtedly suffers from the fact that too few anthropologists know much economics and that this discipline itself is too highly developed to allow much scope to the intelligent amateur. As regards the notion of jural relations, it seems to me that this is an imprecise term, incorporating both moral and legal notions, perhaps the more useful because of this. But a teaching which has to focus upon imparting a knowledge of jural relations as one of its major tasks involves some attention to the basic concepts of jurisprudence. How far are teacher and student prepared to go into this field? How much basic training in disciplines such as political theory, economics, or jurisprudence can be combined with a training in social anthropology must depend to some extent upon the particular academic framework within which the subject of social anthropology is taught.

TEACHING METHODS

In social anthropology, as in other subjects, there appears to be no general agreement as to what should be the balance between classical teaching methods of the formal lecture and small-group, personal discussion. My own experience has been with both, and I think that each has its place. My early training in social anthropology with Malinowski was unorthodox from the lecture point of view. Malinowski did not lecture very frequently, and when he did it was often on a topic quite different from that announced in the program, and often again it was turned into a seminar discussion. With the growth of a sizable undergraduate body the formal lecture has tended to take a more prominent place. Inevitably it has provoked criticism, and of course the need for class work in small groups and personal discussion of a "tutorial" order has been seen. Nevertheless, the case for the formal lecture remains, if only because it must cater for students taking courses in social anthropology as a secondary part of their university work. The value of a lecture is that it allows of the presentation of one or two themes and problems, carefully selected for their teaching interest, and illustrated by material most apt to the point; if so presented, it can give in a synoptic, systematic form, a piece of knowledge which it is difficult to convey in any other way. From a wider field I quote the view of Sir Alexander Carr-Saunders (1960), noted among British educationalists:

The lecture is potentially the greatest medium of education. Those know this if, like myself, they have had the good fortune to sit under a master of his subject who, after careful preparation, addresses his audience, visibly searches for the best order of presentation, seeks the necessary qualifications and appropriate terms, and so makes a personal communication to each member of his audience, arousing in them that tension of the faculties which he himself is experiencing.

The private tutorial has obviously a vital function, and the main difficulty in its wide use is usually an unfavorable staff/student ratio. The seminar is, to my mind, a teaching mode of the greatest value. Having ideally between a dozen and a score of participants, with a theme which can be pursued in its ramifications from week to week, it allows of the exploration of the ideas of the participants as well as those of the leader. In my view the leader should have a definitely activist role, intervening even high-handedly to draw out the implications of a statement or to clear up obscurity. At the same time he must have a respect for the personality of each participant so that even the most naive and timorous can be induced to express their opinions. In my opinion, a seminar for social anthropology students should be primarily a teaching instrument, that is, it should stress less the acquisition of ethnographic facts than the exploration of ideas. From this point of view, a naive or even wrong-headed statement is sometimes more helpful as a lead than a sophisticated, accurate one which provides the answer immediately. The keynote of Malinowski's seminars, which were justly renowned, was always, "What is the problem?", and such *Problemstellung* must always be kept in the forefront of discussion if the standard is to remain high.

MATERIALS

In the early years of teaching social anthropology the question of materials was one of adequacy rather than of choice. There were no text books, and every student was put immediately to reading Malinowski's *Argonauts of the Western Pacific* and Radcliffe-Brown's *Andaman Islanders,* Chapter V onwards. The proliferation of studies, both descriptive and theoretical, has now begun to pose some rather serious teaching problems. Already it is almost impossible to demand of students that they should read all the major works in social anthropology during their university period. This situation arises in part because of the lack of clear distinction between purely descriptive and purely theoretical works. In my view such distinction would be impracticable, if only because it would remove the inducement from many social anthropologists to provide us with their descriptive data. But, because most monographs setting out the results of field research contain some significant contributions to theory as well as a mass of ethnographic detail, it has become impossible to require students to cover the whole range of significant literature. On what basis is selection to be made?

One obvious method is in terms of regional specialization. This allows of the intensive pursuit of a range of problems in terms of a body of material which can be systematically analyzed. Clearly, however, such specialization must be set within a broader theoretical frame. For this, it is necessary as a rule that the student should read also some monographs dealing with other areas, because of their theoretical interest. For example, it should not be possible for a student specializing in the Melanesian field to avoid reading the classic Africanist monographs by Evans-Pritchard, Fortes, and Nadel. If he is to be properly educated in, say, political anthropology, he should also have read a number of the other Africanist monographs.

Another possible method is to rely upon the textbook and "reader" for the major frame of theory and for most illustration outside the particular regional field of specialization. Up to a point this may be necessary, but the difficulty is that the textbook or "reader" illustrations can rarely give enough of the systematic supporting detail to render the treatment of the problem of satisfactorily intellectual interest. The student must be sent back to the original journal article or the original monograph to obtain the correct balance in the theoretical handling of the problem. It has sometimes been argued that undergraduate teaching should be based solely on published material which has been available long enough for the professional evaluation of it to be clear, and that current controversies should be excluded. From the pedagogic point of view such conservatism is probably justified. On the other hand, some current controversies strike deep into the theory of our subject, e.g., a current controversy about the concept of "filiation." Reference to issues immediately under debate can stimulate the interest of students, in making them realize they are taking part in a live subject; moreover, a few of them probably will have the intellectual curiosity to look at current journals, and require some guidance upon what really are the basic points at issue in such controversy.

In general, British university teaching, not only in social anthropology, has tended to be cautious about the use of textbooks. Since a textbook is by its very nature only by accident a contribution to knowledge, the writing of such works may interfere with a scholar's presentation of his own material and ideas. From a teaching point of view again there has been some suspicion of "tabloid" presentation, a suspicion that has been to some extent heightened by outside approaches from people wanting to get a brief and painless introduction to social anthropology without the trouble of going through too much intellectual discipline. Again, the writing of textbooks has not been easy because of the relatively uneven coverage of the major aspects of social anthropology. On kinship and marriage material has been ample; on political anthropology it is rapidly growing; on economic anthropology it is still fairly thin; and on religion it is copious but unsystematic. With the great increase in the numbers of undergraduate students, however, including many who wish to take social anthropology only as a secondary subject, the need for some concise treatment of the major principles of the subject has become more obvious. Moreover, the material at the present time is of a range and quality which allows of significant compression into a reasonable systematic frame. Textbooks, therefore, are tending to multiply and in my view rightly so, provided that they are written primarily to aid students to master the subject and teachers to save time—and not with the primary objective of making money, which may result in a slipshod, ill-balanced product, misleading to students!

The character of the textbook must be to some extent related to the character of the testing of knowledge by examination. Here my experience, and I imagine that of most of my colleagues, has been that we all tend to be less adventurous in the questions we ask of students in a formal examination than in the things we teach them in our lectures and in our routine work. This is partly because teaching is a collective activity, and the testing of the results of teaching has also to take account of other men's work besides our own. Hence, we seek the highest common factor in what has been taught. An examination paper or textbook which betrays too much of the author's personal bias, or too little allowance for that of his colleagues, is a disservice to his subject. Yet in both some degree of individuality in theoretical treatment is to be looked for, and in this need for balance lies a major problem.

PREPARATION FOR TEACHING

I assume that social anthropology will be taught only by those who have had a proper training, primarily in this field. But it has been a complaint that teachers in social anthropology, as in most other university disciplines, receive no preparatory training for their actual teaching task. It is to their credit that, on the whole, they have proved so adequate. Formal training of the kind given to schoolteachers is, in my view, not wholly appropriate to the kind of intellectual development which it is the job of the university teacher to stimulate. Nevertheless, there are some aids—including even technical ones concerned with voice control—which may be cultivated. More attention to the language of teaching as distinct from the language of writing—though both could often be simpler—is likely to pay dividends. Some specific advice on these matters given regularly by senior to junior colleagues when they begin teaching might possibly be a useful practice here.

In conclusion, one thing we must all remember is that the problems of pedagogy are not the same as those of exploring social relationships, and that the anthropologist who wishes to become a teacher must needs consider both.

NOTES

[1] I am indebted to my colleagues, especially to Maurice Freedman, in the Department of Anthropology, London School of Economics and Political Science, for helpful opinion on the first draft of this paper. I am grateful also to Ethel Albert, and other participants in the Symposium at Burg Wartenstein, for their useful later comment.

[2] The Association of Social Anthropologists of the Commonwealth has devoted several sessions of its periodic general conferences to discussion of these problems. In this paper I have drawn to some extent upon the (unpublished) record, *The Teaching of Social Anthropology: Report on a Conference of the Association of Social Anthropologists held at King's College, Cambridge, from September 22 to 25, 1958,* supplemented by a paper by Michael Banton delivered before the Association of Social Anthropologists Conference, April 1960.

[3] Yet I have been told of two schools in London where some social anthropology has been regularly taught to late teenagers with apparent success. (In both cases the teachers had been trained in my own department!) What I do think is of primary importance is that teachers of human geography and allied subjects should have some training in social/cultural anthropology.

REFERENCES CITED

CARR-SAUNDERS, A.
  1960   English universities today. London, The London School of Economics and Political Science.
FIRTH, RAYMOND
  1954   Social organization and social change. Journal Royal Anthropological Institute 84:1-20.

EDWARD M. BRUNER AND GEORGE D. SPINDLER
with the assistance of Fred H. Werner

The Introductory Course in Cultural Anthropology

THIS PAPER tells how the introductory course is currently being taught in thirty-four institutions in the United States. Our information is based upon written responses to questionnaires supplemented by interviews with colleagues, by reflections on our own experiences in teaching, and by the field study of one course. We gathered these data because we felt that an empirical investigation emphasizing what is actually being done in a series of beginning courses would contribute more than our thoughts on what should be done. Although there are many gaps in our data, we believe that we have identified some of the key questions and problem areas in introductory teaching.

Our sample is about equally divided between private and state institutions and includes most of the major anthropology departments in the country. In every institution represented anthropology has been established for a decade or more, and every instructor has a Ph.D. degree in anthropology. The sample is not representative of all the introductory courses now being offered as it is heavily weighted in favor of universities to the neglect of small liberal arts colleges and junior colleges. But we tend to discount the assumed differences between college and university courses, as we have no evidence suggesting that the nature of the course necessarily varies with the size of the institution.

GOALS AND ORGANIZATION

The beginning course is typically taught for a mixed group of sophomores and freshmen, with more of the former than the latter. The class group tends to be heterogeneous and often includes a few upper class-men, but the modal student is the proverbial college sophomore.

In an overwhelming majority of cases the course is taught for the general education of college students rather than for anthropology majors or social science majors. For most students a single introductory course will represent the limit of formal training in anthropology. Instructors appear to have accepted this teaching obligation with apparent enthusiasm and appropriate goals.

As seen by respondents, the primary goal of the introductory course is to enlarge the horizons of undergraduates, to open and broaden young minds. In this objective there was widespread agreement among the vast majority of anthropologists surveyed, although the particular emphasis varied. In rank order the specific purposes of the introductory course were to communicate (1) a sense of the wide range and variability of human culture, (2) an appreciation of culture as a holistic and integrated system, (3) a respect for other ways of life and an understanding of ethnocentrism, (4) a perspective on one's own culture and insights into modern life through the application of anthropological concepts, (5) an awareness of the continuity of man and culture in long-term evolutionary perspective, and, finally, (6) some conception of anthropology as a discipline.

Anthropologists also agree that they are attempting to communicate a point of view rather than any particular set of concepts or body of data. Specific cases and problems are simply media for the expression and transmission of the anthropological point of view applied to the observation and interpretation of human behavior. Such broad notions as "cultural diversity" or "the cross-cultural perspective" may be illustrated with equal effectiveness by reference to a wide variety of particular facts. It is not of great importance whether the instructor draws his examples from Oceania or Africa, or prefers to emphasize economy rather than religion. But it is essential that the concepts be firmly rooted in fact. Although anthropologists do not regard facts as having merit in themselves, they insist upon empirical referents on all issues.

A humanistic emphasis clearly dominates the purposes of many anthropologists in their introductory teaching. In our sample this was clearly characteristic of the majority. This emphasis receives its full flowering in the following:

I am filled with wonder and humility at being human—what does this mean, to be human? And when we see the varieties of human cultures we must learn both to appreciate the values of others, and to treasure our own roots, because they are our roots, and no man can live without his own. I believe anthropology to be the most interesting and intellectually stimulating discipline because it deals with the whole sweep of human history and the deepest human values. But it is also a way of life, because it is nourished by field work—and this too, I try to communicate. I believe the values of anthropology, like those of philosophy, are basic to a liberal education.

It seems that anthropologists are more humanistically oriented in their introductory course than in their advanced courses or in their professional research. Even our most "tough-minded" colleagues turn humanistic in purpose, though not necessarily in method, in the beginning course. We have noted the same trend when anthropologists address themselves to the lay public. Perhaps when the image of anthropology is shaped for nonanthropologists we penetrate to the most fundamental values of our discipline.

Although anthropologists agree on the goals of the introductory course, a comparison of the content of the courses they offer reveals considerable variablity. Part of the variation may be understood by examination of the beginning course in the context of the total undergraduate program. Many different patterns are found. In some institutions two introductory courses are offered concurrently each semester, one entitled "physical anthropology" and the other "cultural anthropology." Usually the cultural course includes archaeology, linguistics, and ethnology, while the physical course is restricted to physical. Other institutions offer a general introduction to anthropology covering all fields followed by a series of advanced level courses on each subfield. In still other institutions introductory anthropology combines prehistoric archaeology with parts of physical and cultural in a course emphasizing an historical, or in some cases, an evolutionary point of view. One such course begins with primate and human evolution, considers race and the rise of civilization, and ends with theories of cultural development.

Because of the variety of institutional arrangements regulating the sequence of courses, the relative emphases of the different subfields of anthropology in the first or beginning course vary widely from one university to another. The modal distribution for all introductory courses in our sample is: 68 per cent cultural anthropology, 15 per cent prehistory, 12 per cent physical anthropology, and 5 per cent linguistics. But one course consists of 90 per cent cultural and 10 per cent linguistics; another 33 per cent cultural, 33 per cent prehistory, and 33 per cent physical; and a third 50 per cent prehistory, 48 per cent cultural, and 2 per cent linguistics. One conclusion from our data is that linguistics tends to be overlooked compared to the other subfields.

If we focus upon the portion of the introductory course concerned with cultural anthropology, irrespective of its place in the total sequence or the amount of time that may be devoted to it, we find at least five essentially different organizations of the subject matter. Some departments base their course entirely upon one of the five alternate organizations; others combine two or more.

Type one considers, in sequence, various aspects of culture such as technology, economy, social organization, government, religion, and language. Most of the courses in our sample as well as the majority of anthropology textbooks are based upon this form of organizaton. It is convenient and flexible. Ethnographic data are utilized from several cultures to illustrate and document generalizations advanced by the lecturer within and between topical areas. For example, the instructor might wish to discuss the relationship between subsistence techniques, size of population aggregate, and systems of social control. He might utilize illustrative data from technologically simple, nomadic hunting and gathering societies like the Arunta, Eskimo, and Northern Ojibwa, and contrast these situations with agricultural, sedentary, East African kingdoms. The procedure is essentially deductive. The analytic conclusions are presented first, then data are found to support them.

Type two is similar in procedure except that the guiding concept is social organization rather than the more global concept of culture. The course is restricted to the comparative study of society and may include such topics as kinship terminology, the nuclear family, the composite family, local groups, political organization, solidarities, and social stratification. Comparative data are presented from different societies in order to develop theoretical points of structural significance. For example, the instructor might compare Hopi, Minangkabau, and Nayar societies in order to illustrate various degrees of matrilineality. No attempt would be made to discuss any one culture as a whole working system, but comparisons would be made between appropriately selected segments of social organization from a number of different societies. Although only a few courses in our sample were devoted entirely to the study of social organization, the topic was the one aspect of anthropology emphasized most heavily in the 34 introductory courses.

Type three differs from the above in that intensive study is made of a limited number of cultures. The goal of presentation is to communicate to students a complex picture of a whole way of life with as much vitality as possible. The culture cases are selected for their diversity and are presented to the student in a variety of ways including lectures, films, records, and tapes. As the students' understanding of cultural diversity grows in scope and depth, the instructor helps the students to group facts and impressions into a coherent cognitive structure. It is at this point that anthropological concepts are introduced. For example, all cultures studied as wholes present systems of values—desiderata in possessions, symbols, personalities, status—that constitute shared motivations for the group. After the student has begun his experience with cases in depth, he can be stimulated to see the relevance of such a concept as values for the understanding of human behavior. The intellectual content of the student's conclusions at the end of the course may not differ from those documented in the deductive method, but the way in which they are attained is quite different. Rather than starting with the generalization or concept as a finished product, the teacher and student preserve the important illusion, from the viewpoint of learning, that the procedure of analysis is at least partly inductive. This procedure approximates in some degree the actual process by which the anthropologist works and may avoid the sometimes misleading finality implied in more strictly deductive procedures.

The fourth form of organization deals with different types of societies in a developmental sequence. One such course has four stages to the sequence—band society, tribal society, archaic civilization, and modern civilization. The goal of the course is to communicate an understanding of the evolution of culture in general as well as of the growth of particular aspects of culture and their functional interrelationships. For example, the transition from food-gathering to food-production was in the main a technological change, but its full significance emerges only from a consideration of the consequences of the shift for the organization of society. Both archaeological and ethnographic data are utilized but not usually in the form of the whole culture cases. Segments of culture are selected from a variety of areas to illustrate points of general importance in the evolutionary framework. The entire course is designed in terms of the instructor's theoretical system.

Type five is a course on the nature of culture and may include such topics as cultural diversity, culture as superorganic, cultural integration, cultural transmission, cultural change, culture as patterned symbols, and culture as an adaptation to the conditions of survival. Such a course tends to emphasize theory. Ethnographic data, used either in the form of segmentalized parts or in the form of case studies, tend to be de-emphasized in favor of the conceptual orientation of the instructor to the nature of culture. The instructor must, of course, have an explicit theoretical framework in terms of which the entire course may be organized.

The five-fold typology is somewhat artificial in that few actual courses are based entirely upon one form of organization. A great many courses also include sections on culture and personality and applied anthropology. The typology may be of some value, however, in indicating alternate ways of organizing the subject matter of cultural anthropology.

To summarize thus far, anthropologists are unified in their statements as to the objectives of the introductory course. They hope to communicate a point of view and a few basic concepts to college sophomores. An analysis of the content and organization of their courses, however, indicates considerable divergence. One question that may be asked is—how are we to explain this divergence.

We attempted to correlate course content with such variables as size of institution, type of university, and number of students per class. As one might have predicted, we were unsuccessful. It is perfectly clear that what determines the content of the introductory course is simply the individual anthropologist. What is taught is dependent upon each instructor's orientation to anthropology. At one point we considered the idea that course content was determined by the graduate school from which the instructor received the Ph.D. degree. We thought of focal centers of anthropological training as similar to focal centers of civilization and of the subsequent spread of particular schools of anthropology. This conception has some validity, but like other extreme diffusionist notions, it ignores local tradition, independent development, and the fact that intellectual interests grow and change.

A second question that may be asked about the divergence in course content is simply, so what? Does it make a difference? As we have already indicated, different instructors may teach the same basic concepts with equal effectiveness by drawing examples from totally different subjects and ethnographic areas. Further, there is no doubt that some of the divergence in course content is essential for effective instruction. Every anthropologist has different research interests and finds that certain problems excite him more than others. A man will be a better teacher if he brings to the classroom his own interests and experiences and if he shares his own excitement with his students. We are suggesting that rather than attempt to cover the entire field, each instructor select those aspects of anthropology about which he is most enthusiastic. By so doing, anthropology is presented as an active on-going discipline rather than as a subject confined between the covers of a textbook.

It is clear that each method of organizing a course in cultural anthropology has advantages and disadvantages, but what is often overlooked is that each organization involves some implicit assumptions about how students learn. It is our impression that not infrequently instructors allow their perception of anthropology to guide their selection and presentation of course content and pay comparatively little heed to the nature of their non-professional student audience. We suggest that each instructor ask himself how best to communicate the concepts he has in mind to students who have not had field work and training experiences similar to his own. The teacher must make every effort to empathize with his audience so that he can make the learning of anthropology a meaningful experience from the students' point of view. In other words, the instructor must decide not only what to teach but also how best to teach it, and possibly most important of all, he must make the effort to become an effective teacher.

We feel that each instructor has a dual responsibility. On the one hand he should introduce his students to that body of formally accepted knowledge which is the discipline's heritage. Undergraduates should become familiar with such topics as the consequences of the neolithic revolution and the various forms of family organization in human society. On the other hand, the instructor should bring it all to life and demonstrate how human beings live, evaluate, and face problems in a variety of cultures in a variety of physical environments, and how anthropological concepts help to understand this variety. He does this by presenting case materials to students which lead them to discover, with guidance, such basic insights as the integration of culture. Each instructor must strike his own balance between the two responsibilities, and each will probably achieve the balance in a slightly different way. The next section considers various techniques of instruction which may help him to achieve his objectives.

READINGS, EXAMINATIONS, AND AUDIO-VISUAL AIDS

Techniques and methods of instruction are so highly personal that many different means may be employed to communicate the same basic concepts. Some instructors use theatrical techniques to arouse and sustain interest; others achieve the same result by lecturing in a conversational manner. Without presuming to discuss the art or style of teaching, this section considers some technical matters under the three rubrics of readings, examinations, and audio-visual aids.

Of the courses surveyed 30 per cent use more than one textbook, 12 per cent use one text, 23 per cent use a text and collateral reading, and 35 per cent use no text. Only a minority (42 per cent) of courses rely entirely upon textbooks. About 75 per cent of the instructors who use textbooks regard them as unsatisfactory. Textbooks are criticized as being too simplified, conventional, unsound, dry, uncoordinated, etc. Most of those who use textbooks do not consider them to be an integral part of the course. In these cases the text is used to stimulate discussion in the sections, to provide ready reference for term papers, and to cover material not included in the lectures. The collateral readings are used in two different ways, to supplement or cover concepts not considered in class or, in the form of full length or short monographs, to expose the student to descriptions of whole cultures.

In 40 per cent of the courses the final grade is based not at all or very little upon objective examinations (true and false, multiple choice, etc.). As one instructor commented, "I strongly disapprove of the so called 'objective' questions . . . because they train the student to think in terms of absolute truth, rather than relative, contrastive truth. They also favor snap verbal responses over the ability to evaluate and balance multiple factors." The final grade is based entirely upon objective examinations in only 10 per cent of the courses surveyed. In one such case the instructor felt that essay questions were impossible to grade uniformly; and further, with a large class and no assistants, he was forced to use objective tests in order to save time. Most anthropologists, however, evaluate their students primarily on the basis of essay questions, book reviews, and term papers or special projects of one kind or another.

Comparing the assigned readings in the thirty-four institutions surveyed, the single most striking fact is the variation in quantity. In university A the students are required to read one textbook. Students in university B are required to read fourteen full-length technical monographs in their entirety in addition to selections from five other books. Almost every gradation between these two extremes is found in our sample. That library resources and the caliber of student may vary from institution to institution is not sufficient to account for such differences in the sheer quantity of assigned reading. Our feeling based upon these and other data is that a great many students in introductory courses are not working as hard or learning as much anthropology as they might.

A certain amount of heat was generated by our inquiry as to the advisability of soliciting course evaluations from students. A slight majority were strongly opposed to the idea, and some found the idea abhorrent. Those who favor end-of-course evaluations by students are quite explicit that their major purpose is not evaluation. They regard student comments as a source of data to be analyzed for clues to student morale and for student perceptions of the course. They are also interested in the extent to which students favor one book or another or in determining which section of the course students find most profitable. Some instructors consider the primary function of the evaluations to be that of providing a channel for the expression of student aggression.

About 75 per cent of the instructors do not utilize field exercises or laboratory demonstrations as teaching techniques. Instructors feel that there is "too much to cover as is" or they are hesitant about releasing "hordes of students" on the town, or they doubt if exercises are profitable in a large class, or they question whether student observations can be intelligently incorporated into the theoretical structure of the course.

The minority who require field exercises show considerable ingenuity. Students in one class write a paper on symbolism based upon their observations of a Russian Orthodox service. In another class students read Rivers' paper on the genealogical method and then collect and interpret genealogies from foreign student informants. One instructor reproduces parts of his field notes and distributes them for students to work on as an exercise in the construction of culture patterns.

This is a problem area of some significance. Chemistry, biology, physics, psychology, and other subjects have their laboratories. Firsthand experience in observing, recording, and interpreting primary data seems no less relevant to the teaching of anthropology. Further, field work is considered by almost all ethnologists to be the touchstone of many of the prime anthropological virtues. Ingenuity is called for here.

Slides, records, tapes, films, and other audio-visual materials are currently used in over 80 per cent of the courses surveyed. Slides appear to be most helpful in summarizing information or in providing direct visual impressions, especially for archaeology and physical anthropology. Films are regarded as useful for conveying some sense of the "cultural whole." The *Ways of Mankind* record series was frequently mentioned and is highly regarded. Very little mention was made of museum specimens for teaching purposes. One instructor, who makes frequent use of specimens, states that when a student holds in his hand a paleolithic axe dating from 50,000 years ago, he experiences a thrill and degree of ego involvement that cannot be duplicated by any other means. A museum may be too costly for many universities, but departments of anthropology might well obtain objects for classroom use.

Ethnographic films, the most important audio-visual aid in cultural anthropology, are used in quite different ways by different instructors. One has his assistant show films when he is out of town; another uses them to liven up the sessions; others make films an integrated and substantial part of the course. In the latter case, much more time is spent giving the ethnographic and conceptual context of the film than in the actual showing. One anthropologist lectures for a few periods on the salient features of the cultural area and of the particular tribe or community covered in the film and assigns readings on the culture when they are available. After the lecture the film is shown and is followed by group discussion in which inferences are drawn concerning such concepts as subsistence techniques, social role, and cultural values.

We feel that here is another problem area in the introductory course. Our guess is that everyone would prefer to add a dimension of reality to his lectures and to the readings on non-Western cultures by the use of more ethnographic films if they were readily available and if they were of sufficiently high quality. Good films, more than any other medium, enable students to participate vicariously in non-Western cultures. But we have relatively few good ones. When such films as "Nanook of the North" and "The Hunters" do become available they are used extensively in introductory courses throughout the country.

COURSE FORMAT

The size of the introductory class varies from a low of twenty-five to a high of three hundred. In one-third of the institutions surveyed there were between twenty-five and forty students per class; in one-sixth there were over one hundred fifty. The modal number of students per class was seventy. The true "mass" course, of from five hundred to one thousand students, although frequently found in other divisions of some universities, is not characteristic of cultural anthropology.

Absolute figures on class size are misleading unless considered in conjunction with data on the course format. We found three essentially different ways in which the introductory course was organized. These differences appear to be determined mainly by university policy. In the first system there is one instructor, one course, and no sections. The professor, usually an experienced member of the department, lectures to all those who enroll in his course. In the second system the total enrollment is divided into a series of concurrently running classes, each taught by a full-time member of the department. The segmentation process occurs as many times as is necessary to keep the number of students in any one class below a predetermined number. In one university each class contained from thirty-five to forty students, while in another institution seventy students per class was considered the maximum for effective instruction.

Before turning to the remaining system we shall consider two variants of the second pattern of organization. In one variant each instructor is completely free to handle his own course. Within the same department there is a series of introductory courses, each offered by a different instructor and each somewhat different in content and emphasis. In the second variant, and we have in mind a particular university, the introductory course has become a departmental project. Most members of the staff offer at least one introductory section a year. Departmental meetings are held in which each instructor contributes information based upon his own specialty, and the entire faculty of the department discuss ways of improving the course. The reading materials, visual aids, and examinations are uniform from section to section. The course is considered successful from the students' point of view, and the cooperative effort is thought to provide a focus for the department.

In the third system the entire class meets together for lectures given by the professor and then breaks up into smaller discussion sections led by graduate teaching assistants. This is the most frequent pattern of organization in those universities where the total enrollment in introductory anthropology is over a hundred. The size of the discussion section is highly variable, ranging from fifteen to seventy.

Discussion sections are apparently a most difficult problem in many of the large audience courses, as indicated by the fact that the majority of instructors in such courses regard the discussion sections as unsuccessful. The anthropologists in our sample clearly prefer to lecture, and many question the value of free-ranging discussion between inexperienced teaching assistants and sophomores who know no anthropology. One felt that discussion sections simply provide a field day for the compulsive talker.

If discussion sections are not highly regarded in some institutions, why then is the system maintained? A primary reason is that sections may offer the only opportunity for students to discuss the lectures and readings in small groups. In very large classes there are many benefits to be derived from some measure of personal contact between student and instructor. The use of graduate students as teaching assistants is a relatively inexpensive way of providing such direct contact. And the short examinations administered periodically by the assistants are also of value.

The main beneficiary of the section system, however, is probably the teaching assistant himself, who obtains both financial support for his graduate studies and some experience in teaching. The former benefit is possibly less important today than it was in the past, considering the number of nonteaching fellowships with relatively large stipends now available from the government and other agencies. The significance of the teaching experience is variable. It may be maximized if the assistantship is offered at the proper stage in the student's graduate career, perhaps during the second or third year, and if the student is allowed to remain an assistant for only one year. Too long a period as a teaching assistant can interfere with the student's progress toward the Ph.D. degree and may, in some cases, become a form of exploitation.

It is most essential that the role of the teaching assistant be very carefully defined and that his responsibilities be commensurate with his abilities. In too many cases the role of the assistant is ambiguous because the instructor does not clearly define the situation and does not provide adequate supervision. The primary responsibility of the assistant is, of course, to his own growth as a professional anthropologist, and it is the instructor's task to insure that the assistantship experience contributes toward that growth. If the training function of the assistantship were made more prominent, the assistant would see his position as a stage in his graduate career rather than simply as a fellowship with responsibilities.

FUNCTIONS OF THE INTRODUCTORY COURSE

Thus far we have considered the introductory course in cultural anthropology primarily from the students' point of view. Our emphasis has been upon the contribution of anthropology toward the liberal education of undergraduates. At this point we shift our perspective to the contribution of the introductory course to the field of anthropology. The beginning course has a number of consequences, or if you prefer, functions, for the department in which it is taught, for the men who teach it, and for the profession-at-large.

As a relative latecomer to many American universities anthropology has had to compete with longer established departments for students, funds, and in some cases, respectability. The power struggle continues every year in universities throughout the country as new departments are created or as they branch off from sociology departments. It is quite clear that in many institutions the greater the student enrollment the higher the standing of the department within the university. An increase in the number of undergraduates who enroll in the beginning course also means more students for the advanced level courses and for graduate school.

The introductory course is not simply a way of building a department—and hence a way of building the profession—but is the major channel for communicating the results of anthropology to the lay public. The beginning course probably has the greatest cumulative effect in transmitting the anthropological point of view to the most people. This is important to anthropologists. If the statements made on the questionnaires are to be taken at face value—and on this point we feel they are—then it is generally believed that our discipline has something vital to contribute toward a liberal education. Anthropologists are convinced of the importance of their message; their conviction, in some cases, approaches missionary zeal. They have much to say and want to reach a wide audience.

We do not suggest that popularity as measured by student enrollment is either good in itself or necessarily correlated with effective teaching. Enrollment figures are undoubtedly influenced by a multiplicity of factors such as type of institution, region of the country, degree of administrative support, distribution requirements, and nature of the student body. Nor do we claim that competition for students is equally prominent in all universities. Our point is simply that an effective introductory course, in many universities, is one route to a strong anthropology department, and that an effective introductory course, in all institutions, is important for the adequate transmission of the findings and insights of cultural anthropology.

GORDON W. HEWES

Course Design

THESE REMARKS are addressed to those faced with the problems of designing new courses or redesigning old ones. A course may be "new" at a given institution, new in the sense that nothing like it has ever been offered anywhere before, or new in the sense that similar courses are just beginning to be established elsewhere. Redesign is involved to some extent whenever the teaching of an established course changes hands. Good teaching of anthropology is probably characterized by continual revision or redesign of courses.

GENERAL DESIGN PROBLEMS

Fundamentally, the design of a course is the process of extracting a manageable unit of academic instruction from the huge, amorphous, and changing body of ideas and information constituting a discipline or cutting across several disciplines. A course has a specified duration and consists of exercises such as lectures, readings, reports, laboratory work, and examinations. At its conclusion the students' performances are normally evaluated according to a system of grades. Course design must, therefore, not only provide for exposure of the subject matter to the students and for employment of methods to motivate them to learn it, but also for ways of assigning reasonably objective grades to each of them. In American colleges and universities, courses are fitted into patterns of requirements and electives, major and minor fields, and are quantified in credit-hours. These details are set down in catalogues and bulletins obtainable from practically all United States colleges and universities. Against this academic background we design and teach courses in cultural or social anthropology.

Although there exists an extensive literature on the educational effectiveness of various design procedures and even more on teaching

techniques, it deals chiefly with primary and secondary schooling. The
fewer studies of college teaching rarely mention anthropology. Professional anthropologists engaged in teaching, though often deeply
concerned with the problem of the effectiveness of their educational activities, have seldom published their ideas. What follows is, therefore,
mostly based on informal conversation and impressions.

Design of the introductory anthropology course has crystallized somewhat, with a tendency to catechismic responses to terms like *potlatch
dolichocephalic, couvade, coup de poing, atlatl, sororate,* and *mana.*
Advanced undergraduate courses in social or cultural anthropology
are far more heterogeneous, with their organization and content mostly
left to the initiative and preferences of individual professors. The
kind of departmental supervision which may be exercised over large
freshman courses is unlikely to be encountered in courses at the third-
or fourth-year level. The impetus for a new course or for revision of
an old one may originate with someone other than the person who will
ultimately teach it, however. An anthropologist who has carried on
fieldwork or research on a given topic may be asked by his colleagues
to work up a course dealing with it. At the opposite extreme, junior
staff members may be assigned a course in the hope that it will help
them fill in a gap in their professional training. If sufficient time is allowed for preparation, this may not be as reprehensible as it sounds.
In any case, new staff members can rarely expect to confine their teaching to topics in which they feel specially competent. The design and
teaching of a new course can be a valuable learning process for the professor.

If a course has been taught before at the same institution, the new
instructor would do well to find out about its format and content, even
if a new approach has been decided upon. Not only may one's anthropologist colleagues have certain expectations about the course, but so may
members of other departments (who may even have been recommending the course to their students). In a large institution, social or cultural anthropology courses are frequently included among the suggested electives in a number of widely separated fields. The course
designer should not only pay some attention to the relation of a particular course to other courses in anthropology, but also, wherever feasible, to the function of the course in the institution as a whole.

As soon as an instructor receives his course assignment—or before
this if he is planning to request a particular course—he should begin
intensive reading on the topic. Reading with an eye to designing an
academic course is rather unlike the reading one might undertake
in connection with research or fieldwork. For the novice teacher, the
amount of material which may be required in a course meeting three

hours weekly for a semester is not easy to assemble, especially if steady lecturing is anticipated. Works which might serve as textbooks or recommended reading may have to be evaluated quite carefully. Library holdings need to be investigated in terms of the probable size of the future class or the kinds of written work that the students may be expected to prepare. It may be necessary to get the library to add expensive reference works or subscribe to new journals, which the individual research scholar could avoid by travel to other libraries or the use of interlibrary loan services.

The plan of the course may emerge from wide reading and cogitation, or it may spring fully formed from a single book. Borrowing a course plan in this fashion is not an unfavorable reflection on the integrity of the teacher, for he is not (at this stage, at any rate) engaged in the preparation of a necessarily wholly original copyrightable book. Anthropologists should be well aware of the rarity of genuine independent invention. Another essential procedure is to review the pertinent recent journal literature (including reviews). Advanced undergraduates in anthropology have the right to expect their instructors to be in contact with current work, however timeless the basic topic may be. Good course design and effective teaching should encourage students to use the journal literature themselves for written reports and background for classroom discussion. The course designer may need to be reminded that excellent material relating to the topic may exist in other languages than English. If he knows of people at other institutions who may have taught a similar course, he might write or confer with them; many experienced professors are very willing to respond to requests for help of this kind.

THE COURSE OUTLINE

By the date that the course is scheduled to begin, a fairly complete course outline should have been prepared geared to the school calendar, taking into account vacations, examination periods, etc. If there is a reading list or set of assignments, these should be fitted into a realistic timetable. Above all, the course-designer should remember that his students are probably taking other courses and will not be devoting themselves exclusively to the one he teaches. Field trips and other special activities also require advance planning. Some professors find that duplicated copies of the course outline distributed to the students help to keep the instructor and his class from wandering too far from the subject matter of the course. Others may find such a device too restrictive.

A reasonable balance between planning and improvisation should be sought. Most good college courses are neither non-directive group-therapy sessions nor a precisely timed set of formal lectures. A well-designed course should allow leeway for occasional unplanned digressions and classroom discussions, for unexpected visiting speakers, and for the instructor to insert new material not anticipated when the course outline was drawn up. On the other hand, the plan should be followed closely enough to enable the instructor to cover what was intended at the outset. There is little virtue in drawing up a careful plan and then getting bogged down in a single portion of it, or in wandering so far afield from the announced theme that not even the most heroic last-minute efforts can bring the theme back into focus. For what it may be worth, it may be noted that the advanced undergraduate anthropology courses taught by Alfred L. Kroeber and Robert H. Lowie were well organized and covered the announced subject matter; one emerged from their courses with voluminous and orderly notes and a mass of factual information. I think this has continued to be the central pedagogical tradition in our discipline.

Design and content are so interrelated that it is difficult to offer advice about one without knowing about the other. One feature of any topic in cultural or social anthropology, however, is constant: it has a history. An initial review of the history of the study of any topic and its place, not only in the larger history of anthropology as a discipline but also in science and the history of ideas in general, seems to be a good beginning. The study of kinship, of magic and religion, of material culture, or of any other topic within cultural anthropology can be initially approached by a consideration of its intellectual history, at least back into the nineteenth century, when our science began to take scholarly shape. This same historical framework can be the basis of a final summing up, toward the last week or so of the course, when it can be used to suggest the possible future development of the topic as a systematic object of scholarly investigation.

DESIGN AND THE INTELLECTUAL LEVEL
OF ADVANCED COURSES

We have been doing a good job of threatening the naïve ethnocentrism of our students, but perhaps less well in challenging their minds. An obvious way to get students to put more into advanced undergraduate anthropology courses is to insist that they write more and better reports, based in part on recent journal literature (which requires more judgment and selection than the use of a single book, however excellent). Another device, which I have been employing lately, is to demand that students who have had, by their third or fourth undergraduate years, course work in a foreign language, use this language in the preparation of written reports. This is a skill that our higher educational system all too often limits to the modern language classroom.

The "whole-culture" approach—in which one or, better, several cultures are described with reasonable completeness—is entirely feasible within the framework of a cultural or social anthropology course devoted to a particular topic such as social organization or religion. There are few topical courses in cultural anthropology that would not benefit from the inclusion—in lectures or readings, or both—of several sample whole-culture descriptions. Since the choice of such samples is very wide, it seems desirable to include not only local, autonomous, simple, or "primitive" societies, but also representatives of the peasant or folk societies which comprise such a large proportion of the world's existing cultural systems. I am not recommending the wholesale dropping of the Arunta, Yahgan, Kwakiutl, Navaho, or Trobrianders, but rather a more balanced diet including communities from the larger, more complex, "modern" civilizations of South and East Asia, the Middle East, West Africa, and Latin America.

Not only the novice teacher is confronted with problems of course design. The veteran professor faces this issue each time he is expected to teach the "same course." If he is conscientious, he will discard his dog-eared, yellowed lecture notes from time to time and make a fresh start, reassuring himself at least that he has not yet succumbed to total academic petrifaction.

Much more rigorous concern with problems of course design than in the laissez-faire tradition of the past looms in the immediate future. A technological revolution in teaching involving closed-circuit televising of courses, teaching machines, and automatized libraries is in the offing. The future position of undergraduate cultural anthropology is probably bound up more than most of us realize with the adaptability of our subject matter to the requirements of the kind of course design now coming to be called "course programming." The handwriting, in light impulses, is already quite visible on the video-screens.

CONRAD M. ARENSBERG

Courses in
Ethnological
Subjects

A DISCUSSION of the special subjects to which ethnological courses have been devoted and of their content and the methods of teaching them must begin with the recognition, already achieved elsewhere in this volume and well-documented in Erminie A. Voegelin's summary of "Anthropology in American Universities" (1950: pp. 350-391), that the number of such courses has always been large. Voegelin's survey shows the standard undergraduate offerings, particularly in independent departments, to have been quite varied. We will name the more usual subject offerings as we proceed. Suffice it to say, in general introduction, that these ethnologic subject offerings have always figured in the curriculum after the introductory courses. In some cases they have had at least as prominent a place as traditional branches of anthropology other than ethnology. Sometimes indeed they have crowded these out. When joined, as they often have been, with area courses, they have made the chief burden of instruction, to the extent that many departments have often been really more departments of cultural anthropology than of general anthropology. Again, ethnological subject-matter courses, while they may have equal billing in curricula with the cognate branches of general anthropology, do not share this eminence alone but are invariably listed with and somehow balanced with area, regional, or civilizational (ethnographic) courses.

In general, they seem to be present in curricula in two classes. The first class, much the larger, is segmentalizing within ethnology. It consists of courses on special subject matters conceived as parts of a nonlocalized, generalizing ethnology. These parts have been sharply different in purpose and coverage from area courses giving the detailed and particularizing ethnographies of selected regions, their tribes, and their peoples. The second class of ethnological subject-matter courses, much smaller or missing altogether, consists of unitary, professional, disciplinary courses treating ethnology as a whole, either as a body of concepts, or as a method of science (e.g., field work). By analogy at least, though it seems not to be so conceived, it offers a unitary specialization for a student major going beyond the introductory course which is parallel to and co-equal with other possible specializations in archaeology, somatology, or linguistics. Oddly enough, however, this neatly logical possibility of curriculum building is nowhere realized, but attention is given chiefly or exclusively to the segmentary courses in ethnology. The unitary courses, if they are represented at all in undergraduate curricula, are to be found in one course in Ethnological (or Anthropological) Theory (or Concepts) and one course in Methods (or Field Work). Even graduate departments show the same relative weighting between the unitary and the segmentary courses in ethnology.

There are good historical reasons. The concepts of ethnology have been derived deductively and even piecemeal from studies of special problems, processes, and loci of culture. Our science has, in many minds quite properly, eschewed too easy generalization, abstraction, and schematizing. Furthermore, traditionally, and perhaps rightly in a science based on field work and participant or close-up observation and minute data-gathering and checking-in-context, the history of the science and the methods of conducting its work have been learned not abstractly but in re-examination of the classic successes of the science and in emulation of them.

Field work techniques are usually a very late acquisition, taken up not infrequently just prior to embarking on one's first field trip. Some of this is changing. But much of the tradition persists: eschewing methodology for its own sake; distrusting grand schemes and abstract generalizations; maintaining a healthy empiricism, which includes no but rather a healthy preference for personal immersion in data and too-tender respect for the pronouncements of the anthropological great for curious exploration of a foreign field; an immensely wide pan-human perspective never permitting completion of our discovery of our data; and a well-warranted horror of overprogramming and over-schematization of research contracted from watching our sister social sciences at work. These attributes of our science have always dictated and continue to dictate that in anthropology theory should be an infrequent course and methodology come very late.

There are further reasons for the overweight of segmentary ethnologic courses. The segmentary courses treat pan-human or first "primitive" and then, by implication, pan-human, universal institutions or aspects of culture in several ways made necessary by the richness and diversity of the data of the science. They separate out universal institutions of mankind seen comparatively for range and variety and evolution: family, law, economics, religion. They separate out processes of culture and its evolution and change. They break away special developments and uses or illuminations of cultural theory: personality, national character, innovation, intergroup relations. The richness and variety of the data are so great and the power of cultural theory so pervasive in modern social and psychological science that we find ourselves in a crisis of self-definition as well as of instruction in anthropology. In physical anthropology, we can leave serology and genetics to the biologists or let them go their own ways. In ethnology, we cannot share our data; we alone are the finders, developers, expounders.

Obviously growth and fission in our science has strongly favored ethnology over the other branches of anthropology. Ethnology has grown very rapidly in numbers of practitioners, of concepts and findings, and of dividing interests unshared with but recognized as important by others, both fellow scientists and the general public. The underlying data of world ethnography which must be presented to make ethnological and cultural theory and discovery intelligible and useful to our world are today so manifold and diffuse and the concepts ordering them are so variegated and graduated that there is danger that by themselves they will preempt what curricular space exists or can be won for our science at large unless very special efforts at balance are made.

The usual programs reported in 1940 foreshadowed the congestions and difficulties of today. They seem to have been largely *ad hoc* blends of the differentiating subject matters and the fortuitous special interests and experiences of the particular cultural anthropologists who happened to have been assembled in a department. Personal interests, experiences, and expeditions often came to be courses, not itself a bad thing in a science relying on personal commitment and example for transmission at the professional level.

There seems to be evidence, in the curricula reported in 1940, and probably the situation is little changed, that the efforts to balance ethnology and the other branches of anthropology had to be blended, as any given department continued to grow, with a continuing effort to keep up with proliferating new developments in ethnology itself.

Thus, one can note a progression of interests: older subject courses, particularly Primitive Religion and Primitive Arts and Techniques, or even Museum Science, have tended to fall away and newer subject courses, Culture Change and Culture Dynamics, or Culture and Personality, even Applied (Cultural) Anthropology, or Anthropology and Contemporary Civilization, or Anthropology and the Underdeveloped Nations, have come up to figure in both undergraduate and graduate programs. In many instances the generous offerings of subject-matter courses, which share curriculum space with area courses and courses on the nonethnological subdisciplines of our field (archeology, physical anthropology, linguistics), seem to attempt a compromise between internal coverage of our science and external extension of the service offered by cultural anthropology. Culture and personality courses serve persons interested in psychology or individual and child development in general; applied anthropology draws in planners and economic developers or public health people; and so on. The device of listing lower-numbered or first-year graduate school courses as open to undergraduates of good standing in their senior (or even, exceptionally, in their junior year, if qualified), probably quite common in departments which have both graduate and undergraduate curricula, makes the possibility of service and drawing power of anthropology all the greater. It also eases the progress of undergraduate majors into a professional graduate specialization in our science. The grave problems of mixed preparation of the audiences of subject-matter courses we must leave to later discussion.

Suffice it to say, then, in historical review of the place of ethnological subject-matter courses in curricula, that there always seems to have been in curricular effort a problem of such balancing and blending. It has continued to be achieved practically in a number of varying ways. Core materials of ethnological importance and core concepts of cultural theory have been central. They have been most often put, it seems, into the fundamental social organization course, making social organization, or kinship, or comparative social organization a nuclear subject matter out of which further differentiation and advance could take place.

The traditional practice indeed suggests that ethnology possesses initial subject matter above ethnographic descriptions which is basic to cultural analysis and comparison and has never lost its importance. This subject matter now seems by common consent to have won itself a central place as basic initial matter for any curriculum of social and cultural anthropology. The newer and internally bifurcating subjects can be ranged beyond it in many ways. The choice of these ways can well continue to represent the trends of the science, so long as the achieved initial and unitary data, methods, and concepts are given recognition. The choice can also reflect a realistic, shifting adjustment of curriculum to the changing interests of changing department personnel.

The best examples of such proliferation and separation of subject matters in ethnological courses are the many curricular programs which offer both a course in cultural dynamics (or culture change), where data and concepts of historically and diachronically oriented anthropology are offered, including a closer look at cultural evolution than the introductory course affords, and a course in social anthropology (or something analogous), which presents a synchronic and detailed analysis of particular cultural wholes in particular societies or of the interconnections of particular institutions. Sometimes it is the course in social anthropology which presents synchronic and analytic internal comparisons of societies and their cultures, separate from the study of temporal successions and processes in culture, and carries the student much beyond the few sketches of whole societies that may have figured in his introductory course. However, we often find the same synchronic comparisons and internal explorations of the interdependencies of institutions, trait complexes, and values separated out and further differentiated in courses dubbed variously Primitive Societies, Folk (or Peasant) Societies, and so on. It is here that the few offerings in Developing Countries or Complex Cultures figure.

This fission of subject-matter courses seems to exist side by side with an older way of presenting the richly proliferating segments of our richly varied data of the world's cultures for analytic treatment and inferential comparison. That is, of course, a continuation of the offerings, beyond Primitive (or Comparative) Social Organization, into courses on particular institutions, either in their putatively primitive forms or in wider comparisons. Primitive Religion, as we said, is less popular as an offering these days, but there are signs of a renewal of interest. Primitive Economics, more and more conceptually oriented, is a rising vogue and seems to have taken the place of an older, more museum-oriented Primitive Arts, Crafts, or Technology. Primitive Political Organization, or Law, or Social Control, is also a rising choice, the more so as it offers a rubric for the inclusion of much matter dealing with the rise of the new African and other ex-colonial nations. Also, it allows common cause, nowadays, with perhaps belated similar efforts of political science and sociology to keep up with a world of newly emergent nations of extra-European civilization and origin. Primitive Science or Thought may be offered where once Primitive Religion or Magic might have been, but the practice seems very occasional and perhaps confined to graduate programs.

Two further types of special ethnological courses must be cited. They are not devoted to an institution (e.g., Primitive Economics), nor to a new subdiscipline (e.g., Culture and Personality), nor to a newly differentiated field of research (e.g., Peasant Societies), nor to a process of either world-wide scope or pressing local or topical interest needing analysis in anthropological terms (e.g., Culture Contact,

Race Relations), the standard occasions for subject-matter offerings in ethnology already touched on. Rather, they include the above-mentioned courses of a more theoretic, disciplinary, or professional interest, far less numerous than the segmentary variety. It may well be that the illustrative material and the concepts used are much the same as in the segmentary courses. The titles, however, suggest a more exclusively professional, a more abstract and summary, and a less service-oriented purpose. These professionalizing courses usually carry names such as Concepts of Anthropology or (History of) Anthropological Theory when they are frankly theoretical or historical, or, with whatever mixture of purposes, whether training of professionals or exposure of students to life situations it is hard to say, they are courses in Field Methods, Field Work, Methods of Cultural Analysis, etc.

Lastly, there is a sprinkling of courses whose titles suggest an overlap between ethnology and other branches of anthropology, such as Language and Culture or Culture and Biology (i.e., presumably human evolution). Space does not permit our treating these here. They are so few as to suggest that they are probably personal solutions of instructors combining the specialties of their own training. On the other hand it may be in some cases that the course in Culture and Biology is another name for the general introductory course offered as a service to other departments or, in smaller institutions, as a requirement in general science.

CRITERIA FOR SELECTION OF SUBJECT-MATTER COURSES

The subject courses in ethnology have now been characterized and something of the history of change in their names and putative contents has been suggested. It is now time for us to consider the probable best solution of the difficulties they present in balance and coverage and in treating differentiation and trend in ethnology. We must then proceed to some suggestions as to the content and method of teaching of the courses considered the best nominations for a balanced, sufficiently extensive undergraduate program of instruction in our science's cultural branch.

Only a small number of courses can be chosen in any curriculum to represent subject-matter diversity in ethnology. There seems little hope that the continuing proliferation of courses can really keep up with the growth of our science and its ethnological interests. Further, there is positive danger that a student who is already coping with anthropology as a whole and is, quite properly, already exposed to its mankind-wide historical and archeological perspectives and its world-wide ethnographic perspectives will have no undergraduate time or attention left for ethnological specialties. There is the further danger that he may lose sight of the essential unities of cultural anthropology. By and large, the introductory course, however successful, can give him only a taste of such unities and of a realization of their position among the other branches of man's story, and this only if, as sometimes happens, it is devoted exclusively to ethnology and ethnography. But it is from first-hand experience with cultural analysis, or first-hand detailed exploration of other and different societies or of other and different comparative institutions, that a genuine appreciation both of the range of variation in human ways, social arrangements, and values and of their complex interdependencies and historical continuities and transitions can be obtained; and they can be given time and scope enough to become absorbed only in one or more full basic ethnological courses. This experience and this exploration can be won, untrammeled by data from other branches of anthropology and clearly built on the initial reformation or ethnocentric, parochial, and ahistorical attitudes the introductory course may have achieved, only in a basic, full ethnological course.

A full, analytic, and rather deep-probing course in one or more ethnological specializations seems necessary to communicate the cannons of objective, value-suspending, comparative description, inductive generalization, and structure-building; culturally foreign and personally self-immersing field work; and orderly, objective, and controlled free-interview or participation-based observation of human realities of action, utterance, and conduct of life. It is upon these that our ethnology is based, and they are our chief message to our age (that man can usefully learn to know himself and the laws that govern him). They can fruitfully be passed over to the student, whether he takes them up himself in a future professional career of his own or whether he merely mingles them with his general undergraduate preparation for responsible national and world citizenship in the twentieth century.

Some hard ethnographic and comparative social-science fact of the diversity and range of human culture and human institutional development must reach the student, in area courses or in a general survey beyond introductory anthropology. Especially in an undergraduate program necessarily limited in the number of courses that can be offered or taken, some such core course is needed that presents ethnology (cultural and social anthropology) by itself, beyond the introductory course, where the student can carry out for himself an objective and comparative analysis of institutions different from those of his own culture.

It seems unwise to present these basic subject matters, concepts and methods in an oblique fashion. Culture and Personality, or Culture Contact and Culture Change, might well, if well presented, impart the same experience. Even a course in Peasant Societies, or Applied Anthropology, or Underdeveloped Countries, if properly presented and understood, can do so. But a danger exists, which the author's personal experience bears out. The special motivations of the students who select such courses, and of the instructors who choose to present them—in the one case, interest in personal problems and adjustments of individuals, in the other social and political adjustments of racial and class conflicts, native and foreign ethnic values, etc.—have a way of obscuring the hard-core learning of the range of cultural variation and the canvas of data-gathering and comparison essential to our science. Realization of diversity, difference, and process in human culture can be got in such courses, and often is. Rigor and objectivity, induction and synthesis with human materials come harder, just because, perhaps, commitment pushes the student ahead faster than his comprehension grows. This experience should not disincline us to exclude individual enculturation (in Culture and Personality courses) from the curriculum, nor incline us to omit culture contacts, clashes, race relations, ethnic successions and accommodations, all of them legitimate problem data for cultural analysis in ethnology and as always prime sources for studies ranging from term papers to Ph.D. theses. It suggests rather that the curriculum should list courses dealing with such matters as permissible only after a basic or core ethnology course has been presented and taken.

Indeed, even on the score of teaching content, the caution is necessary. It is too much to have to explain the differences between Eskimoan small-family and bilateral kinship and patrilineal joint-family and patrigentile organization, or to work out the true natures of caste in India, color in the United States, and Indio-Ladino stratification in Central America at the same time that one is presenting the dynamics of race contact or the conflicts of value and personal motive in American second-generation immigrants or in new African city-dwellers, or the failures of plans for cooperatives. The advanced specializations, service courses, and partial-subject-matter offerings, although they have a definite place in the graduate and in the undergraduate curriculum, ought not to be burdened with core matter or basic instruction, concepts, and methods. They should instead presuppose some world ethnography, some cultural analysis, some inductive data-gathering and collation already assimilated.

An undergraduate concentrator who takes his first introductory anthropology in his sophomore year and a basic ethnology course in his junior year would be ready in his senior year for the further progression of courses. But such progression is still all too rare, and with small numbers, probably impossible. Except for majors, it is out of the question. We will long be burdened, even in graduate school, with having to teach both outsiders and professionals, in such ethnographic subject-matter courses, with all the delays and the splits of attention involved in speaking to audiences half of whom are in possession of the basic facts and concepts and half of whom are not. The only solutions are to require the latter persons to undertake some special reading or to ask a different sort of performance from them, neither ideal.

Lastly, again, it seems an overburdening of course, instructor, and student, particularly undergraduate student, unless the ethnology of the introductory course of his institution was particularly rich, to expect the basic concepts, methods, and data of our science of cultural complexities and diversities, and interconnections and successions, particularly in institutional matters and comparative social organization, to be transmitted in area, regional, or civilizational courses. In such frankly descriptive ethnographic courses, the kinds and identities of cultural data can and ought to be used for characterization, localization, establishment of distribution, and differential occurrence and contrast among the cultures of the peoples of the earth and its regions, including in detail the region special to the course. But American education below college level has practically abandoned both history and geography and till lately skipped *in toto* acquaintance with the extra-European world (Europeans did no better on this second score, to tell the truth), or even extra-United States history. We cannot, therefore, rely on college ethnographic or civilizational courses, however rich, to do more than establish identification. There is simply too much material for a course on India or on the Peoples of the Pacific also to treat *lobola* or *kula*-ring, or to read Lévi-Strauss, or to understand for the first time depth-area trait distributions, or to worry over mythic and symbolic projections of social structure. If the student is an anthropology major, he must use such concepts in understanding India or Oceania and its peoples and their ways. If he is a nonmajor, engaged in a perfectly legitimate search for knowledge of his world of today, he will either be confused if ethnological concepts and comparisons are not used, or overburdened if he must learn them along with the other "facts" of place, people, and condition.

COMPARATIVE-INSTITUTIONAL COURSES AS CORE COURSES

It seems clear then that a core course in ethnology, beyond the introductory general anthropology course, is very necessary. Traditional practice, in which Primitive Social Organization, or Primitive Social Structure took up the role, has much to commend it. Social organization, even for persons not enthusiasts for the social or structural determination or penetration of all facets of culture, cannot and has not normally been taught without some comparative establishment of the full range of technological, familial, kinship, communal, age-grading and sex-typing, religious-organizational and ceremonial, stratificational, legal, juridical and political, and even economic variability in human institutions, human culture. It is, of course, quite possible to lose the way of both instructor and student in the intricacies of kinship systems. Nevertheless, most courses in Primitive Social Organization are forced to include other facets of social organization. Most elementary questions about the reasons for kinship systems establish some at least of their connections with other aspects of the institutional systems. Indeed any good return to firsthand ethnographic description forced by a genuine attempt at analysis so soon immerses one deep in intricacies of overlapping values, roles and functions, entanglements of religious and ceremonial participation, mythic charter, gift-giving and exchanges, juridical dispositions of property, personal obligation, membership rights, etc. that a rounded treatment, at least a rounded adumbration of most of the institutions of a culture, is forced upon instructor and student alike.

Usually, however, design of such a course, whether or not it goes so far as to preëmpt the territories of more specifically institutional courses (Primitive Religion, Primitive Economics, Primitive Political Organization, Law, etc.), and thus devotes sections and readings to each of these things, certainly covers explicitly the institutions universal to mankind. It also asks at least implicitly what functions and institutions are common to mankind's social life at any stage of complexity of society. It thus sets the stage for higher-civilizational developments of state, urban, church and ecumenical organization. In the very acts of establishing the overlaps of functions in primitive society separated in more complex, even peasant, societies, the stage is usually set for exploring what social arrangements are culturally differentiated for all human groups, e.g., age-gradings, or incest, or jealousy, or class-differentiation, or religion and magic, etc., and how different societies, of differing complexity, including our own, handle with culturally derived or emergent rules different universals of individual need and emotion, social and societal concern, interpersonal and intergroup adjustment and coördination.

Specifically, then, such a core-ethnology course, at least beginning with the traditional Primitive (and/or Comparative) Social Organization, as good a rubric for general comparison of cultures as can be found today, would probably best take the following sequence of topics.

1. The universals of culture, the problem.
2. Status and role, the human, primate, mammalian biograms and

their species-based social life, some essentials of coöperative and collective existence in higher animals, band, horde, community, tribe, etc.

3. Incest, family structure and its varieties.

4. Kinship terminology, kinship systems, kinship analysis. Unilateral, bilateral, and other kindreds.

5. Residence, marriage, alliance, property, revenge, juridical relationships, filiations, and corporate rights and obligations, problems of functional, historical, and other analyses.

6. Political, religious, and economic extensions of kinship. The problem of the kin-based society, the acephalous society. The family cult and the rites of passage, totemism and other mythic charters or projections of kinship organization.

7. The community: bees, coöperative exploitation of resources, bands and settlement patterns, public works, the role of irrigation, and the forms of the community. Functions of collective organization: warfare, defense, storage, the management of crisis. Hamlet, village, dispersed settlement; canton, region, and councils.

8. Age-grading and sex-roles. Rites of passage. Formal age grades and associations.

9. Religious, cultic and ceremonial organization. Shamanism, polytheism, monasticism, congregational (ecclesiastical) organization. Form, structure, functions, and varieties, of magical, ceremonial, and religious leadership, belief, and experience. Syncretism and the great religions. The little tradition and the great tradition.

10. Chieftainship, monarchy, the rise of the state. Extracommunal, territorial and regional political organization.

11. Economic organization. Barter, ceremonial exchange, reciprocity, redistribution, fairs, markets, and trade. The debate over primitive economics.

12. Social stratification, stratified clans, part-time specializations. Part-cultures and ethnic specializations. Transhumance, nomadism, special peoples. Guilds, classes, castes, estates, and complex societies.

13. Primitive science, transmission and specialization in knowledge, *expertise,* and education. Expansion of communities of communication. Language and culture, multilingualism, pidgins, and linguae francae. Tribal culture-areal organization, ecumenical movements, acculturations and incorporations of peoples, nativistic and counter-ecumenical movements.

Once such a course was outlined, it would serve as an initial core of ethnological concept and content, capable of introducing either area courses with their identifications, or special-subject courses treating either area courses with their identifications, or special-subject courses treating either processes (Culture Change) or institutions (Primitive Economics) in expansion of the core materials. It would be a simple matter to add, in changing balance and proliferation, the further subject-matter courses we have shown now to contend for attention. Such a core course, expanding and updating the traditional Primitive (now Comparative) Social Organization, would play its proper role in introducing the student, after orientation and indoctrination in the broader introductory course, into the still all-too-broad but now quite precise and specific core-concepts and core-methods of our rich modern ethnology in anthropology.

REFERENCE CITED

VOEGELIN, ERMINIE A.
    1950   Anthropology in American universities. American Anthropologist
                52:350-391.

DAVID H. FRENCH

The Role of
Anthropologist
in the
Methodology of Teaching

THIS DISCUSSION of roles, methodology, and techniques may have implications for the teaching of various fields of anthropology at both graduate and undergraduate levels.[1] As written, however, it is directed toward undergraduate teaching of cultural and social anthropology. Although undergraduate courses frequently have both anthropology majors and non-majors enrolled, it will be assumed here that the needs of the latter are not sufficiently different to require courses to be modified for their benefit. It can be argued that the functions of general education are best fulfilled when students take a wide range of courses, each taught in terms of the rationale of that discipline.

Methodology in the teaching of anthropology will be approached through an examination of the roles of those who participate in educational systems. Techniques, i.e., the tactics of the classroom, are secondary, and the discussion of them will follow later.

In the twentieth century, students in anthropology courses are confronted with two general classes of instructors: 1) anthropologists who are teaching, and 2) teachers who have anthropology as their subject matter. The distinction is based on the primacy of the role of anthropologist or that of teacher for a given instructor. It will be argued here that anthropologists functioning as teachers better serve the needs of all students. Indeed, one could maintain that the kinds of problems these students will eventually confront as citizens require a fundamental understanding of *disciplined modes of inquiry,* rather than an appreciation of information.

THE ROLE OF STUDENT

By and large, the aims of students are antithetical to those of teachers (cf. Waller 1949). They hope to graduate and to gain the opportunities and privileges they regard as deriving from this attainment. They usually also have other aims: establishing friendships, making preparations for marriage, and the like. In general they choose and participate in courses in such a way as to minimize effort and maximize rewards, especially grades. For them, a good course is one which facilitates this "economizing" process. If at the same time the course is "interesting" or "stimulating," then so much the better. Anthropology courses, incidentally, can quite easily satisfy such aesthetic, recreational, or social-emotional motives. The fact that many (but not all) of those enrolled in courses have aims that are secondary from the teacher's viewpoint does not mean that these students are irrational or that they necessarily do not "want to learn."

In so far as any kind of modification is a general aim, the teacher is most likely to make a permanent modification in the students' behavior if he does not play the game their way, but rather manages to induct them into a new kind of role. In a biology course the teacher who succeeds best is one who changes *students* into *biologists,* if only for the period in which they are in the course. Some of these proto-biologists will, of course, take other courses and become more publicly recognized as biologists. For those who do not, the probability that they can read and think more intelligently about biological subject matter in the future would seem to be enhanced by their having played the role, both intellectually and emotionally. For anthropologists, as for those in other disciplines, a middle-range educational goal, therefore, is to transmute students into persons capable of acting *as if* they were professional scientists or scholars: i.e., they envision the same types of problem formulation; they confront the world with specific alternatives that derive from the discipline; finally, they are motivated and supported in such behavior.

A teacher is not simply one who imparts information; he is also a model for one or another culturally regularized role. To the students he may represent nothing more than the role of teacher. He may also represent an academician. It is consistent with the argument being presented here, however, for the principal model to be that of *anthropologist.* It is improbable that the students can act like anthropologists while taking the course unless the teacher is seen as acting like one.

THE ROLE OF ANTHROPOLOGIST

Acting like an anthropologist in the classroom means employing the discipline, rather than social science, behavioral science, one's school, the local urban community, "people," or "humanity," as a major point of reference. To illustrate: students sometimes joke about anthropologists who make frequent use of data from "their tribe" in their teaching. Nevertheless, the use of one's own field data calls attention to the legitimate preoccupation an anthropologist can have with field research and its results. Not only field research but also journals, monographs, anthropological meetings, the history of the discipline, anthropologists as persons, and even selected gossip can serve as reference points. Naturally, the anthropologist-as-teacher chooses appropriate contexts for employing the various types of discipline-oriented materials. As a teacher he has a responsibility to communicate with the majority of his students. This paper, in fact, assumes a degree of competence in teaching, and it does not assume that every good anthropologist will be a good teacher of undergraduates. The significant point is that there should not be a major distinction between the general approach to problems which is employed in the classroom and outside of it. Complex matters may need to be simplified, or postponed until advanced courses, but they should not be distorted so that they are inconsistent with the pattern of activities characterizing the discipline.

If an anthropologist is to maintain the discipline as a point of reference, he should engage in research, be at least moderately oriented toward publication, and maintain contact with other anthropologists. Large departments function in such a way that these activities are a normal part of improving and maintaining one's place in the system. To remain an anthropologist, the member of a small department has greater need to attend meetings, to maintain an active relationship with the scholarly literature, and to preserve his identity as a research worker. For an anthropologist to do his best job as a teacher, not only should he engage in these activities, but it should be known by students that he does so. The student will also learn another aspect of the discipline, viz., that the teacher is not an anthropologist in general but has a specific area of competence within the discipline.

It should be clear that adequate teaching of anthropology depends both upon the presence of a facilitating environment and upon men capable of functioning as anthropologists. Unfortunately, there is no necessary relationship between formal training and this ability. In anthropology, as in other fields, there are men for whom training was simply a means to a non-professional end, i.e., social mobility or occupational

security. These may be more dangerous than those who have no training and recognize it; fortunately, there are as yet few such men in anthropology.

With increases in the number of college students and increases in interest in other cultures and in human development, it has sometimes been
necessary for men without the usual formal training to teach courses
labelled "anthropology." (Less confusion results when such teaching
of the subject matter of anthropology occurs in courses entitled "behavioral science" or "social science," though these courses may have
weaknesses in other respects.) The untrained teachers are in a difficult
position, but one that is not intrinsic to anthropology courses; it would
also be difficult for a chemist to teach creative writing or historiography.
It follows from the logic of this paper that non-anthropologists who
must teach anthropology are best advised to become socialized and en-
culturated with respect to the discipline. This cannot be done entirely
in a library or a single summer course. Attendance at anthropological
meetings and involvement in other activities which will permit them to
learn the role of anthropologist would seem desirable.

TEACHING TECHNIQUES

The discussion of educational *methodology* in the preceding pages does
not give definitive answers to every question about the most suitable
techniques for teaching anthropology. Legitimate alternatives exist,
with the choice depending upon curricular arrangements and the instructor's habits or convenience. Students can be encouraged to act
(which includes "thinking" and perceiving) as if they were anthropologists as well in lecture courses as in those that emphasize discussion. The teacher does not have to have close contact with the students
to serve as a model and to transmute students into anthropologists.

Within the framework of the choices that are made, however, certain
techniques would appear to be better than others. For example, in anthropology, or in any other field, the kind of reading matter provided by
the average textbook increases the probability that students will remain students. Anthropologists may write textbooks, but they don't
read them. The digested facts contained in most texts are as conveniently
forgotten as they are conveniently learned—in part because the very con-
sistency in the point of view of a single book eliminates the tantalizing
discrepancies that can encourage students to become involved in the
current problems of the discipline. Source books or readers are thus superior to texts, especially if it is made clear to the students that the majority of the selections consist of articles written by anthropologists
for anthropologists and published in the regular journals. While the resources of most schools do not permit extensive use of scholarly jour-

nals for ordinary class assignments, some contact with journal literature would seem to be desirable, even in introductory courses.

In addition to scholarly journals, some use of monographs is also desirable. They have an obvious value in the writing of term papers. The student can, however, become aware that the utilization of monographs for obtaining data for papers is not limited solely to undergraduates—professional anthropologists also use them.

A real difficulty in the use of books of readings, journal articles, and monographs is that they do not, in themselves, provide continuity for a course. Lectures, alone or combined with discussion sections, are familiar means for creating the degree of continuity an instructor feels is necessary in a course. Nevertheless, the task of providing continuity or integration—whether within a course or among separate courses—remains to some extent the task of the student.

Like the general form of a course, the types of examinations given depend upon the customs of a school, the instructor's habits, and the availability of time. Consistent with this discussion, the writer admits to a preference for examinations which test more than the information memorized by students. At some point in a course, it would appear to be desirable to ascertain the learner's ability to think like an anthropologist in a partially unfamiliar situation (cf. Bruner 1960:38-40). This does not necessarily require time-consuming "essay" questions, though carefully designed questions of this type may actually be a superior device. A useful type of examination in moderately large courses is to ask the student whether each of a series of statements is "true" or "false" and then to indicate in a few sentences why he made the decisions he did.

If the role of passive student is one of limited desirability, another common classroom role is even more to be avoided. This role is that of "audience member," whether for entertaining lectures or motion pictures. With television and the other recreational media so universally available, young Americans have ample opportunity to *learn* how to look and listen as members of an audience. Most members of most audiences are having emotional experiences, i.e., they may be enjoying themselves, but they rarely learn very much. John Pock has called attention to research findings in this area (e.g., Katz and Lazarsfeld 1955) and has commented (personal communication): "If there is any generalization that can be drawn from contemporary studies in communication, it is that there is no evidence that audiences participate in anything but a passive capacity and with limited, if any consequence." Some teachers remain optimistic, despite such powerful arguments against the use of audio-visual aids. If they are used at all, they should be preceded—and sometimes followed—by readings, lectures, or discussions which emphasize the cognitive content of the material and are directed toward raising audience members at least to the level of students. Advanced undergraduates and graduate students should be better able to experience audio-visual material in the role of proto-anthropologists. This is because they can treat these materials *as data* for analysis, rather than as information to be contemplated, appreciated, or regurgitated. The instructor can further this aim by requiring both rigorous class discussion and examinations on content and significance.

The arguments against the use of audio-visual aids do not necessarily hold for the use of museum resources; passive audience behavior is more easily prevented. Especially if it is made clear how specimens are relevant in actual research procedures, the judicious use of durable museum material enhances certain courses. Parenthetically, a common situation is that state universities and other large institutions have a surplus of museum material no longer of importance in research which can be loaned or donated to schools that lack museums. This is the existing practice in some states, and it might become more prevalent were the smaller schools to take the initiative and request such arrangements.

In the normal operation of any program for the teaching of anthropology, a certain number of students will decide to major in it. Of these, some will begin to act like proto-professionals, and others will remain students. The members of a department of anthropology might be well-advised to pay attention not only to grades and other "objective" results of student activity but also to the frequency with which a given person acts like an anthropologist. An appropriate question might be: can I visualize this young man or woman as a colleague in seven years' time? Even though the instructor has not "worked closely" with students, he should still be able to make careful observations and hard-headed discriminations during those periods in which the potential anthropologist is in action. Such judgments can, of course, serve as a basis for: 1) encouraging proto-anthropologists and discouraging perennial students; 2) aiding the undergraduate anthropologist in his choice of fields and choice of graduate schools; and 3) the writing of more useful or informative letters of recommendation. (Naturally, reliable judgments depend upon the instructor's having an adequate self-image in relation to the discipline in the first place.)

Preliminary role performances, rather than grades alone, can provide criteria for selecting undergraduates for research projects. The writer has had experience with a number of types of undergraduate research, ranging from ordinary term papers to field work with Indians and urban minority groups. Consistent with the viewpoint here, the best term projects carried on entirely at the school would appear to be those that approach most closely the kinds of research and writing carried on by professional anthropologists; this is most easily achieved in connection with advanced courses. Some undergraduates appreciate the opportunity to participate in "real" research projects being undertaken by the instructor. More often than one might suspect, it is possible to "farm out" to them a limited task which can make a small but significant contribution to a research program. This implies that there is no intrinsic contradiction between teaching and research.

Members of the Reed College student body have been sporadically engaging in field research in recent years. Two anthropology majors were recipients of Undergraduate Research Stipends from the Social Science Research Council during the period of operation of that program. Others functioned as research assistants for faculty-centered projects. Fortunately, all of these undergraduates were successful; they gained experience, gathered useful data, and communicated their results through written reports. Sometimes, however, summer field parties are disrupted by students who had received adequate grades to qualify for the training but who lacked the ability to act like anthropologists in the field. Members of such parties should be carefully selected, with special attention being paid to the role behavior that will be expected of them.

CONCLUSIONS

Anthropology as a discipline has long benefited from its association with universities and colleges (cf. Parsons 1959:551-553, regarding the importance of this for sociology). A reciprocal relationship holds: teaching within these schools benefits when the faculty members each hold an identity in a discipline. This is in opposition to the educationist proposition that a good teacher can teach anything well. On the other hand, it may be true that a good student can learn and forget almost anything; sound educational methodology would expect *permanently* useful insights to be derived only from some degree of participation in the role activities of the discipline. Temporarily, at least, the undergraduates should act as if they were anthropologists; this is possible when the teacher exemplifies the complex of activities involved in the role of an anthropologist and when discipline-oriented teaching materials are employed.

NOTE

[1] An earlier draft of this paper was read in a symposium on teaching at the spring meeting of the American Ethnological Society at Stanford, April, 1960. The author wishes to acknowledge the suggestions of participants in the symposium and of his colleagues at Reed College who read that draft; among them were Professor John Pock, Professor David Tyack, and President Richard H. Sullivan. Revisions of the manuscript were undertaken at Harvard University while the author was Visit-

ing Professor of Anthropology and a Research Fellow in the Center for Cognitive Studies. Thanks are due to the Center and the Laboratory of Social Relations for clerical and other assistance and to Professor Jerome S. Bruner.

Many of the propositions advanced in the paper cannot be supported with systematic data. They are based on fourteen years of undergraduate and graduate teaching in three universities (Columbia, Harvard, and Washington) and in a college (Reed). The arguments, which are intended to apply either to universities or to colleges, also depend upon the general adequacy of research and theory in role behavior in illuminating the functioning of institutions and professions.

REFERENCES CITED

BRUNER, JEROME S.
    1960   The functions of teaching. Rhode Island College Journal 1:35-42, 49.
KATZ, ELIHU, AND PAUL F. LAZARSFELD
    1955   Personal influence: the part played by people in the flow of mass communications. Glencoe, Ill., The Free Press.
PARSONS, TALCOTT
    1959   Some problems confronting sociology as a profession. American Sociological Review 24:547-559.
WALLER, WILLARD
    1949   The separate culture of the school. In Sociological analysis by Logan Wilson and William L. Kolb. New York, Harcourt, Brace, pp. 625-632. (Reprinted from The sociology of teaching. New York, Wiley, 1932.)

PART IV

ANTHROPOLOGY
COURSES
ON
REGIONS
AND
CIVILIZATIONS

Introduction

Courses on tribal peoples in various regions of the world have long been an important part of the curriculum in anthropology. In recent years there has been a rapid development of courses on civilizations, in which the historic roots as well as the modern social complexities of civilizations are discussed. The term "area course" is sometimes used to distinguish such courses from "regional courses," which have to do mainly with primitive peoples or only with ancient civilizations. Considerable thought has been given to new ways of teaching by participants in the area programs which have been established in a good many colleges and universities in recent years. Some of the results are given in Bennett's and Marriott's papers. Vogt's paper considers several models for teaching a regional course and gives special attention to a "genetic model" for teaching a course on American Indians. His comment that regional courses are far more difficult to organize and to teach satisfactorily than are other kinds of courses may come as a surprise to those who have no trouble in listing trait descriptions and distributions to fill the students' notebooks in a regional course. It is not that part of a regional course which presents teaching difficulties; it is the development of a satisfactory theoretical frame that requires much thought and planning. In using the frame which Vogt recommends for an American Indian course the teacher can discuss linguistic reconstructions to raise questions of historical relations. For courses on peoples in other parts of the world, some other approach may be preferable.

The two papers on courses about civilizations illustrate other kinds of course design. It so happens that both papers are based on interdisciplinary courses, given jointly by several instructors. Both Bennett and Marriott point out how the anthropologist's typical approach differs from that of the area specialist, who is usually oriented toward the humanities. The area specialist—whether Sinologist, Indologist, Islamist, or other—tends to view the civilization of his specialty as an incomparable creation and devotes his attention to the features of excellence which he discerns in it. The anthropologist not only takes a broader, comparative view but also imparts a sense of concreteness about peoples of other cultures, showing them as human beings whose ways of life can be understood, rather than as exotic and possibly enigmatic abstractions.

Bennett's comments on the intellectual characteristics of the freshman students in his comparative civilizations course are relevant to the teaching of freshmen in any anthropology course. We should take special note of his belief that a course comparing cultures and civilizations is best given for freshmen. The course which Bennett outlines could be an excellent model for an introductory course in cultural anthropology. It might be highly effective to introduce basic anthropological concepts within a general consideration of selected civilizations, as those of the Middle East and of Middle America.

The course which Marriott describes is on a single civilization and is given for more advanced students, but the features of a multidisciplinary approach which Marriott discusses parallel those mentioned by Bennett. In both courses there is the question of the best means of cooperation between area specialists and anthropologists and of a balance between description and analysis. Marriott, like Vogt, emphasizes the importance of enabling the student to do his own analyses of significant problems raised in the course. The India civilization course is the outcome of careful preparation, under foundation auspices, and breaks new ground for effective teaching in area programs. Few institutions will be able to afford so large a number of teachers for so relatively few students. Yet the standards and methods of such experimental courses provide useful models, especially in the rapidly developing field of civilizational studies. With the great increase in anthropological research and writing in this field, courses on civilizations have become an essential element in an anthropology curriculum.

                                                                    D.G.M.

EVON Z. VOGT

Courses
of Regional
Scope

IN THIS PAPER I shall characterize briefly various possible approaches to the teaching of regional courses, and then describe an approach utilizing the genetic model and the method of controlled comparison which Professor Gordon R. Willey and I have been applying to North and South America in our courses at Harvard on the Peoples and Cultures of the New World.[1]

In my judgment, regional courses are far more difficult to organize and to teach satisfactorily than topical or subject courses. In a topical course, such as Kinship or Primitive Religion, the enterprising anthropological lecturer may advance a series of brilliant theories or propositions about the subject matter and proceed to illustrate his propositions with or apply his theories to ethnographic materials that he happened to master in graduate school or that he gathered on his various field expeditions. By comparison, the lecturer in an ethnological area course is genuinely constrained by the empirical data if he provides systemic coverage. He cannot, when he reaches the limits of his control of the ethnographic materials of an area, start lecturing about some tribe on another continent which illustrates a theoretical point or merely strikes his fancy. Not only is the lecturer expected to have masterful empirical control of the data of the ethnological area, but he must be prepared to organize and present the materials in new and stimulating ways. Our students are too bright these days to be satisfied intellectually with an area course that merely covers the range and content of the native culture existing in a given region—they can cover these materials in the published monographs and papers. Rather, an increasing number of students are ready and eager for an analysis of problems and issues in ethnology and cultural history.

VARIOUS APPROACHES TO REGIONAL COURSES

Various approaches are possible in organizing a course that provides systematic and meaningful coverage of an ethnological area. I will discuss three, and then make a case for considering the use of a fourth. A classic traditional method is the *culture trait* approach which was utilized successfully and rigorously by older members of our profession like Roland B. Dixon. What one does is to delimit the ethnographic region under consideration, then divide the cultual content existing in the area into a roster of traits, such as houses, bows and arrows, kinship systems, initiation ceremonies. Each trait, or cluster of traits, is then given exhaustive treatment until the students have become experts on house types or bows and arrows or kinship within the ethnographic area being covered. There is no doubt in my mind that Professor Dixon succeeded in communicating a vast amount of ethnographic knowledge to his students on the traits of an area—in fact, we may not have done as well since on this score. By making rigorous comparisons in the Leslie Spier style one can also use the method to good advantage in untangling certain problems in culture history.

A second traditional method is of course the *culture area* approach, which is probably still utilized in some form most frequently in courses on ethnological regions and culture history. What one does is to subdivide the area under consideration into some kind of meaningful subareas, and then proceed to lecture about the native culture found in each of the subareas. The method almost inevitably emphasizes the ecological adjustments and subsistence systems of the cultures in an area as the basic variable for subdividing the region and for interpreting the major observable variations in culture. There is the further difficulty, which the archaeologists are always quick to point out, that subareas drawn up for the ethnographic present are not satisfactory for prehistoric horizons; hence, moving to consideration of cultural history requires shifting boundaries around, often on a makeshift basis. This difficulty has been partially solved by the recent development and use of the concept of "area co-tradition" (Bennett 1948), which seeks to describe "a culture area with time depth," employing more methodological precision than we have had in the earlier treatments of culture areas. There is not yet agreement among archaeologists as to how and where the concept is applicable (see especially Rouse, 1954; 1957), but it is at any rate clear that an area framework does at least provide a means of reaching systematic coverage and an excellent method for understanding the important ecological relationships of cultures—either in the ethnographic present using a simple "culture area" concept, or still better with time depth using an "area co-tradition" concept.

A third possible approach is to select a series of *culture types* that represent the range of cultures existing within a culture area and then concentrate the lectures and reading on these type cases. Fred Eggan used this method of organization very successfully in his area courses at the University of Chicago when I was a graduate student there, and it is now commonly used in American universities. A recent development of the concept of culture type is found in the work of Julian Steward whose "Levels of Sociocultural Integration" provides us with a more rigorous and sophisticated framework for analysis than we have had previously (Steward 1951). The culture type approach has the advantage of shifting emphasis from the ecological adaptations as the basic variable to a broader view of the cultural systems, and it also permits intensive coverage of particular tribes, giving ample opportunity for the lecturer to analyze the functional interrelationships of the culture for the students. Inevitable choices have to be made in selecting the sample, so that equally intensive coverage of a large number of tribes is of course not possible. Furthermore, I do not think that a typological approach lends itself quite so well to the consideration of problems of culture history in an area as the framework I discuss below.

THE GENETIC MODEL AND CONTROLLED COMPARISONS

The approach which Gordon Willey and I have been using now for some years in our courses on the New World is based essentially upon Romney's (1957) "Genetic Model" and Eggan's (1954) "Method of Controlled Comparison," with some modifications required by the nature of the data in the early archaeological horizons. We assume with Romney that it is fruitful to consider that the various members of a linguistic family have developed from a common ancestral group:

The genetic model takes as its segment of cultural history a group of tribes which are set off from all other groups by sharing a common physical type, possessing common systemic patterns, and speaking genetically related languages. It is assumed that correspondence among these three factors indicate a common historical tradition at some time in the past for these tribes. We shall designate this segment of cultural history as the "genetic unit" and it includes the ancestral group and all intermediate groups, as well as the tribes in the ethnographic present. The genetic unit represents a substantive segment of cultural history while the term "genetic model" refers to the conceptual framework which serves as a tool to order the data . . .

Drawing upon well known methods of historical reconstruction the genetic model focuses attention on the task of locating the region and time in which the ancestral group lived and in tracing their migrations, developments, fusions, and differentiations up to the present . . .

The genetic model complements current theories that make interpretations upon an area based framework. For some problems we must go beyond an area-bound construct. Where meaningful historical units extend outside a traditionally defined area a change in perspective may lead to new results.

Rather than assuming that people have always been pretty much in the same place the genetic model directs attention to such questions as: When did the people who occupy a given region arrive there, from what direction did they come, and what cultural equipment did they bring with them? Meaningful questions about developments within sub-groups may then be posed. (Romney, 1957, pp. 36-37)

The potential that exists in this model for the organization of materials in an area course has recently been increased by a number of developments. The interesting work of Isadore Dyen (1956) in "Language Distribution and Migration Theory" has been followed up by an outstanding paper by Diebold (1960) on "Determining the Centers of Dispersal of Language Groups." It is clear from this work that we are on the threshold of being able to use some exciting new methods for reconstructing with high probability the location of the ancestral homelands of tribes speaking related languages. The development of Swadesh's technique of lexicostatistics (see Hymes 1960) promises to give us at least relative time-depths on when the migrations and differentiations from the proto-group occurred.

To these developments one can add the suggestions made by Eggan (1954) to the effect that we design our ethnological studies to make careful comparisons among groups of culturally related tribes for which the geographical and historical frames are reasonably well controlled.

To use this general model one first attempts to determine the ancestral homeland using "migration theory" and to calculate time-depths for the differentiation of the sub-groups in the language family using lexicostatistics. With enough linguistic data the proto-languate can be reconstructed using the techniques of comparative linguistics. The proto-kin-term system (which is part of the proto-language) can also be reconstructed. Archaeological data (and physical anthropological data on skeletal materials, if available) can then be brought to bear on this reconstructed picture of the proto-group. The outlines or the subsistence system and the settlement pattern can usually be determined; in many cases, inferences as to socio-political groupings and ceremonial organization can also be fruitfully made.

With the outlines of the proto-culture to form a base-line, the problem then becomes one of analyzing the processes of differentiation from the proto-culture that have led in this genetic unit to the observed variations in culture in the ethnographic present. In general there appear to be three sets of factors operating that account for the differentiation that has occurred: (1) shifts in ecological settings as the proto-group radiates out and moves into neighboring and different ecological niches; (2) variations in culture contact with and diffusion from other cultural groups; (3) internal cultural "drifts" that occur in the cultural systems and are analogous to linguistic drifts (Vogt 1960).

The final step in the analysis is to focus on selected tribes within the genetic unit and to provide the student with concepts and data for the understanding of the functional interrelationships within given cultural systems.

Note that the use of this model does not ignore cultural inventories conceptualized as traits or patterns; nor does it ignore the important ecological and subsistence dimension of culture. Rather, these concepts and approaches are utilized in the genetic model to help answer questions about cultural history differentiation, and functional relationships.

Note also that the model has the enormous advantage of potentially using the full range of anthropological data—archaeological, linguistic, physical anthropological, and ethnographic—as it becomes available on a given genetic unit.

USE OF THE MODEL IN AMERICAN INDIAN COURSES

In "Peoples and Cultures of the New World" (Anthropology 110a and 110b) at Harvard, we give two lectures a week and divide the class into sections for intensive discussion during a third hour. Each course should be a full course lasting a year, but we now devote only a term to each—largely because Gordon Willey has been in the field each Spring term. Most of the archaeological and ethnological data are given the students in their reading; the lectures and section meetings concentrate on problems, issues, and matters of interpretation. The first three weeks of each course are devoted to problems of the peopling of North and South America, the early big-game hunting and food-collecting horizons, the domestication of maize, and the development of formative cultures. These prehistoric developments are, for the most part, out of range for the time depths it is possible to probe using the genetic model.

We then shift gears and proceed to use the genetic model. It is of course quite clear at this stage of anthropological knowledge that the model can be utilized in illuminating ways on certain blocks of culture, but not yet on others where archaeological, linguistic, and ethnological data are very complex or still too scanty. In North America, for exam-

ple, we begin in Middle America and cover the Maya, Uto-Aztecan, and
Oto-Manguean cases, with a brief look at the Tarascans as a special, and
still puzzling, case. North of the Rio Grande, the model yields results
in the case of the Athabascans, Algonkins, and Eskimo. We also go as
far as we can with groups of genetically related tribes like the Iroquoian,
Siouan, Caddoan, and Muskogean, although here the problems are admittedly complex. For the Northwest Coast, California, Southwest, and
Plains we use a culture area approach, because in these cases and at this
stage of our knowledge the linguistic and cultural materials are still
probably best covered by a culture area framework.

In the course on South America we also devote the first three weeks
to problems of peopling, the pros and cons of trans-Pacific influence,
and the early archaeological horizons. We then consider the implications of the new Greenberg (1960) classification of the aboriginal languages of South America (see also Tax 1960). Although the Greenberg classification is highly tentative, it provides some exciting leads
for research into the problems of culture history. We consider the three
large groupings of Greenberg—the Gê-Pano-Carib, the Andean Equa-
torial, and the Macro-Chibchan—and where possible use these leads
in organizing the materials for discussion. Some of the intriguing questions that it is now possible to raise are: were the proto-Gê-Pano-Carib
early arrivals in eastern South America who have since developed and
differentiated in that region? If the peoples of Southern America, like
the Ona, Yahgan, and Tehuelche are offshoots from an early Andean
block of languages, when did this migration to the south occur and at
what point is it manifested in the archaeological sequence described
by Junius Bird and others in the Straits of Magellan area? Are Tropical Forest Arawakan and Tupian peoples derived also from an early
movement out of the Andean area, moving essentially from west to east,
and were their movements in part responsible for the presently observed
split distributions of Gê-Pano-Carib? Are the Chibchans all derived
from an early proto-group somewhere in northern South America or
Lower Central America? Perhaps the most intriguing question of all
is based on still preliminary research: it would appear that on many measures the Gê-Pano-Carib tend to emphasize matrilineal organization,
and the Andean-Equatorial tend to emphasize patrilineal organization, and the Chibchan matrilineal. It may be that ecological, subsistence
and division-of-factors account for these differences, but the question
arises whether this varying emphasis might not derive from developments in these systems in early prehistoric times.

It is obvious that much less work has been done in South America of
the type than can answer these questions. The work of Clifford Evans
and Betty Meggars in the Tropical Forest area has been extremely

illuminating, and the work of Irving Rouse and his associates has already reached the point where the use of the genetic model for analysis of the Arawakans is beginning to be fruitful. Hence, we feel that the model points the way for research in the future. We can go as far as we can with it, and then provide more intensive consideration of selected cultures within each of the major groupings: the Southern hunters, the Gê, the Tropical Forest Tupian and Arawakan, the Andean, the Chibchan, etc. I would guess that the next decade will bring exciting developments in both South and North American cultural history and ethnology, especially as more data and more analysis come in from the linguists and the archaeologists to provide background for the ethnographic differentiation we presently observe and to set the stage for more sophisticated functional analysis than we have to date. Whether or not the model will be as fruitful in Oceania, Asia, and Africa as we have found it to be in North and South America is beyond my competence to judge, but I hope that teachers of courses on these other areas will explore its possiblities.

NOTE

[1] I am grateful to members of the Conference on the Teaching of Anthropology, March 2-4, 1961, University of California, Berkeley, and to Gordon R. Willey for criticisms and suggestions on an earlier draft of this paper.

REFERENCES CITED

BENNETT, WENDELL C.
    1948   The Peruvian co-tradition. A reappraisal of Peruvian archaeology, memoirs, Society for American Archaeology 4:1-7.
DIEBOLD, A. RICHARD, JR.
    1960   Determining the centers of dispersal of language groups. International Journal of American Linguistics 26:1-10.
DYEN, ISIDORE
    1956   Language distribution and migration theory. Language 32:611-626.
EGGAN, FRED
    1954   Social anthropology and the method of controlled comparison. American Anthropologist 56:743-763.
GREENBERG, JOSEPH
    1960   The general classification of Central and South American languages. Selected Papers of the Fifth International Congress of Anthropological and Ethnological Sciences, Anthrony F. C. Wallace, ed. pp. 791-794.
HYMES, D. H.
    1960   Lexicostatistics so far. Current Anthropology 1:3-44.
ROMNEY, A. KIMBALL
    1957   The genetic model and Uto-Aztecan time perspective. Davidson Journal of Anthropology 3:35-41.

ROUSE, IRVING

    1954   On the use of the concept of area co-tradition. American Antiquity
              19:221-225.
    1957   Culture and co-tradition. Southwest Journal of Anthropology 13:123-
              133.

STEWARD, JULIAN H.

    1951   Levels of sociocultural integration: an operational concept. South-
              western Journal of Anthropology 7:374-390.

TAX, SOL

    1960   Aboriginal languages of Latin America. Current Anthropology, vol.
              1, nos. 5-6, pp. 431-436.

VOGT, EVON Z.

    1960   On the concepts of structure and process in cultural anthropology.
              American Anthropologist 62:18-33.

JOHN W. BENNETT

A Course in
Comparative
Civilizations

THIS PAPER is based on the experiences of the writer in teaching a freshman course in comparative civilizations at Washington University during the past two years. The course is offered to about 300 students in the liberal arts and is one of three year-courses in the social sciences which freshmen may elect. The course is entitled "Peoples and Cultures of the World," although it has developed into a comparative high civilizations course with a problem orientation, featuring a social science viewpoint. Therefore it serves, to some extent, as an introduction to the offerings of the Department of Sociology and Anthropology. Since one semester features Asian civilizations, the course also provides a freshman level for our Asian Studies program. In this paper I wish to explain the rationale for the course; make some comments on student performance and outlook; and provide a brief description of the course content.

COURSE RATIONALE

In developing the course as it is presently taught, we have been guided by the fact that we, as a Department of Sociology and Anthropology, are responsible for a course with broad liberal arts objectives. At the same time, it is our responsibility to bring to this course our disciplinary knowledge and points of view; indeed, we *must* bring these to the course for the reason that we are trained within them and could hardly do otherwise. We therefore have had to ask ourselves the question posed by Robert Erhrich (1954) as to the role anthropology (and in

191

our case sociology as well) can play in a liberal arts curriculum. Part of our problem is solved by the subject matter suggested in the course title: "Peoples and Cultures of the World"; certainly it is important to introduce our provincial young Americans to ways of life and tradition differing from the Western. An underlying theme of the course is accordingly the comparison of Western-American patterns with those of other cultures and civilizations. This theme is developed particularly strongly in the discussion sections. We emphasize that America's growing international responsibilities and increasing tendencies toward the development of intercultural experiences and perspectives in the modern world require much more knowledge of other societies than was the case in the isolationist past.

In planning this course we have been especially cognizant of the difference between our approach and that which has emerged in some of the universities with well-developed area research programs. In these cases undergraduate courses dealing with comparative civilization materials are usually planned by area specialists, those whose professional work is centered on a specific area, usually the area of a civilization, and the theme of comparison may be subordinated to the concept of cultural autonomy. Such terms as "the Hindu Great Tradition," "Islamic civilization," or "Sinitic co-tradition" exemplify the point of view (see Creel 1959; Singer 1957, for extended discussions). In courses taught from this standpoint it is assumed that great nations or peoples can be taken as relatively autonomous entities, since the customs and beliefs have a distinctive continuity based on relatively independent origins and development. Such courses are usually historically oriented, often have strong literary emphasis, and tend to feature generalizations about the uniqueness of particular civilizations. It is our belief that although the area specialist viewpoint is suitable for more advanced levels of instruction (as we develop it in our Asian Studies program), at the freshman level a problem orientation and an emphasis on comparative development is more suitable for the needs of general education.

Most of the teachers involved in area or civilizations courses seem, on the basis of an admittedly sketchy inquiry, to have emerged from disciplines other than anthropology and sociology (history, political science, and the humanities are the commonest sources). However, as funds have become available from foundations for the planning of area instruction for undergraduates, qualified people from other disciplines have joined forces with the original group (a tendency which has led to changes in the professional area societies). Anthropologists at a number of institutions have joined forces with area specialists in this manner; this seems to be a growing trend.

It is more than likely that when anthropologists cooperate in the teaching of area courses, they will approach the task with a different set of assumptions. The anthropologists may feel, first, that the autonomy of the great civilizations is simply not as great as it is sometimes assumed by culture historians, that in fact as our knowledge of the Neolithic and early Bronze Age accumulates, the similarities, borrowings or at least parallel evolutions among these civilizations have been as great as the independent inventions and unique traditions. Modern anthropologists, or at least some representatives of the field, work with the knowledge that each of the several early urban civilizations originated in quite similar ecological circumstances, and that these similarities were further added to by trade and migration and by comparable institutional developments. Fairservis' emphasis on possible Indo-European or Central Asian horse-aristocrat elements in Shang China is an example of migratory influences, and in teaching early China we find it desirable to consider the human ecology and historical background of Central Asia and the Middle East as a prologue. It often comes as a considerable surprise to students who have had courses in Chinese philosophy previous to taking our course to discover that "unique" China very likely owes something to Southwest Asia, *via* Central Asia.

Second, many anthropologists would question the tendency among some area specialists to generalize about the nature or essence of the great civilization, and to use this as a comprehensive explanation for many aspects of social life. The anthropologist and sociologist will insist, for example, upon a distinction between the culture of the elite and that of the masses. They will point out that what area specialists frequently regard as "civilization" are the customs and beliefs of the elite classes, never including more than a small minority of the population. They also may point out that these elites were not as culturally isolated as is sometimes believed and were in fairly close communication with similar elites in other "great" societies. The peasantry, on the other hand, may well represent unique cultures, insofar as communications between them and other peasantries were nonexistent. Yet peasantry, because of ecological imperatives, often has an underlying similarity the world over that makes it posible and even necessary to consider it as a general category without regard for the different civilizational entities in which it might be located. We find it advisable to analyze the characteristics of peasants-in-general for our freshman before considering Chinese or Mexican peasants.

However, while some anthropologists will disagree with the area specialist's view of cultural autonomy and homogeneity, others might agree on the grounds of the holistic-relativistic conception of cultures —a point of view which has been of enormous importance in the human-

istic and social studies and which also has caused a good deal of confusion owing to misapplication. It is of considerable interest to find that
as this notion is beginning to wane in anthropology, it is reaching a peak
of influence in other fields of study. The opinion of the writer is
that the idea of discrete, maximally-differentiated cultures may have
been appropriate for some cases of tribal societies, but it has little applicability to the historically-complex cases of great high civilizations, with
their extensive inter-influence, and where sharp distinctions must always be made between ideology and practice and between elites and
commoners. In these cases it is always necessary to adopt a view similar
to that of Julian Steward (1955), involving the recognition of "levels"
or degrees of cultural homogeneity or uniqueness characterizing different sectors of the great complex civilized societies.

A third major issue is that of comparison. Here it is doubtful if much
difference of opinion will exist between the anthropologist and the
area specialist. The merits of comparative approaches to civilization
have become known to all, and most area courses now utilize the point
of view. However, it goes without saying that comparative research is
more extensively practiced by anthropologists than by area specialists,
as a matter of professional activity (and more so than by sociologists as
well). The area specialist is generally and quite rightly preoccupied
with his own field, and if he engages in comparison, it is often without
a knowledge of certain useful techniques and ideas developed by anthropologists. One important role for anthropologists engaged in teaching and planning area courses might be to organize the comparative
side of the instruction program and advise the area specialists on the intellectual skills necessary for making accurate comparative judgments
and analyses. Thus, the role of the anthropologist in area course work
should be more than just a specialist on a given culture. He should seek
to make known the distinctive anthropological views and contributions
to the problem of cultural growth and, in general, to the whole problem
of similarity and difference in human societies. If he does not contribute
something of these, then he is not functioning in the course as a professional anthropologist.

Our course in comparative civilizations has "grown"; that is, it was
not planned overnight according to a rational scheme or set of intellectual specifications. Its function at an introductory level for our departmental offerings in the social sciences was an added function, not its
original. Our most general mandate is to furnish young Americans
with a broader world viewpoint on man and society, but we are, as professionals, concerned with seeing to it that they acquire some of the
knowledge of the world gathered by social scientists. We are interested in
showing man's relation to his environment and his continued depen-

dence on this environment in spite of vast technological evolution. We are concerned with the processes of growth and change in physical and cultural man. We are concerned with the social complexities as well as the cultural uniformities of great civilized traditions. And we are concerned with historical contact, change, and influence between and among civilized and pre-civilized societies. In short we find it possible, with some limitations, to introduce the freshman to a considerable sample of the content of anthropology and sociology and other fields, without featuring these disciplines as the professional source of that content. Subject matter is the focus of the course; disciplinary concerns are secondary.

THE FRESHMAN STUDENT

It should be clear by now that we aim at something more than a description of non-Western cultural traditions. We realize that there is abundant justification for "area courses" which seek to do this and no more, but nevertheless we are attempting a more complex task. We demand from our students often more than they can handle with the limited intellectual equipment furnished them by the high schools, and we have found it necessary to break our course into lecture and discussion sessions in order to drive home the ideas. We have also found it necessary to think very carefully about the problem of needs and capacities in our students and to try to relate the level of instruction to these.

At this point we may consider some of the patterns of thought evidenced in student discussion and answers to examination questions. This list is not peculiar to area-course student behavior; it is very likely an outline of the thinking habits of young Americans on most topics. We can, however, relate these patterns to our specific subject matter.

1. *Concreteness.* At the very outset we find that our students find descriptive detail more congenial than interpretive explanation and analysis. They show an inability to handle abstract ideas and generalities and to apply them in particular cases. They find it easier to learn a fact than use an idea. An example can be drawn from our instruction on the role of the scholar-bureaucrat in traditional China. We have found it relatively easy to teach them that the scholar has a "high status," even though it is always a little difficult for them to grasp the idea that the role involved a fusion of the intellectual and politician, since these functions are so disparate in modern society. But they are able to learn this fairly readily. However, when we ask them, "Why were scholar-bureaucrats high in status?" we usually get an answer like this: "Because they were looked up to." We may then ask, "Why were they looked up to?" and draw the answer, "Because people in China were taught to do so." At this point the instructor patiently goes back over the analy-

sis of the interplay of social dynamics and ideology which has been introduced earlier in this or some other context! The example illustrates the acceptance of fact or descriptive detail and the difficulty of analysis. It also illustrates the paradoxical tendency of young Americans to accept the *status quo* but at the same time be unable to understand the nature of a *truly* conservative society (traditional China). It further illustrates the difficulty of grasping the analytical thinking required for making *causal* explanations of social phenomena.

2. *Bipolar thinking.* We find great difficulty among these students with questions of dialectics. They tend to choose one or the other of a polar conceptual pair and accept it as a valid and comprehensive description of the entire topic. An example can be drawn from our teaching on the origins of Japanese culture. We may set them an examination question like this: "Comment on the relative originality or imitativeness of Japanese culture." Here a plurality of students always assumes one or the other; and perhaps the majority of these, following common stereotypes, selects the imitative side. Most answers simply list the borrowed or imitated elements. In lecture and discussion considerable effort is made to get the students to see that there is a reciprocal interplay between borrowing and inventing and that both are always involved in cultural growth, but this idea is difficult for the freshman to grasp. No, Japan must be either one or the other! (It is evident from this how dangerous it may be simply to teach undergraduates "facts" about foreign cultures. They get only that side of the matter and hence may learn nothing of importance.)

3. *Pragmatic bias.* This thought pattern particularly influences the treatment of Oriental religion and philosophy. "Why do people believe in that if it doesn't work?" is a question inevitably asked by students when descriptive summaries of particular beliefs and doctrines are presented. The point of view also affects the understanding of certain types of social structure. Japanese feudal etiquette often gets the response, "What good is all that formality?" A discussion of ancestor veneration in China often pulls the response, "Why do the Chinese worship their ancestors if they know it doesn't do them any good?" (Our answer to this is often a simple, "Why pray at all?")

A more complex issue related to the pragmatic bias concerns progress and development. Here we find ourselves in opposition to other academic disciplines (e.g., economics) from which the students get confirmation of the idea that people are not normal if they don't want industrial development and the joys of modern nationhood. China's attitude toward the West during the Ming dynasty often evokes the response, "If the Chinese didn't want to improve, there must have been something wrong with them." Discussions of the relativity of attitudes toward progress and change also have to deal with the fact that nearly all countries now *do* want to "develop"; hence it is America's mission to develop them; hence, the doctrine of progress is proven.

4. *Limited time perspective.* Our students find great difficulty in conceiving of relative spans of time and in choosing the right words to express these. Such terms as "past," "present," "contemporary," and "ancient" have extremely variable and vague referents for the students and are used in examination questions at the instructor's peril. Much time is spent in introducing the student to relative time conceptions, for example, in the case of Japan. We show how, from the standpoint of a continuous tradition and political unity, it is an ancient society, while from the standpoint of comparison with ancient Mediterranean civilizations, it is very recent.

Aside from these particular habits of thought which impede the understanding of problems and processes, we also contend with numerous ethnocentric attitudes. The low status of the merchants in many ancient societies is often hard for students from a business-oriented society to grasp. The extended family system is especially difficult to understand, and the lack of a clear-cut tradition of romantic love in such societies is another shock to our freshmen. The "mosaic" society of the Middle East is not always easy for our "conformist" generation, with their involvement in the "mass society," to comprehend.

Perhaps one of the most difficult things of all to achieve in courses dealing with exotic civilizations is a sense of concrete reality. We feel that many courses taught from the area-specialist viewpoint actually contribute to a feeling of unreality, since they stress the exotic and eternal elements in these societies, often presented as maximally different from our own institutions. We strive to humanize, or at least to socialize, the conception the student has of exotica. We endeavor to show him that these "strange" ideas and customs have a perfectly familiar and understandable basis in human relations and needs, and of course we find such information in the disciplines of anthropology, sociology, and political science. There is altogether too little information available, however. As a matter of fact, its very absence explains the existence of area courses: if the entire way of life of foreign peoples were incorporated, as a matter of course, into instruction in every field of knowledge, we would not need to offer area courses or even have area institutes. We should keep this in mind at all times; there is too much feeling that area instruction is a special and mysterious task, requiring private talents and special insights, and it is this very emphasis, sometimes present in area instruction, which postpones the accomplishment of a primary goal: to make foreign traditions and ways of life as familiar to the student as his own.

We have discussed some of the freshman's intellectual shortcomings.
Now let us consider his general attitudes and outlook. Few of our freshmen could be described as buoyant, confident, optimistic; the majority
seem confused, hesitant; basically quite serious, yet not sure which
ideas should be grasped and which should be neglected. The majority
seem critical of unalloyed materialism and the more vulgar aspects of
American life, yet their reasons derive from a disguised and modified
Puritanism and not from a sophisticated intellectual outlook. They are
not fitted out with a packaged set of values which we must combat or
accept; they are plastic and can be taught, and their resistances stem
from intellectual unsophistication rather than from doctrinaire opposition.

The great majority of these freshmen are in college in order to *learn*.
They are not yet "spoiled" by the occupation and career-oriented philosophy of the system of majors and minors, professional pretraining and
the rest, which confronts them from the sophomore year on. At the same
time, their intellectual equipment is meager indeed; they have no
broad base of understanding and are therefore ripe for imprinting. A
course with broad objectives like ours can perform a considerable service in this situation. It is especially valuable because it straddles several
fields of knowledge (history, humanities, political science, economics,
anthropology, sociology some aspects of biology and geology) and
thus provides a unifying framework for the many specialized courses
which the student is taking or will take. The objectives of our course
may be defined as *education* (as distinguished from simple learning):
education in the broad current and movement of human history and development, from its biological beginnings to its contemporary industrial
status.

Underlying the student's many prejudices and ethnocentrisms is an
enormous native friendliness and curiosity, which we find it possible to
build upon. They are on the whole favorably disposed toward other
peoples and cultures; in the undergraduate course the battle is not so
much against prejudices as against ignorance. The prejudices that exist
are superficial and flippant, not deeply ingrained nor involved with
personal defenses, as they may become in later years. The students respond readily to an approach which lowers the sights just enough to
make the material linguistically comprehensible but does not con-
descend. In many ways freshmen are more responsive to the material of
the course than upperclassmen are to comparable materials in advanced courses, and it is our conviction that the earlier the comparative
cultures (or "areas") course is introduced, the more desirable the results—providing, of course, that one has a teaching staff willing to do
the work that it takes to bring these materials into the sphere of com-

prehension of very young and unsophisticated students. (See Schoenwald 1960 for some cogent comments on this most neglected side of the undergraduate instruction issue.)

COURSE CONTENT

Our course is divided into two semesters, each of which is designed to be taught independently, and either one coming first. This was done partly to permit flexibility in the assignment of teaching staff, but also as a result of the differences in approaches to the subject matter of the two semesters. One semester is taught by an area specialist in Asian studies[1] (who has, however, a social-science orientation), the second semester by a cultural anthropologist. Both instructors are members of the University's senior staff, and their participation consists of two lectures a week. The several weekly discussion sections are conducted by graduate assistant instructors of high caliber. Lectures are presented to the entire enrollment of 300 students; the group is divided into smaller sections for discussion.

The semester taught by the cultural anthropologist has the following content: The initial frame of reference is evolutionary, the lectures and discussions occasionally based on Huxley's first four essays in *Knowledge, Morality, and Destiny* (1960), which may be used as a text. Man is considered as a whole, in terms of his physical and cultural evolution, with attention to time pserspective, growth trends, and his position with respect to the animal kingdom and the natural environment. After this introduction, the central concept of the course—the "focal regions of civilizational growth"—is introduced, with the help of texts like Childe's *What Happened in History* (1951) and Ashley-Montagu's *Man: His First Million Years* (1957). At this point the course proceeds to an examination of the Middle East, as one of the two "focal regions," using Coon's *Caravan* (1958) for readings, supplemented by Childe (1951) or Frankfort's *The Birth of Civilization in the Near East* (1956). After completing the Middle East, the course turns to Middle America, as the second "focal region," with the help of Wolf's *Sons of the Shaking Earth* (1959). Sometimes auxiliary texts on the American Indian, like Collier's *Indians of the Americas* (1947) are also used. If time permits, African societies are introduced briefly at the end of the course as a case study in incomplete civilizational development. We require the students to buy and use outline maps, and we endeavor to give them a sense of geographical relevance (Ehrich 1960).

The two major focal regions are discussed from several standpoints. We are, first and foremost, concerned with the conditions under which high civilizations originated and developed in each of these regions. Secondly, we are interested in similarities and differences in the origins and growth patterns of civilizations in the two regions and the reasons for these. Third, we are concerned with the regions and their cultures *as such;* that is, from the standpoint of the "area course" concept. However, it is clear from this description that the *emphasis* is upon the central problems of historical and cultural anthropology and not on area subject-matter. Even during the final lectures and discussions for each region dealing with the modern historical and socio-economic picture, we feature anthropological-sociological interpretations of acculturation, modernization, and social differentiation. The general nature of tribal and peasant society is discussed along with the presentation of civilizational growth.

The other semester of the course is concerned primarily with the high civilizations of Asia. This makes it somewhat comparable to the University of Michigan's undergraduate Asian studies course (Crane 1959), in which three Asian traditions are presented. Our course has an important emphasis on Asia as such, on the great Asian traditions. However, its primary objectives are not areal. We consider Asian civilization in order to compare it with Western traditions, and we include the Soviet Union toward the end of the course in order to demonstrate a case of a civilization with features of both the Orient and the West. We also place great emphasis on the differences between ancient and modern civilization and the causes of modernization or of its delay. Almost equal time is devoted to the ancient and contemporary periods of Asian societies, and in dealing with the contemporary period, we are able to introduce considerable sociological material (as contrasted with historical-anthropological) relating to status, social stratification, the development of large organizations, and the like.

The course often begins with the problem of origins, for which Fairservis' *Origins of Oriental Civilization* (1959) is an appropriate text. Fairservis' concern for prehistory and human paleontology provides a useful link to the other semester of the course. The first Asian tradition to be examined is China. A useful text is Bodde's *China's Cultural Tradition* (1957). India is considered next, for which we generally use Nehru's *Discovery of India* (1959). Japan is introduced third, though we have not been as consistent in our use of the tradition of Japan as we have been of that of India and China. Reischauer's *Japan: Past and Present* (1958) is used as a text. For the Soviet Union we have used a variety of readings; perhaps Rostow's *Dynamics of Soviet Society* (1954) has been most frequently adopted.

The courses overlap in the respect that a group of central ideas about the nature of man, social life, and cultural evolution are present in both. However, they are designed to be taught in either order, and either order could be defended. The "anthropological" course can be first if its preoccupation with origins and growth patterns is seen as basic to the other course's interest in civilizations as such. On the other hand, the comparative civilizations course can be first if one takes the position that the students should be introduced to a rich content before the theories are presented. (In practice the order of presentation usually is determined by teaching schedules.)

NOTE

[1] Dr. Stanley Spector. He and our assistants, Peter Rompler, Christopher Hurn, and Sacha Weitman, have helped considerably in the preparation of this paper, although the synthesis is my own.

REFERENCES CITED

ASHLEY-MONTAGU, M. F.
    1957   Man: his first million years. Mentor Books, New American Library.
BODDE, DIRK
    1957   China's cultural tradition. New York, Rinehart & Co.
CHILDE, V. GORDON
    1951   Man makes himself. Mentor Books, New American Library.
    1951   What happened in history. Mentor Books, New American Library.
COLLIER, JOHN
    1947   Indians of the Americas. Mentor Books, New American Library.
COON, CARLETON
    1958   Caravan. New York, Henry Holt & Co.
CRANE, ROBERT I.
    1959   The role of the introductory Asia course in undergraduate education. Journal of General Education 12:164-169.
CREEL, H. G. (ED.)
    1959   Chinese civilization in liberal education. The University of Chicago.
DE BARY, WILLIAM T.
    1959   Asian studies for undergraduates. Journal of Higher Education 30:1-7.
EHRICH, ROBERT W.
    1954   Anthropology in a liberal arts curriculum. Journal of Higher Education 25:357-362.
    1960   Ignorance of elementary geography among college students and student teachers. School and Society 88:65-66. No. 2168.
FAIRSERVIS, WALTER
    1959   The origins of Oriental civilization. Mentor Books, New American Library.
FRANKFORT, HENRI
    1956   The birth of civilization in the Near East. Anchor Books, Doubleday & Co.
HUXLEY, JULIAN
    1960   Knowledge, morality, and destiny. Mentor Books, New American Library.

NEHRU, JAWAHARLAL
    1959   The discovery of India. Anchor Books, Doubleday & Co.
REISCHAUER, EDWIN O.
    1958   Japan: past and present. New York, A. A. Knopf.
ROSTOW, W. W.
    1954   The dynamics of Soviet society. Mentor Books, New American Li-
                brary.
SCHOENWALD, RICHARD L.
    1960   The world of general education. Commentary 30:168-170.
SINGER, MILTON (ED.)
    1957   Introducing India in liberal education. The University of Chicago.
STEWARD, JULIAN
    1955   The theory of culture change. Urbana, University of Illinois Press.
WOLF, ERIC
    1959   Sons of the shaking earth. Chicago, University of Chicago Press.

McKim Marriott

*An Indian
Civilization
Course*[1]

BEFORE VENTURING to participate in any sort of undergraduate "area course," a cultural anthropologist, student or teacher, may well ask what such a course can have to do with anthropology as a generalizing and historical science. If anthropology would deal systematically with social and cultural wholes, and if it would deal comparatively with the general processes of their change and development over the whole variety and depth of man's history, then what educational purpose can be served by restricting a course of undergraduate study to a single civilized area?

The area of each major non-Western civilization may be thought of as one kind of whole culture and society, comparable in its completeness to the primitive wholes which have been the anthropologist's favored focus since Boas and Malinowski. A civilization has all the familiar parts of the primitive whole—it has all the chapters expected of the tribal monograph, and some more as well. It has contents which we can readily identify under the usual rubrics of technology, economy, social organization, religion, system of values; more than these, it is also likely to have cities, government, science, formal history, philosophy, literature, and all the rest of the higher humane inventory. As a class, such civilizations as China, India, or Islam exceed the anthropologist's primitive cultures in complexity and in size of population. They are more extensive both through space and through time. And yet, considering the interconnectedness among their parts, their constancy within certain territories, and their continuity of known history, such civilizations still stand among what an anthropologist may reasonably regard as things conceivable as wholes.

An anthropologist may grant that a civilizational area can be considered as analogous to his familiar unit of analysis in the single primitive whole. However, he may previously have hesitated to use the single tribe or group or tribes—only the Hopi or the several pueblo tribes, only the Arapesh or the tribes of the Sepik River—as the subject matter of an academic course unit for undergraduate teaching. Concentration on the unique phenomenon is a pedagogical technique more appropriate to the humane than to the scientific side of anthropology, for science requires comparison and contrast. How can the student move toward the goal of generalization about society and culture when he has but a single specimen before him? And what of the anthropologist's responsibility for an historical outlook on the larger scene of world culture? If he accepts the single civilization as a course unit, does he not implicitly credit it with a degree of cultural autonomy greater than can be justified by his professional knowledge of cultural diffusion?

Granting that the materials of an introductory course may be civilized rather than primitive, one might find his way back to a generalizing science and a comprehensive history of culture through incorporating the study of several specimens of civilization within the work of a single course. This solution is not unlike a common anthropological course formula: several primitive cultural wholes are compared or surveyed as parts of a larger sector of human variation or cultural history. This is the way to science being followed in Asian civilization courses at Washington University (Bennett, this volume), the University of Michigan (Crane 1959), and elsewhere. It is a possible solution. But since civilizations are units vastly more complex and difficult to grasp as wholes than are tribes, a course dealing with several civilizations during a year's time can examine and compare only relatively limited aspects of these major cultural units. Courses on Asian civilizations at Columbia University have restricted themselves to history and the humanities (de Bary 1959), while courses at the University of Michigan and Washington University have dealt comparatively with selected topics chosen from the social sciences. In such courses, the values of generalization and survey are balanced against the value of intensively examining a civilization as a whole example of human culture and society.

A COURSE ON INDIAN CIVILIZATION

I would like here to discuss an alternative means of return to the scientific interests of anthropology through a kind of single-area course which does seriously attempt to retain the anthropological value of acquaintance with a civilization as a social and cultural whole. This kind of course on Indian civilization exists at several institutions under various disciplinary auspices. I illustrate from my experience with an inter-disciplinary course on the civilization of India at the University of Chicago, a course in which anthropological participation has probably been higher than in most similar courses elsewhere.

The course on Indian civilization from which I draw examples is one of five year-long courses on five different non-Western civilizations offered primarily for undergraduates in the College of the University of Chicago.[2] Juniors in the social sciences, usually prepared by a year's study of American democracy and by another year's introduction to the behavioral sciences, must elect one of the five non-Western civilization courses. Many students taking the course have already spent a year on the history of Western Europe. Undergraduates in anthropology are usually beginning an introductory course on general anthropology during the same junior year. Enrollment in Indian civilization generally includes thirty or forty undergraduates in social sciences, ten or more graduate students in several disciplines, and some undergraduate students in the humanities.

All of the civilization courses at Chicago have multidisciplinary staffs, but the staff of the Indian civilization course is the most diverse. Regular faculty participants include two anthropologists, along with an historian, two or three Indic language and literatures men, and a political scientist. Other lecturers are invited from such disciplines as art history, comparative religions, economics, education, geography, medicine, philosophy, social thought, and sociology. From one to four teaching interns are associated with the course each year to learn its techniques. While such a course could probably be taught well by staff of two or three members, the course's attractiveness as a forum for interdisciplinary contact and pedagogical experimentation dictated a larger staff size at the outset (Weiner 1959).

A week of course work consists of two hours of lectures, an optional hour of films or live demonstrations, and then a culminating 90-minute discussion period. For discussions, the class is divided into sections of ten to fifteen students. One or two discussion sections are led by regular staff members throughout the year; these members also guide the discussion work of teaching interns who conduct the other sections as part of their apprenticeship. The entire staff contributes lectures, assigns and evaluates student papers, constructs and reads examinations, and makes recommendations as to revisions of the course's contents each year.

INDIAN CIVILIZATION AS AN OBJECT OF ANTHROPOLOGICAL STUDY

Concentrating a year-long course on a single civilization aims to capitalize on some distinctive characteristics of civilizations as a genus—

their size, complexity, long known duration, and relations with each other. These characteristics of each of the major civilizations open up opportunities for the anthropologist to undertake new kinds of cultural history, comparison, and even contrastive analysis. Such opportunities exist because any major civilization, as opposed to a small-scale society, is big and complex enough to incorporate diverse ways of life simultaneously, and often to have done so over many centuries as a characteristic tendency. On inspection, then, the reputedly "narrow" area specialist of such a civilized area, if he is a competent scholar, will be found to know not just "one culture," but a great many subcultures which compose the civilization in its many levels, regions, ethnic divisions, and periods of the past. A civilization of so many parts offers rich material for internal comparison.

Whatever the internal diversity of a single civilization, a genuine concentration only on Indian (or Islamic, or Japanese, or Chinese, or Russian) civilization might be suspected of fostering an illusion of cultural autonomy. In fact the reverse is true, for the deeper one digs into a civilization, the less autonomy one perceives. A rapid reading of Indian history tends in fact to raise in most students' minds a preliminary doubt as to whether India is ever definable as an autonomous thing, so many and so significant are the repeated invasions through the northwestern passes and from the sea, as well as Indian imperial sorties into Central and Southeast Asia. Putting this historical observation into ethnological terms, J. H. Hutton (1946:1) agrees that India may be likened to "a deep net into which various races and peoples of Asia have drifted and been caught." The fish-trap theory of India's cultural history has its analogues in the views of experts in the fine arts, drama, architecture, sciences, and technology of India as well. The anthropologist who wishes to stress the genetic continuity of world culture can work comfortably enough within such a civilizational area, for no one can avoid recognizing the external affinities of the Indus cities, or of the culture of the Aryans, Persians, Greeks, Kushanas, Arabs, Mughals, and British, to mention but a few of the more prominent immigrant peoples.

Within Indian civilization, the anthropologist as culture historian finds himself methodologically at home. The area of India in the days of British imperialism used to be saluted as an "anthropological zoo," "a museum of living ethnological fossils," and the like. Being an old civilization with wide peripheries and large internal refuge areas, India displays not only urbanites and peasants but also indigenous tribal cultures of many sorts, some of them resembling the ancestors of today's intelligentsia. If he instigates a course on such a civilization, the anthropologist as "museum" director will wisely fill out his staff with curators of many other disciplines. Or if area specialists of other disciplines happen to have reached the edifice before him, the anthropologist is likely to find several large halls still empty, awaiting his expertise.

SOME PROBLEMS OF A MULTIDISCIPLINARY APPROACH

Description *versus* Analysis

One prominent danger in any multidisciplinary area course is that the task of mastering a mass of descriptive detail will take precedence for many students over the more important aim of analyzing and learning ways of dealing more generally with cultural fact. Social scientist and humanist colleagues of many disciplines in the Indian civilization course agree on deploring the unanalytic tendency whenever they perceive it. At the same time, since each is a practitioner of a different discipline, he does not have open to him the ordinary academic expedient for forcing analysis, which is to press every description into the theoretical mold accepted in his own discipline.

This does not mean that such a faculty is forbidden to formulate problems regarding each body of fact in those terms which disciplinary experience demonstrates to be most relevant and productive. But the faculty makes those formulations as a whole and teaches them as an integrated series. The course is constructed out of a series of six major topics, each of which contains problems set by two or more of the contributing disciplines: (I) definitions of Indian civilization—its nature, boundaries, and continuity through time; (II) the "classical" tradition of the civilization—its development and significance; (III) medieval cultural differentiation and the challenge of Islam; (IV) the civilization as social organization; (V) the civilization in confrontation with the West; (VI) the civilization and problems of nationhood. Thus classical and medieval Indian thought is treated not only as philosophy, but also as history, as social product, and as world view. Social organization is in turn discussed as related to authoritative doctrine and as politically consequential. And so on. The discussion for each week focuses within a topic upon one or two crucial issues which tend to be more nearly disciplinary in conception.[3]

To encourage an analytic rather than a merely descriptive approach, students are offered a minimum of summary analysis along with a maximum of problems to be wrestled with. Basham's handbook of Indology (1954) and Nehru's history (1946) pose problems and provide background for the reading of primary materials. Texts in translation are made abundant (Burtt 1955; de Bary *et al.* 1957; Radhakrishnan and Moore 1957; Van Buitenen 1959; Yohannon 1958), as are documents (Weiner 1961), first-hand field reports (Marriott 1955; Singer 1959), and theoretically oriented essays or brief models of disciplinary analysis (Chicago 1961). So that students will have every opportunity to confront theoretical questions with "inside views," a very large part of the readings (2,100 out of 2,900 pages) is chosen from the work of Indian authors. Socratic methods are stressed in discussion sections (Pickus 1957), and so is role-playing, in which the student is asked to espouse the views of a given author in order better to understand them.

To stimulate an analytic approach, some care is taken over definitions of key concepts. The idea of "civilization," for example, is first introduced in a theoretical and methodological essay especially commissioned for the course (Redfield 1957). The student is provided at the same time with a short cultural history of India (Nehru 1946 or Panikkar 1954), Davies' atlas of Indian political history, and a supply of outline maps. During the first three weeks of the course, he is asked to show the extent of Indian civilization at a variety of dates from 1000 B.C. to the present, and then to defend his choice of boundaries by argument. He cannot emerge from such exercises without some respect for and grasp of the difficult mental operations involved in defining "civilization" politically, socially, and culturally.

An opportunity to move toward understanding other such basic concepts as "social organizaton" can also be offered through the student's own inductive struggle with civilizational data. Contrasting or conflicting readings are deliberately paired off together: David Mandelbaum's (1948) concise model of the Hindu family or A. L. Basham's (1954:153-88) summary of family patterns from classical literature is assigned along with a condensation of Irawati Karve's (1953) survey of the actual great variety of regional kinship systems. The student is asked to determine from study of these contrasting data—ideal and actual, matrilineal and patrilineal, cousin-marrying and cousin-prohibiting, etc.—whether there is an Indian family type, and if so, what it is and why. When the discussion group meets over such a set of readings, there is an intellectual task to be performed.

As in the examples just cited, descriptions of Indian society and culture are presented with maximum concreteness. In preparing his written assignments (four papers during the year), each student is required to acquaint himself thoroughly with (1) at least two major works of the Indian humanities; (2) two social units—villages, cities, castes, sects, etc.—within Indian civilization; 3) two biographies or autobiographies of Indians or Pakistanis; (4) a modern novel by an indigenous author. The student who knows such representative cultural specimens in detail is equipped to play the game of comparative analysis along with his professors. Woe is the lot of the lecturing anthropologist who dares to confront such an informed audience with an overgeneralization based on his limited community study! The varied wealth of information which a student soon comes to possess about the civilization can do much to overcome any naïve tendency to regard it as a unique or unanalyzable whole.

Scientific *versus* Humanistic Analysis

To say that humanists and social scientists are agreed on the importance of an analytic approach to he study of a civilization is not, of course, to say that they are entirely at one on the questions of what to study and how to study it. For example, an anthropologist will certainly support the desirability of including in the syllabus specimens of the philosophy, drama, poetry, sculpture, and music of a civilization. He includes them because those things belong to the whole whose parts he wishes to understand in their relations to ach other. He regards them as aspects of the civilization's natural history and studies them "because they are there."

A humanist, on the other hand, typically employs a different criterion for including materials: he demands excellence. The Indian drama is to be included in a course on Indian civilization not just because drama is "there," but only if the Indian drama is defensible as good drama. An anthropologist might be content with any representative specimen of the medium and might prefer that play whose action reveals more about social customs or values peculiar to the civilization. Not so a humanist, who wants no mere sample of ordinary native form and content, but a play which can be appreciated as one among the world's outstanding pieces of theater. How is the judgment of excellence to be made—perhaps by the standards of Aristotle? (The humanist, not the social scientist, here turns out to be the more severe comparativist!) If so, the entire classical drama of India will be ruled out of the curriculum, since the Indian theater knows no example of tragic plot or tragic character. At this point an anthropologist may well object that Indian drama might more reasonably be judged by the aesthetic standards of Indian civilization, rather than by those of ancient Greece. The upshot of such a debate between social scientist and humanist is that materials on Indian aesthetic theory and literary criticism must also be added to the course. A play meeting their requirements may then be included in the syllabus.

Such an outcome implies several kinds of gain for anthropology: the anthropologist gets not only a specimen of the Indian classical drama, with what its content tells of past customs and values, but also information on Indian aesthetic theory. Still more, he gains an understanding of this aspect of the civilization deepened by the experience of applying the civilization's own standards of excellence.

Similarly in the study of an alien philosophy, a humanist typically is not content with studying it for what it is. He may insist on asking larger questions as to its validity. These questions in turn require, if the anthropologist is also to be satisfied, penetration into indigenous canons of logic and epistemology, and their application.

The dialogue between the anthropologist's relativism and disregard of excellence on the one hand and the humanist's preference for universalistic evaluation on the other hand tends toward a typical compromise: relativistic evaluation. The result for the student is that he learns not only to know about the best specimens of the civilization's arts and thought, and to know whether he likes them, but also to know in what way he might evaluate them if he were a participant in the civilization.

By incorporating the criteria of both humanities and science, a civilization course can thus yield a more sophisticated product in its students, a kind of product which is not likely to emerge from purely anthropological study of primitive cultures. Such a product is not untrue, I think, to anthropology's status as a science, while it is also perhaps truer to man's nature as humane.

Anthropological *versus* Humanistic "Reality"

While he may accede to the humanist's insistence on standards of excellence as relevant to the choice of materials on the arts or thought, the anthropologist may do so with professional reservations. If he has studied aspects of the civilization in the field, he is most likely to have observed, not the most refined art or idea as practiced by its finest exemplars, but instead the common way of life as lived by the lowly and the unrefined. The anthropologist often knows more about the feet of clay than he does about the exquisite head of the humanist's golden idol. His tendency to dwell on the visceral aspects of peasant life as his version of the truer "reality" of a civilization may be found more than a little irritating by the humanist, who (like the ambassador) is professionally concerned with portraying the "higher" and distinctive achievements of a civilization.

As Milton Singer has noted (1961), the anthropologist's concern is commonly with the whole context of human activity; the humanist's is with the text alone. The humanist's tendency to consider abstracted ideation as the significant part of a civilization's "reality" may alarm the earthbound anthropologist, who is well aware how much meanings are generally shaped by social uses. Furthermore, the anthropologist may easily be made to feel uncomfortable about his field observations in a civilization when probed by more specialized scholars, for he may himself never have thought of inquiring from his villagers their views on tragedy, the transcendence of God, or the atomic theory of matter.

The bridging of such gaps between the first-hand observation of the anthropologist and the specialized textual studies of other disciplines must for the most part wait upon the development of textually more sophisticated field studies by anthropologists and upon the closer orientation of other disciplinary researchers to social contexts. Meanwhile, joint participation in a civilization course may be one of the most effective means for promoting discontent with the present unsatisfactory hiatus between text and context, and for stimulating constructive countermeasures on the part of both anthropologists and practitioners of other disciplines.

DEALING WITH CIVILIZATION COMPLEXITY

How to convey a feeling for the genuineness of information about an alien culture is a familiar question in the teaching of anthropology. Solutions are well known to pedagogy: one needs to excite the maximum participation of students through an appeal to many senses, many media of communication, many realistic examples. Information about a civilization such as India's differs mainly in its complexity. At the same time, because Indian civilization is a living civilization, portions of its complex reality can be recreated in the classroom with special ease. One can have movies, performances, art exhibits, feasts, lectures by persons experienced in the culture, and much more.

Thus the staff of the Indian civilization course was faced with the task of conveying to students a sense of the reality and complexity of India's language problem, and wished also to instruct them in some elementary concepts and principles of historical and social linguistics. A live laboratory session was designed to do the job. Speakers of eight Indian languages, graduate students at the university, were invited to appear in pairs before the class. These were native speakers—people with very genuine personal problems of communication. A speaker of one regional language of India was asked to translate each of two English sentences already known to the class, and to read those sentences in his own speech to a speaker of a different Indian language. The second speaker was asked to give in English his understanding of what had been said to him. Students in the class could at once perceive the general lack of comprehension among speakers of the various regional languages, correcting their misimpression that the differences are comparable to differences among American dialects. With a little guidance, students could also estimate degrees of comprehension or lack of comprehension, and thereby infer the relative genetic or geographic proximity of the several languages and linguistic families. Furthermore, the two English passages to be translated were of very different character, the one dealing descriptively with common objects, the other dealing abstractly with a theory. The first sentence tended to bring out the most various vernacular elements, and to be less comprehensible to the speaker of another language. The more abstract sentence generally elicited a high proportion of borrowed Sanskritic vocabulary, and was more readily understood across language boundaries. Students could thus directly perceive the phenomenon of cultural levels in India's language problem.

In general, laboratory sessions like these are best concentrated at the beginning of the course or topic of study where immediate grasp of a complex reality seems essential to further effective learning. Thus, before readings on regional varieties of family and kinship organization are discussed, actual unrehearsed kinship interviews are conducted before the class, again calling on a few of the many enthusiastic volunteers among the Indian graduate student population. Genealogies from individuals of two or three contrasting regions are recorded on the blackboard directly from the informants. It is not unusual in such interviews for an Indian informant to question the anthropologist's whole line of investigation, or to make an impromptu speech against caste or familism, sometimes in opposition to his own elicited experience. All of this adds to the genuineness of the demonstration.

The more abstruse the subject, the greater the need for concrete experience. Before Brahmanical theorizing about sacrificial ritual is discussed in the course, there are not only slides of sacrifices and tapes of the recitation of Sanskrit mantras. There is also an actual staging of a Brahmanical ceremony of initiation or "second birth," with Indians playing the roles of priest and teacher, an American student the role of the youngster being initiated. In all of these attempts to recreate for students a whole, natural context of human activity, I see a kind of contribution which can be made with peculiar appropriateness by the anthropologist.

The very complexity of a civilization can actually help to enhance its reality for students. For example, undergraduates commonly find initial difficulty in suspending their disregard for what they initially perceive as India's penchant for religious and metaphysical speculation. How can a person take seriously a belief in metempsychosis, or astrology, or the dependence of the order of the universe upon sacrificial ritual? At first encounter, the student may think himself engaged in a dialogue between his own "rational" West and the "irrational," misty-minded East. When he discovers that by no means all Indians are or ever were believers in any one set of doctrines, and that religious and philosophical debate within India is multiple and spirited, then the student can begin to draw parallels to more familiar controversies in the West. In Vedantist and Buddhist, dualist and monist, Jain and yogin he can find analogies to Catholic and Protestant, trinitarian and unitarian, realist, and nominalist. What began as a debate between himself and the imagined monolithic Indian holy man shifts rapidly over to a complex and far more convincing conversation among many more credible Indian participants, some of them sure to be partisans of the student's own views.

Again, the student may initially perceive a monolithic India as a "backward" nation, uninterested in material achievement, and preferring things of the spirit—all this in sharp contrast to the student's perception of his own nation as active and progressive. This initial misimpression of India is perhaps best dispelled not by consideration of the national outlook or performance as a unitary quality, but by investigation of the vigorous and sometimes opposite economic demands of India's political pressure groups—capitalist, Socialist, Communist, Gandhian, and non-Gandhian, etc. (Weiner 1961). Once initiated into the internal dilemmas of the Indian economic debate, the student is more likely to find himself sorting out the many conceptions of economic "progress"—and perhaps revising his own—rather than assessing the extent of India's chimerical "otherworldliness." A many-sided conception of civilizational "reality" may prove both most valid for scholarship and most effective for overcoming the sense of strangeness about an alien civilization.

SUMMARY

Those areas of the world which are the sites of major, living non-Western civilizations make appropriate subject matter for the undergraduate learning of many aspects of what cultural anthropology has to teach. A civilization can be conceived as an expanded systemic whole and studied intensively, if one extends and modifies concepts employed in the study of whole cultures of smaller scale. At the same time, a civilization can furnish internally the diversity needed for comparative analysis, and a rich subject matter for study of cultural change and for the history of culture in general.

Since a non-Western civilization is both alien and complex, and since it is best understood with the assistance of many disciplines, a civilization course may tend to lapse into undisciplined general description, The tendency can be reversed by building the course around a series of workable but uncompleted analytic tasks, supplying primary materials and theoretical approaches from several relevant disciplines, but a minimum of ready-made answers. Differences between the universalistic, evaluative mode of analysis favored by humanistic disciplines and the relativistic, non-evaluative mode of analysis favored in the sciences can be reconciled at least internally if evaluations are carried out with regard for the civilization's own humane aims and critical standards.

Observations by cultural anthropologists can contribute importantly to conveying a sense of the living, contextual "reality" of an alien civilization, although there may remain large gaps between the anthropologist's observations and the refined, abstracted concepts studied by other disciplines. The picture of civilized reality which both teaching and research may most usefully strive to create would appear to be the reality of many aspects, as cultivated by many disciplines. To such a realization anthropology can contribute, and from such a realization it can profit.

The unique gains and rewards which are available to the cultural anthropologist, student or teacher, from his work in a multidisciplinary civilization course are many. If a civilization includes great breadth of internal diversity—if every evident cultural theme has many a variation—then the anthropologist must sharpen his methodological tools, for each of his functional statements will be more vulnerable to comparison and challenge. If a civilization has great known historic depth, then the anthropologist may extend his comparisons through time, and will be encouraged to develop diachronic modes of thought about social and cultural systems. If a civilization possesses refined ideational dimensions, then the anthropologist must learn means for attending more subtly to the thought of his people. By participating along with scholars of other disciplines in the common study of a human whole, he discovers the limits of his discipline—limits which he may transform, if he takes up the challenge, into the frontiers of an advancing anthropology.

NOTES

[1] Many of the problems examined in this paper were suggested to me by the above paper of Dr. John W. Bennett.

[2] Initial support for the preparation of readings, training of teaching interns, development of visual aids, etc., in all the non-Western civilization courses at Chicago has been provided through the generosity of the Carnegie Corporation.

[3] Full outlines of course procedures are made available by the Educational Director, The Asia Society, 112 East 64th Street, New York.

REFERENCES CITED

BASHAM, A. L.
    1954   The wonder that was India. London, Sidgwick and Jackson.

BURTT, E. A. (ED.)
1955   The teachings of the compassionate Buddha. New York, New American Library.

CHICAGO. UNIVERSITY. COLLEGE.
1961   Source materials in Indian civilization. Chicago, Syllabus Division, University of Chicago Press. (Mimeographed)

CRANE, ROBERT I.
1959   The role of the introductory Asia course in undergraduate education. Journal of General Education 12:164-169.

DAVIES, C. COLLIN
1949   An historical atlas of the Indian peninsula. Bombay, Oxford University Press, Indian Branch.

DE BARY, WILLIAM THEODORE
1957   The Columbia general education program in Oriental studies. In Introducing India in liberal education, Milton Singer, ed. Chicago, University of Chicago Press.

DE BARY, WILLIAM THEODORE, et al. (EDS.)
1958   Sources of Indian tradition. New York, Columbia University Press.

HUTTON, JOHN HENRY
1946   Caste in India. Cambridge, Cambridge University Press.

KARVE, IRAWATI
1953   Kinship organization in India. Poona, Deccan College Post-Graduate and Research Institute.

MANDELBAUM, DAVID G.
1948   The family in India. Southwestern Journal of Anthropology 4:123-139.

MARRIOTT, MCKIM (ED.)
1955   Village India. Chicago, University of Chicago Press.

NEHRU, JAWAHARLAL
1946   The discovery of India. New York, John Day.

PANIKKAR, K. M.
1954   A survey of Indian history. Bombay, Asia Publishing House.

PICKUS, ROBERT
1957   Socrates in an Indian civilization course. In Introducing India in liberal education, Milton Singer, ed. Chicago, University of Chicago Press.

RADHAKRISHNAN, S., AND CHARLES A. MOORE (EDS.)
1957   A source book in Indian philosophy. Princeton, Princeton University Press.

REDFIELD, ROBERT
1957   Thinking about a civilization. In Introducing India in liberal education, Milton Singer, ed. Chicago, University of Chicago Press.

SINGER, MILTON
1961   Text and context in the study of religion and social change in India. Second conference. Cincinnati, Frank L. Weil Institute for Studies in Religion and the Humanities.

SINGER, MILTON (ED.)
1959   Traditional India: structure and change. Philadelphia, American Folklore Society.

VAN BUITENEN, J. A. B. (TRANS.)
1959   Tales of ancient India. Chicago, University of Chicago Press.

WEINER, MYRON
    1959   The study of Indian civilization at Chicago: needs and choices. Journal of General Education 12:24-28.
WEINER, MYRON (ED.)
    1961   Developing India. 2 vols. Chicago, Syllabus Division, University of Chicago Press.
YOHANNON, JOHN D. (ED.)
    1958   A treasury of Asian literature. New York, New American Library.

PART V

THE
TEACHING
OF
ARCHAEOLOGICAL
ANTHROPOLOGY

T HE EMPHASIS in these papers is on concepts, problems, and themes. The picture they give of the archaeologist is that of the scientist-scholar whose accumulated findings enable him to survey from high vantage ground the grand vista of man's career. Only in subsidiary view does there appear the other aspect of the archaeologist, an image which Woodbury notes is often grossly distorted in popular journals, that of the skilled digger meticulously searching for remains, occasionally discovering treasure, at the bottom of a pit.

The teaching of archaeology is here considered to be absolutely integral with the teaching of all of anthropology, archaeology leavening the other anthropological fields with the necessary appreciation of time, change, and the hard material facts of life, and being reciprocally infused with an understanding of those dimensions of man which cannot be revealed through the excavator's spade. This conception of archaeology enchances culture theory: it is exemplified in the unconventional and interesting design of a course in introductory archaeology mentioned in Kidder's paper. This course opens with a discussion of theories of time and goes on to stages of culture history. Then follows a consideration of intellectual life as it can be inferred from archaeological evidence, and the course concludes with a survey of historical theories and of modern problems, including those of nuclear energy and of population growth. Eyes habitually focused on potsherds could not lift to scan these horizons; teachers completely engrossed in tool taxonomy could not envisage this scale of significance in their subject.

Yet the basic data from the earth are not neglected. Jennings calls attention to the respect for minutiae and for the craftsmanship of science which can be engendered in archaeological courses. Jennings, like the other authors, sets his teaching sights high. The general view is reflected in a sentence from a term paper which I happened to see, written by a student of Jennings. The term paper is a perceptive piece and contains several quotable passages, among them, "Archaeology is, after all else, a methodology for studying the evolution of the mind of man."

Even a paper as intentionally specific as is Baerreis' discussion of teaching techniques concludes with the tonic note that in the process of developing techniques, teachers of archaeology must also be concerned with the presentation of a sound conceptual framework. Such a frame not only enlarges the significance of the teaching, but its absence may corrupt archaeology. Gjessing tells us that this has happened in some European countries where, in the absence of a well-defined theoretical base, archaeology has been used as an extension of national history and has been exploited for chauvinistic purposes. Gjessing, too, advocates the broad view of archaeology and cautions against the pitfall of making chronology and taxonomy ends in themselves. He welcomes the advances in dating techniques made possible by other sciences, as enabling the archaeologist to give more attention to his essential problems rather than having to concentrate heavily on chronology.

The essential problems are outlined in Braidwood's paper. The goal of teaching archaeology, he writes, is to create new vistas of understanding of human history. This history is all of culture history and is not restricted to the evidence from the earth, though the discovery and use of that evidence is an archaeologist's special responsibility. Three main themes are proposed by Braidwood for an "introductory-advanced" course, i.e., a course which is a student's first course in archaeology but which he takes after he has learned some general anthropology. The opening theme places archaeology within the whole study of the human scene, as shown in Braidwood's chart. The second theme embraces the great problems to which the study of archaeology can be addressed; these could effectively be dovetailed with the main topics of a civilizations course, as set forth in Marriott's paper. The third theme, on the *why* of cultural differences, links with similar discussions in papers on ethnological courses. Because the study of civilizations has risen to prominence in the teaching of both archaeologists and cultural anthropologists, there has been a parallel interchange in both fields with other students of civilization. Kidder notes the importance of reciprocal relations with classical and oriental archaeologists, just as Bennett and Marriott made similar note of cooperation with area specialists.

In regard to the best sequence for the study of archaeology, Woodbury, Kidder, Braidwood, and Gjessing agree that a student should have a general introduction to anthropology, giving him an understanding of culture, before he studies the general principles and problems of archaeology in an introductory archaeology course. Beyond that, Kidder recommends that archaeology be taught only as part of regional and area courses, thus preserving the true continuity of archaeological and ethnological interpretations.

The utility of archaeology to anthropology generally is pointed out by Jennings. Among other contributions, some students who are attracted by archaeology become interested in the study of general anthropology. Another kind of utility is the social utility of archaeology discussed by Gjessing. Archaeological writings can provide a people, as do works of history, with an image and an identity; these can be narrowly exclusive, or can take in all of mankind without belittling the group's particular allegiance. These papers on archaeological anthropology leave no doubt as to which is the preferable view.

D.G.M.

RICHARD B. WOODBURY

Purposes and
Concepts

D URING THE LAST FEW DECADES archaeologists have subjected their research to continual scrunity and reappraisal in their desire to improve field techniques, refine analytic and synthetic approaches, and eliminate weaknesses in the means of accumulating, processing, and evaluating their data. But only rarely have they given serious thought to the techniques or possible weaknesses of their teaching of archaeology, beyond urging the addition of new courses and the financing of larger laboratories. Archaeologists have focused their attention on their research, of course, because this is the basis of their reputations and professional advancement. Teaching has often been relegated to the role of a time-consuming chore which could be carried out in a traditional manner, free of scrutiny by colleagues or superiors. Nevertheless, it is through teaching that archaeologists can contribute to the education of the next generation's scholars, administrators, politicians, writers, and citizens. If archaeologists do not speak for themselves, the alternative will be, at best, a continuation of the naïve and distorted public image of archaeology that is supplied to the public by the presumably college-educated writers and editors of influential mass media such as *Life* magazine. In an analysis of thirty-four archaeological articles appearing in a ten-year period of *Life* (Ascher 1960), four "themes" were found that characterized the presentation to the public of the activities and achievements of archaeologists: discovery, usually by chance, of something exciting; the calling in of the archaeologist, as an expert; the archaeologist's use of complex and skilled techniques; the emphasis on the "largest," the "oldest," and so on. The impression given to readers is that "To be an archaeologist, more often than not,

223

is to be an expert on call." This picture of archaeology would be amusing if it were not both pitiful and dangerous, ignoring as it does most of the careful steps by which archaeologists reach conclusions and contribute to the wide-ranging study of man that is anthropology's general realm. While it is true that more and better writing for the general public will also help dispel this inadequate image, it is with college and university teaching that we are here concerned, the channel of communication by which archaeology is daily in close touch with the "educated public" of tomorrow.

GENERAL PURPOSES

One essential preliminary to a consideration of the teaching of archaeology is agreement on the general purpose of all college teaching. This is not the place to discuss the variety of goals that colleges and universities attempt to reach. I will assume here that, in spite of many secondary and tertiary purposes, the basic purpose of college teaching is to prepare a person for dealing with the adult world into which he is emerging in an informed, effective, and satisfying manner. This entails, on the one hand, developing the inquiring mind and sense of moral responsibility of the citizen, and on the other acquiring the academic foundations of technical skills essential for either postgraduate education or a career. Therefore, the essential core of a college education must combine in judicious balance two types of courses: general introductions or surveys, the courses that provide an understanding of mankind and the complexities of the world he lives in; and the specialized courses that lead a student deeper and deeper into a particular discipline. Robert Ehrich, in comments (April, 1960) on an earlier version of this paper, added that another main purpose of a liberal arts education was particularly well served by archaeology—"the development of respect for and the inculcation of a craftsmanlike approach to any subject." He points out the "field excavation and the recognition and treatment of data require technical craftsmanship of a reasonably high order, and the accurate interpretation through sequential and comparative study and through application of theory requires an equally high level of intellectual craftsmanship. It is one of the very few subjects in which we can bring into class some of the concrete data from which we draw our conclusions, and thus make explicit some of the aspects of this quality." (See also Ehrich 1947, 1954.)

Anthropology is increasingly widely accepted in the liberal arts curriculum, beginning at the freshman level, and need not be defended or explained here. And both archaeology in particular, as well as the general field of anthropology, are admirably suited to broaden horizons, give meaning to hitherto insignificant facts, and furnish a basis for future observation, reading, discussion, and thought, regardless of an individual's vocation.

THE RELATION OF ARCHAEOLOGY
TO ANTHROPOLOGY

Although it might seem that the inclusion of anthropology in the college curriculum would assure a presentation of archaeology, this is no more true than is the converse. Whether archaeology is presented will depend on the view of the relationship between the two that is held by the teacher and by the department; the treatment can range from overemphasis to complete omission. New World archaeology has had a long and close interplay of both data and personnel with the general field of anthropology, but Old World archaeology tends to have its strongest contacts with history, art, and philology, although the points of view and theoretical approaches of the two are steadily growing closer. In the United States anthropology has traditionally been considered as combining the study of man from the physical and cultural standpoints. Archaeology is viewed as either a branch of cultural anthropology, devoted to "the diachronic study of human behavior in the perspective of cultural change" (J. H. Rowe, comments on an earlier version of this paper, April, 1960), or as a set of techniques for the acquiring of data from the past which may be used by any of a large number of disciplines (Taylor 1948). The first point of view can be carried to the extreme of seeing archaeology as depending almost entirely on a body of data, concepts, and theories separate from the rest of anthropology; and the second point of view can lead to such emphasis on the niceties of excavation, recording, and analysis that generalizations are never achieved. My own view is that archaeology is clearly a part of cultural anthropology, and not only possesses its own distinctive techniques but also shares a large body of data and many approaches and concepts with ethnology and social anthropology, and thus with cultural anthropology in general. However, the trend away from historical studies, which are the *sine qua non* of archaeology, and recent emphasis on synchronic approaches have resulted in less and less interest in archaeological data by nonarchaeologists. Preferably, archaeology should be neither an independent branch of study nor a mere technique, and the archaeologist must be also an anthropologist (or some other specialist) in order to give his work the fullest meaning. This is a position that by no means all social scientists hold.

Since introductory textbooks are written in terms of each author's view of his specialty's organization and structure, they offer an excellent reflection of the varying point of view held by members of the profession. In addition, of course, they tend to set the framework of future courses and thus perpetuate their author's viewpoints. Therefore it is instructive to examine the position occupied by archaeology in a number of general texts.

Kroeber's *Anthropology* (1923) devotes major sections to prehistoric sequences of both hemispheres and unites them with descriptions of modern cultures in a manner that clearly shows the continuity of the present with the past. His 1948 edition of *Anthropology* does the same thing on a somewhat more extensive scale. By contrast, important general texts by Lowie (1934; 1940), Linton (1936), Goldenweiser (1937), Chapple and Coon (1942), and Gillin (1948) omit virtually all discussion of cultural sequences and of the time depth of culture in general, although a few exceptions to this occur in Chapple and Coon. It is curious that this non-historical treatment of culture was continued by so many authors, since there was a considerable interest in culture history and archaeological progress among many who were not themselves archaeologists. Lowie states, in his autobiography: "Nothing, I have always felt, was more detrimental to my anthropological education than the lack in my graduate years of any up-to-date summary of the elements of culture history in a systematic topical survey. Boas could have supplied the need but never dreamed of doing so, even in his lectures." (Lowie 1959:137.) But the prefaces to both the 1934 and 1940 editions and their contents make it clear that to Lowie "culture history" was not culture's long development through time but rather the elements of which culture is now composed—subsistence, dress, shelter, the family, and so on. Herskovits' 1948 textbook gives to prehistory 16 pages out of 680, and largely ignores time perspective in the rest of the volume. In its 1955 revision, archaeology occupies 20 out of 569 pages. *General Anthropology* (edited by Boas and published in 1938) resembles Kroeber's text in devoting a major section to world prehistory ("Prehistoric Archaeology" by N. C. Nelson, 92 pages, 14 per cent of the text), although it does not attempt to relate past to present cultures. Jacobs and Stern's *Outline of Anthropology* (1947) sketches world-wide culture sequences in one short chapter (23 pages, 8 per cent of the text). Kluckhohn's *Mirror for Man* (1949) devotes a chapter to the methods and significance of archaeology, but in line with the book's purposes does not summarize culture sequences.

A number of textbooks of the last decade contain separate sections of varying lengths devoted to archaeology and its findings: Turney-High (1949), Hoebel (1949 and 1958), Titiev (1954 and 1959), Shapiro (1956), Keesing (1958), and Honigmann (1959). In most of these, the sequences into which archaeological data have been arranged are presented as a discrete body of knowledge little related to the rest of cultural anthropology. By contrast, Beals and Hoyer, in their 1953 textbook and in its second edition (1959), introduce data on the time depth of various aspects of culture throughout their discussions and achieve the first textbook presentation of anthropology to minimize the standard archaeological sequences without neglecting the significance that archaeological conclusions have for any general study of culture. Keesing (1958), while treating of "The Growth of Culture" in a separate chapter, also introduces occasional time perspectives into the rest of the volume. If these books are a reliable reflection of the role that archaeology has played in anthropological teaching, then it would appear that the origins and development of culture are now more widely recognized as important to an understanding of culture than they were two or three decades ago (Kroeber being a conspicuous exception). It may also be that in the future there will be somewhat greater interest in the inclusion of historical perspective in all considerations of culture, and less emphasis on presenting the details of culture sequences, or at least the specialized terminology and criteria for subdivisions of the sequences. It is noteworthy that both Coon and Linton followed their non-historical textbooks with more general works (*The Story of Man* 1954; *The Tree of Culture* 1955) in which the emphasis is strongly historical, with archaeological findings and time perspective introduced in abundance and variety. Perhaps before long a textbook will be equally successful in using our extensive knowledge of the past to illuminate anthropological generalizations.

Thus, the beginning student of anthropology, whether taking a course as the first step towards professional training or as part of a general education, can in the future perhaps be given a fuller sense of the extraordinarily remote and simple beginnings of culture, of its gradual growth, elaboration, and spread, and of the fundamental continuity of the present with the past. Certainly this has both more fascination and more significance than the minute details of tool types, sites, and culture complexes that the specialist must use as a basis for his generalizations.

ARCHAEOLOGICAL CONCEPTS FOR THE INTRODUCTORY COURSE

When we turn from the objectives of teaching archaeology in the undergraduate liberal arts program to the particular archaeological concepts that should be taught, a question already mentioned arises again. How far does archaeology employ a group of concepts specifically its own which should be presented in archaeological terms? A little reflection will show that it shares many important concepts with all of scientific investigation, for example, the distinctions between raw data, description, and generalization, and the use of hypothesis and inference. Even though these are concepts shared by all sciences, archaeology is a particularly suitable academic subject in which they can be explained for the first time, since the concreteness of the data and the relative simplicity of some of it—a stone axe, a kernel of carbonized grain, or a pattern of stone walls—makes presentation of data effective by picture, museum exhibit, or classroom specimen. And the exemplification of such concepts as inference can proceed more easily from a handful of artifacts than from the uncertain observation of the beginner through the microscope or from the entries on a sociologist's questionnaire. Kluckhohn emphasized this as follows:

There is a certain kind of learning which comes from handling objects which is not supplied by any amount of reading or listening to lectures or even looking at pictures. I think our archaeological teaching tends to be significant in proportion to the extent to which the student has this kind of experience. (Personal communication, April 18, 1960.)

Many other concepts that are important to archaeology are shared with the rest of cultural anthropology, such as trait and trait complex, invention, diffusion, and culture area. Some of these are well suited to being introduced to the student in connection with archaeological data, but for most of them other contexts may be equally good. Culture change, including prehistoric acculturation, is especially suited to a teaching approach that combines archaeological data with the whole of anthropology. Those concepts that are most specifically archaeological, such as the taxonomic schemes for classifying artifacts or for designating spatial and temporal units of culture, are probably best presented later than the introductory course, or for the beginning student at least subordinated to a discussion of the more important contributions of archaeology to the study of man.

Lest it seem that archaeology must loom larger in the beginning anthropology course than any of the other equally important subfields, it needs to be mentioned that the widespread interest of students in archaeology makes it quite feasible to present an undergraduate course such as "Introduction to Archaeology." Here, the *techniques* of archaeology, in addition to its basic concepts, procedures, and results, can receive more emphasis. specific data for illustration can be drawn from a single area, or, as in the reader that Heizer (1959) has edited for use in such a course, from the entire world. In either case a substantial amount of culture history can be interwoven with explanations of procedures and methods. Such a course can also be offered jointly with another department, such as classics, fine arts, or history. Even stronger emphasis on technique is available to the interested student in the numerous archaeological field schools that run for about eight weeks during the summer and give regular academic credit. Nearly twenty universities now operate regular programs of this sort.

THE ANTIQUITY OF CULTURE

There are at least two contributions that archaeologists have made to anthropology, and in fact to the general body of knowledge that should be part of every person's intellectual acquisitions at the college level, if not earlier. These are, first, a demonstration of the antiquity of culture, of its initial simplicity, and of the complexity of its growth and diversification; and second, an understanding of the extent to which our own cultural background can be traced back past the classical world of Rome and Greece to its much earlier Near Eastern beginnings.

The first of these topics is often dealt with in introductory courses by means of a quick survey of the Old World paleolithic sequences, usually mainly those of western Europe. However, when presented to a class in advance of a consideration of culture as the central concept of anthropology, such a review can be little more than a confusing collection of names for segments of a chronological skeleton that is never fleshed out in any meaningful fashion. Certainly the mere sequence of periods or tool types is of less importance, and of less interest to the student, too, than such topics as the religious implications of the oldest known graves, or the technological significance of the shift from core to blade tools.

For the most effective presentation, I believe that the introductory course must *begin* with a careful discussion of culture. Keesing, for example, discusses culture immediately after his introductory explanation of anthropology's origins and subdivisions, whereas Beals and Hoijer introduce the concept of culture after almost 200 pages of human biology and fossil man; and Hoebel discusses the concept of culture after he has finished with fossil man and with prehistory also. The course should next combine, as far as possible, the story of man's physical evolution with the story of the origins and growth of culture. In spite of strong centripetal forces tending to drive physical anthropology towards the other biological sciences and away from the social sciences, there seems a constant realization in much of the writing on human evolution of the importance of cultural data and of the interplay between behavior and bodily form. The beginning student's understanding of anthropology will certainly not be furthered by a complete separation of the record of fossil man from the record of his tools.

The relative simplicity of the oldest known material remains of culture should not, of course, obscure the possibility that other aspects of culture were more complex even at an early date. Here the student can appropriately be introduced to the nature of inferences from archaeological data, to the light that modern primitive groups can shed on the past, and to the implications for human society of nonhuman social systems. But the major emphasis should be on the broad and relatively straightforward picture that can be presented of the development of human culture with its varying technologies and economic systems. Whether one prefers Childe's "revolutions" or Braidwood's "eras of food-getting practices" or Redfield's "transformations," they represent important generalizations resulting from archaeological research. To discuss culture, particularly for the beginning student, without the perspective that this chronological information affords is to prune back anthropology to little more than a "primitive sociology" and to ignore one major source for our understanding of cultural and social systems.

WESTERN CIVILIZATION'S NEAR EASTERN ROOTS

The second of archaeology's great contributions to the educated person's understanding of the world he lives in has been its demonstration that civilization did not begin in Greece and that the European cultural heritage has far deeper roots than the standard textbook presentation of history suggests. Our cultural tradition can now be traced back quite clearly to the birth of civilization in the Near East, and the Arabic line of transmission to the modern world is in many ways as important as the Greek. An introductory course cannot present all of the story of the change from food gathering to cultivation and from village to city life, but it can at least briefly emphasize the importance of these transformations and the extent of our debt to the first Near Eastern civilizations.

It is not unusual for students to reach college with only the dimmest impressions of civilization's long growth prior to Greek and Roman times. They have studied history and literature but know nothing of the origin of the alphabet, nor even of writing itself. They are filled with interest in twentieth century technology, but do not know when or where the wheel began, or metallurgy, or mathematics. These are subjects to which the general introduction to anthropology can give only brief attention, but they can make a course on the archaeology of the Old World, in the junior or senior year, full of interest and significance. It should also be suggested that the parallels in Near Eastern and Far Eastern developments and the problem of the nature and extent of contacts between them deserve to be brought to students' attention, if only as an antidote to our ethnocentrism and as a reminder of the incompleteness of some parts of the human story.

THE NEW WORLD

One other archaeological problem of general anthropological significance deserves mention in a beginning course, the independent or nearly independent growth of civilization in the New World. While the details of New World chronologies are of little importance in a beginning course, the fact that civilizations did develop in the western hemisphere is of great importance, as well as great intrinsic interest. New World civilizations show similarities to and differences from those of the Old World that are of prime importance in the anthropologist's search for cultural regularities—one of our acknowledged basic aims. Also, the possibilities of trans-Pacific contact and its significance if demonstrated, are fascinating current problems in our field of which students deserve to know the existence. It would be a dull subject indeed that could be taught as though all the facts were in, the research completed, and the books closed against any further questions, disagreements, or new interpretations. Anthropology should, in fact, be taught with a constant awareness of the challenge that gaps in our knowledge present and of the excitement that new findings consequently can arouse in anyone alert to their implications.

CONCLUSIONS

In sum, then, archaeology has an important role to play in the teaching of anthropology, if this subject is to make the contribution it should to the liberal arts curriculum. Archaeology should be introduced as an integral part of anthropology, a source of data pertinent to every branch of the discipline, and not as a separate body of chronological details relating to a past that has no connection with the present. The most important contributions archaeological data can make to the beginning course are, first, in showing the origins and growth of culture, with emphasis first on its relation to human evolution and then on the basic importance of changing subsistence techniques, and second, in demonstrating the relevance to the modern world of the Near Eastern beginnings of our civilization.

REFERENCES CITED

ASCHER, ROBERT
    1960   Archaeology and the public image. American Antiquity 25: 402-403.
BEALS, RALPH L., AND HARRY HOIJER
    1953   An introduction to anthropology. New York, Macmillan.
    1959   An introduction to anthropology, second edition. New York, Macmillan.
BOAS, FRANZ (ED.)
    1938   General anthropology. Boston, Heath.
CHAPPLE, ELIOT D., AND CARLETON S. COON
    1942   Principles of anthropology. New York, Henry Holt.
COON, CARLETON S.
    1954   The story of man. New York, Knopf.

EHRICH, ROBERT W.
    1947   The place of anthropology in a college education. Harvard Educa-
                tional Review 17:57-61.
    1954   Anthropology in a liberal-arts curriculum. Journal of Higher Educa-
                tion 25, 357-362.
GILLIN, JOHN
    1948   The ways of men. New York, Appleton-Century.
GOLDENWEISER, ALEXANDER A.
    1937   Anthropology. New York, Crofts.
HEIZER, ROBERT F. (ED.)
    1959   The archaeologist at work, a source book in archaeological method
                and interpretation. New York, Harper and Brothers.
HERSKOVITS, MELVILLE J.
    1948   Man and his works. New York, Knopf.
    1955   Cultural anthropology. New York, Knopf.
HOEBEL, E. A.
    1949   Man in the primitive world. New York, McGraw-Hill.
    1958   Man in the primitive world, second edition. New York, McGraw-
                Hill.
HONIGMANN, JOHN J.
    1959   The world of man. New York, Harper and Brothers.
JACOBS, MELVILLE, AND BERNHARD J. STERN
    1947   Outline of anthropology. New York, Barnes and Noble.
KEESING, FELIX M.
    1958   Cultural anthropology. New York, Rinehart.
KLUCKHOHN, CLYDE
    1949   Mirror for man. New York, McGraw-Hill.
KROEBER, ALFRED L.
    1923   Anthropology. New York, Harcourt Brace.
    1948   Anthropology, new edition, revised. New York, Harcourt Brace.
LINTON, RALPH
    1936   The study of man. New York, Appleton-Century.
    1955   The tree of culture. New York, Knopf.
LOWIE, ROBERT L.
    1934   An introduction to cultural anthropology. New York, Rinehart.
    1940   An introduction to cultural anthropology, new and enlarged edition.
                New York, Farrar and Rinehart.
    1959   Robert H. Lowie, ethnologist, a personal record. Berkeley and Los
                Angeles, University of California Press.
SHAPIRO, HARRY L. (ED.)
    1956   Man, culture, and society. New York, Oxford University Press.
TAYLOR, WALTER W.
    1948   A study of archeology. Memoirs of the American Anthropological
                Association, 69.
TITIEV, MISCHA
    1954   The science of man. New York, Henry Holt.
    1959   Introduction to cultural anthropology. New York, Henry Holt.
TURNEY-HIGH, HARRY H.
    1949   General anthropology. New York, Crowell.

ALFRED KIDDER II

Course Design

In the content of the teaching of anthropology, archaeology should be considered primarily as an integral part of that approach to the study of man. Historically, however, archaeology stems from two quite different academic traditions. If we are to be concerned with archaeology in its entirety, we cannot ignore the contributions of the classical archaeologists and of archaeologists trained in Oriental studies. Their offerings are comparatively narrow in geographical scope, but who is to say that their courses dealing with the origins and development of the civilizations of the Old World and of Western Culture are not as stimulating and effective in general education as are the more widely ranging and culturally, as opposed to historically, oriented courses taught by anthropologically trained archaeologists?

In short, archaeology is by no means the exclusive possession of anthropology, and I am convinced that ideally any introductory course should include at least the basic contributions of classical and other Old World scholars. This raises the issue, again in ideal terms, of the training and experience of teachers. I am persuaded, without being sure that it is always true, tht the most effective teachers of archaeology as a part of the general education of undergraduates or in preparation for more advanced work are those who have been basically trained in anthropology and have then been concerned to a considerable degree wtih Old World archaeology. For an Americanist, as I know from my own experience, even a very slight exposure to archaeology in the Eastern Hemisphere at first hand is a great deal better than none. The corollary, of course, is that for Old World specialists (as some of my colleagues have told me), a trip to Mesoamerica or the Andes is most revealing.

233

EXAMPLES OF COURSE DESIGN

In suggesting several workable and tested outlines and ideas on the teaching of introductory courses in archaeology in the undergraduate curriculum, I am assuming that flexibility of course design is necessary for practical purposes and is also academically desirable, for it takes the best advantage of the experience and intellectual predilections of teachers. There is, in fact, no single, rigid model that can be held to be superior either for the introductory or for more advanced courses. I shall present three examples of different approaches to putting together introductory courses with which I have been involved and which I think will illustrate the relatively wide range of possibilities in course design. The first two are one-semester courses, given by close colleague trained in anthropology, and, very importantly in my opinion, each has had archaeological experience in both hemispheres and has done ethnological field work. This experience meets my ideal require ments in this respect for an instructor in such courses.

Course Number 1 entitled, "Introduction to Archaeology," was planned, and for a short time given, in collaboration with an anthropologist whose chief research has been in human paleontology. It opens with a discussion of theories of time: how people have regarded past and future time and how it is conceived in our own culture. This is linked to the problem of the age of the earth, the origin of life, and to geology, paleontology, human evolution, and evolutionary theory. The first phase, Time-Evolution-Man, is followed by a full period of discussion. It is accompanied by appropriate reading assignments, slides and films, as are subsequent divisions.

Phase two, Technology-Economy, deals with the Paleolithic and subsequent Old World stages through the beginning of civilization and the development of urban economy, with briefer comparative discussion of American Indian cultures at comparable stages. Ethnographic sketches of the Eskimo and the Bushmen, with films, serve to bring the lives of hunting people closer to comprehension by a largely urban audience, most of which has no anthropological background. The phase concludes with a short review of archaeological techniques and interpretation, with demonstration at a local colonial site, and a consideration of the physical and economic bases of preliterate cultures and civilizations. It is punctuated by five discussions.

There follows a section on Intellectual Life, which progresses from inferences drawn from archaeology and ethnographic analogy on the social and intellectual life of the Stone Age through the political and social structure, art, religion and philosophy of ancient Old World civilizations, as derived from archaeological and early documentary evidence. The intellectual origins of Western civilization are then discussed, with emphasis on classical cultures followed by views of the Renaissance and the Industrial Revolution through the eyes of the archaeologist.

The final phase, Speculation, is devoted to historical theory, from Gibbon to Toynbee, and the problems of the twentieth century, including control of nuclear energy, control of weather, problems of food, population growth, war, cultural and political conflict, ethics, and related topics that arise in the four discussion periods in the phase.

This course clearly recognizes the relationship of environment, technology, population size, and cultural complexity, and it relates our present condition to what has gone before. It has, on account of its unusually large chronological scope and high percentage of discussion time, to be largely limited to the Old World. It is the kind of course that appeals to undergraduates from many departments who do not intend to proceed in anthropology. It does so precisely because it is not concerned with minute detail and has relevance to modern life. It is essentially philosophical in outlook and derives about as much from history as it does from dirt archaeology. It does not insist that "archaeology is nothing if it is not anthropology," but nevertheless succeeds in implanting a considerable number of anthropologically derived ideas, the most significance of which is probably that of the emergence of overall regularities of culture growth as the origins of the major civilizations of the world become better known.

In this course reading assignments are nearly all in inexpensive editions, many in the Penguin series. They convey a large part of the content, since so much of the approximately forty hours of classroom time is spent in discussion. It seems to approach as closely as any course of which I am aware the goal described by Professor Jesse D. Jennings, in a letter to the author, of giving "the undergraduate the greatest appreciation of prehistory and the greatest understanding of the cumulative effects of past cultures upon life today."

Course Number 2 is more conventional; it is also less encompassing, both spatially and temporally (largely because it is limited to two hours a week). It begins with a discussion of what archaeologists do, and why, and devotes comparatively more time to method in both field and laboratory than does Course Number 1. The scope of its subject matter is confined presently to the Old World, from which selected areas are chosen to illustrate what archaeology can do to elucidate cultural growth and change. Given additional time, the instructor would expand it to include selected American developments to illustrate the possibility of demonstrating worldwide regularities in cultural history. Discussion time would also be expanded.

Both these courses are excellent. Each reflects the experience and intellectual predilections of its instructor, and they both show that it is practically impossible, in one-semester courses, to deal with world-wide, or even hemispheric archaeology on a full-coverage basis.

An example of an introductory course that greatly extends content to cover systematically the entire world is Course 3 (two semesters), in which six of fifty-four lectures are devoted to the scope, history, theory, and method of archaeology, as well as to considerations of geological and biological backgrounds. The remainder of the lectures and reading cover the archaeologically known culture sequences of both hemispheres, but, in contrast to Course 1, do not venture very far toward the relationship of prehistory through early historical times to the present. There are other two-semester courses of this type, but none, to my knowledge are as thoroughly comprehensive. Such courses are really not so much introductions to archaeology as they are courses in World Archaeology. Course 3, for example, is taken by many graduate students with no prior exposure to archaeology. With additional laboratory work, these students are often able to meet minimum requirements for the doctorate with little added work in archaeology. It is debatable whether a course of this kind, with so strong an emphasis on content, is as effective as an *introduction* as are courses that treat content more selectively and emphasize basic theory in greater proportion. For purposes of general education the latter type, except perhaps in the case of the all-embracing type of course taught by an exceptionally gifted person, would seem to be preferable. I believe that in general the major content of archaeology should be, and usually is, left to area courses, in which both the ethnography and archaeology of an area are taught, and to specialized courses (in Mesopotamia, the Central Andes, the Maya, etc.), designed for graduate students and advanced undergraduate majors.

ARCHAEOLOGY IN ANTHROPOLOGY CURRICULUM

The foregoing raises the question of the relationship in curricula, from the arachaeologists' point of view, between introductory courses in general anthropology, in archaeology, and more advanced and specialized courses. It is my impression that in introductory courses in anthropology, archaeology is usually given very superficial treatment. Moreover, it appears that in most instances, prehistory is presented before ethnology, reflecting the usual order of general anthropological textbooks. In cases in which these impressions are confirmed, it would seem that there is certainly a need either for more time to be devoted to archaeology or for a separate introduction to archaeology. If neither alternative is feasible, it would improve and facilitate the teaching of archaeology in introductory anthropology if the usual procedure in such courses were reversed, to give students at least some notion of the lives of hunters, gatherers, and simple farmers prior to exposing them to the bare bones of recoverable material culture. Ideally, introductory anthropology should be a prerequisite for any course in archaeology, but practically, this would often exclude students who, for one reason or another, prefer a fuller treatment of prehistory to a survey of anthropology in their plans for general education.

If it is agreed that most undergraduates should receive most of their archaeological instruction in conjunction with ethnography in area courses, the importance of introductory archaeology becomes evident. In my experience, the product of even a very good course in general anthropology is not well prepared for the archaeological sections of an area course, to say nothing of a specialized course. The Introduction to Archaeology then becomes almost a "must" unless the instructor of an area course is willing to spend time he cannot well afford to orient students in the basic theory and method of archaeology. The introductory course can, and should, be a most useful part of the anthropological curriculum and, if well presented, an equally useful facet of general education.

The question of the nature and number of advanced and specialized courses in archaeology desirable in small departments, combined departments, junior colleges, and small colleges depends so much on the availability of good instruction that it is almost impossible to answer realistically. Generally speaking, I believe that no specialized courses in archaeology alone (other than introductory archaeology) should be offered to undergraduates. In departments of whatever size, archaeology should be taught as an integral part of area courses, which would logically follow introductory anthropology and, ideally, introductory archaeology. In universities, advanced majors with an archaeological bent may be admitted to specialized graduate courses. But for undergraduates, specialized courses tend to fragment the over-all view of archaeological-ethnological continuity. The availability of too many courses can also lead to overconcentration.

CONCLUSION

In spite of my disinclination to advance a single model for an introductory course, I believe that there are certain qualities it should have and concepts that it should present. I feel very strongly that the teacher of such a course should be an archaeologist, or at the very least, that he should have done some field work and have had a part in interpreting the results. Ideally, as I have said, he should be acquainted at first hand with both hemispheres, and if he has had ethnological experience, so much the better. Many excellent teachers, do not fully meet these ideal requirements, but I suspect that the best of them would like to have been able to. To repeat, the introductory course must be flexible, in the sense that it be tailor-made to suit the experience and qualifications of the instructor and the very variable interests and capacities of students at different institutions.

Since much of the basic material of archaeology is strange to students, good illustration is essential. This would seem obvious, but I am sure that many instructors face budgetary restrictions in trying to obtain the best slides and films. More fundamentally, the introductory course should present the aims of archaeology and the methods of attaining them with sufficient selected examples to make them clear. If time permits examples should be drawn from both the Old and the New World.

The relationship of environment, technology, population size, and cultural complexity should run as a theme throughout, forming the basis for comparative views of the past leading to the discernment of regularities in culture growth. I think it highly desirable then to attempt to carry the culture-historical conclusions drawn from the past into the present and even the future, as in Course Number 1, especially if the course is part of a general education program.

Finally, and perhaps from the students' point of view most important of all, the introductory course should allow ample time for discussion; at this stage thorough understanding of the basic concepts is far more important than added content. Judicious selection of areas and periods to be used as examples thus becomes the instructor's major problem in the detailed planning of his outline. Courses designed with these objectives in mind should do much to ease and improve the teaching of archaeology at higher levels, and, hopefully, stimulate the production of more and better archaeologists.

ROBERT J. BRAIDWOOD

Themes and Course Progression

My invitation is to consider ". . . the design of advanced courses in archeology . . ." There is no point in repeating the variety of useful observations, which the other archeological papers contain, but implications which derive from them (or parallel them) will certainly appear here. Whether the archeologist as a teacher is to function as archeologist or anthropologist will not concern me, nor will the philosophical justification for teaching the subject.

I will assume that "advanced" means anything beyond the level of a one-semester introductory course in archeology. In fact, what I shall suggest as a first advanced course might also be used as an introduction for more mature or beginning upper class students in anthropology. I have few fruitful ideas on the design of a course at the really introductory level, beyond remarking that the beginning student's first break with the unfortunate "public image" of archeology should perhaps not be too traumatic, and I join John Rowe in recalling that there are respectable archeologists with courses of their own in fields other than in anthropology.

AN INTRODUCTORY–ADVANCED COURSE

My thinking is primarily ordered upon a chart, published in quite a different context (Braidwood 1957) but very little amended from that used in Robert Redfield's (1946) essay called "Anthropology, Unity, and Diversity." We might, of course, replace the words "historical" and "scientific" on the chart with "diachronic" and "synchronic." In any case, we have a pair of orientations within anthropology upon which two introductory advanced courses might be constructed. Naturally, my concern here is only with the historical or diachronic orientation, and I believe it to be to our advantage that this orientation includes

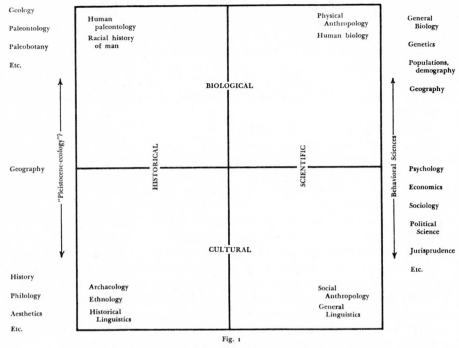

Fig. 1

SOURCE: Adapted from Robert Redfield, *Anthropology: Unity and Diversity* (1946).

both the biological and the cultural aspects of anthropology. This commits us, on one end of the axis, to a consideration of paleo-environments and to human paleontology itself, and, on the other end of the axis, to such subjects as ethnology and historical linguistics as well as to the archeology of the historical ranges of time.

Clearly there is too much content here for a one semester or even a one year course, if each aspect of the content suggested by the historical axis on the chart were to receive equal weight (and if some attention were also to be given to the cognate fields suggested—and to other useful cognates—in the space on the left of the chart). Nevertheless I know of no device more useful, both for one or two introductory lectures and as a general ordering of content, in making clear the role archeology must bear within the totality of the anthropological quest, and indeed of the many facets of the quest itself. Ideally, a course patterned on this historical axis would be given by a pair of instructors, with an archeologist resident throughout, and a human paleontologist resident throughout the earlier portion but perhaps replaced by a resident ethnologist in the later portion. I say "resident" because

I am convinced that the "vaudeville act" kind of course is not good teaching. This need not, of course, preclude occasional round table sessions with—for example—a geologist, a historian, or an esthetician, as well as with other anthropological colleagues. But as Kidder, among others, observes, any course would be tailored by its teacher to his own experiences and capabilities. It will also naturally be tailored to the type of student body and to such traditions of teaching as obtain in a particular department.

A second theme for ordering the content of the introductory-advanced course I suggest would be the selection (again tailored to the teacher's tastes and capabilities as need be) of a set of "the great problems approached by archeology." I give, below, my own reformulation of these [cf., introduction to the general entry "Archaeology" in the *Encyclopædia Britannica* (i.e., editions following 1954), with a bow to Robert M. Adams for clarification due to his thoughts on the matter], but would certainly not maintain that they are the only "great" problems or the best formulation of them.

1. How may we understand the emergence and development of man, or, more properly, of a toolmaking and culture-bearing manlike being?

2. How may we understand the appearance of anatomically modern man and the cultural florescence which seems to have attended upon and developed with his appearance?

3. How are we to understand the origins of food production and rise of an effective village-farming community or its equivalent?

4. How did civilization, manifesting itself archeologically as a more or less urbanized and politically formalized society, with public works and monumentality in art and architecture and usually with writing, make its appearance; how shall we understand certain apparent regularities common to the independent original civilizations?

5. How are we to understand the nature of the early (not so profusely literate) civilizations as they differ from or resemble the later historical or modern civilizations, and what were the mechanics of cultural transmission and of cultural change in their time?

6. Given the enormous culture-historical time depth with which only archeology is prepared to deal, what can we learn of the changing relation between man, society, and culture on the one hand and of environment on the other; what of the generalized cultural processes (diffusion, invention, acceptance, rejection, etc.), which—because of the bearing of this time factor—can be examined in no other way? For the related set of problems under this heading, it would not matter whether civilization proper ultimately had been achieved or not.

What is in mind here is obviously an attempt both to highlight and to cut down to manageable scale an already vast body of archeological literature, much of it detailed and rambling. I see no reason why a modest amount of primary site report reading should not be assigned at the level of each one of these problems, if for no other reason than to give students an appreciation of the contents of the various levels of assemblages upon which interpretation must be based and from which the authors of their secondary or textbook accounts have had to proceed. I would certainly not hold students responsible for the actual nuances of distinction between a Levallois flake and a Gravettian backed blade, for example, but I would see that they learned that such distinction is possible and meaningful. I would certainly be concerned that they sensed the increasing dimensions for interpretation in all bands of the assemblage spectra, as they read at least some selected site reports on the different levels suggested by the problems.

For a third theme, to be interwoven with the foregoing two (the historical axis theme and the "great problems" theme), I suggest a concern with the *why* of cultural differences, in time and in space. This is clearly an echo from a course called "Human Origins" (Tax *et al.* 1947) organized at Chicago in the early post-war years—and there are doubtless other echoes of this course in the introductory-advanced course I propose here. However, the old Chicago course was of three quarters duration and demanded considerable joint staff involvement and a rather elaborate set of teaching aids (which persisted in getting out-of-date!); it would not be a practical solution for many departments of anthropology. Nevertheless, the theme of concern with the why of cultural differences could, I believe, be usefully woven into the fabric of the general content of the course I suggest, and would perhaps be made the subject matter of the final weeks of the course. What is at issue would be a short consideration of the history of ideas about cultural differences and of the criteria usually used to specify them (e.g., technological competence, intellectual-aesthetic achievement, cultural and political domination), and then an examination of the types of reasons or determinisms (e.g., evolutionistic, geographic, racist) used to explain the differences.

It may be noted that this subject matter could follow rather naturally from the generalized content suggested for consideration under the fifth and sixth of the "great problems." However, it seems to me that a more exhaustive treatment of the "why" of cultural differences might well arise again at an even more advanced level of attention to the great problems in anthropology generally.

REGIONAL COURSES

As does Kidder, I would suppose that the next step in advanced courses would be to "regional" ones. I like to keep my own on at least a proseminar basis, and construct them as often as I can upon the presence of a visiting colleague or on the basis of some joint interest in a problem which one of my resident colleagues and I may have. This is not yet an exhaustive treatment of all of the archaeological details of a given region, but rather the details of the region are used as a quarry for ideas against which some general proposition may be tested. As often as not, the ideas involved in the propostion may concern methods or conceptual tools leading to more full-bodied interpretation.

Such "regional" courses doubtless reflect two things in me, personally: (1) a lack of that peculiar kind of general interest and—may I say—omnipotence, which would incline me towards the old style "aims and methods in archeology" type of course, coupled with a conviction that physical methods are best learned in the field (*vive* Point of Pines!); and (2) my enrollments are never large, since the regions of my own competence all involve archeological site reports in foreign languages. This means that whatever the title of the course may be, I have never given the same course twice, and each one is an experiment. In fact, if such courses have any great value, much of it must lie in the fact that they organize themselves about something which I am "hot" on at the moment, and in terms of what I assess to be the capabilities of the participating students.

I am in a very awkward position as regards advice for really detailed substantive regional courses. The first and only one I was ever involved in, Henri Frankfort's seminar on Near Eastern pre- and proto-history to *ca.* 2500 B.C.), took five years. True, it was really exhaustive and resulted in such things as McCown's (1942), Perkins' (1949) and our own (Robert J. and Linda Braidwood 1953, 1960) sub-regional summaries, but a very good deal of detail has been added since the Frankfort seminar met. I am of the opinion that if "region" is to mean a culture area of any significant extent and if the treatment is really to be exhaustive, then at least some other regions of the world would also call for something in the order of five years.

My own way out of this dilemma is to see to it that at least some of my so-called "regional" pro-seminar courses involve the exhaustive search of site reports on sub-regions, with each student in a small group responsible for a different sub-region. Each student is further responsible for making a comparison of his own sub-region with the summary treatments given it by Childe (1952), by the authors in the Ehrich (1954) volume, and in our own summary (1953). Occasionally, individual students may attempt the exhaustive treatment of a pair or more of adjacent sub-areas in a reading course, but—I am sorry to say—I see no practical means of administering a complete and detailed treatment of the whole Near Eastern region over any very significant block of time and development.

The question then arises, would not an up-to-date summary course be better than nothing? I suppose my answer would be that there is already summary—upon the approximate level of a reading of Childe's *New Light,* in the Near Eastern instance—in the equivalent of the introductory-advanced course I suggest here. I would anticipate about the same amount in the course I suggest. In my "regional" pro-seminar courses, we begin to go above the level approximated by Childe's *New Light* and our own summaries, on a sub-regional basis. In Chicago, of course, the students at this level are almost all graduate students (and I would imagine they would be close to this level in any equivalent department) and are certainly anthropology majors if they are not already committed to archeology as a speciality. They hear a great deal and participate a great deal, and presently take on some modest job involving the handling of the field materials themselves. I may be wrong but I think they are getting a continuous sense of summary by further reading and by osmosis. I actually concern myself more about keeping them general anthropologists, at least through the level of the M.A. degree.

A PERSONAL APPROACH

It is doubtless inevitable that any attempt to consider ". . . the design of advanced courses . . ." must become highly personal and also expresses an ideal. Thus, for example, I give no formal training in ceramic technology, although I know my colleague Jelinek concerns himself a bit with it. But it is unfortunate for such of my students who may happen to be away on the occasions of a visit by Matson, when the office buzzes with talk of ceramics. I have the suspicion that some of my colleagues may see little "design" in anything I write here, perhaps beyond the level of the introductory-advanced course. This does not disturb me, but does make me wonder how useful my ideas may be found elsewhere. I am only one of four people who teach archeology, either wholly or in part (and quite often jointly and happily) in a rather large department, with many other colleagues of whom none, to my knowledge, are without some degree of interest in culture-historical problems. I am surrounded by other culture historians (whatever they may call themselves!) in the Oriental Institute, and there is no dearth of primary materials for students to handle. Since Chicago is a private university, we are under no pressure to undertake salvage archeology unless we please to, and can tailor our interests to the problems which fascinate us most. I know many of my good colleagues in both Old and New World archeology do not enjoy such luxuries, and I am somewhat embarrassed by what I write, since I have nothing to depend upon but my own experience and habits.

It does strike me, however, that the goal of teaching in archeology at any level or under any name (I might prefer to be called a paleoethnologist, myself) is to create new vistas of understanding of human history. I appreciate Gutorm Gjessing's reminder (*vide infra*) that this goal is a continuing process, that we must always keep at it as each new generation asks new questions of history. At the most introductory level in pre- and proto-historic archeology, I would suppose, there would best be little more than a narrative account of our current understandings, with only a modest nod toward the nature of archeological evidence and of how it is acquired. But as the introductory-advanced level begins, something akin to the principles of historical criticism must also begin to be established. What, more exactly, is the nature of the archeological evidence itself and what the relative order of its incompleteness? What points of reference in natural history and in the culture history of the ethnological present may be used to give more substance to the interpretation of the primary pre- and proto-historic evidence? I have suggested that students at this introductory-advanced level have their attention focused on certain "great problems" and that here we attempt to explain and demonstrate the useful and justifiable ways in which the primary evidence may be manipulated—from field situation to laboratory to generalizing interpretation. Then I ask that they be allowed to try this process on for size, as they consider the variety of explanations which have been given for cultural differences.

At the fully advanced level, I'm afraid, I have simply asked for more of the same, at a "regional" or even sub-regional level. If the advanced student has horse sense and patience to read and some good field school experience, he will learn field and laboratory techniques and their potentials. My concern is rather with his development of that thing akin to historical criticism, growing hand-in-hand with his ability to interpret imaginatively in all bands of the assemblage spectrum. How shall he best do this? I would submit that it would best be done within the framework of a thorough and continuing education in general anthropology, where (to paraphrase from Wheeler's obituary on Gordon Childe) the study of man is as nearly a science as perhaps that wayward subject admits.

REFERENCES CITED

BRAIDWOOD, ROBERT J.
  1957   Means toward an understanding of human behavior before the present. *In* The identification of non-artifactual archeological materials, Walter W. Taylor, ed., pages 14-16. National Academy of Sciences–National Research Council, Publication Number 565. Washington, D.C.
BRAIDWOOD, ROBERT J., AND LINDA BRAIDWOOD
  1953   The earliest village communities of Southwestern Asia. Journal of World History 1:278-310.

1960   Excavations in the plain of Antioch. Oriental Institute Publications, Number 61. Chicago, University of Chicago Press.

CHILDE, V. GORDON
1952   New light on the most ancient east. 4th edition, rewritten. London, Routledge & Kegan, Paul, Ltd. (Cf., also New York, Grove Press, Inc., Evergreen E-72.)

EHRICH, ROBERT W. (ED.)
1954   Relative chronologies in old world archeology. Chicago, University of Chicago Press.

McCOWN, DONALD E.
1942   The comparative stratigraphy of early Iran. Oriental Institute, Studies in Ancient Oriental Civilization, Number 23. Chicago, University of Chicago Press.

PERKINS, ANN L.
1949   The comparative archeology of early Mesopotamia. Oriental Institute, Studies in Ancient Oriental Civilization, Number 25. Chicago, University of Chicago Press.

REDFIELD, ROBERT
1946   Anthropology: unity and diversity. *In* Human origins: an introductory general course in anthropology, Sol Tax *et al.*, ed. Selected Readings, Series II, pages 8-12. Distributed by the University of Chicago Bookstore, Chicago, Ill. (out of print).

TAX, SOL, *et al.*
1946   Human origins: an introductory general course in anthropology. 2d edition. A syllabus, two volumes of selected readings and a set of maps. Distributed by the University of Chicago Bookstore, Chicago, Ill. (out of print).

JESSE D. JENNINGS

Educational
Functions

As have other teachers, I have been amazed at the fervent interest which some undergraduates show in antiquity, in antiquity for its own sake. This interest is also held by many others, but on the part of these undergraduates it is backed up by a willingness to study and work at learning about it. Curiosity about the past may be one of the basic reasons for the increased demand for courses in general anthropology and, specifically, for courses in archaeology. This curiosity can be readily transmuted into systematic inquiry. The existence of this interest in the past constitutes a justification of the teaching of archaeology at almost any level for its general educational value. If, by satisfying this curiosity about man and his past, one can at the same time impart some depth and breadth and systematic understanding of man's behavior—which is anthropology's primary goal—then good teaching of archaeology is doubly important, not only to the student but also to the anthropologists themselves.

The findings of archaeologists have been fundamental in the development of anthropology as we know it today. Through a concern with historical problems and with the increasingly deep time perspective archaeology provides, there has been an enrichment of general ethnological interpretation and understanding. For example, the American plains area was once viewed as empty of occupants until invaded by Woodland Indians after the arrival of the horse. Through archaeological work, it is now known that the plains cultures have deep roots in a long prehistory, a prehistory well understood in broad outline and in many cases in great detail. Another fact to be reckoned with is that archaeology is learned, taught and interpreted by American archaeologists as inseparable from the other data encountered in anthropology today. Archaeology is the gateway through which many students actually enter anthropology, in that archaeology has given them the first glimpse of the broader field. Another fact is that modern history and modern cultures are better understood when the full extent of human history is appreciated.

The task of archaeological teaching can then be recognized as the introduction or reinforcement of several central ideas. These include the introduction of the concept of culture; presenting archaeology as a part of anthropology rather than antiquarianism or ancient history; the blending of ethnological and archaeological fact so that today's cultures are seen as extensions and developments of an earlier archaeologically ascertained base; and inspection of the concepts of cultural relativism as well as of cultural evolution. It is also possible to examine the misleading concept of culture degeneration or decadence.

There is the opportunity for correlating cultural development as perceived archaeologically with the environmental scene in the kind of study that is being called human ecology. There is the opportunity and the obligation to examine the notion of environmental determinism of culture, the extent to which man himself modifies and controls the external environment and, finally, just what portions of the full range of available resources, in any given environment, man has *chosen* to exploit. The contrast between what is available and what is actually used is the most important aspect of human ecology which can be examined in an archaeological context.

THE PRESENTATION OF CONCEPTS
AND PROBLEMS

We can now move to a consideration of ways in which materials can be presented to meet these objectives. The facts of culture progression from simplicity to complexity ought to be introduced. The inseparability of man and culture as mutually dependent focal points of a unified study must often be exemplified. The fact that minutiae and knowledge of detail are "the basis of all grand ideas," no matter what the field, should be emphasized. Ideas must be based on painstaking assessment of minutiae; the significance of minutiae must never be lost sight of and must be taught both through precept and practice. Another important point would be a deliberate emphasis upon material culture and technology as being of importance in the understanding of the analysis of cultures and culture change. In the field of human ecology there should be a definite effort to introduce data from every other scientific field of relevance. As an example I cite the outlining of the biotic resources of Western Europe as the background for discussion of Magdalenian culture and the subsequent course of the Neolithic; another example would be the limitations climatic factors evidently imposed upon the desert culture of North America.

Archaeology should in all cases be presented as a scientific procedure. This would involve differentiating the archaeologist as a scientist concerned with culture history from his frequent role as technician. All the concepts introduced, such as culture sequence, culture difference, culture contact, should be introduced as principles, facts or processes, not as isolates but as tools for larger interpretative generalization. A course should contain many exercises, either laboratory or contrived, and term papers on various levels. If at all possible there should be museum facilities available. There should be brief experience, either actual or simulated, in the field. Archaeology should provide, through objects or detailed site reports, the specificity which the beginning student often feels lacking in the presentation of general anthropology.

Cultural continuity through all of human history is an important concept to be presented through archaeological data. In reinforcing this idea, all archaeological sequences could be brought forward in time to the point of transfer from archaeological to ethnological/historical data. For example, a teacher using the data of Plains archaeology should begin with the lithic or archaic, move on to the Woodland, then present the many local manifestations of Upper Republican culture and, shifting to Nebraska deal with the protohistoric Lower Loup cultures and finally the historic Pawnee remains.

In any archaeological course about North or South America, much student interest can be generated by pointing out the full effect the varied Indian cultures have had upon American culture of today. Hallowell has demonstrated how dependent current American culture is on the nearly vanished Indian cultures. One could readily point out how the original European settlers of the bleak New England coast survived only because of Indian corn, Indian techniques of planting, Indian housing and medical practice. Or touching upon maize as the basis of all American high cultures, one comes to the present key role maize has in American agricultural economy. The way is then open to full discussion of the influence of the American Indian culture upon current American ideas and values.

FIELD, LABORATORY, AND MUSEUM EXERCISES

The matter of field and laboratory exercises can be considered together. Here one of the greatest teaching assets is being ignored or overlooked. Both field and lab work are usually considered in the province of the specialists or the expert; it has never been seriously tried on the undergraduate level in archaeology, although it is commonplace to do so in other sciences. The advantage of field and laboratory work would seem to me to rest in the teaching of respect for detail and minutiae. No student who has laboriously worked on a student dig over a weekend or in some synthetic situation, such as my own table-top dig, can escape the importance of observations of relationships. Observational and descriptive skills, essential to any good field work, appear to have great carry-over value. Several ethnologists have told me that their experience in recording the findings of archaeological excavation were of greater value to them in later ethnographic field work than anything else they have done in the way of training. This, they aver, was because it focused their attention upon the details of material culture, taught them the fallibility of human memory, and made them respect more than anything else the crucial importance of physical relationship.

In both field and laboratory, however, there are other advantages beyond those of respect for data which can be developed. The way in which archaeological thinking and generalizing can progress from things to ideas, from discrete objects to synthesis, is nowhere better learned than in the laboratory. As one obvious example, I suggest that the sorting of sherds or stone tools leads readily to thinking about the relation of technology to culture growth and complexity. Or from typological segregation of artifacts one can readily move to consideration of constructs versus cultural reality, to the problems of culture base and of culturally significant types. The validity of a statistical method can be tested, or at least examined, in any typological study. On the basis of typology, one can weigh the concepts of culture trait in relation to the notion of trait complex. In short, almost all the assumptions underlying speculation about culture transmission, culture growth, migration, diffusion, or invention can be, if not tested, at least given scrutiny in the laboratory. Exercises such as the one devised by Heizer on the typology of United States coins can demonstrate how much archaeology and ethnology continuously borrow from each other in order to interpret findings.

The traditionally strong role of the museum in the development of anthropological thought has somehow been partially lost. Material culture, however, remains one of the major sources of information about human behavior. I would urge that wherever a museum exists it ought to be utilized in all anthropological teaching. It is easy to do this in the teaching of archaeology, but the role of material objects in all anthropological teaching is a crucial one and should be so recognized. Utilization of material objects in teaching would, of course, reinforce the identification of archaeology with basic scientific methodology. For many teachers a museum is not available; in such cases the laboratory must bear the brunt of this facet of teaching. But with a good museum available, more imaginative and more effective teaching can be achieved. Particularly is this true if specimens are displayed in the more modern contextual way which we have come to expect.

SPECIAL FUNCTIONS OF THE TEACHING OF ARCHAEOLOGY

All these suggestions should contribute to the highly important function of giving the student, through archaeological materials, an intimacy with the past and with the whole world of man and culture. Undergraduates fresh from high school teaching, particularly of history, where individuals and their foibles receive undue emphasis as opposed to the broader sweep of cultural forces, may not be ready for the abstractions encountered in the general anthropology course. But, through the laboratory and field work and museum studies suggested above, the student can get a clear conception of the cultural flow which comprises history. The alternation of abstractions with specifics, which a well-balanced course in archaeology provides, would achieve this valuable function of undergraduate teaching.

Archaeology has traditionally been the portal through which the young student first glimpses the excitement and stimulation of a study of man and culture. One can mention a score of famous American anthropologists whose first publications are in archaeology and resulted from field work which they did. Many persons take their first general anthropology course because of the glamor which they came to associate with archaeology through a high school course in ancient history. Others have sought out beginning anthropology because of reading some such book as *Gods, Graves, and Scholars,* or any of the excellent paperback books on Egypt, Greece, or Mesopotamia. Archaeology has long had this introductory role.

In summary, I am suggesting that the crucial function which archaeology can fill for some undergraduates ought to be recognized and utilized as one of the reasons for teaching archaeology. Part of its bridging value may lie in the glamor of the past which has been mentioned before. Additionally, some students are attracted by the fact that archaeology is concerned, at least in part, with ordering, describing, classifying, and comparing tangible specimens. One of the strengths of archaeology is that its raw data are tangible objects, usually of little intrinsic or emotional value, and so conclusions based on the data can be readily re-examined and sustained or reinterpreted.

Archaeology can fulfill a dual general educational role. It can, by focus on man and culture, introduce the whole broad field of anthropology to persons thitherto unacquainted with it; simultaneously it can, by its utilization of scientific procedures, give an appreciation of the scientific method to students in all areas of knowledge, regardless of whether the full field of anthropology proves to appeal to them.

DAVID A. BAERREIS

Teaching
Techniques

THE PROFESSIONAL ARCHAEOLOGIST learns his discipline through field and laboratory experience, since there is no adequate substitute for what amounts to an apprenticeship under a skilled practitioner. As a teacher, however, he must deal with the diverse course offerings in undergraduate college curricula, both those that are general in character but have some archaeological content and those that are specifically directed toward the field. The students normally include only a small proportion of pre-professional majors, the majority being individuals attracted to the courses because of their intrinsic interest or their value in a liberal or general education. Techniques of teaching must in any case be directed towards familiarizing students with the physical as well as the conceptual components of archaeology.

AUDIO-VISUAL AIDS

The utility of slides and films for instructional purposes is such that perhaps there is less need to point out their merits than to suggest a word of caution against excessive use. It would seem impossible to set fixed limits to the portion of time that might be profitably expended on the use of audio-visual aids. This must depend upon the total class hours available and also upon related considerations, such as the availability of a good teaching museum for assignments that can supplement the regular class hours. Where adequate museum facilities are lacking, the instructor is more dependent upon the resources he can bring in to the classroom.

Useful films of specific archaeological content are available for the general course. Such films include: *Lascaux: Cradle of Man's Art*

253

(Gotham), *The Beginning of History (Stone Age, Bronze Age, Iron Age—International Film Bureau), Zaculeu* (United Fruit), and *The Maya Through the Ages* (United Fruit). These films are examples, not an enumeration of all films available. Of exceptional merit are the films sponsored by the Archaeological Institute of America, which are distributed through the New York University Film Library. These cover Egypt and Greece as well as Point of Pines and Be-Ta-Ta-Kin. Films on archaeological methods can also play a useful role in the instructional program to serve as a guide or to orient the student. Such films have been produced by the University of Illinois (*Digging Into History*) and at Indiana. The H. W. Wilson *Educational Film Guide* provides a convenient reference point for appropriate films. A useful supplement to this was prepared in the American Anthropological Association *Film Index*. Recent announcements of similar projects suggests that additional guides to comparable material may be soon available.

The number of films specifically directed to the needs of archaeological instruction is limited. However, there are other categories of films that may be used for teaching. For example, in an advanced course dealing with the archaeology of a specific locality or broader region, essential characteristics of the environment or terrain can frequently be presented in an effective manner, economical of time, through the medium of film. The student of archaeology must learn to relate artifacts with the customs and practices of living peoples, so that descriptive films dealing with basketry or pottery manufacture and other technological areas may profitably be shown with appropriate sections in the archaeological lectures. And certainly no better appreciation can be gained of the problems facing a hunting people of limited technological development than through the splendid film, *The Hunters,* made under the auspices of Peabody Museum of Harvard University on the Bushmen of South West Africa. The very process of attempting to conceptualize the archaeological implications of such a mode of life in terms of the concrete remains that would be left behind by such a group and the disparity between the concrete remains and the routine of daily activities is valuable from a pedagogical viewpoint. Comparisons with the mode of life of living peoples are also of considerable importance in demonstrating the unity of anthropology and the need to approach a problem from the viewpoint of the several subdivisions within the field. While the archaeologist would ordinarily do this to understand the function of specific tools, it is perhaps not as commonly employed at the level of a total cultural configuration.

The use of appropriate slides has even greater potentialities, in view of relatively lower costs and the possibility of spacing them through the course at precisely the points desired. While illustrations from publications can always be copied at very low cost to suit the individual instructor's needs, such slides frequently lack the appeal of colored slides taken of an actual scene or object. Some years ago, a distributing center for color slides was set up on a non-profit basis in the Bureau of Visual Instruction of the University of Wisconsin.[1] The objective was to procure sets of slides taken by individuals or institutions from which copies could be made and distributed to those desiring them. At present archaeological slide sets are available for Zaculeu (Guatemala), Hopewellian material (Illinois), culture sequences in eastern and southern Florida, areas and period of culture in the Greater Antilles and Venezuela, culture sequences in the Long Island Sound region, Aztalan (Wisconsin), Emerald and Anna Mounds (Mississippi), Gordon Site (Mississippi), Mogollon material from Tularosa Cave (New Mexico), and from the Bull Brook Site (Massachusetts). Slide sets are available from many institutions and private firms, but their high cost can make considerable inroads on a limited departmental budget. The archaeological teaching profession may still find it very much to their advantage to continue the development of a project such as that initiated at Wisconsin. Mention should be made of the filmstrips issued by *Life* (Life Filmstrips, 9 Rockefeller Plaza, New York 20, N.Y.) The costs involved are modest. Topics of archaeological interest, derived from series in the magazine, are included. Since the filmstrips result in individual pictures of smaller dimensions than those produced in the normal 35 mm. slide, some difficulty is encountered in integrating this material with other slide resources.

The availability of good slide series may create the problem touched upon previously, i.e. the extensive use of slides cutting into time needed for lecture purposes. Making slides available outside regular class hours relieves the strain somewhat. At Wisconsin, use has been made of an automatic slide projector.[2] The machine projects 30 slides upon an opaque screen. Normally manufactured for continuous showing of a series, it has been modified to cut off its operation on completion of a cycle. Titles and brief descriptive comments may be prepared in standard slide mounts to add to its instructional value. The contribution of such a machine is twofold. It provides students with an opportunity to see additional visual material after regular class hours, and in a minor way it compensates for the lack of adequate museum facilities. It also allows important material to be seen as frequently as is needed by the student, so that he is not limited to the single occasion on which a slide may be shown in the classroom.

OTHER TEACHING AIDS

The audio-visual aids discussed, useful as they are, constitute but a pale reflection of the value of actual specimens in demonstrations. There is, admittedly, a problem of availability. Without doubt, however, a discussion of the Acheulean industry accompanied by an opportunity to handle an actual Acheulean hand axe presents the salient points far more effectively than a series of slides illustrating the material. It is not simply a matter of gaining a better understanding of the form characteristics of hand axes; the dramatic aspects of handling an actual tool of great antiquity adds a dimension of reality to what may previously have been but words to the student. The actual tools serve as a stimulus to a better grasp of the facts and concepts of prehistory.

Teachers in the New World who have no direct contact with the prehistoric sites of the Old World may feel that such materials are beyond their reach. Yet we read of the large numbers of implements found in sites of Africa and Europe that must have but little value as museum specimens. If the mechanism were provided, surely type collections could be made available for teaching purposes. Another indirect benefit might be achieved in relation to the training of the preprofessional student. Would burins have been so long unrecognized in the New World if there had been adequate collections for students to examine during their period of academic work?

With ingenuity, it is possible that other varieties of teaching aids can be constructed. Table top archaeology, as described by Jesse D. Jennings, is a case in point (1950). Robert F. Heizer[3] reminds us that we should not overlook such economical methods as the use of mimeographed sheets of stratigraphic sections, tables, charts, etc. which can be distributed to students before lecture at appropriate points in a course. Readings and lectures can easily be enriched in this fashion through direct reference to real problems and situations that have been faced in the field or in the analysis of data.

TERM PAPERS, REPORTS, AND EXAMINATIONS

The question to be considered here is whether archaeology in general differs from other scholarly subjects sufficiently to warrant the development of a distinctive pattern of examinations and report writing. For most assignments and examinations, the answer is clearly no. Yet there are some distinctive aspects of archaeology that perhaps require special attention in this connection.

The presentation of archaeological material must almost inevitably at some point revolve around the presentation of information concerning particular implements. It is conceivable that a student may complete a course in which scrapers, celts, and axes have been discussed and still not be able to recognize one if he stumbled over it in a field. There is, therefore, some merit in insisting upon a practical examination involving the recognition of artifact types and an indication of their cultural significance. Such an examination would parallel the practical tests given in a geology course, e.g. in invertebrate paleontology. Assignments involving the sketching or drawing of type implements would, of course, also be made. It is possible that such an approach would have its greatest value to the pre-professional student, but it should be of some value to the general student as well.

A pattern, used in an advanced course in North American archaeology, is to present the student with a description of what was found at a particular excavation and to ask for an evaluation of the finds in terms of determining the cultural identification and temporal placement. By requiring the student to draw appropriate inferences from a body of material, it permits the examination to duplicate the pattern of reasoning involved in a site analysis. Such a task would be appropriate as an assignment apart even from the examination procedure. One might also present the student with an assemblage of artifacts from which he would be expected to draw conclusions of the same kind. Robert F. Heizer suggests a problem which might be assigned to provide experience in artifact classification: a sample of U.S. coins of denominations from one cent to one dollar must be classified and a commentary on cultural inferences derivable from these coins prepared. Seriation problems might similarly be posed for student solution.

FIELD EXCAVATION

The initial concern of providing opportunities for actual participation in field excavations by the undergraduate student is not systematic training in excavation technique, but rather the desirability of providing opportunity for excavation experience at all levels of archaeological instruction, from the beginning through the advanced course. This is a desirable instructional component that should be included at least as an optional feature of the course program, if competent supervision can be provided. As in the case of providing actual specimens for class examination, there is no better way than through participation in archaeological work to gain an understanding of the actual nature of the field both in content and methods. More supporters of archaeological work can surely be secured in this manner than through many hours of formal class instruction. The experience of the Department of Anthropology of the University of Toronto would appear to demonstrate that such work can be effectively organized to handle large numbers of students. A by no means inconsiderable byproduct of such field trips at the University of Wisconsin has been the provision of materials for thesis work by our graduate students. There is an obvious obligation when excavations are conducted, even as a training exercise, for the results of the investigation to be reported in the archaeological literature and thoroughly documented, or the action sinks to the level of site vandalism.

The question of field excavations evokes the further question of systematic instruction in field techniques. Trips of short duration such as those mentioned above do not, of course, provide an adequate background for understanding the ramifications of field technique. This is extremely difficult to teach except in a field situation. The many opportunities that have opened for undergraduate participation as laborers on archaeological projects, such as the expanded river basin work, do not solve the question of adequate training in techniques. Moreover, where the primary objective of a field excavation is a research goal, training aspects must suffer. Teaching field techniques is a full time program, and the research results obtained through the teaching program must be a secondary consideration. It is highly desirable that students be encouraged to attend a summer field session of the kind given by many universities through the summer months, where instructional considerations play a primary role. Such work can, of course, be supplemented by more formal courses in such subjects as surveying, cartography, and aerial photo interpretation, as part of the regular curriculum.

CONCLUDING REMARKS

Literature which might be drawn upon to supplement the preceding discussion is scanty, although some valuable suggestions have been made in a brief discussion by C. W. Weiant (1952). It provides an interesting formulation of an inductive approach to archaeological instruction. The summary presentation of the Program of the History of American Indians (Armillas: 1958) and the constitutent papers upon which this summary is based (see bibliography in Armillas: 1958) not only provide the instructor with convenient bibliographies for class use but also can be used to formulate a series of lecture topics for the archaeology of the New World.

A discussion of techniques of teaching can unduly stress technical aspects of presenting material and the manipulaion of concrete data. But as in other aspects of anthropology, it is the frame of reference or the body of theory that makes the facts meaningful. In developing improved teaching techniques, we should not focus solely upon means of presenting facts but must also be concerned with the presentation of a sound conceptual framework.

NOTES

[1] A preliminary announcement of the project appeared in *American Antiquity*, XVII: 88, 1951. A complete list of slide sets and their cost may be obtained from the University of Wisconsin, Bureau of Audio-Visual Instruction, 1312 W. Johnson Street, Madison 6, Wisconsin. Additional sets for the slide series are welcomed, the original slides being returned when copies are made. A list describing the individual slides is distributed in mimeographed or dittoed form with each set purchased. Copy for the description should be prepared by the assembler of the slide set. The goal of the project was to operate on a cost basis thus making the sets available at reasonable prices.

[2] The model is an Admatic, distributed by The Harwald Co., 1216 Chicago Avenue, Evanston, Illinois.

[3] R. F. Heizer's comments cited here and elsewhere in the paper were given in a discussion of a preliminary version of this paper presented at the 25th Annual Meeting of the Society for American Archaeology, May, 1960.

REFERENCES CITED

ARMILLAS, P.
    1958   Program of the history of American Indians. Part one: Pre-Columbian America. Social Science Monographs II: Pan American Union, Washington.
    1960   Program of the history of American Indians. Part two: Post-Columbian America. Social Science Monographs VIII: Pan American Union, Washington.

JENNINGS, J. D.
    1950   Table top archaeology. Archaeology 3:175-178.

WEIANT, C. W.
    1952   An inductive approach in the teaching of archaeology. American Antiquity XVII: 251-253.

GUTORM GJESSING

Archaeology,
Nationalism,
and
Society

ARCHAEOLOGY EMERGED as one of the spring flowers of national romanticism in the latter half of the eighteenth century, following in the wake of J. J. Rousseau. As an empirical science it was born in Denmark in the first decades of the nineteenth century, when C. J. Thomsen discovered the factual reliability of the old Renaissance idea of the sequence of stone, bronze, and iron ages. With his famous "three-period system," which is still the cornerstone of prehistoric chronology in most of Europe and over large areas of extra-European Old World, he made the first step towards archaeological systematization (Thomsen 1836). On the whole, Scandinavian prehistorians, primarily in Denmark and Sweden, took such a leading part in the early development of scientific archaeology that prehistorians of any standing in other European countries had to learn at least one of the Scandinavian languages. Scholars such as C. J. Thomsen, J. J. A. Worsaae and Sophus Müller in Denmark, Hans Hildebrand and Oscar Montelius in Sweden, Oluf Rygh and Ingvald Undset in Norway, made fundamental strides forward in building up archaeological theories and methods.

History always conveys the values of the historian's own time. As a French historian once exclaimed: "L'histoire est toujours à faire," or in J. Franklin Jameson's phrasing: "Each generation views the past in its own way, asks questions concerning it which preceding generations have not asked, and requires that history be written anew in such

a manner as to answer them" (1909:109). During the decades immediately preceding 1800 and more strongly yet in the course of the nineteenth century, as we well know, a tremendous wave of nationalistic
emotion and aspiration rolled over Europe. It inspired painters and
poets as well as historians and politicians and resulted in a series of
wars of national liberation. An intense desire to preserve and make
one's national traditions overt and conscious was part of the same drive.
Archaeology grew as an extension backward in time of national history.
Alfred L. Kroeber spoke of this aspect of European archaeology (and
of anthropology as a whole), as a point of contrast to American anthropology: "It might even be said without undue unfairness that one typical American attitude is explicitly antihistorical" (1954:364). He
even suggested that Americans tend to be proud of not having much
history. This may be true, but on the other hand national, romantic feelings are tremendously complex and irrational. Europeans living in the
United States and looking at the country from what Redfield called the
"outside view" (1955:81) may possibly find Kroeber's characterization slightly oversimplified, interpreting the general American attitude
to history and traditions as one of ambivalence rather than of rejection.
In other words, there may well be a strong need for re-creating historical traditions, manifest in Gothic churches and public libraries, or
in Grant Wood's wonderfully satirical painting, "American Gothic."

The national feelings nurtured by archaeology do not make cultural or ethnic discriminations within the country in question, generously overlooking such trifling details as ethnic or cultural disconti-
nuities. As example from my own country is the mesolithic Komsa culture from Finnmark in northernmost Norway (Böe and Nummedal 1936). Norwegian archaeologists are inclined to trace its history
through North Russia to Asia and to date it to early post-glacial times.
It has even been suggested that the culture might be autochthonous,
having survived the last glaciation on land which is now covered by the
Arctic Ocean (Nordhagen 1933:118). Our Danish colleagues, on the
other hand, claim it to be an outgrowth of early Danish cultures and
are consequently dating it to very late mesolithic times. Obviously national prestige is unconsciously at work in both countries, although
nobody in either country dares to hint that there is any ethnic continuity from mesolithic times to the formation of the present population.

The important fact is that archaeology has had, and still has, its social
utility in creating and strengthening feelings of national values and traditions, "the more so" as Professor Clark puts is, "that upon this its advancement must ultimately depend" (Clark 1939:189). This interdependence between archaeology and society is indissoluble. V. Gordon Childe said that as an archaeologist he was concerned with con-

crete, material objects, but as a *prehistorian* he always and exclusively had to consider his research objects as concrete expressions and embodiments of human thoughts and ideas, in short, of knowledge (Childe 1957:7). There is no need of any Whorfian meta-linguistics to see the relationship between our archaeological thinking and our civilization's realm of conceptions and ideas. Retiring into the "Ivory Tower" may seem to be an effective escape from engagement in the problems of a turbulent world, but in the end it is a delusion.

In all the new European states that emerged from World War I, archaeology had a great efflorescence. Excellent work has been done in Finland and the Baltic states as well as in Poland, Czechoslovakia, and Hungary. Further, in spite of Israel's weak economy and the constant danger of war, an impressive amount of the most fascinating archaeological work is being done, and funds are being lavishly spent on excavations, publications, and exhibitions of archaeological results abroad.

In my opinion it is extremely important that this point be made quite explicit at an early stage of teaching, in order that students may be alert to the danger of perversion to conscious, political aims of the social-political function of archaeology. When tradition is becoming conscious of itself, it turns into traditionalism, and national feelings turn into nationalism or even chauvinism, if not brought under intellectual control.

In 1912 Gustaf Kossinna published his famous book, *Die Deutsche Vorgeschichte eine hervorragende nationale Wissenschaft*. It was the outcome of nearly twenty years of thinking. His, may I say, antiscientific view had already been made public in 1895 in his Cassel lecture, which seven years later procured him a chair as the first professor of German prehistory (Clark 1939:204). Even between the two world wars, during the Weimar Republic, Kossinna had many proselytes, especially in Germany, of course, but in other countries, too.

"It can't happen here!" But it assuredly can. The danger is always present. It would be escapism to believe that political exploitation of archaeology is confined to totalitarian states. The government of my own small democratic country in certain situations does not hesitate to use archaeology directly as a political tool, as I know from my own experience. During the Finno-Russian War of 1939-40, at which time I was in charge of the archaeology of North Norway, I was asked by our state-owned broadcasting company to give a lecture on the first settling in Finnmark by Norwegians. The idea originated with a former foreign minister and expert on international law and was explicitly intended as an anti-Soviet political action.

The danger is not less today than before World War II. Governments probably will have fewer scruples in directing our science into political channels. This is only partly due to the militarization of science in general. It is also due to the whole ideologico-political situation having reached such a point that even for individual scholars the border-line between science, ideology, and politics has been disturbingly blurred. This danger is as much present in the United States or Latin America or anywhere else as it is in Europe. This is the bearing of the comments I made on Kroeber's conception of an "anti-historical" America. Increased funds for excavating, research work and publications are always tempting, but there is danger in the first step. In the twinkling of an eye, archaeology and political propaganda may get so tangled together that it may be extremely difficult, if not impossible, to unravel them.

The tendency is far more apparent in totalitarian states. Any revolutionary government will have to create solidarity and loyalty toward the regime by any means at its disposal. The effect of archaeology as enhancing national prestige and identity, is in principle the same that I mentioned above for the new states, although in totalitarian states, the research will be more consciously and explicitly politically directed.

In all Communist states, archaeology has had a remarkable renaissance, and there have been extraordinary achievements in the field. The Soviet Union, Rumania, China, and to a certain extent even East Germany (the four areas which I know from personal experience) are multi-national states, e.g., Germans, Poles, and Czechs in East Germany. Consequently, ethnic as well as sociological problems have been given a prominent place at the front of the archaeological stage (cf. Childe 1951). One purpose is to create loyalty toward the nation and Party, so archaeology in these countries does not necessarily mean propaganda to justify expansion outside existing national boundaries.

Justification of expansion was very clearly the aim in Hitler's Germany and Mussolini's Italy. Archaeology was consciously intended as an instrument to realize Il Duce's dream of reviving the greatness of the Roman Empire and der Führer's dream of a European New Order under the active leadership of *das grossdeutsche Reich*. Kossinna's *hervorragend nationale Wissenschaft,* therefore, was enthusiastically welcomed. German prehistorians were never so intensely interested in the archaeology of European countries outside Germany as they were during the Third Reich. The Belgian professor S. J. de Laet writes: "We have not in our countries forgotten the *Germanenforschung* of the Nazis and certain grand works on the Frankish colonization in our regions which had no other purpose than that of furnishing a 'scientific' basis which could justify a political annexation of our countries by the German Reich" (1954:154).

There is no need to elaborate this point any further. But I sincerely feel that it is of great importance to point to this grave danger and to emphasize that it is by no means confined to totalitarian countries. If we want academic pursuits to be free in the future and if we want to keep archaeological thinking intellectually sober, it is of fundamental importance that we lay the dangers and temptations open to our students. The danger of being unconsciously waylaid by nationalistic political propaganda, in fact, is the greater, because with us it most often derives from "unconscious preconceived ideas, which are a thousand times the most dangerous of all," and because archaeology, at least in European countries, is still considered an extension of national history and therefore has no well-defined theoretical basis. Moreover, archaeology still has to rely very much on its popularity in order to procure its source material. Consequently, the temptation to submit to current popular opinions is the greater. Therefore also, archaeological theoretical concepts are much less well developed than, say, in cultural or social anthropology. One of the means of counteracting nationalistic or even direct political abuse of archaeology would be to change it into a more or less generalized theoretical science. "There is no science but the science of the general" (Poincaré 1952:4).

The taxonomic period in the development of archaeological research was certainly a necessary stage. To be able to classify and systematize the material, taxonomy was and still is indispensable, and it is not likely that any archaeologist will deny this. It must, however, be admitted that very many of us have fallen into the taxonomic pitfall and have made chronology and taxonomy ends in themselves. Walter W. Taylor somewhat ironically remarked:

They have accused the archaeologist of tatting endless rosettes of the same old ball of "material culture" and maintained that his findings are next to useless for the purpose of history and culture study. It seems that the archaeologists are becoming as Tolstoy once said of modern historians, like deaf men answering questions which no one has asked them. In their broader implications these accusations are all too true. (1948:95)

My own feeling is that this not too commendatory characterization perhaps might strike European archaeologists harder than the American ones at whom it was aimed, although the reaction against this type of archaeology had already clearly set in during the nineteen-twenties. In any case, it is fairly clear that the "past" which the archaeologists claim to reconstruct does not consist of "taxonomic rosettes" made purely for their own sake, nor is it limited to economic techniques only.

Moreover, the situation of archaeology today is in many respects different from what it used to be. So many chronological techniques and devices have been developed by natural sciences, such as quaternary geology, pollen analysis, dendrochronology, radio-carbon dating, etc. and with results far surpassing our own methods in accuracy, that the archaeologist should now be able to spend considerable time and effort solving his own and essential problems. This does not mean that he can do away with the morphology of artifacts (the term "typology" in European usage has the restricted connotation of the Montelian "typological method," so that I prefer the term "morphology"), but it does mean that he is not bound to concentrate on chronology to the same extent as before.

If archaeology is to be considered part of anthropology, teaching it should contribute to integration. But integration is a two-way process. Teaching therefore should not merely draw from cultural and social anthropology but should also supply these branches of the discipline with contributions of value. Since any socio-cultural entity is in continuous process of change, and since any change entails the concept of time, one of our chief contributions can be the strengthening of control of the dimension of time. This has to be given without losing the integrity of archaeology as a science, but also with some restraint to prevent the development of a too particularistic or sectarian inventory of archaeological concepts.

To my mind, then, teaching archaeology should have two leading principles. One is the interdependence between the theoretical and the practical aspect. The other follows the elementary logical principle of the relation between whole and parts, namely, that if a property is contained in the whole, it also will be inherent in the parts. The opposite conclusion is not necessarily correct: a property contained in the parts does not necessarily belong to the whole. This means in practice that teaching should proceed from the general to the particular. In point of fact, this is the general process of all real extensions of knowledge: the first step is the stage of perception, in which the sensed data are arranged in synthetic systems, and the next stage is the verification or nullification of the system by observed data. The process may be stated thus: human knowledge arises from sense perceptions, passes through a stage of synthesis, then returns to observed facts (Gjessing 1956:153). Only by performing the analysis in this way is it possible to interpret single objects in terms of culture history. Following this principle, teaching can best be organized in three stages: (1) introductory courses of general anthropology, including ecology and some elementary principles of scientific method, with a certain emphasis on the archaeological and, hence, on the culture historical aspect; (2) general principles and methods of archaeology, focussing on one or two larger areas; (3) specialization in a more or less restricted field, according to the student's particular interests.

REFERENCES CITED

Böe, Johs., and A. Nummedal
1936   Le Finmarkien. Instituttet for Sammenlignende Kulturforskning. Serie B-XXXII, Oslo.
Childe, V. Gordon
1951   Social evolution. London, Watts.
1956   Society and knowledge. New York, Harper.
Clarke, J. Grahame
1939   Archaeology and society. London, Methusen.
De Laet, S. G.
1959   Archaeology and its problems. London, Phoenix House.
Gjessing, Gutorm
1956   Socio-culture. Studies honouring the centennial of universities Etnografiske Museum. Vol. I, Oslo.
Jameson, J. Franklin
1909   Year book of the Carnegie Institution of Washington, No. 8.
Kroeber, A. L. (ed.)
1953   An encyclopedic inventory. In Anthropology Today. Chicago, University of Chicago Press.
Nordhagen, Rolf
1933   De senkvartaere klimavekslinger i Nordeuropa og deres betydning forvkulturforskningen. Instituttet for Sammenlignende Kulturforskning. Serie A-XII, Oslo.
Poincaré, Henri
1952   Science and hypothesis. New York.
Redfield, Robert
1955   The little community. Chicago, University of Chicago Press.
Taylor, Walter W.
1948   A study in archaeology. American Anthropologist Memoirs No. 69, Menasha, Wisconsin.
Thomsen, C. J.
1836   Ledetraad for Nordisk Oldkyndighed. Copenhagen.

PART VI

THE
TEACHING
OF
LINGUISTICS
IN
ANTHROPOLOGY

Introduction

ADAPTING TEACHING to the specific conditions of instruction is a generally acknowledged principle of pedagogy. The authors of the three papers of this section have provided abundant, concrete details for alternative course objectives, readings, and designs. Yet, the richness and level of detail have not set up barriers against transfer of their proposals to other situations, but rather suggest various means of adaptation. Linguistics teaching is concerned with a body of problems and concepts as a set of skills or tools. The papers of Dell Hymes and Kenneth Pike were prepared for a symposium on the teaching of linguistics in anthropology at a meeting of the Central States Anthropological Association at Bloomington, Indiana, in April, 1960, and Floyd Lounsbury's paper for the symposium at Burg Wartenstein in August, 1960.

Taking as his main concern the "study of speech and language within the context of anthropology," Hymes classified under ten headings specific objectives, problems, and concepts that link the study of language and speech to anthropology. One of the objectives of linguistic anthropology, as of other anthropological specialties, is the correction of student misconceptions and stereotypes. The cross-cultural variability of speech and language can be taught in the process of examining their relations to world-views or to social structure and personality. Relating language change to culture change or the history of the study of language to the history of anthropology is mutually enriching to both special fields, descriptively and conceptually.

The interchangeability of methods and concepts among different branches of anthropology is regarded as an index of the unification of anthropology in each of the papers on the teaching of linguistics. Much the same view, with additional illustrations, is presented by William Laughlin in his paper on teaching physical anthropology and in some of

271

the papers on curriculum in Section I. It is noteworthy that unity is looked upon as a goal to be reached by specific theoretical and methodological achievements, not as an already-existing state of anthropology. Interdisciplinary integration of linguistics with other fields of inquiry is treated by Pike apropos the adaptation of linguistics to the varied needs and interests of students. This adds to the ideas and illustrations contained in Section IX on the relations of anthropology with other subjects.

Balancing concepts and problems with information and skills, or mediating between the demands of breadth and depth, is a precarious enterprise. Lounsbury's paper presents the case for what is probably a minority opinion in this volume, viz., the priority of depth over breadth at each level of instruction. This is taken in part to mean that each linguistics course must be primarily a tools course, with the broader view deferred until some restricted technique or topic has been mastered. The method is intended to provide students with a sense of accomplishment of the kind that can come from mastery of a skill, but also with a broadening of horizons and with the experience of discovery. That linguistic subject matter should be used to impart the sense of discovery was suggested also by Carl Voegelin, in his introductory address at the above-mentioned 1960 symposium in Bloomington. Pike, too, draws attention to the importance of leading students of linguistics to discover things for themselves.

In his presentation of course designs, Pike considers not only the requirements of different student levels and interests, available hours for instruction and other variables of institutional settings, but also he weighs the advantages and disadvantages of alternative ways of teaching linguistics and suggests concepts and readings appropriate for each of several course designs. Skills other than the purely linguistic are required for student efficiency, e.g., the ability to absorb and organize large masses of material and to do different types of reading (close analysis, skimming). One of the devices which he describes is no doubt applicable to many other types of subject matter: students are required to identify an author's "criteria of elegance" and to examine their works with a view to judging their success in meeting their own standards. This helps students to organize the content of what they read and at the same time it enables them to appreciate differences of style in theory and problem solving directed to the same data.

The acquisition of linguistic skills is, not surprisingly, taken as a primary though not as an exclusive goal of linguistics courses. To the variety of patterns presented by Lounsbury and Pike for courses at different levels may be added the one-year, introductory course design sketched elsewhere by David Olmsted, in illustration of a course design for a specialty to be taught in a small or combined department. Linguists alone among anthropologists appear to be content with textbooks and other published resources in their field. The secret of their success is not immediately apparent but would be well worth fathoming.

E.M.A.

Dell H. Hymes

Objectives and
Concepts of
Linguistic Anthropology

T HE MOST GENERAL QUESTION about objectives is—Why should we teach linguistics in anthropology? One's answer will of course vary with one's answer to the question—Why teach anthropology itself? However we differ in answering the larger question, there is general agreement in American anthropology that the reasons for teaching anthropology imply the teaching of something about language and thus of something about linguistics. (For British anthropology, see Robins 1959.) Speech is so fundamental an activity of man and language so integral a part of culture that no anthropology worthy of the name could pass either by. As regards content, our subject would be incomplete without them. For theory and method, speech and language provide useful, sometimes crucial examples of general problems—of how men differ, or of how they are alike; of how cultures work, or of how they change; of the scope of anthropology, or of the skills of the anthropologist. Some teachers may include speech and language out of a sense of duty or professional piety (students should know about the phoneme as they should know about the Pleistocene), but ideally the objective of teaching anthropology is to convey to students a sense of fundamental problems and a vision of the unity of anthropology.

This statement of general objective should be a truism. Specific objectives, on the other hand, are many and complex. They vary with time and place and depend on the particular institution, especially on the position of anthropology in it and on the linguistic training available outside anthropology. These latter two factors vary so much that it

275

seems impossible to speak directly of objectives for particular institutions and teachers. But one can discuss the range of objectives and concepts that a full anthropological program might contain, as a context for the logistics of individual situations, after first considering the position of the teaching of linguistics within anthropology and without.

The objectives of anthropologists in the teaching of linguistics and the objectives of others who teach linguistics overlap but need not be identical. Anthropologists cannot expect other departments to provide all the linguistic training their students need but must exercise responsibility for some special teaching of linguistics within anthropology. As with so many subjects studied by both anthropology and other disciplines, there is overlap rather than total inclusion of one by the other.

No special discipline exhausts the interests of the anthropologist. In principle committed to coordinating all knowledge about a subject, anthropology has its particular technical skills, history, ideology, emphases and professional organization. Thus, while the sum total of the special disciplines might seem to leave nothing for anthropologists to study, they continue to find useful work. All this applies to the study of speech and language. Anthropologists make their own contributions of data and of theory, and their concerns give rise to questions which nonanthropological specialists in linguistics may not at the time be asking or to emphases which the latter may not care to make. Linguistics as a discipline is in fact a congeries of subfields, whose orientations are conditioned by particular bodies of data, national backgrounds, leading figures, and favorite problems (cf., Malkiel, Ms.). Depending on the representation of these special fields, the teaching of linguistics varies greatly from one institution to another, and some offerings will be of more relevance to anthroplogy than others.

Conversely, anthropological interest in languge does not exhaust that of the linguist. As a matter of general intellectual principle, of course, nothing linguistic is alien. Yet at any given time and place, anthropology's active interest is far from covering everything within the manifold domain of linguistics. In short, the anthropological interest is always selective. It groups facets of language that might not otherwise attract attention together, facets of language which anthropologists often encounter, and which, if encountered by others, often lead them into anthropological territory.

There is, then, a special field, linguistic anthropology, conditioned like other subfields of linguistics and anthropology, by certain bodies of data, national background, leading figures, and favorite problems. In one sense, it is a characteristic activity, the activity of those whose questions about language are shaped by anthropology. Its scope is defined not by logic or nature, but by the range of active anthropological interest in linguistic phenonema. As indicated, its scope may include some problems that may fall outside the active concern of some linguists, and it always uniquely includes the problem of integration with the rest of anthropology.

I would define *linguistic anthropology* simply as *the study of speech and language within the context of anthropology.* When we teach about language in anthropology, we engage in linguistic anthropology in this sense. We are not teaching linguistics as it would or might be taught by a specialist who knows nothing of anthropology, just as in other cases we are not teaching economics, political science, or history of religions as these might be taught by their specialists. We are teaching as anthropologists concerned with subjects relevant to questions which we, as anthropologists, ask. Rather than adding one quantum of discipline A to set beside quanta of disciplines B, C, and D, we are trying to look at the subject matters of all those disciplines from some general point of view.

This being so, we should approach a subject matter such as language in certain ways. First, we should stress the fundamental questions which speech and language pose for anthropology, rather than sheer information content. A student who takes only a single course may still retain an anthropological point of view about language long after he has forgotten the answers to the final examination. Second, we should approach such questions from general ground held in common with the rest of anthropology, rather than from the specific terms in which a problem is couched for specialists. For example, language is important to the question of cultural factors in perception, and such concepts as the phoneme could be approached from that point of view (Brown 1956; 1959:22-55).

The matter of fundamental questions and common ground implies something about personnel. For teaching about languages beyond the introductory course, it is essential that the instructor be someone whose experience includes linguistic research, and in some cases this is sufficient. There are clearly isolable technical skills, such that an anthropologist will be termed a "linguist" for having them and which can be imparted entirely outside an anthropological context. Yet, it is also essential that some of the teaching of anthropology students about language be by someone whose experience includes anthropological research. For effective communication and training, the instructor must be able to assume the roles both of linguist and of anthropologist. This means that one objective of teaching linguistics in anthropology must be to provide teachers who have this dual qualification.

Let me turn now to specific objectives of teaching those facets of language which are of special concern to anthropology. Some grouping is necessary, and I shall use ten headings: (I) Nature of Language, including common misconceptions and stereotypes; (II) Cultural Focus and Semantic Field; (III) World View; (IV) Social Structure and Personality; (V) Speech Play and Verbal Art; (VI) Processes of Change; (VII) Results of Change; (VIII) Systematic Theory; (IX) Field Work; (X) History and Delineation of the Field. As to the distribution of topics among levels of courses, from the viewpoint of a subdiscipline there seem to be three types of students. The "interested bystanders," students from other fields and anthropology students who do not require a special knowledge of linguistics, should have some overview of the Nature of language (topic I) in an introductory course, together with as much of topics II-VII as fit the capacities of the course and instructor. The "participant observers," anthropology students who do not plan to specialize in linguistic work, but who will find it helpful or essential (this would exclude only those who are not prospective fieldworkers, historical anthropologists, or contributors to general theory), should have more substantial presentation of topics I-VII, perhaps something of VIII-X as well, in a "Language and Culture" course, or distributed among topical and areal courses, as particular peoples and problems make it appropriate. On the graduate level they should certainly have something of VIII-X. The "persons-in-the-subculture," students specializing wholly or partly in linguistic work, whether domiciled within a department of anthropology or a department of languages or linguistics, should be able to organize individual counterparts of the present paper.

(I) NATURE OF LANGUAGE

An important part of anthropological teaching is combating misconceptions and stereotypes about other peoples, especially so-called "primitive" peoples, and seeking to convey an objective approach to cultural and racial differences. This applies to notions which are still widespread about so-called "primitive" languages, which supposedly eke out their limited vocabularies with gesture; which, being unwritten, supposedly change rapidly; which presumably have no or few "abstract" terms; which are perhaps even "grammarless." The teaching of anthropology must continue to raise the question—Are there languages which are primitive in any of these senses?—and show that the answer is, No. (See Boas 1911; Kroeber 1911, 1948; Sapir 1921:221-235; Strehlow 1947; Hill 1952; Beals and Hoijer 1959:566-569; Nida 1947: sections 1, 3; and the writings of Benjamin Lee Whorf 1956 *passim*.) That mistaken notions of primitive languages persist, even in some linguistic circles, is shown by Entwhistle (1949) and by remarks about primitive languages which required strong refutation from Bernard Bloch at the Seventh International Congress of Linguists in London in 1952 (Proceedings 1956:96, 392, 411; 394-396). It is necessary to continue to stress the difference between the political and the scientific importance of a speech community, pointing out that the diversity of the world's languages is an irreplaceable laboratory for understanding the nature of language and hence something of the nature of man.

The notion of primitive languages leads to questions of evolution and typology. What is the range of diversity in languages? Boas (1911: 15-43) has shown that generalizations derived wholly from European languages are inadequate in the face of the diversity of American Indian languages. His examples and those in Sapir's *Language* (1921:43-156) have been a source for many textbook writers. Sapir's chapters are a brilliant world survey, anticipated in his 1911 article, "The History and Varieties of Language" (reprinted in Fried (ed.), 1959:163-186). Sapir and Swadesh (1946) highlight diversity in obligatory categories by presenting translations of the same English sentence into five radically different languages. Whorf's articles, especially "Science and Linguistics" and "Languages and Logic," are effective. (The former has been reprinted in Maccoby, Newcomb, Hartley (eds.,) 1958, as well as in Carroll 1956.) Whorf's "A Linguistic Consideration of Thinking in Primitive Languages" (Carroll 1956:65-86) concludes with a statement of the scientific importance of the diversity of the languages of the world. Nida (1945) gives a well-organized account of how languages may differ, oriented to the translator and field worker. His books (1947; 1952) provide many examples and discussions.

Another issue is—Are there general principles and universal features within the diversity? (See below, typological classification.) In what sense are all languages equal? In what sense are some languages more highly evolved than others? In important part, these are matters of refuting misconceptions about primitive languages (*v. supra,* especially Sapir, Whorf, Beals, and Hoijer). Sapir keynoted the approach with the classic statement, "when it comes to linguistic form, Plato walks with the Macedonian swineherd, Confucius with the head-hunting savage of Assam" (1921:234).

The standard view that languages do not show evolutionary advance is presented well by Greenberg (1956:56-65, reprinted in Fried (ed.), 1959:187-198; and 1959:61-75). My view is that the concepts of evolutionary advance, adaptation, competition, etc. apply to language, and that this will come to be generally accepted (cf., Ginsberg 1939: 465; Hymes 1961c; Murdock 1959).

The difficulty here, as in so many other areas, is that a stereotyped error has been met by a refutation which has become stereotyped in turn. Many unsophisticated people still make the original error, so that to point out the inadequacy of the refutation is to seem to lend aid and comfort to an enemy; yet, unless the conventional refutation is transcended, important problems remain uninvestigated. We must discuss writing as an intrinsic part of language coordinate with speech in modern life, yet not agree with those who scorn unwritten tongues, or think speech inferior to writing. We must discuss vocabulary as an intrinsic part of language, yet not support those who misconceive languages as just collections of words and without denying the beauty and the autonomy (for some purposes) of grammatical form. When we read Sapir's *Language* today, we must remember that it was a splendid tract on behalf of grammatical form, one his age and audience needed, but in scholarly circles the battle is now won. If, as Sapir wrote, we must not confuse a language with its dictionary, neither can we afford to ignore that a language *is* in part its dictionary. We must discuss evolutionary differences among languages, such as in size and utility for science of their vocabularies (as now extant), yet not perpetuating notions of "primitive" languages without grammars, with inadequate vocabularies eked out by gesture, with no abstract terms. (See also Brown 1959:264-298.)

For this group of questions and concepts, I suggest the tag: "Diversity, Equality, Relativity." The fundamental questions here are what to make of the world's linguistic diversity and how to conceive its relation to our own language. There is evident common ground here with questions in the rest of anthropology.

All this leads into the question, What is the nature of language? One of the most important objectives is to convey an appropriate conception of the nature of language, and there are at least three good ways of doing this in an anthropological program. One is to contrast the key properties of human language with forms of communication among other species. This fits well with an approach which stresses evolutionary concepts (see Brown 1958:ch. 5; Greenberg 1956, 1959; Hockett 1958, 1959, 1960). A second way, which can be related to the first, is to consider the child's acquisition of language, stressing the remarkable nature of the new ability it acquires and contrasting this to the prelinguistic stage (see Brown 1958:ch. 6; Luria 1959; Luria and Yuovich 1959). This fits well with an approach which stresses psychocultural concepts, socialization, and the like. A third way is to focus on general concepts of descriptive linguistics, such as phoneme and morpheme (and transformation, tagmeme, and distinctive feature), perhaps in contrast to the received notions about language likely to be held by students, or in terms of a concept of language as a system, contrasting "etic" and "emic" approaches as Sapir did in "Sound Patterns in Language" (Mandelbaum (ed.) 1949:19-25; for 'etic' and 'emic,' Pike 1954:8-28). This fits well with an approach which stresses concepts of pattern and structure, and it leads most directly into further linguistic training. These three ways are not mutually exclusive. Whatever the primary approach, the concept of a language as a system, not merely a collection of words, must be somewhere included, as must some version of the distinction between language and speech (*la langue* and *la parole*). (Consult Gleason 1961; Hockett 1958; Jakobson and Halle 1956.)

(II) CULTURAL FOCUS AND SEMANTIC FIELD

I single out these two concepts because they play such a large part in anthropological interest in vocabulary and meaning and because they so directly relate language with the rest of culture, both in field work and in theory.

Since before Boas first mentioned the Eskimo words for "snow," anthropologists have taken elaboration of vocabulary as an indication of cultural inerest and have often cited it in discussion. The question here is—To what extent and in what way is a language an index of its associated culture? I should like to stress that the answer is interesting and not obvious. If a language were exactly a mirror of a culture, so that for every concept or category held by the members of the culture there were a dictionary entry, then ethnography would not merely require lexiocography but would become identical with it. Doing linguistic work would depend upon its convenience, and, if inconvenient, might be dispensed with, since the results would only be isomorphic after all with the ethnography done without its aid. In point of fact not all cultural categories and concepts are linguistically expressed. In relation to its culture a language is a sort of selective "meta-language," a cultural way of communicating about much, but not all, of the culture. Thus the question—To what extent and in what ways is a language an index of its associated culture?—should be of considerable interest. The problem relates to concepts in both a psychological and an evolutionary perspective. (See Boas 1911:21-24; 1934, especially the introduction; Evans-Pritchard 1940:41-48; Herskovits 1949:548-551; Marsh and Laughlin 1956:38-78; Sapir, "Language and Environment," in Mandelbaum (ed.), 1949:89-103 and in de Laguna (ed.), 1960:434-450.)

The concept of semantic field involves particular areas of lexicon, such as kinship, place names, color terms, and numerals. It links the structural approach of the linguist with the ethnographic interest of the anthropologist. It thus seems the best framework within which to present semantic analysis to anthropologists. The fundamental question is—To what extent and in what ways is the vocabulary of a language structured? On an advanced level, this question leads directly to current research. On an intermediate or elementary level, the question can help

disabuse students of mistaken conceptions of absolute meanings and
equivalence of meaning across languages. Under this heading could be
introduced any consideration of certain traditional linguistic areas,
such as onomastics and Wörter-und-Sachen studies. (See Conklin 1955;
Frake 1961; Haugen 1957; Malkiel 1957.)

(III) WORLD VIEW

Under this heading I intend the aspect of culture sometimes designated by such terms as world view, ethos, cultural pattern, configuration
theme, logico-meaningful integration, values. The fundamental question is—To what extent and in what ways is a language related to the
world view of those who speak it? Daniel G. Brinton included in the
study of language, besides phonology and grammar: "The determination of the psychical character of the tribe through the forms instinc-
tively adopted for the expression of its thoughts and reciprocally the
reaction exerted by those forms on the later intellectual growth of
those who are taught them as their only means of articulate expression"
(1890:37). This statement brings out the twofold nature of the question, the first aspect being that to which Dorothy Lee has addressed herself and the second aspect being prominent in some of the writings of
Benjamin Lee Whorf.

Brinton's statement has the virtue of recognizing the reciprocal relationship between language and thought as mutually shaper and shaped.
Where one strikes a balance between the two as to relative weight will
vary. The essential thing is not to forget either pole, by espousing complete linguistic determinism or by denying it completely. A conceptual
distinction important in striking a balance is that between *habitual*
and *potential* behavior. On the one hand, the potential range of perception and thought is probably pretty much the same for all men,
and speakers of a language often make new discriminations and find
linguistic expression for them. Thus, in the face of the known facts of
linguistic change, linguistic determinism cannot be absolute. On the
other hand, we would be immobilized if we tried to notice, report, or
think all possible discriminations at each moment, and we usually
rely on those habitual discriminations to which our language is
geared. Thus, a good deal of what we notice, report, and remember is
linguistically shaped, and there is historical and experimental evidence
for this (e.g., references in Hymes 1961b, pp. 324-337). It is worth noting that Whorf's major article for fellow anthropologists dealt with the
relation of language to *habitual* thought and behavior, and that some of
his trenchant statements of linguistic relativity do not in fact assert its
absoluteness but assert that its importance must be recognized if it is
to be transcended.

Sapir's views on this matter are well known. For an apparent change of view, it is interesting to compare Sapir 1921:221-235 and the posthumously published, "The Relation of American Indian Linguistics to General Linguistics" (1947), with the often-quoted opening paragraphs of "The Status of Linguistics as a Science" (Mandelbaum (ed.), 1949:160-166), and "Conceptual Categories in Primitive Languages" (1931). Boas' view, apparently consistent throughout his career, that language has some effect on culture but culture the controlling effect on language, is stated in his introduction to the *Handbook of American Indian Languages* (1911). In their early writings both Boas and Sapir stressed the likelihood of anachronism in relating grammatical patterns for an historical, developmental perspective. It is noteworthy that both Sapir (in Mandelbaum (ed.), 1949:160-166) and Whorf in Carroll (ed.) 1956:134-159) begin with *lexical* examples, and that in this article written for a professional audience and in tribute to Sapir, rather than for a lay audience, Whorf treats the connection between Hopi grammatical categories and culture as a matter of historical development and interinfluence under favorable conditions of stability.

A good summary of the development of recent interest in the problem is Hoijer (1953). The soundest and best-documented study which deals with categories and broad cultural themes is Hoijer (1951). There is a high proportion of grain among the chaff in Hoijer (ed., 1954) and two of the best chapters, Hoijer, "The Sapir-Whorf Hypothesis," and Hockett, "Chinese vs. English: An Exploration of the Whorfian Theses," are reprinted in M. Fried (ed.), 1959:219-231, 232-248. Hoijer broaches the problem of semantic characterization of a language, as does Stanley Newman, "Semantic Problems in Grammatical Systems and Lexemes" in Hoijer (ed.), 1954:82-91; Hockett focuses on the lexical level as more precisely definable. Whorf's writings are available in Carroll (ed., 1956), already cited. Some of Dorothy Lee's work is now available in a paperback, *Freedom and Culture* (1959).

On an advanced level, it is important to note that methods for the semantic characterization of a whole language have only begun to be adequately developed. As a descriptive concept which can be noncommittal regarding linguistic determinism and relativity, that of the *cognitive style* of a language might be useful (for the term and a survey, see Hymes 1961a).

(IV) SOCIAL STRUCTURE AND PERSONALITY

The fundamental questions here are: To what extent and in what ways is a language related to the social structure of those who speak it? To what extent and in what ways is a language related to the personalities of those who speak it? Whereas the preceding two headings have been concerned with language as a "countersign of thought," here it is a question of language as a "mode of action," to use Malinowski's phrases (Malinowski 1921). The key concept here is *variation*. We might adopt Whatmough's term, *selective variation,* to denote the selective use of the resources of a language in correlation with particular social institutions, social settings, groups, roles, and personalities (Bright 1960, Gleason 1955:284-300, Whatmough 1956). All this is variation, of course, regarded in terms of the ideal of a homogeneous linguistic system. From the point of view of the speech activity, it has its own structure. Linguistics has handled this area only partially, with such concepts as style, speech level, dialect, idiolect, and expressive language.

A central concept under this heading should be that of *speech functions.* Under this concept should be delineated the components of a speech situation, or speech event, which, since each can vary independently of the others, must each be taken into account. A set of such components gives a framework for analyzing, explaining, and predicting speech events, and hence for describing speech activity in relation to social structure and personality. The literature on the subject of speech functions is varied and unintegrated, and most classifications omit pertinent factors. An expansion of a classification by Roman Jakobson may prove adequate. (See Hymes 1962 for detailed analysis of the use of such a scheme.) As components of a speech situation or speech event, this scheme would distinguish (1) sender, (2) receiver, (3) code, (4) topic, (5) message form, (6) channel, as does Jakobson, and add (7) scene. As adjectives to designate the associated functions, we may use (1) expressive, (2) rhetorical or persuasive, (3) metalinguistic, (4) referential, (5) poetic, (6) channel and (7) situational or contextual. In using this classification heuristically, we ask with regard to each component what can be told about it from the speech event, or, what difference would be made if it were different while the other components were held constant.

Thus, regarding (1), the *expressive* function, what can be told about the sender of the message, from age, sex and natonality to motive and attitude toward any of the other components; what would be different about the speech event were the sender someone else? Regarding (2), the *rhetorical* function, what can be told about the receiver of the message, from age, sex, and nationality to what he or she will do in response to the message, to how he or she will perceive the other components as a consequence of the message; what would be different were the receiver someone else? Regarding (3), the *metalinguistic* function, what can we tell about the code which the speech event presupposes?

This is often the focus of the linguist and of the child or foreigner learning the language. What would be different were some other code used in the same situation? Regarding (4), the *referential* function, what can we tell about that to which the message refers; what would be different were this different? (See Brown 1958 for a fine discussion relevant to anthropology.) Regarding (5), the *poetic* function, what can we tell about the form of the message; what else would be different were it to have some other form? Here attention is drawn to the shape of the message itself and to any devices which are in fact used to draw attention to the shape, such as rhythm and choice of sounds. Regarding (6), the *channel* function, what can we tell about the channel, which may be various forms of transmission by voice, writing, or musical instrument? What else would differ if the channel were different? This may be the perspective of the communications engineer or of the anthropological analyst of speech surrogates. (See Stern 1957.) Regarding (7), the *situational* or *contextual* function, what can we tell about the setting, linguistic or extralinguistic? What else would be different about the speech event were the setting different?

We can use a scheme of speech functions heuristically in two ways. We can note features which associate with a certain function and isolate them as such: expressive and rhetorical features, features diagnostic of certain types of speakers and hearers, or speaker-hearer relations; metalinguistic devices for communicating about the code; features which have reference and features which do not; features which contribute to poetic form; features restricted to a given channel; features diagnostic of certain situations. We can also view the whole of the speech event from each function in turn, seeing the whole of it, for instance, as variously expressive of the sender.

A great deal of the material which hangs about the edges of a formal description of the structure of a language can be handled in terms of such a framework. A conceptual scheme of this kind helps bridge the gap between the linguist's description of language and the anthropologist's description of behavior of which speech is part.

An important point under this general heading is the universal importance of speech to human social life. The universality of this importance must not blind us to the variation in the role of speech in different societies and personalities. Speech is but one mode of communication and action among others, and there are few if any situations in which its use is universally necessary. Cultures differ in the value they attach to speech activity and to their language and in their conceptions of them. Societies differ in the behavior settings in which speech is required, optional, or forbidden; in the way in which speech enters into the definition and evaluation of groups and roles. Personalities differ in the way in which speech enters into the socialization process which shapes them, and in the ways in which speech is part of the expression and perception of personality. Not only are there cross-cultural differences in these things, but there are significant class differences within our own society. An important concept to convey would be that speech activity, like sex and religion, must be treated as a cross-cultural variable. (For fuller exposition, see Hymes 1961c.)

The questions to which this concept gives rise have been little investigated systematically but can be of great interest to students from many social science disciplines. Most of the literature provides examples rather than principles or generalizations, though general points or classifications or dimensions are given in most of the papers cited above. Under this general heading would come paralinguistics (Trager 1958; Danchy, Hockett, and Pittenger 1960; and references in both); some aspects of bilingualism (Haugen 1956; Weinreich 1953); some aspects of dialectology (Mc David 1946, 1948, 1952-3, reprinted in Allen (ed.), 1958; Pickford 1956); (Gumperz 1958, 1962); such topics as male and female forms of speech, honorifics, respect forms and other aspects of social variation in speech and language (Bloomfield 1927; Brown and Gilman 1960; Casagrande 1948; Emeneau 1941; Evans-Pritchard 1948; Garvin and Riesenberg 1952; Haas 1944; Martin (Ms.); Nadel 1954; Newman 1954; Sapir in Mandelbaum (ed.), 1949:206-212; on kinship terminology, see Goodenough 1956 and Lounsbury 1956); speech and personality (for general discussion and references, see Hymes 1961b); and much of what has been dubbed ethnolinguistics.

(V) SPEECH PLAY AND VERBAL ART

The fundamental question here is—To what extent and in what ways is speech manipulated for its own sake, or for the kinds of effect which the culture recognizes as play and aesthetic? Two important concepts are: (1) interest and enjoyment in speech play and verbal art, together with standards of excellence, are universal; (2) the medium of verbal art is itself already culturally structured. Thus the study of a body of verbal art must take account of the structure of the language which is its mode of existence. Here the relations between anthropology and an important part of folklore can be brought out and work on style can be introduced. On speech play, see Conklin 1956, 1959; Haas 1957. On verbal art, see Shimkin 1947, especially for variety and richness in a simple society and raconteur's activity; Emeneau 1958 for a brilliant account of the structure and functioning of an oral poetry; Lord 1960 on the characteristics of the oral poet's performance and art, especially regarding epic; Austerlitz 1958, Lévi-Strauss 1955, and Sebeok 1953, 1956, for linguistically oriented modes of analysis; Jacobs 1958 and

Propp 1958, for detailed analysis of a body of narrative; Bascom 1955, for "verbal art" as a generic concept; and Boas 1925 (collected in *Race, Language, Culture* 1940:491-502), and Radin 1955:1-28, for general treatments. Newman 1940 is a brilliant characterization of Yokuts vis-à-vis English.

(VI) PROCESSES OF CHANGE

Two fundamental questions are—How does a language change? and How is linguistic change related to cultural change? Although language change is an instance of cultural change, I know no careful working out of a conceptual scheme for cultural change that is applied as well to language. On an advanced level, an interesting test of the scope of a theory of cultural change would be such appliction to language, and, conversely, it would be interesting to find the level of generality at which concepts of linguistic change had to be formulated to apply generally to culture. On an introductory or intermediate level, many specific concepts of the processes of linguistic change are well known and can be well exemplified. Some broad concepts which might be emphasized are: (1) Linguistic change is both an instance and an index of cultural change; (2) the explanation of linguistic change must be sought partly outside of language; (3) there is a distinction between historical linguistics and language history; (4) a language adapts, evolves, and encounters evolutionary competition, both as to content (especially vocabulary and syntactical usage) and as to the range of functions it serves.

This topic should include not only the technical concepts of historical linguistics, such as sound change, analogy, and borrowing, but also the problems and concepts of language history, such as are concerned with linguistic nationalism, the development of standard languages, diglossia, problems of literacy, the use of the vernacular in fundamental education, some aspects of bilingualism and dialectology, the formation of trade jargons and creoles, and efforts toward a universal language or an international auxiliary language.

On processes of change, a general treatment relating language and the rest of culture is Hoijer 1948. For more detailed treatments, see Bloomfield 1933:369-495, Hockett 1958:365-538, Sapir 1921:157-220, Sturtevant 1947:65-168 (now in paperback). On linguistic acculturation in particular, see Casagrande 1954, 1955, Dozier 1956, Haugen 1953, Herzog 1941, Swadesh 1948. Casagrande and Haugen give general formulations and numerous references, as does Weinreich 1953. Casagrande emphasizes historical inference, Haugen the bilingual medium, Weinreich the theoretical and analytical considerations. Haas 1951 documents an interesting process of change from

several languages. On trade jargons and creoles, see Cole 1953, Hall 1955.
Reinicke 1938, Weinreich 1958, in reference to a controversy between R. Hall and D. Taylor (one which I feel is as yet unresolved).

On linguistic nationalism and the development of standard languages, see Garvin and Mathiot in Wallace (ed.), 1960:783-790; Garvin 1959 (in a symposium on "Urbanization and Standard Languages"
to which the issue is devoted); Deutsch 1953; Ferguson 1959a, 1959b;
Bloomfield 1933, Ch. 3: 4-10, 19, 27: 4-6; and Unesco's *The Use of Vernacular Languages in Education* (a valuable document which should
be reprinted).

On international languages, Jespersen 1928; and Sapir in Mandelbaum (ed.), 1949:110-121, represent the two outstanding linguist proponents, whereas reviews by Martinet (of Interlingua-English; Interlingua) 1952 and McQuown (of H. Jacog, A Planned Auxiliary Language) 1950 present the criticisms and reservations of most linguists today. Jespersen's book is also a stimulating history; see also Jacob 1950,
and Guerard 1922. The movement for an international auxiliary language continues to be active, with new plans, studies, and scattered successes in scientific and practical sectors, but no survey is available.

(VII) RESULTS OF CHANGE

A fundamental question here is—What contribution does linguistics
make to the rest of historical anthropology? We can outline two kinds
of useful results, "chronicle" and "content." Under the concept of
"chronicle" is included showing the fact of an historical connection
between two linguistic groups, estimating the time depth of the connection and inferring the likely place of the connection. Such work
might be illustrated with the fact that Navaho, Hupa, and Chippewyan
are related with certain other languages in the Athapaskan family, that
their common ancestor was probably spoken something like 2,500
years ago, and that this was probably somewhere in the vicinity of far
northwestern Canada. Or it might be shown that "wine" was borrowed
by English speakers from Latin, and that this must have been before
the invasion of the British Isles, and hence somewhere in the northern
part of the continent of Europe.) The comparative method, reconstruction, lexicostatistics, and glottochronology, family tree vs. wave theory principles of interpretation, inference of homeland from language
distributions or reconstructed vocabulary, and questions of "substra-
tum" belong here if they have not already been treated with processes
of change.

Under the concept of "content" comes the information about the
culture history and past cultural inventory of speakers of a language
which can be inferred from loanwords, innovations, and reconstruction

of the vocabulary of the proto-language. This can lead to a conceptual model which is shared by all of historical anthropology. The fundamental question is—How are resemblances and differences (among historical units such as cultures, races, languages) to be interpreted? The answer involves distinguishing four kinds of source for resemblances and relating these to three kinds of classification of the units which show resemblances.

Resemblances are either due to an historical connection or not. Resemblances which are not due to historical connection may be *generic* (inherent in all units within the frame of analysis) or *convergent* (due to chance or some recurrent tendency such as sound-symbolism). Resemblances due to historical connection may be *genetic*, transmitted continuously from a period of a common ancestor, or *diffusional*, transmitted from one unit to another subsequent to any period of a common ancestor. This is a conception of resemblances as a sort of tree with branching choice-points, since we often proceed by successively sorting out, first, the historical from the non-historical resemblances, and, second, the genetic from the diffusional resemblances, because genetic classification is fundamental to other historical work.

This brings us to the three kinds of classification. A *genetic classification* considers only resemblances due to a genetic historical connection, without regard to proximity in space or time. An *areal* classification considers resemblances due to either kind of historical connection, and with regard to proximity in space and time. A *typological* classification considers selected resemblances, without regard either to historical connection or proximity in space and time. However, the latter kinds of consideration enter into typological classification if it seeks a representative sample.

As indicated, such a conceptual model relates linguistic work to kinds of problems in other branches of anthropology. On an advanced level, it might be considered how the methods pertinent to each branch are used and grounded, in order to understand how the results of data gathering and analysis in each branch depend on these, and in order to explore resemblances and differences in the underlying logic of the methods. This would facilitate unifying historical anthropology, both in the integration of results and in the integration of concepts.

Anthropologists usually desire graduate students to know the results of genetic classification for their area of specialization in some detail and all students to know the broad outlines of genetic classification for the languages of the world. Outline information is readily available in a number of textbooks, of which Gleason 1955:350-372 may be specially cited. Detailed information on an area of the world requires research or consultation with a specialist, since in most areas of anthropological interest the genetic classification is controversial and in course of development. As to the other modes of classification, beginning students and non-majors may perhaps best be left with a sense of the ordering power of genetic classification and the regularities on which it is based, together with an awareness of the nature of areal and typological classification, and a realization that the significance of these latter two modes is likely to increase. If concrete illustrations are desired, Emeneau 1956 is excellent for areal relationship, Greenberg 1954 (perhaps supplemented by Kroeber 1960) for typological indices. In using and evaluating genetic classifications, it is wise to distinguish between *proof* and *establishment*. To prove a relationship is to rule out chance and borrowing as sources of resemblances, showing that genetic connection is the only probable explanation. Often the amount of data and/or research permits no more than such an affirmation of the fact of relationship. To esbalish a relationship is to provide the systematic and detailed analysis of resemblances which can be the basis for such contributions as time depth, reconstruction of vocabulary, etc. Scholars differ as to where to draw the line between establishment and proof. The job of establishment is never complete, as continuing Indo-European work attests.

As general discussions of this topic, see especially Greenberg in Kroeber (ed.), 1953:265-286; Sapir 1921:211-235; and Swadesh 1959.

On fact of relationship, there has been an American anthropological literature of increasing interest and importance. Of contributions concerned with method and principles, note Greenberg, cited above, and 1956:35-45; Hymes 1959; Lamb 1959; McQuown 1955:501-511, 556-566; Swadesh 1951 reprinted in Fried (ed.), 1959:199-218.

On establishment, see Bloomfield, Sapir, Sturtevant, and Hockett, as cited in VI above, and Gleason 1915:333-349; Hockett 1948; Sapir in Mandelbaum (ed.), 1949:73-82.

On time perspective and time depth, see Hymes 1960; Sapir in Mandelbaum (ed.), 1949:389-462. On inference of homeland from language distributions, see Dyen 1956, or the explication by Diebold 1959; from reconstructed vocabulary, see Thieme, "The Comparative Method in Linguistics," (to be in Hymes (ed.), *Reader in Linguistic Anthropology* (Ms.). On reconstruction of cultural vocabulary, see Swadesh 1959, cited above Thieme, just cited; and Sapir in Mandelbaum (ed.), 1949:213-224.

On areal classification, see Emeneau 1956; Trubetskoy 1949:343-350; Voegelin 1945. On typological classification, see Boas 1911:74-82; Greenberg 1954:192-200, 1956:86-94, and 1957:68-77; Hockett 1954; Sapir 1921:127-156; Ullmann 1953.

The remaining topics (VIII, IX, X) are primarily for graduate instruction, since they assume professional commitment on the student's part.

(VIII) SYSTEMATIC THEORY

There has been much interest in the extension or generalization of linguistic methodology to other aspects of culture. Except to mention its existence and importance, this topic is best reserved for students with a good background in anthropology or linguistics, preferably both. [The principal references include Goodenough 1951:51-64 and 1957 in Garvin (ed.), 1957:167-173; Kluckhohn 1958, 1959; Lévi-Strauss 1945, 1957; Pike 1954, 1955, 1956, 1960; Uldall 1957; Hall 1959.]

Interest in the writings in this area comes most readily to students who have experienced the operation of linguistic method, or have been persuasively exposed to its results. In an anthropological context the teaching of linguistic operations has a value beyond that of practical application to language data, for knowledge of such operations is proving to be the main avenue of entry into general anthropology for certain logical and qualitative methods of analysis of restricted sets of data. As usually taught in the United States and England, linguistic operations are a paradigm of the inference of structure, pattern, and system from raw data. It is a paradigm which it is difficult to communicate except through the experience of performing the operations themselves and of reflecting on the alternative modes of structuring that the data and operations permit. All the writings above have value for the student of anthropology, but perhaps the best introduction to the extension of linguistic operations comes from the recent work in areas of vocabulary, such as Conklin 1955 (color terms), Frake 1961 (disease terms), Haugen 1957 (orientation terms), Joos 1958 senses of a single term), and the work in kinship, especially that of Goodenough 1956, Lounsbury 1956, and the discussion of it in relation to an anthropological theory of meaning by Wallace and Atkins 1960 and Wallace 1961.

(IX) FIELD WORK

In field work the prime questions which guide the linguistic training of prospective ethnographers are—How to collect verbal data accurately? How to organize it usefully? How to find out meanings? In most texts and courses the objectives and the correlated concepts are in what I would call the middle range. They presuppose the collection of the data, but do not get to the handling of dictionaries, tests, and meanings. But the anthropological field worker faces first the task of making an accurate record, and then of dealing with this record not only as raw material for a grammar but also as cultural information. Here I would like to cite Pike's *Phonemics* (1947) for its practical advice on phonet-

ic mastery, and Nida's *Morphology* (1949) for its practical advice on
getting and handling meanings. These objectives are not now in the forefront of linguistic discussion, and appropriate concepts are discussed only
here and there in the literature. As general intellectual equipment of the
anthropologist in this regard, three conceptual points can be singled
out. The first is the distinction Hockett calls *gathering* vs. *collation*
(Hockett 1958:102-111). The anthropologist should know that for
his field work needs, success in the gathering stage may suffice, and
so he need not be inhibited into linguistic inactivity by uncertainties
which properly pertain to collation. That is, if he discovers that /p/ and
/b/ contrast initially in forms such as /pil/:/bil/, but there is not a contrast among labial stops after initial /s/-in a form such as /spil/, then
he can make an adequate record. He need not decide definitively whether the second unit in /spil/ is to be interpreted as /p/, /b/, an archi-
phoneme /P/, or part of the intersection of a voicing-irrelevant sequence /SP/ and a voiceless component.

The second point is that an anthropological conception of the description of a language is threefold—grammar, texts, and dictionary—
and that the training of anthropologists for linguistic work must deal
with all three. (Sapir 1930-1931 is the outstanding American example.
On method, see Garvin 1955, Nida 1958, and other references in
Hymes 1959b.) This threefold conception goes back at least to Schlei-
cher's pioneer field work in Lithuanian a century ago but sometimes
is lost sight of.

The third point is that semantic description is part of linguistic description. This point need not follow from the second, since texts might
be obtained only to check the distribution of forms and dictionary be
treated as a residual list of forms and glosses. The anthropologist's concern with language as part of culture, or with learning a language as
a tool for cultural investigation, requires careful semantic description.
And insofar as the linguistic material obtained by an anthropologist is
to serve historical linguistics, semantic detail for as much of the lexicon
as possible is invaluable, e.g., it may provide the crucial links in etymol-
ogies. [See also sections II, VIII (end).]

(X) HISTORY AND DELINEATION OF THE FIELD

Within a general program, there must be a place for the history of anthropology and of the study of language as part of it. The subject is
too little studied for there to be a standard source on which to draw.
Yet at least in graduate instruction some answer should be considered
to certain fundamental questions.

The first question is simply—What has been linguistic anthropology? Here a roster of names may help, from Gallatin, Hale, Gatschet,

Brinton, and Powell, through Boas, Lowie, Radin, Sapir, and Kroeber, to contemporaries. The second question is—Why is the study of language a part of anthropology? I would suggest that in an historical answer, the reasons fall into three broad categories: culture history, field work, and theory. As to historical perspective, language classification was early seized upon for the ordering of ethnological data (e.g., Powell 1891; Swanton and Dixon 1914; cf. Kroeber 1905). The results of historical linguistics have always been of interest in anthropology (e.g., Kroeber 1941) and the work itself continues to attract younger anthropologists (e.g., Burling 1959; Goodenough, Ms.). With regard to field work, the published arguments have not been whether, but how best, to use language. Whatever their differences on other points, Boas and Sapir, Malinowski, Kluckhohn, Herskovits, and Nadel have all agreed that linguistic control is essential in field work (see Hymes 1959b) and, as is well known, some problems are scientifically unapproachable except with the aid of linguistics (e.g., folk science, narrative style, person perception—anything to which authentic texts or native verbal behavior is essential). With regard to theory, it is of course always true that if language is part of culture, then culture theory must somehow apply to and account for language. The degree of active interest in this truth has varied more than interest in the linguistic aspects of historical anthropology and field work (cf. especially Boas 1911; Goodenough 1957; Kluckhohn 1959, 267 ff.; Lévi-Strauss 1945; Pike 1954).

Let me consider here why the history of anthropology is a vital part of the teaching of anthropology, with reference to its linguistic component. One practical reason is that the history of one's field plays an ideological role in current disputes, so that knowledge of it is essential to balanced judgment. Recent discussions of Boas sometimes miss the mark by overlooking the major role that linguistic work had in his career. A second reason is that continuity and cumulativeness are desirable in a science. This is possible only if we have and inculcate historical perspective, if we show the concern for the history of our field that we hope others will show when we have become part of it. A third reason is economy of effort. A good many things turn out to be new bottles for old wine. If it had been remembered that the problems posed by Whorf go back in American linguistic anthropology through Boas and Brinton to von Humboldt, then we might have a record of steady contribution to their understanding, instead of neglect, then flaring of interest, then again neglect. We tend to be intolerant of our own profession past, just as some of us are sympathetic to every religion but Christianity. But we ought to be able to judge our predecessors in their own context, as we judge the Eskimo or Trobrianders. And doing so may lead inquiry back to roots in American culture, when we recall that some of the questions asked in linguistic anthropology were once posed by Jefferson, Gallatin, and Thoreau (see Hallowell 1960:17, 25-30).

In the teaching of linguistic anthropology, as in the study of it, there is an embarrassment of riches and a poverty of organization. Kroeber's counsel is appropriate, when he observes in some of his last papers, that:

I feel that the study of both culture and language is in crying need, in its own right, of far more systematic classification of their multifarious phenomena. Perhaps we have had a surplus of bright ideas and a shortage of consistent ordering and comparison of our data. (1960a:17)

Also:

The situation is made more difficult by the fact that anthropologists still tend to value personal expertise, technical virtuosity, cleverness in novelty, and do not yet clearly recognize the fundamental value of the humble but indispensable task of classifying—that is, structuring—our body of knowledge, as biologists did begin to recognize it two hundred years ago. (1960:14)

The organization of the present paper represents a stage in my own efforts to structure anthropology's investment in the study of language. I hope that it may assist the efforts of others.

REFERENCES CITED

AUSTERLITZ, ROBERT
    1958   Ob-Ugric metrics. Finnish Academy of Sciences. Helsinki, FF Communications 174.

BASCOM, WILLIAM
    1955   Verbal art. Journal of American Folklore 68:245-252.

BEALS, RALPH L., AND HARRY HOIJER
    1959   An introduction to anthropolgy. New York, Macmillan Company.

BLOOMFIELD, LEONARD
    1927   Literate and illiterate speech. American Speech 2:432-439.
    1933   Language. New York, Henry Holt.

BOAS, FRANZ
    1911   Handbook of American Indian languages. Smithsonian Institution. Washington, BAE-B 40, part I.
    1925   Stylistic aspects of primitive literature. Journal of American Folklore 38:329-339.
    1934   Geographical names of the Kwakiutl. Columbia University Publications in Anthropology 20.

BRINTON, DANIEL G.
    1890   Essays of an Americanist. Philadelphia.

BROWN, ROGER W.
    1956   Language and categories. Appendix to J. S. Bruner, J. Goodnow, G. A. Austin, A Study of Right Thinking. New York, Wiley.
    1958   Words and things. Glencoe, Free Press.

BROWN, ROGER W., AND ALBERT GILMAN
  1960   The pronouns of power and solidarity. *In* Style in language, T. A. Sebeok, ed. New York, John Wiley.
BURLING, ROBBINS
  1959   Proto-Bodo. Language 35:433-453.
CARROLL, JOHN B.
  1956   Language, thought, and reality: selected writings of Benjamin Lee Whorf. New York and Cambridge, John Wiley and The Technology Press, M.I.T.
CASAGRANDE, JOSEPH B.
  1948   Comanche baby language. International Journal of American Linguistics 14:11-14.
  1954-55 Comanche linguistic acculturation. International Journal of American Linguistics 20:140-51, 20:217-237, 21:8-25.
COLE, DESMOND T.
  1953   Fanagalo and the Bantu languages in South Africa. African Studies 12:1-9.
CONKLIN, HAROLD
  1955   Hanunoo color categories. *In* Selected writings of Edward Sapir. D. Mandelbaum, ed. Berkeley and Los Angeles, University of California Press.
  1956   Tagalog speech disguise. Language 32:136-139.
  1959   Linguistic play in its cultural setting. Language 35:631-636.
DANEHY, J. J., C. F. HOCKETT, AND R. E. PITTENGER
  1960   The first five minutes. Ithaca, New York, Paul Martineau.
DEUTSCH, KARL
  1953   Nationalism and social communication. New York.
DIEBOLD, A. WHITNEY, JR.
  1959   Determining the centers of dispersal of language groups. International Journal of American Linguistics 26:1-10.
DOZIER, EDWARD
  1956   Two examples of linguistic acculturation. Language 32:146-157.
DYEN, ISIDORE
  1956   Language distribution and migration theory. Language 32:611-626.
EMENEAU, MURRAY B.
  1941   Language and social forms: a study of Toda kinship terms and dual descent. *In* Language, culture and personality: essays in memory of Edward Sapir. L. Spier, A. I. Hallowell and S. S. Newman, eds. Menasha, Banta.
  1956   India as a linguistic area. Language 32:3-16.
  1958   Oral poets of South India—the Todas. Journal of American Folklore 7:312-324.
ENTWHISTLE, W. J.
  1949   Pre-grammar? Archivum Linguisticum 1:117-125.
EVANS-PRITCHARD, E.E.
  1940   The Nuer. London, Oxford.
  1948   Nuer modes of address. The Uganda Journal 12:166-171.
FERGUSON, CHARLES
  1959a   Diglossia. Word 15:325-340.
  1959b   The Arabic Koine. Language 35:616-630.

FRAKE, CHARLES O.
    1961   The diagnosis of disease among the Subanun. American Anthropologist 63:113-132.

FRIED, MORTON
    1959   Readings in anthropology. New York, Thomas Y. Crowell.

GARVIN, PAUL
    1956   Problems in American Indian lexicography and text edition, Anais doXXXI Congo. Internacional de Americanistas (São Paulo), 1,013-1,028.
    1957   Report of the seventh annual round table meeting on linguistics and language study. Washington, Georgetown University.
    1959   The standard language problem: concepts and methods. Anthropological Linguistics 1:28-31.

GARVIN, PAUL, AND MADELEINE MATHIOT
    1960   The Urbanization of the Guarani language. *In* Men and cultures, selected papers of the Fifth International Congress of Anthropological and Ethnological Sciences, A. F. C. Wallace, ed. Philadelphia, University of Pennsylvania Press.

GARVIN, PAUL, AND SAUL RIESENBERG
    1952   Respect behavior on Ponape: an ethnolinguistic study. American Anthropologist 54:201-220.

GINSBERG, MORRIS
    1939   The problems and methods of sociology. *In* The study of society. F. Bartlett *et al.*, eds. London, Routledge

GLEASON, H.A., JR.
    1955   An introduction to descriptive linguistics. New York, Holt.
    1961   2d edition of 1955.

GOODENOUGH, WARD
    1951   Property, kin and community on Truk. Yale University Publications in Anthropology No. 46.
    1956   Componential analysis and the study of meaning. Language 32:195-216.
    1957   Cultural anthropology and linguistics. *In* Report of the Seventh Annual Round Table Meeting on Linguistics and Language Study, P. Garvin, ed. Washington, Georgetown University.
    1960   Paper on historical phonology of Nakanai, presented at annual meeting, Association for Asian Studies, New York City, April.

GREENBERG, JOSEPH
    1953   Historical linguistics and unwritten languages. *In* Anthropology Today, Kroeber *et al.*, eds.
    1954   A quantitative approach to the morphological typology of language. *In* Method and perspective in anthropology. R. Spencer, ed. Minneapolis, University of Minnesota Press.
    1956   Essays in linguistics. New York, Wenner-Gren Foundation on Anthropological Research, Viking Fund Publications in Anthropology, 24. University of Chicago Press.
    1957   The nature and use of linguistic typologies. International Journal of American Linguistics 23:68-77.
    1959   Language and evolution. *In* Evolution and anthropology: a centennial appraisal. Washington, Anthropological Society of Washington.

GUERARD, ALBERT
  1922   A short history of the international language movement. London.
GUMPERZ, JOHN J.
  1958   Dialect differences and social stratification in a North Indian village.
          American Anthropologist 60:668-682.
HAAS, MARY R.
  1944   Men's and women's speech in Koasati. Language 20:142-149.
  1951   Interlingual word taboo. American Anthropologist 53:338-344.
  1957   Thai word games. Journal of American Folklore 70:173-175.
HALL, EDWARD
  1959   The silent language. New York, Doubleday.
HALL, ROBERT A., JR.
  1955   Hands off pidgin English. Sydney.
HALLOWELL, A. IRVING
  1960   The beginnings of anthropology in America. In selected papers from
          the American Anthropologist 1888-1920, F. de Laguna, ed. Evanston,
          Row, Peterson.
HAUGEN, EINAR
  1953   The Norwegian language in America. 2 vols. Philadelphia.
  1956   Bilingualism in the Americas: a bibliography and research guide.
          American Dialect Society 26. Alabama, University of Alabama Press.
  1957   The semantics of Icelandic orientation. Word 13:447-460.
HERSKOVITS, MELVILLE
  1949   Man and his works. New York, Alfred A. Knopf.
HERZOG, GEORGE
  1941   Culture change and language change: shifts in the Pima vocabulary.
          In Language, culture, personality, L. Spier, A. I. Hallowell, S. S. New-
          man, eds. Menasha, Banta.
HILL, ARCHIBALD A.
  1952   A note on primitive languages. International Journal of Linguistics
          18:172-177.
HOCKETT, CHARLES F.
  1948   Implications of Bloomfields's Algonquian studies. Languages 24:117-
          131. Reprinted in Readings in Linguistics, M. Joos, ed. Washington,
          American Council of Learned Societies, 1957.
  1954   A manual of phonology. Indiana University Publications in Anthro-
          pology and Linguistics, 11.
  1958   A course in modern linguistics. New York, Macmillan.
  1959   Animal "languages" and human language. In The evolution of man's
          capacity for culture, J. N. Spuhler, ed. Detroit, Wayne State Univer-
          sity Press.
  1960   The origin of speech. Scientific American 203:89-96 (September).
HOIJER, HARRY
  1948   Linguistic and cultural change. Language 24:335-345.
  1951   Cultural implications of some Navaho linguistic categories. Language
          27:111-120.
  1953   The relation of language to culture. In Anthropology Today.
  1954   Language in culture. ed. Chicago, University of Chicago Press.
HYMES, DELL H.
  1959a   Genetic classification: retrospect and prospect. Anthropological Lin-
          guistics 1:2.50-66.

1959b   Fieldwork in linguistics and anthropology (Bibliography). Studies in Linguistics 14:82-91.

1960   Lexicostatistics so far. Current Anthropology 1:3-43.

1961a   On typology of cognitive styles in language. Anthropological Linguistics 3:1.22-54.

1961b   Linguistic aspects of cross-cultural personality study. *In* Studying personality cross-culturally, Bert Kaplan, ed. Evanston, Row, Peterson.

1961c   Functions of speech: an evolutionary approach. *In* Anthropology and education, Fred Gruber ed. Philadelphia, University of Pennsylvania Press.

1962   The Ethnography of speaking. *In* Anthropology and human behavior, T. Gladwin, ed. Washington, D.C., Anthropological Society of Washington.

Ms.   Reader in linguistic anthropology. New York, Harper and Row.

JACOBS, MELVILLE

1958   The content and style of an oral literature. New York, Chicago, Viking Fund Publication in Anthropology 26, University of Chicago Press.

JAKOBSON, ROMAN, AND MORRIS HALLE

1956   Fundamentals of language. 's -Gravenhage Mouton.

JESPERSEN, OTTO

1928   An international language. London.

JOOS, MARTIN

1958   Semology: a linguistic theory of meaning. Studies in Linguistics 13: 53-70.

KLUCKOHN, CLYDE

1958   The scientific study of values. University of Toronto Installation Lectures/1958.

1959   Common humanity and diverse cultures. *In* The human meaning of the social sciences, D. Lerner, ed. New York, Meridian Books.

KROEBER, ALFRED L.

1905   Systematic nomenclature in ethnology. American Anthropologist 7:579-593.

1911   The languages of the American Indians. The Popular Science Monthly 78:500-515.

1941   Some relations of linguistics and ethnology. Language 17:287-291.

1960a   Statistics, Indo-European and Tasconomy. Language 36:1-21.

1960b   Evolution, history, and culture. *In* Evolution after Darwin, S. Tax, ed., Chicago, vol. 2.

KROEBER, ALFRED L., *et. al.*

1953   Anthropology today. Chicago, University of Chicago Press.

LAMB, SYDNEY M.

1959   Some proposals for linguistic taxonomy. Anthropological Linguistics 1:2.33-49.

LEE, DOROTHY

1959   Freedom and culture. Spectrum Book Co. (paper). Englewood Cliffs, New Jersey, Prentice Hall.

LÉVI-STRAUSS, CLAUDE

1945   *L'analyse structurale en linguistique et en anthropologie.* Word 1:2.1-21.

1955   The structural study of myth. Journal of American Folklore 68:428-444.

1957   *Anthropologie structurale.* Paris, Plon.

LORD, ALBERT

1960   The singer of tales. Cambridge, Harvard University Press.

LOUNSBURY, FLOYD G.

1956   A semantic analysis of the Pawnee kinship usage. Language 32:158-194.

LURIA, A. R.

1959   The directive function of speech. Word 15:341-352.

LURIA, A. R. AND F. IA. YUOVICH

1959   Speech and the development of mental processes in the child. London, Staples Press.

MALINOWSKI, BRONISLAW

1921   Meaning in primitive languages. Appendix A to The Meaning of Meaning, C. K. Ogden and I. A. Richards. London, Kegan Paul. (Variously reprinted).

MALKIEL, Y.

1957   Review of Herculano de Carvalho, Coisas e palavras. Language 33:54-73.

Ms.   Distinctive traits of Romance linguistics. *In* Reader in linguistic anthropology, D. Hymes, ed.

MANDELBAUM, DAVID (ED.)

1949   Selected writings of Edward Sapir. Berkeley and Los Angeles, University of California Press.

MARSH, GORDON H., AND WILLIAM S. LAUGHLIN

1956   Human anatomical terms among the Aleutian Islanders. *In* Selected writings of Edward Sapir, D. Mandelbaum, ed. Berkeley, Los Angeles, University of California Press, 12:38-78.

MARTIN, SAMUEL

Ms.   Speech levels and Social structure in Japan and Korea.

MARTINET, ANDRÉ

1952   Interlingua. Word 8:163-167.

MCDAVID, RAVEN I., JR.

1946   Dialect geography and social science problems. Social Forces 225:168-172.

1948   Postvocalic /r/ in South Carolina: a social analysis. American Speech 23:194-203.

1952-3   Some social differences in pronunciation. Language Learning 4:102-116.

McQUOWN, NORMAN

1950   A planned auxiliary language. Language 26:175-185.

1955   Indigenous languages of native America. American Anthropologist 57:501-570.

MURDOCK, GEORGE P.

1959   Evolution in social organization. *In* Evolution and anthropology: a centennial appraisal. Anthropological Society of Washington. Washington: 126-143.

NADEL, S. F.

1954   Morality and language among the Nupe. Man 54:55-57.

NEWMAN, STANLEY S.
1940   Linguistic aspects of Yokuts narrative style. *In* Yokuts and Western
            Mono myths, A. H. Gayton and S. S. Newman, eds. University of
            California Publications, Anthropological Records 5:1-110. Reprinted
            in The California Indian, R. Heizer, ed.
1954   Vocabulary levels: Zuni sacred and slang usage.
            Southwestern Journal of Anthropology 11:345-354.

NIDA, EUGENE A.
1945   Linguistics and ethnology in translation problems. Word 1:194-208.
1947   Bible translating: an analysis of principles and procedures, with spe-
            cial reference to aboriginal languages. New York, American Bible
            Society.
1947   Linguistic interludes, sections 1, 3. Glendale, California, Summer In-
            stitute of Linguistics.
1949   Morphology. Ann Arbor, University of Michigan Press.
1952   God's word in man's language. New York, Harper.
1958   Analysis of meaning and dictionary making. International Journal of
            American Linguistics 24:279-292.

PICKFORD, G. R.
1956   American dialect geography: a sociological appraisal. Word 12:211-
            233.

PIKE, KENNETH L.
1947   Phonemics. Ann Arbor, University of Michigan Press.
1954   Language in relation to a unified theory of the structure of human
            behavior, Part I. Glendale, Summer Institute of Linguistics.
1955   Language in relation to a unified theory of the structure of human
            behavior, Part II. Glendale, Summer Institute of Linguistics.
1959   Language in relation to a unified theory of the structure of human
            behavior, Part III. Glendale, Summer Institute of Linguistics.
1956   Towards a theory of the structure of human behavior. *In Estudios
            Antropologicos publicados en homenaje al doctor Manuel Gamio.*
            Mexico, D.F.

POWELL, JOHN WESLEY
1891   Indian linguistic families north of Mexico. 7th Annual Report,
            Bureau of [American] Ethnology. Washington, Smithsonian Institu-
            tion.

PROCEEDINGS, VII INTERNATIONAL CONGRESS OF LINGUISTICS
1956   London.

PROPP, V.
1958   Morphology of the folktale, Indiana University Research Center in
            Anthropology, Folklore, and Linguistics No. 10. International Jour-
            nal of Linguistics 24.4.

RADIN, PAUL
1955   The literature of primitive peoples. Diogenes 12:1-28.

REINICKE, JOHN
1938   Trade jargons and Creole dialects as marginal languages. Social
            Forces 17:107-118.

ROBINS, R. H.
1959   Linguistics and anthropology. Man 59:175-178.

SAPIR, EDWARD
1921   Language. New York, Harcourt, Brace.

1930-31   The Southern Paiute language. A Shoshonean language: texts of the
          Kaibab Paiutes and Uintah Utes: Southern Paiute dictionary. *In*
          Proceedings, American Academy of Arts and Sciences 65:1.1-296;
          2.297-356, 3.537-730, Boston.

1947   The relation of American Indian linguistics to general linguistics,
          Southwestern Journal of Anthropology 3:1-4.

SAPIR, EDWARD, AND M. SWADESH

1946   American Indian grammatical categories. Word 2:103-112.

SEBEOK, THOMAS A.

1953   Structure and content of Cheremis charms. Anthropos 48:369-388.

1956   Sound and meaning in a Cheremis folksong text. For Roman Jakob-
          son 430-439. 's-Gravenhage, Mouton.

1960   Style in language. New York, Cambridge, John Wiley and The
          Technology Press, M. I .T.

SHIMKIN, DIMITRI B.

1947   Wind river Shoshone literary forms. Journal Washington Academy
          of Sciences 37:329-352.

SPIER, LESLIE, ALFRED IRVING HALLOWELL, AND STANLEY S. NEWMAN

1941   Language, culture, and personality: essays in memory of Edward
          Sapir. Menasha, Banta.

STERN, THEODORE

1957   Drum and whistle "languages": an analysis of speech surrogates.
          American Anthropologist 59:487-506.

STREHLOW, T. G. H.

1947   Aranda traditions. Melbourne, Melbourne University Press.

STURTEVANT, EDGAR L.

1947   An introduction to linguistic science. New Haven, Yale University
          Press.

SWADESH, MORRIS

1948   Sociologic notes on obsolescent languages. International Journal of
          American Linguistics 14:226-235.

1951   Diffusional cumulation and archaic residue as historical explana-
          tions. *In* Southwestern Journal of Anthropology 7:1-21.

1959   Linguistics as an instrument of prehistory. Southwestern Journal of
          Anthropology 15:10-35.

SWANTON, JOHN R., AND ROLAND B. DIXON

1914   Primitive American history. American Anthropologist 16:376-412.

TRAGER, GEORGE L.

1958   Paralinguistics: a first approximation. Studies in Linguistics 13:1-12.

1959   The systematization of the Whorf hypothesis. Anthropological Lin-
          guistics 1:31-35.

TRUBETSKOY, NICOLAI

1949   Phonologie et geographie linguistique: *In* Principes de phonologie.
          Paris.

ULDALL, HANS

1957   Outline of glossematics, Part I. Copenhagen, Nordisk Sprog- og
          Kulturforlag.

ULLMAN, STEPHEN

1953   Descriptive semantics and linguistic typology. Word 9:225-240.

VOEGELIN, CHARLES F.

1945   Influence of area in American Indian linguistics. Word 1:54-58.

WALLACE, ANTHONY F. C.
    1961   The psychic unity of human groups. *In* Studying personality cross-
              culturally, B. Kaplan, ed. Evanston, Row Peterson.
WALLACE, ANTHONY F. C., AND T. ATKINS
    1960   The meaning of kinship terms. American Anthropologist 62:58-88.
WAX, MURRAY
    1956   The limitations of Boas' anthropology. American Anthropologist
              58:63-74.
WEINREICH, URIEL
    1953   Languages in contact. New York. Linguistic Circle of New York.
    1958   On the compatability of genetic relationship and convergent devel-
              opment. Word 14:374-379.
WHATMOUGH, JOSHUA
    1956   Language: a modern synthesis. London, New York, Secker & War-
              burg, St. Martin's Press.

FLOYD G. LOUNSBURY

Methods and
Course
Progression

THE COMMENTS which are set down here pertain to two topics: (1) some principles of general applicability (not restricted to linguistics) which may determine strategy in the conduct of a course, and (2) the goals of certain types of courses in linguistics.

Some of these comments may appear dogmatic and opinionated. If this is so, I shall have to confess to holding my opinions strongly. But they are not, I feel, based solely on whimsy or private prejudices. A certain amount of experience in teaching—some of it floundering, some of it incorporating deliberate experimentation—lies behind them.

ON METHOD: SOME GENERAL CONSIDERATIONS

The Priority of Depth Over Breadth

There is wide disagreement on this question. Many hold that breadth should come before depth, that one should attain a wide general knowledge before focusing on a single field, and that one should have a general view of the field before going deeply into one aspect of it. Applied to curriculum this results in the proliferation of "survey" courses that skim shallowly over a wide range of presumably (but not always apparently) interrelated subject matter. It even results, in some universities with which I am acquainted, in "interdisciplinary" courses for undergraduates before they have attained any technical competence whatever in any single branch of one discipline. These supposedly make a student "broad" rather than "narrow." They ward off, it is said, the undesirable effects of early specialization. One thing is sure: they delay the acquisition of technical skills.

I am an extreme partisan of the opposite point of view. The programs to inculcate breadth at the expense of depth, as I have seen them, accomplish little more than to encourage amateurishness. At worst—and this is often—they breed bewilderment and discouragement. The objects of science are not such that they can be apprehended by the bird's-eye-view method. I do not believe that their "totality" can be grasped without some mastery of their details. Professions to the contrary, it seems to me, are delusion or pretense. I believe that one who has mastered one small part of a subject is in a better position to grasp something of the nature of the whole than is one who looks at the whole without any such firmly established roots and vantage point within it.

To the extent that the conceptual tools and analytic methods appropriate to one specialty within a field bear any similarity to those applicable in another part of the same field, this position is surely tenable. A mastery of those in one area gives the student at least some basis for insight into the problems of another related area. Again, to the extent that the phenomena (and data) of one area have some kind of relevance to those of another area, this position is also defensible.

Breadth is essential and certainly should not be lost sight of as a goal in education. I believe, however, that it is most effectively achieved when there are points of depth to work out from. We are concerned with how we may best help our students to attain it, without superficiality, from the courses and other forms of instruction which we make available to them. Placing a primary importance on depth and technical mastery in a special area does not necessarily prejudice the attainment of breadth. Rather, it may assist it.

The Importance of the Experience of Discovery

A course which is to cover a certain syllabus of material may tend toward one or another of two quite different methods of procedure. I have seen examples of each type. At the one extreme are those conceived of, we might say, as a "Gray Line tour" through the points of scenic and historic interest in a given area. At the other extreme are those conceived of more as an "expedition," setting out to explore a *terra incognita,* with high hopes of discovery. Of the latter type, I should add, I have seen some succeed and some flounder. As between the two types however—the "tour" or the "expedition"—the latter can be by far the more rewarding experience.

There is no substitute for the experience of discovering things for oneself. Knowledge and understanding gained in this way are more deeply lodged, more highly prized, and more readily available for future use.

Of course we must reckon with the cumulative aspect of science. The student cannot recapitulate, by personal rediscovery, the whole development of a science or even the content of a normal course syllabus. A large part of it must inevitably be accepted at second hand. But whenever an instructor has the opportunity for a choice between (a) presenting results cut and dried or (b) setting the stage and preparing the student to discover these results for himself, the choice, I believe, should be the latter.

It is especially important that the student be led to the crucial concepts of a discipline by this route. Even the acceptance of completely formulated results can be made to seem like a fresh discovery if the student has been permitted to work his own way at least part way along the path of discovery that leads to them. Then, when he comes upon them, they come as an answer to his quest. He is prepared to appreciate their significance and is ready to apply them.

The Importance of Relevance

Information has value only when relevant. Relevance is not a property of information as such, but is rather a property of the recipient and the situation in which he finds himself in at the moment. We should say "relevance to . . ." or "relevance for . . . ," rather than simply "relevance."

A student will find the concepts, theories, and data which are presented to him in a course far more meaningful if they relate to an interest of his or to a problem on which he is working. Without such context the information may seem pointless. With such a context, on the other hand, a student is much more receptive. He apprehends the significance of the material more readily, may often find it exciting, and—most important—acquires the ability to use it productively and to retain it.

This does not mean that an instructor need modify his syllabus and standards in order to suit the interests and readiness of his students (although, when these are known, it is advisable to exploit them to whatever extent possible). Rather, it means that one should take care to develop course materials and assign tasks in such a way as to *lead students into problems* first. The problems should be of such a nature as to furnish the context within which the facts, theories, concepts, and methods which are the object of the course will have relevance. It is especially important that technical concepts and methods not be presented in a vacuum.

The Superiority of Problem Orientation

A student in a worthwhile course must normally digest and remember a great deal of factual data. But if this is the apparent aim and net result of the course, it will have failed in its proper aims as part of either a scientific or a liberal education. It is necessary to inculcate in the student a sense of scientific problem and an understanding of the principles of disciplined inquiry. While this is a matter which more properly belongs under the heading of "aims" rather than of "methods," it is nonetheless relevant here in the list of considerations which should determine method. If an instructor takes care not to lose sight of this aim in his course, and if he is successful, the pay-off in student response can be great.

The Importance of a Sense of Accomplishment

Probably the greatest reward that can come to a student from a course of study is the awareness of growth in his intellectual abilities and of mastery of skills which give him power over materials before which previously he was helpless. A general sense of "appreciation" of a field, or knowing about it, does not give this reward. "Survey" courses never give it. It can come only with the acquisition of genuine technical skills.

There is a marked tendency in some schools to differentiate courses on the basis of a division of function: some are surveys for the general appreciation of a field, some are basic-information courses devoted to the acquistion of classified factual knowledge, and some are tool courses devoted to the acquisition of specific technical skills. All three of these, surely, are necessary ends. The wisdom of dividing them among separate courses, however, is open to serious question. My own feeling is that every course should be a "tool" course in a very real sense and should give the students a technical skill which they did not have before. With the acquisition of skill comes the feeling of accomplishment. Nothing is more pathetic on the educational scene than the student who has "taken" course after course but has missed this sense of accomplishment.

The Importance of the Opening of Horizons

It is difficult to express adequately one's thoughts on this subject. The opening up of one's horizons of thought is probably the most deeply reaching—and most transforming—part of one's education. Anthropologists in particular, I believe, have richly enjoyed this experience. One who has been through it and been affected by it is usually able to lead his students—or some of them—to the edge of their known worlds of ideas and either excite them or shock them by the view of what may lie beyond.

THE AIMS OF INTRODUCTORY COURSES

The Focus of a First Course in Linguistics

In posing the question of aims for a first course in linguistics it is instructive, I think, to consider what have been the points of special appeal in this field for those who, as students, were attracted to it to the extent of being drawn into it professionally.

For many a student with scientific leanings the first and decisive attraction came with the discovery, in language, of the "lawful" nature of a form of human social behavior. This has often come as something of a revelation, for our customary backgrounds of knowledge (as students) and our inherited preconceptions about the nature of things do not usually prepare us for it. We are prepared instead to expect natural law in the realm of physical phenomena, but to expect either chance or volition in those phenomena in which man and society are involved.

For some the first glimpse of law in this realm came with the discovery of the "regularity of phonetic change"—often in a very special single example of it, that which is known as "Grimm's law." Later on one comes to take the phenomenon of "regularity" in this aspect of linguistic change for granted, as natural, and as though it could hardly have been conceived of otherwise. But still, one does not easily forget the impression it first made on him when it was totally unexpected.

For others the first glimpse of law in this realm came with the discovery of the "unconscious patterning of behavior" in language—often in the special instance of phonemics, as Sapir described it in some of his famous papers. Again, one comes to take this for granted as one goes on in the field and as linguistic theory evolves, but the powerful first impression is hardly forgotten. In fact, one experiences it anew every time he solves a difficult structural problem in a language and discovers the "pattern," unexpected and surprising, within which the bewildering data finally make sense.

A third topic capable of making a considerable impression on students is the so-called "linguistic relativity "principle. The essence of this view was already current in nineteenth-century philosophical discussions of language, but its impact upon anthropologists and linguists, especially in America, came later as it was made more concrete by Boas and as it was put especially vividly by Sapir and Whorf. Contemporary developments in structural semantics—especially in the field of lexi-

cography, and as brought into relation with other cultural forms—
have contributed further to the understanding of this principle. They
are equally effective with students.

These topics represent three somewhat different subdivisions of
the field, having to do respectively with language change, the structure
of form, and the structure of meaning. All of them are effective eye-
openers for students. All are good topics for inclusion in a first course in
linguistics. The course need not, and cannot, cover all of them in an intensive manner. It is important, however, that *one* such topic be gone
into deeply and thoroughly so that a student can know the feeling of
accomplishment that comes with technical proficiency. Others of these
or similar topics can be introduced as relevant contexts are afforded,
not for the purpose of equally intensive work at this point, but rather
for broadening the student's view and giving him a glimpse of other
facets to the study of language. With one point of some depth in the
field, the attempt at breadth should be somewhat more fruitful than
otherwise. It is also important that each such topic be introduced
in such a way and in such a context that the student may experience
something of the excitement of discovery as he comes upon it.

The sections which follow pertain to certain special types of introductory courses.

Survey Courses

As indicated earlier, I have a rather negative feeling toward introductory survey courses, i.e., "samplers."

Professor Pike, in his paper, raises the question of what should be the
nature of a first course in linguistics for undergraduates. He poses the
question thus:

> Should the first course for undergraduates give lectures on the range and
> treatment of concepts in the field, or should it rather teach the students
> to apply a few of the basic concepts to actual data? Should it be a course
> in reading *about* linguistics, or one in *using* linguistics? The decision to be
> reached here is whether the first course should be—say—entitled "An Intro-
> duction to Linguistic Science," or whether it should be a course in applied
> phonetics, or phonemics, or some other branch of linguistics. (p. 2)

Pike considers the pros and cons on each side in his paper, and offers
many helpful suggestions. On the subject of survey courses I quote further from his paper. In fairness to him, however, and also to any
who feel more sanguine about survey courses than I do, I should warn
that I am quoting out of context those parts which suit my purpose
here. He says:

> A disadvantage of starting with a survey course is that the student may

find himself overwhelmed with concepts which appear to him to be of no immediate relevance. He misses, also, the early thrill of discovering for himself some of the structure of a language. . . . It is also possible for a beginning student to get enamored with theoretical discussion before he has built into his intellectual system the brakes on speculation supplied by recalcitrant data. There is also considerable frustration on the part of the lecturer if he finds himself—because of the many topics to be covered—forced to give a single lecture or two, say, to phonetics, one to phonemics, one to lexicostatistics, and so on. The skim is so thin that the basic attempt to get the concepts deeply engrained in the student fails—or an illusory success is given which may in fact be disadvantageous. (p. 5)

My own preference is to reject the "introductory survey"—especially the type which is offered as a one-semester course—in favor of a more intensive course, of a year's duration, where the student learns to *use* linguistics and applies its methods to actual data.

An Intensive Course in Linguistic Analysis

There are now available several excellent textbooks for use in intensive courses in linguistic analysis. This new and happy circumstance has greatly simplified the task of teaching these courses. Some of these texts —the best of them—contain more material than can be covered intensively in a year's course. This is all to the good, however. It calls only for a comment on the use of such texts. The course should focus on one area of linguistic analysis for thorough mastery by the students. The remainder of the topics may be surveyed then more briefly and without view to equal mastery of these yet. This is again to advocate the cultivation of breadth when it becomes possible to work out from some one point of genuine depth. It should be noted also that even the best of these texts require that the instructor supply a great amount of supplementary material—both of problems and work in the literature on linguistic theory—in the particular area chosen for intensive work in the course.

Now, a word or two concerning the possible choices of areas for intensive work. It has been customary for some decades for linguists to choose, as their starting point in instruction, the microstructures in language and to work *toward* (but never reach) the macrostructures. There is a good historical reason for this. It is the microstructures—the molecular phenomena in language—which first yielded to scientific analysis. There is, or has at least seemed to be, a naturally determined order of discovery in the hierarchy of linguistic structures. I think it will not be long before we can, if we wish, reverse this sequence in the teaching of linguistic analysis, i.e., we may possibly begin with the analysis of larger units and the higher-level organization in language, and work toward the smaller and deeper. This will need some experimentation. It is now not too early to begin this. I should expect certain advantages to derive from it, one of which would be a more apparent relevance of linguistic studies to other more general interests and goals in education.

Another comment may also be made along this line. It is also customary for courses in linguistic analysis (in America at least) to be concerned almost exclusively with linguistic forms and to avoid the subject of meaning except for the posting of danger signals all around it. Here, also, I believe the time is ripe for a change. To be sure, there is not yet anywhere nearly so much that can be taught with confidence concerning the scientific study of meaning and the analysis of semantic structures, but—and this should be stressed—there is at least the beginning of something. The approved negative attitude toward the subject is perhaps nearing the end of its usefulness. I would not yet remove all of the "danger" signals, however.

One further observation might be made, concerning the choice of problem materials. Inasmuch as many courses in linguistic analysis are taught (in America) by anthropologists or by people in the fields of non-Western languages, there has grown up a marked tendency to use, for purposes of problem material, data drawn heavily form American Indian languages, Asian or African languages, etc. To some extent this is excellent because of the shock value that these data have. But there is a negative side to this also. For the majority of students, as I have learned, it fails on the criterion of *relevance*. Many of them (undergraduate non-anthropologists) simply are not ready for this kind of material in large doses. They do not find in it the relevance to their needs, their interests, and their other studies, such as will motivate them strongly to study linguistics.

It would be highly desirable, I believe, to work out an introductory course in linguistic analysis in which the majority of the problem materials would be drawn from the two or three languages of greatest practical relevance for the majority of students. These might well be English, French, and German, but varying, of course, with the particular geographic area and the kind of academic institution. It would be well to take students by the problem method systematically through the structures of these languages, starting perhaps preferably with the larger structures and working toward the smaller, and always treating the material as an object of scientific inquiry. The purely practical side-benefits for students could be immense while they were being led into scientific linguistics. Some problem material from exotic languages should surely be included. This can have all the greater impact, and be all the more relevant, if placed against a background of some genuine understanding of our Western languages.

This procedure would doubtless place a handicap on some of us who teach linguistics. Many of us (especially the anthropologist-linguists among us) have simply not pursued English, French, or German with the same unrelenting scrutiny and analysis with which we have pursued the exotic languages in which our research interests (as anthropologists) lie. Nor are we motivated to do so, when the time required for it would have to be taken away from our own special research areas. Besides this difficulty there is another (especially for Americans). We often lack proficiency in the use of these languages, beyond that minimal proficiency needed to comprehend articles of a technical nature in our professional field. We would be rather hesitant to expose our somewhat shaky knowledge before students, some of whom might by chance be modern-language majors and have better practical control over the languages than we. The flight into exotic language materials in linguistics courses is often a flight into safety for the instructor.

"Language and Culture" Courses

These are the special problem of linguists who teach in anthropology departments. Nearly every anthropology department (in the United States) wants one. Some even want two of them—one for undergraduate students and one for graduate students who are specializing in anthropology. The conceptions of what such a course should accomplish for the students seems to be rather surprisingly uniform among the nonlinguist anthropologists. Rarely, however, do the linguists who teach them have the same view of the function of such a course.

Often the "language and culture" course is a single-term course. Often it is the only linguistics course which an anthropology student (even at the graduate level) will take. The expectations of the department may drive the instructor—especially if he is young—to including a bit of all sorts of things. The student may get from it a few or several of the following: some half-true platitudes about the nature of the "symbol," a bit of the "Whorf hypothesis" (without any understanding of how to formulate a concrete hypothesis of this genre and submit it to test), an attempt to understand the notion of the "phoneme" (surely doomed to failure), a bit of "glottochronology" (without any basis for applying critical judgment in this business), the notion of "drift" (one of the foggiest notions to have appeared in linguistics), family-tree classifications of the languages of the major ethnographic areas (without any notion of what the phylogenetic model means when applied to languages, or what constitutes proof of relationship), etc. The course can easily become one of the worst type of "sampler" survey courses, giving the student no mastery over anything, no sense of accomplishment, and no equipment or enough time to enable him to make any discoveries for himself. Neither does it give the instructor any sense of accomplishment. He derives only frustration from it. Yet, somehow, in spite of these faults, a certain number (a small number) of students do become interested in linguistics by this route, begin to read and study further on their own, and go on to take intensive work in other courses—and, in the end, become linguists. Possibly such courses are not actually quite as bad as their instructors, in their frustration, feel they must be.

It does not take very many flings at this kind of a course before the instructor readjusts his sights, drastically cuts down on the aims at coverage in the course, and develops something else out of it. The solutions may vary.

I will describe one solution—that which I have adopted for an undergraduate class going under this title. It is a possible solution where a college encourages or will tolerate a certain number of low-enrollment seminar-type courses for advanced undergraduates. It is a combination of a lecture-type course and a seminar-type course.

The obligation to give the students some breadth and appreciation of the field as a whole is discharged by giving a weekly hour-lecture on one single linguistic topic of some relevance to anthropology. Each week is a different subject, and each one must be entirely self-contained—as if one were giving a special lecture for a meeting of an anthropology club or a linguistic club. The student is not required either to do any reading on the subject of the lecture or to answer an examination question on it. The only requirement is that he be present.

The student's own work in the course is to dig deeply into a single relevant subject of his own choice. A list of possible subjects is distributed to the class at the beginning of the term, together with the title and reference to *one* introductory paper (or chapter of a book) on each subject, and a bibliography of further materials on each of the same subjects. The student may read several of the introductory papers in the process of making up his mind (in the first week or two) as to which of the subjects he will go into intensively. Having made the decision, he has the bibliography of further materials to work on.

The class lectures on selected topics utilize one third of the class time normally allotted to a course (three hours per week, fifteen weeks per semester). The remaining hours are made available to the students for individual or small group consultations on their projects.

Since they have choice, the projects can relate well to their other interests. They have the opportunity to acquire depth and some degree of competence in a single special area through this seminar or individual-study aspect of the course, while a breadth of a sort is given in the lecture part of the course. Their grades are based solely on their own intensive work and the papers that they write on the basis of it. Papers are to represent the results of analysis, rather than merely a review of literature.

Topics vary widely, depending on the interests and previous course work of the students. The choice of topic is carefully supervised by the instructor. Topics include: grammatical analysis (immediate-constituent and paradigmatic analysis), distributional analysis, analysis of the referential structures of kinship terminologies, analysis of the structure of logographic writing systems, lexicostatistic studies, projects in comparative linguistics, projects in typology, studies of primitive or folk traditional verbal compositions, etc. The restrictions on choice are the following: There must exist a sufficient theoretical literature on the subject to make it a profitable undertaking; it must not be a subject on which the instructor is unable to advise; it must have some relevance to some branch of anthropology.

This procedure solves the problems of relevance and motivation for the student. It enables him to end the course with a feeling of having learned and accomplished something. He has enjoyed the experience of discovering things for himself. It handles the problems of depth and breadth in a fairly satisfactory way. It does *not* make a complete linguist out of the student, but this is not to be expected from any single course anyway. Some have a course in linguistic analysis before entering; some go on to take one afterwards.

Needs of Graduate Students in Anthropology

Graduate students in anthropology must receive a somewhat more balanced course in linguistics than that just outlined for an undergraduate course. Here one needs a year's course which is a compromise between a survey and an intensive course. I am still in favor, however, of fitting the linguistic training of a graduate student in anthropology to his other interests in the field of anthropology. An archaeology student might be more interested in the results of historical and comparative linguistics, lexicostatistic estimates of time depth, linguistic taxonomic methods, etc. A social anthropology or ethnology student might profit from learning something about the dimensional analysis of paradigmatic systems, the insolation of units, the linguistic approach to kinship systems, and so on. Much of linguistic method is either transferrable or suggestive of methods for the analysis of data pertaining to other aspects of culture. Anyone who is contemplating field work, of course, should also learn phonetic transcription, the effective use of tape recorders, phonemic principles, and linguistic analysis. Those choosing linguistics for specialization should learn all of these and more. There are also linguistic topics of relevance to physical anthropology.

The prospects of comprehensive examinations, unfortunately, are rather more in students' minds in the first two years than are the points of relevance of their study programs to their future research. It is the comprehensives that necessitate a more carefully balanced course for graduate students in anthropology than would otherwise be either to their taste or my own taste. I do not know whether this is a good thing. My inclination otherwise would be to give students more individual leeway.

KENNETH L. PIKE

Choices
in Course
Design

T HERE IS NO ONE "CORRECT" way to design a course for teaching linguistics. Differences in audience, goals, contents, textbooks, and theoretical outlook combine to make it impossible to prescribe any single course which will simultaneously satisfy all practical and theoretical considerations. In this article, therefore, we discuss the problem of course design in reference to a few basic decisions. These particular ones reflect my own experience and theoretical bias.

Specifically, for undergraduates, one must determine whether needs are to be met (1) for persons wishing some introduction to linguistics, only as part of a broad general educational curriculum or for the distribution requirements of such a plan, (2) for serving as cognates related to—but not central for—some other discipline, or (3) as preparation for professional work in linguistics.

LINGUISTICS FOR UNDERGRADUATES

In the past, linguistics has been in the universities aimed almost exclusively at the graduate student. There is no theoretical reason, however, why linguistics cannot be aimed at students early in their college careers. My own students have ranged from those working on their doctorate, through those working on their masters degrees in linguistics, to substantial numbers who ranked as upper division students in undergraduate school. In addition, I have been briefly involved in teaching a bit of linguistics to an experimental group of junior high school students—with results which show that initial grammatical and pho-

315

nemic theory as well as phonetics and dialect mimicry can be profitably taught to interested junior high youngsters.

CONCEPTS OR PRODUCTION

Should the first course for undergraduates give lectures on the range and treatment of concepts in the field, or should it rather teach the students to apply a few of the basic concepts to actual data? Should it be a course in reading *about* linguistics, or one in *using* linguistics? The decision to be reached here is whether the first course should be—say— entitled "An Introduction to Linguistic Science," or whether it should be a course on applied phonetics, or phonemics, or some other branch of linguistics.

If the course is an introduction to linguistic science, it would presumably help the students understand the place which linguistics plays in relation to other disciplines. It would let him get some appreciation for the history of linguistics as it has developed over 2,500 years. It should enable him, in addition, to understand something of the nature of the chief concepts utilized in linguistics—concepts such as the phoneme, allophone, morpheme, allomorph, tagmeme, transform grammar, historical and comparative linguistics, cognate set, diachronic phonemics, family tree, lexicostatistics, dialect geography, isogloss, transition area, semantic field, over-all pattern, decoding, encoding, and so on. The introductory course might aim at fulfilling requirements of a general education curriculum or of providing a cognate for persons from other disciplines.

Various textbooks are available for such a course. Until recently the standard text was Bloomfield (1933). This still is excellent to use for its introductory material on languages of the world, for a summary of certain problems of meaning types, for a summary of the comparative method, and for a summary of dialect geography. More recently, however, a well-written introduction has been prepared by Gleason (1961) which is much easier for the student to read. Gleason's book, in addition, brings the students' approach up to date in reference to communication and Bloch-Trager phonology. A further text by Hockett (1958) is also being used in introductory courses. It is more detailed in certain areas than Gleason and emphasizes differently certain concepts in the field —it may be especially useful, for example, in reference to over-all pattern, internal reconstruction, and various historical matters.

A disadvantage of starting with a survey course is that the student may find himself overwhelmed with concepts which appear to him to be of no imediate relevance. He misses, also, the early thrill of discovering for himself some of the structure of a language—an experience which may come, say, with a concentrated course on phonetics and phonemics. It is also possible for a beginning student to get enamored with theoretical discussion before he has built into his intellectual system the brakes on speculation supplied by recalcitrant data. There is also considerable frustration on behalf of the lecturer if he finds himself— because of the many topics to be covered—forced to give a single lecture or two, say, to phonetics, one to phonemics, one to lexicostatistics, and so on. The skim is so thin that the basic attempt to get the concepts deeply engrained in the student fails—or an illusory success is given which may in fact be disadvantageous.

My own preference, therefore, is to try to insure that the student looking forward to a career in linguistics either take some tool course in phonetics and phonemics at the same time as he is taking a broader introduction, or that he take some tool course before immersing himself in the wider field. A thorough grounding in phonemic principles can through analogies make more rapidly intelligible many problems in historical linguistics, grammatical structure, and even in ethnolinguistics.

The general introductory course, however, may be given using a text such as that of Gleason, which gives reasonably wide coverage but which at the same time provides a supplementary "work book" so that a small number of phonemic and grammar problems are given along with the conceptual introduction. This, it seems to me, should be insisted on for any students who do not expect to go beyond the introductory course.

For graduate students an introductory course may have similar objectives to the one just discussed. Further supplementation, however, may be needed in terms of readings in the literature. To such problems we now turn.

INTENSIVE OR EXTENSIVE READING ASSIGNMENTS

Before discussing tool courses in anthropological linguistics we wish to discuss the possibility of training in the general concepts of linguistics beyond that which can be obtained in introductory courses. This is most frequently handled as a high-level graduate seminar for people who are working on research problems, or are preparing for preliminary examinations for the doctorate. Although this material can be engineered down to an undergraduate level—adjustment being made as to amount of material and sophistication of discussion required—I think that this should not be attempted extensively before the student has had opportunity himself to try out linguistic tools on informant data directly—or should be concomitant with research on such prime sources. If this can be arranged, however, a course of readings may be profitably attempted at either level of experience.

Under these conditions I prefer that one should neither put all his available time on a rapid widespread reading of a large mass of articles, nor on the other hand devote the whole semester to an exegesis of a half a dozen of the most important articles. Rather, in my view, the student is best advised to invest half his energies in a very light skimming of a large number of articles, and the other half in an intensive study of an exemplary few.

The content of such a course could be taken from Joos' *Readings* (1957) as an easily accessible set of articles for rapid perusal. The individual instructor will find it necessary to supplement these readings, however, in accordance with his own particular convictions about the crucial developments in linguistic theory or special aims of the seminar. British instructors would find the readings restricted on an irrelevant—that is, a national—base. My own choice in these matters is reflected in an annotated bibliography prepared for graduate students by Pike and Pike (1960). Classification of the entries allows choice of area for intensive study by particular students, whereas asterisks on selected articles in each section allow assignment to all students of a minimum number of enough articles to lay the groundwork for fruitful discussion in class. Persons interested in the application of linguistics to language learning problems might wish to supplement with the set of Readings reprinted from Language Learning (1953) or the set reprinted by Allen (1958).

In such a program the undergraduate student—and often the beginning graduate—needs help in learning how to skim an article rapidly. I have found it convenient to request half-page book reports on each of —say—fifty articles. For each he is asked to state in one sentence—preferably in the words of the author—the purpose of the article. In addition, a one-sentence summary of the general approach, general content, or general results is to be given. It is helpful if the student has been urged to select some particular topic on which he focuses his attention, so that he gets used to the idea of searching a wide variety of literature for items relevant to his point of interest. He should comment on any material which, in the article, bears on this topic (or a term paper may be required to discuss the literature on this topic). Finally, he may be asked to make a note of any item which annoys him, as appearing to be inadequately treated—with the idea that such notes eventually point the way to research topics for future writing.

While skimming such materials the student needs help in trying to organize the frightening mass of material. Otherwise his knowledge becomes a hodgepodge, and the student remembers too little to be effective. I personally find that one effective organizing principle is to try to get the students, during the semester, to react to each of a dozen or two authors as persons writing in reference to tacit *criteria of elegance*. If the students can, as it were, look at a problem through the eyes of such an author and determine whether it is elegant according to his tacit or explicit criteria, they build up a feeling of an approach toward problems which is ever so much more retainable, and ever so much more productive, than a mere attempt to remember contents of articles. Such an attempt as this has been successful if and only if at the end of a semester a student can *sympathetically* take a topic *ad hoc* and give a fairly shrewd judgment as to the way such a problem would be attacked by the leading figures in the field today.

The student should be helped to see, for example, that in any materials prepared by Harris the tacit criteria of elegance make it probable that a quasi-mathematical formulation will be attempted. With Fries, on the other hand, no major study is satisfactory unless it is related to a massive amount of data, carefully collected and inductively studied. For Bloch, elegance would appear to involve a postulational system of simplicity and careful progression—and so on. My students find that I am interested in integrating all manner of bits of structure into a hierarchy of systems rather than leaving them in disparate compartments; and that I not only want theoretical material to be developed far enough to be applicable in field situations, but also want field discoveries to lead to attempts at theoretical statements which encompass them.

The *detailed* analysis of a few specific articles, on the other hand, helps the student to understand the nature of coherent writing. It is designed to help him learn to "work through" careful, close-knit arguments and to detect gaps in them. In an article worked through with care, he is expected to check all illustrations, follow all arguments, be able to reproduce the line of argument, and pick up misprints in the data. He may even see, more clearly than the author himself, some of the problems involved, since the student may begin far in advance of where the author did at the time of writing.

Although such a course is so extensive as to be frightening to the graduate as well as to the undergraduate, I have found both types of students much excited by an attempt to enter sympathetically into the points of view of Sapir, Bloomfield, Fries, Hjelmslev, Firth, Trager, Bloch, Harris, Nida, Chomsky, and others.

LINGUISTICS AND INTERDISCIPLINARY INTEGRATION

The learning process goes deep when the student is interested. To the extent that the instructor is convinced—as I am—that language to some degree is a clearing house for conceptual classification of a man's experience, to that degree we may assume that at some point—if one can trace it far enough—any interest of the student will come in contact with some linguistic problem. By exploiting these interests in term papers, we can take care of variant student interests without proliferating courses beyond those which the administrative set-up allows. On an undergraduate level, such excursions may prove to be rare and not very profound. Nevertheless, they might well serve as the stimulus which would lead some honors undergraduate on to graduate school, doing research in an interdisciplinary area of considerable importance to us all.

Archaeologists, in a course on phonemics, have been encouraged to correlate time-depth suggestions from lexico-statistical techniques with their own time-depth suggestions from their archaeological data, as well as with studies of dialect geography and comparative linguistics. A teacher of high school French has been encouraged to study the type of pronunciation mistakes made by his pupils. Students majoring in a language have been encouraged to work on the language which is their major, attempting to apply to that language techniques of intonation analysis, or of tagmemics, or of phonemics, etc. that may be new to them. Cultural anthropologists in a course on field methods in linguistics have occasionally tried to apply "phonemic" concepts (Pike 1954) to non-verbal areas, e.g., to the structure of hopscotch.

Schools vary greatly as to the amount of time which can be made available on an undergraduate level for anthropological linguistics. This affects the amount of interdisciplinary components which can be included in the training. In Michigan, in 1959-60, the undergraduate program in linguistics—though modifiable in accordance with the aims of the student—included prerequisites of sixteen hours in a foreign language and the concentration program, which required twenty-six hours in language and literature, nine hours in linguistics proper, and nine cognate hours. The language and literature selections could be from English, German, Chinese, and so on. The cognate courses—no more than two from a single department—could be chosen from anthropology, philosophy, psychology, sociology, or speech.

The student interested primarily in cultural anthropology needs to be able to transcribe data from a preliterate culture. From language study, furthermore, he may obtain crucial data for understanding kinship terms and other anthropological data. He should be interested in philosophical matters of world view in relation to language, and in parallels in structure between society and language, or between nonverbal behavior and verbal behavior, in view of his search for an understanding of components of man. (Extensive discussion of many of these matters and bibliography is found in the articles by Hymes and Lounsbury in this volume.)

Students of modern languages, on the other hand, may be especially interested in the general nature of language and in principles of language learning. Breadth of linguistic background here gives a richness to teaching which at certain stages proves to be as eminently practical as it may at first appear irrelevant.

Missionaries need both the general tools for analyzing a language as such and cultural studies to enable them to understand in sociological or anthropological frameworks the linguistic items which they collect.

Students of philosophy need emphasis both upon the cultural universals of language structure and on the variability of language in reference to distribution classes of words, sentence structure, and the correlation between meanings and linguistic form. Otherwise they are prone to make judgments about philosophical universals which are falsely based, lacking an understanding of language variability. The current interest of some philosophers in the writings of linguists seems to be concentrated upon the Whorf hypothesis. This emphasis, I believe, is on much too narrow a front to be lasting; it tends to be overly specific in indicating perceptual detail conditioned by language detail. The more deep-seated problems would seem to me to involve the manner in which the general structural characteristics of language are paralleled by other behavioral and societal structures, and which together with them reflect cultural universals. These, in turn, should help us see more clearly some of the built-in components that every man inevitably brings to his observing of the world. For discussion and bibliography, see Pike (1960:97-98, 101-104, 115-118, 123-124).

The psychologist will want emphasis upon the psycholinguistic units of behavior. The relationships between perception of visual objects—and limitations therein—and perception of verbal matters and their limitations are beginning to get attention and should be pointed out to the beginning student in psychology as possible areas of development for graduate work. Note, for example, Brown and Lenneberg (1954) and Miller (1956); and compare components of Barker and Wright (1955) with my attempts to show parallels between verbal a nonverbal segmentation (Pike 1954, 1960; see also in 1955:35-36; 1960: 63-64, 111, 116).

DEGREE OF PROFICIENCY FOR UNDERGRADUATES

If a school has budgeted only one semester hour for linguistics, about the best the instructor can do is to give a general course containing about three lectures on consonants, three on vowels, one on tone, three on phonemics, three on morphology, two on syntax, and one on general background. A text for such a series of lectures might be that of Nida (1950). A dozen or two of such courses are taught to undergraduates

around the country—especially in church-related schools for missionaries—and have proved very helpful.

My experience would suggest that roughly three hours of phonetics
per week for a semester should, however, take the beginning undergraduate or graduate student through enough exercises to give a quick
coverage of the various kinds of sounds which he must be prepared to
meet at various places in the world and to give him assurance that he
can start working by himself on the sounds of a language. It should be
emphasized, however, that this is but a beginner's knowledge. A student of "B" caliber, after this training, still turns out a transcription
which, to the specialist, appears shockingly deficient. In the American
training system, however, it is highly unlikely that more time than this
can be allotted. In the British system in training for a phonetic diploma on a graduate level, numerous courses in phonetics are added
one to the other, along with laboratory phonetics of an articulatory type,
which prepare the student much more thoroughly than we can currently hope for in courses in the United States.

If less time than this is allocated to phonetic drill, aims must be cut
accordingly. With fifteen contact hours of phonetics, for example,
sound types can be briefly reviewed, but the "B" student is likely to
have little confidence in working and is scarcely more than introduced
to the symbols.

The time needed to get across to the student the basic phoneme
concept is much longer than the field specialist is likely to anticipate.
Again, for the "B" student, the process takes nearly a semester. When
students are followed into the field it becomes evident that such a
course is none too much if the student is expected to have understood
the principles in a manner which will allow him to apply them to the
specific data which he finds. A semester course of three hours in phonetics and one of three hours in phonemics is highly desirable, though
often unattainable.

In Michigan, for many of our students—mostly graduates—we have
worked out a compromise: In a single three-hour credit course, two regular class hours weekly throughout the semester are spent on phonemic theory and exercises while the third is spent on phonetic theory.
Two additional "noncredit" hours are spent on phonetic drill in small
sections of about ten students each. This does fairly well for the better
students but should be considered a minimum for field preparation.

The problem of time needed in preparation for grammar analysis
is similar to that for phonetics and phonemics. A minimum is a one-
semester course of three hours per week in which techniques are given
for the analysis of morphology and syntax. Some students do fairly
well after this amount of classroom experience. The majority, however,

need twice that amount of time—divided perhaps between a course on morphemics for a semester and a course on syntax (or with a second course on field methods in linguistics, slanted towards syntax).

In addition, time must be taken in further training courses or in other departments if the student is to be introduced adequately to the relations between language and culture, to concepts and techniques of dialect geography, historical linguistics, and to special conceptual tools such as those of lexicostatistics. It is evident that the amount of time required is too great to allow the material to be given in an undergraduate program.

It should be emphasized that in linguistics, as in other disciplines, it is by no means always an advantage to try to give to the undergraduate the maximum possible amount of technology in his professional field. Rather, his bachelor's degree should first of all be a broad cultural one, with much of his professional training left to a graduate program.

I have noted that some students who as undergraduates received extensive training in linguistic technology have failed to develop the research independence which is essential to a professional scholar. Such persons may need to go to graduate school to get the broader cultural experience which in most instances is easier to obtain as an undergraduate.

Specifically, one of the most difficult problems of training a person for professional linguistics is that of getting him ready to write an acceptable essay. It is by no means to be taken for granted that the person who can develop insight into the structure of a language can also present that data in a way satisfactory to his colleagues. The two technologies are quite different. It is a serious mistake, therefore, to overemphasize linguistic technology in the undergraduate days to the extent that the student fails to develop the capacity to write a good theme.

CONTENT OF THE TOOL COURSES

Under the assumption that at some time in his career the anthropological linguist needs tool courses governing theory and technology of phonetics, phonemics, morphemics, syntax, language and culture, and comparative work, we now discuss specific detail which may be treated profitably in such courses. (Content of an introductory course was discussed in §1; of a reading course in §3.) Where courses must be combined, the same general content usually is relevant, with exercise material and explanatory notes correspondingly shortened.

Phonetics

The student needs to be made aware of the articulatory mechanisms in the mouth and throat. I prefer to do this by using a combination of two approaches—a static and a dynamic one. The static approach works through face diagrams, including sounds made with an egressive or ingressive moving column of air initiated in the lungs, in the throat, or in the mouth (Pike 1943). By a dynamic approach I mean the study of the changing of articulators as they lead to changing sounds (Pike 1947:10-11, 41, *et al.*).

This general view may then be followed up with lectures and drill on specific sounds. Contrastive materials are best introduced as a list of syllables contrasting in initial consonant or vowel alone. Once such a contrast in mastered, it can be given in dictation in one- or two-syllable words from actual language material. If the material includes minimal pairs, this gives a psychological support which is very great. Drills to help the student pronounce these sounds are found in Pike (1947: 12-43). A planned course sequence, with dictation drills of a simple type and with brief lesson plans, can be found in Eunice Pike (1946).

To this sequence there needs to be added drills on large-unit phonetics—on syllable types, stress-group types, breath-groups, and the kinds of junctures which come between them (see Pike 1955:41-70; Trager and Smith 1951).

Segmentation theory of physiological and acoustic action at the vocal cords is in preparation by Morrison (1961). This will give us some of the articulatory basis of voice quality insofar as it is initiated in the larynx. General symbols for voice quality, on the other hand, can be found among my intonation studies (Pike 1945:101-02), with some later studies by Trager (1958) and others (some bibliography in Pike 1960:52b). Persons interested in dialects, in stage work, or in speech as a clue to psychological state, should be encouraged to do extra work at these points, along with study of dialect records and mimicry of recorded conversational material.

Additional drills are needed for tone and intonation. Unless the student can control his own English intonation he is unlikely to handle successfully drills in lexical pitch. Drills in English intonation may profitably include (1) the reading of texts marked for pitch, (2) reading such texts on a monotone, (3) listening to texts so as to identify errors introduced by the teacher, one per phrase, (4) reading a text with the same intonation type applied repeatedly to each phrase of the text, and (5) taking from dictation simple contrastive intonation patterns. Some intonational drills are extremely valuable early in the phonemics course in order to get a student ready to enjoy the contribution which linguistics can make to his understanding the presence of unsensed structures within his own culture. The discovery of items new to him about his own language makes him ready to learn more.

It is advisable to have experience in instrumental study of articulatory movements. Little of that is now available in this country—though

Great Britain continues to hold the tradition strong—and our American phonetic studies are suffering as a result.

A person specializing in phonetics should also be able to handle the acoustic spectograph and interpret its recordings. This might be included in the beginning courses for an occasional undergraduate as cognate work, but more frequently would be found in special courses on the graduate level. If he wishes to be able to keep his own machinery in good working order, he needs extensive graduate training in electronics as well.

Phonetic study is now beginning to have intricate correlation with the work of physiologists, both in terms of action potential—studying the electrical energy released at the time of speaking—and in muscular studies of various kinds. These cannot be included in a beginning program and of themselves constitute a graduate sequence of some magnitude, much of it available only in Europe.

Phonemics

The boundary line between courses in phonetics and in phonemics is not easy to draw. Ideally they should be taught simultaneously, with some overlap, or combined in a single extensive course. The reason for this is that a heavy dose of phonetics without phonemic controls may lead the student to an unfortunate attitude towards the structure of language. He may feel that a phonemic unit is somehow not "accurate" and thus fail to sense the essential nature of units as points of contrast in a matrix of contrast, rather than as absolute bits.

Early in the beginning of the course students should be given some kind of demonstration to show them how linguistic theory works in practice. I have often found students unhappy unless early in a course we have given some demonstration, with an informant, of analysis of phonemes, morphemes, and tagmemes. With it, enthusiasm often builds up while they wait for their chance to do the same thing later in the semester.

In a course in phonemics I continue to utilize a text we prepared some time ago (Pike 1947). It centers analytical techniques around four easily remembered general principles. Some suggested changes in course sequence and detailed lesson plans are available in supplementary manuals (see Evelyn Pike 1954, 1955). Most scholars would want to supplement the 1947 text to bring the theoretical statements up to date. Principally they might want to emphasize the possibility of multiple descriptions of a single set of data, and to keep more separate the grammatical and phonological materials. Readings in Trager and Smith (1951) or in Hockett (1958) are useful here When teaching from the older text, I myself supplement it with lectures from my materials of 1955 (especially Chapters 8 and 9) and 1960 (Chapter 15), in order to show the interaction of the phonological, lexical, and grammatical hierarchies.

An alternative approach to the basic needs of a phonemics course is an inductive one. Some instructors prefer to handle the course by analyzing during the semester the sounds of—say—three languages, using informants. The sounds are written on the board phonetically, and tentative phonemic analyses made as the instructor goes along.

For those experienced analysts who dislike to be tied to the theory of a textbook, the inductive method is much more interesting; they prefer an informant approach which allows them to vibrate between various kinds of theories as the particular data seem to respond to these, rather than submitting to the artificial controls of a specific technology. Since teacher interest is contagious, the approach most enthusiastically supported by the instructor is likely to become the one best for the class. The inexperienced teacher, on the other hand, is far better off utilizing a textbook approach where theoretical controls are built into a sequence provided him. Experienced teachers also often prefer the textbook approach for beginners at the undergraduate levels, since it is graded in difficulty, and a student comes out with a more specific technology and a conviction that he has systematically studied the method.

A third very useful approach is one based on models. The instructor assigns a number of the best descriptions of the phonemics of languages and has the students study them in great detail. Here the person is looking at a kind of end product which he himself wants to produce. In this sense it is very direct. A few models which reward careful study are found in Joos' *Readings* (1957). A useful selection should include one emphasizing contrastive features of the Jakobson type (for example Wong, on Mandarin 1953, with addenda 1954), syllable structure (a good short study is one by Clark 1959), a special analytical problem (Longacre on tone 1952), English phonemics (Trager and Smith, for over-all pattern 1951), the prosodic approach of British scholars (Firth 1957), acoustic analysis (Lehiste and Peterson 1959), and so on.

This approach has the disadvantage, however, that the student may find that the beautifully lucid published articles bear little resemblance to the scrawled mass of phonetic notations of his beginning work. In the long run, student needs are best met by a combination of a pedagogically oriented sequence of exercises, inductive demonstration, and a study of published model descriptions.

Morphemics and Syntax

The problems of teaching morphemics are related to those of teaching phonemics, as the concepts of phoneme and morpheme are related. The concepts should be equated across the two fields, whenever possible, in pedagogical presentation. Contrast, complementation, variation, and so on, should be shown to operate on a similar conceptual basis in the two areas. This relationship allows the student to get reinforcement of the new material from the old and to learn the new with less difficulty.

For morphemics, as for phonemics, my preference is to teach undergraduates by means of graded exercises. A standard text for this kind of morphemic analysis has been that of Nida (1949). For a shorter course some exercises may be found also in Gleason's workbook (1955).

As for phonemics, so for a course in morphemics, pedagogical alternatives to the exercise approach include both an inductive approach by analysis of languages in the classroom or an approach through the reading of models. The most fruitful current morphological models for a beginner, in my judgment, are an article by Cox (1957) and the tagmemic (née grammemic) study by Shell (1957). Many special studies are available, reflecting different theoretical points of view and treating very specific problems. A selection is found in Joos (1957).

The techniques for analyzing syntax have seldom been treated in separate courses. Suitable pedagogical materials have not been readily available, nor has the theoretical background been far enough advanced to make it feasible. With the development of tagmemic theory (Pike 1954, 1955, 1960; Longacre 1960) and transform grammar (Harris 1952; Chomsky 1957), our pedagogical treatments of grammar have advanced substantially.

The most encouraging part of this development is the attention which can be given to syntax, teachable to the undergraduate student on a level of difficulty comparable to that facing him in the study of morphemics and phonemics, and (in tagmemics) with concepts correlated with these. A pedagogical text applying the tagmemic approach to both morphology and syntax is Elson and Pickett (1960). The most comprehensive models using the two treatments are for tagmemics, Pickett (1960) for transform grammar, Lees (1960).

On theoretical grounds some European scholars would prefer, as theoretical background to analysis, materials of Hjelmslev (1953), or those of Firth reflected in analyses by Mitchell (1953) and others. Pedagogically also, other alternatives are available.

As for phonemics, so for grammatical analysis, an inductive approach or a study of models can be utilized. The advantages are—as in phonemics—directness, flexibility, and realism. The disadvantages tend to be discursiveness, inconsistency and incompleteness.

Field Methods

Courses in field methods should in principle be an inductive application of principles taught in courses concerning phonology and grammar. They add experience in the recording, storing, and processing of data. See Nida (1949:175-221) for suggestions concerning grammatical material.

A course consisting exclusively of the students watching the instructor analyze can be extremely boring to the student. Interest must be maintained by arranging for the students to take part. Here, too, boredom sets in quickly if each student seeks information only on points of immediate interest to him. It seems that the instructor must direct the course of investigation, in order to preserve unity of aim, At the same time he must constantly be ready to raise and discuss points of theoretical interest based upon difficulties in the data and upon live options given by differing available approaches to linguistic theory.

When students in the course have not had adequate background training in phonemics, morphemics, and tagmemics a course offered in field methods must have a different character. In this instance the theory and technology lacking in the training must be woven in.

Language and Culture

Content for a course on language and culture can ideally cover several areas—though any one or two of them might take the full time for a semester course. (See articles in this volume by Hymes and Lounsbury for suggestions.)

Comparative and Historical Materials

Traditionally, no tool courses have been provided for the study of comparative and historical materials with techniques comparable to those for phonemics. It would, seem that the time has come to develop them. (See Hoenigswald 1960 and, for lexicostatistic pedagogy, Gudschinsky 1956.) I have personally found the group of materials on the Proto-Popotecan family to be useful as a model. The work of Gudschinsky (1959) is, because of its charts, the easiest for students to follow.

The significance of comparative and lexicostatistical work in reference to migration theory is treated by Dyan (1956). Brief surveys of techniques of dialect geography can be found in Bloomfield (1933:321-450) and Hockett (1958:471-84), and, applied to one dialect of the Proto-Popotecan family, in Gudschinsky (1958).

A NOTE ON CONCENTRATED SUMMER INSTITUTES

Some readers may be interested to know the particular fashion in which materials discussed above are integrated in the intensive sessions of the Summer Institute of Linguistics at Norman, Oklahoma.

The first-year courses cover eleven weeks, with students in class five hours daily, five days per week. In general, one hour each week day is devoted to phonetics, one to phonemics, two to morphology and syntax. A fifth hour picks up tag ends of literacy (Gudschinsky 1951); discussions of semantics problems in translation (Nida 1947); translation theory in reference to tagmemics (Pike 1957); language in relation to culture, with a special reference to translation; monolingual demonstration; and anthropological attitudes necessary in dealing with informants, in special relation to Bible translation (the major interest of most of the students in this particular institute).

An initial period of four hours of bilingual demonstration interrupts the routine early in the summer. A further two-week field experience is provided on the campus at the end of the summer. For the latter, informants are available—especially from American Indian groups. Most of the students attempt to present written observations of phonetics, phonemics, morphology, and syntax. Some of them, however, are in sessions of a language-learning type, in which they try to apply techniques of learning a language to see how much of the language they can learn in the allotted time.

In the second summer, informant work is carried on throughout the course. At the beginning there is an intensive week for learning to speak a few phrases and constructions in the language. This is followed by routine informant work for grammatical and phonemic analysis. Whereas during the first summer attention is focussed heavily on the basic textbooks of a technological type, during the second summer focus is lifted to models written by different scholars. Here the purpose is to get the student to be aware of different theoretical trends, and to be more independent and flexible in his attack on any particular problem.

Competent students who begin linguistics with these courses find themselves equipped with a technology adequate for initial field work. Those who desire to become professionally prepared, however, are encouraged to go on to full graduate school programs to get the breadth of experience which is not available in this institute and which is necessary if a person is to be efficient and resourceful in the face of difficult field problems.

REFERENCES CITED

ALLEN, HAROLD B. (ED.)
    1958   Readings in applied English linguistics. New York, Appleton-Century-Crofts, Inc.
BARKER, ROGER G., AND HERBERT F. WRIGHT
    1955   Midwest and its children: the psychological ecology of an American town. Evanston, Row, Peterson and Company. (Date supplied by publisher.)

BLOOMFIELD, LEONARD
    1933   Language. New York, Henry Holt and Co.
BROWN, ROGER W., AND ERIC H. LENNEBERG
    1954   A study in language and cognition. Journal of Abnormal Social Psy-
                chology 49:454-62.
CHOMSKY, NOAM
    1957   Syntactic structures. 's-Gravenhage, Mouton and Company.
CLARK, LAWRENCE E.
    1959   Phoneme classes in Sayula Populuca. Studies in Linguistics 14:25-33.
COX, DORIS
    1957   Candoshi verb inflection. International Journal of American Lin-
                guistics 23:129-140.
DYAN, ISIDORE
    1956   Language distribution and migration theory. Language 32:611-626.
ELSON, BENJAMIN, AND VELMA B. PICKETT
    1960   Beginning morphology-syntax. Santa Ana, California, Summer In-
                stitute of Linguistics.
FIRTH, J. R.
    1957   Papers in linguistics 1934-1951. London, Oxford University Press.
GLEASON, H. A.
    1955   An introduction to descriptive linguistics. New York, Henry Holt
                and Co. Revised 1961.
    1955   (reprinted Nov. 1957) Workbook in descriptive linguistics. New
                York, Henry Holt and Co.
GUDSCHINSKY, SARAH C.
    1951   (revised 1953, 1957) Handbook of literacy. Santa Ana [Glendale], Sum-
                mer Institute of Linguistics.
    1956   The ABC's of lexicostatistics (glottochronology). Word 12:175-210.
    1958   Mazatec dialect history: a study in miniature. Language 34:469-481.
    1959   Proto-Popotecan: a comparative study of Popolocan and Mixtecan.
                Indiana University Publications in Anthropology and Linguistics,
                Memoir 15.
HARRIS, ZELLIG S.
    1952   Discourse analysis. Language 28:1-30, 474-494.
HJEIMSLEV, LOUIS
    1953   Prolegomena to a theory of language. Indiana University Publica-
                tions in Anthropology and Linguistics, Memoir 7.
HOCKETT, CHARLES F.
    1958   A course in modern linguistics. New York, The Macmillan Com-
                pany.
HOENIGSWALD, HENRY M.
    1960   Language change and linguistic reconstruction. Chicago, The Uni-
                versity of Chicago Press.
JOOS, MARTIN
    1957   Readings in linguistics. Washington, American Council of Learned
                Societies.
LANGUAGE LEARNING, SELECTED ARTICLES
    1953   Series I, English as a foreign language. Ann Arbor, Research Club,
                1522 Rackham Bldg.
LEES, ROBERT B.
    1960   The grammar of English nominalizations. Indiana University Re-

search Center Publications in Anthropology, Folklore and Linguistics, Publication Twelve.

LEHISTE, ILSE, AND G. E. PETERSON

1959   Vowel amplitude and phonemic stress in American English. Journal of the Acoustical Society of America 31:428-435.

LONGACRE, ROBERT E.

1952   Five phonemic pitch levels in Trique. Acta Linguistica 7:62-82.
1960   String constituent analysis. Language 36:63-88.

MILLER, GEORGE A.

1956   The magical number seven, plus or minus two: some limits on our capacity for processing information. Psychological Review 63:81-97.

MITCHELL, T. F.

1953   Particle-noun complexes in a Berber dialect (Zuara). Bulletin of the School of Oriental and African Studies 15:375-390.

MORRISON, MAY

1961   An acoustical description of laryngeal vocal quality. Research in progress.

NIDA, EUGENE

1947   Bible translating. New York, American Bible Society.
1949   Morphology, the descriptive analysis of words. 2d edition. Ann Arbor, University of Michigan Press.
1950   Learning a foreign language. New York, Committee on Missionary Personnel of the Foreign Missions Conference of North America.

PICKETT, VELMA B.

1960   The grammatical hierarchy of Isthmus Zapotec. Language Dissertation No. 56. Baltimore, Waverly Press, Inc.

PIKE, EUNICE V.

1946   Dictation exercises in phonetics. Santa Ana [Glendale], Summer Institute of Linguistics.

PIKE, EVELYN G., AND STAFF

1954   Laboratory manual for Pike's phonemics. Santa Ana [Glendale], Summer Institute of Linguistics.
1955   Instructor's supplement for laboratory manual for Pike's phonemics. Santa Ana [Glendale], Summer Institute of Linguistics.

PIKE, KENNETH L.

1943   Phonetics: a critical analysis of phonetic theory and a technic for the practical description of sounds. Ann Arbor, University of Michigan Press.
1945   The intonation of American English. Ann Arbor, University of Michigan Press.
1947   Phonemics: a technique for reducing languages to writing. Ann Arbor, University of Michigan Press.
1954,   Language in relation to a unified theory of the structure of human
1955,   behavior. Parts I, II, III. Glendale (now Box 1960, Santa Ana, Cali-
1960   fornia), Summer Institute of Linguistics.
1957   A training device for translation theory and practice. Bibliotheca Sacra 114:347-362.

PIKE, KENNETH L., AND EUNICE V. PIKE

1960   Live issues in descriptive linguistic analysis. Second edition. Santa Ana, California, Summer Institute of Linguistics.

SHELL, OLIVE A.
    1957   Cashibo II: grammemic analysis of transitive and intransitive verb
               patterns. International Journal of American Linguistics 23:179-218.
TRAGER, GEORGE L.
    1958   Paralanguage: a first approximation. Studies in Linguistics 13:1-12.
TRAGER, GEORGE L., AND HENRY LEE SMITH, JR.
    1951   An outline of English structure. Studies in Linguistics, Occasional
               Papers 3. Norman, Oklahoma, Battenburg Press.
WONG, HELEN
    1953   Outline of the Mandarin phonemic system. Word 9:268-276.
    1954   Addenda et corrigenda to "Outline of the Mandarin phonemic sys-
               tem." Word 10:71.

PART VII

THE
TEACHING
OF
APPLIED
ANTHROPOLOGY

Introduction

In clinical disciplines such as applied anthropology, Laura Thompson observes in her paper, practice usually moves ahead of theory. This has been true in applied anthropology at least since World War II, when a good many anthropologists were drawn into work on practical problems. Theoretical views of the nature of applied anthropology have varied widely; some practitioners put its potentialities for hypothesis-testing above its clinical, problem-solving aspects.

The papers in this section reflect the interest which has arisen in the teaching of the subject and the differing opinions about that teaching. Four of the papers were first presented at a symposium during the 1960 meetings of the Society for Applied Anthropology. Kenneth Little's paper was written for the international conference at Burg Wartenstein. Three of the authors, Rapoport, Thompson, and Barnett, teach an undergraduate course in applied anthropology. Richard Adams, who organized the symposium, recommends that studies in applied anthropology should be used liberally in undergraduate courses, but that a separate undergraduate course in the subject is not advisable. All five authors agree that there should be little difference between the training of an anthropologist who is going into an academic post and one who is preparing for work in the applied field.

Operational procedure in applied anthropology is illustrated by Rapoport's paper. Rapoport observes that in these papers on teaching we become our own "clients" and ask ourselves for evalutions and recommendations for action to improve our teaching. Since no conclusive data on which to base recommendations are available, he presents an exploratory discussion. In the course of it he gives a clear and concise outline of the principal methods of teaching; his evaluation of them can be useful to teachers in every field of anthropology.

Rapoport puts his finger on a feature of applied anthropology which raises special problems. The clients of a practitioner want suggestions for policy and action. Such recommendations entail value choice; ordinarily, anthropologists avoid commitment to values other than those of the scientific method. That academic anthropologists do, in fact introduce certain values into their teaching, negatively about chauvinistic ethnocentrism and positively about respect for other cultures, is illustrated in more than one passage of this volume and is discussed in Ethel Albert's paper. Nevertheless, as Rapoport notes, a crucial challenge arising in applied anthropology courses is that of "translating scientific knowledge in a value-neutral framework into specific action implications."

Laura Thompson faces this challenge boldly. She sees applied anthropology as a key discipline and a course in applied anthropology as an important contribution to a student's liberal education. Her outline of the educational value of such a course touches on some of the central problems of our civilization. She refers to such problems as that of understanding the dynamic nature of cultures including our own, of predicting group behavior, of grasping the new importance of planning, and not least of all, of molding an ethic based on science.

Applied anthropology must be applied in the present and for the future; at the present time western technology and forms of government are so pervasive that, as Little mentions, training in applied anthropology must include training in studying large-scale societies. While an applied anthropologist may focus on a little community or on a particular social or economic group, he must be constantly aware of the forces which impinge upon it from the larger setting.

Anthropologists in a good many countries are being asked to help prepare students for work in the newly independent and "underdeveloped" countries. Kenneth Little's paper refers to this kind of training. It is likely that the demand for this service will continue to grow. Similar service courses are given by anthropologists who teach in such professional schools as those of public health, education, and foreign service, as the papers of Section IX indicate.

Applied anthropology covers so wide a range, including many problems which are within the special competence of other toilers in the applied vineyards, that Barnett would have a course in applied anthropology concentrate on problems involving the anthropologist's specialty of cultural diversity. Barnett outlines several models of course design and points out that the nature of the field calls for more attention to short-term than to long-term change, more to motivation and values than to tradition and structure. We may add that the analyses of motivation and changing events should be presented against the background of tradition and long-range stability.

Adams' discussion of the use of studies on applied anthropology in teaching reflects a characteristic of the field. It is one of the most versatile, wide-ranging, and eclectic branches of anthropology, since its practitioners feel free to use whatever ideas and methods may be helpful for the practical problem, rather than operating within the academic bounds and literature of the discipline. Anthropologists are generally eclectic in their research and teaching, whatever their special field of work. When they turn to applied problems this eclecticism is given free rein, subject only to the requirements of the problem. Studies done in this manner are particularly useful for the student whether he reads them in preparation for a professional task or in the course of his liberal education, because they demonstrate how knowledge and methods from different disciplines can be marshalled for an empirical purpose.

D.G.M.

ROBERT N. RAPOPORT

Aims and
Methods

I N ANTHROPOLOGY, of all the liberal arts fields, it has always seemed to me particularly inept to cite the old saw that "those who can't do, teach." Since Malinowskian times, "doing" (at least what anthropologists "do") has been higher in the profession's scale of values than teaching or scholarly reflection. When "schools" have accumulated around the great men of our field, they have tended to be based on the hard bed-rock of personally gathered field data. In those cases where the field experience was linked to the affairs of such persons as colonial or trusteeship administrators, the additional interest was present of application of the anthropological findings to practical action. In any case, the methods used by the professional anthropologists in their university teaching have remained sacrosanct professional prerogatives, not themselves subject to the dispassionate scrutiny their users advocate. As we now become our own clients and ask ourselves for evaluations and recommendations for action to improve our educational programs, we see that we present a difficult case. In the absence of conclusive evalutive data based on controlled, theory-guided experimentation, the best start is an exploratory discussion.

The present discussion will be limited to the fields in which social anthropologists have contributed. It will: (1) delineate the special character of teaching goals in applied anthropology for undergraduates; (2) explore the merits of conventionally used teaching methods for these goals; (3) indicate some less conventional approaches that would seem relevant to these goals; and finally (4) describe critically some of the problems of selecting and using various teaching methods. This is seen as a prelude to further study of the problem.

THE GOALS OF TEACHING APPLIED ANTHROPOLOGY

To a great degree the goals of teaching applied anthropology coincide with those of other courses in social anthropology, i.e., the imparting of a body of knowledge and of a particular perspective in viewing cultural phenomena. There are, however, some distinctive features of the aims of applied anthropology courses, stemming partly from the type of students usually found in them and partly from the special character of the field itself.

To begin with, any course of anthropology for undergraduates, even undergraduates majoring in anthropology, must be seen as composed of a much larger proportion of students who will *not* become professional anthropologists than who will (Kluckhohn 1960). This fact has immediate relevance for setting the general teaching goals of anthropology in the undergraduate curriculum—bringing them toward alignment with other liberal arts courses. The dominant goals here are to contribute to the development of "well rounded," "free," and "thinking" citizens. Applied anthropology, as such, may be part of this general pattern, especially if the course is heavily attended by a large cross-section of students (as, for example, when taught by a famous figure and addressed to such popular topics as "Anthropology in the Modern World").

More often, however, applied anthropology courses vary from this pattern in important ways. The courses tend to be small in size. Furthermore, a different kind of student is often strongly represented in the class—viz., the prospective professional in one of the fields that characteristically or potentially applies anthropology. These students intend to go on to legal, administrative, or industrial schools following their graduation and seek, prudently, to absorb a social science perspective *before* becoming engulfed in specialized training.

The presence of this group brings to the forefont another facet of educational goals. Rather than stressing professional "doing" of anthropology on the one hand, or the well rounded "knowing about" anthropology on the other, it is the "capacity to apply" anthropology that becomes relatively more important. Any particular teacher may deemphasize this aspect of applied anthropology—its "art" in Adams' terms (Adams 1960)—in favor of its more purely scientific aspects. However, in undergraduate teaching especially, the interests of the students may prompt a different distribution of emphasis than might hold for graduate professional training.

Policy and action, frequently the dominant preoccupation of applied anthropologists' subjects and clients, imply value choice. Academic anthropology, on the other hand, assiduously avoids commitments to values other than those of the scientific method. To develop an understanding of this process of translating scientific knowledge in a value-neutral framework into specific action implications is, therefore, a crucial challenge arising in applied anthropology courses.

The goals of teaching applied anthropology to undergraduates might thus be seen to include the following elements:

a. To impart a certain amount of substantive content from the field of anthropology in its academic and applied dimensions.

b. To engender a social scientific orientation; in anthropology this is seen as a balance between the necessary detachment from one's own and other cultures on the one hand (so that they may all be seen as equally valid human variants) and the necessary empathic involvement in particular cultures on the other hand (so that their unique perspectives can be understood in their own terms).

c. To develop a capacity to move from the general to the specific as well as the reverse; and to see, in particular situations, the relevance of social science postulates for policy and action.

With reference to these goals there are indications that teaching methods are differentially effective. Each course is likely to be oriented in some degree to all of the above goals, though particular courses will vary in the type of combinations and emphases they select. It is therefore hypothetically appropriate to use more than one method in any given course.

CONVENTIONAL METHODS

It would seem that conventional undergraduate teaching methods—*lecture, teaching aids* (e.g., films), *reading assignments,* and *examinations*—are best suited for serving the first aim outlined above. The lecturer, as an authoritative representative of his field, delivers, in organized rhetorical packages, accumulations of his erudition—hopefully adding to what the Herbartian educators used to call his students' "apperceptive mass." Large groups of students can thus be delivered substantive packets of information. (Relatively few of the students will be geared to gaining the further potential advantage of this method—namely, the identification with a scholarly figure engaged in the exercise of one aspect of his craft.) The reading assignment places further bodies of stored information at the disposal of the teacher for adding to the student's cognitive awareness of the contents of the field. Teaching aids must not be dismissed as necessarily minor ancillaries to the lecture method. Films and other documents may become principal teaching instruments in such areas as studies of culture at a distance. Nor should the potential teaching functions of examinations be lightly dismissed. Although most teachers use examinations, and even mid-term quizzes and reports as evaluative devices, at least one teacher of applied social science reports a preference for early administration of examinations, precisely for the maximization of their value as teaching devices. They stimulate discussion that carries well into the course, and this dicussion (especially in small classes) affords the teacher further materials for evaluation of students' abilities.

Another method conventionally associated with undergraduate teaching—especially in the physical and biological sciences—is the *laboratory* (or field trip). In anthropology, especially social anthropology, this method is ordinarily reserved for graduate training, often connected with work toward the dissertation. Linguists have long used native speakers for language training, and this method has more recently been brought into the classrooms of social and applied anthropology courses (cf. Whyte and Holmberg 1956). Similarly, the *discussion group* in its most productive form is usually associated with graduate teaching, especially in the seminar form, and is often seen as an ancillary method in undergraduate teaching. This is probably due to the twin considerations of the large size of many undergraduate courses and the sheer volume of information to be transmitted. While this method does not seem so well suited for the conveyance of a large amount of organized content, it is considered valuable in helping the student properly to internalize the information. By verbalizing his reactions to the contributions of others, the student is thought *ipso facto* to contribute to the development and consolidation of his own thinking on the subject and to his general capacity to use human interaction as a way of learning.

Most courses have more than one method associated with them but are characterized by the dominant method employed. Thus we speak of lecture courses, seminars (reports and discussions of students' work), reading courses, or field work (lab) courses.

There is a good deal of evidence that at least as important as the method used is the teacher's style or technique in using it. Take Firth's comment on Malinowski as a teacher:

. . . what he really liked was the seminar, the informal discussion group, with someone else giving the paper. Bending over his sheaf of notes at the head of the table or sunk in his deep armchair, nothing would escape him— no loose phrase, no shoddy thinking, no subtle point of emphasis. With a suave question, a caustic word, or a flash of wit, he would expose a fallacy, probe for further explanation, or throw new light on something said. At the end, after inviting opinion from all sides, he would draw together the threads in a masterly way, lifting the whole discussion to a higher theoretical level, and putting it in a perspective of still wider problems. He was always constructive. One of his gifts was so to transform what had been said as to bring out its value as a contribution to the discussion. He made each member of the seminar feel that, fumbling and inept as the words had been, Malinowski perceived the ideas and gave them all or more than they deserved. (1957, p. 8)

Classically, educators have tended to lean toward one or the other side of what is seen as a basic rift in approaches—i.e., the permissive (democratic, student-centered) approach on the one hand, and the directive (autocratic, subject-centered) approach on the other. Professor I. A. Richards, illustrating the subject-centered approach, sees the goal of teaching to be the subjection of the human psyche to the sovereignty of reason and urges teachers to don a mask of knowledgeability, refraining from *public* self-doubting. He scoffs at the idea that professors must get to know their students personally and individually, stating:

People will tell you that a good teacher must do this and that, have a deep interest in every one of his students, must know them intimately and be really concerned with their intellectual, moral, and other kinds of development. I think this is no more than the reflection of the student's favorite myth that knowing the professor socially would be helpful. I have known superb teachers who to the end of their days could not tell one student from another, orally, optically, or even intellectually." (1951, pp. 11.)

The professor, as in Coleridge's famous verse, does best, says Richards, to address "all in each in all men" among his students.

In contrast, Dr. Charles Slack, a teacher of applied social science in the field of juvenile delinquency, says that he gets the best results out of teaching undergraduates by initially at least keeping *all* authoritative viewpoints out of the course—his own or those of published professionals. He feels that the fresh perceptions of students provide a creative infusion of new life into the ossified thoughtways of such fields as the treatment of schizophrenia or of juvenile delinquency. He feels, furthermore that by forging their own ways of thinking about problems to which they are exposed students achieve a deeper and more significant learning experience.

Most anthropologists seem to favor an intermediate position. Like Leland P. Bradford of the Bethel Training Laboratory, they seem to acknowledge that their goals include more than merely cognitive learning, but include the deeper and broader goals of personal and professional development (Bradford 1958). Arensberg, for example, describes his method as follows:

The students and I, in common analytic discussion of the cases, arranged by me in order of complexity, with me giving the facts in summary, or a student doing it, they discovering the principles, move from simple empirical principles (also presented in ancillary literature) to complex structural modelling of culture contact, culture borrowing, and planned intercultural transfer of techniques (technical assistance, schemes of rehabilitation, development). (Personal Communication 1960)

Studies aiming to evaluate the relative merits of democratic vs. autocratic techniques of teaching have not been conclusive in their findings. College students vary as to their preference for one or another style, as do the teachers themselves, but studies to date have not shown clear-cut relationships between these experiences (whether preferred or merely endured) and academic performance (Allport 1951, Wispe 1950). There is some indication that the dimension of teacher-skill is more important than that of method-choice. Furthermore, some studies indicate that the kinds of gains to be anticipated through the use of student-centered techniques are not those picked up by conventional examination performance, but include such clinical psychological gains as increase in "growth," "insight," and the like (Murphy and Ladd 1944, Cantor 1946).

In anthropology, especially in applied anthropology, the stress laid on other goals than the accumulation of information prompts an interest in the more student-centered methods of teaching. There seems to be an increased emphasis on the development of non-conventional methods to maximize these goals.

NONCONVENTIONAL METHODS

The newer methods of teaching, which tend to bring into focus goals other than mere conveyance of substantive information, often comprise explications and developments of techniques that were present but implicit and not systematically developed in traditional classes.

Thus, while an experienced traditional teacher states that he likes to leave his classes with a "challenge" at the close of his lecture (Dunlop 1951), a modern, self-conscious teaching methodologist says that he uses as a basis for his teaching method the Zeigarnik effect (Melbin 1960). According to this postulate of learning theory, uncompleted tasks are recalled better than completed ones. As in psychoanalytic theory, where the "unfinished business" of childhood is seen as compelling the individual to repeat his search for the solutions, the immature student, who is shown perspectives bearing on the solution of an "applied" problem but is not given a "pat" answer, hypothetically learns more by forging his own solution. In Festinger's terms, he acts to remove the "cognitive dissonance" that is set up in him (Festinger 1957).

In order to cultivate the capacity to empathize with alien cultures, some teachers have experimented with techniques of role playing to draw individuals' awareness and identification away from the values and objects of their own cultures onto those of exotic groups. Keesing, for example, used foreign students in the Training Program for Overseas Administrators to role-play various typical situations to be found in administering alien populations. He reckoned that this was very helpful in teaching his students to appreciate the problems and cultural perspectives of members of cultures very different from those of the students (Keesing 1949). Whiting has used sociodramatic role-playing to teach ethnography for several years and reports success along the dimentions of learning that concern us here (Lurie and Whiting 1954).

Experiments have also been attempted with the use of field experience in conjunction with university courses. Leighton and his associates actually took classes into the field for peripatetic first-hand demonstrations of field work in the cultures of the American Southwest (Leighton, Adair, and Parker 1951).

Appreciation of contrasting cultural orientations tends to imply the placing of one's own cultural commitments in a different perspective. The cultural relativistic approach, favored in varying degrees by most contemporary anthropologists, requires that this new perspective lead the student to view his own culture as one in a great spectrum of human types, each of which must be understood in its own terms but none of which he must consider superior in any absolute sense. This process of becoming able to place one's own culture in the dispassionately perceived range of human types is called by Spindler "objectification."

As a personal experience, "objectification" tends to be painful, for the alienated person within our culture (as are some rebellious adolescents not uncommonly found in undergraduate classes) as well as for the untroubled ethnocentric one. Several observers of teaching approaches engendering this reappraisal of the range of cultural values and the place of our own in it have noted student defensiveness. Wispe in his study of two kinds of discussion groups, found that though permissive groups are popular with many students, others, perhaps more immature, were found to crave directiveness from their instructors and tended to be very hostile toward the permissive instructor (Wispe 1950). While permissiveness and cultural relativism are not necessarily tightly linked orientations, there are other indications that the student hostility is a function of the social science content as well as the situation in which some may have wished to "escape from the freedom" of an unstructured class. Cyril Sofer, whose observation stems from the study of a social science teaching program to students of a London technical college, notes this reaction to the content of the courses he observed and concludes that the "capacity (for a teacher) to tolerate long periods of spoken or unspoken criticism without becoming hurt, upset or angry, or diverted from one's purpose, is a *sine qua non* for successful teaching and advisory work" (Sofer 1959). Sofer was mindful of the fact that social science ideas impel students toward revising their appraisal of their own values and activities, and that this could be very threatening to students' personal defences.

We thus find some experimentation with methods self-consciously engendering a detached view of one's own culture, a capacity to empathize with alien cultural orientations, a comparative lack of directiveness in drawing conclusions or formulating practical implications—each of which can arouse defensive reactions among students but all of which may be effectively harnessed in teaching applied anthropology to undergraduates.

Any particular course in applied anthropology will combine conventional and unconventional teaching methods to suit the specific goals, student composition, teacher style, and university context. Principles for making wise choices among the available alternatives remain, however, relatively inexplicit—based on intuition, tradition, or other such factors uncertainly linked to rationality. As a gesture toward the accumulation of case studies evaluating particular teaching methods (on the basis of which more rational choices may be made in the future), I contribute a case study.

AN EXPERIMENTAL INNOVATION IN METHODS
FOR TEACHING APPLIED ANTHROPOLOGY

My course in applied anthropology (Social Relations 117 at Harvard) is a rough experimental attempt with a small class (15-20 students) of intermediate range (about one-fourth graduate students, the rest undergraduates) to combine several teaching methods toward the end of maximizing the multiple teaching goals stated above.

The course is based on three general beliefs—each of which I entertain very tentatively, pending further research. First, I believe that a number of unconventional methods are particularly valuable in pursuing the goals of teaching applied anthropology to undergraduates. Second, I believe that the enthusiasm for these new methods should not entail the abandonment of the tried and true conventional methods which have specific places in the course organizaton. Third, I believe that the large university and its adjacent community offer a rich, little-tapped mine of potential teaching-laboratory situations which provide valuable educational resources for both student and teacher.

The course uses three basic methods:

1. *Lectures:* In these I survey the concepts and contents of applied anthropology. I seek to communicate substantive contents of work in several of the fields in which anthropology has been applied and the idea of a relativistic orientation. The readings that are assigned concur-

rently with the lectures supplement this with case materials. For example, in the field of technological development, I assign the Spicer volume (1953); in public health the Paul volume (1954) and in the field of hospital studies several specimens (e.g., Caudill, 1958; Rapoport, 1960).

2. *Field experience:* Each of the students is assigned to an actual research project on applied social research. The first year I attempted this, I assigned students to various ongoing projects in the Boston area. Ideally a reciprocally rewarding working relationship was to develop in which the student provided research assistance while the project director provided a "live" situation for learning. Here the aim was to cultivate the empathic capacity of the student by getting him to appreciate the specific subcultural perspectives of the various parties involved in applied research—the researcher, the subjects, and the client. Because of the problems of providing a uniformly valuable supervised experience (cf. below), I changed my procedure the following year to have fewer projects, in all of which I was more closely involved myself.

3. *Student-centered discussion groups:* Students discuss their field assignments in the light of the lectures, reading, and later in the course, their field research experiences. In these discussions attempts are made to work back and forth between abstract theoretical perspectives, and the requirements of action in the specific case. Three kinds of student-centered discussion groups have been tried: the group consultation (in which the student was attempting to formulate his research problem and design with the participation of his peers), the role-playing feedback (in which the report back to the class at the end of a field experience took the form of role-playing in which individual students enacted the roles of researcher, client, and subject) and terminal research report (similar to the conventional seminar report and discussion).

One problem encountered early in experimenting with this combination of teaching methods was the differing willingness of students to undertake field investigations. While I tried to warn off those who were not prepared to do a field project (the field projects were very time-consuming as well as frightening to some), some students inevitably remained in the course who, though they might be capable of good academic work, did not seem able to carry through a satisfactory field experience. One who was working with me on a study of foreign students never mustered courage to get in touch with the student assigned him, despite a great deal of support, special introductions, etc. Another made a special arrangement with me to do preparatory library work for a project he was to undertake the following summer. I hesitated to force this timid student into a field situation but attempted subsequently to show him how unrealistic his doubts and anxieties were, in the light of the experiences of his fellow-students.

The variable character of projects was also an initial problem. The directors were individuals of different experience and different inclination to make the clerkship a rewarding one for the student apprentice. Also the research installations provided uneven opportunities for involvement. Projects were in different phases of planning, execution, and analysis and were functioning within different contexts of restriction, confidentiality, and security regulations. Ideally in the terminal feedback phase of group discussions these variations were to be put to good use, illustrating the varieties of research conditions under which one might work. However, in some cases individual students, lacking the over-all perspective that could later be generated in class discussion, found their own small segments of the work difficult. One student, for example, was very put out by the restricted task of punchcard data processing to which he was assigned. He complained that he would not learn anything from this experience and asked to be reassigned. The following year, I decided to reduce the number of field projects in which the students participated, and to play a closer supervisory role in all of them.

Finally, I would like to mention the economic problem. In order to make a course of this kind work out well an unusual expenditure of time is required for both instructor and students. The number of students that can be handled in this way is limited even in an environment so rich in potential field training situations as the Boston area.

I believe that despite the difficulties, some of which are mentioned above, the type of teaching approach advocated is unusually rewarding for all concerned. Had I used a single approach, e.g., the lecture method or the case discussion method, I would have given myself fewer problems. However, I also believe that neither the students nor I would have learned as much. Aside from what I learned about current research projects in the Boston area and about Harvard students and how they function, I learned something about teaching methods of applied anthropology. The conclusions I have come to, relative to making a course of the type described above work out well, include the following:

First of all, it is important to give a great deal of attention to the selection (or development) of field projects. A minimum, but not necessarily sufficient requirement is that a professional social scientist be present to provide supervision for the student. Assigning students to projects that lack such professional supervision would not only slight the student's tutorial guidance but would omit that aspect of the field situation that exposes the student to a view of the functioning social scientist in his on-going role relationships with client and subject populations.

Once suitable individuals and projects are located, briefing should be fully carried through—so that the collaborating professional knows what he is expected to give to the student and what he may expect from the student, and so that the student may know what he is expected to get from the project and what he is expected to give to it. Difficulties may arise, for example, if the student expects access to confidential materials or "sensitive" contacts while the professional collaborator expects to use him as a coding clerk. My own view has been that the student's participation, even in the most pedestrian tasks for on-going projects, allows for a valuable learning experience, if properly handled. However, "proper handling" involves a good deal of work toward finding compatible "fits" between the students and the available project positions.

In general, I have found that three kinds of working arrangements have proved viable for the students:

a. to do autonomous small projects within the framework of a larger project (e.g., one student did a study of girl delinquents, using the card files of Walter Miller's delinquency project which had data currently under analysis with other foci in mind);

b. to work as an assistant to a professional engaged in a particular task or project (e.g., a pair of students assisted Murray Melbin in coding and tabulating data on turnover in the aides role in McLean Hospital);

c. to work as a team on an autonomous project (e.g., three students under my supervision, interviewed a small series of advanced foreign students on their experiences with technical cosultation in their home countries and presented a group report. This has now been adapted for publication. [Rapoport 1963]

Out of these experiences with appropriate arrangements I expect each student to get an idea of the characteristics of field research situations; how a research problem gets defined (and its relation to the definitions that the practically-oriented client formulates); the choice of methods with reference to the research problem; the conduct of the research (e.g., interview methods; public relations; the analysis of the findings; and, especially important in the applied fields, the drawing out of implications deriving from the research). Obviously, in any given field experience connected with a course of this type, a student will only get direct exposure to a limited number of these research dimensions, but I expect each student to be alerted to the whole range of problems.

Once the student is placed in a field clerkship, it is important to follow through on his progress. This is valuable, I feel, not only from the point of view of providing whatever tutorial counselling and practical assistance may be necessary, but also from the point of view of watching for the difficulties that students tend to get themselves into. These difficulties are very often not to be dealt with by deft rescue action, but didactically by assiting the student to face and work through the factors that have generated the discord. From this, the student may learn something about the management of role relationships in a field research situation.

One precaution that may have already become rather obvious is against attempting to do too much in a single course. Some middle ground should be found to avoid the limitations stemming from overspecialization on the one hand and the superficiality stemming from overgeneralization of the other. The scope of any particular course will, naturally, depend partly on the propensity of the teacher and partly on the place of his course in the over-all curriculum.

In conclusion, I should like to reiterate that while the word *method* connotes orderliness and rationality, we ought not draw the conclusion that uniformity of method is an imperative in this or any other field of teaching anthropology. The choice of methods will vary according to the particular teacher's skills and preferences, the student body, course specifications, and the university setting. The systematic reporting of experiences with various methods, as here attempted, does not purport to describe an "ideal" pattern in any absolute sense. It serves rather to clarify the characteristics and potentialities of particular methods so that they may become part of a well-defined repertoire for professional choice which will vary according to the specifications of the teaching situation.

NOTE

[1] This paper was first presented at a symposium on Undergraduate Teaching of Applied Anthropology at the meeting of the Society for Applied Anthropology, Pittsburgh, May 31, 1960. Many friends and colleagues have contributed to this paper through their discussions with me. Particularly fruitful have been my talks with Murray Melbin, Rhona Rapoport, John Whiting, Cora Du Bois, and my students in Social Relations 117.

REFERENCES CITED

ADAMS, RICHARD
    1960   Personal Communication.
ALLPORT, GORDON W.
    1951   How shall we evaluate teaching? *In* A handbook for college teachers:
               informal guide, Bernice B. Cronkhite, ed. Harvard University Press.
ARENSBERG, CONRAD
    1960   Personal Communication.

BRADFORD, LELAND P.
1958   The teacher-learning transaction. Adult Education, vol. 8, no. 3.
CANTOR, N.
1946   The dynamics of learning. Buffalo, New York, Foster and Stewart Publishing Company.
CAUDILL, WILLIAM A.
1958   The psychiatric hospital as a small society. Harvard Press.
DUNLOP, JOHN T.
1951   Teaching the social sciences. In A handbook for college teachers: informal guide, Bernice B. Cronkhite, ed. Harvard University Press.
FESTINGER, LEON
1957   A theory of cognitive dissonance. Evanston, Illinois, Row, Peterson and Co.
FIRTH, RAYMOND
1957   Introduction. In Man and culture: an evaluation of the work of Malinowski, R. Firth, ed. London, Routledge and Kegan Paul.
HALL, E. T., JR.
1959   The silent language. New York, Doubleday and Co.
KEESING, FELIX M.
1949   Experiment in training overseas administrators. Human Organization, vol. 8, no. 4.
KLUCKHOHN, CLYDE
1959   Anthropology in Harvard College. Harvard foundation for advanced study and research news letter. Cambridge, Mass.
LEIGHTON, ALEXANDER H., J. ADAIR, AND S. PARKER
1951   A field method for teaching applied anthropology. Human Organization, vol. 10, no. 4.
LEWIN, KURT
1948   Resolving social conflicts. New York, Harper and Bros.
LAURIE, NANCY O., AND J. W. WHITING
1954   A technique for teaching ethnology. American Anthropologist, vol. 56, no. 3.
MELBIN, MURRAY
1960   Personal Communication.
MORSH, JOSEPH E., G. BURGESS, AND PAUL N. SMITH
1955   Student achievement as a measure of instructor effectiveness. Bulletin No. TN 55-12. Lackland Air Force Base, Texas, Air Force Personnel and Training Research Center.
MURPHY, L. B., AND H. LADD
1944   Emotional factors in learning. New York, Columbia University Press.
PAUL, BENJAMIN D.
1955   Health, culture and community. New York, Russell Sage.
RAPOPORT, ROBERT
1960   Community as doctor: new perspectives on a therapeutic community. Springfield, Ill., Tavistock-C. C. Thomas.
1963   Some notes on para-technical factors in cross-cultural consultation. Human Organization (in press).
RICHARDS, I. A.
1951   The teaching process. In A handbook for college teachers: informal guide, Bernice B. Cronkhite, ed. Harvard University Press.

SOFER, CYRIL
   1959   New ways in management training. London, Tavistock Publications.
SPICER, EDWARD
   1952   Human problems in technological change. New York, Russell Sage
             Foundation.
SPINDLER, GEORGE D.
   1955   Education and anthropology. Stanford University Press.
   1959   The transmission of American culture. The Burton Lecture 1957.
             (Distributed by the Harvard University Press for the Graduate
             School of Education of Harvard University.)
WHYTE, WILLIAM F., AND ALLEN R. HOLMBERG
   1956   How do we learn languages. *In* Special Issue of Human Organiza-
             tion *on* Human problems of United States enterprise in Latin Amer-
             ica, vol. 15, no. 3.
WISPE, LAUREN
   1950   An evaluation of methods of teaching in introductory social science.
             Department of Social Relations, Harvard University. (Ph.D. Thesis)

LAURA THOMPSON

Concepts and
Contributions

APPLIED ANTHROPOLOGY, in the United States at least, is a rather
recent development within the discipline of anthropology as a whole.
We may forget, in view of the rapid development of applied anthropology and its subdivision into many specialities, that it is less than
twenty years since we founded the Society for Applied Anthropology,
and less than thirty years since we began writing very much about applied anthropology of any sort.

Impetus was given to development of the applied aspects of anthropology in this country by conditions during World War II and immediately afterwards. The national emergency drafted into work on
diverse, urgent practical problems first-class anthropologists who would
not otherwise have entered this field. Applied anthropology mush-
roomed into several subdivisions, including administrative anthropology, industrial anthropology, educational anthropology, medical and
psychiatric anthropology. Many senior anthropologists thus acquired
some experience in this new field, not only those who were making a
life career of applied anthropology, but also those who preferred to return to academic anthropology when pressures were relaxed.

If the development of the discipline had been more gradual, there
might be less confusion now about its status and function in the profession as a whole and about the definition of its areas of problem. Actually, before a single textbook had been published in applied anthropology and before consensus could develop as to this field and how to
define it, courses in applied anthropology were being taught as part of
the curriculum in many anthropology departments.

Even today, except in certain types of industrial anthropology, the

353

theoretical bases, methodologies, and operations of the applied anthropologist in the several fields of applied anthropology have not been formulated adequately and presented for training purposes. We do not have an adequate text, so far as I am aware, in this over-all field, although of course excellent presentations of several aspects of it have been published; as, for example, by Barnett (1956), Leighton (1945), Mead (editor 1953), Opler (1956), Paul (editor 1955), and Spicer (editor 1952).

What Is Applied Anthropology?

In an attempt to dissipate some of this confusion, let us note some recent trends in applied anthropology. Modern applied anthropology differs from so-called academic anthropology in several very important respects. An analogy to medicine may help to clarify the issue. Applied anthropology in its various branches may be thought of as the "medicine" of anthropology, if one thinks in terms of the medical profession at an earlier period in its development. At the present stage in the development of applied anthropology, the successful practitioner has to function in several roles. Not only is he required to diagnose the problem and recommend treatment, as did the old-fashioned general medical practitioner, but he must also develop the instruments of diagnosis and do the research or laboratory work to discover the remedy. Frequently, he is also expected to superintend, if not actually to administer, treatment.

As in medicine, every problem in applied anthropology, by its very nature, is a situational or "field" problem in the traditional sense; that is, inevitably it involves an on-going life situation. It focuses on a group of human beings behaving in a real life context—in other words, a *clinical* context (Thompson 1959). This means that the applied anthropologist is functioning in a natural laboratory situation, rather than an artificially contrived laboratory, or in the library or armchair type of research.

Methodological Objectives

A further source of difficulty in understanding recent trends in applied anthropology is that the applied anthropologist is given a practical problem involving group behavior by the administrator who has engaged his services. The administrator may be a government official, public health officer, physician, psychiatrist, or industrial manager. As a scientist, the applied anthropologist cannot work directly on the practical problem. He must first translate it into a scientific problem to be solved by the methods of science. This may be considered the basic methodological objective of the applied anthropologist and also the crucial step in the construction of his research design. It requires considerably more skill than formulation of a scientific problem of the academic type. Difficulties in this area may be expected to decrease, however, as we come to understand the significance of this procedural step and acquire the experience to handle it. Modern applied anthropology may thus move from the level of "trouble shooting" to the acknowledged status of a professional discipline which, like medicine, will represent the applied, clinical aspect of several fundamental sciences.

MAIN CONTRIBUTIONS OF APPLIED ANTHROPOLOGY TO A LIBERAL EDUCATION

A Dynamic Concept of Culture

One of the contributions which the study of applied anthropology may make effectively to a liberal education is a working concept of culture as dynamic. In thinking over the development of applied anthropology as a systematic discipline and its rapid subdivision into many branches, I am struck with the importance of a dynamic approach toward the study of culture and especially toward the analysis of culture change, as basic to the whole movement. Modern applied anthropology could not have developed to its present status within the lifetime of today's senior anthropologists had we not begun to question the relatively atomistic view of culture expressed in much of the work of the American Historical School and other traditional approaches to the study of cultural phenomena. We had, for example, explicitly to reject a working concept of culture that tended to view the whole as a sumtotal of discrete component traits, with the notion that the process of culture change involved merely the addition and/or subtraction of some of them.

Until we learned to focus on, and to develop, theories of culture process adequate to the nature of our problems, a systematic discipline of applied anthropology could not emerge. There could be only "trouble shooting" and kindred activities. Now we postulate that all cultures are constantly changing, and granted this assumption, we are preoccupied with the pace and rhythm of culture change in situational context, its differential nature, and its relationship to stress either from within or without the cultural group. And, as applied anthropologists, we are concerned with differentiating between classes of stress and the several degrees within each class, and with their effects on the culture of the particular group or community under consideration.

Since, in clinical disciplines such as applied anthropology, practice usually moves ahead of theory, the new views regarding cultural dynamics have frequently been implicit rather than explicit in the literature. But fruitful theories regarding the dynamic nature of culture process are gradually being formulated. These are proving successful in resolving practical problems translated by the applied anthropologist into scientific problems involving phenomena of culture change. As a result, we may expect in the near future a strengthening of the discipline and clarification of its goals, working hypotheses, methods and operations. Such clarification should improve the teaching of applied anthropology.

Clinical Prediction of Group Behavior

Perhaps of greater significance than the above, as a potential contribution to a liberal education, is the applied anthropologist's constant and unequivocal concern with prediction of the behavior of groups under certain circumstances. Predictive ability is the most difficult tool demanded of the applied anthropologist, and it is a crucial skill, since on it depends his maturation as a scientist.

The problem of prediction of group behavior within the framework of anthropological theory and methodology is in need of study and clarification. Anthropologists employed by the armed forces were asked to predict the behavior of communities or ethnic groups familiar to them as a result of field experience, but inaccessible at the time. Since many of the suggestions involving such predictions were subsequently implemented, the situation afforded a good testing situation. I suggest that, if the record could be assembled and declassified, the predictive abilities demonstrated would be impressive. Many of these subsequently validated predictions, however, were not based on the usual method of extrapolation. Rather, a clinical method, not yet clearly defined, was used. This involved: (1) a dynamic working model of culture viewed as an emergent; (2) a penetrating, detailed, firsthand knowledge of the changing culture of the community under consideration, including its traditional ecology and values and frequently also its group personality structure. Let us note, also, that it was the urgent need to solve real and critical practical problems in a national emergency involving high stakes that elicited these successful efforts in applied anthropology.

Planning and Development Models

Another contribution that may be made to a liberal education through the study of applied anthropology is clarification of the community planning and development problem. Almost every problem in applied anthropology involves planning and development at some level. In our space age, there is a need for a clear view of this problem on the part of the educated person in his role as a citizen of his community and nation. Especially does the young man or woman growing up in the contemporary situation need some well-informed help in achieving his or her own viewpoint on planning and development on an international scale, and even in global perspective.

The work of applied anthropologists, social philosophers, and others concerned with applied social research suggests two main approaches to the community planning and development problem. The first may be called the "blueprint" approach, whereby planning and implementation form two distinct and usually sequential operations. Karl Mannheim (1940) explored many facets of this viewpoint. The *means* of achieving the ultimate objectives may vary from authoritarian to grassroots democratic in type, but if the *ends* are fixed in advance, we may class the planning project as "blueprint" in type. A. H. Leighton's *Governing of Men* (1945) is an excellent example of this kind of planning. Virtually all Point Four and economic development projects are of this type. This approach apparently takes as its model the procedure of the architect and city planner. Hence, it is not surprising that some brilliant work has been done in applied anthropology by professional city and regional planners. The project of Albert Mayer (1958) on rural communities in India is a case in point.

An alternate planning and development model has been called "social action research." I believe the potential of this model is little understood among planners, not to mention laymen and students. According to the social action research approach, planning and implementation form a single operation. Both ultimate and immediate goals are flexible and sensitive to the needs in the changing real life situation of the ongoing ecosystem. The members of the group take responsibility for the entire operation. They may proceed by trial and error and may profit directly by their failures as well as their successes, and they may adjust their goals accordingly.

An ancient custom of the Papago Indians will illustrate this type of planning—a tribe which has lived in its southern Arizona desert niche for millennia. Traditionally, all the males in a Papago village met nightly in the village round house. Led by the village chief, they discussed community problems, from how to defend themselves against Apache raids to what to do about drought (Underhill 1939; Joseph *et al.* 1949). In attempting to solve a community planning problem among the Hopi Indians, I finally selected this planning model (*Culture in Crisis* 1950).

Scientifically-based Norms and Goals

Another contribution which the study of applied anthropology may make to a liberal education, and one closely related to the above, is clarification of the problem of community norms and goals in an ecocultural context. By clarification, I mean illumination by means of concrete case studies to the end that the liberal arts student may gain a theoretical grasp of the problem, and also learn to apply this knowledge to his own on-going, real-life situation.

Our space age, with its global perspectives, seems to be moving in the direction of developing a universally applicable set of community norms based on the findings of modern science. These concern the physical health of the individual, his emotional equilibrium, his nutritional balance, his social behavior in relation to the prevailing mores, etc. The standards may or may not emphasize ecocultural differences between groups, but they attempt to achieve universal acceptability on the basis of scientific research.

We are also working on the problem of developing cross-cultural norms of community health and balance which may have universal validity. Such norms have already been developed, of course, for natural ecological communities. They are accepted and in constant, successful use in sustained yield forestry, wild life management, soil and moisture conservation, etc. Many students, however, do not realize that the universally-accepted group of norms of applied biology are mainly based on an organismic approach. This postulates a universal directiveness built into all organisms at every level, beginning with the cell and manifest even in the ecosystem as a whole. Basic to this approach is the hypothesis that the organism directs its activities toward ultimate biological goals of self-actualization—including, of course, maintenance, reproduction, and completion of the life cycle through succeeding generations. Functional ecology, the basis of the successful, modern natural rescources conservation movement, assumes implicitly that this principle of directiveness toward ultimate biological goals manifests itself also at the group level. Ecology further postulates the evolution of the biotic community toward a climax type of balanced organization and, after loss of its balance under stress, self-recovery, and search for a new climax.

Modern stress theories, developed in the areas of psychosomatic medicine and psychiatry, manifest a surprising similarity to these older hypotheses of the organismic biologists. Living representatives of the latter include such distinguished names as Edmund Sinnott, Julian Huxley, E. S. Russell, and Alfred Emerson. It is interesting to note that applied anthropologists are developing a similar theory in relation to the evolution of human communities (Thompson 1960, 1961). Its application to human groups is yielding norms which seem to have significance in regard to the problem of *human* resources conservation.

Relation of Concepts to Hypotheses

Regarding the working concepts from applied anthropology mentioned above, we emphasize here that their meanings should be implicit in the deductive working hypotheses of which they form a part (Northrop 1947). The student should be given adequate instruction not only in concepts of culture viewed as dynamic process but also in the functions of such concepts in relation to deductive working hypotheses concerning the nature of man, the nature of organism and life, the nature of the universe, etc. In connection with the discussion of norms and goals for example, he might be introduced to the emerging concept of the "healthy or balanced community" and how this may be related to a dynamic theory of culture. Also the concepts of "goal-directed behavior" and "human conservation" could profitably be related to such a theory of culture. In this way he will be able to tie in the teachings of applied anthropology with the philosophical framework he should be developing in the course of his liberal arts education.

SUCCESSFUL TEACHING METHODS

In view of the absence of adequate textbooks and teaching materials in applied anthropology, these working concepts can be presented successfully, according to my experience, by student-centered teaching methods as formulated, for example, by Thomas Gordon in his *Group-Centered Leadership* (1955). Students respond favorably to a class project having as its aim to develop an outline for a general textbook in introductory applied anthropology, together with some general principles to guide the practitioner. The case study method may be used (e.g. Mead ed. 1953, Spicer ed. 1952).

So presented, undergraduates seem to experience no special difficulty in understanding the objectives and concepts discussed in this paper. In fact, I believe that younger students frequently have less resistance to the new approaches and concepts of applied anthropology than older, more theoretically-committed graduate students. Regarding the problem of undergraduate versus graduate courses, in view of the history of applied anthropology the problem of undergraduate training in this discipline cannot be separated, I believe, from that of training in applied anthropology in general. I therefore suggest that the main objectives, working concepts and problems of applied anthropology be presented at the undergraduate level as part of a general survey of the whole field of anthropology. Professional training and apprenticeship, by means of first-hand field experience in a community with an unfamiliar culture, probably should not be expected until the student has enrolled for a professional degree at the graduate level.

If applied anthropology is indeed the key to discipline, some believe it to be, this specialization will continue to attract students—even quite superior ones—interested in the subject itself, the way of life it necessitates, and the creative challenge it affords. As its practitioners gradually develop and formulate their theoretical approaches, methods, and findings, and demonstrate their predictive skills, applied anthropology cannot help but gain in stature in the profession, as well as outside it.

NOTE

[1] An early draft of this paper was presented at the Symposium on the Teaching of Applied Anthropology in Undergraduate Courses to Liberal Arts Students at the Annual Meeting of the Society for Applied Anthropology in Pittsburgh, May 30, 1960. An expanded, revised draft is being published elsewhere.

REFERENCES CITED

BARNETT, H. G.
    1956   Anthropology in administration. Evanston, Ill., Row, Peterson.
GORDON, THOMAS
    1955   Group-centered leadership. Boston, Houghton Mifflin Co.
JOSEPH, ALICE M. D., R. SPICER, AND J. CHESKY
    1949   The desert people. A study of the Papago Indians. Chicago, University of Chicago Press.
LEIGHTON, A. H.
    1945   The governing of men: general principles and recommendations based on a Japanese relocation camp. Princeton, Princeton University Press.
MANNHEIM, KARL
    1940   Man and society in an age of reconstruction. New York, Harcourt Brace.
MAYER, ALBERT, AND ASSOCIATES
    1958   Pilot project India: the story of rural development at Etawah, Uttah Pradesh. Berkeley and Los Angeles, University of California Press.
MEAD, MARGARET (ED.)
    1953   Cultural patterns and technical change. A manual prepared for the World Federation for Mental Health. Paris, UNESCO.
NORTHROP, F. S. C.
    1947   The logic of the sciences and the humanities. New York, Macmillan.
OPLER, MARVIN
    1956   Culture, psychiatry and human values. Springfield, C. C Thomas.
PAUL, B. (ED.)
    1955   Health, culture and community: case studies of public reactions to health programs. New York, Russell Sage Foundation.
SPICER, E. H. (ED.)
    1952   Human problems in technological change: a casebook. New York, Russell Sage Foundation.
THOMPSON, LAURA
    1950   Culture in crisis: a study of the Hopi Indians. New York, Harper and Bros.

1959 The clinical situation in psychotherapy, dependency government, and applied anthropology. Human Organization 18:131-134.

1960 Applied anthropology, community welfare and human conservation. In Selected papers from the 5th International Congress of Anthropological and Ethnological Sciences, A.F.C. Wallace, ed. Philadelphia, University of Pennsylvania Press.

1961 Toward a science of mankind. New York, McGraw-Hill.

UNDERHILL, RUTH

1939 Social organization of the Papago Indians. In Columbia University Contributions in Anthropology, vol. 30. New York, Columbia University Press.

KENNETH LITTLE

*The Context
of Social
Change*[1]

ANTHROPOLOGISTS possess an approach and a method of studying social relations which can be employed in all forms of culture. Anthropological experience, therefore, should be of assistance not only to governments and agencies concerned with the administration of so-called backward peoples but in the social development of modern communities. The question that arises, however, is in what ways can such advice be useful to those seeking it and to what extent should anthropologists be involved in its application.[2]

THE SCOPE OF APPLIED ANTHROPOLOGY AND THE ANTHROPOLOGICAL ROLE

Many of our colleagues consider that the anthropologist who agrees to study a given problem should do no more that supply basic information about it.[3] They argue that to offer advice is to identify oneself with social policy and hence to compromise one's scientific position. Others, while admitting the difficulty of prediction, feel nevertheless that if the anthropologist is in a better position than anyone else to point out the possibly unforeseen consequences of a particular policy, it is his duty to do so.[4]

Quite apart, however, from the scientific and ethical problem of whether anthropologists are justified in acting as consultants and advisors to colonial governments, international organizations concerned with community development, and to big business, there is the wider educational function of our subject. This has been specifically recog-

363

nized in the training program of various colonial governments. Thus, it has long been the practice in, for example, Great Britain and France, to send junior officials for special instruction in the native laws and customs of the peoples they are to administer. Many of the territories where European district commissioners and *commandants* used to hold sway are now self governing, but this does not mean that their successors and the new corps of community developers which are taking over will not require a similar training. On the contrary, the very rapidity of change in those countries calls for a greater rather than a lesser degree of anthropological understanding on the part of the layman. Hitherto, it is true, many of the *intelligentsia* who led the movement for self-government have been inclined to look askance at anthropology, regarding it as the handmaiden of colonial rule. However, there are already signs of a different attitude, and the likelihood is that anthropologists will be much in demand once the newly independent governments concerned are in a better position to make use of their services.

One of the main tasks in such countries being to reconcile an older wtih a newer mode of life, anthropology's role is fairly obvious. However, it is not only African pastoralists and Indonesian peasants and the like who are undergoing transition. Our own Western society, too, is changing rapidly, and there is an equal need to "manipulate" social relations in a skillful and understanding way, particularly in certain professions and occupations. There is, for example, the work of teachers in educating their pupils, of doctors and nurses in caring for their patients, of business managers concerned with labor relations and economic productivity, and the combatting of poverty and crime by welfare workers. All these are matters requiring sociological insight.

Specific reference has been made to anthropology's educational function because of its bearing upon practical affairs. It is necessary at the same time to make a clear distinction between the layman's use of anthropology and the role of the anthropologist per se. The implications of the two are professionally and technically quite different, as may be seen if we compare the position of, say, a government official charged with organizing a mass literacy campaign, with that of the anthropologist asked merely for advice about the matter. Ideally, both such persons would seek to learn as much as possible about the social organization and customs of the traditional community concerned. However, for practical purposes, any educational and administrative experience the government official possessed would probably be more important for the job than anthropological qualifications. An anthropological interpretation of the problem would undoubtedly be useful, but only that part of it in accord with official policy and the educational requiremens of the situation would be of practical value.

If my reading of this situation is correct, the moral for the teaching of applied anthropology is clear: it is not to confuse anthropological aims with those of other vocations and occupations. It may be useful, and relevant, for the anthropological student proposing subsequently to work in the field of public health, town planning, or community development to gain what knowledge he can of such matters during his course. However, it is no part of a department of anthropology's responsibility to supply this information or to teach social welfare. On the whole, since the student's time is limited, it will be more profitably spent in learning to become a good anthropologist. The better he is at his own job, particularly fieldwork, the better his chances of dealing successfully with whatever practical problems he is invited to solve.

APPLIED ANTHROPOLOGY IS BASICALLY ANTHROPOLOGY

This is to argue that there should be little difference between the training of the applied and of the academic anthropologist. However, there is, in fact, a good deal of variation in the scope of the subject as taught from country to country, and in different departments in the same country. Quite often, anthropology is taken to mean archaeology, material culture, general linguistics, and physical anthropology, as well as cultural or social anthropology. Although there is doubtless a case for including all these subjects within the education of the academic anthropologist, for practical purposes the problems facing applied anthropology are primarily sociological, requiring a much greater knowledge and understanding of a people's culture and social structure than of any other factor. For this reason it is suggested that applied anthropology should be taught specifically in terms of cultural or social anthropology.

Another reason for this apparent specialization has already been mentioned. It derives from the almost omnipresent phenomenon of culture contact and consequent process of social change, for, as Malinowski has put it, "the figment of the 'uncontaminated' Native has to be dropped from research and study." The methodological implications of this situation may be less significant if one's concern is mainly to reconstruct the traditional culture. For the applied anthropologist, however, the conclusion is obvious: he must seek to understand not only indigenous society *per se,* but its relationship with modern institutions of administration, industry, educaton, etc. How otherwise is he to advise his government or anybody else about the matters in which they are interested—the repercussions on the native economy of introducing novel methods of agriculture; how precisely to increase literacy without undue disturbance of family life; on what basis to organize a co-operative movement; how to reconcile indigenous forms of initiation with Western ideas of hygiene and morality, etc.?

Any such advice necessarily involves prediction, and this can only be made after a most complex and careful analysis of a very wide variety of factors, including a clear identification of social processes.[5] The latter, at the present stage of our discipline's development, consists very largely in learning the kinds of necessary connection between social facts and changes which are to be looked for. It involves finding a place in the scheme for the new social phenomena which, like messianic movements, educated elites, voluntary associations, etc., are the result of cultural contact.[6]

CURRICULA FOR APPLIED ANTHROPOLOGY

The last-mentioned point—the necessity of the anthropologist having knowledge of the working of modern institutions—brings us to the question of curricula. More and more opportunities are arising for anthropologists to apply their science to the problems of our own society. Quite apart, therefore, from the contemporary requirements of research in the traditional field there can be no false dichotomy between what is "sociological" and what is "anthropological." Part of the task now is to provide insight into the social origins and movements of our own times. Consequently, such authors as Durkheim, Marx, Merton, Pareto, Simmel, and Weber will have to be read as carefully as Firth, Linton, Lowie, Malinowski, and Radcliffe-Brown.

This is not to detract from anthropology's time-honored foundations. There is a wealth of ethnographic material from African, American Indian, and Oceanian peoples and the excellence of this information ensures that general principles of social structure and social organization and of cultural differentiation can best be learned from primitive society. Social stratification, on the other hand, is better exemplified on the whole by the more complex societies of the West, both modern and historic, as well as by civilizations in the East. In the latter regard, in addition to studying particular Western institutions, such as the organization of local government, work, and religion, it might also be helpful if certain so-called social problems, such as delinquency, were included.[7]

Further, a knowledge of the social factors involved in race relations is particularly relevant to anthropological work in virtually all colonial and "under-developed" areas. The latter course should aim at clarifying the scientific meaning of "race"; should examine racial contacts in a comparative basis, including countries where race is *not* a social factor; and discuss theories of racial and other prejudice, including anti-Semitism. Study of the sociology of so-called minority groups will

probably throw light also upon problems in which the applied anthropologist is directly interested; for example, the very determined resis-
ance of some non-literate peoples to Western forms of social change.

In the latter regard it follows logically that the general phenomenon
of social change should constitute an overlapping as well as parallel
course to race relations. Major attention should be given, but not entirely confined, to anthropological analyses of culture contact. The
latter have the great advantage of being based upon empirical material, but the approach of other social scientists and of historians is also
relevant. In addition, such a course should review the development of
European colonization and expansion overseas.

The question of fieldwork has also to be considered. Fieldwork is
even more important to the applied anthropologist than to his academic
colleague. It is neither practicable nor necessary for the latter personally to visit every society he draws upon for comparative or theoretical
purposes in his writings. The applied anthropologist, however, is expected to provide practical advice, and so it is essential for him to base
his recommendations upon direct observation and personal knowledge
of the particular situation. His actual participant-observation has practical as well as scientific implications, because in the course of it the investigator gets to know his informants personally and not merely as
sources of information or as actors in a social situation. What he learns
about their individual characters, personalities, and interests may have
special value when it comes to forecasting future action in which these
persons will in all likelihood be involved. Fieldwork also provides a read-
ier insight into other imponderable factors, such as technology and geography, likely to affect the subsequent situation. It goes without saying that training for these tasks should be in line with the rest of the
curriculum and should include the methods of studying large scale societies as well as comparative linguistics and the usual anthropological
techniques of participant-observation and of investigation in depth. In
this regard, therefore, the student should be taught the use and limitations of questionnaires and other formal methods as well as random
sampling and elementary statistics, etc. He should also be set and required to report upon a practical problem necessitating actual methods of field enquiry.[8]

There is also the question of supplementary or supporting courses
to social anthropology itself. The answer to this would seem to depend
upon whether the students concerned are already anthropology graduates with the intention, perhaps, of applying their anthropology to
a particular field. They might be specifically interested, for example,
in problems of nutrition or of literacy. In the latter case, the additional
subjects to be studied appear fairly obvious. As a general background

to anthropological training itself, however, the best principle to proceed on is that the student should appreciate the significance of Western legal and other institutions for grafting on to alien cultures. Economics and politics have an obvious bearing on this matter, whereas economic history will illuminate some of the recurring trends that the anthropologist finds in the contact situation, particularly the so-called Industrial Revolution. Last, but not least, the history of European colonization and expansion overseas is a necessary background to general anthropological study, if not already included as part of the course on social change.

ANTHROPOLOGY IN COLONIAL AND "BACKWARD" TERRITORIES

This brings us to the question of what anthropology can provide for those who have to deal with practical problems of administration, community development, public health, etc. among primitive and "backward" societies. In this case, as already stressed, the objective is not to produce anthropologists, but to help the administrators and other officials concerned to gain an anthropological insight into their work and into their relationships with the communities with which they deal. This does not necessitate an elaborate study of sociological theory, but it does involve some theoretical appreciation of the organization and functioning of social groups as well as the meaning of alien cultures. The present writer's experience is that the best and most convenient way of fostering this understanding is by use of examples from a number of different primitive societies. Societies of Eskimo hunters, East African pastoralists, and Polynesian fisherman are culturally homogeneous enough to be studied as wholes and to demonstrate the interrelatedness of the various social factors.[9] Once the latter lesson has been assimilated, specific attention can be paid to the particular region where members of the class are to live and work. This further course should dwell on what is known about the history of the indigenous population and of their culture and social organization, including systems of land tenure. It should also consider in detail the effects of Western contact upon the traditional way of life and should include discussion of possible future trends in the political and other institutions of the peoples concerned.[10]

ANTHROPOLOGY FOR THE LAYMAN

The first part of the latter curriculum, consisting of an elementary exposition of anthropological principles and of the meaning of "culture" and "social structure," is also relevant to various professions and oc cupations in our own society. As mentioned on an earlier page there are such people as the doctor, the school teacher, the personnel manager, and others to whom it will be an advantage to be able to think sociologically about their particular problems. The amount of relevant material which has been gathered by anthropological methods is growing steadily. Thus, in addition to the earlier studies of the Lynds, Lloyd Warner and his associates, Homans, Whyte, Shaw, etc., in the United States, a large amount of fieldwork has lately been carried out by British anthropologists and other investigators using similar techniques. For example, studies made by Bott (1957), Firth and his associates (1956), Frankenberg (1957), Young and Wilmott (1957), Marris (1958), and Townsend (1957) provide for industrial society the same kind of basic information about kinship and community as is yielded in more traditional fields.

It is suggested, therefore, that use could profitably be made of these data to link up with the courses provided for quite a wide range of non-anthropological studies, including such subjects as economics, law, education, architecture and town planning, social work, and modern history, as well as medicine and psychiatry.

Depending upon the student's prospective specialization and upon other considerations, the anthropological offering might also include at least two further courses. The first of these would be concerned with the sociology of selected professions, for example, school teaching. It would examine, as far as the empirical data allow, the aims and the scope of this profession, would consider its organization, and pay special attention to the various ways in which teachers interact with the wider community. The second course would be concerned with the special social problems of our times, e.g., delinquency, broken marriages, etc. It would discuss these matters in terms of social groups and social behavior and not, needless to say, as examples of social abnormality. It would also examine such problems as far as possible in the light of comparative social institutions and would seek to show their relationship to different social systems.

CONCLUSION

This paper has examined the position of applied anthropology in relation to the anthropological curriculum. It has sought to show that for practical purposes there is very little difference between the training of the applied and the academic anthropologist. In the course of their work and their study, nowadays, both of them are involved in or concerned with situations of so-called acculturation and social change, and both of them require knowledge of their own society's institutions if they are to make progress in their careers and in their research. For the work of the applied anthropologist, however, it is particularly important that

he should have means of studying culture contact and change dynami-
cally and as a method of predicting social processes.

NOTES

[1] The writer of this article has never had the experience of teaching people how
to apply anthropological principles to their work in other fields. He has, however,
taken an active and direct part in organizing courses and in the instruction of
students in training for various non-anthropological occupations in the British
colonies. These students have included Colonial Service cadets (mainly British)
undergoing a year's post-graduate course prior to their posting to such places as
West, Central, and East Africa, South East Asia, and the Pacific; senior Colonial
civil servants taking "refresher" courses in anthropology and related subjects; non-
European students in training as social welfare and development officers in British
colonies in Africa, the West Indies, and the Far East; groups of African and West
Indian teachers preparing themselves for administrative duties in their respective
territories; and occasional British and other European students, mainly missionaries.

[2] One of the best expositions of the applied anthropologist's role is to be found
in Godfrey Wilson's article, "Anthropology as a Public Service," *Africa*, 1940,
13:43-61. See also L. P. Mair, *Studies in Applied Anthropology*, London, 1957,
passim; E. E. Evans-Pritchard, "Applied Anthropology," *Africa*, 1946, 16, 2:92-98;
S. F. Nadel, in "Problems of Application: Results" in *An Appraisal of Anthropology
Today*, Sol Tax, *et al.*, ed. Chicago, 1953, p. 182, and a series of articles entitled
"Values in Action: a Symposium" *Human Organization*, 1958, 17, No. 1.

[3] Very much of the work carried out by anthropologists in Africa on behalf of
the British government falls into this category. Cf. Daryll Forde, "Applied Anthropology in Government: British Africa," Inventory Paper for Wenner-Gren Foundation. International Symposium on Anthropology. New York City, June 9-20,
1952.

[4] Raymond Firth believes that anthropologists are better employed in this way
than in presenting policies. Cf. "Some Social Aspects in the Colombo Plan" *West-
minster Bank Review*, May 1951, pp. 1-7. More recently, Firth has suggested that
the anthropologist has a role as a "social catalyst." He helps the people he is
studying to explore the possibilities of a situation and decide for themselves what
is best to be done in the light of the fuller knowledge he can give them (*Social
Change in Tikopia*, 1959, p. 27). Firth's colleague, James Spillius, has illustrated
this argument by an account of the transformation of Tikopia islanders in plantation labor. The part played by the anthropologist was confined to interpreting the
objectives of each party—the Tikopians and the European managers of the planta-
tions—to the other without identifying himself entirely with either side (cf.
'Polynesian Experiment,' *Progress*, The Magazine of Unilever 46:91-6, No. 256.
See also Spillius' article, "Natural Disaster and Political Crises in a Polynesian
Society; an Exploration of Operational Research," *Human Relations*, 1957, 10:3-27,
113-25, esp. 5-6, 11).

[5] The importance of testing whether anthropological theories are relevant to the
real world has been emphasised by Clyde Kluckhohn. Summary Report, *Wenner-
Gren American Anthropological Association Conference, op. cit.*

[6] Present space does not permit discussion of the theoretical problem involved,
i.e. that of finding a suitable frame of reference within which the factors concerned
may be satisfactorily studied and resolved. It was considered in the present writer's
original paper, cf. *British Journal of Sociology*, December 1960, 11:332-347.

[7] The relevance of Western social institutions for field study and research has been stressed by numerous writers, including Schapera, *op. cit.*, and M. J. Herkovits, *Acculturation,* 1938, New York, p. 18.

[8] The latter subjects mentioned, i.e. race relations, social change, and fieldwork methods, are not generally included within the anthropological curricula of British universities. There is teaching in race relations, however, at both the London School of Economics, London University, and Edinburgh University. The former department of anthropology also offers courses entitled, respectively, Anthropology and Social Problems, Problems of Applied Anthropology, and Social Implications of Technological Change; whereas Edinburgh offers courses entitled, respectively, Problems of Social Change and the Social Implications of Technological Change. Edinburgh also offers a course entitled Methods of Social Research, including field-work techniques, elementary statistics, etc.

[9] This point is made and exemplified usefully in UNESCO's *Cultural Patterns and Technical Change,* Margaret Mead, ed. 1955.

[10] Courses somewhat on these lines are given for the benefit of British Colonial Service cadets in the Faculty of Archaeology and Anthropology, Cambridge University, and in the Institute of Social Anthropology, Oxford. The Department of Social Anthropology, Edinburgh University, also offers an elementary course including regional discussion of social change, for the benefit of overseas students and of European students in training for administrative posts in education or as missionaries.

REFERENCES CITED

BOTT, ELIZABETH
 1957 Family and social network: roles, norms and external relationships in ordinary urban families. London Tavistock Publications.

FIRTH, RAYMOND (ED.)
 1956 Two studies of kinship in London. London, Athlone Press.

FRANKENBERG, RONALD
 1957 Village on the border: a social study of religion, politics and football in a North Wales Community. London, Cohen and West.

MARRIS, P.
 1958 Widows and their families. London, Routledge and Kegan Paul.

TOWNSEND, P.
 1957 The family life of old people: an inquiry in East London. London, Routledge and Kegan Paul.

YOUNG, MICHAEL, AND PETER WILMOTT
 1957 Family and kinship in East London. Glencoe, Ill., Free Press.

HOMER G. BARNETT

*Materials
for Course
Design*

I~~N DESIGNING A COURSE~~ in applied anthropology several alternatives present themselves, as they do in the planning and presentation of any other course. Some of them will be found to be incompatible with any given instructor's conception of the subject and others will be unsuited to the teaching commitments of a department. It is assumed, however, that a general statement of the problem is called for in the present instance. Hence, it is the purpose of this paper to indicate some of the questions which must be answered in organizing course material and to suggest alternative possibilities.

SCOPE

One factor which will inevitably affect the design of a course in applied anthropology is the designer's conception of what constitutes anthropology. This will affect not only the content of the course but the very question of whether there can be one; that is, whether there is anything anthropological that can be applied, and if so, whether it can be taught. Doubt has been expressed on both counts, and with good reasons. It would seem, however, that those reasons stem from the traditional view of anthropology as an academic discipline, and that a relaxation of this constraint can be beneficial to both the theory and the practice of it. In other words, there are equally good reasons for maintaining that the assumptions, the concepts, and the empirically derived findings concerning the nature and function of social and cultural systems can be applied to specific problems in interpersonal relations, and that

373

they, and the conditions under which they are applicable, can be taught just as any other system of strategies and techniques can be taught. I venture to say, however, that something in addition to the holistic concept of society and culture will be necessary for this excursion outside the confines of academic discourse. In order to accomplish it more attention than in the past must be given to motivations, attitudes, and values and less to structure; more to swiftly changing events and less to long-term trends and basic stabilities; more to what knowledge can be applied and less to what it should be called.

At the same time, some limitations on subject matter must be imposed; and since the proposed course is within the scope of anthropology, an instructor must ask himself what its specifically anthropological component can be. The answer to this question can be found to the satisfaction of most members of the profession in the historical role of their discipline. In the main, it has made its place among the social sciences through its emphasis on the comparative study of human group behavior. Consequently, if the designer of a practical problems course considers it important, as I do, to maintain this distinction and to contribute to it, he will be well advised to place an emphasis upon, if not to deal exclusively with, problems which require an awareness of social and cultural diversity as a critical element in their solution. This limitation does not preclude issues involving labor and management or minority groups within a single culture framework, but it gives them a secondary place in the course design and may tacitly and appropriately consign them to other applied disciplines which are equally, or better, qualified to deal with them. It should certainly not exclude those instances in which a specifically anthropological orientation is called for in dealing with problems created by regional differences in a national culture.

Even this reduction in the scope of the course leaves a number of activities in question. Should, for example, the research and advice of physical anthropologists and linguists in the service of government and industry be included? Is a man who works on the identification of the skeletal remains of unknown soldiers or on the specification of the clothing and armament of those yet to become unknown an applied anthropologist? Is the linguist doing intelligence work to be included? These men, with their training in cultural anthropology, as well as in their specialties, have no counterparts in other disciplines; and to the extent that they draw upon that training, there seems to be as much reason for reviewing their efforts as for reviewing those of the cultural anthropologist who attempts to get across the concept of value systems to a class of Harvard pre-medical students or a team of public health workers in Mexico. Perhaps ideally there should be a weighting of examples from all the specialities within what is recognized as anthropology in proportion to the actual number of practitioners, although variation can be expected here, depending upon the purpose of the course.

Before leaving the subject of scope, it might be appropriate to suggest that students of applied anthropology cannot be reminded too often of the importance of applying their wisdom to themselves. It seems that anthropologists, for all their knowledge of such matters, have no fewer inter-personal difficulties than do other people, and as a group they have not been remarkable for their ability to cope with them. Some have found it easy enough, for example, to advise a colonial administrator on ways to improve his relations with the natives in his charge without being able themselves to maintain an effective working relationship with the administrator. This is not simply a matter of personality adjustment. It may be that, but frequently it is much more; and it is that component of the situation than an anthropologist, pure or applied, is alleged to know something about. Colonial administrators, senators, and businessmen occupy statuses that demand the performance of certain roles; and unless the practitioner of applied anthropology is prepared to assail the entire status system represented by any given individual, he will do well to live with it as best he can—and hope that he will be treated with equal understanding. This lesson can be injected at various points along the way in a course, or it can be treated as a special topic. Learning it is essential to the anthropologist working with non-anthropologists, and it is a salutary experience for others as well (Barnett 1948, Leighton 1949:129-173, McAuley 1953:518).

PROBLEM AREAS

Another variable that must make a difference in course design is the organization of its content. Any one of several schemes, or a combination of them, is possible and effective. One approach would emphasize the range of problems that have engaged the attention of action-oriented anthropologists with both a theoretical and a practical aim in mind; theoretical because the discipline presumes to cover the gamut of human behavior, and practical because the extent of its application is very likely unknown to students, some of whom may find somewhere in it an opportunity for a career. In each problem area the information on work done may be separated from programmatic statements. There are practical as well as logical reasons for maintaining the distinction, especially if one wants to stress the fact that anthropologists have acted on their own advice as well as given it to others. Cross-cultural health programs provide an example. In some instances anthropologists have participated in the promotion of these projects, either by assisting in a survey of some complex of customs, such as

food habits, or by analyzing reactions to a program to alter them
(Anonymous 1947, Adams 1953, McDermott, *et al.* 1960, Paul 1950).
In others they have provided source material for such purposes as the
preparation of manuals for the guidance of medical personnel and discussions of the difficulties of implementing action programs (Anonymous 1958a, Adair and Deuschle 1958, Foster 1951, Wellin 1958).
In recent years they have given considerable attention to mental
health. Emphasizing the importance of social and cultural variables,
some of them have concerned themselves with the sources of psychic
stress and with therapeutic devices in non-western societies;; others have
dealt with emotional disturbances generated by acculturation; still others have brought the comparative viewpoint to bear upon their work
with or study of mental disorders in our own society. They have also participated in international congresses on mental health (Caudill 1953,
Opler 1959).

Other broad areas of interest can be reviewed in similar fashion.
In the field of industrial relations a variety of specific studies are available for an analysis of method and theory. These include research on
work groups, industrial communities, labor unions, communication
channels, socio-technical systems, work psychology, and acculturation.
There are summaries of work done on these problem as well as more
general treatises (Richardson 1955). Anthropologists, sociologists, and
labor relations specialists have joined their efforts in some instances;
in others anthropologists have attempted to present their analyses in
terms that are meaningful to a businessman (Hoslett 1951; Keesing,
Siegel, and Blodwen 1957).

Socio-economic problems even more clearly within the domain of
anthropology have emerged the world over with the introduction of
western technology and its products into non-industrialized societies.
At times anthropologists have been engaged by governments to make
studies of land tenure, labor migration, or subsistence patterns of native groups to provide background data upon which to base administrative policy (Rodnick 1936, Schapera 1952). In other cases they
have participated in the planning of economic development projects
(Erasmus 1952).In still others they have served as consultants to tribal
groups or have assisted them in the implementation of plans to meet
their changing needs (Euler and Naylor 1952, Maude 1949, Van Ball
1953). In by far the greater number of cases however, anthropologists
have reported on the consequences of planned or unplanned economic
changes, presenting them for the record or assessing them from the
standpoint of a theory of change (Belshaw 1959, Fisher 1953, Mandelbaum 1953, Nash 1958, Richards 1948, Schapera 1928).

Anthropologists have brought their understanding of cultural variability to bear upon problems of formal education within and outside our society. Most often they have addressed themselves to efforts to educate members of nonliterate groups. Some have been employed as consultants to educators in colonial areas; others have been commissioned to undertake studies of native systems of instruction preliminary to the formulation of an educational policy (Wedgwood 1950). Rarely have they had, or taken advantage of, the opportunity to put their views into effect by teaching or designing curricula, but instances are not entirely lacking (Castro 1949, Wist 1935). Several have written of the general principles involved in cross-cultural education (Mead 1946). More opportunity for the effective dissemination of their views on this subject has been offered through participation in conferences with educators and administrative personnel in which educational philosophies and the means of their realization have been discussed (Keesing 1941). On the American scene they have had comparable experiences. A few schools of education have appointed anthropologists as teachers of prospective teachers, and a few public shcool systems have incorporated the study of culture into their curricula at the instigation of anthropologist (Hoebel 1955). However, as in the case of nonliterate societies, formal and informal conferences calculated to encourage an exchange of viewpoints between anthropologists and educators have been more common than participation in teaching programs.

A remarkable opportunity for the application of anthropological theory was opened up with the passage of the Act for International Development by the U. S. Congress in 1950. That law initiated the so-called Point Four Program for technical and financial assistance to foreign countries seeking to improve standards in health, education, government, agriculture and many other aspects of national life. Comparable programs have been undertaken by the United Nations and by sovereign governments in the interest of their less developed regions. A few American universities have also engaged in more restricted technical assistance projects (Anonymous n.d., Anonymous 1955, Holmberg 1956). The significance of these developments for applied anthropology have been outlined in several places (Gladwin 1960, Tannous 1951). Anthropologists have engaged either in the planning or in the execution of projects abroad, as well as among dependent groups in their own countries (Anonymous 1951, Adams 1953, Barnett 1956, Halpern 1958, Sasaki 1960). They have also evaluated government projects at home and abroad from an anthropological standpont (Barnett 1958a, Erasmus 1954, Foster 1951, Führer-Haimendorf 1958, Spicer 1952).

Another extensive problem area is the one created by newly emerging patterns of leadership, realignments of interpersonal association, re-

definitions of kinship and other aspects of social and political structure
undergoing change. There are, in fact, many anthropologists who regard
this province as the only one with which their discipline equips them
to deal. In other words, they claim competence in dealing with the problems of agriculture, economics, and health only insofar as these problems require an understanding of the organization of human groups
with common interests and established rules of mutual behavior. The
British social anthropologists have concentrated on this area of research
(Mair 1957).

There are several other problem areas in which anthropologists have
applied their professional knowledge in the capacity of decision makers,
or advisors, or detached observers. They include disaster studies,
urbanization, displaced populations, community demoralization, warfare, anthropometry, and human kinematics (Anonymous 1956; Dupree n.d.; Gutkind 1960; Keesing 1952; Leighton 1946, 1949; Macgregor 1946; Mason 1950; Newman 1953; Peirce 1960; Spillius 1957;
Wallace 1956).

OBJECTIVES

Another way to organize the material of a course is with respect to the
objectives of the anthropologist. Obviously this approach cannot be
completely divorced from the one just outlined, for problem solving is
an objective. Nevertheless there can be a different orientation, with the
emphasis placed on aim rather than subject matter. Thus, the purpose
of some anthropologists has been to alert professionals in other fields to
the importance of the cultural approach in dealing with people. If an
instructor wishes to extend this aim to its limits he may include cases
of anthropologists holding appointments in schools of education and
medicine where they teach prospective professionals and to some extent influence the thinking of their colleagues (Hoebel 1955, Paul
1956). More clearly in line with anthropological interests are instructional programs for professionals whose jobs require them to work
with people with cultures distinctly different from their own. Instances
that come immediately to mind are courses of study for colonial administrators. Years ago the Dutch established curricula in anthropology
and other subjects for their civil servants destined for the Indies. More
recently, other governments have adopted the plan. Thus, the British
have their Devonshire Training Scheme and the Australians maintain
a School of Pacific Administration for the training of their colonial
officers. School teachers assigned to native areas are given comparable
instruction in both of these countries (Barnett 1956:49-57).

Although Americans have not yet accepted the idea that it is essential for their official representatives abroad to have a prior understand-

ing of the culture of the country to which they are assigned—much less of the method and theory behind this understanding—there have been sporadic efforts on the part of some governmental agencies to provide such training for certain of their personnel. Descriptions of specific programs of this nature are available as well as assessments of the reasons for their inadequacies (Cleveland, Mangone, and Gerard 1960; Hall 1956; Kennard 1948). One prominent reason has been that the trainees have regarded the instruction as too academic and theoretical. An obvious but not an easy remedy has been to arrange for administrators, educators, and other career specialists to experience direct contact with people of other societies under guidance; in short, to take them on an extended field trip the significance of which they are prepared to understand (Leighton, Adair and Parker 1951).

During World War II the United States military services established Foreign Area and Language Studies program with units at several universities staffed by instructors who, in many instances, were linguists and cultural anthropologists. The students were armed service personnel selected for overseas duty with Military Intelligence branches, the Provost Marshal General's Department and the Signal Corps. A common interest of these arms and services was that the soldier become fluent in one or more modern foreign languages, know the area in which the languages were used, and have insight into the elements which could favor or endanger relations between the Army and the peoples of the overseas area. There were some specifically anthropological techniques and concepts injected into the teaching of the men, one being open-ended interviewing, another and more radical one the use of native language informants instead of the traditional language teachers (Fenton 1945).

A related but different complex of wartime efforts involved anthropologists in the preparation of foreign area reports to the armed services for a variety of purposes. Some material was for the use of intelligence agencies, some for military government in occupied areas, some for operations on the home front. It included a number of "survival manuals" drawing upon native lore to avert unnecessary disaster to castaways and downed airmen, advice on the provisioning of troops through cooperation with natives at advanced outposts, answers to questions about alien customs, ethnographic and linguistic data on projected areas of occupation, and pocket guides to everywhere (Anonymous 1944, Anonymous 1943-44, Emory 1943). In addition to providing these kinds of information, which drew upon already existing knowledge, anthropologists have also worked on problems arising from international conflict. (Anonymous 1953, Mead and Metraux 1953). There have also been analyses of psychological warfare and war psychology from the standpoint of the social scientists (Gillin 1953, Mead 1943).

More recently, and on an entirely different front, anthropology has come to be recognized as an important adjunct to the training of missionaries. For ages successful evangelists have known the value of understanding the customs and languages of the people whom they seek to convert; but this appreciation is now being formalized in ways that are meaningful to anthropologists and in part due directly to their efforts. Courses on culture and society are being given in seminaries and in summer institutes for experienced missionaries (Anonymous 1958b, Ewing 1957). There is also an increasing concern that the missionary comprehend the nature of cultural and social change (Considine 1960).

Another major purpose of applied anthropologists has been to help reduce intergroup tensions. They have done this either through acting as advocates for one of the claimants in a dispute, as expert witnesses, as research consultants, or as intermediaries between groups. During the land claims litigation involving the U. S. Government and various Indian tribes, anthropologists served as expert witnesses, some for the government some for the Indians (Ray 1955). When the Japanese on the Pacific Coast were interned shortly after the outbreak of World War II, research units staffed by anthropologists were set up at the detention centers, in part to study the effects of evacuation, in part to maintain communication between the internees and the administrative authorities, and in part to discover what administrative actions would or would not work under the prevailing conditions (Embree 1944). Comparable research and adjustive functions have been assumed by anthropologists with reference to complaints of minority and nonliterate groups (Barnett 1956:158-170, Hawthorn 1952, Leighton 1946, Perham 1947:217-218). They have also attempted to promote mutual understanding between friendly nations through writing, lecturing, or diplomatic representation (Mead 1948). In fact, at one time, with the establishment of the post of a cultural attaché, it seemed that a new career for anthropologists had developed in this field of cross-cultural interpretation (Embree 1949, Valliant 1945).

PRINCIPLES

Another organizational scheme would be with reference to the principles that have been found to be, or are hypothesized to be, effective in solving problems or reaching objectives of the kind outlined above. It is not entirely distinct from the other two schemes, for many if not most of the reports of activities cited in them embody propositions that are believed to be generally applicable. Yet it can be different, as is indicated by the fact that this approach is the one that most anthropologists have in mind when they express misgivings about the feasibility of a course of study or a program of action that can properly be called applied anthropology. Although, for reasons already mentioned, much remains to be done in applied theory construction and its implementation, there is nevertheless a more respectable inventory of working hypotheses concerning the influencing of social and cultural change than is generally recognized within the profession or outside it. Many of the hypotheses, including those all of us use in our daily contacts with other people, are so commonplace that their true character as powerful means to predetermined ends are not professionally acknowledged. Others derive from more systematic study and abstract analysis, hence are more in the nature of what is expected of scientific principles, but they are borrowed from psychiatry or social psychology and may, therefore, be rejected as non-anthropological. But, regardless of source, whether from common sense or anthropological generalization, they can be used and their use can be taught.

One way to present them is with reference to the theoretical system that has generated them. There are, for example, many imperatives to action implicit in Tylor's definition of culture as "that complex whole which includes knowledge, belief, art, morals, law, custom and any other compatibilities and habits acquired by man as a member of society." They stem from the social genesis of culture and from the interlocking of its parts (Beaglehole 1957:117-118). These and yet other considerations must be taken into account when culture is viewed as the fulfillment of universal human needs the very universality of which makes it possible to graft an alien institution onto the stock of its indigenous functional equivalent (Malinowski 1945:64-72). In theoretical constructs that are definitely psychological the propositions advanced concerning the nature of change, and therefore for the guidance of one who seeks to promote it, are stated in terms of the cognitive and affective properties of individuals singly or in groups. Belief systems, interpersonal relations, attitudes, and personality organization become important considerations, as do the behaviors activated by stress, deviancy, and reward. Within this framework there are clearly discernible differences in the character of the principles adduced from the data on change (Barnett 1953:291-409, Fisher 1953:141-142, Leighton 1946: 247-367, Mead 1953:286-318).

An alternative or additional approach would make use of case studies of change in which observers have analyzed the data with reference to the general principles involved. There are a fair number of such studies, and it might be useful to classify them for instructional purposes. Comprising what is perhaps the largest category are those analyses which describe the difficulties encountered in specific programs owing to a neglect or ignorance of cultural differences. Their authors stress the importance not only of being aware of the possible conflicts produced by the introduction of an innovation but the crucial effects of the manner of its introduction. Pertinent factors include the status of agents of change, the means by which they communicate their intentions, and the images they create of themselves (Adams 1953, Mandelbaum 1953, Whyte and Holmberg 1956). Not far behind in number are those case studies which describe failures to introduce change. They overlap with the first group, for many of the causes are the same: stereotyped thinking, imposed wants, breached communication, incompatible institutions and goals (Aberle 1950, Honigman 1951, Miner 1960, Streib 1952). Some case studies apply general principles to an analysis of reactions to specific programs of change. They seek to disclose the conditions for the acceptance or rejection of something new, or attempt to characterize degrees of receptivity in terms of kinds of innovations or socially defined groups of individuals (Erasmus 1952). Still others assess the merits of one type of implementation procedure relative to another, noting the assumptions upon which they rest and the consequences to be expected from each (Barnett 1958a). Finally case studies may be presented to a class as problems to be solved in the light of the students' knowledge of principles previously discussed. The situations may be hypothetical or actual. The instructor may prefer to originate them; if not he can draw upon a prepared set (Spicer 1952).

Alternatively, a study of principles may be approached through a review of the kind of predictions they permit. Some of them are believed to have universal validity, based as they are upon broad assumptions concerning the nature of society and culture. In the context of change they are frequently stated as reliable guides to action (Linton 1952:75-77). Others, while still general in character, take the form of prognostications; that is, they state that if certain conditions or symptoms are present particular consequences will follow attempts to introduce a change (Herskovits 1952). Some advance recommendations or rules for making changes acceptable (Leighton 1946:355-367, Mead 1953: 291-295).

In addition to general prescriptions for action there are reports of proposals made with respect to specific problems. In most instances, they are, by their nature, recommendations to governments or other sponsoring agencies. Innumerable reports of this sort have been made by administrative officers, but those submitted by anthropologists are especially relevant (Gluckman 1943, Kaberry 1952, Mayer 1951). A strategic variation on the more usual method of recommending solution to a problem involves a projection of the consequences of alternative courses of action with the decision left to administrative officials. This procedure derives from a particular view of the role of an applied anthropologist as well as from an estimate of his predictive resources (Barnett 1956:129-140).

OTHER APPROACHES

The remaining approaches will be outlined more briefly. One is to describe and illustrate the consequences of particular biases in the application of anthropological concepts; that is, to adopt what may be called the "school" approach. This has already been suggested with the mention of theoretical systems in the preceding section; but it can be emphasized and amplified. There is more than one way to do this. Attention can be focussed on individual commitments to theory and practice. Some anthropologists, for example, argue for the desirability if not the inescapability of "interventionism" in the affairs of others if the social scientist is to take any action at all (Holmberg 1955). Others call for objectivity and abstention from the setting of goals by the anthropologist in an action situation (Barnett 1958b). Still others maintain that goals must be set by the anthropologist in cooperation with the people to be affected, either on a trial basis or by advance planning (Tax 1958, Thompson 1950). Then there have been differences of opinion about whether the social scientist should function as a clinician or as an engineer in effecting change (Gouldner 1956).

A treatment according to national predisposition is also feasible. What, for example, has been the conception and practice of applied anthropology in Great Britain, in the United States, in Holland, in Russia, and the United Nations? This is an enlightening approach, for there are really significant differences. They arise from different theoretical presuppositions and from national ethos as well as from different types of involvements with native peoples. There are also different degrees of awareness of, and regard for, developments in other countries among the followers of the several national anthropological traditions. There are, consequently, degrees of isolation and cross-fertilization, degrees of tolerance and mutual benefit.

Another profitable approach, especially for students interested in entering the applied field as a career, is to explore the as-yet unrealized potentialities of the discipline. Data on this aspect of it are available from at least three points of view. In one the author considers the entire range of social science, assessing its accomplishments in general and in particular, describes its drawbacks and the obstacles it encounters in being accepted as a science, and indicates ways and means by which its utility can be expanded (Leighton 1949, Schramm 1954). In another, anthropologists analyze the effectiveness of their discipline, sometimes taking a critical view of its accomplishments, sometimes suggesting where and how it can contribute more than it does (Adams 1954, Chapple 1954). Third, there are non-anthropologists who on the one hand take issue with anthropological claims to greater usefulness and on the other suggest areas of more effective cooperation with their disciplines (Fleck and Ianni 1958, Landy 1958, Pierce 1960, Teicher 1951).

Finally, there can be an effective combination of any two or more of the preceding approaches. As has been mentioned, they overlap each other. Any one of them will cross-cut others and therefore expose more than is indicated by its label. At the same time separate beginnings can be made in order to emphasize the range, flexibility and the richness of the subject. Then areas of convergence can be pointed out to show that there are unifying interests which make it a subject and not a congeries of individual preoccupations. I have found this the most satisfying approach, for it minimizes bias and provincialism in the presentation and permits students to draw their own conclusions and make their own choices among alternatives. It can be accomplished in a single school term or extended over the academic year, depending on the number of cases, problems, and other elements included in the review.

CLASS COMPOSITION

So much for the organization of the content of the course. Another variable affecting its construction is the purpose it is expected to accomplish. Is it to provide students with skills and knowledge to be used to answer practical questions; that is, answers on which a course of action will be based? Or is it to assist in the mastery of a speciality, one of the subdivisions of the broad field of anthropology on a par with folklore, linguistics, and primitive economics? Or is it simply but importantly to contribute to a student's liberal education, along with history and international relations? The answer to these questions will dictate not only the level of discourse—that is, the assumptions that can be presupposed and the number of technical terms that can be used without explanation—but also the content and approach of the course. All three purposes can be accomplished at once, but not very satisfactorily. For this reason as well as for his own satisfaction, an instructor will very likely want an enrollment of students with backgrounds as homogeneous as possible. This could mean that he would prefer to accept only anthropology majors; or in those institutions where anthropology and sociology and perhaps other disciplines are closely integrated, students with a more generalized but common social science background. The establishment of such a requirement would make instruction much easier, but there are other considerations which should and sometimes must be taken into account.

First of all, the number of majors in a department or a division will affect the number of students who can be expected to enroll in a course in applied anthropology. The subject is not yet a required one, and small departments may feel compelled to choose between offering it only in certain years when a new crop of majors comes along, or accepting non-majors in it. The same alternatives may be forced upon larger departments because the subject is new and instruction in it is untried, or because it is considered to be unacademic and therefore not quite respectable. Students are the more likely to adopt a superior attitude toward such a course, because no small number of those to whom they look for guidance and favor hold this view and communicate it in one way or another to them.

But the necessity of compromise is not the only reason for planning a course to accommodate students with heterongeneous backgrounds and different objectives. Heterogeneity of a kind can, in fact, be an asset to a class. This is particularly true if it derives from practical experience and not simply from what some other professor has said. A class which includes practicing missionaries, extension agents, and school teachers who know their jobs but want to learn to work more effectively through gaining a better understanding of people can have a quality of reality that very often is lacking. Or, if it is not lacking, it tends to get biased in favor of the experiences of the instructor, which may or may not be good, depending on the point of view.

In my experience mixed classes of this kind have been the most challenging and productive. The genuine interest that is manifested and the liveliness of the discussion resulting from different student backgrounds more than compensates for any disadvantages arising from their differential preparation for the course. Moreover, the concepts and theories of the applied anthropologist are not so abstruse or technical that they cannot be understood by any intelligent senior or professional person. They can be unsettling or unacceptable or both, but they can be comprehended with a little extra effort by both student and instructor.

REFERENCES CITED

Anonymous

1943-1944 Publications of OPSOE, occupied areas section. Office of the Chief of Naval Operations, Navy Department.

1944 Living off the American tropics. Information Bulletin No. 10. Arctic, Desert and Tropic Information Center. Office of Assistant Chief of Air Staff, New York.

1947 Report of the New Guinea nutrition survey expedition. Sydney, Australia, Government Printer.

1951 The Haiti pilot project. UNESCO Monographs on Fundamental Education, No. 4.

1953   Russian Research Center, Harvard University, Dunster St. Cambridge
            38, Mass. Five Year Report and Current Projects.
1955   The Haverford Gold Coast training program. (mimeographed).
1956   Social implications of industrialization and urbanization in Africa
            South of the Sahara. London, UNESCO, International African
            Institute.
1958a   Manual for rural community health workers in Thailand. Health
            Division, United States Operations Mission. Bangkok, Thailand.
1958b   Catalog Issue. The Chicago Lutheran Theological Seminary.
(No date)   The Cornell action-research project in India. (mimeographed).
(No date)   Employment opportunities in the Central Intelligence Agency.
            Washington, D.C.

ABERLE, DAVID F.
1950   Introducing preventive psychiatry into a community. Human Or-
            ganization 9:5-9.

ADAIR, JOHN, AND KURT DEUSCHLE
1958   Some problems of the physicians on the Navajo reservation. Human
            Organization 16:19-23.

ADAMS, RICHARD N.
1953   Notes on the application of anthropology. Human Organization
            12:10-14.
1954   On the effective use of anthropology in public health programs.
            Human Organization 13:5-15.

BARNETT, H. G.
1948   On science and human rights. American Anthropologist 50:352-355.
1953   Innovation. The basis of cultural change. New York, McGraw-Hill.
1956   Anthropology in administration. Evanston, Illinois, Row, Peterson
            and Co.
1958a   The case against proffered aid. In Foreign aid reexamined, James
            Wiggins and Helmut Schoeck, eds. Washington D.C., Public Affairs
            Press.
1958b   Anthropology as an applied science. Human Organization 17:9-11.

BEAGLEHOLE, ERNEST
1957   Cultural factors in economic and social change. In Underdeveloped
            areas, Lyle Shannon, ed. New York, Harper and Brothers.

BENNETT, WENDELL C.
1947   The ethnographic board. Smithsonian Miscellaneous Collections 107,
            No. 1.

CAUDILL, WILLIAM
1953   Applied anthropology in medicine. In Anthropology Today. Chi-
            cago, University of Chicago Press.

CASTRO, ANGELICA
1949   The Institute for Literacy of monolingual Indians. Indigenista
            Interamericano 9, No. 1:71-78. Mexico, D.F.

CHAPPLE, ELIOT D.
1954   Contributions of anthropology to institutional psychiatry. Human
            Organization 13:11-15.

CLEVELAND, HARLAN, GERARD J. MANGONE, AND JOHN CLARK ADAMS
1960   The overseas Americans. New York, McGraw-Hill.

CONSIDINE, REV. JOHN J. (M.M.) ED.
1960   The missionary's role in socio-economic betterment. New York,
            Newman Press.

DUPREE, LOUIS (ED.)

(No date) Anthropology in the armed services: research in environment, physique, and social organization. Social Science Research Center. Pennsylvania State University, University Park. (mimeographed).

EMBEE, JOHN F.

1944 Community analysis—an example of anthropology in government American Anthropologist 49: 277-291.

1949 Some problems of an American cultural officer in Asia. American Anthropologist 51:155-158.

EMORY, KENNETH P.

1943 South sea lore. Honolulu, Bernice P. Bishop Museum. Special Publication 36.

ERASMUS, CHARLES

1952 Agricultural changes in Haiti: patterns of resistance and acceptance. Human Organization 11:20-26.

1954 An anthropologist views technical assistance. The Scientific Monthly 77:147-158

EULER, ROBERT C., AND HARRY L. NAYLOR

1952 Southern Ute rehabilitation training. Human Organization 11:27-32.

EWING, REV. J. FRANKLIN (S.J.)

1957 Anthropology and the training of missionaries. Catholic Educational Review 55:300-311.

FENTON, WILLIAM

1945 Reports on area studies in American universities. University of California. European and Far Eastern A.S.T.P. Ethnogeographic Board. Washington, D.C. (mimeographed).

FISHER, GLENN

1953 Directed cultural change in Nayarit, Mexico. Middle American Research Institute. Tulane University, New Orleans. Publication 17.

FLECK, ANDREW C., JR., AND FRANCIS A. J. IANNI

1958 Epidemiology and anthropology: some suggested affinities in theory and method. Human Organization 16:38-40.

FORDE, DARYLL

1953 Applied anthropology in government: British Africa. In Anthropology Today. Chicago, University of Chicago Press.

FOSTER, GEORGE

1958 Problems in intercultural health programs. New York, Social Science Research Council, Pamphlet 12.

FOSTER, GEORGE (ED.)

1951 A cross-cultural anthropological analysis of a technical aid program Washington D.C., Smithsonian Institute, Institute of Social Anthropology.

FÜHRER-HAIMENDORF, CHRISTOPH V.

1958 The west in the "underdeveloped" countries. Swiss Review of World Affairs. December:16-18.

GILLIN, JOHN

1953 How effective can cultural anthropology be in group relations? Social Forces 31:299-304.

GLADWIN, THOMAS

1960 Technical assistance programs: a challenge for anthropology. Fellow Newsletter, American Anthropological Association 1, No. 10:6-7.

GLUCKMAN, M.
  1943   Administrative organization of the Borotse native authorities.
            Rhodes-Livingstone Communication 1. Livingstone, Rhodesia.
GOULDNER, ALVIN
  1956   Explorations in applied science. Social Problems 3:169-181.
GUTKIND, PETER C. W.
  1960   Congestion and overcrowding: an African urban problem. Human
            Organization 19:129-134.
HALL, EDWARD T., JR.
  1956   Orientation and training in government for work overseas. Hu-
            man Organization 15:4-10.
HERSKOVITSS, MELVILLE J.
  1952   The problem of adapting societies to new tasks. In The progress
            of underdeveloped areas, Bert F. Hoselitz, ed. Chicago, University
            of Chicago Press.
HOEBEL, E. ADAMSON
  1955   Anthropology in education. In Yearbook of anthropology, New
            York.
HOLMBERG, ALLAN
  1955   Participant intervention in the field. Human Organization 17:17-19.
  1956   From paternalism to democracy. The Cornell-Peru Project. Human
            Organization 15:15-18.
HALPERN, JOEL M.
  1958   Aspects of village life and culture changes in Laos. Council on Eco-
            nomic and Cultural Affairs, Inc. New York.
HONIGMAN, JOHN J.
  1951   An episode in the administration of the Great Whale River Eskimo.
            Human Organization 10:5-14.
HOSLETT, S. D.
  1951   Human factors in management. New York (revised ed.).
HAWTHORN, HARRY B. (ED.)
  1952   The Doukhobors of British Columbia. Report of the Doukhobor
            Research Committee. University of British Columbia, Vancouver,
            B.C., Canada.
KABERRY, P. M.
  1952   Women of the grasslands. London, United Kingdom Colonial Re-
            search Publications 14.
KEESING, F. M.
  1941   The South Seas in the modern world. New York, John Day: 81.
  1952   The Papuan Orokawa versus Mt. Lemington: culture shock and its
            aftermath. Human Organization 11:16-22.
KEESING, F. M., BERNARD J. SIEGEL, AND BLOWDEN HAMMOND
  1957   Social anthropology and industry: some explanatory workpapers.
            Stanford University, Department of Anthropology.
KENNARD, EDWARD
  1948   Cultural anthropology and the foreign service. The American For-
            eign Service Journal. November.
LANDY, DAVID
  1958   The anthropologist and the mental hospital. Human Organization
            17:30-35.
LEIGHTON, ALEXANDER
  1946   The governing of men. New York, Princeton University Press.

1949   Human relations in a changing world. New York, E. P. Dutton and Co. 138-142, 147, 174-179.

LEIGHTON, ALEXANDER, JOHN ADAIR, AND SEYMOUR PARKER
1951   A field method for teaching applied anthropology. Human Organization 10:5-11.

LINTON, RALPH
1952   Cultural and personality factors affecting economic growth. In The progress of underdeveloped areas, Bert F. Hoselitz, ed. Chicago, University of Chicago Press.

MACGREGOR, GORDON
1946   Warriors without weapons. Chicago, University of Chicago Press.

MAIR, L. P.
1957   Studies in applied anthropology. London School of Economics Monographs on Social Anthropology 16. London, Anthone Press.

MALINOWSKI, BRONISLAW
1945   The dynamics of cultural change. New Haven, Yale University Press.

MANDELBAUM, DAVID G.
1953   Planning and social change in India. Human Organization 12:4-12.

MASON, LEONARD
1953   The Bikinians: a transplanted population. Human Organization 9:5-15.

MAUDE, H. E.
1949   The cooperative movement in the Gilbert and Ellice Islands. Noumea, New Caledonia. South Pacific Commission, Technical Paper 1.

MAYER, P.
1951   Two studies in applied anthropology in Kenya. London, United Kingdom Colonial Research Studies 3.

McAULEY, JONES
1953   Anthropologists and administrators. South Pacific 6:518.

McDERMOTT, et al.
1960   Introducing modern medicine in a Navajo community. Science 131: 197-205, 280-287.

MEAD, MARGARET
1943   Anthropological techniques in war psychology. Bulletin of the Menninger Clinic 7:137-140.
1946   Professional problems of education in dependent countries. The Journal of Negro Education 15:346-357.
1948   A case history in cross-national communications. In the communication of ideas. Lyman Bryson ed. New York. Chapt. 13.
1953   ed. Culture patterns and technical change. Paris, UNESCO.

MEAD, MARGARET, AND RHODA METRAUX (EDS)
1953   The study of culture at a distance. Chicago, University of Chicago Press: v.

MINER, HORACE
1960   Cultures change under pressure: A Hausa case. Human Organization 19:164-167.

NASH, MANNING
1958   Machine age Maya. Memoir 87, American Anthropological Association.

NEWMAN, RUSSELL W.
    1953   Applied anthropology. *In* Anthropology Today. Chicago, University
                of Chicago Press.
OPLER, MARVIN K. (ED.)
    1959   Culture and mental health. New York, Macmillan.
PAUL, BENJAMIN (ED.)
    1950   Health, culture and community: case studies of public reactions to
                health programs. New York, Russell Sage Foundation.
    1956   Anthropology and public health. *In* Some uses of anthropology: theo-
                retical and applied. Washington, D.C., Anthropological Society of
                Washington 49-57.
PERHAM, MARGERY
    1947   Native administration in Nigeria. London, Oxford University Press:
                217-218, 221.
PIERCE, BERNARD F.
    1960   Anthropologists as human factors engineers. Human Organization
                19:47-48.
RAY, V. F.
    1955   Anthropology and Indian land claims litigation. Ethnohistory 2,
                No. 4.
RICHARDS, AUDREY
    1948   Hunger and work in a savage tribe. Glencoe, Illinois, The Free Press.
RICHARDSON, F. L. W., JR.
    1955   Anthropology and human relations in business. *In* Yearbook of An-
                thropology.
RODNICK, DAVID
    1936   Report on the Indians of Kansas. Applied Anthropology Unit, U. S.
                Office of Indian Affairs.
SASAKI, TOM T.
    1960   Fruitland, New Mexico. Ithaca, New York, Cornell University Press.
SCHAPERA, I.
    1928   Economic changes in South African native life. Africa, No. 1:170-188.
    1952   Anthropology and the administrator. South Pacific 6, No. 1:294-298.
SCHRAMM, WILBUR
    1954   Utilization of the behavorial sciences. Report of a planning review
                for the behaviorial sciences division of the Ford Foundation. (mimeo-
                graphed).
SPICER, EDWARD H. (ED.)
    1952   Human problems in technological changes New York, Russell Sage
                Foundation.
SPILLIUS, JAMES
    1957   Natural disaster and political crisis in a Polynesian society: an ex-
                ploration of operational research. Human Relations 10:3-27, 113-124.
STREIB, GORDON F.
    1952   An attempt to unionize a semi-literate Navajo group. Human Organ-
                ization 11:23-31.
TANNOUS, AFIF I.
    1951   Positive role of the social scientist in the Point Four program. The
                Scientific Monthly 72:42-49.
TAX, SOL
    1958   The Fox project. Human Organization 17:17-19.

TEICHER, MORTON I.
1951 Anthropology and social work. Human Organization 10:22-24.

THOMPSON, LAURA
1950 Action research among American Indians. Scientific Monthly 70:34-40.

VALIAN, GEORGE C.
1945 Shadow and substance in cultural relations. Scientific Monthly 60: 373-378.

VAN BAAL, J.
1953 The Nimboran community development project. Technical Paper 45. South Pacific Commission.

WALLACE, ANTHONY F. C.
1956 Tornado in Worcester. Committee on Disaster Studies Report 3. National Academy of Sciences-National Research Council, Publ. 178.

WEDGEWOOD, CAMILLA
1950 The contribution of anthropology to the education and development of colonial peoples South Pacific 4, No. 5: 77-84.

WELLIN, EDWARD
1958 Implications of local culture for public health. Human Organization 16:16-18.

WHYTE, WILLIAM F. AND ALLAN R. HOLMBERG
1956 Human problems of U. S. enterprise in Latin America. Human Organization 15:1-15.

WIST, BENJAMIN O.
1935 Ethnography as a basis for education. An experiment in American Samoa. Social Science 10, No. 4.

RICHARD N. ADAMS

General Use of
Studies in
Applied Anthropology

Courses in the application of anthropology in programs of directed culture change (such as those outlined in the papers by Robert Rapoport and Homer Barnett, *supra*) have a very real value for the graduate or professional student. I agree with Kenneth Little's contention, however, that the best training in applied anthropology is a thorough grounding in anthropology, specifically social anthropology. I would, perhaps, take the argument a little further, and hold that for *undergraduates,* courses that are specifically concerned with the application of anthropology are positively undesirable. My reason for this is that in our present state of knowledge a low level course in the "application" of complex materials is as inappropriate to anthropology as it is to law or medicine; it provides the student with a false sense of knowledge and control over materials that warrant professional attention.

This does not mean, however, that the wide variety of materials resulting from applied projects should in any sense be denied any student. Rather, to follow on Little's argument, these materials should be introduced wherever apt as a part of the more general courses in the total curriculum. It is the purpose of this paper to suggest some specific ways in which applied studies may fit into other courses so that the student can see anthropology in action. We will limit our discussion to papers and reports derived from projects in directed culture change, whether or not an anthropologist actively participated on the project.

It has been my experience that for students a description of how a

393

real person met a situation and resolved it is much more meaningful than the often displaced, third-person reports of an ethnography. Most instructors use their own field experiences to carry this "intimate" or "human" touch, but cases from attempts by others to intervene in the life of a group can do the same thing. One value of most of the cases that are presented in the two standard casebooks (Spicer 1952, and Paul 1955) derives from the fact that they place the reader in the position of the field worker and demand that *he* try to resolve the situation better than did the authors. In most of the specific suggestions to follow, a major asset of the materials is that they bring this sense of immediacy to the classroom situation.

Before going into illustrative cases, two cautions should be observed. First, applied studies often draw from a wide variety of conceptual categories and theories. While this is healthy, and should encourage the instructor to take the opportunities to introduce his students to such ideas, in fact instructors are not always sophisticated in the range of theory that a particular analyst has used. Furthermore, where such sophistication is present, the squeeze of time in a given course may make it advisable for the instructor to avoid cases that require going too far beyond the major theoretical categories used in the course. Thus the work of Leighton (1946) on Japanese relocation can serve as rich material, if the instructor is willing either to rephrase the material or to involve his class in Leighton's theoretical formulations. Such obstacles, however, are usually not serious, since most anthropologists have become familiar, at least on a working basis, with a variety of psychological, sociological, ecological, and economic concepts. Indeed, any contemporary socio-cultural analysis that is limited to the terms developed within cultural anthropology is a very restricted thing.

Another disadvantage lies in the fact that many of the analyses, whether done by professional anthropologists or not, are not sufficiently detailed or sophisticated to enable an instructor to pick from them materials that can be used clearly in undergraduate introductory or intermediate level discussions. This, however, is a problem inherent in any attempt to use materials collected for one purpose in the context of another.

We will now turn to specific suggestions for cases to be used in the regular course offerings of a department. Our discussion will be handled under three rather general topical headings, since it cannot be anticipated that departments will have exactly parallel course offerings. It must be remembered that our discussion is intended for courses at the undergraduate level and that utility for any wider application would be purely incidental.

AREA STUDIES

Courses in the cultures of contemporary areas became particularly important during World War II, and most colleges today continue to maintain a few such offerings. It is not surprising that some of the major area surveys, both broad and narrow, were designed as part of practical projects. Most such surveys are either concerned with an entire nation or country, or with a specific regional or ethnic component.

Among the first may be mentioned the "country monographs" of the Human Relations Area Files, the various products of the project in contemporary cultures initiated by Ruth Benedict and continued under the stimulation of Margaret Mead (Benedict 1946, 1952; Mead and Metraux 1953, and the bibliography therein), and the Central American surveys carried out under the auspices of the World Health Organization (Adams 1957). Concerning regions and ethnic areas there is a much wider selection. The Mexican *Instituto Nacional Indigenista* (various) has published a series of survey studies of the Indian groups of that country; the "Research in Indian Affairs" program of the Bureau of Indian Affairs and the University of Chicago stood behind a series of studies (Kluckhohn and Leighton 1946; Leighton and Kluckhohn 1948; Macgregor 1946, 1955; Thompson and Joseph 1945; Joseph *et al.* 1951; Thompson 1951, 1952); and the Ethnographic Survey of Africa continues to issue a variety of summary papers on local regions (International African Institute, various). Examples of more restricted surveys include those of the Venezuelan Andes (Consejo de Bienestar Rural, n.d.), and the Cameroons (Ardener *et al.* 1960). For some areas it is impossible to obtain a general areal picture if one does not have recourse to applied work. But this should never allow one to overlook the fact that the particular orientation of the investigators has led them to seek certain kinds of material; few such surveys are balanced in the way a reader might wish, and none is ever "complete."

MODERN WHOLE CULTURES

While the classic field of social anthropological study is that of the small community, tribe, or society, studies in recent years have by no means been so limited, and some anthropologists have become involved in issues embedded in the larger colonial, national, and international contexts. It is not odd, then, that products of applied programs provide us with some of the major endeavors into the understanding of national cultures and international social relations. The best general review of some of these studies is to be found in the various papers in Kroeber (ed. 1953), specifically those of Mead (1953), Forde (1953), Held (1953),

Metraux (1953); and in the additional papers by Barnett (1956), Gladwin (1956) and Macgregor (1955). Among the pioneering works in this area, Brown and Hutt (1935) and Malinowski's posthumous volume (1945) should be consulted.

Among the areas that have been especially explored in the course of applied work have been the specific functioning, or dysfunctioning, of development and culture change projects; the "diffusion of ideologies"; and the whole series of complexities involved in the subject of cultural integration. The last of these includes other material as well and will be discussed separately.

Studies in the area of culture change tend to suffer special biases when carried out by the proponents of a special ideology or line of action. It is not entirely reasonable to expect an analytically balanced study of religious missionizing by missionaries; or of local political events by governmental officials of the great powers; or indeed, of the impact of any program of culture change by its proponents. However, there are studies that do provide insights into the complexities of some such projects. The work of the committee on food habits of the National Research Council (1943) is a very good instance (in an area, incidentally, where anthropologists have been slow to follow). The UNESCO concept of "fundamental education" was observed by Fisher (1953) in Nayarit, Mexico, and a number of projects received the attention of anthropologists and other experienced persons in the casebook edited by Teaf and Franck (1955). Public health work has been an area of particular attention, and the work of Saunders (1954) and Clark (1959) represent two attempts to deal with cultural variables in U. S. Spanish-speaking populations. Dube (1958) has taken up more general community development in India.

On a more specialized area, the contacts of nationals through educationally inspired programs have been examined by Beals and Humphrey (1957) for Mexican students in the United States, and by Bennett et al. (1958) for Japanese in the same context. The return of nationals has been studied by the Useems (1955) in India, and the direct operation of United States universities in other countries by Adams and Cumberland (1960) for Latin America.

Direct intervention of anthropologists in community change situations is rare, but important instances are to be found in the reports of Holmberg (1960), Gearing et al. (1960), and those by the Mexican Instituto Nacional Indigenista, already cited. Anthropologists have served as consultants in various capacities to government administrators, and in this field, the work of Barnett (1956) is an important contribution, as well as those already cited in the Kroeber (1953) volume.

The ticklish problem of describing degrees of ideological change in conjunction with the total cultural situation has been approached by Useem (1952), Wax (1953), and in a volume issued by the Council on Foreign Relations (1960).

CULTURAL INTEGRATION

If any single topical area can be chosen as the core of applied anthropological concern, it is probably cultural integration. It is a subject that must be handled in all introductory courses and is analyzed in various more specialized contexts in other courses. It is the anthropologist's peculiar virtue (and problem) that he tries to bring to the analysis a framework of understanding that will try to account for the multiplicity of factors that may be operative in a single situation. It is here (as well as in other ways) that the two casebooks (Spicer 1952, Paul 1955) presently available provide an important and varied diet. In both instances the editors have tested their materials pedagogically and provide a wide range of materials and problems. Until others are prepared, the cases in these two books can provide the general instructor with some telling instances of the nature of, as well as illustrating misunderstandings about, cultural integration.

Even though the theoretical formulations used in the Spicer and Paul volumes may not be congenial to all instructors, the cases supplied frequently illustrate the miscarriage of configuration analysis. For example, Lewis (1955) presents an excellent example of an error often made in studying communities. This author shows how he assumed that a physical community would manifest a "community" spirit in terms of cooperation, and how in fact the direction of change he had desired was thwarted owing to his misunderstanding. The case described by Apodeca (1952) illustrates how difficult it is to bring oneself to the different dimensions used in the cultures of other people. In this instance an extension worker took all sorts of precautions concerning the introduction of a new corn, but his professional predispositions led him to overlook a central feature of the culture of the people in this respect.

Some cases are particularly useful simply because they bring up for open discussion features of the student's culture that he may be reluctant to approach directly and which, therefore, will be obscure to him. The cases by Stycos (1955) and Schneider (1955) deal with birth control and abortion and do so in such a way that the instructors can illustrate the obstacles, conflict, and confusion that occur in cross-cultural vision. These are merely illustrations of how these cases may be used; the instructor should be familiar with these cases, even if he has no access to the other kinds of sources mentioned in this paper.

Most of the materials cited earlier involve problems in the understanding of cultural integration, and should, therefore, also be consulted for illustrations along this line. To these may be added some general sources that the instructor may explore for further instances. The collection by Teaf and Franck (1955) has already been cited, and to it may be added that by Shannon (1957). The journals that most consistently carry materials of these kinds are *Human Organization* (formerly *Applied Anthropology*) and *Economic Development and Culture Change*. There are also many papers scattered in regional journals and series, such as *Africa, Journal of African Administration, Social and Economic Studies* (Jamaica), *Man in India, Eastern Anthropologist* (India).

SUMMARY

While there is serious doubt whether courses on applied anthropology should be taught at the undergraduate level, materials from reports of efforts at directed culture change can profitably be integrated into the regular course work. They serve to bring a sense of immediacy and direct insight into the workings of culture and society. The Spicer (1952) and Paul (1955) casebooks provide a wealth of such materials, and there are many other specific cases to which one may turn if time and facilities permit. Recourse to works such as these, combined with an analysis of the factors at work, can encourage the student to appreciate an empirical and scientific approach to the study of man. It will do so, however, not by misleading students into thinking that they can readily solve other people's and other nation's problems for them. Rather it brings the realization that problem of man have commonalities and differences and that the delineation of these is the only way to guard against oversimplification and mistakes.

REFERENCES CITED

ADAMS, RICHARD N.
  1957   Culture surveys of Panama-Nicaragua-Guatemala-El Salvador-Honduras. Pan American Sanitary Bureau, Scientific Papers No. 33. Washington.
ADAMS, RICHARD N., AND CHARLES C. CUMBERLAND
  1960   United States University cooperation in Latin America; a study based on selected programs in Bolivia, Chile, Peru, and Mexico.
APODECA, ANACLETO
  1952   Corn and custom. *In* Human problems in technological change, E. Spicer, ed. New York, Russell Sage Foundation.
ARDENER, EDWIN, SHIRLEY ARDENER, AND W. A. WARMINGTON, with a contribution by M. J. RUEL
  1960   Plantation and village in the Cameroons. London, Oxford University Press.
BARNETT, H. G.
  1956   Anthropology in administration. Evanston, Row Peterson Co.

BEALS, RALPH, AND NORMAN HUMPHREY
  1957   No frontier to learning; the Mexican student in the United States. Minneapolis, University of Minnesota Press.
BENEDICT, RUTH
  1946   The chrysanthemum and the sword. Boston, Houghton Mifflin, Co.
  1952   Thai culture and behavior. Southeast Asiatic Program Data Papers, No. 4, Cornell University Southeast Asia Program. Ithaca. (Unpublished wartime study dated September, 1943).
BENNETT, JOHN, HERBERT PASSAN, AND ROBERT K. McKNIGHT
  1958   In search of identity; the Japanese Overseas scholar in America and Japan. Minneapolis, University of Minnesota Press.
BROWN, G. GORDON, AND BRUCE HUTT
  1935   Anthropology in action: an experiment in the Iringa District of the Iringa Province, Tanganyika Territory. London, Oxford University Press.
CLARK, MARGARET
  1959   Health in the Mexican-American community. Berkeley and Los Angeles, University of California Press.
CONSEJO DE DIENESTAR RURAL, CARACAS
  n.d.   Problemos economicas y sociales de los Andes Venezolanos. Parte 1. Caracas.
COUNCIL ON FOREIGN RELATIONS
  1960   Social change in Latin America today. New York, Harper Brothers.
DUBE, S. C.
  1958   India's changing villages. Human factors in community development. London, Routledge and Kegan Paul.
FISHER, GLEN
  1953   Directed culture change in Nayarit, Mexico; analysis of a pilot project in basic education. Middle America Research Institute, Publication 17, Tulane University. New Orleans:65-176.
FORDE, DARYLL
  1953   Applied anthropology in government: Brithis Africa. In Anthropology today, A. Kroeber, ed. Chicago, University of Chicago Press:841-865.
GEARING, FRED, ROBERT McC. NETTING, AND LISA R. PEATTIE
  1960   Documentary history of the Fox project, 1948-1959; a program in action anthropology, directed by Sol Tax. Chicago, University of Chicago Press.
GLADWIN, THOMAS
  1956   Anthropology and administration in trust territory of the Pacific Islands. In Some uses of anthropology: theoretical and applied. The Anthropological Society of Washington. Washington, D.C.:58-65.
HELD, G. JAN
  1953   Applied anthropology in government: the Netherlands. In Anthropology today, A. Kroeber, ed. Chicago, University of Chicago Press: 866-879.
HOLMBERG, ALLAN R.
  1960   The research-and-development approach to change: participant intervention in the field. In Human organization research: field relations and techniques, Richard N. Adams and Charles C. Cumberland, eds. Homewood, The Dorsey Press:76-89.
INSTITUTO NACIONAL INDIGENISTA (MEXICO)
  Various   Memorias. Mexico. As of 1959 there were eight volumes, some general, some about specific groups or communities.

INTERNATIONAL AFRICAN INSTITUTE
   Various   Ethnographic survey of Africa. London. 7 vol. to date. Each volume is
           devoted to an arbitrary region and surveys are published in series
           within each volume.

JOSEPH, ALICE, ROSAMUND B. SPICER, AND JANE CHESKY
    1951   The desert people. Chicago, University of Chicago Press.

KENNARD, EDWARD A., AND GORDON MACGREGOR
    1953   Applied anthropology in government: United States. *In* Anthropology
           today, A. Kroeber, ed. Chicago, University of Chicago Press: 832-840.

KLUCKHOHN, CLYDE, AND DOROTHEA LEIGHTON
    1946   The Navaho. Cambridge, Harvard University Press.

KROEBER, A. L. (ED).
    1953   Anthropology today. Chicago, University of Chicago Press.

LEIGHTON, ALEXANDER
    1946   The governing of men: general principles and recommendations
           based on experience at a Japanese relocation camp. Princeton, Prince-
           ton University Press.

LEIGHTON, DOROTHEA, AND CLYDE KLUCKHOHN
    1948   Children of the people. Cambridge, Harvard University Press.

LEWIS, OSCAR
    1955   Medicine and politics in a Mexican village. *In* Health, culture and
           community, B. Paul, ed. 403-434.

MACGREGOR, GORDON C.
    1946   Warriors without weapons. Chicago, University of Chicago Press.
    1955   Anthropology in government; United States. *In* Yearbook of anthro-
           pology, W. L. Thomas, ed. 421-433.

MALINOWSKI, B.
    1945   The dynamics of culture change. New Haven, Yale University Press.

MEAD, MARGARET
    1953   National character. *In* Anthropology today, A. Kroeber, ed. Chicago,
           University of Chicago Press:642-667.

MEAD, MARGARET, AND RHODA METRAUX (EDS.)
    1953   The study of culture at a distance. Chicago, University of Chicago
           Press.

METRAUX, ALFRED
    1953   Applied anthropology in government: United Nations. *In* Anthro-
           pology today, A. Kroeber, ed. Chicago, University of Chicago Press:
           880-894.

NATIONAL RESEARCH COUNCIL
    1943   The problem of changing food habits. Bulletin of the National Re-
           search Council No. 108. Washington.

PAUL, BENJAMIN (ED.)
    1955   Health, culture and community. Case studies of public reactions to
           health programs. New York, Russell Sage Foundation.

SAUNDERS, LYLE
    1954   Cultural differences and medical care: the case of the Spanish-
           speaking people of the Southwest. New York, Russell Sage Founda-
           tion.

SCHNEIDER, DAVID M.
    1595   Abortion and depopulation on a Pacific island. *In* Health, culture
           and community, B. Paul, ed. 211-238.

SHANNON, LYLE W.
1957   Underdeveloped areas; a book of readings and research. New York.
SPICER, EDWARD H. (ED.)
1952   Human problems in technological change. New York, Russell Sage
            Foundation.
STYCOS, J. MAYONE
1955   Birth control clinics in crowded Puerto Rico. *In* Health, culture
            and community, B. Paul, ed. 189-210.
TEAF, HOWARD M., JR., AND PETER G. FRANCK
1955   Hands across frontiers: case studies in technical cooperation. The
            Hague and Ithaca, New York, The Netherlands Universities Foun-
            dation for International Cooperation.
THOMAS, WILLIAM L., JR. (ED.)
1955   Yearbook of anthropology, 1955. New York, Wenner-Gren Founda-
            tion for Anthropological Research.
THOMPSON, LAURA
1951   Personality and government. Mexico, Instituto Indigenista Inter-
            americano.
1952   Culture in crisis. New York, Harper Bros.
THOMPSON, LAURA, AND ALICE JOSEPH
1945   The Hopi way. Chicago, University of Chicago Press.
USEEM, JOHN
1952   The development of democratic leadership in the Micronesian Is-
            lands. *In* Human problems in technological change, E. Spicer, ed.
            261-280.
USEEM, JOHN, AND RUTH USEEM
1955   Western-educated man in India. New York, Dryden Press.
WAX, ROSALIE H.
1953   The destruction of a democratic impulse: a case study. Human Or-
            ganization 12:11-21.

PART VIII

GRADUATE
TRAINING
IN ANTHROPOLOGY

Introduction

O F THE THREE PAPERS in this section, Eggan's is mainly on graduate training in the United States, Fortes' and Beattie's papers are mainly on that training in England and in Commonwealth countries. All three center on cultural and social anthropology. More discussion of graduate work in America and in other fields of anthropology would have been desirable here, although there are valuable comments on these matters in a number of the papers on undergraduate teaching.

Graduate and undergraduate studies are obviously closely linked. The graduate training which an anthropologist has had directly influences the kind of undergraduate teaching which he does. But the reverse has not been equally true. Anthropologists' experiences in teaching undergraduates have not notably influenced graduate programs, mainly because these programs are designed for training in research, not for teaching. Yet some feedback has occurred. A graduate student is usually required to study various anthropological subjects as preparation for the courses he may later have to teach. And he is apt to learn something from the unsentimental appraisal of the teaching practices of his teachers in conversations with his peers.

Fred Eggan outlines the common three-stage pattern of the Ph.D. program for anthropologists in the United States. A graduate student begins by acquiring a broad base in the several fields of anthropology. In the second stage he does intensive study on the subject or subjects of his special interest, and in the third stage he conducts research, usually field work, and writes his dissertation. In Great Britain, as Beattie points out, the first and second stages are largely within the undergraduate or diploma curriculum, and the third stage is the substance of the graduate program. Thus the phrase that a graduate student has "fulfilled all the requirements for a Ph.D. except the dissertation" seems strange to English anthropologists, who set scarcely any other signifi-

405

cant requirement. It should be noted that a broad acquaintance with general anthropology is offered at Cambridge in the first year of the undergraduate program in anthropology and at Oxford is required of those who take diplomas or certificates in anthropology.

A difficult problem in American graduate training is that of providing a broad base of anthropological knowledge for beginning graduate students. There is little good in putting students through a review of what they have already learned. This is especially pointless for those who know what they want to do, are eager to get on with it, and who should be taken as quickly as possible onto the exciting trail of new ideas and discoveries. For those who have been undergraduate majors in some other subject—not an undesirable condition at all, as several authors in this volume have noted—some general preparation is indicated. But this should not require that a graduate student become an undergraduate again, taking only undergraduate courses and examinations. Such role regression unduly delays and may undermine the initiative needed by research students; it may even stultify the interest which brought them into the discipline. These students should acquire the necessary background through reading and attending lectures at their own pace and should demonstrate the adequacy of their preparation by passing a graduate examination rather than by amassing undergraduate course credits.

In the next stage, of intensive study of selected subjects or fields, a graduate student can get particular benefit from informal interchange of ideas with his teachers and with fellow students. This is the period when the student comes to grips with the topics and concepts on which he will do most of his research and teaching. Fortes emphasizes that the basic attitude necessary for anthropological work cannot be taught didactically but must be assimilated from teachers and literature in this stage, which he terms "pregraduate education." The exchange of ideas with one's fellow students is most important. A favored pub, or its equivalent as a classless meeting place, has been the setting for much effective education among several generations of graduate students in anthropology.

Practice in writing is an important feature of this stage, whether it is in the form of the long essays recommended by Fortes or the shorter essays mentioned by Beattie. As important as the writing itself is the assessment and discussion of the writing by teachers and fellow students. Through such writing and discussion, the graduate student makes his way from what Fortes terms the "essentially reproductive examination tasks" of his previous studies toward "the productive activity of research" in which he must use the knowledge which he has acquired.

Both Eggan and Fortes note that many of the most productive an-

thropologists did very little in the way of preparatory reproductive tasks in anthropology. Boas plunged his students directly into advanced analysis, and they "were expected to pick up their knowledge
of general anthropology on their own." They did. Malinowski's students "were thrown straight into the millstream of current controversy"
and might embark on research with only a superficial acquaintance
with the literature and history of anthropology. Under each of these
teachers, graduate training in anthropology did not suffer. Even allowing for the subsequent development of the subject and the very different kind of selection of students, one may wonder about the imposing
series of hurdles which an American graduate student must usually
cross before he is allowed into the heady fields of research. These may
serve the profession as *rites de passage;* do they also serve education
and research in anthropology?

Fortes sets forth recommendations for the research stage. In a graduate student's first research project, he observes, theoretical catholicity
is smothering. The student, under the guidance of his mentor, must set
a firm and limited course for his research, using only selected concepts
and methods, working toward specific and attainable objectives. Some
anthropologists prefer a more open and flexible approach, but a graduate student who is suddenly confronted with the myriad complexities of a living society, can greatly benefit by having a clear chart of
objectives and direction within which he can work.

The award of the doctorate, as Eggan reminds us, marks the beginning of a research career, not its end. In most cases it also marks the
beginning of a teaching career. The problems combining the two pursuits are not easy ones, especially for new Ph.D.'s. Eggan's suggestion of instituting interneships, under which a young anthropologist can
teach and do research under favorable conditions, offers a possible solution to the dilemma which often awaits the successful student at the
end of the formal program of graduate studies.

D.G.M.

FRED EGGAN

The Graduate Program

I<small>N THE</small> U<small>NITED</small> S<small>TATES</small> professional training in anthropology began essentially as a graduate research enterprise for the most part, and has gradually expanded and filtered down through the educational system. Hence, the teaching of anthropology has been profoundly modified by the character of graduate training in anthropology, and the models for the curriculum have come from the graduate school—at least until very recently.

American anthropologists, in contrast to their European colleagues, are virtually unanimous in viewing anthropology as a broad interrelated field of the sciences concerned with "man and his works." Four, and sometimes five, sub-fields or disciplines are usually recognized: archaeology or prehistory, linguistics, physical anthropology, ethnology, and sometimes social anthropology. The major American university departments of anthropology are generally large, with specialists in several of the sub-fields. Normally there is an undergraduate "major" or concentration in anthropology as well as a graduate program, and the number of students in both is growing rapidly.

The growing diversity of staff and the increasing numbers of students introduce problems of organization and control which were not present in earlier decades. Anthropology is being taught in over a hundred institutions at the collegiate level and further expansion is in immediate prospect. There is likewise a greater range of research activities; though most research is still carried out at the major university and museum centers, there is a growing interest on the part of governmental and business organizations. Hence the training of anthropologists offers important problems which are just beginning to be faced in graduate instruction.

THE DEVELOPMENT OF ANTHROPOLOGY

The formal training of anthropologists began in the 1890's in the United States but was initially of central concern to only a handful of institutions. During the 1930's there was an acceleration of graduate training, and in the postwar period there has been a continued expansion.

The emphasis on *professional* training for anthropological research began essentially with the advent of Franz Boas, though the Peabody Museum at Harvard and the University of Pennsylvania were earlier in the field. Boas' conception of anthropology developed out of his own researches among the Eskimo and on the Northwest Coast and out of a growing interest in the nature of the relationships between race, language and culture. The early pattern at Columbia University followed that of the Ph.D. program in the German universities, with primary emphasis on the doctoral thesis and its defense.

The early departments of anthropology were closely associated with museums, and the latter absorbed most of the Ph.D.'s who were produced. Graduate students were self-selected, often coming in from other disciplines. The teaching of anthropology remained marginal except for the few university centers, and many anthropologists did no formal teaching, or did it relatively late in their careers.

During the 1930's anthropology began to develop a social science orientation in many institutions, partly as a consequence of the depression period and partly as a result of the impact of new developments in social anthropology concerned with functionalism. Joint departments of anthropology with sociology, or occasionally with other social science disciplines, became more common during this period, and graduate programs were developed in many of our major state universities, as well as in private institutions.

These developments during the decade of the 1930's shifted the centers of research from the museums to university departments of anthropology. During this period modern archaeology came of age, and in physical anthropology the spotlight shifted from human evolution to problems of race. The increased interest in social problems led to a greater emphasis on undergraduate programs and to a greater need for teachers of anthropology. During this period the number of institutions giving the Ph.D. degree doubled, and the number of doctoral degrees awarded increased some five-fold.

In the postwar period the rapid expansion of anthropology has continued, but with a number of new directions and opportunities. The number of universities offering the Ph.D. degree in anthropology had again doubled by 1954; and more doctorates were awarded in the first postwar decade than in the previous fifty years (see Beals, 1960). A greatly increased number of research opportunities, both pre-doctoral and post-doctoral, have been made available by private foundations in the 1950's, and more recently by the National Science Foundation; and job opportunities with governmental agencies operating in newly developing countries are increasing in number.

It is this acceleration in the rate and scope of development of anthropology in the United States which presents us with problems for which we have to find new solutions. The problems involved in our doctoral programs were recently discussed at some length in the Ph.D. Curricula Conference held in Washington, D.C., in November, 1958, and I have drawn on the "Summary Report" (Foster 1958) in sketching the various stages of graduate training as developed in our major centers for anthropological training.

PATTERNS OF GRADUATE TRAINING

Despite the new developments in recent decades it is clear that the major focus of graduate training in anthropology is still on preparation for research. Teaching is seldom considered an important problem—one learns to teach by practice, or by being a "teaching assistant," or merely by observing one's professors and resolving to do better. As a result the graduate student seldom suffers from "cultural shock" on his first field trip, but his first teaching assignment is frequently a highly traumatic experience.

The common pattern of graduate instruction in most American institutions is to begin with a broad base in "general anthropology," and later to narrow one's interests to a single subfield or discipline and to specialize in that and closely related fields. During this period of specialization the student is expected to discover a topic or "problem" that is of particular interest to him and on which he would like to do research and write his doctoral dissertation. Preferably the thesis should be based on field or laboratory research, though library theses are often acceptable. After the thesis is finished the student looks forward to securing a teaching position in a university or college which will allow him some opportunity for further research and writing and the possibility of advancing his career.

Stated in this simple fashion such a "career line" seems logical and straightforward. One learns about the whole field first, then one makes a selection for more intensive research. But most of the anthropologists of the older generation had no such "logical" training. Students of Boas might be plunged into advanced statistical methods or Kwakiutl linguistics, or whatever Boas happened to be interested in at the moment, and were expected to pick up their knowledge of general anthropology on their own. When he felt they were "ready," he sent them into the field with a problem. Lowie (1959) has written feelingly about this procedure in his recent autobiographical account of his training and career. And many of the second generation of graduate students have had parallel experiences, taking advanced and introductory courses simultaneously, assuming that wrestling with Kroeber's *Anthropology* can be considered "introductory."

The "pyramidal" approach to anthropological specialization is in large measure a means of coping with larger numbers of graduate students. When there are only a few graduate students it is relatively simple to handle them individually and let them go at their own pace. There is no precise order that is relevant to learning anthropology, though some orders may be more efficient than others. A considerable amount of the integration has to take place within each individual's skull, and experience and maturity increase one's skill in judgment. In the centers with a large number of graduate students there is a greater tendency to regulate and supervise the initial periods of graduate training. But advanced graduate students are generally handled individually and given considerable freedom of action. I would guess that the amount of time spent by the faculty on the training of students is directly proportional to the stage of advancement reached. Even so, much of a graduate student's training is secured through interaction with his peers. Graduate anthropology clubs offer opportunities for informal discussion and debate and more recently have supported a number of mimeographed journals as an outlet for written papers and reports.

One of the major differences between American and European practice appears to be with regard to the status accorded graduate students in anthropology. In many United States universities, the advanced graduate student is treated as a "junior colleague" and encouraged to join professional associations and to present papers at regional meetings. Correlatively, there is less emphasis on the "master-apprentice" relationship. At Chicago, where our orientation is almost entirely toward graduate studies, we attempt to extend the conception of "junior colleague" to all graduate students, but with varying results. At the earlier stages of graduate training many of the students seem to need, or prefer, a moderate amount of guidance.

Few American institutions have a strong conviction with regard to the specific character of pre-graduate training which is desirable for graduate work in anthropology. Some departments demand an undergraduate major, but the majority seem to prefer a broad general education, along with evidence of both interest and ability. Since the Ph.D. program is generally fairly long, there is adequate time for instruction in anthropology after entrance into the graduate school.

Where undergraduate programs parallel graduate programs, though at a lower level, the bright student is frequently bored with the repetition involved.

The problem of selection of graduate students in anthropology is both difficult and serious. Anthropology, with its wide scope—ranging all the way from the biological sciences through the social sciences to the humanities—has traditionally attracted students with varied inerests. But as anthropology becomes more organized and conventional the unusual student may not be so welcome as he once was. At the graduate level motivation and interest are probably of greater significance for success than are undergraduate grades, hence personal interviews and recommendations are particularly important.

A few institutions severely restrict the number of graduate students in anthropology and attempt by rigorous selection procedures to pick out candidates with a high probability of success. But the majority of institutions with Ph.D. programs take in a wider group of potential anthropologists and apply selection procedures at the M.A. level, or some related stage.

In general the M.A. degree in anthropology has had varied meanings and little currency. In some institutions it is awarded automatically at a certain stage of training; in others it may be given as a consolation prize. It generally does not specify the acquirement of any particular skills, and it opens few doors to employment. With the current extension of teaching opportunities in anthropology to liberal arts colleges, state teachers colleges, and junior colleges, and the prospective shortage of trained teachers, there is a need for the re-examination of the M.A. degree for potential use in these situations. But this problem is more acute in other disciplines and will probably be solved, if at all, on a more general basis, possibly by providing a degree intermediate between the M.A. and the present Ph.D.

The M.A. program usually involves a year or more of graduate work devoted for the most part to "general anthropology," and ordinarily includes a research paper or master's thesis. Sometimes the departmental staff collaborates on a year-long core course covering a range of topics, or there may be introductory courses in each of the recognized fields. At Chicago after the war we experimented with an integrated series of core courses, each interrelating different points of view and bodies of data, and taught cooperatively. These were our most exciting—and demanding—courses, and the few undergraduates who ventured into them were often out of their depth. At the end of the first year participants took a six-hour examination covering "general anthropology" which was also utilized to determine whether the student should be allowed to continue to the doctorate. More recently we have extended the M.A. program to two years, to allow for better coverage, some specialization in one's field of interest, and acquisition of a foreign language, but some of us feel this is too long a period, and we are currently discussing how it can be reduced.

The M.A. thesis in most departments of anthropology is normally based on library research, though occasionally it is based on a summer's field research or on participation in some faculty member's research project. The topic may grow out of a successful term paper in some class or be assigned by an advisor or staff member. The thesis, however it is developed, is of very great importance in both the training of the graduate student and in evaluating his potentials for doctoral research. One problem is to keep the master's thesis within reasonable bounds—there is a tendency to let it develop into a small edition of a Ph.D. thesis without increasing its value in prognosis.

The major departments of anthropology generally utilize this level to assess their graduate students in terms of their potentials for successful doctoral work. Up to this point students have generally proceeded through a common program and may be judged relative to one another. Beyond this level each student will require an increasing investment of time and energy on the part of one or more staff members. Likewise, it should not be forgotten that the student himself is investing the most important years of his life in the joint enterprise.

A number of institutions make it a practice to hold an assessment session by the whole staff. At Chicago we go over each student after the "qualifying" examinations and attempt to estimate the probability of successful doctoral work, utilizing not only the examination record but course work, written papers, and performance in class or elsewhere. The excellent and the poor students are relatively easy to sort out—it is the student with a variable record, or with a B average, who is difficult to advise. Here we frequently wait for the M.A. paper before making a final decision. In general we present a written prognosis to the student but give him an opportunity to make up his deficiencies or to show us that we are in error. But he is on probation, and the burden is on him to demonstrate his ability. We have found one useful further test to be a ten-day written paper on a problem for which there is no easy answer and with free access to the library and other resources.

Our qualifying examination is thus primarily used for admission to candidacy for the Ph.D., and the award of the M.A. degree is incidental. Our M.A. is likewise ambiguous. For it may be given to a superior student with excellent research promise, and to an average student who has "passed" the qualifying examination, but not at a high enough level to warrant encouragement for the doctorate. The first student, incidentally, is reasonably prepared for introductory undergraduate teaching in Junior Colleges, but the same cannot always be said of the terminal M.A.

Once a student is admitted to candidacy for the Ph.D. degree, he begins the most important stage of his graduate training. His program should now be arranged to facilitate the mastery of his chosen field and the acquisition of the skills necessary for research. One important aspect of anthropology is the large number of productive combinations among its various fields or subdivision. New ones are continually emerging, and it is this intensive interaction, among other things, which keeps anthropology a viable unit, despite its increasing complexity. There are likewise productive combinations with fields outside of anthropology: here the student has varying degrees of freedom depending on the department.

This advanced training stage normally takes one or two years and includes "tool" courses, advanced courses and seminars, and preparation for field or laboratory research. The "tool" courses vary with different fields but involve training in techniques. The seminars are concerned with the important problems in the discipline, and student reports offer opportunities to assess strengths and repair weaknesses. Field methods courses are becoming more common as an "introduction" to field work.

During this period one or more staff members take responsibility for guidance. My own philosophy is that the student should select his own doctoral thesis subject, since he is going to have to do the hard work involved, but I find much variation on this question. Generally the student presents a formal thesis proposal for faculty comment and criticism, and a committee is normally set up with responsibility for guidance and preliminary approval.

The question as to whether a Ph.D. dissertation should be based on field research or on library resources depends on a number of factors. Other things being equal field research is to be strongly preferred and for most fields of anthropology is indispensable. Field work adds an essential ingredient to the student's training, something equivalent to the year of interneship for the M.D. or the personal training analysis of the psychoanalyst. It is a period when the student is largely on his own, with the opportunity to make mistakes and to be frustrated, but also with the opportunity to achieve personal successes and to come to grips with reality. Here supervision should be available when needed, but general reminders and encouragement are usually enough for the superior student. Where a library thesis is necessary for some reason, the student should be strongly urged to secure field experience post-doctorally. This does not mean that library theses may not make equally good contributions to knowledge, but only that they do not make the same kind of contributions to the training of a professional anthropologist.

The length of time to be devoted to the initial field research varies with the situation and the problem. There is a general feeling that it should last about a year, thus giving an opportunity to observe the full calendar round of activities. But there is currently a belief among some American anthropologists that the initial field research might be reduced to six or eight months, for purposes of writing a thesis, with later additional field trips post-doctorally. The tendency to greatly lengthen the field research period is felt to be undesirable at the pre-doctoral level, though it has certain advantages for the superior student.

The period following the return of the student from the field is a particularly important one. This is the period during which he begins to realize his potentials, and his maturation often takes place with great rapidity. His primary task is to organize his data and write his dissertation, but he may also find part-time activities as a teaching assistant to be extremely valuable. Here, also his major advisers need to exert detailed supervision over his writing and his seminar reports. At this stage "apprenticeship" is a proper relationship as there is less danger of developing a "carbon copy" of the professor.

Our conception of the training of Ph.D.'s includes a conviction that new problems and new methods will continue to be developed so that we expect our students to be better trained than we were and to be interested in different problems as well. This diversity of interest is both a strength and a weakness. We often make advances, but we don't systematically follow them up and fill in the gaps. We also tend to consider the doctorate as evidence of promise of research ability rather than its complete fulfillment. The thesis is thus the first step in an independent research career rather than a capstone. In America one's reputation is seldom made with the doctoral dissertation but waxes or wanes in terms of subsequent research activities and accomplishments.

On the horizon is a program of post-graduate training for selected Ph.D.s', as well as summer institutes of various kinds for specialized training or research. Systems of internships have been tried out in a number of governmental enterprises and are in operation in some of the area programs. The South Asian program at Chicago has had one or two Ph.D.'s as internes each year with great success. The Center for Advanced Study in the Behavioral Sciences at Stanford, California, offers promising young scholars an unparalleled opportunity to spend a year with their peers and their seniors in behavioral science disciplines. And within a few years the major graduate training centers in the United States will very likely be heavily involved in postgraduate institutes and other activities, such as the Peace Corps. How these will affect anthropology is not yet clear, but I would predict that it will have a central role.

RELEVANCE OF GRADUATE TRAINING

In this brief survey you will have noted that I have paid little attention to the administrative and financial problems that normally loom large in discussions of graduate training. There are no ready answers to how many foreign languages should be required, or how the advisory system should be set up, or what kinds of examinations should be given, or how the graduate student should be supported. We have experimented with all kinds of examinations, including treating the final oral examination as a social occasion, only to find (as we might have expected) that the students felt they were missing something important by not going through the full *rite de passage*.

Looking at graduate training as a whole there are two aspects which are of particular importance. There is first the mastery of what is generally known with regard to anthropology. It is this "general anthropology," along with a respect (and sympathy) for alien ways of life and a nonethnocentric attitude, which is particularly relevant to undergraduate teaching. The facts of anthropology can be distilled from the textbooks, and this is a useful exercise. But teachers who have arrived at the general synthesis through themselves having put some of the parts together are an important step beyond the textbook, since they can show students how the conclusions have been arrived at and the nature of the evidence involved. And if respect for alien ways of life is to be a reality it has to be implemented by some first-hand experience.

Secondly, there is the primary concern in advanced graduate training in anthropology with the unsolved problems on the frontiers of knowledge. Here there are not only as yet no answers, but often the right questions have not even been asked. But there is intense curiosity, and part of the excitement lies in seeing new relationships and testing new hypotheses or hunches. Here, also, one follows the problem in various directions until one runs up against a wall of ignorance. It is at this point that one wishes the scope of anthropology to be even broader than it is.

The problem we face is how to get both of these components into the undergraduate teaching program. The excitement of research cannot be extracted from the monographs in which it is entombed, and the attempts at popularization of anthropological research by outsiders usually miss the point. Even such dramatic discoveries as radiocarbon dating and glottochronology seem dull when reduced to a formula.

If we are to put both these components into undergraduate programs it will probably have to be done through fully trained anthropologists. We do it now in a few liberal arts colleges, but it is more difficult to accomplish with the large undergraduate classes in state universities. Some type of research opportunity may also have to be provided for selected undergraduates.

It seems clear that anthropology is destined to take over the role formerly occupied by the classics in a liberal education. As we once looked to Greece and Rome for cultural contrast and ancestral legacy, so we are beginning to look to mankind generally for a more adequate portrayal of our cultural heritage in its full development and diversity. And this can be a most important part of our education for living in the modern world.

If enough fully trained anthropologists are to be available for all these tasks we will need to develop more efficient methods of graduate training, or else greatly increase the number of graduate students. The "normal" program for the Ph.D., as listed in the university catalogues, is generally three years beyond the B.A. For anthropology it is considerably longer, involving as it does field research and a writing-up period after the basic training is acquired. At Chicago some years ago we surveyed our own Ph.D.'s and found that the average length of time was close to seven years, a figure which appalled us, but which we find is about the national average.

It is this investment of time and the resulting costs, that makes it difficult to provide adequately trained anthropologists at all levels; or to adopt a laissez-faire attitude towards the graduate student. The current prospects for expansion in anthropology suggest that we do not need to worry about an overproduction of Ph.D.'s for some time to come. We have also attempted to bolster our overlong program by providing better support for the graduate student and his growing family. But we also need a realistic appraisal of our various needs, and to cut our graduate programs, in part, to their measure.

Teachers with undergraduate majors in anthropology *could* raise immeasurably the present low level of "social studies" in junior high schools and, ultimately, in the grades. M.A.'s specially prepared for teaching could revolutionize the same subjects as now taught in high schools and some junior colleges. Advanced graduate students could be very useful in junior colleges and liberal arts colleges while they are completing their research—as well as after. The teacher's colleges need even better prepared teachers if anthropology is to filter through to the ultimate recipients.

All that stands in the way are vested interests and problems of status—as well as money. A few such institutions as the above have been able to attract first-rate scholars and hold them. But in many cases they utilize only a few of their skills and much of their training is wasted.

It should be possible to develop some rational allocation of our limited resources to carry anthropology even farther into our educational system than the college undergraduate level.

REFERENCES

R. L. BEALS
1960 Current trends in the development of american ethnology. *In* Selected Papers of the Fifth International Congress of Anthropological and Ethnological Sciences, Anthony, F. C. Wallace, ed. Philadelphia.

GEORGE FOSTER (CHAIRMAN)
1958 Summary report. Wenner-Gren-American Anthropological Association Ph.D. Curricula Conference. Washington, D.C., November 23-24 (Mimeographed).

ROBERT H. LOWIE
1959 Robert H. Lowie, ethnologist: a personal record. Berkeley and Los Angeles, University of California Press.

MEYER FORTES

*Graduate
Study and
Research*

KNOWLEDGE IN ANTHROPOLOGY, as in all science and scholarship, grows by the processes of discovery to which we give the name of research. Such research may take the form of winning new territory by means of established strategies and tactics, as the Lynds (1929) did in Middletown and more recently, to cite instances at random, Pitt-Rivers (1954) did in Spain, Bott (1957) in London, Frankenberg (1957) in Wales. Previously unknown features of custom and social organization are thus brought into our ken. The studies I have mentioned have broadened our orthodox anthropological horizon to include regions of western civilization not previously perceived in the anthropologist's idiom and have thrown up for our instruction novel institutions, like the Pentre football club (Frankenberg 1957). But knowledge also grows from the re-exploration of occupied territory by means of new techniques and new theories. The re-studies of well-described areas and communities evaluated in Oscar Lewis's excellent paper (1953) and exemplified by Firth's new book (1960) are instances. New techniques, new concepts, new frames of reference, new problems, are prerequisites if re-investigation is to be of value, and these might just as easily arise through borrowing from other disciplines of social and psychological science as through the elaboration or revision of parts of our own corpus of theory.

THE FRAMEWORK OF RESEARCH

New developments in theory and method may be the fruits of field research. They may, however, equally arise from theoretical study and

421

thought and especially from re-analysis of existing ethnographical and allied literature. As to the first of these arm-chair sources of theoretical progress, I need instance only the collection of essays recently brought out by Hallowell (1955). The second is well exemplified by Murdock's now classical book on *Social Structure* (1949) and Lévi-Strauss's *Les Structures Elémentaires de la Parenté* (1949), each of which reanimates the comparative method with an infusion of modern techniques of investigation or of theoretical speculation. I think it is fair to add British contributions which have made some of the pace for the post-war expansion of theory such as *African Political Systems* (Fortes and Evans-Pritchard 1940) and *African Systems of Kinship and Marriage* (Radcliffe-Brown and Forde 1950).

Varied as are these aspects and tendencies of anthropological research they are closely interlinked, advancing along a comprehensive front, albeit with unequal speed in different sectors. And to this unitary movement of advance there corresponds a single, though very loosely organized, army of research workers.

Where, then, in the over-all pattern of research and in the composition of research cadres, is it most useful and profitable to fit the graduate student in? Should every graduate student start in the ranks, working on some routine task under leadership or should the abler ones be placed straight away in the elite stream? Should graduate students be sent out to frontiers where new territory is being won or should they be given all the new tools to experiment with in well-occupied territory? What does experience of graduate student research teach us and what may we aim at? Should the accent be on the contribution a graduate student can make, at however lowly a level, to the general body of anthropological knowledge, or on his professional and technical initiation without counting the cost in finance or in the waste of materials?

Let me say at once that I know it is impossible, and possibly irrelevant, to try to give precise answers to these questions. Everybody responsible for training and directing graduate students in research knows that he must take each case on its merits, nursing a student along, restraining him, or letting him have his head, at different stages of his development. Purism is out of place. The well-tried ideas and methods and the latest fashions inevitably get mixed up in his equipment. And he often, if not always, derives more stimulus and instruction from his peers than from his teachers. All the same, it is useful for the teacher to have a map of sorts in his mind if he wants to be a helpful guide.

PRE-GRADUATE EDUCATION

What do we mean by a graduate student? In the United States he is often quite a young man (or woman—but I shall use the masculine pronoun to stand for the class as a whole) who is just beginning his specialized training in anthropology. He may during his college years have done some work on a fairly elementary level in one or other branch of the subject or he may have been exposed to a portmanteau course giving him a broad and general view of the whole study of race, culture, and society in time and space.

But often and, may I add, to the advantage of his own development and of the subject, he will have had his college education in other fields of study than anthropology. Not till his third year, as I understand it, will he have enough competence in his special field of anthropology to undertake research. At least this is surely true of social and cultural anthropology. Judging by programs of undergraduate study in my own department at Cambridge, very junior students can take part in archaeological excavations with advantage. But this merely serves to remind us of some basic differences between anthropological studies that start from the living community as their source of material and those that depend on the physical relics of extinct communities for their data.

In Great Britain the graduate student in anthropology is coming to be, more and more, like his peer in the more orthodox academic disciplines. Some students still embark on an anthropological career, as many in our generation did, after an education—often after some research or practical experience—in other fields of study than anthropology or in a colonial civil service, in medical practice, industry, or school teaching. But an increasing proportion are coming up through undergraduate honors courses in anthropology or the social sciences. Like physicists, economists, and historians, they have had their basic training before they achieve the status of graduate studentship and embark on the studies that will lead to a doctor's degree. They have this basic training as undergraduates.

I want to emphasize this, for its contrast with the *ad hoc* preparation received by some of the great men in our subject in the past, and by some of my contemporaries. It will be enlightening for some historian of anthropology in years to come to trace the effects on their anthropological work of Frazer's classical education, Radcliffe-Brown's schooling in the rigorous intellectual climate of Cambridge philosophy at the turn of the century. Malinowski's training as a physical scientist, Seligman's in medicine, and so on. In my own generation in British anthropology, Evans-Pritchard took his first degree in the Oxford School of History, Firth moved over from economics, Leach was an engineer and mathematician, and I drifted in from an arduous quinquennium of research in statistical and experimental psychology. It may be significant, to our successors, that Forde, Schapera and Gluckman, Little and Monica Wilson, to mention only that age grade, anticipated the trend of today by receiving a part at least of their anthropological training as undergraduates.

Many of us who did not, learned our job at the bench, so to speak, working directly under the master's eye.This meant that we learned it back to front. We were thrown straight into the millstream of current controversy. We went out to the field or embarked on library research with but a superficial acquaintance with the classical literature of anthropology or the history of its development. The emphasis of our training was operational—how to get at the facts in the field, how to think about them, how to analyze and present them in the framework of current theory. The pattern is that of the natural sciences. A young physicist does not need to read Newton's *Principia* in order to do original research. Young psychologists of today, I find, may have heard of William James but don't think it necessary to read his works before embarking on research. In the natural sciences the young research worker starts from the current state of affairs. Everything that has not been superseded, whether in theory or in method or in the matter of experimental data, is embodied in the current body of accepted knowledge, the orthodoxy of the day.

Undergraduate—or pre-graduate, as I would rather say to accommodate the variety of arrangements we find in practice—anthropology must and can take a different shape, though the natural science pattern is much in evidence. Hence the student who goes into research after a pre-graduate education in anthropology can be expected to have a fund of skills, knowledge, and attitudes very different from that of an immigrant from another academic discipline. How much, as opposed to what, we can expect will depend on the length and the degree of specivilization of the pre-graduate course. The extreme case is perhaps exemplified in my own department, where undergraduates can spend two entire academic years specializing in one branch of anthropological studies, and, indeed, are obliged to have a preparation of this kind in order to be accepted for postgraduate degrees.

What then may we expect of the anthropologically educated pre-graduate? First, as to attitudes. I take this first because I believe it to be crucial for productive anthropological scholarship and research. It is a matter of the orientation, the perspective, the value bias, call it what you will, conducive to that combination of disinterested sympathy, dispassionate curiosity, integrity, and the respect for alien ways of life that give balance and sanction to the anthropologists' studies. This attitude cannot be taught didactically. It has to be assimilated from the literature and from teachers. This is where a broad pre-graduate anthropological education is an advantage. For in such a course the net can be cast wide. The aim should be to make the student aware, on the one hand, of the great diversity and complexity of human culture and social organization, on the other of the common human tendencies, needs, and ideals served by diverse forms of customs and institutions. Well chosen ethnographic reading, supplemented by museum collections,[1] is the best medium for this purpose; and in this connection, my own experience is that it is more instructive and less distracting to pay too little rather than too much attention to our own civilization. The student should moreover learn that culture and social institutions provide means of dealing with ugly human propensities and difficulties in social relationships as well as realizing beneficial ends and higher values.

But this is not enough. A pre-graduate course should also familiarize the student with the diverse theoretical and philosophical interpretations of human social life and culture that have been attempted, or at least with the most important of them. He must make some acquaintance with the work and thought of the classical authorities of the past, Morgan and Frazer, Maine and Durkheim, Boas and Tylor, down to Malinowski, Sapir, Radcliffe-Brown, and so on, as well as with the ideas and theories of their successors. Thus he will know about—though he cannot be adept in all—the various theoretical systems and frames of reference currently on trial. And one other element of orientation is essential. A student must grasp the fundamental principle that the distinctive subject matter of cultural and social anthropology is the living community. He must understand why records, relics, and remains of social life in the past can never take the place, for the anthropologist, of the living community as the source of his data and as the touchstone of his abstractions and theories. With this sort of background he will have some inkling of the fact that human nature is a patchwork of good and evil traits. He will understand how, wondrously varied and diverse as are the cultures and social systems of mankind, they all subserve the same general ends of social existence. Above all he will begin to realize why there is an inevitable gap between the realities of social life and the theories and interpretations which have been devised to represent and explain them.

There are some simple tests of how well a student has learned these lessons. His enthusiasm should be beyond doubt, but not at the expense of his critical faculties. If he still bothers himself with the question whether social anthropology is a science or an art; or if he has an exaggerated respect for what he believes are objective rather than subjective methods; or if he turns nativist, despising his own and extravagantly admiring exotic cultures; or, worse still, if he turns the other way in aversion from and contempt for other civilizations; then his anthropological education has been a failure, or at least incomplete, and he is not yet ready to undertake research.

This is a pretty comprehensive background to demand, you may say;

but you must remember that I have in mind the student who has had two years of specialized pre-graduate study, sometimes after a year of introductory study over a wider range of anthropological subjects, or a year in some other academic subject. And less than such a course of study is, in my view, inadequate as preparation for research in the field or in the library.

What, then, can we mean by knowledge and skills, in contradistinction to the orientation and the attitudes I have summarily referred to as the background? It is largely a distinction of emphasis. But let me make it clearer by some examples. We do not normally expect pregraduate study to include learning a language needed for field work or even for library research. But we can expect the student to have a sufficient grounding in linguistics to facilitate mastering an unwritten living tongue or a literary foreign language. Again, it would be too much to expect a pre-graduate course to provide enough statistical training for sophisticated demographic or survey research. But we can expect such a course to provide enough elementary statistics to give the student an understanding of the kind of problems and hypotheses that must be investigated by numerical and quantitative methods.

But the most important skills for which the foundations should be laid in a pre-graduate training are conceptual and theoretical. To put it at its lowest, a student entering on graduate research should have enough knowledge of anthropology to use technical terms with accuracy. But something more than this is surely desirable. One way of putting it would be to say that he should be equipped with a set of conceptual—and, therefore, internalized—models with which to match the descriptive and analytical statements he encounters in the literature, and later, the facts of behavior he will observe in field work.

The current jargon-word "model" is appropriate; for what I wish to indicate by it is something quite different from a definition that can be found in a text-book or a *vade mecum* like *Notes & Queries in Anthropology*. What I have in mind is the more complex pattern of conceptual and operational skills mobilized when we identify, describe, and follow out the ramifications of a custom or institution in the field or in the analysis of data. To take a trivial example, the student should be able immediately to "spot" matrilineal descent in a particular community's social structure and to establish its critical attributes and connections with other institutions, applying theoretical expectations derived from the "model" he has in his mind of the general class of social fact epitomized in the concept. Now such models cannot be built up into the outfit of skills and knowledge which is the indispensable requirement for research merely by the study of textbooks and general treatises. The only way to do it is by intensive study of ethnographic sources in the manner of a natural scientist in his laboratory or a linguist with texts. But as with the natural scientist, two conditions are necessary for success in this undertaking. The student must have a relevant theoretical chart by which to steer his course and he must have the guidance of an experienced pilot, that is to say, of a practitioner expert in the handling of that particular theoretical chart.

I think it is worth discussing this issue at somewhat greater length. What I am describing is a state of total preparedness as opposed to command of a battery of discrete techniques. There are, in fact, very few specialized technical skills that can be usefully inculcated for research in social and cultural anthropology. One can give a student some tips about so-called interviewing techniques, but if he has not an aptitude for talking to, and far more important, for listening to people, he will be chronically handicapped in field work. One can, as I mentioned earlier, teach him the fundamentals of linguistics and statistics. One can advise him on the use of mechanical aids like tape recorders and cameras. But all this is incidental to the main requirement, which is the fund of knowledge and the system of theoretical expectations to which I have given the label of conceptual models. More than that. He must have at his disposal a more elaborate array of models, in fact, models of major sectors of social structure and of whole social systems and, of course, of the systems of custom the cultures embodied in them.

To put this in practical terms, the research worker must be equipped to recognize parallels and contrasts, identities and divergencies, between what he himself discovers in the field or in the library and peoples, cultures, societies documented in the literature; and to do this efficiently he must have a grasp of the hypotheses and generalizations, the descriptive and analytical procedures, the organizing theoretical schemes embedded in the sources of his models, as well as a comprehension of the ethnographic facts as facts. He must not only be able to "spot" a matrilineal descent system when he somes across one in his field work, to revert to our trivial example; he must also have a range of models at his disposal so that he can recognize "Trobriand" or "Hopi" or "Nayar" etc. characteristics in it and thus be prompted to look for contexts and institutions which may not be apparent at first sight. Furthermore, he must be in a position to choose a theoretical formula to guide his follow-up enquiries. For as is now commonplace, cultural and social facts have many facets, and the aspect that is seen by a particular research worker depends to no small extent upon the theory with which he operates. No student of contemporary social life in a missionized African society will expect Frazer's hypothesis about the progressive supersession of magic by religion to hold. If he has studied the great *corpus* of Tswana ethnography

which we owe to Schapera, he will not be surprised to find a high incidence of church allegiance associated with eclipse of the traditional
religion—but also with a vigorous persistence and even growth of
magic and sorcery.[2] If he has assimilated the theoretical lessons of the
"Manchester School"—the work of Gluckman (1955), Turner
(1956), Mitchell (1956) and others—he will consider whether or not
the persistence of magic and sorcery is related to the persistence or
proliferation of conflict situations between persons and groups.

Am I not demanding too much of the pre-graduate training? This
is a matter of definition. What I am calling the pregraduate stage will
certainly spill over into the first year or two of graduate work, in the
English rather than the American sense of the term. For it is in the
productive activity of research rather than in the essentially reproductive examination tasks that a student's ability to use his knowledge is
most effectively shown. We all know that the best examinees don't necessarily make the best research workers. But what I want to emphasize, as a personal opinion, is that this is no more than a spill-over. The
solid foundations must be laid before a student attempts even the most
elementary form of research. Professor Monica Wilson recommends
that "before a graduate student embarks upon research, he should
have a training in a field other than anthropology but relevant to it,"
and she instances economics and linguistics. This is undoubtedly desirable, though it cannot everywhere be met.

THE FIRST STAGE OF GRADUATE STUDY: THEORY AND PRACTICE

This brings us to the heart of the matter. Three issues arise.
First, with what sort of theoretical map or maps do we provide our
graduate student? Second, how do we steer him through the changing fortunes of his research? And last, the question previously raised,
where do we place him in the over-all pattern of research? In other
words, what tasks do we set a graduate student, what equipment do
we deem essential for him to have in order to cope with them
and how do we supervise and direct his work?

As I have already urged, pre-graduate study should acquaint the
student with the major theoretical tendencies in social and cultural
anthropology and their premises in social theory and social philosophy. Before he embarks on research, the student should be acquainted
with the distinctions of purpose and procedure between historicist
and functionalist methodologies. He should understand why the kind
thinking exemplified in, shall we say, Kroeber's or Leslie White's theories are in certain respects antithetical to the methodologies of Malinowski and Radcliffe-Brown, and he should be clear about the dif-

ferences between the theoretical systems of the latter. He should know enough about Marx, Durkheim, Weber, and their precursors and successors to perceive their influence on anthropological theory. Again, he should be sufficiently familiar with the "culture-pattern" and "collective character" experiments in the analysis and description of culture to appreciate their divergence from and links with functionalist ideas. And in addition, he should at least have heard of the attempts that have been made to explore the psychological and psychogenetic variables in custom and social organization.

But should he be launched into research with all these maps in his pouch and left to try them all or find out for himself which is appropriate where? I think this would be fatal. Theoretical catholicity in a graduate student engaged on his first research project smothers it, if not to death at any rate to banality. It is the teacher's responsibility to induce—he cannot impose—choice of a theoretical system which will pay off best for the research proposed, and it is his duty also to influence the student not to stray to his inevitable disadvantage from the straight though not necessarily narrow course plotted by the system he has adopted. I am convinced that nothing is so confusing to a graduate student beginning research as the licence to pick and choose indiscriminately among a welter of theories and hypotheses presented to him as all of equal value. It is better if he has no theories and aims simply to set down in his own language what he sees and hears as a naive observer. The results may be of negligible scientific utility but will, at least, be honest.

Good graduate student research, then, in my opinion requires a well-defined and limited theoretical approach, consistent adherence to it, and attainable objectives. To put this in another way, the student must have a limited kit of conceptual tools, but he must be able to use them skilfully; he must begin his investigations with a limited and coherently interrelated set of questions in mind; and he must be capable of denying himself the luxury of following up trails which lead to problems outside the scope of his theoretical equipment. And this is where the internalized models I spoke of earlier become relevant. The paramount concern of social and cultural anthropology is with the phenomenon of custom. We structuralists are sometimes accused of flouting this principle. In fact our ethnographic and theoretical work shows beyond any doubt that our concern is with the analysis and elucidation of the springs of custom. But our procedure is to seek in the first instance to establish the matrix of social relations within which living custom has its being, from which it derives its functional significance, and to which it gives texture and symbolic meaning. And if this goes for structural studies, how much more does

it not hold for the other accepted frames of reference followed in anthropological study. I stress this here in order to make the point that
it is essential for the research student to be thoroughly imbued with
this conception of his subject matter. He must have it engraved on
his mind that his main task is to observe and record the minutiae of
custom and conduct in their context of social relations. And facility
for this—to the extent that it can be acquired and is not an inborn gift
—is best achieved by the close study and assimilation of ethnographic
monographs in which the theoretical point of view the student is going to follow is shown at work through the medium of good descriptive data.

But if there is one lesson that has been borne in on me as a result
of fifteen years of supervising graduate student research, it is that
reading by itself is not enough. The parallel with psychoanalysis is
illuminating. Reading all the books does not by itself make one master of the theory and equipped to put it into practice. Our experience
with graduate students embarking on research is that their reading
has to be crystallized and transformed into applicable skill by special
seminar work under direction of a practitioner of the theory. I think
of it as a form of apprenticeship.

Let me explain more fully. We are now discussing the man who
has taken his first degree with something like two years of specialized
study and is about to engage in research. Let us call him a research student and let us consider first the man who has not yet decided on the
ethnographic region or the focal problem to which he will be devoting three or four years of research. How shall we direct his initial
period of apprenticeship? One way might be to attach him for a month
or two to a team or a senior research worker engaged on a long-term
project of field work, be it in a tribal area, an Indian village, an
American city or an English suburb. A prescribed and limited task
within the wider program would be allocated to him. He would try
out such techniques as taking genealogies, collecting census data, interviewing informants, observing and describing social activities. He
would thus, it could be argued, be learning how to do field research
by trial and error, and this would be the easier, because his error can
be corrected on the spot and his trials are not expected to make a responsible contribution to the project.

I put this in a hypothetical form, but it is a procedure often followed. In my view it is of little value and may even be disadvantageous to the research student. For if those he works with are experienced field workers, he may get discouraged through comparing his
clumsy efforts with their expert performance. On the other hand, he
may quite as easily develop a delusion of success if his infant efforts

seem to him to go well, and he may come away with inflated ideas of his own skill—and with distorted ideas about the simplicity of field research. I have met both of these products of premature, short field expeditions and summer vacation, urban social studies.

The alternative I prefer is for a research student at this stage to be allotted a subject for library study. He is directed to examine his published sources as if they were field records. He works under the supervision of a teacher who prescribes an established, or at least known hypothesis as his starting point, and descriptive papers and books which best present the hypothesis as his models. This exercise should take two or three months; it should demand close examination, collation, and analysis of the ethnographic data. Finally, an essay should be produced to be read and discussed in a research student or staff seminar, and then re-written in the light of the criticism. An example of such an exercise undertaken at Cambridge is an essay of the order of 25,000 words on joking relationships, the result of several months of work, in which the student analyzed a series of papers and monographs on East and West Africa to test Radcliffe-Brown's hypotheses. This can be called an exercise in comparative method. Another is that of a student who has meticulously re-examined the whole Trobriand *corpus* to elicit the critical structural norms of Trobriand marriage, using as her models some of the African studies on this topic of the last decade or so.

You will observe what I am laying most insistence on—attention to ethnographic detail. I consider this to be by far the most important benefit of the exercise. It gives the student a foretaste of what he will be expected to aim at in his field work. Its second value is the opportunity it gives the student of putting his internalized models to the test, and finding out how far he has succeeded in building up habits of anthropological perception and thought conformable with the theoretical system he is trying to apply. That is why we prescribe accepted, if you like, well-worn problems and reputable, well-evaluated sources. Sometimes a student makes small but interesting theoretical discoveries. This is an encouragement to him. What is more important, he often finds deficiencies in the sources. By discovering for himself what are the gaps and lacunae, as Malinowski called them, in the field reports of even the greatest of our authorities, the research student is made aware of omissions he must guard against in his own work. Please note, in connection with this, that the sources students are advised to consult are the original books and papers, not digests. We insist on reading and mastery of a selected range, often quite small, of the original publication. We do not encourage students to pick out the nuggets they think they need by searching no farther than the

index of a book. Nor do we require them to search for material over
a large or world-wide sample of societies. From this point of view a
series like the Ethnographic Survey of Africa is primarily of bibliogra-
phic use, and the Human Relations Area Files would not serve the
main purpose.

I turn now to the man who has selected—more likely has had selected for him—the tribe, area, community, problem, etc. which he
will study in his field work. I take it for granted that no graduate student's training in social anthropology is complete without field work
and the writing up of a field study. If the student knows where he is
going, the program I have outlined is modified. In the first place, he
is advised to begin to learn the language he will need in his field work
and may have to attend classes for this purpose. Second, he will be directed to read widely in the regional literature of his area—geographical, economic, historical as well as ethnographic works. Ideally,
he should go out to the field, be it a tribe in Africa or a village community in India or an industrial suburb in England, with an apperceptive mass, to borrow an old-fashioned psychological term, of general regional information which will help him to see where his area
fits into a wider picture of time and place. This takes time, six
months at least; for he will also have a theoretical exercise to do, but
in his case it will be tied to the region he is destined to work in. Most
important of all, he will be expected to produce a fairly detailed plan
of field work, presenting the significant geographical, historical, and
ethnological facts for the area and outlining the kind of enquiries he
hopes to pursue. He is warned that it is most unlikely that he will actually adhere to this plan, but he soon learns that it is a valuable technique for crystallizing his reading on the area and getting his theoretical aims into focus.

Unfortunately we cannot nowadays always follow this program
with students who receive field research grants for particular areas or
are hired by overseas research institutes immediately after they complete their pre-graduate degrees. By their own admission, their field
research suffers in consequence, but we have to bow to the hard facts
of finance.

One or two points remain to be underlined. The principle of avoid-
ing theoretical confusion should, in my view be strictly adhered to.
Research students at Cambridge are not, for example, given instruction in the methods and concepts pertaining to such specialized frames
of reference as that of the "Culture and Personality" school. We
hold them fairly strictly to structuralist theory and its close congeners.
We believe that a good student will find his own way to other disciplines and theoretical approaches if his research leads in those direc-

tions. We believe that structuralist theory provides the best conceptual apparatus and the most satisfactory models for the initial "opening up" of an analysis of any social system. Once that is accomplished, the student can follow his own inclinations and the logic of his research and attempt other methods of analysis. Another precaution I personally adhere to is to go slow on "hot" controversial issues with beginners in research. The latest fashions have as seductive attractions for keen and ambitious research students as for humanity in general. But they can be dangerous. Dazzled by an unclarified new theory, the research student doing his first field job is prone to fail in his primary task of getting the descriptive facts in depth and in context. In my judgment it takes two or three years for a new idea to be digested and put in its proper place in the total system of anthropological thought; and before that has been done beginners in research must be cautiously introduced to it.

You will observe that I say nothing about what might be called the "public relations" side of preparation for field research—how to get along with government officials, how to establish a "role" for the anthropologist in the community he is studying, and other matters of like sort. I regard them as peripheral, like learning to drive a car and use a camera. Our experience is that the best way of dealing with them is to leave it to the research student to soak up clues, in part from the literature and largely from fellow students who are recently back from the field. This is one reason why a seminar for research students should include both prospective field workers and students engaged in writing up field results. The personality of the student is, of course, a major factor. Three cases have come within my purview in recent years of inadequate field research being apparently due to the student's incapacity to establish rapport in his community. The cause, in each case, was without a doubt personality defects in otherwise able and even brilliant men. Some failures are inevitable in an enterprise so largely governed by personal qualities as is anthropological research.

FIELD WORK

Our research student is now ready to take the field, and the first problems are, where shall he go and what kind of study shall he undertake? There are two extremes among research students. On the one hand there is the man or woman who, through a quirk of temperament or an accident of personal history, early becomes passionately absorbed in an area, a type of society, or a way of life and tenaciously pursues the aim of carrying out field work to fulfil his passion. I have such a man in mind. He set his heart on studying hunting and collecting societies living in severe ecological conditions, read all the relevant literature and finally persuaded interested bodies to find the money for two years of field work among one such group. At the other extreme is the man who has no predilections, perhaps believes that a properly trained anthropologist should be capable of carrying out field work in any community he happens to strike, and is willing to go where an opportunity offers. This student will often, perhaps even usually, do much better field work than the first student, for he is more detached and has a broader perspective of cross-cultural equivalences. He is liable to be influenced by his teachers to follow up work they have done. Or he accepts the opportunities provided by recruitment for research projects conducted by bodies like the East African and the Rhodes Livingstone Institutes or planned by national bodies like the Social Science Research Council. Some of the best field work done by British anthropologists since the war has been carried out under the auspices of local research institutes.

The two Institutes I have mentioned—and others could be added—represent what is in my opinion the optimum arrangement for a first field project. Each has operated with a broad and flexible program which included tribal ethnography; urban communities; economic, political, and religious problems; traditional cultures; and changing cultures—in fact the whole gamut of topics that are in the forefront of modern theoretical developments. In both organizations the young field worker has been given maximum freedom to conduct his enquiries on his own and in whatever ways he deemed appropriate, but general supervision by a senior scholar has been at his disposal whenever he needed advice or help, and a central institution has provided occasions and a place for him to meet other research students and field staff for the exchange of ideas and the ventilation of difficulties. Common interests, common aims, and to a greater or lesses extent common theoretical ideas, thus emerge, and the effect is visible in the publications that result. Note that this pattern is not teamwork in the strict sense, nor is it inter-disciplinary. It is perhaps best described as collaborative research and therein, I suggest, has lain its strength and productivity. Teamwork, whether inter-disciplinary or uni-disciplinary, implies that the over-all field, that is the total community under study in all its aspects, is partitioned by geographical, or structural, or conceptual criteria and each of the segments thus demarcated is handed over to one or more research workers as his or their special province, the intention being eventually to pool observations by different hands to arrive at a definitive picture. My own limited and now out-of-date experience of teamwork on the Ashanti Social Survey (since, however, confirmed by private information about more recent experiments of the same kind) has convinced me that it is often a disadvantage for a student to begin his research career as a member of such a team. Whether he works in it as a rank and filer, or as an n.c.o., charged with such limited tasks as interviewing a sample of housewives or recording daily routines, or what you will, or whether he is treated as a junior officer with some latitude to act on his own initiative, the loss to him as an anthropologist is the same. For the fundamental defect of teamwork, for an anthropologist, is that he is not directly and responsibly concerned to know the whole society and its entire culture.

I do not say that it is possible for any student of a society, living or extinct, to achieve absolutely exhaustive knowledge of it. That is not the point. What I am arguing is that what distinguishes the anthropologist's way of perceiving and thinking about society and culture is his concern with the whole, with what Redfield called "the humane reality," by which I think he meant the total social system, not a particular aspect or segment. It is imperative, I suggest, for the research student to be orientated from the outset of his career to relate customs, institutions, social relationships, economic practices, juridical norms, religious beliefs, etc., which he necessarily encounters in particular, piecemeal situations, to the hierarchy of contexts that makes up the total social and cultural system. He must apply his internalized models from the outset to look for where things fit into the whole system, even though his concept of the whole is bound to be nebulous for a long time, and probably incomplete always. To achieve and maintain this organicist perspective—if we want to give it a name—he must work with a whole society or such part of a bounded political or geographical or cultural system as is itself a whole society on a smaller scale. The best instances of the latter are the rich and rewarding studies that have been carried out in the past few years in Indian villages. They are quite different from such studies as that of Raymond Smith in British Guiana (1956), where the village is not a microcosm of the largest, allinclusive social system but only an economic and local constituent of the whole.

My conclusion is that the research student embarking on his first field job should ideally be placed in the position where he is bound to study a whole social system. This is why the simpler, more homogeneous "tribal" societies provide the best training ground for induction into field research; and this is why the tradition, going back to our founding fathers, both in Europe and in the United States of, basically, one man one tribe at one time, has been so fruitful.[3]

To revert to more practical matters, it is now generally accepted that the minimum period of field study likely to be effective is a full calendar year. In fact the habit is spreading of stretching field work to two or even three consecutive years with very short breaks in between. My experience at Cambridge is not favorable to this development. Even in the most salubrious climate, the relative isolation and intense application called for in field work seems to result in diminishing returns after about fifteen months. I am still in favor of the arrangement so profitably followed by the International African Institute, among others, in the thirties, by which research fellows were required to return to metropolitan headquarters for a spell of preliminary digestion of their data between two field trips of around a year at a time.

This brings up a question I alluded to earlier. What is the balance of advantage for a student to work in new ethnographical territory as against further fieldwork in an area or a people already well described in the scientific literature? The advantage of the latter is that it often facilitates supervision, especially if the student is following on work previously carried out by his supervisor. The advantage of the former, for the able student, is that it is stimulating and encouraging to find out things which are new to the supervisor and to the anthropological world. In practice, of course, it is really a matter of degree. Some of the New Guinea tribes now being investigated for the first time by the research students of the Australian National University were not even known to exist a decade ago. Yet their cultures and forms of social structure are not so remote from those of groups already known as to make comparisons impossible.

I have referred to the supervision of the research student during his first field trip. However well equipped he may be, intellectually and scientifically, initial field work is part of, albeit the final part of, his apprenticeship. It will go more smoothly and more productively if he can have recourse to a more experienced scholar from time to time for comment, guidance and moral support. This, as I indicated, is one of the major advantages of research institutions and universities that are within easy access of the field worker, as of course, is quite normal in countries like the United States, India, South Africa, and Latin America. The British student who goes out to areas remote from home centers must rely on supervision by correspondence; and here it is a very great advantage and in fact virtually essential for the student to have access to a senior scholar who has worked in the same or a related area. The most helpful supervisor is one who is able to visualize the conditions in which the student is working and who has some basis on which to guess, if not to forecast precisely, what possible twists and turns may lie ahead for him in his field work.

A first field project is best treated as a stage of the student's apprenticeship. This does not finally end until he returns to his base to write up the results. I am sure it would be generally agreed that this is by far the most important stage of a research student's training. Our practice, in Cambridge, follows the standard pattern of placing each student under an individual supervisor, who may or may not be the same as the supervisor responsible for his field work. We also have weekly seminars of graduate students and staff to discuss and comment on papers presented by each student in turn. This is the stage at which theoretical guidance becomes of paramount importance. Hence, it is sometimes more useful for a student to have access to a supervisor who is not an authority on his ethnographic region but is able to see the theoretical issues clearly, and carries enough weight to prevail upon him to stick rigorously to a chosen frame of analysis and method of exposition. At this stage, when the student has his own field material to use as a touchstone, it is proper and even necessary to let him loose on currently controversial ideas that are related to his thesis subject. Seminar discussion based on comparing experiences from different areas is an indispensable corrective to natural tendencies towards irrelevant or careless thought and presentation. But careful, chapter-by-chapter supervision is the key to turning the promising apprentice into a competent craftsman. All this again takes time. I find that the procedure which pays best is to get the student to begin by writing straight off the cuff a general descriptive account of the society or community as a whole. I tell the student not to refer to his field records but to write the account in narrative form straight from memory and to cover all the conventionally distinguished aspects of social and cultural life. This task may take a month. But out of it usually grows a central problem which the student finds himself interested in as a thesis subject; and it emerges in the correct anthropological form, within the context of the total social structure and the total culture of the community, insofar as these have become known to the investigator. This makes it easier to see that the student does not lose sight of "function," "structure," "meaning," "context"—call it what you will—that stands for the crucial anthropological approach in extending knowledge of man, society, and culture. This is the emphasis in what is, to my mind, still the finest description of field work method as it should be followed by a social anthropologist—I mean of course, the first chapter of Malinowski's *Argonauts of the Western Pacific*.

NOTES

[1] The specimens, being treated not as objets d'art or as technological exhibits, but as what I would call congealed culture—physical embodiments of knowledge and skill, belief and value, myth and story in their total setting of time and place.

[2] Professor Monica Wilson has drawn my attention to recent studies which show that traditional religious beliefs (e.g. ancestor worship) are by no means extinct among the Tswana.

438 MEYER FORTES

³ As has been indicated earlier in this paper, I do not mean to imply by this that isolated tribal communities are the only type of community suitable for anthropological study. I am arguing only that they provide the best training ground for social anthropology.

REFERENCES CITED

BOTT, ELIZABETH
    1957   Family and social network. London, Tavistock Publications.
FIRTH, RAYMOND
    1960   Social change in Tikopia. London, G. Allen and Unwin.
FORTES, MEYER, AND E. E. EVAN-PRITCHARD
    1940   African political systems. London, Published for the International African Institute by the Oxford University Press.
FRANKENBERG, RONALD
    1957   Village on the border. London, Cohen & West.
GLUCKMAN, MAX
    1955   The judicial process among the Barotse of Northern Rhodesia, Glencoe, Ill., Free Press.
HALLOWELL, A. IRVING
    1955   Culture and experience. Philadelphia, University of Pennsylvania Press.
LÉVI-STRAUSS, CLAUDE
    1949   Les structures élémentaires de la parenté. Paris, Presses universitaires de France.
LEWIS, OSCAR
    1953   Controls and experiments in field work. In Anthropology Today. Chicago, University of Chicago Press.
LYND, ROBERT S., AND HELEN M.
    1929   Middletown. New York, Harcourt, Brace & Co.
MITCHELL, JAMES CLYDE
    1956   The Yao village: a study in the social structure of a Nyasaland tribe, Manchester, England, Manchester University Press.
MURDOCK, GEORGE P.
    1949   Social structure. New York, Macmillan Co.
PITT-RIVERS, JULIAN A.
    1954   The people of the Sierra. New York, Criterion Books.
RADCLIFFE-BROWN, ALFRED REGINALD, AND DARYLL FORDE
    1950   African systems of kinship and marriage. London, New York, Published for the International African Institute by the Oxford University Press.
SCHAPERA, ISAAC
    1956   Government and politics in tribal society. London, Watts. (Has a comprehensive bibliography of Schapera's writings.)
SMITH, RAYMOND T.
    1956   The Negro family in British Guiana: family structure and social status in the villages. London, Routledge & Kegan Paul.
TURNER, VICTOR W.
    1956   Schism and continuity in an African society: a study of Ndembu village life. Manchester, Manchester University Press.

JOHN H. M. BEATTIE

Techniques
of Graduate
Training

I HERE DISCUSS some of the techniques or methods commonly used in training graduate anthropology students. I confine myself to social and cultural anthropology. Seminars and examinations are among the more important of these techniques, but formal lecturing, and individual supervision or "tutorials" of varying degrees of formality, also play a significant part in training, and I consider these also. So far as I can, I concentrate on the "practical" aspects and implications of these various forms of teaching activity, since issues of principle fall within the scope of other contributions to this section. But the utility of training techniques cannot be evaluated without reference to the ends which they are intended to achieve, so some brief reference to these must be made.

DEFINITION AND ORIENTATION OF GRADUATE TRAINING[1]

Graduate training I take to mean any teaching of anthropology to graduates, and to include preparation for graduate diplomas and certificates in anthropology, as well as for intermediate research degrees (M.A., M.Litt., M.Sc., B.Litt., B.Sc.), and for the doctorate. But I concentrate mainly on training for the Ph.D. degree, and, as far as Great Britain and the British Commonwealth are concerned, with preparation for the doctorate in *social* anthropology. I make the general assumption (though it is one which needs some qualification) that persons who are admitted to prepare for a research degree in anthropology already have or are supposed to have a sufficient knowledge of the subject generally, for example a first degree in it, or a graduate diploma.

There are, however, significant differences among British universities, as well as between them and American universities, in the extent to which graduate training is regarded as culminating in the doctorate, or as leading to several different possible terminal qualifications. In some British departments (Oxford is an example) it is possible to take a graduate diploma or certificate course, which is a one or two years' general course, specializing in social anthropology, archaeology, or physical anthropology, but including work in the other two fields as well, as an end in itself. Many people, such as administrators and missionaries, do this. Also, an intermediate degree (B.Litt. or B.Sc.) can be taken as an end in itself, and many students stop (or are stopped) at this point, some for years and some forever. In some British and Commonwealth universities no diploma courses are provided, or if they are they are rarely taken, and in yet other universities no intermediate post-graduate degree is given, so that virtually all students are Ph.D. candidates from the start of their post-graduate work. Where this is so (as in Cambridge, for instance), a person who is admitted to prepare for a doctorate in anthropology is required to show evidence of adequate promise as a scholar (for example a good degree in another subject) and also sufficient general knowledge of anthropology (for example a first degree or a diploma in it) to qualify them to carry out research in this field. In the absence of some such qualification, a pre-doctoral candidate is ordinarily required to take an undergraduate or a diploma course successfully, or to work for an intermediate research degree, before being admitted to read for a Ph.D.

In general, leaving aside the considerable group of graduates who seek only diplomas, certificates, or intermediate research degrees, the aim of graduate training is to achieve a doctorate. But what sort of doctorate? There is a very great difference between the idea of what a Ph.D. should be which is held in British and Commonwealth anthropology departments and the idea of what a Ph.D. should be which is held in American and Continental universities. The main difference is that the British and Commonwealth doctorate is awarded exclusively on research, while the American and Continental doctorate, though of course requiring research too, is also—perhaps pre-eminently—based on knowledge in the whole field of anthropology, usually including, *inter alia*, physical anthropology and archaeology. In order to obtain a Ph.D. in social anthropology in England and in the Commonwealth universities, a candidate, once admitted, has to (1) fulfill the purely formal requirement of residing for a certain number of terms in the university, (2) maintain contact with an academic supervisor who will give him such advice and direction as he requires, and (3) submit and usually defend in *viva voce* examination a thesis or dissertation, most commonly based on field work. The thesis must show an adequate standard of scholarship and originality, and, in the vague phrase often used, it must represent "a genuine contribution to knowledge." Once a student is registered for a Ph.D., he has no further examination in general anthropology at any level, nor is he required to fulfill any class or seminar requirements. The assumption (not always warranted) is that only students who have shown themselves, by an earlier degree or otherwise, to be competent in general anthropology, are admitted to read for a Ph.D. Outside Great Britain and the Commonwealth, however, a Ph.D. in anthropology is generally regarded rather as the culmination of a course of general anthropological training. Research, usually field research, is required, and a dissertation must be presented, but a Ph.D. candidate must also qualify at a moderately high level in such other subjects as archaeology, physical anthropology, and linguistics, and he must also satisfy certain class and seminar requirements by physical attendance and maintain certain standards in class work. Thus, in effect, a British Ph.D. student is regarded as a scholar whose training in general anthropology, social or otherwise, has been completed, and who is now permitted, with (ideally) a minimum of supervision, to engage in independent research on an approved topic. When he submits himself for examination for the doctorate he will be judged only upon the results of this research.

These differences reflect both different notions of what anthropology is and different ideas about what a Ph.D. in anthropology is for. While in America anthropology is commonly regarded as "the general study of man," covering "all aspects of man and his activities,"[2] in England social (or cultural) anthropology has increasingly come to be regarded as a social science in its own right, logically (though not historically) no more tied to physical anthropology or archaeology than to a number of other social sciences, such as history, economics, human geography, and even theology and law. Combined with this there is some difference as to what a Ph.D. in anthropology should be qualified to do. In England there is very much less emphasis on teaching as the main function of a Ph.D. than there is in America; while the doctorate is increasingly coming (perhaps unfortunately) to be regarded as an essential qualification for a university post, it is not yet quite this; the emphasis is still on preparation for research rather than on preparation for teaching. Also, not only are there very many fewer teaching posts available in Great Britain and the Commonwealth, but the teaching range demanded in anthropology departments is a good deal more limited; for example a man with a Ph.D. in social anthropology is not ordinarily required to teach physical anthropology or archaeology; these are taught by specialists in these fields. It is thus a great deal easier for young British anthropologists to press on with research in their chosen fields during their early years than it is for their American colleagues.

Important though these differences are, and significantly though they affect training techniques, they can be overstressed.[3] A general knowledge of anthropology (however the word be understood) obviously is required wherever the subject is taught, and a capacity to carry out original scholarly research is everywhere a desideratum for the degree, even though the emphasis laid on this requirement varies. So a comparison of the means adopted is by no means useless. I accordingly discuss formal lecturing, academic supervision and "tutorials," seminars, and examinations in the different contexts in which they are used. I also say something about informal student-staff relations, for in my view these are among the most important training techniques at graduate level.

FORMAL LECTURING

Formal lecturing has its main importance at the undergraduate and "diploma course" stage; it plays less part (little or none in British and Commonwealth universities) in teaching at Ph.D level. In England, the lower level lectures for graduates are usually given to small groups, often on fields or problems in which the lecturer has special competence, and they are attended by those graduate students who think that they may benefit from them. Where, as in Oxford and London, there is a graduate diploma course, lectures are given in general anthropology, ethnology, and (for social anthropology students) in such topics as sociological theory, comparative religion, kinship systems, social change, and the detailed ethnography of selected regions, as well as in archaeology, prehistory, and physical anthropology. Even at the diploma course level attendance is optional, though candidates are strongly advised in their own interests to attend some of the courses. Once a student has successfully completed a diploma course and, perhaps, an intermediate research degree and is registered for a doctorate, he is not ordinarily expected to attend any lectures, and he would be unlikely to do so unless he were specially interested in a particular course.

I think that most teachers of graduates would agree that there is little point in giving them material in lectures which they can just as easily get out of books. Thus the only lecture courses which a postdiploma student in Oxford would be likely to attend are those based on the lecturer's unpublished fieldwork, or on a particular problem area (primitive religion, say, or prescriptive marriage systems) in which the lecturer is himself carrying out research. In British and Commonwealth universities graduate anthropology lectures are usually addressed to very small classes (rarely more than a dozen or so), and they are directed to people who already know, or are presumed to know, a good deal about anthropology. Thus Cambridge admits two to four graduate students annually, Edinburgh four or five, Manchester five or six, Canberra about six, Oxford six to twelve.[4] This of course means that in Britain and the Commonwealth less reliance has to be placed on formal lecture courses, since a wider range of less formal teacher-student contacts is feasible, for example through seminars and individual supervisions. In a subject where a wide range of subjects has to be covered and, especially important, where many required texts are in very limited supply, a good deal of essential information can only be conveyed to a relatively large student body through the medium of formal lectures. However tedious this may be for students —and I think there can be no doubt that the uninterrupted attention required, except where the lecturer is of outstanding brilliance, *is* tedious—there does not seem to be any alternative method of dealing with large classes, so long as wide coverage is demanded, and essential texts (above the elementary text-book level) are expensive or, as in the case of some journal material, practically unavailable.

If it is accepted that formal lectures are rather a means of imparting information than a technique for stimulating thought, they are obviously least useful where the information they purvey is readily obtainable elsewhere. In British social anthropology departments it often, perhaps usually, is not; text books in the subject are few and not widely used, so that general reviews of the field of social anthropological studies are usually given in lecture courses, generally at an undergraduate or pre-doctoral level. Also, a high proportion of lectures in most British and Commonwealth departments, especially those of most interest to graduate students, consist in presentations and analyses of the lecturer's own unpublished field material. The fact that formal lecturing plays little or no part in preparation for a doctorate in British universities (though of course it is of major importance in undergraduate teaching) may be said, finally, to reflect the narrower range of study required of students at the Ph.D. stage in Great Britain and the Commonwealth.

SEMINARS AND TUTORIALS

Whereas formal lecturing especially characterizes undergraduate teaching, seminars are universally used in graduate training. Here the aim is not, or at least not primarily, to impart information, but rather to afford students an opportunity to formulate and defend their own points of view, to encourage quick and constructive thinking, and to develop a capacity to criticize and submit to criticism intelligently. Everywhere, formal lecturing is increasingly replaced by seminar teaching as the research student advances; in England, as has been noted, any kind of formal or "group" teaching is virtually absent from the latter stages of preparation for a Ph.D.

There are, it seems to me, three issues in regard to seminars on which some variance of opinion is possible: the first is the optimum size of classes, the second is the degree and kind of staff participation advisable, and the third is the amount of preparation desirable. On the first point, I suppose that most teachers would agree that the smaller the seminar the better, for in a small group members can quickly get to know one another, so that the shyer ones will feel less inhibited; intellectual contact with other minds is more thorough-going and intense because less broadly distributed, and so more rewarding for members; and there is full opportunity for all to participate adequately. I have the impression that American anthropology departments are more consistently successful in keeping the size of seminars down than British ones; in the United States the policy seems generally to be to have many small student seminars rather than a few large ones. In some English universities at least, seminars are fewer but larger; thus a weekly seminar held in the Institute of Social Anthropology at Oxford may have up to twenty or thirty people present, both students and staff (there are smaller seminars, however), and attendance at University College, London, seminars may run up to sixteen or more. Obviously, whatever their other merits, nothing like complete participation in discussion can be achieved in groups of this size, which often tend to assume the character of more or less formal lectures followed by questions rather than the informal give-and-take of seminar discussion. But English anthropology departments also run small-scale seminars, often for small groups of graduate students interested in a restricted field. Thus in Oxford small groups have met regularly to discuss East African age-sets, for example, or Mediterranean studies.

On the second point, the degree of staff participation in seminars, I have the impression that the distinction between "staff seminars" (where all staff and a few picked or specially interested research students attend), and student seminars, where only one or perhaps two staff members are present, is less clearly made in Britain than it is in America. The fact that large scale staff seminars are rarer in American anthropology departments is no doubt partly due to the wide range of special interests covered in graduate courses; it is difficult to select topics broad enough to interest equally all staff and students. In some British graduate departments, however, where the emphasis is almost exclusively on social anthropology, staff seminars have been extensively and very fruitfully employed, though not unnaturally it sometimes happens that the main beneficiaries are the staff rather than the students. Manchester runs a particularly successful joint staff-student seminar. It is, however, evident that where a number of interested faculty members are present, the discussion will be mainly carried on by them (to the benefit, no doubt, of such students as may be present), and that maximum student participation is best ensured in the small-scale seminar, where only one staff member attends to guide the discussion and to stimulate the shy or backward. Both types of seminar evidently fulfill useful though different functions, and an important incidental merit of the larger-scale staff-student seminar is that it provides an opportunity for students to meet and hear scholars from outside the department, with whose writings they are, in many cases, already familiar. This is of value, of course, to undergraduates as well as graduates, but the stimulus to student effort at all levels thereby afforded needs, perhaps, fuller recognition. It is, in any case, important to distinguish large-scale staff and student seminars from small-scale student classes, and to recognize what each can and cannot do, and it may be doubted whether the distinction has always been clearly made or its implications recognized.

There is a good deal of variation in practice, if less in principle, as to the amount of preparation which should be undertaken for a seminar, not only by the person who is to present a paper or topic, but by all the members of the group. Much depends upon the degree to which the seminar is regarded mainly as a teaching technique rather than as a forum for discussion among professionals (who may be presumed anyway to be more or less briefed on the topic under discussion). In American universities, where seminars are in large degree means to the acquisition of required information, there is, I believe, very much more stress on preparation by all participants. Of course it is plain that even where the stress is primarily on discussion and the exchange of ideas, the more informed the participants are, the more useful their contribution is likely to be. The implications of this platitude, obvious though they are, are not always acted upon even by professionals.

Should post-graduate seminars be primarily oriented to ethnography or to anthropological—or sociological—theory, or more or less equally to both? The question itself, of course, implies the debatable assumption that these two things can usefully be distinguished. But a difference of emphasis is possible, and although the general view seems to be that equal weight should be given to both aspects, British and Commonwealth anthropology departments tend, perhaps, to favor a slightly more theoretical orientation in their seminars than American ones.[5] The "theorists'" point was that while ethnographic information can be provided in formal lectures, or through textbooks, consideration of the kinds of comparative theoretical framework by means of which field data may be interpreted is a more complex matter, demanding in the absence of any authoritative and universally accepted anthropological "theory," a good deal of discussion and thought. Material of this kind is thus especially suitable for seminar treatment. I share this view, though of course the point needs to be made that anthropological theory without any kind of real content is as barren as —perhaps more barren than—bare ethnographic information devoid of any kind of systematic (i.e., theoretical) organization; evidently both must be combined. Nonetheless, it may reasonably be held that a seminar, at any level, will operate more profitably if it is directed to the consideration of some specific theoretical and comparative problem rather than merely to the presentation of fieldwork. It may be that attachment to the idea of the "culture area" as a basis for anthropological thinking accounts for the more ethnographic emphasis in some American seminar activity (if I am correct in asserting such an emphasis). Certainly theoretical problems will—or should—arise anyway, but the presentation of a theme in terms of some theoretical interest is likely to avoid waste of time and to develop a more explicit concern with relevance to a selected theme or themes, a concern which is urgently needed even in the work of many professional anthropologists.

Comparable with the "small seminar" type of pupil-teacher contact is what I consider to be the most important medium of graduate teaching, that is, personal, face-to-face contact between one teacher and one research student, or perhaps two; where there are more than this the situation approximates a seminar rather than a tutorial. There is a wide range in the kind of contact possible. At one extreme is the formal weekly "tutorial," at which the student reads a prepared essay on a selected topic to his supervisor, who then criticizes and discusses it; this is the undergraduate pattern at some British universities, and is also sometimes used in graduate teaching (but at Oxford, for example, only up to the diploma level). The "term papers" required in some American departments, which are criticized by the teacher in tutorial or seminar, embody the same teaching technique. At the other extreme is occasional informal discussion and consultation with a supervisor by a student who is engaged in writing up his own research. This is the procedure usually adopted in the preparation of a thesis, though varying use is made of it, both from university to university, and even within the same department, since a great deal depends on the initiative and needs of the student. Thus in Oxford we have found that some research students make very much greater claims on their supervisors than others do; by and large the better the student, the more independently he will work, and the less of his supervisor's time he will demand. Of course there is a limit to the independence desirable; students have been known to submit theses without any, or with only the most limited, reference to their supervisors, and this has not always had very happy results. This "tutorial" or supervisory teaching technique is, I think, employed everywhere, though to varying extents and with varying degrees of formality. In Oxford a graduate diploma student has an hour's tutorial weekly during term; a B.Litt. student usually sees his supervisor two or three times a term; a D.Phil. student, on the average, somewhat less frequently. Comparable periods are given to "tutorial" teaching in Manchester, University College, London, and elsewhere in Britain.

Evidently, the amount of time that can be given to this form of instruction depends both on the teacher-student ratio and on the extent of other teaching activities. There is no doubt that especially for research students these individual "man to man" contacts can be the most valuable of all teaching techniques, assuming the adequacy of staff, both in quantity and quality, for they make heavy demands on time and competence. In general, the more advanced the student is in his particular research, the smaller the size of the group from which he will gain maximum benefit. A group of research students working in the same field may benefit greatly by group discussion; but a man well advanced on his own dissertation needs individual discussion of his particular research problems with the right supervisor.

But who is the right supervisor? In the "one teacher—one pupil" situation, the interests and abilities of the teacher assume proportionately higher importance, especially where the thesis is being prepared on the student's own fieldwork. Thus, for example, in Great Britain a man preparing a thesis on fieldwork in East Africa would ordinarily be supervised by a staff member who has had experience in that area, one whose field was South East Asia by a South East Asian specialist (or the nearest available), and so on. But although the principle involved here may seem to be self-evident, there is something to be said for having an advanced student, working on his own field material, supervised by a staff member whose field experience is in an entirely different area. The latter's different background and orientation, and the more critical and comparative approach that this may imply, could be no less valuable than local knowledge. No firm generalization is possible here, since the suitability of a supervisor to a particular student and his project is a complex matter to be decided *ad hoc* in the circumstances of particular cases, and often virtues will have to be made of necessities. But, it is perhaps worth adding that at this level especially the teaching process is a two-way one; the thinking of both supervisor and student may be reciprocally stimulated. As an Africanist, I think that I would be willing to supervise a man working on field material from another part of the world, provided that I could rely on a colleague (or on the student himself) in matters of bibliography and of comparative ethnography.

The difference between informal supervisions of the kind that take place between an advanced research student and his supervisor, and the sort of informal contacts that may occur over a morning coffee break, for example, or even in the local "pub" at the end of the day, may not be great. Casual teacher-student contacts of this latter kind can be extremely valuable, and I think that every post-graduate department, when it can, should provide for students and staff to be brought together informally as much as possible. Of course, this is not always practicable; where there is a large undergraduate school, where there are too many students for much individual contact to be feasible, or even where there are no physical facilities in the department for such informal contact, there is not much that can be done. But I think that many of us feel that these casual and unscheduled contacts between staff and graduate students (as well as between the students themselves) are sufficiently important to merit being classified as a technique of graduate training, and that where possible ample provision should be made for them.

A merit of such semi-formal or informal contacts is that they provide a useful additional means for teachers to determine students' interests, needs, and reactions, for these are often more readily expressed in such casual, "social" contexts than in the more formal teacher-student relationships. It can hardly be doubted that there is a need to consult graduate students (whatever may be said of undergraduates) as to what they want from their training; if they do not by this time have some fairly clear ideas of their needs they can hardly be suited for advanced research. In Oxford the better graduates, even at the diploma course level, are quite explicit about the kinds of seminar topics, lectures, etc. they want, and of course this information is helpful to the staff, whether or not they do anything about it. No doubt the situation is the same elsewhere. But it is a matter for discussion how far students, even research students, should be given "what is good for them" and how far they should be allowed to follow their own interests and ignore what does not interest them. Here it is sufficient to underline the obvious truism that it is useful for teachers to know what their students' interests (and, no less important, their "dis-interests") are, and that this can only adequately be done though sustained personal contact.

EXAMINATIONS

It is, perhaps, questionable how far examinations (at least terminal ones) can properly be regarded as "techniques of graduate training." They are, however, part, usually the final part, of the whole process by which a graduate is turned into a professionally qualified anthropologist. I am here concerned mainly with the Ph.D. examination. Generally speaking, the purpose of an examination is to assess the kind and degree of capacity which a candidate possesses. There are different types of examination, and these often test different capacities. So much is platitude, but the implications of these facts in graduate anthropology teaching perhaps deserve some consideration.

As far as the Ph.D. is concerned, any of three types of examination are commonly used, often a combination of some or all of them. These are, first, the scrutiny of a thesis or dissertation, usually followed by a *viva voce* examination on it; second, a written examination paper or papers, on general anthropology, on a specialized field or fields, or occasionally, on the dissertation itself; and third, oral tests, again on any or all of these themes. All of these examination types may serve different ends, and it is worthwhile taking a look at their use in graduate anthropology, especially at the Ph.D. level. Everywhere, the submission of a thesis or dissertation is a requirement for the doctorate, as it is for lower research degrees, where these are awarded. Policy varies, however, in regard to whether or not the candidate is subjected to oral examination on his thesis. In British and Commonwealth universities such a *viva voce* examination, concerned entirely with the subject matter of the thesis, is the only formal examination which a Ph.D. candidate has to take. Even it is sometimes dispensed with in some Commonwealth universities; for example doctoral candidates in anthropology are not usually required to take an oral examination in the universities of Cape Town or Sydney, though one may be arranged if it is requested by an examiner in a particular case.[6] In Canberra there is usually an oral based on the thesis. Even in Great Britain the importance attached to the oral examination varies; in Edinburgh, for example, it plays a relatively minor part, while in Oxford and London it is a much more serious affair, is sometimes public, may occupy two hours or longer, and is looked forward to with considerable apprehension by most candidates. The situation is thus somewhat different from that in America, where the much wider scope of a Ph.D. would seem to imply the attaching of rather less relative importance both to the thesis and to oral examination of a candidate specifically upon it.

Almost everywhere, however, oral examination plays some part in the process of creating Ph.D.'s in anthropology. It has often been argued that people of high ability are sometimes unable to do themselves justice in oral examination, owing to temperament and "nerves," so that this form of test puts them at a disadvantage. In my very limited experience, given sympathetic and perceptive examiners, this is not very often the case. It might even be argued that in anthropology candidates who are contemplating field work, as most are, such temperamental susceptibility is a serious weakness, so that an oral examination performs a valuable function in disclosing it. For it is not merely a test of the candidate's knowledge and intellectual ability, it is also a measure of his readiness of wit, presence of mind, common sense, and stability "under fire." All these are desirable, if not essential, qualities in anyone who wishes to undertake social anthropological fieldwork in an unfamiliar culture. Of course, this aspect of the oral examination argues primarily its importance at the pre-doctoral or "screening" stage, and I think that most universities (except such exclusively post-graduate ones as Canberra, where much stress is laid on the quality of a candidate's written work) make use of it at these earlier stages, either in "screening" or in orientation tests. In Oxford an oral examination on the three major branches of anthropology forms an important part of the graduate diploma and certificate examinations (whatever the student's specialization); and oral examination is also required for the intermediate research degrees of B.Litt. and B.Sc.

With regard to the part played by written examinations in graduate teaching, I have already remarked that in most British and Commonwealth universities no specific written examination is required for the doctorate, though it may be (usually on the candidate's thesis or in fields cognate to it) for intermediate research degrees. In American universities, however, written examinations play an important, sometimes a major, part, not only at preliminary or intermediate stages of postgraduate training, but for the Ph.D. itself. It is sometimes held that a man who can write a first class examination can also, with guidance, write a good dissertation. I am not sure that this is self-evident, though it is probably valid when phrased negatively; a man who cannot write an adequate examination paper is unlikely to be able to write a good thesis. As far as written question papers themselves are concerned, there is a gradation between the simplest type of written examination (of the "right or wrong" variety) and the writing of an essay or thesis around a problem, and it is probably correct to say that on the whole there is, or ought to be, a gradual process up this scale as a student advances. At a graduate level most examination papers in anthropology are of the "short essay" type, and at least a large proportion of the questions are general rather than specific, so that the candidate is required to demonstrate a capacity to organize the information he possesses around a theme, also to show ability to express himself clearly. This last is obviously an important and essential quality in every scholar's training; and the right kind of examination is an important test of it, as also, of course, are the weekly essays which a student is required to produce in the earlier stages of his course, for example, during the diploma year in Oxford. The examination for this last involves, as well as practical examinations in material culture and physical anthropology, and a *viva voce* examination, six three-hour papers, on four of which four questions only are to be answered, on one of which (a general anthropology paper) more than four may (but need not) be answered, and one of which consists simply of one question, often an isolated quotation (a choice is given) on which a full length essay has to be composed. This, of course, puts the occasional foreign student with a weak command of English at a disadvantage, and allowances have to be made. But it is certainly true that teaching people to express themselves clearly and effectively is still one of the most important tasks in graduate training. This perhaps should not be the case, but a look at much published anthropological material will show that it is so.

With regard to Ph.D. examinations, a matter on which there is a good deal of divergence, not only between British and American practice but also among British universities themselves, is the composition of the body of examiners. These may vary from two to five or more; they may or may not include an external examiner; and, with regard to the examination of a candidate's thesis, his supervisor may either be required to act as examiner or he may be prohibited, except in the most exceptional circumstances, from doing so. On this latter point, British universities seem fairly evenly divided as to whether a Ph.D. candidate should be examined by his supervisor; in all, or practically all, American universities his supervisor is required to serve as one of his examiners, usually the chief one. The difference in policy here, insofar as it is not a function of historical causes, may reflect the different approaches to the Ph.D. examination discussed earlier. Where the examination of a thesis is the crucial and in effect the only test upon which the merit of a candidate is judged, then it seems logical that his examiners should not include the staff member or members most closely concerned with the writing of it. Where, on the other hand, the Ph.D. examination is rather regarded as the concluding stage in a continuing series of tests and assessments in which the supervisor has all along been concerned, there is no logical reason why he should be excluded from it. Objectivity is assured by the inclusion in the examining committee of at least one examiner from outside the department, perhaps (as is the usual British practice) from outside the University altogether. It may not be going too far to say that by and large most American universities themselves assess the merit of their candidates, whereas the British practice is to submit their Ph.D. theses to the scrutiny of an outside scholar, who examines jointly with a member of the candidate's own department, in some cases his supervisor. Thus I think that policy with regard to the participation of outside examiners is also connected with the way in which the Ph.D. is regarded. But it may also reflect the greater distances in the American continent, which make (or made until recently) this sort of interaction between universities impracticable because of the time and expense required in traveling between one university and another.

There are other techniques of post-graduate training besides those considered here, and even about the latter there is certainly very much more to say. A comparison of Ph.D. failure rates, for example, might seem to provide a useful means to determining the success or otherwise of the training techniques used; thus according to my information failure rates are consistently higher in American universities than they are in England. But any analysis based on data of this kind would require the greatest caution, for two reasons in particular. The first is that in Great Britain the main stress is on "screening"; only students well advanced in the subject, and of them only those judged likely to make the grade, are admitted to read for a Ph.D. In America, on the other hand, the primary emphasis seems to be on "weeding" rather than on "screening." Thus although admission rates are often high there is a considerable process of attrition along the way. This must involve some wastage of teaching skills and effort, expended upon the students who are not going to make the grade. A second reason why particularly careful analysis of failure rates would be necessary is that the term "failure" itself may be (and often is) differently interpreted. It may mean, for example, failure in the final examination, reference back for reëxamination, or failure to reach the stage of thesis submission at all—even, in America, the final general examination. These ambiguities no doubt account in part for the difference between American and English failure rates which I have noted.

All that has been attempted here has been to identify the more important post-graduate training techniques, to indicate, in the broadest terms, some of their possibilities and limitations, and to suggest that differences in their use are to some extent conditioned by different ideas about what the objectives of graduate training should be. It may well be that there is room in anthropology teaching for a more critical assessment of the modes in which the various training techniques or types of "learning experience" (lectures, classes, seminars, informal discussions, and so on) are oriented towards the different kinds of objectives at which graduate training, whether explicitly or implicitly, is aimed. As my concern has been rather with means than ends, I have characterized these objectives—the acquisition of information in order to impart it to students, the development of the capacity to plan and undertake research, preparation for fieldwork—only in the very broadest terms. It is true that there is some consensus everywhere as to the ends of graduate training (after all every graduate department wants to turn out good scholars, able to think systematically and write clearly), but there are also considerable variations in aim, and I have drawn attention to some of these. Their fuller consideration and analysis is an essential logical preliminary to the comparative assessment of the techniques employed.

NOTES

[1] I gratefully acknowledge the willing co-operation of a number of colleagues in America, Europe, and the Commonwealth, who went to considerable pains to respond very fully and helpfully to my uninformed inquiries about training methods. I wish also to record my indebtedness to the Center for Advanced Study in the Behavioral Sciences, Stanford, California, during the tenure of my Fellowship at which this paper was prepared.

[2] Typically, physical anthropology, archaeology, ethnology, social anthropology, and linguistics.

[3] I am not here concerned to argue the virtues of either of these different approaches; they reflect differences both in tradition and in aim, each has its merits and demerits, and the line between "ignorant specialism" and superficial generality is not always in practice easy to draw. There seems, however, to be a tendency among some American anthropologists to cut down somewhat on general anthropology at the Ph.D. level, so laying more stress on specific research as against general anthropological knowledge. Cf., for example, G. A. Foster and Sol Tax, as reported in the *Summary Report of the Wenner-Gren—American Anthropological Association Ph.D. Curricula Conference* (Washington, D.C.) November, 1958:11, 29.

[4] These numbers are now tending to increase. But in America graduate classes are usually larger; for example Columbia admits 40 to 50 graduate students each year, Harvard about 25, Berkeley 20 or more.

[5] Of seven representatives of British and Commonwealth departments who commented on this point, three attached some primacy to theory; of five Americans only one did.

[6] This dispensation may, in some cases at least, reflect the difficulty of obtaining the physical presence of an external examiner where distances are great and regional specialists not readily available.

PART IX

INTERDISCIPLINARY
RELATIONS
IN
TEACHING
ANTHROPOLOGY

T HE AUTHORS of the papers in this section addressed themselves to the questions of what work in anthropology could best be taken by students in other fields and, conversely, what studies in other fields can be recommended for undergraduate majors in anthropology.

In considering the relations of anthropology with the social sciences, Casagrande notes that, with the increasing interest in studying the social, political, and economic changes now sweeping across the world, anthropologists are drawn into closer contact with other social scientists. One might add that this soon leads one to the question of applied anthropology and contacts with policy making and its execution as manifest in such professions as law, social work, education, medicine, and public health. Basic theoretical problems are also at issue, and Casagrande recommends a course in anthropology for other social scientists so that they may better take into account the socio-cultural context of the behavior which they study.

In connection with biological sciences Spuhler and Livingstone see anthropology chiefly as the beneficiary of cross-disciplinary study, for its concentration on a single species makes it suitable as a place for applying general principles derived in wider interspecies contexts. This is the obverse of anthropology's relations with other social sciences where anthropology usually has the broader perspective because of the more culturally diverse societies from which its data are collected. According to Spuhler and Livingstone the physical anthropologist should be familiar with the results (but not necessarily all the techniques) of biological research. One might well argue similarly that other social scientists should be familiar with the concepts of anthropology, although most will never use its methods of field work.

Despite the clear differences between those who consider anthropology as a social science and those who emphasize its alignment with the humanities, adherents of both views see anthropology as performing a similar educational function. Leslie, in recommending a course in anthropology for students of the humanities, expects it to give them knowledge of other traditions than those of the elite classes of Western societies.

Anthropology's contextual analysis is a main lesson which anthropologists of all kinds expect their subject to convey. This applies not only to students of the social sciences, biology, and the humanities, but also forcefully to the professions. Kimball, in his course for graduate students in education, aims to give his students an appreciation of the cultural context within which American education functions. He uses material from American colonial history as well as from prehistory, presenting the subject matter inductively. He sees the natural science approach in anthropology as providing insights valuable for educators, and for all professions.

Paul discusses an interdisciplinary lecture and seminar course on the human community for students of public health. Paul deals more with the content and methods of the course than with its purposes, and takes for granted the value of the anthropological approach for public health practitioners. Most graduate students of public health are mature individuals who have had varied experiences and who are already internationally oriented. The contrasts between these students and those described by Kimball span the types of graduate professional students for whom a course in anthropology may be desirable; the different approaches of Kimball and Paul suggest the variety of methods by which a course in anthropology can be taught in training for different professions. When the role of anthropology in medical education was discussed several years ago, some of the participants believed that the anthropological point of view should be introduced into the curriculum even when no specific courses on the subject are included (The Teaching of Anatomy and Anthropology in Medical Education, published in Part II of the Journal of Medical Education, October, 1956).

Hoebel and Rossow point out that in the conduct of foreign relations the professional must focus on the process of communication between cultures but must retain his preference for his own culture. Hence a foreign service officer needs an introduction to such anthropological theory and methods of analysis as can be adapted to his purposes rather than extreme area specialization. In respect to law, Hoebel and Rossow state that anthropology can make its contribution at two levels. At the introductory level, anthropology shows the interrelating functions of social action as aspects of total social systems. At a more advanced level, a course in the anthropology of law can present the concepts of social control, norm formation and the legal buttressing of selected norms.

In anthropology's relation with other disciplines, the usefulness of anthropology is in the application of the culture concept and of anthropological modes of societal analysis. The contributions from other fields to anthropology are diverse and include theories of other biological and social sciences, methods of the humanities and law, and materials from all the disciplines and professions which deal with man.

G.W.L.

JOSEPH B. CASAGRANDE

The Relations
of Anthropology
with the
Social Sciences

IN THIS PAPER I can only scan a very large topic—the reciprocal relations between anthropology and the social sciences, with primary emphasis on problems of undergraduate instruction in these fields. First, I should like to make some general observations on the place of anthropology among the other branches of knowledge, then focusing down to the social sciences, note briefly a few convergent and divergent trends. Finally, I should like to state several assumptions I shall make about the aims of anthropological teaching, the desiderata of cross-disciplinary training and the nature of our undergraduate audience, before discussing some specific ways in which I think the mutual interests of anthropology and the social sciences may be served in the classroom.

THE PLACE OF ANTHROPOLOGY AMONG THE FIELDS OF KNOWLEDGE

It has often been remarked that anthropology spans virtually all the established fields of knowledge, embracing in both subject matter and in its total approach to the study of man the natural sciences, the biological sciences, the social sciences, and the humanities.[1] Indeed, without pressing imperial claims, it can be said that anthropology, perhaps with philosophy, stands to all of these as a sort of supra-discipline. The various arts and sciences, dealing in specialized ways with but *aspects* of human behavior and experience, can from the perspective of the sociology or anthropology of knowledge themselves be seen as shaped by and taking color from the Western cultural tradition in which they have developed. Although the sciences are rapidly becoming world-wide in scope, they are in this view still ethno-sciences.

Anthropology can be regarded as a field of knowledge *sui generis,* to which is devoted a relatively small, largely self-identified world association of scholars bound together by a common interest in the total history of man and in his nature as both a biological and cultural creature. Where others have taken man and his works asunder anthropology has always sought to keep him whole. Ours is a field with few boundaries and many frontiers, ranging freely over other areas of study and making alliances with scholars and scientists of all complexions; it is not out of mere courtesy that anthropology is a member of all three of the national councils—The American Council of Learned Societies, the Social Science Research Council, and the National Academy of Sciences-National Research Council. We need not swear single allegiance to any one of the several groupings of the traditional fields of knowledge. For historical, intellectual, and practical reasons our relations with all of them are broad and deep, and it becomes us to cherish all of these ties rather than renounce or disparage any of them.

ANTHROPOLOGY AMONG THE SOCIAL SCIENCES

One may agree with Kroeber (1959:404) that "anthropology was originally not a social science at all. Its father was natural science; its mother, esthetically tinged humanities." However, once it had come of age anthropology formed a liaison with the social sciences that one must at least liken to a common law marriage. In recent decades there has, I believe, been a deepening rapprochement between anthropology (particularly cultural anthropology and those major branches of the discipline that have come to be called ethnology and social anthropology) and the other social sciences. It would take us too far afield to spell out in detail the nature of these interrelationships and to trace their historical development,[2] but let me mention briefly several recent trends that I believe have contributed to the increasing mutuality in the relations of anthropologists with other social scientists. Assuming this over-all trend is real and not a figment of my imagination, it constitutes one very persuasive reason why students in anthropology and the social sciences ought to become better acquainted with each other's fields.

First, one might note the development, particularly since World War II, of interdisciplinary and area research wherein the resources of a number of disciplines in various combinations are brought to bear on a particular problem or to gain broad understanding of a particular world area.[3] Related to this have been a variety of efforts to forge and foster an integrated social science. One might mention here the establishment of the Department of Social Relations at Harvard University, and of the Center for Advanced Study in the Behavioral Sciences, the recent launching of the journal, *Behavioral Science,* the rise of the Society for Applied Anthropology, an organization characterized by its interdisciplinary membership, the publication of symposia volumes such as that edited by John Gillin (1954), the efforts to develop integrated social science courses such as that instituted in 1949 at Northwestern University, and the work of organizations such as the Social Science Research Council, which through a number of interdisciplinary committees has sought to bring the combined capabilities of a number of social sciences to bear on problems such as economic growth and comparative politics.[4] Some may regard such efforts as premature or even ill-advised, but one cannot deny their existence or their vitality. Although there is no space for documentation here, perhaps the most compelling evidence of the increasing tempo of this scholarly interchange is to be found in the greater awareness on the part of individual social scientists of developments in related fields, their efforts to secure further training, often at the post-doctoral level, in them, and their productive use, in their own research, of theories, concepts, methods and techniques borrowed from other disciplines.

A particularly potent force in establishing closer working relationships between anthropologists and other social scientists is a direct consequence of the times we live in. I refer to our common stake in studying the social, political, and economic changes that are sweeping across the world. The catch phrases—economic development, political modernization, the newly developing or underdeveloped areas— have a familiar ring. I am sure I need not underscore the tremendous practical as well as theoretical importance of understanding the processes of change that are at work in the world.

Moving out from their diverse traditional bases—the sociologist, economist, and political scientist from the parochialism of studying their own or Western institutions, and the anthropologist from his almost equally traditional concern with studying the smaller scale societies of primitive and nonliterate tribal peoples—social scientists are today increasingly confronting each other in the peasant villages and pre-industrial cities of the world—in India, the Near East, Africa, Southeast Asia, Latin Ameria. The economists, political scientists, and sociologists for their part want to know what the anthropologist can tell them about the cultures of the peoples they encounter in these exotic places, what insights the concept of culture can give them, how they might go about doing field work in areas where their accustomed documentary sources are not so readily available. And the anthropologist in his turn relies on his colleagues' experience in the collection of data on national institutions and the analysis of social trends in these often complex and highly differentiated societies.

Lest, in calling attention to these interdisciplinary urges, I draw a distorted picture of contemporary anthropology, it should be noted that in anthropology as in probably all fields one may observe both centripetal and centrifugal tendencies—both a reaching out to other fields and an abiding concern with core problems. Anthropology has always been diffuse in its interests and difficult to contain, yet it has at the same time displayed an urge toward autonomy. This urge is especially strong today, precisely at the time when anthropology and the social sciences are finding a larger common meeting ground. The press toward autonomy is, I think, apparent in several current developments. It can be seen in the tendency for anthropology to seek departmental independence. This comes about most typically through a process of progressive fission. Although there are exceptions, the pattern seems to be for a host department (usually sociology) to add an anthropologist or two, then for it to become a joint department of sociology and anthropology (usually named in that order) and finally, at a later stage, for anthropology to become established as a separate department. This process, I would maintain, cannot be rationalized on scientific grounds alone. It is in part a consequence of rivalry and academic power politics,[5] but even more significant for the often outnumbered anthropologist, it meets his deep need to be unequivocally identified with his primary reference group, a need that is perhaps most keenly felt in small schools where there are only one or two anthropologists.

There has also been a resurgence of interest in topics such as kinship and cultural evolution that have long been of central concern to anthropology. And within the field itself, as other papers in this volume have shown, the major subfields of archaeology, ethnology, linguistics, and physical anthropology have become tightly united under the flag of culture.

These dual tendencies are, I believe, a sign, not of weakness, but rather of maturity and vigorous strength. While some are exploring and pushing out on new frontiers, there is still someone at home tending the shop.

THE UNDERGRADUATE AUDIENCE AND SOME GENERAL OBJECTIVES OF CROSS-DISCIPLINE STUDY

I wish in this section to state a few assumptions and prejudices about the nature of our undergraduate audience and about general desiderata of training in fields allied to one's own. First, I do not believe that introductory anthropology should at the undergraduate level be taught as a service course; *i.e.,* that it should be slanted to any special interest group. Nor is it in any event practicable to offer service courses in smaller colleges. I strongly feel that emphasis should fall on broad liberalizing objectives such as have been eloquently enunciated by other contributors to this volume. Since we all are, I think, basically agreed on these general objectives there is no need to rehearse them in detail here. The student in social science should benefit in at least equal measure as others from the often eye-opening, systematic exposure to the various transmutations of human experience, and from a deepening awareness of the concept of culture and its power in shaping human ends.

The usual undergraduate audience for introductory courses is a very mixed bag. Introductory and survey courses, in anthropology as well as in other social sciences, are bound to attract students in a wide variety of fields, from those in preprofessional curricula to those destined to major in home economics, physics, psychology, or English literature. Even if it were deemed desirable, one could not hope to design a course that would *in toto* serve the special needs of students in even a major grouping of disciplines such as the social sciences. Moreover, most students enrolled in introductory courses are apt to be underclassmen, many of whom will not yet have chosen a major; only in retrospect will they be able to see what in fact was relevant to their major field of study or in preparation for their chosen careers.

A series of separate papers would be required to specify in detail the particular values that work in anthropology might have for students in each of the several social sciences, and conversely to indicate the value of courses in other social sciences for anthropology majors. In this brief paper I can mention only a few of the reasons for urging students to expose themselves to these sister disciplines. However, first let me describe in more general terms what I feel the student should ideally gain from work in *any* other field.

I would suggest that it is important to learn not facts or the content of a discipline so much as its distinctive modes of thinking and inquiry, the theoretical frameworks employed, and from a more philosophical perspective, the particular image of man that emerges from a discipline's working assumptions and its "way of knowing."[6] At least as important then as learning the results of work in other fields is learning the kinds of questions that are posed, the concepts and methods employed, and the ways in which evidence is obtained, analyzed, and marshalled to answer these questions.

One must probably acknowledge that most introductory courses are not well suited, nor is the time when they are usually taken propitious, to acquaint the student with the basic tenets and procedures of

a discipline. More advanced "integrative" courses, particularly those
on research methods, theory, experimental design, and the history
and modern viewpoints of a discipline, are doubtless better tailored
to give the student the deeper insight into a field of the sort suggested
above. Here there is certainly scope for the creation and development
in anthropology as well as in other social sciences of new courses that
will seriously take into account the oft-expressed need of the advanced
student from an allied field who, say, has had one or two introductory
level courses, to gain economically in a single intensive course the kind
of over-all perspective on a field I have indicated.[7] If the position I
have taken here has any validity, one might urge students to look for
the courses (and, importantly, the instructors) that can meet these
broad objectives. It also suggests that students be encouraged to select a sequence of courses designed to get this kind of depth in a single
related field, perhaps in the form of a minor, rather than sample a buf-
fet of survey courses.

ANTHROPOLOGY COURSES FOR THE SOCIAL SCIENCE STUDENT

Let me now turn to consider what the student in other social science
fields can in general obtain from anthropology, beyond the broadly
liberalizing values we have already noted, and to the particular kinds
of courses they might profitably take. Of prime importance is the attainment of a vivid and deep appreciation of the culture concept as the
broadest framework or matrix for the understanding of human behavior. In short, the student must be taught *to take culture into account,*
and to see whatever aspect of behavior with which he may be especially
concerned in the total context of the sociocultural system wherein it
is embedded. Thus one of anthropology's major values for the other
social sciences lies in its capacity to *correct, amplify,* and *integrate* the
more particularistic approaches of the several social sciences. This function has been well and pointedly stated by Redfield:

So with respect to the more specialized social sciences the influence of the
anthropologist is to correct and enlarge the understanding achieved by the
more segmental and analytical approaches through consideration of the entirety. This entirety, seen as social structure, a system of social relations, or
more commonly as culture, is again offered by the anthropologist in correction and amplification of the analytically and experimentally conceived science of psychology. (1953:732-33)

In this connection the *testing* function of anthropology and its findings is of especial significance. If the goal of psychology, sociology, economics and political science is to generate propositions of general relevance for all mankind, then these propositions must be tried out
against the ethnographic record. It is only by such comparative scrutiny

that a truly universal science of man can painstakingly be developed.

On the methodological side, contact with anthropology will for many social science students constitute their introduction to comparative method and, if only at second hand, to techniques of field research. However, much of what they might learn of these two time-honored anthropological methods will often be only implicit in the course materials; as a group we anthropologists have been remiss, for we have failed to systematize and codify our methodological and analytic procedures.[8] Here, too, there is room to develop new courses and teaching materials.

In cross-cutting disciplines, in addition to teaching what is distinctive to each, one might pay particular attention to what could be called "linking concepts," *i.e.*, those that are actually or potentially useful for two (or more) disciplines. Prime examples of linking concepts are status and role, which serve effectively as a tri-disciplinary conceptual and theoretical bridge among psychology, sociology, and social anthropology. Personality, social structure, social system and other more global concepts as well as concepts of more limited scope, such as reference group, might also fall into this category of "linking concepts."

It is difficult to offer any general prescription about what students in a given social science should take what courses in anthropology. The recommendations one might make must depend on the student's particular interests within his own discipline (whether he is interested, say, in clinical, experimental, social, or industrial psychology), his career objectives, and not least, what courses and what instructors are available on his campus. In many cases the ideal solution would be to offer individually designed independent reading courses with frequent tutorial conferences with the instructor, but this practice would be feasible in only a few exceptional institutions.

Of direct relevance for students in many of the social sciences interested in the ramified problems of economic and political development would be courses in acculturation, cultural dynamics, and social and cultural change, all areas in which anthropologists have special competence. Similarly, a course in applied anthropology would be valuable for those planning overseas careers in government, business, or in an international agency. (It has recently been estimated that one out of three students currently enrolled in institutions of higher education will spend a major part of his adult years abroad.) And if such students have already chosen the part of the world in which they hope to be employed, they would have an obvious interest in area courses.

One useful model for the more direct confrontation of anthropology and the other social science fields is provided by the widely prevalent course in personality and culture in which, depending upon just how it is handled, materials from several fields of psychology (personality theory, clinical, social, psychiatry) and anthropology, and often also sociology and social psychology, are brought to bear on the topic. In somewhat analogous fashion courses in economic anthropology and political anthropology might bring the approaches of both disciplines to bear on these institutional aspects of culture. Similarly courses in social organization, social structure, or those dealing with cultural or societal types might be expected to elicit the joint interest of sociologists and anthropologists.

SOCIAL SCIENCE COURSES FOR THE ANTHROPOLOGY STUDENT

It is equally difficult, and for many of the same reasons, to make general recommendations about particular courses anthropology students should take in other social science fields. Nor is it very helpful to gratuitously admonish anthropology students to become generally knowledgeable about developments in all the social sciences. Nevertheless there are a few broad guidelines that can be noted. Thus, unless they have quite specific interests, one might urge students to look first to psychology, social psychology, and sociology, as the disciplines most closely allied to anthropology and from which, as Cora Du Bois notes, we have borrowed most heavily. Indeed, the disciplinary ancestry of some of our most productive theories and concepts, such as status, role, institution, and socialization is almost hopelessly tangled. Again, beyond the introductory level, I would stress courses in theory, research methods, and in the intellectual histories of these auxiliary fields. In one way or another the undergraduate student in anthropology should gain some familiarity with figures in sociology such as Max Weber Durkheim, Simmel, Marx, George Herbert Mead, Cooley and W. I. Thomas, and among contemporaries, with Merton and Parsons, and in psychology with the personality theorists covered in such a book as that by Hall and Lindzey (1958), and with the major contributors to Gestalt psychology and learning theory.

Among the more widely offered courses in sociology those in demography, social change, the urban and rural community, minority groups, social movements or collective behavior, and survey research methods are broadly relevant to anthropological interests. In psychology, courses in personality theory and assessment, social psychology, child and developmental psychology, learning theory, psychological tests and measurement, comparative psychology and motivation and emotion deal with material highly germane to anthropology. In this connection one might note a very general fault of anthropologists —the uncritical use of projective and other psychological tests. More adequate training of anthropologists in psychological testing might have resulted not only in better data but also perhaps in the development by anthropologists of new and more appropriate instruments. With other contributors to this volume I would urge that all undergraduates secure training in statistics and other quantitative methods. The most relevant courses are in most institutions those taught in the departments of sociology or psychology, and we shall doubtless for some years to come send our students to them until courses in quantitative methods are regularly offered in anthropology departments.

In political science the most relevant courses, in addition to those dealing with the government and politics of particular world areas, would seem to be comparative politics, contemporary political theory, and where offered, courses dealing with the politics of emerging nations. Of especial interest to students who wish to work in applied areas would be courses in the broad field of public administration. In economics, courses in economic development, comparative economic systems, and in labor and industrial relations might be recommended. And if one includes history among the social sciences, I should urge the anthropology student to take a course in historiography, particularly in the evaluation and use of documentary sources.

SOME STRATAGEMS FOR THE CLASSROOM

If we can agree that the above are some of the desiderata of cross-disciplinary training, one might then ask what strategies can we employ in the classroom, what other kinds of courses can we design to achieve some of these goals, what arrangements might we make? In the balance of this paper I want to consider briefly what is done or might be done (1) in introductory courses, (2) in special and advanced courses, and (3) in integrated courses.

In large introductory lecture courses in which students are also assigned to discussion or quiz sections, it would be possible to assign students to special sections on the basis of their particular interests. Thus, students majoring or declaring an intention to major in, say, psychology or political science, might be grouped together and perhaps given special readings or other assignments in addition to the regular course work. There are, of course, disadvantages and hazards in such a procedure, not the least of which is the difficulty of deciding just who should be assigned to such special sections, particularly in the case of freshmen and sophomores who may be far from settled on a major. If the luxury could be afforded, one might also offer an introductory course for upperclassmen, i.e., *after* the choice of a major has been made. Such a course presumably might be of special interest to social science majors, some of whom may, in those colleges where a minor is required, elect anthropology as a minor. A course of this sort taught on a more advanced level than the usual introductory offering might then be more effectively tailored to the needs of the students, but still not a service course in the usual somewhat pejorative sense of the term.

The prevailing pattern in courses such as personality and culture, or in other courses such as economic anthropology, that bridge two disciplines is for them to be taught by anthropologists within anthropology departments and largely to anthropology students. Doubtless such a course is best taught by one person highly competent in both contributory fields and who can move easily between them. However, few are fully competent in two disciplines, and an alternative way to offer a course, say, in political anthropology, would be to have it given jointly by a political scientist and an anthropologist for students of *both* disciplines. One can in such a course imagine an intriguing kind of interdisciplinary dialogue in which instructors and students alike would be concerned with the explication, for themselves and each other, of their characteristic approaches. Such a course might take up problems of the classification and comparison of political systems, of the analytic distinctiveness of political behavior, of the utility of political theory for anthropology, etc.[9] Similarly, courses bringing together economists and anthropologists or psychologists (from either the experimental or the psychiatric-clinical side) and anthropologists might also prove to be stimulating enterprises for both students and teachers. Such a course would be frankly experimental and doubtless could only by grace of rare dedication and much good will be sustained over any length of time. Although better suited to graduate level instruction, a course organized along these lines might well afford a memorable intellectual encounter for a group of selected undergraduates.

To carry the approach suggested above one step farther, it would be highly interesting and instructive to devote a course to the detailed examination of an institution or set of institutions from the points of view of *several* social science disciplines. Thus one might look at Inca political and economic institutions from the points of view of social anthropology, political science, and economics; or one could similarly examine several aspects of the relationship between the local community, seen as a sub-society, and the larger society of which it is an integral part. It would be, I am sure, very difficult to bring off a successful course of the kind suggested here; and it would be an extremely searching test of the ingenuity and competence of the instructor or instructors who might boldly undertake to do so.

THE INTEGRATED SOCIAL SCIENCE COURSE

The integrated social science course is a thorny subject, certainly large enough for separate discussion in another paper. The organization and administration of such courses presents both intellectual and practical problems difficult enough of solution to give pause to even our most sanguinely interdiscipline-minded colleagues. It is ironic that we often expect our students after taking a prescribed assortment of courses in several social science fields themselves to achieve an almost miraculous integration of them when we, their teachers, are indifferent, incapable or not inclined to do so.

One hears many arguments pro and con the integrated course—that this way lies intellectual salvation (or chaos), that it eliminates tedious duplication of material now given in introductory courses in several fields (e.g., cultural anthropology, sociology, and social psychology), that it is premature to attempt such a course, that only *after* being exposed to the separate disciplines can one expect the undergraduate to integrate them, etc.

One of the first and most carefully planned integrated courses is that inaugurated at Northwestern University in 1949. Titled, "An Introduction to the Sciences of Human Behavior," the course is sponsored by the departments of anthropology, sociology, and psychology and is designed to combine introductory materials from these three fields into a one-year sequence. A detailed description of the course and a discussion of some of the problems encountered in giving it are available elsewhere.[10] However, an observation by Merriam seems especially apropos: "The tendency of the student is to attempt to see the points of view *as* different and to pigeonhole them into the convenient categories of the three disciplines and, try as we may, we cannot always override the tendency. Integration remains our biggest problem..." (1959: 42-43).

In reviewing Northwestern's experience with the course, Kimball Young, one of its founders, makes a series of observations which he feels may well apply to other interdisciplinary courses. His comments are so pointed they deserve to be quoted at length:

(1) Such courses must grow up from departments concerned. No administrative fiat can create them. (2) It takes time to build such joint courses. We spent more than a year in discussion and planning before the course was begun. It certainly was not too much. We might well be farther ahead had we taken still additional time to develop a common frame of reference and to coordinate our concepts and content. (3) Such courses are seldom if ever put into final form; there must be continuous discussion and improvement. (4) No course can rise higher than the personnel which teaches it. Congeniality among the staff members—senior and junior alike—is essential. There is, moreover, always the danger that the initial enthusiasm which helped launch a joint course may later be dissipated. (5) The necessary high morale for such programs, however, can be kept up if the administrators of our colleges and universities give such courses continuing and ample support. The status of the staff must at all times be adequately recognized and protected by promotions and increases in compensation in line with the institutional policy for all departments. If this is done, the recruitment of

personnel for such programs will be simplified and the quality of those concerned with the course improved. (6) In planning for such interdisciplinary courses, it is unwise to try to cover all the social sciences. It is wise to try the program with two or three of those most closely related. Only in this way will there be adequate time to develop the joint program. It is wasteful of time and energy to spread one's effort too thin over a large area. (1959: 55-56)

Patently, the institution of such a course is not something to be taken lightly.

From a somewhat different perspective, John Messenger (1959) has described his experience in teaching anthropology as part of a general education course in social science at Michigan State University. He notes that in addition to teaching the basic concepts of anthropology, sociology, social psychology, economics, and political science, the course attempts to show the student how science can be used to analyze human behavior. One of the principal justifications for the social science course and the other broad survey courses in the humanities and the sciences, Messenger feels, is to introduce the student at an early stage in his college career to all the fields of knowledge and thus put him in a better position to choose a major. The latter observation, I think, deserves more than passing notice.

CONCLUSIONS

It is probably fair to state that the tendency in higher education and particularly in graduate study is increasingly to narrow its scope by scrutinizing more and more intensively fewer and fewer areas of knowledge. In anthropology as compared with some fields this to be sure still gives us ample room to maneuver. Graduate study is essentially and, if deep competence is to be gained in a single discipline, perhaps inevitably, parochial. As in other fields increasing numbers of students in anthropology now enter graduate study with an undergraduate major in the field. While this may shorten their professional training, it also limits the breadth and variety of prior training and interests that has so long characterized recruits to the field. If this is indeed the case, then it seems to me that the need for students to enlarge their disciplinary horizons is even greater at the undergraduate level. It is at this stage that exposure to other fields is most apt to "take" and to set patterns of interest that persist into graduate work and later professional activity. In the long run one of the most promising ways ultimately to bring about greater collaboration among the various students of human behavior is to establish early the habit of taking other approaches into one's ken. But whether or not a student goes on to professional or graduate study he will, I strongly feel, come away with a deeper understanding of man and the vicissitudes of the human situation if they are seen in the broader perspective of the several sciences devoted to his study.

NOTES

[1] For further comments on the nature of anthropology and its manifold relations with other established disciplines see Redfield (1953); *An Appraisal of Anthropology Today* (Sol Tax et al., 1953), pp. 151-159, and the remarks by Kroeber, pp. 358-360; and also Kroeber (1936 and 1959).

[2] For detailed consideration of these relations see Ogburn and Goldenweiser (1927), Gillin (1954), Lévi-Strauss (1954).

[3] Luszki (1958) discusses problems of interdisciplinary research. For a general discussion of area research see Steward (1950).

[4] Two recently published volumes illustrative of the work of such interdisciplinary SSRC committees are Almond and Coleman (eds., 1960) and Moore and Feldman (eds., 1960), sponsored respectively by the Committees on Comparative Politics and on Economic Growth.

[5] As in any close relationship, that between sociology and anthropology has been notably ambivalent, as Bennett and Wolff (1955) have so vividly documented. In part, this very ambivalence may reflect a need on the part of both sociology and anthropology to establish their identities as separate and respectable disciplines.

[6] Here I would join with Ethel Albert in emphasizing the general utility and relevance of courses in the philosophy of science such as Ernest Nagel might teach, or on the sociology of knowledge as Robert Merton would present it.

[7] At the risk of seeming immodest I should like to describe briefly a course I have been experimenting with. Entitled Cross-Cultural Analysis, the course is devoted to a comparative analysis of recurrent problems inherent in the biosocial nature of man, particularly as these are reflected in stages of the life-cycle from birth through death. Attention is also given to the cross-cultural treatment of other "crisis" situations such as illness, deviancy, and abnormality, and the handling of aggression. The various topics are all discussed from the dual point of view of society and the individual, drawing on the theoretical work of Radcliffe-Brown, Malinowski, Bateson, Merton, Linton, van Gennep, Kardiner, and Nadel among others. The approach is frankly pedagogical, the aim being to acquaint the students with problems of the comparative method, with the ramifications of the cultural embeddedness of customs and institutions, and it attempts to bring a variety of theoretical formulations to bear on a series of crucial and intrinsically interesting common human concerns.

[8] An exception is the recently published book edited by Adams and Preiss (1960), which provides an excellent introduction to field research methods.

[9] David Easton, in his article, "Political Anthropology" (1958), touches on a number of questions that could be examined in a course in this institutional area.

[10] "Anthropology in the Interdisciplinary Program," by Alan P. Merriam, and "Some Problems of Interdisciplinary Courses in the Social Sciences," by Kimball Young, in *Teaching Anthropology*, Logan Museum Bulletin No. 8, Beloit College, Beloit, Wis., 1959.

REFERENCES CITED

ADAMS, RICHARD N., AND JACK J. PREISS (EDS.)
    1960   Human organization research: field relations and techniques. Home-

wood, Illinois, Dorsey Press for the Society for Applied Anthropology.

ALMOND, GABRIEL, AND JAMES S. COLEMAN (EDS.)
    1960   The politics of developing areas. Princeton, Princeton University Press.

BENNETT, JOHN W., AND KURT H. WOLFF
    1955   Toward communication between sociology and anthropology. *In* Yearbook of anthropology—1955, William L. Thomas, Jr., ed. New York, Wenner-Gren Foundation.

EASTON, DAVID
    1958   Political anthropology. *In* Biennial Review of Anthropology, Bernard J. Siegel, ed. Stanford, Stanford University Press.

GILLIN, JOHN (ED.)
    1954   For a science of social man: convergences in anthropology, psychology, and sociology. New York, Macmillan.

HALL, CALVIN, AND GARDNER LINDZEY
    1958   Theories of personality. Boston, Wiley

KROEBER, A. L.
    1936   So-called social science. Journal of Social Philosophy 1:317-340.
    1959   The history of the personality of anthropology. American Anthropologist 61:398-404.

LÉVI-STRAUSS, CLAUDE
    1954   The place of anthropology in the social sciences and the problems raised in teaching it. *In* The university teaching of social sciences: sociology, social psychology, anthropology. Paris, UNESCO.

LUSZKI, MARGARET BARRON
    1958   Interdisciplinary team research: methods and problems. New York, New York University Press for National Training Laboratories.

MERRIAM, ALAN P.
    1959   Anthropology in the interdisciplinary program. *In* Teaching anthropology. Beloit, Logan Museum Bulletin 8.

MESSENGER, JOHN C., JR.
    1959   The teaching of anthropology in a general education program. *In* Teaching anthropology. Beloit, Logan Museum Bulletin 8.

MOORE, WILBERT E., AND ARNOLD S. FELDMAN (EDS.)
    1960   Labor commitment and social change in developing areas. New York, Social Science Research Council.

OGBURN, W. F., AND A. A. GOLDENWEISER (EDS.)
    1927   The social sciences and their interrelations. New York, Houghton.

REDFIELD, ROBERT
    1953   Relations of anthropology to the social sciences and to the humanities. *In* Anthropology today, Alfred L. Kroeber, ed. Chicago, University of Chicago Press.

STEWARD, JULIAN H.
    1950   Area research: theory and practice. New York, Social Science Research Council Bulletin 63.

TAX, SOL, et al., (EDS.)
    1953   An appraisal of anthropology today. Chicago, University of Chicago Press.

YOUNG, KIMBALL
    1959   Some problems of interdisciplinary courses in the social sciences. *In* Teaching anthropology. Beloit, Logan Museum Bulletin 8.

J. N. Spuhler and
F. B. Livingstone

*The Relations
of Physical
Anthropology
with the
Biological Sciences*

P

HYSICAL ANTHROPOLOGY is the study of the biology of human populations in all its aspects, including especially the variability, genetics, adaptation, ecology, behavior, and evolution of human populations past and present. Unlike general biology it is oriented to the study of a single group of organisms: it is human population biology. And unlike other divisions of human biology such as anatomy, embryology, or physiology, it is oriented to the population and not to the individual.

THE SCOPE OF PHYSICAL ANTHROPOLOGY

The specific organism-oriented aspect of physical anthropology leads immediately to a difference which makes it unique among the biological sciences: physical anthropology is concerned with the only living species whose behavior is fully cultural and is mediated by symbols. Thus physical anthropology has strong ties with those behavioral sciences which deal with man's cultural behavior.

Both in research and in teaching there have been three general problems of primary interest in physical anthropology during the past 100 years: (1) macroevolution of man and the primates, (2) microevolution and classification of the living varieties of man, and (3) compar-

475

ative growth and development of man, especially in the post-natal period.

Our primary purpose is to discuss the relations between the curriculum in physical anthropology, which, in this country, is usually taught in departments of anthropology, and the curricula in the other biological sciences. In addition, however, we wish to make some observations about the relations of physical anthropology and general anthropology and about the use of statistical methods in physical anthropology.

PHYSICAL ANTHROPOLOGY AND GENERAL ANTHROPOLOGY

Because they are anthropologists, physical anthropologists should be well versed in the other fields of their discipline, and they should also be familiar in a general way with the other fields of social science such as sociology, human geography, and history. We emphasize social science as an integral part in the training of physical anthropologists, because they are the only biological scientists who regularly receive formal training in the social sciences. We would agree with McCown (1952) and with Hulse (see his paper in this volume) that a major function of physical anthropology is to interpret the biological nature of man in its cultural setting.

There is another, perhaps equally important, reason for some emphasis on social sciences in the training of physical anthropologists. Biological determinism of social and cultural behavior is a common element of American and Western opinion or belief. As Alfred Tozzer (1933) so nicely demonstrated, the stressing of biological determinants and the neglecting of cultural determinants prevail in American biographical literature. Most biographers credit every characteristic of a great man to a biological predecessor—his fortitude he got from his father, his wisdom from his grandfather on his mother's side, and so on. Many of the schemes proposed by planners, including some biologists, for the improvement of society are based on similar reasoning—with the right biological ingredients, we could all be Lincolns, Beethovens, or whomever we choose.

And, unfortunately, the "biology mainly counts" view is sometimes given too much weight in "scientific" interpretations of human variation. A prominent part of the exhibit in the British Museum (Natural History) in commemoration of the Darwin centennial was devoted to an "explanation" of the association between the "th" sound and blood group O in Europe. The "explanation" (following the distinguished plant geneticist, Darlington 1947) was posed in terms of "race" as diagnosed by blood group O frequencies and the biological ability to articulate "th." The association is there. However, a glance at the world distribution of blood group O and of the "th" phoneme, as well as general principles, suggest the association is non-causal and of trivial interest. Our knowledge about the genetic mode of inheritance of the O genotype and about the cultural mode of inheritance of the "th" phoneme provides a more general and a more convincing "explanation."

While we think physical anthropologists properly should join other biological and social scientists in the job of public education regarding the relationship of cultural, social, and biological factors, we also think this task is all too often approached in a merely negative way. Too many of our courses in physical anthropology are almost exclusively devoted to telling the students what is wrong, what is in error, in human biology. The public results of this sort of negative pedagogy over the past hundred years suggests the effort is largely wasted. The intelligent college student is left with neither an accurate nor a useful notion of human population biology in courses or textbooks which put much effort in pooh-poohing the concept of "race," then turn about and present in some detail a racial classification (perhaps disguised as a classification of "ethnic groups"), and then make no further use of either set of materials. There is in fact a lot of misinformation in the corpus of public knowledge about physical anthropology. In our opinion this may be transformed into better sense most rapidly by anthropological curricula which accentuate the positive rather than the negative aspects of "racial" or "ethnic" biology of man.

Since man is a cultural animal we emphasize that instruction in cultural anthropology and in other social sciences is of great importance in the training of a physical anthropologist. But the biological sciences will always remain the core subjects of physical anthropology.

THE BIOLOGICAL CURRICULA FOR PHYSICAL ANTHROPOLOGISTS

It is convenient and representative to divide certain of the many subjects of biology into five major groups:

1) Structural biology—e.g., human anatomy, comparative anatomy,

2) Regulatory biology—e.g., human physiology, comparative physiology, general physiology,

3) Developmental biology—e.g., descriptive embryology, experimental embryology, human growth, gerontology,

4) Genetic biology—e.g., formal genetics, chemical genetics, population genetics,

5) Environmental biology—e.g., ecology, ethology.

The study of evolution fits in all five categories. Evolution is a central theme in physical anthropology. This is one reason why it is difficult to state briefly an opinion about the biological courses most needed in training physical anthropologists. As carried out in this country, the training of a biologist nearly always requires specialization, often in only one of the above major groups. Given our demand that the students of physical anthropology have extensive training in the behavioral sciences and especially cultural anthropology, how do we select from the curricular riches available in general biology?

Again we must insist that physical anthropology is about *human* biology. It is concerned with (1) biology and (2) man. In our teaching we need to put emphasis on both aspects. We need to make our courses respectable as general biology, and we need to be knowledgeable about the specific biology of human populations.

Teachers of physical anthropology thus have a double job. This is partly, but only partly, because we are set in a conventional way of assigning fields of knowledge to specific university departments. Our European, African, and Asian colleagues have curricular problems, but because these physical anthropologists are usually associated with departments of anatomy, the problems are somewhat different. Our students should have the opportunity of gaining a detailed knowledge of the biology of man, and perhaps of some other primates, but may be excused for lack of detailed knowledge of nonprimate organisms from phages to frogs.

Although physical anthropologists need not know the details about other organism oriented subjects, they ought to know about general biology; and this means about general biology in the 1960's, not in the 1930's. Physical anthropologists are keen and quick to report *their* subject has changed remarkably during the last ten, or twenty, or thirty years, and some of the materials beyond thirty years ago they tend to use only as history or as bad example. However, physical anthropologists are less keen and quick to pick up the changes in general biology, which itself has changed perhaps more fundamentally and profoundly during the past ten years than has physical anthropology. For example, the genetic study of micro-organisms broke the boundary between cellular and genetic biology on one side and chemistry and physics on the other. Those physical anthropologists who continue to cover the basic concepts of genetics using only Mendel's peas for illustration are doing their students and the themselves a disservice. We, like other general biologists in the 1960's, should present the basic ideas of genes and phenotypes in terms of DNA, RNA, and notions about genes making enzymes which make proteins which make things like bone, teeth, hair, and cellular antigens.

A few years ago some of us interested in the teaching of physical anthropology engaged in an unresolved argument about whether our students should take the full undergraduate series of courses in physics and chemistry. In the traditional path of chemistry instruction, students do not reach topics holding direct interest for physical anthropology until they go through the whole series, introductory inorganic, qualitative, quantitative, organic, biochemistry. Obviously this sequence is not possible for most students who want to study anthropology and to start professional work after not more than, say, seven years at a university. Fortunately, the long way is not necessary for everybody. Most teachers and students of physical anthropology in the 1960's can learn enough about organic chemistry by reading an introductory text like John Read's, *A Direct Entry to Organic Chemistry* (1948). Naturally, we need to clarify what we mean by "enough." Much of the traditional course and laboratory work in chemistry up through organic is "how to do it." We should never require a student to take a "how to do it" course if in his anthropological career he will never "do it"; and especially not if the general ideas can be learned in three weeks rather than in three or four semesters. In a similar manner the physical anthropologist can become familiar with the concepts in other fields of basic science and thus maintain our traditional broad scope without being encumbered by years of technique training which specialists in these fields go through.

Returning now to the curricular riches of biology, is there anything within this vast realm which is necessary for all physical anthropologists? This depends, of course, on the problems, aims, and current content of physical anthropology, and these are difficult to characterize. Even if we use the succinct but well-worn definition that physical anthropology is what physical anthropologists do, it is not much help. A glance at journals or at the interests of the list of members of the American Association of Physical Anthropologists indicated such divergence that it is difficult to find any common interests, goals, or methods. What then can we say about the biological training which would be useful or essential to active or passive participation in this field?

Because of the diversity of interest, the least common denominator of our science is quite general; for present purposes we may define this L.C.D. as human biological variability, both past and present. For the most part this variability is populational and genetic, not environmental or developmental. (Here we are trying to characterize physical anthropology as a general area of study; we would suggest that a census of publications or courses shows that topics like nutritional anthropology, or those concerned with ontogeny and growth, are important but currently minor parts of the general area.) With this in mind, what biological training is to be recommended?

The vast scope of the theoretical and factual content of physical anthropology, together with the multiplicity of techniques utilized, precludes successful attempts either to teach or to learn it all, and this applies particularly to techniques. Those now being used in anthropological studies include electrophoresis, chromatography, blood grouping, anti-globulin tests, anthropometry, osteometry, X ray, photography, the surgical techniques of experimental morphology, carbon 14 and potassium 40 isotope dating, histo-chemical staining, the handling of chromosomes, stratigraphic techniques, and so on. If mastering a technique is to be worthwhile, it should be used occasionally, if not often, in research and study. Aside from some fundamental techniques of anthropometry and a few basic laboratory procedures (like "don't sterilize polyethylene bottles in an autoclave"), we feel there is no one set of techniques which should be mastered by all physical anthropologists. Techniques are a means and not an end in themselves. A student of physical anthropology should be made aware of the many techniques which are available to him; he should know enough about techniques to understand case histories in observational and experimental human biological science, but he should not be expected to master more than a few of them. When he decides which problems to pursue, he should know how to find what means to use.

The *results* established by the many techniques are, however, another story. If a physical anthropologist wishes to understand the changes in anthropoid structure and function which have taken place as a result of the acquisition of culture by the hominids, he should have a comprehensive background in physiology and anatomy. But for the most part the results from biochemistry, serology, hematology, and other biological disciplines have been used by physical anthropologists only for specific anthropological problems. For example, genes are said to have anthropological value—whether they were identified by serological, clinical, or other techniques—if they appear to be related to the so-called races of man. And one can still read, too frequently, that the Diego factor or some other gene has "anthropological value" because it appears to be restricted to a single race or because of its non-adaptive character it can be used to trace migrations. Thus, within the sphere of human biology, physical anthropology has become associated with the identification of races and their migration. This, we suggest, is of limited value. We should be interested in all genes, although more intensely in those which attain appreciable frequencies in some populations.

If our function is to interpret or attempt to provide explanations of human variability, then obviously we must know the facts of human variability. But more importantly, we should have a strong theoretical background. Although we have described physical anthropology as an interpretative profession, it is also true to a great extent that we have made few contributions to biological theory, but instead have borrowed theories from other branches of biology to interpret or explain the facts of human evolution. For the most part the facts of human variability are taught in courses in physical anthropology, but to obtain a theoretical background it may be necessary to look to other biological fields. This theoretical training should include genetics, ecology, and the biological theory relating to speciation, migration, and selection, and it should be specifically in these fields which are population-oriented, not individual-oriented. This training does not necessarily have to be in the form of courses in other departments but can be found in inter-departmental seminars, association in research with other biologists, reading courses, or even in some instances in courses offered by anthropology departments. Additional familiarity with facts, content, or a particular technique can be obtained in the department which specializes in that particular area of human biology, but we think the theoretical orientation is a prerequisite for all physical anthropologists. And we think hindsight indicates that many of the discarded theories of the past in interpreting either the fossil record or modern variability have been for the most part a result of unfamiliarity with the theoretical content of the rest of the biological sciences.

We have said nothing about specific items and topics of curriculum in physical anthropology. This is deliberate. In our opinion one can start from many different points of departure and still give an excellent introductory or intermediate course in physical anthropology. Let it start with the specific interest of the instructor, e.g., in why (or how) a specific femur has a large third trochanter. But let it then do justice both to modern physical anthropology and to modern general biology. Do not stop with the circular explanation that this is a large third trochanter, because the man who carried this femur was a member of a group of men who had propensities for large trochanters.

For a proper understanding of almost any problem in physical anthropology, the student needs an elementary knowledge of human structural, regulatory, developmental, genetical, and environmental biology. The proper results of physical anthropology are always multivariate and often quantitative. And this brings us to the need for quantitative method and theory in comparative human biology.

STATISTICS AND PHYSICAL ANTHROPOLOGY

From its beginnings physical anthropology has been data rich and theory poor. From the beginning we have employed techniques which produce data in bulk, but we have not applied theory which produced wide interpretations or general conclusions. Over the past one hundred years, thousands of anthropologists have accumulated meticulous data on thousands of human populations; most of the studies have involved complex multivariate systems of measurements and observations. Even when reduced to measures of central tendency (which is the usual case for publication), the sheer volume of data defies absorption or interpretation by the unaided human nervous system. Here one should remember the massive tomes like those of Krogman (1941) on growth, Mourant (1954, 1958) on blood groups, or of Hrdlička (1935) for the anthropometry of Indian populations in the American Southwest.

It is now abundantly clear that complex multivariate systems (which most physical anthropologists feel impelled to study) cannot adequately be analyzed and interpreted by a seriatim method where differences between means of characters are judged or tested by taking the characters one at a time. All anthropological measurements are inter-correlated, and the isolated probability statements of significance tests are not appropriate measures of biological or classificatory distance. Fortunately the statistical methods of, and the computing machines for, multivariate analysis are well developed and are easily available in most colleges where physical anthropology is taught. The methods and machines have been developed mainly from analysis of the data of business transactions and large engineering projects. Their proper use for anthropological problems often requires minor refinements. Our students should be able to understand and to suggest these needed refinements. This requires some training in statistics. The minimum amount is a basic course in statistics, at least the level presented in some elementary work like Moroney (1953).

PHYSICAL ANTHROPOLOGY FOR OTHER BIOLOGISTS

What contribution may anthropology make to the education of other biologists?

It is true, and we think not unfortunate, that human biology has received more from general biology than it has returned. The same conclusion holds for any other species-specific biology. The importance of our subject for general biology is precisely that it *is* species-specific. The content of human biology differs from that of other-species biology in that it contains elements not present in the same form and richness in any other species—in particular it contains culture, which is a biological adaptation, with non-genetic, symbolic modes of transmission which greatly supplement somatic evolution.

This circumstance would lead one to expect that physical anthropology might make its most welcome contribution to the highly specialized, highly technical parts of human biology. This seems to be the case. For example, the professional schools in medicine, nursing, dentistry, and public health seem much more concerned that their students receive some preprofessional training in physical anthropology than graduate departments in, say, botany or zoölogy. Some of the great teachers of anatomy in medical schools (e.g., Keith at London, Todd at Western Reserve, Jackson and Scammon at Minnesota) included a great deal of anthropology into their anatomy lectures and demonstrations. The recent trend toward introducing human genetics into the medical and dental curriculum has increased the awareness of and need for physical anthropology as an element of human biology.

We have emphasized the content of physical anthropology which has to do with the genetic variability in, within, and between human and hominoid populations past and present. We have acknowledged our indebtedness to other branches of biology which discover, diagnose, describe, or deal in any way with this content. In some instances, physical anthropologists also have made direct contributions to these areas of knowledge. Today, however, field work in human biology is often a team affair. What then does the physical anthropologist do for the team? In our experience, and we think generally, the anthropologist will be the field or laboratory worker who relates the biological results to cultural variables, or, perhaps, to anthropometric, nutritional, or still other human biological factors in a general context.

Good courses in physical anthropology will benefit any student in general or human biology who wants controlled and tested information on the biology of human and other primate populations which takes particular cognizance of the facts that the species-specific behavior of man involves certain unique elements, including a type of behavior and biology mediated by symbols, a type of behavior and biology much more varied and complex than that of other species, and a type of behavior and biology which includes a capacity for extraordinarily rapid change.

REFERENCES CITED

DARLINGTON, C. D.
    1947   The genetic component of language. Heredity 1:269-286.
HRDLIČKA, A.
    1935   The Pueblos, with comparative data on the bulk of the tribes of the Southwest and Northern Mexico. American Journal of Physical Anthropology 20:235-460.
KROGMAN W. M.
    1941   Growth of man. Tabulae Biologicae 20:1-963.

McCown, T. D.
   1952   The training and education of the professional physical anthropolo-
             gist. American Anthropologist 54:313-317.
Moroney, M. J.
   1953   Facts from figures. London, Pelican, 472 pp.
Mourant, A. E.
   1954   The distribution of the human blood groups. Oxford, Blackwell,
             438 pp.
Mourant, A. E., A. C. Kopeć, and K. Domaniewska-Sobczak
   1958   The ABO blood groups. Oxford, Blackwell, 276 pp.
Read, John
   1948   A direct entry to organic chemistry. New York, Harper Torchbooks.
Tozzer, A. M.
   1933   Biography and biology. American Anthropologist 35:418-432.

CHARLES LESLIE

*Teaching
Anthropology
and the
Humanities*

THE CHARACTER of anthropological studies is obscured by the fact that they are taught in the social science divisions of American colleges and universities and in many schools combined with sociology courses in a single academic department. A few years ago Bennett and Wolff estimated that 70 per cent of all academic anthropologists taught in combined sociology-anthropology departments (1955:340-341). Yet, in an essay on the history of anthropology Sol Tax concluded that, "In tradition, spirit, and method anthropology is not particularly a social science, and neither administrative convenience nor the need to classify is likely to make it one" (1955:321).

Describing the character of anthropological studies, Robert Redfield pointed to "the polarities of the anthropological field . . . simply apparent in the opposition of physical anthropology to cultural anthropology." He formulated these polarities in a more general manner by saying that, "anthropology is organized around an interest in man seen as something with the characteristics of all life, and around an interest in man seen as something human—a quality not shared, or very little shared, with other forms of life" (1953:729-730). The first of these polarities includes the study of fossil man and human evolution, the biology of human races, the development and diffusion of forms of human adaptation, the ecology of social groups, and many other subjects within archaeology, ethnology, and physical anthropology. The mode

485

of research associated with these subjects gives both polarities of anthropology a scientific character very different from that of the social sciences. An examination of this difference shows the relationships between anthropology and the humanities, and the main values of courses in anthropology for students of the humanities.

Anthropologists traditionally study remote communities in which they observe and collect a great variety of materials, and they seek to understand these communities in historical and functional perspective. In contrast to the research of economists, sociologists, and psychologists, this kind of work is not highly analytic and mathematical, nor is it guided by experimental methods and abstract theoretical models. Anthropologists are naturalists, and the tradition in which they work was shaped in the atmosphere of museums of natural history. According to Collier and Tschopik, "museums played a dominant role in the development of anthropological research, theory, and teaching in the United States" (1954:772), and, in both Europe and America, the leading universities which train professional anthropologists either possess their own museums of anthropology, or maintain close relationships with independent museums of natural history. But, as Kroeber remarked, apropos the classification of anthropology with sociology in academic bureaucracies, "There have never been any museums of sociology" (1954:764).

Between 1890 and 1920, when anthropology was being established as an academic discipline, the concern of museum research was to record information about rapidly disappearing primitive cultures, to accumulate basic data on human evolution and the biological characteristics of racial groups, and to collect archaeological materials from prehistoric cultures. The need to record, collect, and accumulate anthropological documents gave much of the work of that period a radically empirical quality. More recent research maintains this strain of empiricism, but the greater part of contemporary research is guided by developing theoretical knowledge, and by improved methods of field research. For example, within the natural science polarity of anthropology, the neo-Darwinian theory of evolution guides the study of fossil man, new theoretical developments in animal ethology are causing a renaissance of research on primate behavior, and more sophisticated methods of ecological analysis are being developed in ethnology and prehistoric archaeology.

One of the pedagogical values of this research is that work within a vital natural science tradition can be taught to students who do not have the special skills and habits of mind necessary to grasp the ongoing development of highly analytic and experimental sciences. One of the pleasures of teaching students of the humanities the natural science subjects of anthropology lies in the fact that they do not have to be "watered down." Anthologies of readings for introductory courses have been composed of recent articles from professional journals, and students may be assigned current professional monographs in anthropology courses that carry few, if any, prerequisites. Thus, students who do not themselves expect to become scientists can experience some of the excitement of materials on the growing edge of scientific research.

Sir Charles Snow has described the contemporary specialization of scientific and humanistic learning as leading to the development of two cultures, one centering around "the literary intellectuals," and the other around "the scientists, and as the most representative, the physical scientists" (1959:17-18). That the two cultures have distinctive conventions and ways of thought is inevitable. What is to be regretted is their ignorance and scorn of each other. Anthropology is not a bridge between humanist culture and the world of the theoretical-experimental sciences. Humanists, if they are to learn anything about the culture of physical scientists, must study the physical sciences, just as the physical scientists will have to go directly to philosophy, literature, and the other arts for humanistic culture. In a civilization divided by the two cultures the value of anthropology for general education is that it is a field of learning in which the naturalist tradition of scientific culture takes human nature and the varieties of human culture for its subject matter.

The existence of the two cultures nourishes the idea that scientific and humanistic approaches to the study of man are inevitably antagonistic. As a matter of fact, the naturalist tradition in anthropology and the tradition of humanistic studies complement each other. Since both traditions are related to museums, the point may be illustrated by comparing an art museum to a museum of natural history. The museum of natural history is a prism in which all life is refracted: the humble artifacts of primitive cultures have their place in the spectrum of existence, with the relics of other animal existences ranged in orders on one side, and the knives of Aztec sacrificers and utensiles of Inca rulers ranged in another order and direction. The art museum also resembles a prism, and in it each great civilized style is a refraction of the human spirit brought to a daring height and purity of expression. Both kinds of museums reveal the historicity of human life, and, though they excite the imagination in different ways, they compel recognition of the plural forms and relativity of human cultures.

Because the humanistic disciplines are mainly concerned with the fine arts, literature, and philosophy, their conception of culture is normative and highly selective, and their historical perspective centers upon the traditions of elite classes within civilized societies. The contrast between this point of view and that of anthropology—like

the contrast between the art museum and the museum of natural history—can excite students of the humanities to fresh considerations of
the meaning of history and of life, for the anthropological point of view
gives impartial consideration to all cultural traditions, and places them
in the long time perspective of human evolution.

While the naturalist tradition of anthropological research stems
from the first of Redfield's polarities, it also guides the work of anthropologists whose interests center in man seen as something distinctly human. In cultural anthropology the emphasis upon field research, and in linguistic anthropology the emphasis upon natural
speech communities rather than the conventions of written languages,
are naturalistic emphases. But rather than leading to a view of man that
is an alternate and complementary view of that of the humanities, the
naturalist tradition in the second polarity of the anthropological field
has led to a convergence of anthropological and humanistic studies.
This convergence is demonstrated by the long and distinguished list
of anthropologists who can appropriately be called humanists. This
list includes Frazer, Sapir, Radin, Malinowski, Kroeber, Benedict, Redfield, Kluckhohn, and Herskovits, to name only a few. And, from the
side of the humanistic disciplines, the list of scholars whose works con-
verge with anthropology includes Jane Harrison, Cornford, Bergson,
Cassirer, Northrop, Huizinga, Frankfort, Von Grunebaum, and a
great many others.

The classification of anthropology with the social sciences obscures
the convergence of anthropological and humanistic studies, just as it
obscures the natural history polarity of the field. Ruth Benedict asserted that "the very nature of the problems posed and discussed in
the humanities is closer, chapter by chapter, to those in anthropology
than are the investigations carried on in most of the social sciences"
(1948:585). The problems that Benedict referred to were those that
arise when anthropologists "include the mind of man within their definition of culture." They have to do with the ways in which men create
the variety of human cultures, and the ways in which these cultures in
turn create different kinds of men. Because anthropologists are naturalists they study these problems in the context of actual cultures which
they attempt to know intimately, and in all of their complexity and
ambiguity. In this respect anthropologists have more in common
with cultural historians, literary critics, moral philosophers and other
humanists than they have in common with sociologists, psychologists,
and economists, who construct theoretical models of isolated aspects
of human behavior and study reality through the lens of questionnaires, controlled experiments, and statistical measures.

Even though the comparative study of economic, political, and legal institutions, of social structures and of culture and personality has brought anthropology into fruitful contact with some parts of psychology, sociology, economics, and political science, the work of anthropologists is usually more humanistic than that of their colleagues in the social sciences. Basing their contributions to the social sciences largely upon field research, anthropologists emphasize contextual analyses that show the interrelationships of institutions within particular historical complexes. Thus, anthropological studies of economic or political institutions often contain information on folklore, religion, the emotional attachments between parents and their children, and many other topics which economists or political scientists consider outside their disciplines. And anthropologists, besides using the causal and functional modes of interpretation common to the social sciences, frequently describe cultures as logical or symbolic systems, or as aesthetic unities. By organizing their descriptions around conceptions such as ethos, cultural plot, moral postulate, symbolic value, and style of life, anthropologists look toward the modes of analysis of the humanistic disciplines (Redfield 1953:733-736). Finally, the most influential research in social and cultural anthropology is written in a style close to that of the cultural historian and literary essayist. If for no other reason, many of the distinguished contributors to the social science aspect of anthropology could be called humanists, because their books and essays form a literary genre—one thinks immediately of the writing of Malinowski and Sapir, of Mead and Benedict, of Gluckman or Firth (Leslie 1960:79-91).

Because anthropology and the humanities have much in common, anthropology teachers should encourage their students to acquire special knowledge of the humanistic disciplines. The ways in which this is done should grow out of the individual interests of students. It would be wrong-headed to think that all anthropology students ought to take a specific number or kind of courses in philosophy, literature, or the other humanistic disciplines. One student might study the archaeology of classical antiquity in order to compare the ancient civilizations of the Mediterranean to those of the New World, another student might study the works of classical scholars such as Jane Harrison or Cornford in order to compare their methods to those of ethnologists and social anthropologists, and still another student might study Latin and Greek civilizations to deepen his understanding of the intellectual tradition within which his own conceptions of man are formed. For equally varied reasons other anthropology students will study musicology, moral philosophy, or the cultural histories of Islamic, Chinese or Indian civilizations. And similarly diverse interests will bring students of the humanities to courses in social anthropology, ethnology, linguistic anthropology, and archaeology.

The convergence of anthropology and the humanities threatens the image some anthropologists have of themselves as scientists and of their field as "the science of man." In their teaching these anthropologists underplay the work of their humanist colleagues both in anthropology and in the traditional humanistic disciplines. The result is that not a few students acquire a false conception of the anthropological field, and students majoring in anthropology become unreasonably critical of materials that could be of great value to them. The problem stems from "academic home-guardism" (Riesman 1958:66-119), as well as from the two culture division of modern intellectual life, and it will not be eliminated until these aspects of our civilization become things of the past. But it can be counteracted by teachers who realize that anthropology is not an academic discipline with fixed methodological boundaries, but an open field of research in which the naturalist tradition of scientific enquiry finds common ground with the humanities. And because these teachers will be anthropologists fully aware of the importance of contextual analyses, they will also realize that no teaching and no learning has vitality that is separated from the living culture in which it occurs. They will seek, therefore, to be cultured men and women who are familiar with the creative arts of their own community.

REFERENCES CITED

BENEDICT, RUTH
    1948   Anthropology and the humanities. American Anthropologist 50:585-593.

BENNETT, JOHN W., AND KURT H. WOLFF
    1955   Toward communication between sociology and anthropology. *In* Current Anthropology, William L. Thomas, Jr., ed. Chicago, University of Chicago Press.

COLLIER, DONALD, AND HARRY TSCHOPIK, JR.
    1954   The role of museums in American anthropology. American Anthropologist 56:768-779.

KROEBER, ALFRED LOUIS
    1954   The place of anthropology in universities. American Anthropologist 56:764-767.

LESLIE, CHARLES
    1960   The comic muse in cultural anthropology. Appendix, Now We Are Civilized. Detroit, Wayne State University Press.

REDFIELD, ROBERT
    1953   Relations of anthropology to the social sciences and to the human-

ities. *In* Anthropology Today, A. L. Kroeber, ed. Chicago, University of Chicago Press.

RIESMAN, DAVID

1958 Constraint and variety in American education. New York, Doubleday Anchor Book.

SNOW, CHARLES P.

1959 The two cultures. Encounter XII, No. 6:17-24, and XIII, No. 1:22-27.

TAX, SOL

1955 The integration of anthropology. *In* Current Anthropology, William L. Thomas, Jr., ed. Chicago, University of Chicago Press.

Solon T. Kimball

*Teaching
Anthropology
in Professional
Education*

During the past few years there has been a gradually increasing awareness of the contribution which anthropology can make to graduate professional education. Its evidence may be seen in the inclusion of data derived from anthropological sources in texts and materials used in graduate instruction. Equally substantial proof is found in the dozen or more anthropologists who hold full or part-time appointments in graduate schools of medicine, public health, nursing, social work, education, or theology. Anthropological influence has also been significant in a few graduate schools of business.

Although the total number now engaged in graduate professional teaching is small at present, we may expect that the relative significance of anthropology in such programs will show a continued and possibly accelerated expansion. Not only will these schools seek to add anthropologists to their staffs, but also relevant anthropological materials will continue to find their way into teaching materials.

The grafting of an academic discipline onto professional root stock creates some special problems. It should be remembered that professional activity is primarily the practice of skills in the performance of service to others. Training is for the purpose of perfecting the arts of practice. Training also includes imparting ethics, theory, and, in some instances, the findings of science. It is in the area of theory and scientific results that some academic disciplines have contributed to profes-

493

sional training. In medicine, for example, the biological sciences constitute a firm basis of the medical arts. Psychology, and to a lesser extent the other social sciences, have provided foundations to educational practices. Social work has drawn upon several fields. Thus, the pattern of the relation of anthropology to professional training has already been established by precedent.

The anthropologist will be expected to transmit those aspects of his discipline which are relevant to the problems of training and practice in a profession. He can do this through teaching, research, and publication, and through such personal influence as time and place permit. Although these several activities can hardly be separated, our primary focus is that of the teaching of anthropology, and it is to that phase of the problem which I now turn.

By necessity, most of my comments will be based upon my own experience of the past several years in a program of graduate teacher training at Teachers College, Columbia University. I am aware that the conditions and needs will vary from those of my colleagues in professional education elsewhere. Nevertheless, I suspect that there are sufficient similarities in the expectations of the institutions in question, in the degree of student sophistication or its absence in the subject, in the problems of choosing, adapting, and interpreting anthropological data, and in the relations with teaching colleagues who are primarily professional in their outlook, that the problems we have met are much alike although our solutions may have been vastly different.

It is not my intention, however, to examine all of the aspects of teaching anthropology in a professional school. Instead, I wish to concentrate upon the contribution which anthropology can make to methods of teaching and to the area of general education or, if one prefers, liberal arts education. (In this sense, I refer to the nontechnical presentation of subject matter which has as its goal increasing knowledge, widening perspectives, and, hopefully, contributing to the capacity to interpret intelligently events in the world.) These are major objectives in my one-semester course entitled "Anthropology and Education," which each year enrolls about 400 students. My other courses are more technically or professionaly oriented and will not be discussed.

The sequence in which the several aspects of the teaching of anthropology in graduate professional education may be examined appears to me to have a certain logic. For example, the conditions of teaching in a graduate professional school is bound to affect organization, objectives, and content of a course. In addition, the background and future expectations of students will have their effects. These are limiting conditions which have a direct influence on the other aspects and should be described first. Objectives, basic concepts, and content constitute an additional three factors which are related, not alone to each other, but also to the conditions of teaching. Finally, the mechanics of course organization, including teaching techniques, form another and related segment. It is proposed that each of these be considered in turn.

LIMITING CONDITIONS

Those who teach foundation subjects—psychology, history, philosophy, and the social sciences—know that the student in a professional program can devote to them only a limited number of hours outside his special field. Anthropology is one of several such courses from which the student may choose. Under these conditions one assumes that few of those who enroll in anthropology will do further work in this field. Thus, a course in anthropology is not intended to serve as an introduction to the field, as a preliminary to advanced work, or for the purpose of recruiting students. Freed of these objectives, there is greater latitude for inclusion and exclusion of materials to approximate the tradition of liberal education, although choice is always made in the context of relevance to educational problems.

Academic background, professional aspirations, and intellectual characteristics are factors to be considered in course organization and content. A tabulation of students for the academic year 1959-60 revealed that four-fifths received their bachelor's degrees from a liberal arts college or university. The remaining fifth were graduates of teachers colleges. Distribution of students based upon area in which undergraduate degree was received gives the following percentages: arts and humanities, 30 per cent; social sciences, including psychology, 23 per cent; nursing, 20 per cent; education, 15 per cent; science, 10 per cent; other, 2 per cent. The overwhelming proportion of students from liberal arts colleges and universities, with a preponderance of degrees in the arts and sciences, should provide a student group possessing a broad academic base for professional training. It is my impression, however, that they have not received the kind of integrated cultural perspective which educators seek in liberal arts training.

Further analysis of student characteristics, based upon degree sought and field of professional study, revealed considerable diversity in professional goals. Nearly two-thirds were candidates for the M.A. degree, most of them being in the first year of graduate study. Of the remainder, slightly more than one-fourth were candidates for doctoral degrees; the others were seeking special certificates or were unclassified. The heterogeneity of academic background, level of graduate training, and professional goals does little more than hint at the qualitative characteristics of students. Although these are far more difficult to assess, a statement of impressions based upon several years' experience should serve, at least, as the point of departure for further study.

The questions asked, the point of view presented in papers, and

written replies to a solicited request for reactions to the course reveal
an almost universal and deeply imbedded system of middle-class values.
It is not surprising to find the students are committed to equality, democracy, and the superiority of Western and, in particular, American
culture. They have been heavily impregnated with a psychological and
atomistic view of the world. For them the significant item of interest
in the human world is the individual, and the understanding of oneself
and others is a primary goal of learning and experience. They have
weakly developed capacities for thinking systemically or scientifically.
In fact, scientific learning is equated with the acquisition of knowledge;
method or philosophy is hardly appreciated. Few of them have had
training in research methods, nor do they show evidence of possessing
systematic criteria for evaluative criticism. It is my belief that these
students are fairly representative of others who have completed an undergraduate education. They reflect the failure of a piecemeal and specialized course program to develop intellectual depth. The deficiency
is not so much in knowledge or skills as it is in an absence of a conceptual
system and associated intellectual tools for interpreting the events
of the world. On the other hand these students are a pleasure to teach.
They are intelligent, cooperative, and receptive; and happily, only
rarely do I encounter one who is the captive of dogma.

An assessment of general and specific expectations may also be risky,
but some observations which apply to a majority should be offered.
There are two main aspects of professional training, the development
of skills and the inculcation of moral and ethical standards governing
professional practice. It is legitimate to ask the extent to which method
and subject matter of anthropology could do either. The objectivity
which anthropology requires in cross-cultural analysis, or in the examination of customs and social groupings, also requires that the learner
eliminate his ethnocentric biases. Anthropological relativism or determinism could conceivably weaken moral perspectives. Moreover, no
direct connection between method, theory, or subject matter and
pedagogical skills is easily discernible. It is my belief, however, that it
is precisely in the areas of professional morality and of teaching skills
that anthropology has much to offer, and that its presentation within a
humanist and general education tradition will produce the best results. One measure of achievement would be to examine the objectives
sought, concepts utilized, and content included. It is to these aspects
that we now turn.

OBJECTIVES, CONCEPTS, CONTENT

A concern with educational problems has been expressed by American anthropologists from time to time over the past several decades.

Interest in the processes of cultural transmission alone should have proved a sufficiently strong bond with educators to have produced some fruitful cross-stimulation. Until recently, unfortunately, the results of the occasional contacts have been meager, at least in comparison with the influence of psychology. One difficulty has been the problem of deciding what aspects of anthropology have relevance for education and their subsequent adaptation and even translation for use by educators. This difficulty is in process of being overcome.

A significant forward step was the Stanford conference in 1954 on anthropology and education organized by George Spindler. His "overview" (Spindler 1954) of the conceptual and historical relations between anthropology and education included an enumeration of fields and interests in anthropology which possess relevance for education. The major areas as I have abstracted them follow:

1. As a basis of *general education*—"an introduction to a new perspective on human life." Relativity and universality.

2. Biological base of behavior—race, evolution, growth patterns, maturational sequences, sexual differences, and glandular processes.

3. Personality in culture.

4. Cultural dynamics—the processes of growth, change, stability.

5. Growth and adaptation of the child—socialization. Transmission of skills, knowledge, attitudes, and values.

6. Cross-cultural education—comparative study of educational processes.

7. Social structure—class, group alignments, prestige ranking, status and role, social control.

The point of view represented and the topics included are those which can and must be presented in graduate course work for educators. There are, however, some areas of theory and method which, I believe, also deserve major consideration. These are:

1. Methods of systemic analysis—community, institutions, autonomous groups, personality.

2. Event analysis—regularities of human behavior in time-space context.

3. The method of natural history—inductive empiricism based upon methods of classification and interdependencies of components.

4. Commitment and perception—cultural and individual aspects.

These additional aspects are necessary ingredients if students are to have the basis for understanding the distinctive world view from which anthropologists operate. Findings may have ends in themselves but they cannot serve the larger objective alone. We must also transmit an understanding of the theory and processes which we utilize in our analyses. Only then will the larger conceptual framework which examines the individual in his physical, psychical, social, and cultural contexts become meaningful; cultures will be seen as wholes, and the relation between individual, group, and culture made explicit.

The crucial test in determining the validity of any method used in the organization and presentation of data is, of course, whether it achieves the objectives and produces desired results. My immediate objective was to demonstrate the use of anthropological data and theory for purposes of general education. A related goal was to demonstrate the relevance of anthropology to problems of contemporary civilization.

For students seeking professional careers in education, an understanding of the cultural context within which American educational institutions and processes developed is particularly appropriate. This goal can be met in part by the applicaton of anthropological method to the analysis of Colonial and Post-Colonial periods in American history. The presentation includes description of settlement patterns, their European cultural antecedents, environmental, technological, social, and cultural characteristics and variations. Particular attention is directed to educational institutions and practices and to their interconnections with other aspects of social and cultural systems. For most, the cultural interpretation of history represents a new approach as does the kind of specificity which delineates regional differences and their meaning. The historical perspective which emphasizes the interconnection between cultural aspects is, however, related to other distinctly defined anthropological purposes. Of major theoretical significance is the concept of *system* contained with an examination of *culture as a whole*. There is demonstration and insistence upon treating cultural items in *context*. *Continuity* of culture is exemplified in reference to European antecedents. *Diversity* and *variation* may be observed in the *comparative* analyses of regional agrarian patterns. Some aspects of *cultural dynamics* are derived from an examination of changes which flow from adaptation to new environmental and social conditions If is also possible to show how understanding American culture in its original and developmental stages has relevance for contemporary problems. If an appreciation of the value of history is one of the by-products, this in itself is a worthy contribution.

Another topic used to explicate other aspects of anthropological method is that of the study of European pre-history. Further justification for the inclusion of this subject can be found in the assumption that a liberally educated person should know something about the cultural origins of civilization. But the method of presentation serves several other purposes beyond those of merely presenting facts. Once again, the vehicle chosen is utilized to carry a particular theoretical burden; in this instance, the method of natural science with emphasis upon man and culture in time and space. Data from the Paleolithic and Neolithic are utilized to show how they can be organized in categories based upon similarities and differences. The method of organization demonstrates the operation and utility of principles of taxonomy. Interrelationships between technology and environment, and between both of these and characteristics of population are described. Through the use of these categories and others, there is presented the cultural *macro-system* and the interdependencies of its components. The processes of *inference* through comparison are utilized. The emphasis upon systemic analysis shows how the methods of inductive, empirical science may be used to organize data about the universe and, at the same time, how it provides a method for eliciting their meaning through functional interrelationships.

The objective of this latter analysis is to provide conceptual tools which permit a logically consistent understanding of man and culture in time and space, to see the relation between different levels of cultural development, and to comprehend the processes of change. These intellectual tools make possible comparisons with methodological systems of other disciplines as well as with the world-embracing schemes developed by particular individuals. For example, the scientifically based approach of anthropology may be contrasted with and used to interpret methods and results of such diverse theorists as those represented by Marx, Freud, Spengler, Sorokin, or Toynbee. The applicability of the methods of an empirical, inductive science to the interpretation of cultural evolution and world history is certainly a significant contribution to general education.

METHODS OF TEACHING

In professional education where considerable emphasis, properly and by tradition, is placed upon moral and ethical standards of practice, it is of utmost importance that the practitioner view the world in an empirical, inductive manner. Otherwise, there is the danger that rigid adherence to learned precepts will hamper the individual in his response to the variety of changing conditions he must meet. Thus, there is an unusual opportunity for the anthropologist in his teaching methods to exemplify the very system of thought which he represents. He can provide a model, not alone for interpreting professional experience, but for all subject matter areas which provide general education to the student.

Few individuals possess the capacity to view themselves and the world around them either objectively or as parts of interrelated systems. Their formal education has prepared them to seek explanations of events within an already formulated system of thought and perception. Intellectually, they have been isolated from new insights through adherence to established formulas, dogma, or other rigid systems of beliefs. In considerable measure, the kind of teaching they experience contributes to this condition. The emphasis upon fact and the equation of detail with knowledge have perverted their capacity to be receptive to the concept of a world organized in systems. The deductive process limits, if it does not determine, how new experience is to be categorized and understood. Unfortunately, most teaching in general education and the liberal arts as it is now practiced is cast in this mold.

An earlier statement asserted that one of the major contributions of anthropology to pedagogy could be the transference of its scientific methods to the art of teaching. This means, specifically, the presentation of empirical data inductively for the purpose of deriving general explanatory statements about the universe, or some part of it. Under such a procedure the facts are seen to be justified, not in themselves, but as they constitute the essential detail for grasping the nature of a system. Systems, in turn, are not to be treated as conclusions or results, but as expressive of the internal dynamics which govern stability and change. Comprehension of the processes of human beings as physical and psychic entities, and of the cultures and societies which they create and transmit, remains the ultimate goal.

Before we examine the problem further, it is best to remind ourselves that anthropology utilizes the natural science approach (Kimball 1954, 1960). In this tradition, it is inductive and empirical in its operation. Its practitioners proceed from a series of assumptions and a body of theory which believes regularities in behavior can be made explicit through system analysis. Furthermore, it is not necessary to formulate hypotheses before initiating research as is the custom with other social sciences. Anthropological research may be justified on the grounds of gathering more data, examining a problem, or for purely exploratory purposes. This activity, however, is never random. It is always formulated, at least by implication, within a framework of larger problems to which the discoveries may add new insights.

The question we now pose is the extent to which the anthropologist can transfer to the classroom his procedures of gathering data in the field; the process by which he sorts, combines, and interprets his facts; and his theories of behavior and grouping. If the transfer were successful, classroom presentation would simulate data collection and analysis. The student would move toward results and conclusions utilizing the same intellectual operations as the instructor.

We should keep in mind that we are concerned with two interrelated but separate problems. The simulation in data presentation of anthropological operations is one; the other is the transmission of the skill of presenting subject matter inductively. Once again I must let my own experience serve as the basis for evaluation. Most, but not all, of the topics are presented within the inductive framework. Age and sex analysis seems to be presented more easily through deductive method. It is assumed that it is unnecessary to establish the validity of the categories. But with personality, small group, and social class analysis, it is possible to use an almost pure form of inductive logic. In small group analysis greater emphasis is given to the method of organizing facts than to the substantive results. In this latter instance it is the intention to demonstrate a technique of teaching.

Systematic examination of the results of this approach have not been attempted. But significant changes in point of view or professional practice should not be expected from such a brief encounter. If there is to be serious testing of the effects of inductive teaching, an experimental and research program should be established with these objectives in mind.

CONCLUSION

Its utilization of natural science method and its concern with humanistic aspects of behavior give anthropology a particularly wide scope in comparison with other disciplines. There is no broader coverage than its focus upon man and his works. Its concern with cultural relativity and pan-humanism and its method of cross-cultural analysis contribute to acquiring a wider perspective of the human condition. In subject matter, approach, and point of view, anthropology seems unusually suited for meeting the needs of a general and humanistic ingredient in graduate professional education.

Its contribution to the technical aspects of professional practice can also be considerable. The utilization of inductive analysis in teaching techniques is of immense significance in a culture where the explosion of knowledge mandates that principles of oranizing new information and experience exceed in importance the stacking of facts upon each other. Other applicabilities rest in such areas as personality, small group, social structure, and cultural dynamics. But let us always remember that the greatest impact occurs from an intellectual transformation which our theory and analytical processes initiate but which is not innate in our subject matter.

REFERENCES CITED

KIMBALL, SOLON T.
   1955   The method of natural history and education research. *In* Education and Anthropology, George D. Spindler, ed. Stanford, Stanford University Press.
   1960   Darwin and the future of education. The Educational Forum 25:59-72.

SPINDLER, GEORGE D.
   1955   Anthropology and education: an overview. *In* Education and Anthropology, George D. Spindler, ed. Stanford, Stanford University Press.

BENJAMIN D. PAUL

*Teaching Cultural
Anthropology
in Schools
of Public Health*

DURING THE LAST DECADE, cultural anthropologists and other social scientists, long habituated to academic environments, have been
radiating into a new environmental niche, the graduate professional
schools. Particularly marked has been the movement into the training
grounds of the health professionals—schools of medicine, nursing, and
public health. The magnitude of this migration reflects new interests and
awareness of new fields on the part of social scientists. It also reflects a
deepening discontent, on the part of medical educators, with the nearly
exclusive emphasis heretofore placed on the "scientific" or technical
aspects of their subject matter and a corresponding quest for new
sources of insight into the behavioral aspects, the side that was once
taken for granted as the "art of medicine."

Social science research and teaching are increasingly seen as pertinent to the practice of medicine, the organization of medical services,
and the implementation of public health programs. Still newer and
more limited is a disposition to see social science as an important part
of the so-called basic or preclinical sciences which form the foundation
of medical educaton. One indication of this emerging trend is the establishment of a full department of behavioral science at the new University of Kentucky Medical School, with a social scientist as professor and
chairman. Courses presented by members of that department are part
of the basic science curriculum in the first year.

503

In recent years, support for social science research and training in health schools has been generously supplied by such funding sources as the U. S. Public Health Service and its National Institutes of Health, the Rockefeller Foundation, the Commonwealth Fund, the Kellogg Foundation, and the Russell Sage Foundation. The latter exercises an influence far out of proportion to its size by virtue of its well-formulated program of grants for the postdoctoral training of young social scientists to work effectively with practitioners of the health, welfare, and legal professions.

The number of anthropologists, sociologists, and social psychologists in the field of health and human behavior has grown from a handful to several hundred during the decade of the fifties. A fair estimate is that over fifty of these are cultural anthropologists. Of the social scientists in the health field, more are located in universities than in governmental and private agencies; more are engaged in research than in teaching. Nevertheless, the number of social scientists now teaching in health schools is considerable. The state of affairs varies according to the type of health school. The situation in medical schools, as in schools of nursing, is variable and complex but falls outside the scope of this paper. Perhaps the most receptive environment for social scientists in general and for anthropologists in particular is encountered in schools of public health. It is also the type of environment most familiar to the writer, who has spent ten years building a Social Science Program at the Harvard School of Public Health.

SCHOOLS OF PUBLIC HEALTH

The twelve schools of public health in the United States (California, Berkeley, California, Los Angeles, Columbia, Harvard, Johns Hopkins, Michigan, Minnesota, North Carolina, Pittsburgh, Puerto Rico, Tulane, Yale) differ from medical schools in five important ways. Each affects the climate for teaching. In the first place, schools of public health, in greater degree than medical schools, accent the promotion of good health as well as the prevention of disease rather than its treatment. This accent invites instruction on the nature of values, motivation, communication, and persuasion—subjects familiar to social science.

Second, in public health, the community rather than the individual is regarded as the "patient." In addition to its traditional preoccupation with the quantitative aspects of the community (biostatistics and epidemiology), public health is paying increased attention to the qualitative aspects—the structure of the community and how it functions. This interest makes students welcome instruction in such social science topics as group process, social organization, and cultural pattern.

Third, public health is multidisciplinary in character owing to the variety of situations for which students are prepared and the range of specialists required on the public health "team." Varying with the school, the proportion of physicians in the student body ranges from a sizeable minority to a majority. In any case, the class typically includes as well, such specialists as behavioral scientists, biochemists, dentists, engineers, health educators, nurses, nutritionists, social workers, statisticians, and veterinarians.

Fourth, schools of public health tend to be postgraduate. To qualify for admission to the School of Public Health at Harvard for instance, nearly all students must already hold a graduate degree—medical, master's, or doctoral. At all schools, most students remain one year to earn the degree of Master of Public Health, although a number stay on to work for a doctorate. At Harvard, students average about thirty-three years of age. Most of them have professional public health experience and arrive with an appetite for social science concepts to order their experiences and formulate their problems.

Finally, most schools of public health are heavily international in orientation. About a third of the students come from a great range of foreign lands; many come from responsible positions in the organized health systems of their home countries and return to posts of equal or greater importance. And a good share of the American students have worked abroad or expect a future assignment overseas. With a lively awareness that economies and customs differ, students are particularly receptive to anthropological instruction in cultural variability. For many, it is a relief to discover a frame of perception which reveals group differences without the distortion of ethnocentric judgments.

These five distinctive features—emphasis on prevention, community approach, interdisciplinary nature of the field, postgraduate level, and international orientation—help explain why most United States schools of public health have recently added anthropologists and other types of social scientists to their staff. The teaching phase of the Social Science Program at the Harvard School of Public Health, which has had more time to develop than like programs in other schools, now consists of an introductory course on "The Human Community" and two elective offerings.

"THE HUMAN COMMUNITY"

A product of ten years of trial and evolution, "The Human Community" is now one of the ten basic courses at the Harvard School of Public Health. It aims to review the salient aspects of man's sociocultural environment, to familiarize students with some social science concepts relevant to their profession, and to make these generalizations meaningful by relating them to actual experiences encountered by students or recorded by others in published case studies. The concepts are presented in lectures; personal experiences and published case histories are discussed in seminars. The course totals 40 hours and extends over the eight weeks of the first quarter. Students attend one two-hour and one one-hour lecture each week and divide into small discussion groups for two additional hours each week.

Weekly lecture topics include: man and culture; demography; social stratification; public opinion and communication; community structure and process; organization and groups; family and life cycle; ecological, social, and cultural change. A review of biological evolution opens the course. To begin on the organic level is to meet most of the students on familiar ground. This introduction also supplies a backdrop for the concept of culture and sets up the distinction between biological inheritance and social inheritance. Culture is explained as a product (and a determinant) of man's evolution, as being subject to regional variation, and as exhibiting system properties. Health programs are seen as instances of directed culture change and health workers as agents of change. Program effects are analyzed in terms of selective acceptance, reinterpretation, and unforeseen consequences—all related to the patterned and systematic nature of culture.

The subject matter of "The Human Community," which is wider than anthropology alone, is presented by an anthropologist, a demographer, a sociologist, and a social psychologist. Of course, resort to multiple lecturers has its strengths and weaknesses. As a specialist, each lecturer is likely to speak with competence and authority. By contrast, an anthropologist who is called upon to cover the gamut of social science concepts is less likely to do so good a job. With multiple lecturers, however, the course as a whole is apt to be disjointed, suffering from gaps, repetitions, and inconsistencies. These weaknesses are particularly evident in cafeteria-style courses where speakers are brought in from the outside with little opportunity to coordinate their efforts or sense the orientation of the students. Anthropologists in academic departments are especially likely to be lured into giving single lectures in health schools. Their contribution is often regarded as an exotic dish to spice up a cafeteria course, but with little relevance to the main purposes of the instruction. Nevertheless, cafeteria lectures often represent a transitional stage in the process by which a medical or public health school decides to add a social scientist to its own teaching staff.

In "The Human Community," we attempt to capture the benefits of the multiple speaker method without paying the customary price. We try to avoid the pitfalls by limiting the number of lecturers, having each give a series of lectures rather than a single talk and, especially, by drawing only on members of our regular social science staff at the

School and using the same team of teachers from year to year in order to extract the greatest gain from joint planning and experience.

For the weekly seminar session, the total class of some 60 students is divided into five sections. Students who endure long lectures in large classes welcome the variation of seminar sessions, where they can talk as well as listen and where they can become familiar with the rest of their face-to-face group. The need for such variation is especially marked in the case of older students with years of experience in the field.

Although student opinion never favors contracting the lectures, it nevertheless judges the seminars the most gratifying part of the course. Three seminar features are largely responsible for this favorable judgment. One is the varied composition of each seminar section. Sections are balanced so that each group has about the same ratio of physicians to nonphysicians, North Americans to foreign students, and so on. If the class contains several nurses, or several students from India, for instance each is assigned to a different section. The mixed composition insures the expression of a rich variety of viewpoint and experience. The variety is particularly valuable for members of a profession committed to working in mixed teams and intercultural situations.

Another favoring feature is the availability of suitable case studies for seminar discussion. The volume, *Health, Culture and Community* (Paul and Miller, eds. 1955), includes 16 case histories of public responses to health programs in Africa, Asia, the Pacific, Latin America, the United States, and Canada. These cases were originally assembled by the writer to meet a need for teaching materials in health schools and were committed to print only after they were tried out in public health seminars and revised in the light of such trials. The cases differ widely in content, but they all illustrate the interplay of sociocultural factors, proceed from particulars to generalizations, and follow a standard format. In preparation for each seminar meeting, students read two specific cases selected to illustrate a range of concepts including those developed in lectures during the same week. The cases provide a firm point of departure for the seminar discussions; students comment, criticize, and offer comparable or contrasting instances drawn from personal experience. The format of the published cases (The Problem, The Situation, Implications, Summary) helps them organize and analyze their own experiences, some of which are submitted as written assignments and orally summarized near the end of the course.

The reading assignment for the first seminar session includes a memorandum setting forth some of the values in contemporary American culture. Coming at the outset of the academic year, when many students are still adjusting to a new cultural setting, the values memorandum invariably provokes an animated interchange. It helps American and foreign students realize that their professional judgments are apt to be influenced by the values implicit in their particular culture.

A third noteworthy feature of the seminar sessions is the fact that the five sections are led by staff social scientists capable of keeping the conversation on a sociocultural plane and of linking the content of the discussion to concepts presented in the lecture room. Each seminar leader is teamed with a public health faculty member (usually a physician with overseas experience), who serves as a partner to the social scientist and as a "resource person" for the students. Of course, such an arrangement depends on the availability of professional personnel in quantity. At present, about a dozen social scientists (and two physical anthropologists) work at the Harvard School of Public Health, most of them full time, on research projects or a combination of teaching and research.

The lectures in "The Human Community" are reinforced not only by case studies, discussions, and accounts of personal experience, as already noted, but also by the distribution of extended summaries several days after each lecture. These are freshly prepared each time by a social science teaching assistant who attends all the lectures for this purpose. An awareness that reliable summaries will be supplied, if it does anything, seems to make students more, rather than less, attentive in the lecture room. Foreign students are especially grateful for the supplement to their classroom impressions and their own notes. The summaries also assist course coordination: lecturers can read what predecessors said; seminar leaders can learn what students heard in lectures; examiners can know that their questions are fair.

FOLLOW-UP COURSES

Qualified students interested in social science can follow up "The Human Community" by taking one or both of the electives given during the second half of the school year. One is an intensive seminar on "Research Methods in Community Health," which meets four hours per week for 15 weeks. It is designed primarily for doctoral candidates and other students expecting to conduct or administer research involving health behavior and health organization. Given jointly by a sociologist and a biostatistician, the course emphasizes survey research techniques and statistical analysis; it includes sessions on anthropological interviewing and field observation. The directors of research projects which are part of the School's Social Science Program aid in the teaching effort by presenting problems of technique and design encountered in their projects, which variously take as the unit of study the person, the family, the organization, and the local community.

The other elective, meant for students who wish to learn more about the anthropological approach or about health research in international situations, is a seminar on "Health and Illness in Cross-Cultural Perspective" (HICCUP). Each weekly session features a different guest speaker, usually an anthropologist from outside the School who has done work in the health field. This seminar series suffers only slightly from the typical drawbacks of the cafeteria offering, since it is not an introductory course and since ample discussion time allows the class to satisfy its need for continuity and comparison. The HICCUP seminar is cross-listed as a course in Harvard's Department of Social Relations and so attracts graduate anthropology, psychology, and sociology students in addition to public health students. The combination is mutually enlightening. During the discussion period, members of the one group are repeatedly intrigued and informed by the unexpected comments coming from the other group.

THE OUTLOOK

Attitudes of the public health faculty toward instruction in the social sciences range from indifference to encouragement; attitudes of students are prevailingly enthusiastic. When these students assume responsible positions in professional schools and health agencies, they are likely to seek additional social scientists as teaching and research colleagues. As compared with their public health mentors, they will be more familiar with the capacities and limitations of social scientists and thus better prepared to work with them effectively.

There is also a complementary task to be done, that of preparing social scientists to work more productively with public health specialists. This need is now being met in part by a number of training programs supported by grants from foundations and the government. To help meet the expected demand for properly oriented social scientists to work in the health field—and anticipating that health schools and agencies will soon establish better career lines than now exist—the Social Science Program each year has attracted one or two young social scientists, mainly cultural anthropologists, to the Harvard School of Public Health, where they earn a professional master's degree to supplement their Ph.D. degree, thus combining two skills in one skull.

OTHER HEALTH SCHOOLS

The attention given in this review to public health schools should not obscure the fact that medical and nursing schools are similarly stirring with social science activity. Social scientists today are attached to about half the 85 domestic schools of medicine. The ratio is not as high as in schools of public health, most of which have social scientists, but in absolute numbers the medical schools are well in the lead. The majority of these social scientists are doing research, not teaching medical students; many work in affiliated hospitals or occupy other research stations in the outfields of the medical training grounds. Those that teach, though not the rule, are nevertheless not rare.

Leaving aside a few innovating medical schools (e.g., Kentucky and Stanford), social scientists who teach medical students are concentrated in two departments: preventive medicine and, especially, psychiatry. These are usually classified as clinical rather than basic science subjects, and the anthropologist or sociologist, trained as he is to think in terms of group rather than individual behavior, undertakes a challenging task when he tries to demonstrate the applicability of his concepts and generalizations to individual clinical cases. In all likelihood, the task of making social science subject matter meaningful to medical students will become easier as social scientists become more familiar with the subculture of the medical world, on the one hand, and as medical schools continue to overhaul their curriculum and reorganize their departmental structure, on the other.

Leaders of the nursing profession have been even more preoccupied than medical educators with the necessity of understanding the "total person" and extending "total patient care." Whether she works in a hospital ward, a health agency, a public school, a Navaho reservation, or an industrial health program, the nurse usually comes in closer contact with people than the physician. Characteristically she serves as the communication link and mediator between physician and patient. For these and other reasons, nursing educators have long insisted on making social science a part of every nurse's training. A recommendation to this effect was published in 1937 by the National League for Nursing. Most schools have made efforts to implement this recommendation, although some hospital schools of nursing have taken credit for "social science" teaching when in fact they were offering courses on such subjects as history of nursing and professional adjustment.

At the outset the nursing student, reared in the philosophy and precepts of an egalitarian society, may well resist thinking about patients in terms of their ethnic, social, or religious backgrounds. Influenced by the philosophy that the true healer knows no race, creed, or color, nursing instructors often warn their students not to pry into the backgrounds of their patients and to treat all alike regardless of who they are. Because of this reluctance to make group differences explicit, it helps to begin a course in behavioral science by supplying anthropological perspective, noting man's long history on earth, explaining the concept of culture and the nature of cultural universals as well as cultural variability, and documenting the fact that "human nature" is not everywhere the same. Anthropology can lend dignity to class or ethnic differences and thus enable nurses (and medical students as well) to acknowledge and respect these differences without feeling that they are falling victim to invidious prejudice and stereotypes.

REFERENCES CITED

ANDERSON, ODIN W.
  1952   The sociologist and medicine: generalizations from a teaching and research experience in a medical school. Social Forces 31:38-42.
BIRDWHISTELL, RAY L.
  1949   Social science and nursing education: some tentative suggestions. Fifty-Fifth Annual Report of the National League of Nursing Education and Record of Proceedings of the Fifty-Third Convention. New York, National League of Nursing:315-329.
BLOOM, SAMUEL W.
  1959   The role of the sociologist in medical education. Journal of Medical Education 34:667-673.
BLOOM, S., A. WESSEN, R. STRAUS, G. READER, AND J. MYERS
  1960   The sociologist as medical education: a discussion. American Sociological Review 25:95-101. (A panel discussion.)
BROTHERSTON, J. H. F., MARGOT JEFFERYS, AND RAYMOND FIRTH
  1955   Anthropology and public health: record of a seminar held weekly January-March, 1954. Public Health Department, London School of Hygiene and Tropical Medicine, and Anthropology Department, London School of Economics and Political Science. (Mimeographed ms.)
BROWN, ESTHER LUCILE
  1948   Nursing for the future. New York, Russell Sage Foundation.
EATON, JOSEPH W.
  1956   The social science content of a medical curriculum. American Sociological Review 21:614-617.
FOSTER, GEORGE M.
  1952   Relationships between theoretical and applied anthropology: a public health program analysis. Human Organization 11:5-16.
FOSTER, GEORGE M. (ED.)
  1951   A cross-cultural anthropological analysis of a technical aid program. Smithsonian Institution, Washington, D.C. (Mimeographed ms.)
JACO, E. GARTLY
  1960   Problems and prospects of the social sciences in medical education. Journal of Health and Human Behavior 1:29-34.
JOURNAL OF DENTAL EDUCATION
  1960   Why not a department of social dentistry? 24:197-213. (A series of four papers.)
JOURNAL OF HEALTH AND HUMAN BEHAVIOR
  1960   Part Two: Training for social science knowledge in medicine. 1:26-55. (A series of six papers.)
MACGREGOR, FRANCES COOKE
  1957   Social sciences and nursing education. American Journal of Nursing 57:899-902.

1960   Social science in nursing. New York, Russell Sage Foundation.

PAUL, BENJAMIN D.

1954   Introducing social science methods in public health teaching. Harvard Public Health Alumni Bulletin 11:18-21.

1956   Medicine's third dimension. Journal of the National Medical Association 48:323-325.

PAUL, BENJAMIN D., AND WALTER B. MILLER (EDS.)

1955   Health, culture and community. New York, Russell Sage Foundation.

RONEY, JAMES G.

1960   Social sciences in the teaching of public health. Journal of Health and Human Behavior 1:47-52.

RUSSELL SAGE FOUNDATION

1958-59   An appraisal of the problems of collaboration. Annual Report: 1958-1959. New York, pp. 8-16.

SAMORA, JULIAN

1960   The social scientist as researcher and teacher in the medical school. Journal of Health and Human Behavior 1:42-46.

STAINBROOK, EDWARD, AND MURRAY WEXLER

1956   The place of the behavioral sciences in the medical school. Psychiatry 19:263-269.

STRAUS, ROBERT

1959   A department of behavioral science. Journal of Medical Education 34:662-666.

TROUPIN, JAMES L.

1960   Schools of public health: a world picture. World Health Organization, Expert Committee on Professional and Technical Education of Medical and Auxiliary Personnel. (Mimeographed ms.)

E. Adamson Hoebel and
Robert Rossow

Anthropological Studies
for Students of
Law and Government

I N THIS PAPER we shall first consider the specific possibilities in anthropological studies for students preparing for the law and the cor-
relative possibilities in legal training for students of anthropology. Secondly, we shall discuss the relevance of anthropological studies
for students who are preparing for professional careers in governmental
service and again correlatively undertake to examine the areas of study
outside of anthropology that would strengthen the backgrounds of anthropology majors who may later enter into one or another of the administrative branches of government.[1]

I

Since the early 1930's all major law schools have become alert to the
need for a broad social science orientation for students of law. Law is
no longer looked upon by the more alert teachers of law as a self-contained body of doctrine. It is accepted that law is a social phenomenon
and the functions and purposes of law are societal. The law schools
have been looking to the social sciences for constructive assistance in
the preprofessional and professional training of their students and are
disappointed that in the large their expectances have not been met.

Anthropology can make its contribution on two levels. The first
turns upon the quality of its introductory course in cultural anthropology. Such courses can make a basic contribution to law training only
when their emphasis is upon the interrelating functions of social actions

as aspects of total social systems. This means that ethnographic facts should be introduced as reality-giving means rather than exotic ends in themselves.

Of course, a much more specific contribution can emerge through the offering of a sound course in law and anthropology. Such a course requires the same type of emphasis as that just stated for introductory cultural anthropology. To make it available to law school students it is usually necessary to waive such prerequisites in lower-level courses as may exist. Law students have demonstrated that they can cope with the anthropological concepts and data that are encompassed in the course. It is necessary at the very outset to present a comprehensive theory of culture which embraces the general idea of social control, norm formation, and the selection of norms for legal buttressing as one phase of norm-maintenance and realization of the ends and goals of societies.

It is also desirable to include summaries of the more significant theories of sociological jurisprudence in order to relate the anthropological approach to general legal theory. Further, it is desirable to introduce and clarify a number of basic jurisprudential concepts from Anglo-American and Continental legal thinking as working tools and to enhance the relevance of the data from primitive societies to the student's own world of experience. The subsequent content of the course may then center on the systematic analysis of a series of socio-legal systems selected from the ethnological literature with emphasis upon them as parts of total social systems and cultures. Only those societies should be selected from the literature which provide a good body of case materials. Today there are more excellent field studies that meet this criterion than can be handled in a one-term course. A final integration in terms of the functions of law is then called for.

Law students, who generally approach social science courses with a good deal of skepticism, uniformly end up with enthusiastic appreciation. They hold that the study of the anthropology of law so presented makes their legal studies meaningful in a way that no other course has done.

The anthropological offering can be developed to even higher and more intensive levels of investigation through the usual seminar device of examination of the legal systems of special areas, such as Africa or Islam.

In the training of anthropologists, competence in law as a collateral field has unfortunately been grossly neglected. A committee of the Association of American Law Schools has recently been dedicated to the task of helping to correct the gap at the lowest level through the promotion of courses on law and on law and society as a phase of liberal arts education on the undergraduate level (Berman 1956). It is the committee's hope that law professors will proffer such courses. The very least anthropology departments could do would be to encourage the development and introduction of such courses in their own collegiate curricula and to see that their own undergraduate majors enroll in them.

On the level of professional training, it is not generally realized that the enlightened law school will gladly accept social science graduate students for enrollment in specific courses. Anthropology graduate students who wish to develop a degree of special competence for the anthropology of law should be encouraged to consult with the dean of their university's law school about this possibility. First year law courses in civil procedure and torts are particularly appropriate, as is, of course, the law school's course on jurisprudence. A number of law schools will arrange a graduate school minor in law for social science majors. It cannot be too strongly emphasized that any anthropology student, whether he has a special interest in the anthropology of law or not, will profit greatly from the analytical training offered in any well-taught law school course. For regardless of subject matter, the best law courses drill in a strong habit of intellectual skepticism tied to the development of truly sharp analytical skill such as every anthropologist ought to have.

II

The primary defining attribute of the profession of foreign affairs is the fact that it operates in a cross-cultural context. Whether one is a Foreign Service Officer dealing with political and economic affairs, a USIS officer working in the information and cultural fields, or engaged in some other overseas function, the cross-cultural context of operations serves both to differentiate one from others engaged domestically in similar pursuits, and to provide the unifying definition of a profession. Regardless of functional assignment, the foreign affairs professional is essentially engaged in interpreting situations, trends, and events that arise in an alien cultural context into terms meaningful in the cultural context of one's own government. He is also conversely interpreting the attitudes, postures, and objectives of his own government into terms that relate to alien institutions. In the American system of government, the actual policy-making which figuratively separates these two aspects of the professional role, is extra-professional and reserved to officials responsible to domestic political processes. Yet the role defined above for the professional is obviously critical in both the formulation and execution of policy. It has a specific definition, it requires special training and skill, and quality of professional performance can be measured with fair objectivity. It therefore satisfies the usual definitions of a profession.

The training arm of the State Department, the Foreign Service Institute has since its founding in the late 1940's been fully appreciative
of the cultural approach to Foreign Service operations, and has stressed
the concepts and methods of cultural anthropology especially in the
training of officers in language-and-area specialties. As a result, the culture concept is quite widely understood throughout the ranks. Similarly, anthropologists have been most responsive in attempting to help
meet the training needs of government, though again they have been
called on mostly in connection with language-and-area specialty training. The more general significance of the cross-cultural context of foreign affairs has not been fully appreciated or specified, however, either
within the profession itself or in the academic world. It is this theme
that will be stressed in the comments to follow.

All this is not to say, of course, that anthropology alone can provide
an adequate pre-professional preparation for foreign affairs. The
range of functions and activities involved in international relations is
so broad that a wide-spectrum inter-disciplinary approach is called
for. Pertinent fields would range from law, politics, and economics to
language, literature, and philosophy, and would include a heavy emphasis on history. Ideally, however, the culture concept should be
thoroughly infused in the courses in these fields and the comparative
approach stressed. This is not to advocate the type of "comparative"
course, all too common in undergraduate curricula, which covers wide
areas in superficial and nominal terms. Bilateral comparisons are sufficient for the purpose, so long as the theme of cultural variety is conveyed
and sustained. All this of course is beyond the control of the anthropologist, but it does suggest a caveat that is pertinent to all disciplines involved, including anthropology. The ideal inter-disciplinary approach
here envisioned will be unachievable in the degree that any disciplinary xenophobia or parochialism is permitted to express itself.

Turning now to the contribution that anthropology itself can make
to pre-professional training for foreign affairs, one must at the outset
recognize that the latter requires an orientation and emphasis somewhat different from the usual academic approach to anthropology. Generally speaking cultural anthropology is objectively oriented, focusing
its attention on specific culture groups, usually alien. For the foreign
affairs professional this is not so simply the case. Instead he finds himself operating in between cultures, and—especially at the higher levels
of responsibility—having often to interpret and evaluate among a number of cultures simultaneously. This suggests that he must focus rather
on the *process* of communication between cultures, on the techniques
of interpreting one to another. Also, by the very nature of his role he

must maintain strong roots in and a distinct preference for his own culture. While accuracy of cross-cultural interpretation is the prime professional criterion, these requirements of versatility and bias limit the degree to which he can afford to immerse himself in a particular alien culture, limits not felt in the same degree by the anthropologist.

Let us consider these points in turn. The constant in-between position of the foreign affairs professional, and his consequent focus on communication processes and interpreting techniques, bespeaks his need for a thorough grounding in the theory of culture and its key concepts and also some capacity to handle the methods of anthropological observation and analysis. The need for an understanding of theory is so obvious to this audience that it need not be further labored. On the matter of methodology, however, some comment is called for. The anthropologist, as a true scientist, seeks accuracy above all else, and is prepared to sacrifice time to that end. He is also able to select his fields of observation, and naturally and properly tends to select those wherein the methods at his disposal will give him sharply accurate results. Unfortunately, the problems that arise in foreign affairs dictate the fields that must be studied and analysed regardless of the adequacy of available methods to the task, and also these problems will not wait. Conclusions must be drawn, recommendations made and action taken almost always on the basis of very incomplete data and only limited certainty. Nonetheless, much of the methodology of anthropology can be very usefully applied in the field of foreign affairs, if only it can be selected and adapted to meet the demands of speed and versatility of application. Such a modified methodology would not lead toward the perfectionism of science but would certainly improve on the largely intuitive methods of observation and appraisal commonly used in foreign affairs today.

The next point concerns the relation the foreign affairs professional must maintain toward his own culture. This of course is a matter that involves the whole process of enculturation of the individual. But here again anthropology can make a major contribution by facilitating a balanced objectification of the mother culture. The first step toward the inculcation of a professional attitude is to break the crust of naive ethnocentrism, yet this operation must be performed without damaging the roots of loyalty and preference for the mother culture, and this task can best be performed in the context of anthropology. This has been demonstrated in experience with mid-career training of Foreign Service Officers. In a sequence of "mid-career courses" these mature officers, few of whom had had any prior exposure to anthropology, have been given *inter alia* an intensive introduction to theory of culture, followed by a sampling of some of the culture patterns important in today's international relations, most of them more or less exotic. All this was duly accepted by the students as useful and illuminating. At the end of the series, however, they were asked to apply the analytical methods they had learned to the study of American culture using their own class as a laboratory and their fellow students as informants. As an added variant they were sometimes asked also to analyze the Foreign Service as a professional sub-culture. These exercises could usually be counted on to produce a wave of real revelation as the full meaning of the culture concept dawned, and it was realized that their own patterns of value and behavior were of the same culturally determined fabric as the alien, and thus susceptible to objective analysis by the same methods. It requires recourse to other disciplines to develop fully an objective understanding and appreciation of the mother culture, but the anthropological approach seems to afford an almost unique way of producing that fine balance of detachment and preference relative to it so necessary in the practice of foreign affairs.

Finally, there is the question of specialization of the foreign affairs professional on a particular alien culture, the so-called language-and-area specialization. Until a decade or so ago there was very little of this kind of specialization within the profession, and also a shockingly limited capability on the part of American universities to provide such training. Happily this situation has been much improved in the meantime. The profession needs much more of this sort of specialization, but at the same time a caveat must be uttered. There exists a limit beyond which such specialization by the foreign affairs professional is more damaging than beneficial. That limit is pretty far down the road of specialization but it is nonetheless there, and should be recognized and understood. The only limit the anthropologist need impose on his own specialization is that he maintain his scholarly objectivity. The constraint imposed on the foreign affairs professional is considerably greater in view of his assigned role as interpreter *between* cultures and his required preference for his mother culture. Moreover, the higher his professional level of responsibility the more he will have to deal in a multicultural, rather than bicultural, context. Now it is common experience that deep and prolonged preoccupation with a single field of attention and study will basically influence and modify one's general outlook. This is not just a weakness in the individual that can be modified by the exercise of self-discipline. It is inherent in the nature of human behavior, as well illustrated in a number of experiments in social psychology. It is thus inevitable that specialization will tend to produce its own bias, and that eventually a point can be reached where this bias will interfere with the professional requirements of mediation, loyalty and versatility. A certain amount of such bias is entirely tolerable, indeed normal and necessary. In fact it is recommended every foreign affairs professional undergo a full specialization in depth in at least one language-and-area in the course of a career; without such an experience he cannot fully appreciate the professional function, and also, of course, such specialists are operationally needed. The specialization should not begin until after a long apprenticeship during which cultural and functional variety is stressed. As a rough and impressionistically based rule it may be suggested that the period of specialization can last some ten to twelve years before the point of seriously diminishing returns is reached. Thereafter despecialization is called for, both in the interest of maintaining the professional utility of the individual, and also because operations demand that senior officers operate more in a multicultural context. Now this is not the primary concern of the anthropologist, but it would be well for the latter to bear this peculiar limitation on specialization in mind as he endeavors to help the foreign affairs profession meet its pre- and postprofessional training needs, and as he may be called upon to advise students on such matters.

To summarize these general observations, it seems clear that the concepts and methods of cultural anthropology concern the very essence of professional operations in foreign affairs, and anthropological studies and data are a most important item of consumption therin. Thus there can be no question that anthropology has a very great contribution to make in both pre- and post-professional training for foreign affairs. The anthropologist can maximize this contribution, however, if he will bear in mind in the shaping of his curriculum some of the special requirements of foreign affairs, and make allowances and adaptations in the light of them. These special factors include the pressures of time and circumstance characteristic in foreign affairs, the intermediate role of the profession, the requirement of both objectivity and bias toward the mother culture, and the need for versatility.

There remains finally the question of what specific courses can best meet these needs. Beyond the basic offerings in cultural anthropology and the customary area courses, specialized courses in cultural dynamics and culture theory would be highly appropriate. Personality and culture should be particularly apposite, as would also be case-centered courses in culture change and applied anthropology. Of enduring value would be a good grounding in linguistic analysis and study in language and culture.

NOTE

[1] The views and opinions presented herein do not necessarily reflect those of the United States Government or the Department of State.

REFERENCE CITED

BERMAN, H. J.
    1956   On the teaching of law in the liberal arts curriculum. Brooklyn, The Foundation Press, Inc.

PART X

ACADEMIC
ENVIRONMENTS
IN THE
TEACHING
OF
ANTHROPOLOGY

Introduction

THE ACADEMIC ENVIRONMENT for the teaching of anthropology, like the natural environment of evolving man, is itself subject to change. The late Professor Felix Keesing, in a delightfully personalized account of an anthropologist's career, which he gave at the Berkeley conference, described three stages of departmental development. First, with a staff of one or two, the teacher must be something of a generalist, but he can retreat to his study, work, and forget administrative problems. Second, with a bachelor's and possibly a master's degree in the anthropology program, he must provide for two classes of majors: those going on to graduate work and those taking anthropology as an interesting, humanistic experience. Third, with the doctoral program, the department head must deal with the different problems of old profs, junior staff, and graduate students.

Olmsted's account of teaching in a small department corresponds to the first stage depicted by Keesing. A chief problem is how much specialized material to introduce into the curriculum and how to do it. Wagley's paper deals with a different dimension. Only field work can serve as a way of identifying both teacher and student with the process by which new knowledge is gained. Several of those who spoke at the Berkeley conference (including Casagrande, DuBois, Spindler, and Vogt) advocated field work for preprofessional and other highly motivated students. Wagley describes a way to meet this need for at least a few students. The question remains, to what extent one can afford the time for such intensive work with undergraduate students, many of whom will not become professional anthropologists, while increasing numbers of graduate students need the same kind of experiences and individual attention. Since actual work with peoples of strongly contrasting culture is clearly not possible for most undergraduate students of anthropology, some teachers attempt to convey the flavor of field work

523

through the device of role-playing in class and by field work projects in the local community.

The description of anthropology in the junior college provided by Nelson suggests that one problem of the junior college teacher is the lack of opportunity to participate in professional activities at any of the levels described by Keesing. Enrollments in anthropology courses in junior colleges represent a sizable fraction of all anthropology enrollments. The teachers generally carry many more hours per week of teaching than are customary in four-year colleges, frequently in courses of two or even three disciplines. The satisfactions of scholarship—even the indirect ones of the administrator who must gain them largely through the accomplishments of his colleagues—are generally thought to be out of reach in the junior college environment. The problem, as some anthropologists view it, is that many of the teachers in junior colleges have not shared in the field work experience and, therefore, cannot transmit the anthropological ethos. This may be remedied, now that provision is being made for summer institutes involving laboratory and field training of anthropology teachers. Furthermore, the library resources, audio-visual aids, and standards of teaching which Nelson believes to be desirable for junior college use are of the same kind as those recommended for anthropology courses in general. Indeed the environments of anthropological teaching in institutions of different sorts may be more notable for their common problems and common potentialities than for any fundamental differences among them.

G.W.L.

HAROLD NELSON

Teaching
Anthropology in
Junior Colleges

A STUDY OF the teaching of anthropology in the United States cannot be considered complete without the inclusion of junior colleges. the following figures will indicate the significant role of junior colleges in American higher education from a statistical point of view. In the 1958-59 academic year there was a full-time enrollment in the junior colleges of the United States of 291,635 students (American Association of Junior colleges 1960:276-279) as compared to the total undergraduate (four-year) enrollment of American colleges and universities of 2,872,045 (U.S. Office of Education 1959:7).

Where statistics are available for comparison with enrollment in lower division, i.e., freshman and sophomore years, the junior college enrollment is impressive. In California, long the vanguard of junior college development and growth, there were in 1958-59, 91,162 full time students enrolled in junior colleges as compared to 54,874 full-time students in lower division in all of the four-year institutions in the state (Master Plan for Higher Education in California 1960: Table 2:51, 4:7), or 62 per cent of all lower division students in California were enrolled in junior colleges. Projected enrollment for 1975 estimates 288,950 full-time students for junior colleges and 130,450 lower division students for all four-year institutions in the state (California Master Plan 1960: Table 7:62, 4:20), or 69 per cent of all lower division students will be enrolled in junior colleges. The California Master Plan Committee believes that the growth of junior colleges may be even greater than their estimated projection figures.

In a recent study, Lantz (personal communication) estimated that in the academic year 1957-58, there were 2,377 anthropology students enrolled in twenty-two junior colleges in California. In the fall semester of 1961, thirty-seven junior colleges in California had 4,663 students enrolled in anthropology. In other states, junior colleges have a large proportion of students enrolled in lower division. In Mississippi half the students who go to college first attend its junior colleges, and the New York State Department of Education estimates that by 1970 at least 50 per cent of its first-year college students will be accommodated in junior colleges (Fine 1960). In sum, there is an impressive number of students attending junior colleges in the United States, in total numbers as well as in proportion to the over-all college lower division enrollment. All indications point to the increasing participation of junior colleges in higher education.

To understand teaching anthropology, or any subject, in the junior college, it is necessary to understand something of the philosophy of education that has been associated with the junior college and that has been enunciated rather clearly in a number of studies over the past forty years. Public education, according to educationists, is dedicated to the proposition that as much education as possible for everyone is not merely desirable but necessary in our kind of society. This is explicitly stated by the American Association of Junior Colleges, which, according to its executive secretary,

pledges complete support to a policy of education throughout the United States so organized and financed as to extend full and equal opportunities whereby each individual may develop his capacities for his own benefit and for the best interests of the nation as a whole. (Bogue 1950:51)

The junior college is open to everyone, since the principle of education for all effectively negates selective admission. Most, if not all, states follow the policy presented in the California Education Code.

The principal of any two-year junior college shall admit to the junior college any high school graduate and any other person over 18 years of age who in his judgment is capable of profiting from the instruction offered. (California State Department of Education 1957: Sec. 8821)

This section is interpreted by administrators, according to the "Restudy of the Needs of California in Higher Education" (1955:114), as opposing selection of students through admission procedures based on academic ability. Furthermore, the "shall admit" provision in Section 8821 of the Code statement, says Clark,

is regarded by junior college administrators as a mandate that places the burden of proof on the official who would reject a student. A case would need to be made, it is argued, that the prospective student could not profit from any work of the junior college. This constitutes an effective block to any tendency to select. In effect, the junior college is expected to admit all applicants, without regard to ability, type of curriculum completed in high school, or any other aspect of background. It is to have an open door. (1960: 44-45)

Given the policies of education for everyone and rejection of, for all practical purposes, no one who wants to enter, the junior college student body has a very wide range of academic skills and abilities. In California, an investigation (California State Department of Education 1955:104 ff.) clearly indicates that in the three-segment system of higher education in the state, the student body of the University is high in academic ability, the state college student body lower, and the junior college student body below the national norm for college students. However:

Although the median general scholastic aptitude of junior college student bodies taken as a whole was lower than that of the state colleges and the University of California, a number of junior colleges did have a significant number of able students. (California State Department of Education 1955: 106)

These are the 30 per cent of junior college students who will transfer to a senior college.

Grace V. Bird, of the Office of Relations with Schools of the University of California, made a study of junior college transfer students entering Berkeley and Los Angeles campuses as juniors in the fall of 1953 (1957). She compared these with the native students, that is, those who entered the University as freshmen two years earlier. Transfer students were divided into (1) eligibles, those who upon graduation from high school were eligible to enter the University directly but for some reason entered a junior college instead, and (2) ineligibles, those who were ineligible to enter the University upon graduation from high school. Miss Bird found that in their first semester at Berkeley, eligible transfer students had a grade point average of 2.45,[1] whereas the native students' average was 2.63, and the ineligible transfers earned 2.07, considerably less than the other two groups. However, by the end of their second semester, eligible transfers averaged 2.62, almost reaching the 2.68 of the native students, and the average of the ineligibles rose to 2.26. During the third semester, eligibles gained only a fraction, rising to 2.68, while native students rose to 2.71, and ineligibles continued to gain slightly, going to 2.38. At the end of their fourth semester at Berkeley, the eligible transfer student average of 2.84 surpassed the native student average of 2.78, and the ineligibles had risen to a respectable 2.60 (Bird 1957:Table I). How-

ever, the final semester averages represent a greater selection among
junior college transfers. These students, at the end of their final semester of undergraduate work, showed a greater drop out rate than native students. Of the ineligibles 55 per cent had withdrawn from the
University before graduation, of the eligibles about 30 per cent. Twenty
per cent of the native students withdrew during the same period of
time, but records indicate that low grades were not the reason for their
dropping out, though they probably were for the transfer students.
The record at the Los Angeles campus, with only slight differences,
showed the same pattern of transfer students falling behind in their
first semester at the University and gradual increases in grade point
average each subsequent semester. It seems quite clear that many
junior college students are capable of performing at the university level.

Recent studies have pointed up the multiple-function purpose of the
junior college. Henry (1956:69) lists four major purposes of the public junior college: preparation for advanced study; vocational education; general education; and community services. Other studies include guidance as an additional function. The administrative and
academic structure of the junior college is organized to meet all of these
functions, not only the one of preparing students for transfer to four-
year institutions.

The junior college, then, is likely to be an institution with a student
body of which two-thirds intend to transfer to a senior college but only
one-third actually do so, with a large adult education program usually
concentrated in night classes, with a vocational program in trades and
services occupations, and with a general education program for many
who will terminate their education with the junior college but who
do not take vocational courses. The teacher in the junior college
is faced not only with a wide range of academic skills and abilities but
with a wide range of student goals as well.

2. CURRICULUM DESIGN FOR JUNIOR COLLEGES

The two functions of a junior college of particular interest in the teaching of anthropology are preparation for advanced study and general
education. Courses offered in the junior colleges are affected by these
two functions, especially the first. Junior colleges, in preparing transfer
students, tend to gear their curricula to those universities and colleges
which the bulk of their transfer students plan to attend. This often
extends to offering the same lower division courses as the nearby senior
college, and designating these courses by the same numbers. Thus,
the anthropology courses most frequently offered in the junior colleges
of California are physical anthropology and cultural anthropology
(Lantz 1959:Table IV). In the past several years a number of junior

colleges have instituted a course in prehistory and culture growth, which appears to be slowly gaining acceptance.

This choice of courses reflects the influence of the University of California and the state colleges, which tend to limit their lower division offerings to the three courses mentioned above. Courses that do not correspond to those offered at the senior college may not be acceptable for transfer credit and it is unlikely that students intending to transfer would sign up for them. It is conceivable that a junior college might work out an agreement with a senior college for elective credit for lower division courses the latter did not offer. If such an agreement were made, lower division courses could be offered in such areas as primitive religion, the nature of culture, or various ethnographic areas.

The general education function of junior colleges raises the question whether it is possible or desirable to design a course for students of different educational levels and career goals. General education has been defined as "that part of education which is concerned with the common knowledge, skills, and attitudes needed by each individual to be effective as a person, a member of a family, a worker, and a citizen" (Johnson 1952:20). Implicit in its philosophy is the assumption that general education will be especially valuable for those who cannot or do not wish to transfer to a four-year college. The problem is: should a lower qualitative level of education be provided for these students? Those who answer affirmatively have suggested a multiple-track system in which students who are incapable of passing college transfer courses would be placed in easier, nontransfer courses. Diluting or simplifying courses to enable lower caliber students to obtain a so-called college education is, it seems to me, a repudiation of the meaning of college education. If a student passes college courses, it is assumed that he has met certain minimum standards of academic achievement. If he is incapable of doing so, then he simply is not a college student and should not be so designated by the questionable practice of easing standards.

This is not to say that differing abilities, needs, and goals are to go unrecognized. It is possible, and indeed commonly practiced, to provide alternative forms, for certain courses. For example, in Santa Monica City College, there is one course in zoölogy for premedical students and another for those in liberal arts who do not need the same kind of material. This kind of curriculum design can be arranged without compromising standards.

Another method of recognizing individual differences is to institute an accelerated program to encourage better students. Honors programs are widely established in American education. Although the procedures vary with each school, the usual practice is to select a few students who have given some indication of superior ability in their first semester and in their second semester assign them additional reading or a special project. They need not meet with the regular class but meet regularly instead with the instructor, write papers, and discuss topics pertinent to the course. The merit of these two plans is that different goals and abilities can be met without sacrificing quality and standards.

3. LIBRARY, LABORATORY, AND AUDIO-VISUAL RESOURCES NECESSARY IN A JUNIOR COLLEGE

A junior college cannot acquire a library collection of the same size and scope as that of a senior college, but a good representation of anthropology books, monographs, and journals is possible, desirable and necessary.

For cultural anthropology there should be a number of books dealing with theory and concept. Such general books as *Anthropology Today, Mirror for Man, Study of Man, Current Anthropology,* and introductory texts by A. L. Kroeber, M. J. Herskovits, Robert Lowie, E. A. Hoebel, and others are essential. Books are needed also in special areas of anthropology, such as social organizaton, religion, art, linguistics, and technology. A wide selection of ethnographic monographs should be provided, so that the student may become familiar with source material. Each of the geographic regions of the world should be represented. If an instructor wishes, a special collecton should be assembled of monographs on a specific culture area such as Africa, Oceania, or Central America.

A physical anthropology collection should include a selection of books on evolution, fossil man, and race. A serious problem for a beginning physical anthropology course is that so much of the material on fossil man is published in journals that are beyond the reach of lower division students. Junior colleges can nevertheless subscribe to a limited number of technical journals even though they are oriented toward the professional rather than the beginning student. To make such material available to junior college libraries, perhaps in the form of selected readings, merits consideration. Since a great deal of material covered in physical anthropology is taken from other disciplines, such as geology, paleontology, genetics, and biology, it is useful to give students a list of books in these areas for further reading to fill out the material given in lecture and text.

A minimum journal collection should include the *American Anthropologist, Southwestern Journal of Anthropology, American Antiquity,* and the *American Journal of Physical Anthropology.*

A bibliography designed especially for junior colleges would be most useful, if only because in many of them, anthropology is taught by individuals who have not been trained in the discipline. (See below.) Such a bibliography should be annotated, divided into sections, e.g. on evolution, fossil man, race, genetics, general texts, monographs (by culture area), and special subject books. Suggestions might also be made for a minimum collection, depending perhaps on the kinds of courses offered, and for larger collections where more courses are offered.

Libraries are well established as essential to all schools, but a resource associated with departments of anthropology in most universities and many colleges, the laboratory, is not usually found in the junior college. Although a research laboratory may not be feasible, space for storing skeletal material, casts, charts, and so on is necessary. If a working area were made available in such a storage space, it might be possible to give additional work to those students especially interested in physical anthropology.

A museum may also be impractical for a junior college, although display space may be found for exhibiting artifacts from various culture areas of the world. An arrangement might be made with a nearby university or museum for the loan of some of its material for display purposes, and perhaps the American Anthropological Association or some other central agency could publish a list of business houses where such material may be purchased. An excellent source of artifacts would be an archaeological site the junior college personnel and students might be digging.

For physical anthropology many displays are possible and material is available. Exhibits of primate skeletal material, for example, could help the student to understand the relationship between anthropoids and hominids. Life science and geology departments often set up exhibits that are helpful to anthropology students. More generally, assistance is available to faculty and students through what has become well known as audio-visual aids: maps, charts, casts, photographs, movies, film strips, and slides.

There are many uses for charts in the classroom, and these can also be made in wall size or binder size or both. A taxonomic chart of the animal kingdom, emphasizing the primate order; a time chart showing the various geologic and zoölogic divisions; a paleolithic culture chart; and charts of various aspects of genetics, such as skin color, blood type, and color blindness, are among the possibilities. There is need for a kinship chart that could be used to illustrate kinship principles to an introductory class.

Good use can also be made of reproductions of artifacts for the classroom or for display. Plastic reproductions of paleolithic flakes, blades, and cores, of Folsom points, and many other kinds of artifacts should be available for junior colleges, since these institutions are unable to obtain them as easily as university museums do.

Unlike maps, charts, and casts, films are of questionable utility in the junior college classroom. Since the teacher does not have an audio-visual center at his disposal, it is necessary for him to set up projector and screen, show and rewind film, and so on. Hence, showing a twenty-minute film may consume the better part of the class hour. If the film has not been produced by an anthropologist, it may be necessary for the instructor to spend whatever time is left explaining the errors in the film, and if the film has sound, it is difficult to comment while the film is running. Though films may be a valuable adjunct to teaching, there are not many that are anthropologically reliable. It is probably better teaching practice to show no film at all than to show one that has little bearing on anthropology.

Film strips are also useful, although many of the disadvantages noted above apply here as well. An advantage of a film strip is that the instructor, without the interference of a sound track, can explain or discuss the picture on the screen and hold it there as long as he wishes. Like movies, film strips are rarely suitable for anthropology classes, with the possible exception of those produced by *Life* magazine.[2]

An area of audio-visual resources that has not been developed as much as it should be is tape and record. Little else is available than the *Ways of Mankind* records (Goldschmidt 1954), which are very good, and a few Ethnic Folkway records, mainly music.

Audio-visual aids are necessary, and if utilized properly can add interest and understanding to anthropological concepts. In order that teachers may make the most effective use of this kind of material, a central agency such as a State Board of Education, library association, or anthropological association should publish and keep current an annotated catalog of available materials and their cost and source.

4. RELATIONSHIP BETWEEN ANTHROPOLOGY COURSES AND OFFERINGS IN OTHER DEPARTMENTS

Borrowing appropriate audio-visual resources from geology, chemistry, zoölogy, art, and other departments may lead to a fruitful exchange of material and ideas. This is all the more desirable, since anthropology uses concepts and data from many other disciplines. The anthropology instructor may wish to call upon other members of the faculty to give short lectures in his classes when the subject of the lecture bears upon other fields. Someone from chemistry could deliver a fifteen minute lecture on Carbon 14 dating or the instructor in ceramics on the making and baking of pottery.

It might be advisable, especially in the junior college, for informal meetings to be held for instructors whose course material is within the province of anthropology, in order to bring them up to date. History of Civilization instructors, for example, could thus become acquainted with the most recent theories and data dealing with the paleolithic or neolithic. Or, conversely, anthropology instructors could be informed of the current Pleistocene glacial theories. Such meetings are advisable in the junior college, because so many instructors are teaching anthropology courses for which they are not adequately prepared. (See Section 6.) They may be able to learn the basic material of the course they teach, but in the peripheral areas of geology, chemistry, psychology, or biology, they may require assistance.

5. RESEARCH AND COURSE PREPARATION FACILITIES FOR JUNIOR COLLEGE TEACHERS OF ANTHROPOLOGY

Most junior colleges are not oriented toward, or even sympathetic to, research. Clark found that at San Jose Junior College,

. . . it is not to be expected that the typical staff member will be oriented to scholarship. The values of the system are against it. Even more than in those four-year colleges that prefer not to have their instructors engaged in research, the junior college expects work to be oriented to students. Research and writing are not encouraged and the load of other activities leaves little time. (1960:122)

Should an instructor pursue research, he may find himself the object of pressure, subtle or explicit, reinforcing the philosophy that junior college instructors are teachers, not researchers. Clark found that

The ideal junior college teacher, as reported in the junior college literature, is free of many characteristics of the academic person. In one study, poor junior college teachers were characterized by administrators in seventy-two different colleges as "warped scholars instead of teachers," "coming from the graduate schools and tending to be crushed under the weight of pedantry," "subject-matter conscious," and similarly. See David B. Pugh and Roy E. Morgan, "Faculty Needs and Requirements," *Junior College Journal,* vol. 13, pp. 427-435, May, 1943. (1960:123n)

Junior college teachers are expected to use whatever time they have left after teaching fifteen hours a week in such activities as assisting students, keeping attendance records (very little clerical assistance is available), grading papers (readers are not usually provided), sponsoring some extracurricular activity, and keeping up if possible with current publications.

I would not argue transforming the junior college into a research institution, since this is impossible, impractical, and undesirable; nor would I argue that the attitude of the university toward research ought to be blindly accepted by the junior college. Nor is it necessary for the anthropology instructor to participate in research to be a good teacher (see Rowe 1960:19 ff.), but it is unfortunate that the dominant attitude in the junior college is negative toward research. He who is interested in research, it is felt, cannot be interested in teaching, and teaching is the business of the junior college instructor.

It need not follow, of course, that a reduced emphasis on research must lead to a negative attitude toward research, nor need it follow that a negative attitude toward research must lead to an anti-intellectual climate. Yet, in the junior colleges, there *is* a negative attitude toward research; there *is,* with a few exceptions among the faculty, an anti-intellectual climate; and there *is* little interest in subject matter but much emphasis of teaching methods and techniques. Emphasizing methods and techniques may be appropriate in the elementary grades or high school, but in college courses, content should take precedence. The intellectually oriented teacher must seek to counteract the stultifying effect of the anti-intellectual, non-academic climate of the junior college and of its concern with means rather than content. The prevailing attitudes, more than limited research opportunities, have a negative effect on teaching in the junior college.

Research is not impossible for junior college teachers. The determined instructor can request a leave of absence or sabbatical leave for research purposes. Instructors of anthropology who have not majored in the subject or who have taken very little graduate work in it should be encouraged to increase their control of the field. The National Science Foundation provides funds for work of this kind. Although there are provisions for graduate study and research, they are infrequently utilized, for there are few benefits to be derived from it other than personal satisfaction. Promotion does not depend upon it, stature on the campus does not depend upon it, and the junior college instructor cannot usually publish enough in any case to gain eminence in the field. A change in attitude is necessary before existing facilities can be fully used by junior college teachers. Once the orientation to research and professional growth is viewed as part of teaching, rather than, falsely, as in opposition to it, still other means than research can be devised to enable junior college teachers to participate actively in their specially chosen field of interest.

University departments might consider giving an upper division course or a graduate seminar at night for nearby junior college instructors who cannot enroll in day classes. Junior college anthropology instructors in a regional area might form an association to discuss both problems peculiar to the junior college and subjects of academic interest. This could be organized as a subsection within a regional anthropological association or as a separate group, but care should be taken to prevent isolation from instructors in four-year institutions.

Facilities for course preparation are more satisfactory, since this is considered a proper function of the junior college instructor. Many junior colleges have developed syllabi for all their courses which are available to new instructors and may be available to instructors in other schools as well. It would be of assistance to all teachers of anthropology if regular sessions at association meetings, regional and national, were devoted to discussion of teaching. A summary of such discussion, published in the *American Anthropologist,* might interest the profession at large in teaching problems and might also attract nonprofessional teachers of anthropology to read the journal.

6. IMPROVEMENT OF THE TEACHING OF ANTHROPOLOGY IN JUNIOR COLLEGES

The most important single need for improving the teaching of anthropology in the junior college is for qualified instructors. An effort is made by junior college administrators to hire teachers with a master's degree in the field in which they are to teach, but administrators often seek people who claim competence in three or four fields. Or, once a teacher is hired, he may be assigned to teach outside his own field. Such a practice may occasionally be necessary for a number of reasons but too often emergencies become permanent assignments.

The survey by Lasker and Nelson in the companion volume to this book brings out clearly the lack of training in anthropology of those who teach anthropology in the junior colleges of California. It is probably much the same elsewhere in the United States. Of fifty-two individuals teaching anthropology in the junior colleges surveyed, ten had their highest degree in anthropology, eleven in sociology or social science, seven in history, five in education, four in psychology, four in geography, and eleven in a scattering of other subjects. Almost all of these were master's degrees, but there were eight doctorates, half of them in anthropology, and three B.A.'s. The field of anthropology is too broad and too technical for any but the exceptional individual to teach it without adequate formal preparation. Adequate preparation should be interpreted as, at a minimum, a master's degree in anthropology.

Another means by which the teaching of anthropology may be improved in the junior college is through coöperation between junior and senior college personnel. Such cooperation can help by bringing more knowledge of the subject to the junior college instructor, by keeping him up to date, and by helping senior college personnel understand junior college problems. Meetings of both groups and free discussion between them could bring an awareness of needs, goals, aims, and purposes to both sides.

To understand junior college teaching problems, senior college personnel must understand the junior college—its function, its academic climate, the kind of courses offered, the kind of teachers hired, and the philosophical orientation and training of its administrators. Junior college administrators, conscientiously and sincerely concerned with providing a high level of education in the junior college, have developed a philosophy of education that differs from that of adminstrators in four-year colleges. Clark reports on this for San Jose Junior College, but it is probably applicable to administrators at most junior colleges:

It can also be seen that the college's administrators possessed . . . an administrative background predominantly, if not entirely, in the elementary or secondary school. All the college officials gained their general administrative outlook, formed habits of work, and learned procedure in such units, principally in junior and senior high schools. None had college administrative experience. With such uniformity of background, the know-how brought to bear in the administration of the college had to be that of the public school and not that of four-year college or universities. (1960:105)

The position of administrators in junior college is admittedly a difficult one. Bound to a public school philosophy of education through academic training and experience and to the interests of the local citizenry whose taxation largely supports the junior college, administrators are, at the same time, aware that a junior college should maintain certain academic standards. Perhaps this problem may be largely resolved if or when junior colleges are separated from the public school system and are given more state, rather than local, financial support.

It is important for anthropologists at senior institutions to participate more actively in the program of anthropological education given at junior colleges, because junior colleges are increasing in number and enrollment, with consequent increases in the number of students matriculating at four-year institutions who have taken their lower division work at junior colleges and because the number of students taking courses in anthropology has been rapidly increasing. If anthropologists at senior colleges are concerned with the quality of their anthropology majors, both undergraduate and graduate, they should be concerned with the basic courses these students take in the junior college. And as professionals responsible for the status of anthropology and the dissemination of anthropological knowledge, anthropologists in senior institutions should be concerned with the anthropology taught in junior colleges.

I would suggest the following means by which anthropologists in senior institutions could assist in improving the quality of anthropology taught at junior colleges. The list could probably be extended.

1. Cooperation with junior college instructors on determining material to be included in anthropology courses.

2. Meetings with junior college instructors to discuss recent research, concepts, and data.

3. Coöperation with junior colleges to encourage further education, research and study for junior college instructors.

4. Coöperation in the establishment of academic standards for junior college teachers of anthropology.

5. Exchanging ideas with administrators in the junior college on educational and scientific goals.

The improvement of teaching of anthropology in the junior college cannot be achieved by junior college anthropology instructors alone; they need the assistance of anthropologists at senior institutions.

NOTES

[1] At the time the study was made, the scale used was $3 = A$, $2 = B$, $1 = C$. At the present time, the University uses the scale, $4 = A$, $3 = B$, $2 = C$, $1 = D$. The report figures have been transferred here to the new scale.

[2] Life Filmstrips, Time Incorporated, New York 20, New York.

REFERENCES CITED

AMERICAN ASSOCIATION OF JUNIOR COLLEGES
  1960 Junior college directory, 1960. Junior college journal 30:207-306.
BIRD, GRACE V.
  1957 Comparison of persistence and performance of native students and junior college transfers entering the university as juniors, fall 1953, Berkeley and Los Angeles. Distributed in mimeographed form by the Office of Relations with Schools, University of California, Berkeley 4, California.
BOGUE, JESSE PARKER
  1950 The community college. McGraw-Hill Book Co., Inc.
CALIFORNIA STATE DEPARTMENT OF EDUCATION
  1948 A report of a survey of the needs of California in higher education, submitted to the liaison committee of the regents of the University of California and the California state department of education. Sacramento. (Also known as the Strayer report.)
CALIFORNIA STATE DEPARTMENT OF EDUCATION
  1955 A restudy of the needs of California in higher education, prepared for the liaison committee of the regents of the University of California and the California state board of education. Sacramento.
CALIFORNIA STATE DEPARTMENT OF EDUCATION
  1957 Education code. Sacramento.
CALIFORNIA STATE DEPARTMENT OF EDUCATION
  1960 A master plan for higher education in California, 1960-1975. Pre-

pared for the liaison committee of the State Board of Education and The Regents of the University of California, Sacramento.

CLARK, BURTON R.
1960   The open door college: a case study. McGraw-Hill Book Co., Inc.

FINE, BENJAMIN
1960   The amazing rise of junior colleges. San Francisco Sunday Chronicle, January 24, 1960.

GOLDSCHMIDT, WALTER (ED.)
1954   Ways of mankind. Written material published by Beacon Press. Records available at National Association of Educational Broadcasters, University of Illinois, Urbana, Illinois.

HENRY, NELSON B. (ED.)
1956   The public junior college. The fifty-fifth yearbook of the national society for the study of education, prepared by the yearbook committee, B. Lamar Johnson, chairman. The University of Chicago Press.

JOHNSON, B. LAMAR
1952   General education in action. American council on education. Washington 6, D.C.

LANTZ, CHARLES C.
1959   Digest of responses to anthropology—sociology questionnaire circulated to public junior colleges in spring 1958. Distributed in mimeographed form at conference on anthropology, Los Angeles State College of Applied Arts and Sciences, October 3, 1959.

MEDSKER, LELAND L.
1960   The junior college. McGraw-Hill Book Co., Inc.

ROWE, CHANDLER W.
1960   Anthropology in the liberal arts college. In Teaching anthropology, Andrew H. Whiteford, ed. Logan Museum publication in anthropology, Bulletin No. 8. Beloit College, Beloit, Wisconsin.

UNITED STATES OFFICE OF EDUCATION
1959   Opening fall enrollment, 1958. Circular 545:7, September.

DAVID L. OLMSTED

*Special Problems
of a Small
Anthropological Staff*

THE TEACHING of special fields of anthropology in a small department (one with three or fewer anthropologists) is similar to teaching anthropology in a department that embraces other fields as well. Indeed, the small anthropology department often grows out of the combined department. The problems of teaching in nonanthropological fields are comparable to those of teaching outside one's specialty but within anthropology. Most of what is said below about the latter is also applicable to the former, though there is probably a considerable difference in the degree of difficulty. The problems connected with teaching the special fields of anthropology in a small department are of two kinds: (1) presenting one's own specialty on a reduced scale appropriate to the miniature setting and (2) attempting a well-rounded program by offering courses in areas outside one's primary interest or—dare we admit it?—competence.

TEACHING ONE'S SPECIALTY

In discussing the first of these problems, I shall restrict myself to an illustration from linguistics.. I speak only for myself, since others get good results from courses organized quite differently from mine.

Once beyond the most elementary propositions about language, its cultural nature and social functions, I find the interesting and important problems are beyond the student who knows nothing of linguistic analysis. The student cannot discover for himself what is most exciting about the relationships within the structure of a language and between

539

it and other systems. Therefore, in considering what to include, I have always opted for some analysis. Even in the limited time available, the student can be taken to a fairly high level in some lines if others are set aside. Here, as elsewhere, my choice has always been for rigorous development in a few areas rather than superficial treatment of, say, twice as many. Thus, if phonetics is presented typologically, ignoring the theory and practice of identification and segmentation of phones, the student can satisfactorily be made ready to understand phonemic analysis.

Here we come to the heart of the undergraduate course. Phonemics and morphemics are the only aspects of analysis worth teaching the undergraduate student in any detail. Discourse analysis and immediate constituent techniques are too forbidding, considering the returns, to be allotted time at this level of instruction.

Very similar assumptions and techniques are involved in linguistic analysis at both phonemic and morphemic levels. Thus one can be taught as an extension, with appropriate modifications, of the other. Moreover, phonemic analysis and morphemic analysis are the most original and generally applicable contributions of linguistics to the study of behavior. A thorough knowledge of their principles and techniques is indispensable to work in all other branches of linguistics.

There is another equally cogent reason for teaching analysis as quickly and thoroughly as possible. It appears difficult for students accurately to evaluate techniques of analysis without actually being taught to perform and apply them. No amount of hearing about them at second hand seems to provide students with a basis for independent judgment. Instead, they tend to manifest either wide-eyed acceptance or scornful rejection. Both of these attitudes have had injurious effects on recent studies of human behavior within and outside of anthropology. I assume that we aim to turn out a student who will be able to decide for himself what kind of contribution linguistics will make to his studies of man. It is paradoxical but, I think, sound to argue that his decision will rest on firmer foundations if he has carried out analyses of real languages instead of being told of the benefits of doing so.

In twelve to fourteen weeks (three hours a week), the student can be given a rigorous introduction to the material in Bloch's *A Set of Postulates for Phonemic Analysis* (1948); learn the derived implications for morphemic analysis; and, in addition, do all the phonemic and morphemic problems in Gleason's *Workbook* (1955).

From this point forward, the course can be directed toward any topic in linguistics. My second semester is devoted to language development in the child, dialect geography, internal reconstruction, and comparative linguistices, including the ethnological inferences that can be drawn from historical linguistics. The students are expected to read, in addition to the relevant chapters in Hockett (1958), selections from George A. Miller's *Language and Communication* (1951), Kurath's *Word Geography of the Eastern United States* (1949), Roger Brown's *Words and Things* (1958), John B. Carroll's *The Study of Language* (1953) and selections from the works of Sapir and Bloomfield. They are expected to solve problems in the dialect geography of American English, and the comparative linguistics of Niger-Congo, Romance, Germanic, Algonquian, and Hokan.

As this course description indicates, the aim of the course is to develop understanding of what is most characteristic in the analysis of diverse linguistic structures and of some of their better-known relationships with other cultural phenomena. It does *not* aim to prepare the field anthropologist; after this course, students are still rather poorly prepared to record a previously unfamiliar language.

The foregoing summary of one course in anthropological linguistics is not intended as a recommendation that others should follow suit. The topics to be included in any course depend on offerings in other departments, the preferences of the instructor, and the place of the course in the aims of the department. If the aim were to turn out semiprofessional anthropological field workers, a field course would perhaps be preferable. If the aim is, as at the University of California at Davis, to teach a well-rounded program in anthropology as a contribution to a college education, concentration on the intellectual—as opposed to the rote learning—aspects of the subject seems indicated.

It seems unlikely that small departments can give undergraduates detailed work in linguistics or physical anthropology. Therefore, it is up to graduate departments of anthropology to offer full programs in these fields and to provide at least a modicum of each for all graduate students. The small department should be able to do better in cultural anthropology and, usually, archaeology. Graduate departments might well insist on considerable basic work in the latter two, since the majority of their students will probably teach in small departments for some time to come. Field training on any appreciable scale is feasible in a small department only in archaeology; in other areas, it is best left to the graduate institution.

TEACHING OUTSIDE ONE'S SPECIALTY

The two beginning courses—Introductory Physical Anthropology and Introductory Cultural Anthropology—are general education service courses that every anthropologist in a small department should be able to teach. These courses can contribute to the general education of the undergraduate as much as any course in the curriculum.

A question of interest, not only to the anthropologist, but also to the rest of the faculty and to the administration, is: granted any anthropologist should teach and any anthropology department should offer the introductory courses in physical and cultural anthropology, to what extent should one teach upper-level courses outside his specialty? I think we can eliminate the graduate level at the outset. Graduate courses should be taught by specialists only. If specialists are not available, the institution cannot properly offer graduate work in their subjects. The rub comes at the upper division level of the undergraduate curriculum. If the college is organized so that junior and senior year students concentrate or major in some subject, then it seems clear that without a recognized major, no subject will play the educational role that its teachers usually feel it should have. The rule seems to be: "no major, no students." I need hardly attempt here to catalogue the advantages claimed for anthropology as part of a general education. I believe in those advantages strongly enough to recommend making some sacrifices to the end of securing an established place for the subject in the advanced course offerings of any four-year college. Those sacrifices clearly involve, for a while at least, teaching outside one's field of specialization.

If the first battle is won, and it is decided that there is to be a major in anthropology, another decision has to be made in small departments. This decision concerns breadth versus depth within the major, given limited resources. Is it better to try to cover the principal fields in anthropology or to concentrate on one or two? It is my impression that the first is better for the students and the second is preferred by the faculty. The argument against trying to present a rounded picture of anthropology usually involves the assertion that one's teaching is better in his specialty than outside it. I am not completey persuaded on this point, except where the faculty member teaches outside his specialty unwillingly. If he is uninterested in teaching the course outside his specialty, his teaching is likely to be substandard. Within broad limits, good teaching is fostered by encouraging the faculty member to teach what he wants to teach. This should present no difficulties in a small department if close attention is paid to this point in the hiring process. It does not seem too much to ask that each of us work up a course or two outside our specialties. It is a central assumption of my argument that most of the specialized branches of anthropology have still not gone so far that, with interest and applicaton, the nonspecialist cannot teach them.

The breadth-depth problem is acutely presented by Ethel Albert who writes (in an editorial letter), "do you [as a specialist in linguistics] think a nonlinguist could or should teach the introductory linguistics course you outline?" My answer is: not unless he thinks he can. Obviously, it will depend on his training and interest. But motivation is even more crucial, for the amount of time that will be required is considerable. Nonetheless, it should be quite possible as a temporary arrangement, for there is nothing occult about linguistics (or any other branch of anthropology) except insofar as nonspecialists decline to know it. I call the arrangement temporary, since, unless his research interests take a permanent turn, the nonspecialist may grudge the time needed to continue keeping up with the literature. On the other hand, he will come away a more resourceful anthropologist, whose teaching, even in his own specialty, should be enriched. This transfer should be effective among all the branches of anthropology, though the advantages have to be weighed against the time lost from one's own specialty. However, the self-imposed necessity to organize a field for teaching should result in permanent changes, internal to the anthropologist, valuable enough to compensate for the losses.

Isolation from fellow specialists, inadequate library facilities and time spent on other courses may place the small-department scholar somewhat out of touch with his special field. Cutting these losses is a formidable task. The scholar in a liberal arts college where research is not a primary criterion of retention and promotion is not under quite the pressure that faces the member of a small or combined department in an institution where the research aspirations are high. Reduced teaching loads and outside grants help, though they are often most difficult to obtain precisely where most needed.

THE HIRING PROCESS

The two most important contributions the senior staff member ordinarily makes to the educational institution are building a good library and recruiting an excellent faculty. Both activities have direct and indirect effects far beyond the tenure of the senior faculty member. The qualities desired in a new department member depend on the department's aspirations, its function in the college or other unit, the strengths and weaknesses of related departments on the campus and the specialities of its present members. Thus the desired qualities cannot be laid down *ex cathedra*. However, it seems wise to try to recruit new faculty so as to give respite to department members who have been teaching outside their own fields. By the same token, it would seem unwise to hire a man in expectation that he would have to face a prolonged period of teaching outside his specialty. That activity, like garlic, is superb in moderation but offensive in excess.

Chandler Rowe has argued that the large university departments preparing the majority of graduate students too often do not turn out general anthropologists and that small-department teaching tends to complete their education. I agree with this, as with much else in his stimulating article, "Anthropology in the Liberal Arts College" (1960). All too often, the departments tend to be departments of cultural anthropology, whose students tend to perpetuate the same pattern in the smaller departments to which they go out to teach.

I think I have indicated my own biases—for a program in general anthropology, for not anticipating graduate work, for urging but not requiring teaching outside one's specialty, for hiring with these aims in view. Others may not agree, and perhaps it is just as well: why argue for a uniform organization of the small department when there is no evidence that one type is better than another? If a man is worth hiring, he should be worth consulting. There is no a priori reason why, even in the same department, one man should not spread his efforts while another concentrates his, so long as each is pulling his share of the load assigned by the institution.

In conclusion, I like to think that teaching outside one's specialty makes it easier to keep the whole of anthropology in view. Certainly, it is increasingly difficult to keep up with research in all of the subdivisions of the field; perhaps in the teaching demands of the small department there is a mild antidote to the fever of specialization.

REFERENCES CITED

BLOCH, BERNARD
    1948   A set of postulates for phonemic analysis. Language 24.1:3-46.
BROWN, ROGER
    1958   Words and things. Glencoe, Free Press.
CARROLL, JOHN B.
    1953   The study of language. Cambridge, Harvard.
GLEASON, H. A., JR.
    1955   A workbook in descriptive linguistics. New York, Henry Holt.
HOCKETT, CHARLES F.
    1958   A course in modern linguistics. New York, Macmillan.
KURATH, HANS
    1949   A word geography of the Eastern United States. Ann Arbor, Michigan.
MILLER, GEORGE A.
    1951   Language and communication. New York, McGraw-Hill.
ROWE, CHANDLER
    1960   Anthropology in the liberal arts college. In Teaching Anthropology, A. H. Whiteford, ed. Logan Museum Publications in Anthropology Bulletin 8, Beloit, Wisconsin.

CHARLES WAGLEY

Field Research
and Anthropological
Teaching

ANTHROPOLOGY is a relatively recent newcomer on most American campuses. Both the subject matter and the people who teach it are somewhat "off-beat" in terms of our traditional university curriculum and academic personnel. The subject matter ranges widely, trespassing upon the domains of other sciences and dealing with customs and behavior strange to our tradition. The teacher of anthropology often comes to his campus fresh from a year or two in Africa, India, the South Seas, or Brazil. He is often absent from the campus, not reading in a European library, but living at some strange address not easy to reach even by airmail. He talks of a favorite tribe or village with a strange name rather than of the more familiar names and places of our own cultural tradition. He may have invested years in acquiring the knowledge of some strange language, and he may know more about the history of his special area of interest than that of Europe. He is apt, at first, to be taken as a "strange bird" by his colleagues and students, although anthropologists are being accepted increasingly as members of the academic fraternity. Some have even become deans and provosts.

FIELD RESEARCH FOR THE TEACHER

Anthropologists are by tradition oriented toward field research. With few exceptions they find their data in the field, as did the naturalists of the nineteenth century such as Darwin, Bates, and Von Humboldt. Until recently, anthropologists seldom talked about teaching. It was something done in between field trips. Yet there are characteristically "mis-

545

sionaries," anxious to transmit to their students the subject matter
which they themselves discovered only by chance. Thus, they often
make excellent teachers. In America, Linton, Kroeber, Kluckhohn,
Redfield, Sapir, Lowie, Boas, Benedict, and others who are still with
us, thought of themelves far less as teachers than as researchers, proud
of the pioneer fieldwork data and theories they had published.

Yet some of the most inspired and inspiring teachers on American
campuses have been anthropologists. The recent Ph.D. in anthropology comes into teaching looking for converts. But, to maintain that level
of enthusiasm for his subject matter, he must continue to participate
in the on-going research in his field, be it Central American archaeology, primate behavior, or African ethnology. Some anthropologists
have come to study American small towns, immigrant groups, the
growth patterns of children, and regional archaeology. These anthropologists have their laboratories near at hand. Increasingly, however,
anthropologists have specialized in Melanesia, Africa, India, Latin
America, and other regions distant from the campus where they teach.
They cannot collect research data at home during the academic year.
Unlike the laboratory scientist who can set up his apparatus next door
to his office, the anthropologist needs to be frequently absent from the
campus to further his research and to keep abreast of the developments
in his own field of interest. He cannot wait six years for his sabbatical
leave; not even three years for a semester off. The creative and active
anthropologist needs a leave of absence more often than his more tra-
ditionalist colleagues.

This does not mean that a college or university with a developing
department of anthropology must finance expensive expeditions. Today, there are many sources of funds for field research, such as the Fulbright program, the National Science Foundation, the National Institutes of Mental Health, and others. Colleges and universities must come
to realize, however, that if they wish to have an active, productive, and
enthusiastic staff, rather frequent "leaves without pay" must be authorized for anthropologists. An institution with an anthropology department of three or four staff members might consider adding yet
another anthropologist. This would not mean an increase in annual
budget, since it is to be expected that one of the anthropologists in such
a department would be on leave without pay during any one academic
year. This would seem preferable to the frantic search for a visiting lecturer which department heads are compelled to undertake regularly.

In addition, it must be remembered that anthropological research
does not end in the field. Anthropologists return from their field trips
with masses of raw data: field notes, potsherds, measurements, and the
like. As most of us are aware, the analysis and writing up of this ma-

terial is generally more time-consuming than the collection of the data itself. This is a fact often ignored by the foundations that support field research and by the universities where we teach. Every anthropologist knows of some body of important field data lying unpublished in a colleague's files. Often, this is due to the heavy teaching load imposed upon the scientist. Thus, even though anthropologists may seek rather frequent leaves of absence for field work, they cannot be loaded with summer-school teaching or heavy teaching obligations during the regular school year. Like historians, chemists, psychologists, and other research-oriented scholars, anthropologists want time for research and writing during the academic year, and should have it if they are to remain intellectually alive.

FIELD RESEARCH FOR STUDENTS

Just as field research is important to the intellectual life of the anthropologist, so it should also form an important part of his teaching methods. Laboratory experience is mandatory in most science courses; even in the humanities and in some of the social sciences, students are expected to learn how to deal with the raw data of the discipline either by working with primary sources in the library or through the medium of field studies. Laboratory experience—participation in the process by which new knowledge is gained—should be of even greater importance in anthropology, which has traditionally placed so much emphasis on firsthand field experience. Field research experience is an accepted part of graduate training in anthropology; all graduate departments urge— some even require—students to do field work, but anthropologists, as yet, have not regarded field research as an integral part of the undergraduate teaching of their discipline. In fact, some doubt was even expressed by several anthropologists at a symposium sponsored by the Project on Educational Resources in Anthropology as to the advisability of attempting to offer field-work opportunities to undergraduates, in terms of time, effort, finances, and other practical considerations. Today, I believe that we can transmit the anthropological field experience to undergraduates and that such an experience should be part of the program of any developing anthropology department. Anthropological field research can be a rich experience not only for the student aiming to become a professional anthropologist but also for those who will enter other fields of endeavor.

a. Archaeology, Linguistics, and Physical Anthropology

It is comparatively easy to give some sort of field experience to undergraduates in the subdisciplines of archaeology, physical anthropology, and linguistics. Under the supervision of a trained archaeologist, undergraduates can carry out excavations in local sites almost anywhere in the United States; even in New York, undergraduate and graduate students have in recent years carried out field excavations over the weekends in nearby New Jersey and New York State locations. Summer field courses in archaeology and opportunities for student participation in field excavations are offered by a number of colleges, universities, and museums each year. With our multi-racial and otherwise varied population, no physical anthropologist should have any problem devising a field-research problem for his students near or on his own campus. Likewise, linguistic informants speaking a variety of languages can be found nowadays on practically every American campus. Field research experience in social or cultural anthropology presents inherent difficulties, however, especially if it is to be carried out under ideal conditions among a people who have a culture dramatically different from our own. Even in those fortunate locales such as New Mexico and Arizona, where Indian communities are within easy reach, "installing students in native communities and putting them to work with informants can be a ticklish business" (Casagrande 1961).

b. Ethnology and Social Anthropology

As Joseph Casagrande suggests in the paper cited above, some aspects of ethnographic field methods can be simulated in the classroom or carried out on the campus or in nearby communities. Ethnographic films can be used to train the student in anthropological modes of observation.

One may also bring informants into the classroom, whether these be native peoples residing nearby, foreign students, or merely classmates. In these anthropological dialogues the student may learn by attending to the way in which information is elicited from the informant by an experienced anthropologist, and by himself putting precept into practice. Finally, one can assign students the task of doing field-like investigations on the campus, in the community, or in their home towns during recesses. While each of these devices approaches the field situation . . . all fall short of the ideal of total immersion in the life of another people with all of the intellectual and emotional challenges that trying to live and learn among them present. In the last analysis there is no substitute for the field. (Casagrande, *op. cit.*)

To date, most field-training opportunities in social and cultural anthropology have been limited to graduate students. For many years, the Laboratory of Anthropology at Santa Fe, New Mexico, offered summer field experience to graduate students under the supervision of highly competent, professional anthropologists. For many years, beginning in the early 1930's, Burt and Ethel Aginsky conducted a Science Field Laboratory among the Pomo Indians—mainly, it seems, for graduate students (Henderson and Aginsky 1941). Graduate students have had supervised field experience in a number of team projects such as the Ramah Navajo project of Harvard University, Cornell's field stations in Peru, Thailand, and India, the Puerto Rican project carried out by Columbia University under the supervision of Julian Steward, and others too numerous to mention. The anthropological field experience has been offered to professionals in other fields as part of their training for overseas assignments (see Bunker and Adair 1959).

To date, however, few undergraduates have had the opportunity to participate in anthropological field research. There are isolated cases of anthropologists who have enlisted the assistance of their best undergraduate students on ethnographic field trips. For four years, the Social Science Research Council offered summer fellowships to college juniors to do social science research under the supervision of an experienced research worker. According to Joseph Casagrande, who administered this program, only seventeen of these awards were made in anthropology. The discontinuation of this program does not reflect dissatisfaction with its results, but rather simply lack of funds; in fact, according to Casagrande, many of the faculty supervisors felt that "the undergraduate was perfectly capable of performing at an almost professional level given the right kind of scope and stimulation" (*op. cit.*). With the rapid expansion of anthropology in the college curriculum and the increased number of undergraduate majors in anthropology, it would seem logical that the field experience which anthropologists value so highly in their professional life should become an integral part of our pedagogic methods.

THE COLUMBIA-CORNELL-HARVARD FIELD STUDIES PROGRAM. An experimental program designed specifically to incorporate field research into the undergraduate teaching of anthropology has recently been established on a cooperative basis by Columbia, Cornell, and Harvard universities. It is hoped that in one form or another this program will become a permanent part of the curriculum in the anthropology departments of these universities and that it may serve as a model for other colleges and universities which are currently developing anthropology departments.

During its first season, the summer of 1960, this program sent eighteen undergraduates in teams of six to three field stations located in Vicos (Peru), San Cristobal de las Casas (Mexico), and Riobamba (Ecuador). The program was then extended for three years by a grant from the Carnegie Corporation. The aims and organizaton of this program are described in the announcement circulated at the three participating universities:

The Summer Field Studies Program is designed to introduce advanced college students to a foreign culture under the guidance of professional anthropologists. Qualified students receive intensive preparation during the spring semester and are then sent to join field teams at special field stations maintained by Columbia, Cornell, and Harvard University in Ecuador, Peru and Mexico, respectively. Each team consists of six students and is accompanied and counselled by an anthropologist familiar with the region. The members of the team take up residence in selected small towns and villages. For approximately three months, they both live among and study the members of these communities, participating as much as possible in the daily round of activities, while at the same time carrying out systematic inquiries about some specific aspect of rural life. Although all student participants are expected to become familiar with the basic concepts and methods of cultural anthropology, they need not be committed to a career in the social sciences. The program proceeds on the assumption that an intensive cross-cultural experience is valuable to students who are preparing for a wide variety of professional careers. It has been found that with proper supervision, interesting and useful research functions may be fulfilled by the students, regardless of their academic specialty.

The fundamental aims of the Program are: (1) to expose American College students to the realities of cultural contrasts; (2) to enrich the students' understanding of international affairs, especially as these relate to the rural segments of under-developed regions; and (3) to encourage an appreciation of the goals and research procedures of cultural anthropology and of the social sciences, in general.

Each university provided staff for the parallel training seminars held during the spring semester for the members of the field teams, as well as staff for the field program. Each student was expected to have a working knowledge of Spanish before beginning field work, but a prior knowledge of the language was not mandatory. Thus, a few students selected for participation took an intensive course in Spanish during the spring term. Although such a program naturally attracted candidates specializing in anthropology, students with a serious interest in Latin American studies, international relations or any of the social sciences were invited to apply. In 1960, twelve of the eighteen participating students were anthropology majors; the others came from such diverse fields as economics, international relations, pre-medicine, and history. The summer field program is offered as a regular course in the summer sessions of the three participating universities. Costs of the summer program, including travel and maintenance, range from $900 to $1200; scholarships providing up to full costs are available. Candidates for this program are limited during this experimental period to regularly enrolled undergraduates of the three participating institutions. In keeping with its inter-university character, each field team is made up of students from all three universities.

Space limitations prevent me from going into the details of field arrangements, individual and group projects undertaken by the students, and the individual reactions of students and teachers during this first season. Both the student participants and the faculty supervisors, however, unanimously agreed on the success of the program. In August, 1960, Joseph Casagrande, then on the staff of the Social Science Research Council, was asked by the inter-university committee administering the program to visit the three field stations and to evaluate the program, so that improvements might be made in future years. Describing this program in the paper cited above, he states:

... to me, the special value of such a field experience for the college student lies in its total educational potential. It is a completely absorbing experience, engaging almost every aspect of the student's intellect and personality. It has a total impact that can rarely if at all be matched by the usual college course; it comes at a time when many students make a choice of career. But whether that choice is anthropology or another intercultural field or not, a summer experience of the kind I have described is a unique and worthwhile educational objective in its own right.

All of us who are concerned with this program realize that it is costly and that the opportunity cannot be offered to many students. A large field team would defeat the very purpose we set for ourselves, namely, to immerse the student in a foreign culture. Such a program is difficult to staff, for it depends on prior knowledge of the field situation by the supervisor, who may feel that the presence of a group of students may be detrimental to his own research. Possibly, no single university would want to maintain such a program; but by interuniversity cooperation the burden can be divided and the talents of a larger number of anthropologists can be made available. In a day when our government is organizing the Peace Corps to send large numbers of young people to work in underdeveloped areas, when the Junior Year abroad is being resuscitated, and when intercultural understanding and foreign experience are being emphasized, it seems clear that anthropology departments should extend their undergraduate teaching into the field. Some form of field training, perhaps similar to the Columbia-Cornell-Harvard Field Studies Program, may be the particular contribution of anthropology to this national need for specialists in many fields who are capable of working effectively in foreign areas.

The point of view has been taken here that the most inspiring and creative teaching is accompanied by research. If student and teacher find themselves involved in a research situation in a foreign culture, then I believe that the anthropological concept of culture will be communicated with maximum clarity. Anthropology is a relatively new academic subject; it should experiment with teaching in new ways and in new locales. We live in an age when cultural differences are face-to-face, conscious realities to large masses of people, and when the concept of culture is pertinent to many fields of endeavor. We must continue to train a solid corps of professional anthropologists while we teach the anthropological facts and the anthropological point of view to a wide university audience. This can only be done in those institutions which recognize the rather unique features of anthropology as an academic profession, and by anthropologists who continue to maintain the rather unique *élan* of their trade.

REFERENCES CITED

BUNKER, R. M., AND JOHN ADAIR
      1959   First look at strangers.
CASAGRANDE, JOSEPH B.
      1961   Undergraduate field training in ethnology. (Unpublished.)
HENDERSON, W. M., AND B. W. AGINSKY
      1941   A social science field laboratory. American Sociological Review 6:
                41-44.

PART XI

PERSPECTIVES
ON
ANTHROPOLOGICAL
TEACHING

Introduction

THE PAPERS of this final section consider the teaching of anthropology in a wider context than that of classroom, curriculum, and college. What contribution, these authors inquire, can the subject make to the thought and life of the students, and through them to the direction of the whole society? Ethel Albert shows that anthropological teaching can scarcely avoid ethical issues. To the degree that anthropological concepts either disturb or reinforce the student's previously held notions about such matters as human differences, alien cultures, the individual and society, to that degree will the study of anthropology affect his outlook and behavior.

For some students, Robert Ehrich notes, anthropology not only provides a background for a new philosophical approach, it also gives them a meaningful and satisfactory way of putting together the bits and pieces of knowledge about man which they have acquired in other courses. There is little disagreement on this point from anthropologists. But some of Ehrich's comments on specific teaching procedures run counter to views expressed by other authors in this volume. Thus Ehrich's recommendation that anthropologists not dissipate their energies unduly in teaching the lethargic majority among college students but concentrate on the few who are, and will be, the intellectual elite, has brought forth debate. In symposium discussions where this issue was raised, some commented that there was no effective way of identifying such an elite among undergraduates; others said that all college students comprised a kind of elite as against the majority of the population who are not college educated; still others held that even if a college elite can be identified and given special attention, there still remains the high importance of transmitting anthropological ideas into the general society and culture. On other matters, Ehrich's view that the introductory course is primarily a vocabulary course, initiating the student into the

concepts for which the professional jargon serves as shorthand, is different from other recommendations on the introductory course which
emphasize that selected concepts should be taught, with professional
terminology given sparingly at this level. Nor do many teachers of introductory anthropology agree, according to Bruner and Spindler's survey, with Ehrich's comment that there are now available enough synthesizing and coordinating publications to relieve the teachers of the need
for fulfilling these functions.

Yet, there is general and strong agreement with Ehrich's recommendations that we should treat the members of our classes as students and
not as pupils; that we should tell them not only what we know, but
also show where we are groping and trying to find new knowledge.
And, importantly, we should encourage them to join in the continuing
quest for new knowledge. A great many anthropologists, certainly in
the United States, proclaim the final proposition presented in Ehrich's
paper, that the training of future anthropologists should not be considered the principal form of teaching activity, and that anthropologists have a vast, necessary, and solid contribution to make to liberal arts
education.

Verne Ray examines the nature of a liberal education and the proper place of anthropology in it. There is no difference, he finds, between
the study of anthropology as part of a liberal education and as preparation for a professional career. A good undergraduate program of studies in anthropology is, in itself, a liberal education. All those who share
the anthropologists' view of the field as being powerfully universalistic,
holistic, time-full and time-free, cannot but agree. But some other statements in Ray's paper were questioned in symposium discussions. One
can readily understand that some teachers take issue with Ray's comment
that the large university is better than the small college for one objective
of liberal education because it offers a greater range and variety of teachers who exemplify, for the students, models of liberally educated men.
Verne Ray's recommendation that undergraduates be given research experience was questioned, not on grounds of desirability, but of feasibility. As for the imperative necessity that the anthropology teacher also
be an active research worker, this too was accepted as a desirable standard
but one not immediately possible in some institutions, particularly in
junior colleges.

Margaret Mead brings together, in a vigorous concluding orchestra-
tion, some of the main themes expressed in other papers. Anthropology,
she relates, is peculiarly fitted to fill a tremendous need in liberal education. It tries to conjoin, rather than fragment, knowledge of man. It
can be taught so as to give understanding of the farthest past of man
and yet with close relation to life today. Mead defines the essence of a

liberal education as learning to share the full identity made possible
by one's civilization. Anthropology's inclusive and integrating approach offers a broad avenue for such learning. The integration is inherent in the anthropologist's experience in field work. The result of this
experience, together with the basic assumptions about man which anthropologists share, is that ". . . when the anthropologist teaches, he
does not preach, he simply embodies the attitudes toward all human
beings which are intrinsic to his work."

The model of field worker, the author says, can easily become the
model for the educated man. Not all teachers of anthropology need be
field workers themselves, but they must have been taught by anthropologists who are, else they cannot communicate the fundamental values
of anthropology. Margaret Mead tells that these values are essential
for wisdom, perhaps for survival. Anthropologists hold them, not as distant ideals, but as of the very essence of the work we do.

                                                        D.G.M.

ETHEL M. ALBERT

*Value Aspects
of Teaching
Anthropology*

ANTHROPOLOGY, like any lively discipline, is constantly in process of redefinition. Teaching provides in effect an operational definition of its scope at any given time. It also influences the kind of research that will be done in the future and hence what will be taught as anthropology in the still further removed future. Viewing in a single perspective the papers assembled in this volume, we cannot fail to note the variations in institutional settings, student interests and abilities, course offerings and other conditions in which the subject is taught. Diversity also marks the philosophies and methods of education which are put forward. And we are made aware anew of the range and complexity of anthropology and of the internal and external relations of its constituent specialties. At the same time, commitment to the conception of anthropology as a unitary science of man is evident in many of the papers. It appears not only where we would expect it, in papers specifically directed to curriculum integration, relations with other subjects and trends in anthropological teaching, but also, and most significantly, in papers on physical anthropology, archaeology, area courses, linguistics, and applied anthropology. Throughout, the striking heterogeneity of the field of anthropology is balanced by a not less striking uniformity of the "anthropological point of view."

THE ANTHROPOLOGICAL POINT OF VIEW

Preoccupied with fine points of difference when we function primarily as theorists, we may overlook what is obvious to us as teachers, the con-

559

trast between any anthropologist's conception of man and the ideas of most beginning students. The magnitude of a contrast is, as we know, relative to the framework of comparison. In the context of teaching anthropology, variations of viewpoint among anthropologists—at least among those within the sphere of influence of western culture—take on the appearance of different interpretations of essentially the same set of concepts. It is, then, not really venturing very far to suggest that there are distinctive core conceptions of man and of methods of studying man that constitute "the" anthropological point of view.

Often referred to but rarely defined, the anthropological point of view cannot be caught, like a fly in amber, once for all time. As anthropology grows and changes, so too does its point of view. Account must be taken of the continuing expansion of the boundaries of anthropology, of the development of its theory, and of responsiveness to changing conditions of teaching and research. A meaningful conception of man and of method cannot be contained within a single fixed statement. Moreover, rigidity of statement is inappropriate because of variations of viewpoint among anthropologists. Generalizations which lend themselves to often widely different interpretations of detail are required to represent faithfully the core concepts and their variations. The anthropological point of view, then, may best be regarded as a developing conceptual framework within which communication can occur among anthropologists of diverse interests, theories and methods—and, hopefully, among students of anthropology in India or Norway or the United States.

Full statement of the anthropological point of view would require analysis of the shared store of data, concepts, methods, and problems represented by the history and literature of anthropology. Others, far more competent for the task, have treated such fundamental concepts as culture and evolution, the importance of field work as a touchstone of research and teaching, the holistic approach, the relations between data and theory. Here, the place of values in the anthropological point of view in teaching has been selected for special attention.

Concern with ethical and other value issues is part of the anthropological tradition. It is evident in many of the papers in this volume, perhaps most explicitly in those on applied anthropology, and was prominent in a number of E.R.A. symposium discussions. We have come to expect diversity, and we are not disappointed. The range of viewpoints about the value involvements of teaching anthropology matches closely the variation in the general literature of the philosophy of social science on the subject of values and the study of man. Attending chiefly to the relatively restricted subject of teaching provides a precious and rare control on value analysis, in the form of data on the actual conditions in which issues and solutions occur. Anthropology provides a method whereby disagreement can be converted into variation. Far from destroying unity, variation enriches and enlivens it. Awareness of the experiential components of value issues provides another safeguard: not the content alone of value judgments but the cultural and historical contexts as well must enter into the analysis.

In what follows, I am indebted for much information about the teaching of anthropology and for many useful ideas to the authors of the papers of this volume and to participants in the E.R.A. symposia. This general acknowledgment is intended to take the place of specific references, which proved impractically cumbersome. The variety of points of view and concepts to be treated are well known in anthropology, e.g. relativism and objectivity. The general procedure will be much the same throughout, viz., listing variations of viewpoint among teachers of anthropology on selected value issues, examining them for the core concepts of which they are variations, and interpreting their significance for the anthropological point of view.

Relativism, as it has developed in anthropology, is a natural bridge between the conceptual and ethical components of theory and teaching. It is used here as the starting point for locating the value involvements of teaching anthropology. An examination of several interpretations of both cultural and ethical relativism and identifications of the relevant core concepts are the concerns of the first section of this paper. To appreciate the potential and actual effects of anthropology courses on students, it is necessary to take into account the diversity of students' values and of their conceptions of human nature and cultural diversity. It is to this variable in teaching that the second section of the paper is devoted. There follows an examination of the value involvements of communicating anthropology as a body of objective knowledge. The paper concludes with a consideration of the significance of the anthropological point of view for relating so-called humanistic values and the value of scientific inquiry in a unified study of man.

RELATIVISM, CULTURAL AND ETHICAL

Presenting anthropological materials to non-anthropologists imposes the necessity not only of selecting data and concepts from an overflowing storehouse but also of deciding how to deal with prevailing popular notions of man and of cultural diversity. The equestrian American Indian in feather bonnet and the African dancing to the savage beat of drums have somehow to be brought down, or up, to the level of mere mortals like ourselves. Combating ethnocentrism or provincialism has been named frequently as one of the main objectives of teaching anthropology, at least of the beginning course.

Relativism is sometimes treated as the whole substance or essence of the anthropological point of view, especially in its corrective aspect. As we know from Herskovits and other writers on the subject, however, usage indulges us the confusing habit of using the word "relativism" to refer to markedly different concepts. In the context of the teaching of anthropology, the first ambiguity that attracts notice may be phrased as a question: do anthropologists intend to correct students' ideas about culture or their attitudes toward cultural diversity or both? The relevant distinction is between relativism as a theory of cultural diversity or variation and ethical relativism as a theory of the nature of values. The relationship between the two types of relativism has long been problematic. It is not at all certain that we can here derive any other benefit from re-examining it than a view of the diverse interpretations in the theory and practice of teaching anthropology.

In its extreme form, relativism directed to correcting bias may be a "reverse ethnocentrism." Western culture is represented as oppressive, vulgar or worse; non-Western cultures, without distinction as to social structure or geography, as exemplars of human excellence and innocence. To be sure, no contributor to this volume has stated this as his position. But we are indebeted to John Bennett for having pointed out that if honesty rather than prudence had prevailed, some of us would have had to report that a negative attitude towards our own culture is our way of trying to neutralize the ethnocentric attitudes of our students. Bending over backwards, we may find it somehow easier to find a "functional" explanation of cannibalism and infanticide than to make excuses for drag-racing and other quaint customs at home. Some touch of xenophilia is probably a prerequisite for field work, or its inconveniences and hazards would not be so easily brushed aside. A warm identification with the adoptive culture of one's field work may vivify discussion and lectures. If it takes the form of a new culture-bound distortion, our xenophilia is as incompatible with good anthropology and good teaching as the ethnocentrism that is to be rooted out of student thinking.

In the use of anthropology for training foreign service officers, public health workers, and teachers (see Section IX), as well as in liberal arts general education, the correction of ethnocentric bias is probably a distinctive and indispensable contribution of anthropology. Regarded as an objective of teaching, opposition to ethnocentrism should not and neet not be a potentially vicious relativism that destroys for teachers and students alike the sense of the value of one's own culture, or a paralysis of evaluation that results from confusing value judgments with bigotry. There are indications in this volume and in the anthropological literature more generally that relativism is used increasingly to designate an attitude of respect towards all cultures, one's own and others', today's and those of the past. "Tolerance," "sympathetic curiosity," "liberal values" are among the near-synonyms employed to identify a balanced view that excludes both strong ethnocentrism and strong xenophilia and to suggest the sense of each individual's participation in the whole panorama of human existence. In this interpretation, relativism has been found useful for showing students their place in the pattern of their own culture (cf. the paper of Solon Kimball), or the place of Western culture as one among many (cf. the paper of Cora Du Bois).

A positive attitude toward cultural diversity and freedom from ethnocentric bias are sometimes presented as primarily a humanistic ethic. They are also easily attached to the teaching of scientific objectivity as part of anthropological method. The suggestion is made in several papers that the inductive approach and the sense of order characteristic of anthropological method can be directed to promoting an equable view of cultural differences. The argument runs that any scientific course can implant in a general way the ideal of objectivity, but anthropology can drive home the additional lesson of an unprejudiced view of cultural differences, i.e., of both cultural and ethical relativism.

While the explicit ethical objective of correcting student bias seems appropriate to many teachers, others, perhaps not less relativisitc in their thinking, prefer an ethically neutral presentation of subject matter. Descriptive data, whether flattering or "offensive to western morals," are presented without explicit reference to values, or full descriptive and theoretic materials on controversial or politically sensitive topics are presented without more ado than neutral materials. "Value-free" teaching, however, by no means necessarily leaves student attitudes unaffected, nor is it necessarily value-free in every sense. The absence of explicit statements opposing ethnocentric attitudes is by no means the same as the absence of the objective of changing attitudes. Objectively presented concepts and data can, though they need not invariably, bring about modifications in student values through changing their store of information. We shall revert to this below. Here, it is sufficient to note that relativism is given diverse interpretations by different teachers of anthropology.

Cultural relativism—or, if we adopt the late Clyde Kluckhohn's suggestion for reducing verbal confusion, cultural relativity—we take to be a theory of the relativity of custom to culture and more generally of the interrelatedness of phenomena in patterns or systems. Differences of viewpoint as to correct statement and interpretation of cultural relativity do not concern us here. Rather, unlike ethical relativism, cultural relativity in some form appears to be integral to what is taught as anthropology. We are then led to ask why there should be general agreement about the importance of the culture concept and of cultural relativity in anthropology teaching, whereas there is rather clearly marked difference of opinion as to ethical objectives and ethical relativism. Questions as to the possible ethical involvements of teaching anthropology are not unlike those of teaching other subjects in the college curriculum, and they fall generally into the vexatious category of the problem of the relation of facts to values.

As an indisputable fact, cultural variation has the same double-edged quality as any other fact: it is suitable for the purest of research and at the same time conformable with a wide variety of philosophical and ethical predilections. Neither in practice nor in logic does cultural variation—or any other fact—uniquely imply ethical relativism or tolerance—or any other value; and neither in practice nor in logic does the fact of cultural variation—or any other fact—dictate a theory of patterned variation—or any other theory. A system of ideas consists of an assembly of premises—concerned with facts, theories, values, definitions, rules, and methods—that, because they are the foundation of the system, are by definition not subject to proof within the system. What distinguishes one system from another is the particular selection of unproved and unprovable postulates. Thus, if we view them impartially, factual judgments will be seen to behave sometimes like women of easy virtue; they will take up with any theory, scientific or ethical, that comes along, not joining them in the holy wedlock of necessary logical connections but in the easy camaraderie of mere non-contradiction. Facts show their mettle when we want to refute a theory—we can almost always disprove a hypothesis. They cannot be relied upon to supply incontrovertible positive proof, either of scientific theory or of value theory.

The fact of cultural variation has been combined with a variety of premises, factual, theoretical, and valuational, to produce nearly the whole gamut of political-social-ethical theories of the Western tradition. Interpretations accepting diversity as right and good are as old as the relativistic slogan of the much-maligned Sophists, Man is the measure of all things. Restrictive interpretations are as old as the absolutism of Plato's totalitarian republic. If we add to the fact of variation the value of tolerance, we come out with the conclusion that variation should be accepted as good. If we add to the fact of variation the premise that only one way is good, others bad or inferior, we come out with some restrictive or absolutist ethics.

Separate premises are needed to translate value theory into practical policy. According to the liberal interpretation of cultural variation and of the desirability of respecting cultural integrity, all men are equal and should enjoy equally the rights of man. A different syllogism has been composed in the Union of South Africa: if each culture is a unique entity, if its integrity should be respected, then to protect African culture from further violations of its integrity, it should be kept totally apart from western culture. There is, of course, more to the question than this, but the cute alteration of the meaning of cultural variation and tolerance for diversity is a good reminder of the complexity of the relations of facts and values.

We may now draw some tentative conclusions about the significance of relativism as part of the anthropological point of view in teaching and in theory. Students are offered a great deal more than the obvious fact of variation and the almost equally obvious fact of culture as structured or patterned. They are presented with a complex set of premises that are fully compatible with but not logically implied by the facts of cultural variation. Moreover, the full import of these premises is appreciated only when it is realized that they are revisions and corrections of theories of an earlier day, gone now from anthropology but still current in political and popular thinking. Cultural relativity, then, draws some of its meaning from opposition to ideas of fundamental biological differences among different-appearing peoples and to the interpretation of cultural differences as determined by supposed biological differences. For present-day students of anthropology, variation is to be interpreted within the framework of the evolution of man as a single biological species; cultural variation and biological variation are to be regarded as independent, interacting variables.

The relativistic interpretation of the "integrity" of culture as ordered cultural variation involves the concept of pattern, or structure, or system, or concomitant variations—that is, variation is viewed as systematic. The appropriate manner of viewing diverse cultural patterns or systems can be given "neutral" statement as a research directive: all men and all cultures are equally necessary and appropriate objects of inquiry, and all are to be viewed objectively. The comparison of cultures is then not invidious comparison, and differences among cultures are not ranked as higher and lower, nor different cultures as better and worse. Cultural differences, rather, are viewed as descriptively significant and as systematically related or relatable, and this is all the meaning they need have in anthropology.

In some twenty-five centuries of use, the concept of relativism has had more than ample opportunity to acquire a great variety of meanings, some overlapping and some directly opposite in sense. As a consequence, many of us are uncertain, when we use the word, to which concept or concepts we are actually referring. Semantic reform is at best a feeble remedy. Yet, we may spare ourselves and our students much fruitless verbal dispute if we take into account that a word that means almost anything means almost nothing. We might do worse than to resort to the simple semantic strategy of replacing the word relativism by a phrase that identifies the particular variant we mean—ethical relativism, or humanistic tolerance for diversity, or scientific objectivity or cultural varation, or the relativity of individual cultural items to the pattern of culture, or, to cite Herskovits' distinctions, methodological or philosophical or practical relativism.

STUDENTS' INFORMATION AND VALUES

Both theoretical and ethical issues of teaching anthropology depend for completeness of statement upon information about students. We start with the disadvantage that there are no systematic data on the effects on students of the different modes of anthropological teaching. However, in the teaching experiences described in papers and symposia, there is sufficient variation to justify some hypotheses.We may assume at the outset that in anthropology as in any other discipline, students as a group do not necessarily learn precisely what their teachers teach. This is likely to be the case whether data and concepts or values and attitudes are presented to them. Further, the effects of teaching anthropology, with or without explicit ethical orientations, probably depend heavily upon the values, information, and professional and other objectives which students bring with them into the classroom. These in turn are affected by their cultural affiliation, regional and national.

It is not clear to what extent experience with different types of students accounts for differences of opinion as to the objectives and methods of teaching which appear in this volume. There seems no reason to assume that the intellectual and moral benefits of anthropology are automatically conferred by the simple act of teaching it, irrespective of where and to whom it is taught. There is reason to doubt that education, by improving the intellect, improves the moral character, though this is to question one of the oldest and most honored educational theories of our culture. Some results of sociological research on the effectiveness of movies and other devices directed to changing ethnocentric attitudes may apply here: materials presented tend generally to confirm pre-existing views of most persons, and to change the views of a few, some in the direction intended, but others in quite the reverse way.

It may be true, as a number of anthropologists have suggested, that one can teach the same course to undergraduates in a junior college, a four-year liberal arts institution, students preparing to teach or to enter some other profession, those interested in applied anthropology, and so on. It may even be that substantially the same material and concepts are appropriate for those contemplating a career as a missionary or as a technician in a so-called underdeveloped area. We would hesitate a long moment, however, before going on to say that the "same" course can be given in Cape Town or Dakar or Delhi, in New York, in the Deep South, and in California. To put it another way, if the same course were offered, it would almost surely not have the same effects in all the places named. This is in effect to say that variability in the cultural and personality characteristics of students may require a diversification of pedagogical strategies to communicate the same core concepts of anthropology, and it may also impose limitations on the possibility of changing student attitudes.

Again, lacking the necessary data, we cannot even guess at the overall statistical distribution or specific contents of changes in student attitudes at the end of a first course in anthropology. It may be, as William Laughlin suggested at the Burg Wartenstein symposium, that tolerance for other cultures that becomes visible after students have taken an anthropology course is a crystallization of a predisposition in that direction, not a creation of the course itself. In the same discussion, Raymond Firth pointed out that information furnished in a course in anthropology can be used for purposes quite different from those of the teacher: the more one knows about a society, the more good perhaps can be done, but also the more harm can be done. Monica Wilson, drawing on her knowledge of Cape Town, suggested that where there is a deep cleavage of ideals, teaching the language of local peoples would be much better than teaching a distorted anthropology course. Vinigi Grottanelli, who teaches anthropology in two different types of university in Rome, reported marked differences in reactions to substantially the same anthropological materials from students specializing in the humanities and from those in the sciences, as well as from liberal arts students generally and from those preparing for missionary duty. The latter are notably less receptive to the idea of tolerance for cultural differences.

Ethnocentrism may be, as Herskovits has said, a universal attitude that cannot be rooted out. It is not, in any case, an evil in itself but rather in its consequences when it is used to justify harsh and repressive social and political measures and in its undesirable intellectual character when it is based on mistaken ideas of man and culture. Physical anthropology, perhaps more than any other branch of contemporary anthropology, is involved in the social-ethical aspects of racist belief, since racist ethnocentrism claims support from a now outmoded interpretation of the cultural and biological significance of visible physical variations of man. It is then all the more interesting that teachers of physical

anthropology, as well as of race relations, where the data and theory of
physical anthropolgy obviously take a prominent place, should be approaching consensus that the most effective teaching, for both scientific
and social-moral purposes, is concentration on the data and theories of
modern physical anthropology. The force of the new information rather
than explicit social-political pronouncements is considered effective in
modifying attitudes.

In elaboration of the view that attitudes can be changed by teaching
theory and data only, Ray Birdwhistell has recommended that where
race is a source of tension, it is best to avoid explicit value judgments
and to present instead straightforward data on population composition, food sources, economic competition, and so on. He was of the
opinion also that emphasizing explicitly the social-ethical issues is not
much more desirable in places where liberal views are held, for this
tends to increase polemical involvement at the cost of communicating
theoretical and factual aspects of anthropology. An increasing number
of teachers are accepting the suggestion made some years ago by Sherwood Washburn, to abandon the practice of refuting racism by demonstrating that caucasoids are more ape-like than other human groups.
William Laughlin has argued that ethnocentric attitudes can be effectively changed in courses in physical or social anthropology or race
relations when, without explicit attacks on racism, there is a detailed
presentation of morphological, genetic, and historical description, together with analyses of the relationships among race, language, and
culture that reveal these as independent variables.

We may conclude that although descriptive data as such are mute,
they can change the meaning of what students already know and challenge existing ideas, thereby helping to create a new outlook. The notion that even cannibals and headhunters marry and mourn their dead
and revere their gods is in fact new to students who have previously
heard only of the unusual or quaint features of other cultures. So, too,
is the realization of the implications of the fact that all peoples have
language, technology, religion, a kinship system, and regard their own
culture as right and natural. Awareness that culture, in all its immense
complexity, is man-made may take the sting out of invidious comparisons, by calling attention to the fact that culture is a human invention, not a free gift or spontaneous biological growth.

It is not only the general student who stands in need of supplements
to his information about man and culture. As Gabriel Lasker pointed
out in the above-mentioned symposium, biologically oriented physical anthropologists must be taught enough about race relations to
awaken in them an awareness of the social implications of their scientific
work. In all this, the principle is the same: student attitudes and values

may be effectively altered without explicit treatment of social or ethical issues, but rather by direct presentation of relevant theory and data. Conversely, realization of the social consequences of advances in knowledge is part of an education in anthropology.

Ethnocentrism and provincialism present somewhat different pedagogical problems, and each is subject to variation. Liberal humanistic views are part of the historic American tradition, so that we may not be prepared for some of the effects of anthropological data on some of our students. The idea of fair play, the awareness that no human beings are perfect, or a religious commitment to the brotherhood of man may exist as contentless principles, or be interpreted to mean that it it not nice to speak ill of anyone. Unflattering details about any culture, western or noble savage, may be rejected as incompatible with such principles. Or it may come as an agreeable surprise to students to discover that American Indians and Africans have elaborate systems of kinship, religion, and other institutions, but culture shock may attend the discovery of America as a culture rather than as a dream. For a surprising number of overprotected young people, American culture seems to be understood as some sort of sinless Garden of Eden, governed by a principle of life adjustment which is consecrated equally by the Constitution and the New Testament. It is not opposition to ethnocentrism that is in order here, but rather the application of the anthropological point of view to the reduction of both "idealistic" naïvete and provincialism. Here again, as in teaching about race, data and concepts of anthropology can much affect attitudes even though no explicit teaching of attitudes is engaged in.

Keeping in mind the variability of students, when we wish to estimate the possible influence of anthropology, we must take into account the occasional student who seems specifically unteachable in anthropology, as some reportedly are in mathematics or foreign languages; a few who seem unteachable in any serious subject; and, at the other end of the scale, those who are brilliant students of chemistry or logic but regard anthropology as no better or worse than other subjects that are acceptable for fulfilling broad liberal arts requirements. We may attempt in vain also to make any impression on an easy-going tolerance for cultural differences that is not distinguishable from the indifference of a deep-lying provincialism.

The data of anthropology can have a seductive, anecdotal quality. It may create or maintain in some students a fascination with the exotic for its own sake and a sense of the dullness of one's own culture by contrast. Perhaps the best sort of "reverse ethnocentrism," it is awkward to deal with in students, because it is so much a part of the appreciation of diversity which motivates professional anthropologists to seek

it out and to document it with such loving care. Strictly, we should be
at a sufficiently great distance to see that what is picturesque or exotic
to us is only humdrum routine to the peoples we study. But we do not
mean to take the fun out of anthropology. It is probably from among
the students who find cultural differences exciting and challenging
that new anthropologists are recruited.

Given the variability of students' information and values—and of
their social, economic, ethnic, and other cultural characteristics—we
must expect diversity in the results of teaching anthropology. We cannot predict accurately if we accept the essentially prescientific notion,
in teaching or in any other serious enterprise, that "like causes like."
Changes in student values may follow upon the learning of the most
strictly objective body of facts; a well-worked out attitude towards
cultural diversity may be presented together with the data and concepts, yet leave students unmoved from an initial ethnocentric position. Affectionate regard for our adoptive field-work culture, or an attitude of respect for all cultures, or objective anthropological data and
concepts will look very different, according to the point of view of the
observers, the students. Flexibility, generally accepted as an appropriate
principle for course design and for other aspects of the teaching of anthropology, appears also to be relevant to the determination of ethical objectives—that is, the decision as to whether or not they are to be
explicit; the specific form they will be given, relative to the specific
teaching situation. My personal preference is to start my courses with an
objective, ethically-neutral analysis of cultural values and beliefs, but
to be prepared for symptoms of ethical disturbance, and to orient discussion of ethical consequences to the specific syndromes that develop.
The decision to take account of ethical factors in teaching anthropological subject-matter is in no small part the outcome of the considerations
that follow.

OBJECTIVITY AND VALUES

From both sides of the teacher-student relationship, we have strong
indications that ethical interpretations are logically independent from
and more variable than the objective content of anthropology. To replace this essentially negative conclusion by a positive statement of the
ethical involvements of anthropology, it is hardly necessary to protest,
is difficult. The interrelations of the conceptual, social and ethical factors
in teaching and in theory are unclear. This is the case not only in anthropology but also in the wider philosophic and academic sphere.

At least three channels of investigation invite exploration of the
anthropological problems of relating objective knowledge to values.
First, like every other specialization at the time of its separation from

the undifferentiated body of tradition, anthropology has inherited ethical preoccupations as internal to its theoretical development. Second, in contemporary discussion of the relations between facts and values, or science, ethics, and humanism, the issues involved in estimating the effects of objective information upon values and attitudes are obscure. As we have already noted, the relevant data are materially incomplete; and, what is perhaps more to the point, discussions of facts and values are often conducted as though there were no relevant data. It is perhaps for this very reason that there is so much confusion and disagreement. Third, in different frames of reference, the interrelations between information and values take on different characteristics. Thus, if we consider the conceptual content of the anthropological point of view, it is, like any objective construct, ethically neutral. By contrast, if we look at it in its cultural-historical context, it has, like any new truth, great potential and actual social-ethical consequences.

Anthropology, like every other scientific specialization, is involved in ethical issues not only because they are part of its heritage but also because its objective content either contradicts or otherwise alters prevailing ideas about man which are used to justify certain social and political practices. Because scientific facts are rarely if ever value-free in their social-cultural consequences, a preference for objectivity is, in social-ethical terms, a value choice. Accepting objectivity is a value commitment. Accepting the anthropological conception of man and culture has ethical consequences, at least in part because value judgments depend upon facts and because in western culture "right" belief and method—or "orthodoxy" or "truth"—have moral significance and political implications. Each of these sources of ethical and value involvement of anthropology has direct and indirect effects on teaching, and each will now be examined in greater detail.

All the branches of contemporary anthropology have in common the task of separately and jointly correcting earlier theory. The task is shaped by the fact that anthropological unity, two short generations ago, was maintained by an assumed intercorrelation of racial, linguistic, social, and cultural variables. At the same time, resolutions of social and ethical issues and recommendations of policy were, and in some quarters still are, regarded as an integral part of anthropological theory. In the past as in the present, agreement about anthropological data and their theoretical interpretation did not carry with it agreement about ethics. The contrast between Hobhouse and Westermarck is a case in point, and both these writers and their successors have a place not only in the history of anthropology but also in the history of ethics and moral philosophy. When contemporary anthropologists, as theorists and as teachers, take up the issues presented in early theory, they are con-

fronted with a mixture of purely technical and clearly ethical or philosophical elements.

The ethical theories and policy preferences of the early evolution-
ists were in general benevolent and humane, and not at all like the repressive ideas now associated with race theory. This circumstance
makes it more rather than less difficult to disengage the ethical from
the conceptual components of anthropological theory. Rejecting the
theory that there is a correlation between race and language is primarily a theoretical matter, but there is also social-political and ethical involvement. For, to reject a biological-racial theory of culture is to ex-
plode the supposed factual foundation of certain types of repressive
social policy. Such political-social-ethical refutation may not be the
immediate objective of scientific inquiry, but it is a definite entry of
the theoretical into the ethical and social realms precisely because there
is a political or ethical interest in the facts.

It takes more perception than most students have to distinguish
between the correction of technical theoretical errors and the choice
of a particular policy or ethics, or to discern the difference between
the polemical method characteristic of discussions of ethics and policies from the scientific dialectic of correction by appeal to data and
logic. Further, the more influence any work has had in reshaping theory, the more its polemical passages are out of date and a disturbing
influence in the straightforward presentation of the new theory and
data it helped to discover. Whether one is of the opinion that the classroom is the place only for refuting theoretical errors or also for explicit
opposition to ethnocentric or other ethical attitudes, the ethical and
policy issues are bound to present themselves, since they are an integral
and sometimes extensive part of the contents of many works which must
be included on any reading list of theory. Dell Hymes' paper contains
some illuminating observations on the consequences of using historically important materials for the teaching of anthropological linguistics.

It is possible to make a virtue of the necessity of using anthropological classics in which a mixture of theoretical advance and ethical polemic plays an important part. The history of change in anthropological theories presents a number of valuable lessons in method. Wariness
of the merely obvious, by whatever means communicated, is well worth
teaching. Students can be taught to be careful how they interpret what
they see, by being shown that literally superficial characteristics such as
skin color or bodily size are not usually systematically or causally related to other visible differences, e.g., in customs or language. A grasp
of the process whereby exploded associations are replaced by new and
more reliable ones can help students to understand the methodological
rule that data are no better than the method and theory that employ

them, and it can also provide appreciation of the difficulty and tentativeness of the scientific procedures needed to establish hypotheses and achieve objectivity.

Generally, the scientific progress of a discipline is measured by the extent to which policy concerns are removed from the center of inquiry and attention concentrated on verifiable, ethically neutral concepts. When we are all in agreement about the merits of objectivity, we may overlook the fact that it is a value choice. "Truth" is a value so obvious that we look right through it. "Scientific truth" as the objective of the methods of logic and observation is also a value choice. When we take into account the diverse ideas of the nature of truth and of ways of reaching it contained in the religious, political, and other belief-systems which determine the commitments of students, we must reckon with the potentialities for affecting social and ethical attitudes of the apparently value-innocent offer of an objective subject matter.

There is abundant lyrical nonsense about the absolute freedom of science from any value involvement whatever—as though this were somehow to its credit. Notions of this kind are the result of examining the content but ignoring the context of scientific statements. The assumption that facts and values are mutually incompatible is accepted with alarming ease by college students. It is perhaps a convenient way to avoid the tangled ethical issues of our time, but it places sicence in the false position of a superorthodoxy. To be sure, an objective statement is not in itself a value judgment. However, inquiry has no direction, unless scientifically obtained truth is assumed to be the goal. Without a commitment to the value of objective truth, there would be no reason to choose the more rather than the less probable hypotheses, no reason to prefer verified theories to intuition or authority or mystical revelation.

There is a tendency to lump together all sorts of values—ethical, social, political, and intellectual. Presumably, what is usually intended when it is said that science is value-free is that commitment to the value of objective truth implies a commitment to refrain from manipulating data to protect against refutation some pre-selected political or ethical position or a factual hypothesis. A distinction between intellectual and social, political and ethical values is as necessary as a distinction between internal scientific context and external social context for locating the value involvements of anthropology, or of any science.

Precisely because objectivity excludes service to a chosen social policy or ethic, the neutrality of scientific truths with respect to social and ethical issues is problematic. As we know, the results of science and sometimes its pursuit as well can be directed to virtually any social goal, without restriction of moral qualities. There is not yet any known

formula for limiting the uses of the results of objective inquiry to benevolent purposes, either in the general public or, as we have seen above,
in those who learn some anthropology. Because there is so much variation in society, in policies and in ethics, we must expect that a single
body of ideas will meet with very different receptions. If anthropology
teaches us anything, it is the indispensability of social-cultural context and variation in determining what any phenomenon—including
science generally and anthropology in particular—really and fully "is"
and how it functions.

Placing strictly objective goals in the center of anthropological theory
and teaching does not remove but rather relocates involvement with
social and ethical issues. The present position of anthropology, as of
other studies of man, bears an interesting resemblance to the position
occupied earlier by the physical sciences and, more recently, by biology.
A glance at the struggles of those sciences whose novelty has by now
worn off may shed some light on the present situation of anthropology
as a new science. It is a tautological truth that any idea that is really
new is at variance with established, accepted ideas. We are far from understanding the general process by which cultural innovation occurs,
and reliable knowledge about the ways new facts influence values and
other aspects of culture must await further study. Cora Du Bois' suggestion that science be studied as a cultural phenomenon rather than
as a (typically Western) supra-orthodoxy is surely timely, if we are
interested in discovering the nature of the relations between knowledge,
valuation, policy, action, and institutional change. Whatever the process,
the fact of change, of great effects from seemingly small causes, and of
the influence of "ideas" on the structure of societies and of their belief and value systems, is nonetheless clear enought for all to see.

Today, for teachers and students and the general public—in the
Western world at least—the assertion that the earth is a spheroid that
revolves about the sun is a commonplace fact, bare of ethical, emotional,
or social significance. But as we well know, when the notion was new,
it was spurned as inconsistent with direct visual experience; it flew in
the face of "common sense"; it made it impossible for Columbus to
collect a crew except by impressment; it imperiled the salvation of the
souls of any who accepted this heretical contradiction of received religious doctrine; and, since "wrong belief" was heresy and heresy was
a capital crime, it imperiled life itself. The wish to keep facts separate
from values or science separate from ethics may be a consequence
of the struggles and risks of those who first accepted modern physics
and evolutionary theory. The scientific and philosophical literature of
those times was replete with political and ethical polemic. Some of it
was very bitter indeed. Again today, "pure" physical science is plunged
deep in ethics and politics.

Even when it avoids open polemic, a presentation of new concepts takes on the appearance and function of polemic simply by being different from accepted or authorized belief. An innovator may be disinclined to attack, but he may find himself obliged to fight in self-defense. One way or the other, ethical disputation becomes part of establishing a new science, for if it does not fight, it dies. This does not mean, of course, that everyone in it is necessarily and always actively engaged in promoting the new concepts outside the bounds of the profession. The simplest solution to the problem of the "public relations" of scientific inquiry is that actually in force: when each one follows his special interest and talent, both internal scientific development and external defense are taken care of. Sometimes but not always both functions may be the concern of one and the same person.

Analogy is admittedly a weak support for any argument. Still, it may well be for the future of anthropology as it has been in the past for other disciplines, that the public position will be strengthened in proportion to the quality of its internal development, and, given the probably justified pragmatic temper of the non-academic world, in proportion to its effecitveness in bettering the human condition by applying theory in practical situations. Other sciences have promoted their internal growth by meeting opposition and by taking new theoretical directions suggested by practical problems. Anthropology need not and usually does not spurn these opportunities for growth.

As a point of contact between the internal theoretical developments of anthropology as an objective discipline and its external relations as a new discipline presented to an uninstructed audience, the classroom affords an excellent site for examining the assumptions and commitments of anthropology. Within the closed professional circle, a statement of the anthropological point of view may be as objective, as ethically neutral, as disinterested as it can be made. Communicated to students or other non-anthropologists, it at once takes on value significance from the consequences of its novelty.

Seen as a social-cultural process, teaching is a confrontation of students with value choices in regard both to method and to content. A complex methodological rule for research and teaching, objectivity is a commitment to a value position as much at variance with popular uncritical acceptance of ideas as is the content of the anthropological conception of man and culture at variance with popular ideas about man.

Refining or replacing comfortable old beliefs is part of the task of the educator. The preparation of students for receiving and absorbing new knowledge is often defective, despite the fact that progress in knowledge is taken for granted and understood as involving change. Yet, young people may first be taught that there is a Santa Claus and then have to unlearn it as they grow up; first be taught the Platonic myth of absolute truth, then have to be shocked or pushed or pulled out of it; first be taught that "life can be beautiful," then have to learn the "hard facts of life." By contrast, students brought up in a realistic and scientific manner may be far better prepared, if not eager, for new knowledge and able to use it constructively without wasting time and emotion on ridding themselves of myths. Or, students who have early determined on a definite career in the sciences or the humanities, while they need substance added and refinements of their preconceptions, can undergo a fundamental alteration of their ideas or values with some assurance that continued association with the academic world will provide a substitute for earlier ideas that is better than what was lost. With the general student in college for a general education, who has neither special training in the kind of flexibility new knowledge requires nor special professional interest, there is a special difficulty. The more earnest and open to education these rudderless students are, the harder is their lot. Disorientation, at least temporarily, is the true tuition they must pay to acquire the frame of mind of an educated individual. Contradiction of cherished ideas and ideals is unavoidably traumatic. At least for a time, the serious but unprepared student is likely to founder in that wretched sort of relativism that is nothing but the loss of an absolute belief.

Given the sort of meek acceptance of authority inculcated in some of our students, together with the disposition to a blind respect for "the facts," new information is disruptive until it has been integrated into a coherent framework of ideas and values. It is not easy to find suitable positive values to fill the void left when the presumed factual foundations of earlier values are gone and the values with them. There is probably nothing that can quite take the place of a sense of absolute certainty, preserved by unquestioning, uncritical acceptance—least of all the principle of scientific inquiry that requires abandoning hope of a final absolute truth which, once attained, relieves us from doubt and terminates the necessity for further searching. It is a touch paradoxical that the prerequisite and most permanent acquisition of the educated person is a readiness not merely to admit but to insist upon "ignorance," in the form of a commitment to open, continuing inquiry.

Objectivity and scientific scepticism can be shown to be, not the absence of convictions and values, nor a refusal to make judgments, but rather a positive way of exchanging old ideas or policies for new and better-verified ones. A wholesome fear of finality and absoluteness may come from examples of the horrors that have been committed by men who were absolutely sure, but in the light of subsequent evidence, not far from absolutely wrong. Changes from one theory to another in science have been confused by the innocent and ignorant with inconstancy of heart or inconsistency of thought. The constant rule, respect for evidence and logical organization, is a necessary point of reference, a new security with new intellectual and practical risks to replace absolute belief and its peculiar risks. If rejecting absolutes is relativism, then we must remember that relativism is not so much a point of view as a point of departure for the construction of positive knowledge and values.

ANTHROPOLOGICAL SCIENCE AND HUMAN VALUES

The conceptual and value components of the anthropological point of view as interpreted here may be summarized in the following statements: (1) The object of anthropological inquiry is the study of man, conceived as a single biological species characterized by systematic cultural variability. (2) Objectivity is a general though minimal methodological commitment. (3) Objective methods are comaptible with a variety of social-ethical objectives, which may be directly or indirectly aimed at in the teaching of anthropology. (4) Objective inquiry is determined by a value choice from among alternative methodologies. (5) It has value involvements that result from the social consequences of the dissemination of new knowledge, and these feed back into its conceptual development and intensify or complicate social-ethical involvements. To this may now be added: (6) As an objective inquiry into human nature and variability, anthropology is not an ethical theory nor does it imply any specific ethical or social-political policy; however, no serious ethical theory can be constructed that ignores or contradicts the results of anthropology. These may be modifying the humanistic tradition of Western culture towards greater precision and effectiveness. And (7) For purposes of constructing a unified and comprehensive study of man and culture, anthropology utilizes the most diverse methods and techniques, data and concepts, including those derived from other disciplines.

The constructive capacity of anthropology to correct and add to students' information and concepts is its educational reason for existing. Its capacity and obligations relative to the value issues raised by discrepancies between popular ideas and anthropological information, concepts and point of view are not so clear, either for teaching or for theory. For, the fact that anthropology has unavoidable ethical and other value involvements—and we take this as fact—does not change the logical and historical separateness of anthropological theory and value theory. A good case has been made out for the view that in teaching anthropology and its method, one teaches at the same time a particular set of values, notably, tolerance or respect or open-mindedness and a

humanistic or benevolent interest in human welfare. While I share the
values and consider them wholly compatible with the method, content,
and point of view of anthropology, I cannot share the view that they
are part of or identical with anthropology or scientific method more
generally. There are strong resemblances of pattern between objectivity and tolerance or a humanistic viewpoint, but there are no proofs
of the kind required by science. That advances in knowledge offer an
opportunity to refine value theory, that new knowledge may provide a
better foundation or an inspiration for a system or theory of values,
that anthropology may gain insights or take direction from value theory is not unlikely. To question the contention that anthropology contains a theory of values held by all anthropologists is by no means to
deny that the discipline can directly affect certain contemporary value
viewpoints and can in principle contribute heavily to some future development of value theory.

Simply by being what it is—the scientific study of the human—anthropology has a corrective effect on the pernicious dichotomy of science and humanism dignified by C. P. Snow under the rubric, "the two
cultures." The classification of anthropology as at the same time natural science, social science, and humanities, although it presents certain
difficulties, holds the promise of the sort of integration of student outlook described by Margaret Mead, Robert Ehrich, and Verne Ray.
Here, it is sufficient to indicate the importance of the steady pressure
exerted by anthropology against the stereotyped contrast of science and
humanism that is more fashionable than it is meaningful.

We are not deceived by the great popular acclaim of science into
thinking it is well understood by students. Some of them, no doubt,
enjoying exceptional home training or an outstanding high school background, have a firm grasp on the general pattern of scientific method
and attitudes. Not a few have a curiously distorted image that is the
reverse of the sober academic reality. A notion of science as absolutely certain, as expert and authorized to speak on every subject, and
as a mysterious craft known only to the initiates, is a reflection of the
same uncritical attitudes exacted from the young in other matters. It
is hardly good preparation for learning or using science.

A complicating factor is the reappearance, since the invention of the
atomic bomb, of a familiar figure in Western culture, the Faustian man
of knowledge who frightens the uninformed and threatens the innocent with the diabolical product of his learning. As teachers, we may
then bask in the reflected glory of the mad psychiatrist who has taken
the place of the Svengali of our youth, the diabolically clever specialist
in brain-washing or world-destroying machines, and, occasionally, the
cold, impersonal genius who is all brain but no heart. It is small won-

der that some students find it difficult to associate anything scientific with anything human or humane, that they sometimes close their minds to the impression of new knowledge and are timid of reaching decisions where experts disagree. Or, if they aspire to a scientific career, it is to some unreal "dehumanized" enterprise which Darwin and Einstein would not recognize as science.

The stereotype of the humanities—soft, sentimental, and easy—is, as we know, as far from the facts as the stereotype of science. The vision of philosophy, literature, art, and anthropology as one of the humanities as effortless, unstructured, and informal is poor preparation for the rigorous training and exacting standards that govern production and scholarship in humanistic studies. There is much in humanistic scholarship that is quite as cold and impersonal as the work done in laboratories. The humanities, as a division of liberal studies, are not as such humanistic, or humane, or humanitarian. To state it otherwise is to play with words. And to pretend that science and humanities are opposed is to ignore the nature of their similarities and differences.

As a class of philosophical values oriented primarily to man, rather than to nature or to deity, humanism is not the exclusive property of any group. There are humanistic scientists and scholars in the humanities, and there are also non-humanists in each field. Some prefer a model of science from which all trace of human invention and problem has been removed, some prefer to place the humanities at so lofty an altitude that all things merely human are alien to them.

The presence of humanistic values in the viewpoints of various anthropologists cannot be accounted for by the fact that anthropology may be classified among the humanities. In some respects, the reverse may be the case. For, from McKim Marriott's statements about the different approaches to area courses of anthropologists and scholars in the humanities and from other sources, it appears that the humanistic disciplines tend to look at man through the opposite end of the telescope from anthropology. The one seeks the rare human accomplishments worthy of designation as classical; the other is directed to the fullest possible representation of the whole range of human activity. From this inclusive conception of the domain of anthropology, a new meaning for humanism as an outlook on man may develop, perhaps benevolence tempered by knowledge and steadied by scrupulous objectivity. Those of us who are humanists will surely bend our efforts in some such direction. Different from inquiry into human values, humanistic or otherwise, the anthropological theory of human nature is an indispensable corequisite or prerequisite to such inquiry. The primary, defining concern of anthropology in theory and in teaching is the development of the science of man.

To give substance to a scientific conception of man is an arduous undertaking. Perhaps it is a task that will never be finally completed. Human interest in man goes back as far as our records take us. Changing methods and concepts reflect and help to shape the changing culture in which they appear. The old chestnut in the logic textbooks, featuring man as a featherless biped, is not much worse for contemporary anthropological purposes than the staid Aristotelian definition of man as the rational animal. Oriented to discovering the characteristic which distinguished man from all other animals, the traditional definition by genus and differentia moves away from the broad, inclusive needs of anthropology.

In effect, we are teaching that each human being is a fair and representative sample of mankind, and that each specific culture is a fair sample of generic culture. The challenge to inquiry is the location of significant defining characteristics amidst so much diversity and the inclusion of diversity in the definition of man. The challenge in teaching is to communicate the realization that the conception of man grows larger in proportion as the level of detail become more minute, and to make the meaning of variation clearer and more orderly by bringing the full range of diversity into view. Anthropology teaches a view of man as literally all men, and of all men as bearers and inventors of culture whose diversity is patterned variation of the same basic elements. The principle that men are equal, or are brothers, or are in essence the same, is very old in Western culture, and so too is the realization that there are differences among men. That the biological unity of man and the patterned variability of culture are equally necessary and complementary parts of a definition of man is new.

The full implications of the anthropological point of view are becoming apparent as anthropological inquiry translates the conception of the unity of man into the conception of the unity of anthropology and in turn of all the sciences of man. It is probably a direct consequence of the ideal of studying man and culture in their totality that the boundaries of anthropology have been constantly expanding and its relations with other disciplines increasing in magnitude and variety. In principle, all methods and all data relevant to man are the concern of anthropology. While there are marked differences among anthopologists as to the scope and methods which they consider appropriate for their own research, there is at the same time a nearly unanimous agreement that alternative approaches are consistent with the objectives of anthropology as a whole.

Anthropology as a discipline can accomplish many things which are beyond the powers of any individual in it. The problems created by proliferation are, like many other problems, much harder to solve in the general statement than in specific and concrete cases. Confronted by the necessity of designing a course or a curriculum or guiding graduate students in their classwork and research projects, anthropologists have come to terms with the tension between the ideal of unity and the facts of diversity of theories, methods, and relations with other disciplines. The construction of a pattern of specialization to fit the specific interests of students and teachers has repeatedly been recommended as the most feasible approach. This is the solution proposed in papers concerned with the question of what subjects outside anthropology should be required of majors in the field, or with the staffing and structure of interdisciplinary courses, or with alternative designs for an anthropological course or curriculum.

Variation of patterns of specialization according to individual student interests is not a centripetal force. It is rather the means by which the general ideal of unity is progressively more precisely and completely realized. No better precaution is needed in permitting each interest to be pursued than the traditional requirement that its results should pass the test of contributing to our knowledge of man. And no better assurance of the continuity of the effort can be asked for than that provided by the process of teaching. Each of us may hope that we have left the field at least a little richer than we found it and that we have provided the means by which our students can do better than we have.

ROBERT W. EHRICH

*Anthropology as
an Integrative
Factor*

SINCE THE TERM "liberal arts education" has almost as many shades of meaning as there are practitioners in its own black arts, it remains for each of us to try to make explicit what he thinks he is trying to do each time he stands before a class.

As a whole the tripartite division of our educational system should make sense, although in practice it often does not. It seems obvious that the elementary schools should concentrate on instilling a facility with the basic techniques of our relatively literate, crowded, and complex society, i.e., reading, writing, spelling, arithmetic, and the like. Although the secondary schools should see to it that the grasp of these areas is widened and deepened, their primary job is to impart a solid foundation of information. It is the function of the college to expand this informational background and to grapple with it conceptually. There must inevitably be some overlapping between these stages. It is essential, however, to inculcate throughout the entire process a respect for intellectual craftsmanship and the realization that, although an informed opinion is worthy of attention, an uninformed one is not.

If we accept the principle that the college student's work should become increasingly more conceptual during the course of his four years, the objectives of a college career come into sharper focus. In this day and age, the student's ultimate goal should be an understanding of the recognized and unresolved questions, what is being done about them, what techniques are being used to answer them, and why these particular means are being employed.

583

If his major objective is to see clearly what we know we do not know, rather than what we think we know, he has taken the first step toward living intelligently with confusion, and this is merely another way of saying intellectual maturity. To achieve this goal, however, one must have a firm grasp of what we think we know, or he cannot really understand the questions. Much of the basic material, then, remains the same, but its presentation must not only supply information, it must also delineate the lacunae. In other words, the ideal liberal arts education should produce graduates who are not only intensely aware of what is going on in the world around them but who also have a sufficient background of information, speculative thought, and historical perspective to understand, to evaluate, and to take intelligent action on the basis of a balanced judgment and an informed point of view.

To anthropologists the role of anthropology in such a context is so obvious that any extensive elaboration becomes embarrassing. However, because anthropology touches on and overlaps so many fields, it does help to coordinate material from a variety of discrete courses in other disciplines, and it lays the background for a philosophical approach of its own. Most, if not all, of us have had upperclassmen who, on completing an introductory course in anthropology, have stated unequivocally that much of their college work had finally fallen into a clear and comprehensible pattern for them. They have become aware that, although anthropology is distinctly an anthropocentric subject, even the patterns of philosophical and speculative thought are not only the products of, but are also themselves, cultural phenomena. Furthermore, although fully as anthropocentric as its sister behavioral disciplines, the greater emphasis of anthropology on comparative studies has helped them to become considerably less ethnocentric in outlook. It is this sort of thing that should be our major goal.

With the present massive stampede into the colleges and with the general development of mass higher education, we must clarify for ourselves what our main job really is. The overall raising of the level of the informed and so-called educated college public is, of course, a prime objective of the democratic process and of mass education and should be the routine by-product of our routine teaching. We must, however, remember that we live in a republic, not a true democracy, and that higher education, undemocratic as this may sound, has as its primary function the development of an intellectual elite. It is on this group that we should concentrate our main effort. The majority will fall back to mental lethargy and the inertia of the daily round. It is with the few that our painfully expended energy may be transformed or maintained and not dissipated. Although the following observations are advanced with both objectives in mind, the latter consideration is uppermost.

Whether an institution offers only a limited amount of introductory anthropology or a well rounded major, the principles should remain the same. A soundly conceived program should not only contribute to the general education of an individual, but it should also be solid enough so that those who may want to go on in the field can do so without being at a competitive disadvantage in graduate study. Anthropology, although a very wide and rather amorphous field, has a certain conceptual and philosophical unity, of value to a wide range of students. The liberal arts oriented students fall into the categories of those who take only the introductory courses, those who may follow up with a few more specialized courses in the pursuit of personal interest or as functionally related adjuncts to their major fields of concentration, and those who make anthropology their major subject as part of a general educational background with no thought of entering the field professionally.

In all disciplines the introductory course is the most important one, for it is primarily a vocabulary course, initiating the student into the specialized terminology of a new field and into the complex concepts for which the professional jargon serves as a shorthand. If it is meaning that we try to communicate, an initial grasp of our semantics is vital. An introduction to anthropology should, therefore, maintain full coverage in an adequate balance between physical and cultural anthropology, no matter what the bias of the instructor or the limitations of time upon him. This holds whether we have merely a few lectures in a composite course, a one semester course, or a two semester sequence.

Sturtevant (1958:11) has made the point that it is often advisable for a student to take his major in another field before doing graduate work in anthropology. His predicate is that anything one brings to the study of anthropology is an advantage. With regard to the scheduling of even an introductory course in an undergraduate curriculum this principle applies, and the student can certainly get much more out of such a course if he takes it with at least three or four semesters of college work behind him. Here we are referring to the informational background theoretically given in high school but necessarily supplemented during the first two years of college. Conversely, of course, a solid grounding in anthropology gives an excellent background for future specialized work in a variety of other fields.

In giving such a course we must remember that, since many of us were in college, the role of the professor has changed. Not long ago there was relatively little synthesized material, either data-oriented or theoretical, and a professor's job was to bring together and coordinate obscure and recondite material and to present it in a relatively coherent manner The spate of comprehensive introductory works, readings, special studies, and the like since World War II have necessitated a marked change, and our present function is one of interpretation and critical evaluation. It is in this context that we must outline controversy, unresolved questions, and the vast lacunae in our data and in our thinking. While this may seem to be *lèse majesté* or, at the very least, bad educational practice in the elementary and secondary school sense, we should never hesitate to admit that we wish we knew what we were talking about. We should treat the members of our classes as though they were students, despite the conditioned reflexes that make them pupils. We may, in this manner, mitigate some of the intellectual harm that has already been done to them.

For these reasons I hold no brief for specific limited assignments, the rigid adherence to a text, or even periodic quizzes to make certain that assignments are carried out. We should proceed on the assumption that the students who come to us are able to read, that an assigned textbook is supplementary reading, and that the nature of anthropology is sufficiently complex so that a student who wishes to do well must necessarily do additional reading in some of the suggested reference material. We should make explicit and adhere to the proposition that the law does not insist that the student come to college, that he comes for his own ends, that we cannot give him anything but that we can help him take, and that we cannot teach in the sense of imparting knowledge but that we can help him learn. Since our role should not be that of mental policemen, we should construct our examinations in such a manner that the student must synthesize or evaluate the material instead of simply regurgitating it. As teachers we should have no truck with statistically scored, short-answer tests, for our examinations should be an integral part of the course work. If the administrative schedule or class numbers make this approach a crushing burden, we should drive for more time or more assistance. This is one area in which we should not compromise. If we value the contributions that anthropology can make to the philosophical insights of a student's four years in college, we should make certain that the student has the opportunity to see this kind of relationship for himself. General essay questions at the end of a course, when we ask a student to tie things together, should be, and often are, illuminating educational experiences and not just mental probes.

In our more advanced courses we are dealing with much the same sort of thing but in a more restricted sense, for what one actually covers in a classroom is still bound to be a superficial treatment of a vast body of data. The real function of a problem-oriented research paper then becomes a mechanism by which the student gradually becomes aware of the great submerged portion of the iceberg that lies beneath the synthesized coverage of classroom and text. Thus the so-called "more specialized" courses are actually more intensive introductions to narrower areas.

In the current educational jargon "general education" is now used to denote either the required distribution courses or core curriculum on the one hand, or the more composite generalized or integrated divisional courses such as "social science" on the other. Anthropologists frequently carry part of this "integrated" load and they do have much to contribute, if and when such courses are a part of the curriculum. If one believes firmly in the inductive process, however, these general courses put the cart before the horse and educationally are all wrong, for they are normally thrown at the entering freshmen who have no body of information to serve as reference points for understanding or evaluating the abstract doctrines imposed upon them. It is obviously impossible to lay any kind of a foundation in several disciplines within the span of a single course. As a capstone course in the senior year this approach would make some sense; on a freshman level it makes none.

In two previous papers (Ehrich 1947, 1954) I have suggested that anthropologists can strengthen their offerings, their faculty position, and their contribution to the education of students by exploiting some of the areas which fall between those covered by the various academic disciplines, or those subjects which may involve more than one field. They may be able to accomplish this either by conducting such courses jointly with members of other departments or alone but with interdepartmental cooperation. As examples one may cite such diverse partnerships as Human Evolution (with Geology and Biology), Human Ecology (with Biology), Culture and Personality (with Psychology), Archaeology (with Classics or History), Primitive Art (with Art), Folklore (with Literature), and numerous others as possibilities and as realities in one institution or another.

In any event, it is my contention that a really integrated approach comes from concrete subject matter and from the interest of the instructor and does not result from an artificial theoretical construct which is the misconception of unity conferred by the erroneous rubric of "Social Science," or the mistaken notion that areas of peripheral overlap between the several disciplines provide a common core.

The major integrative function of anthropology lies within its own subject matter, beginning with the introductory course, and continuing on the more specialized level of advanced courses where data, process, and theoretical interpretation are joined to those of history, the behavioral disciplines, and the natural sciences. While we may have to participate in the amorphous integrated courses in order to eat, it should be with the full realization that our purpose in them is to make what is inherently an intellectually shoddy instrument a little better in quality. Perhaps our major contribution lies in the culture concept, which often appears to be a sort of revelation to some of our colleagues in other fields as well as to our students.

This turn of the discussion brings us to the question of whether we should advocate and work toward the making of an introductory course in anthropology a requirement for all students. Although I would very much like to see each student exposed to the field, and although I am fully aware that this would provide more warm bodies in the classroom and consequently more jobs for anthropologists, I personally would not like to see this happen. When one deals with a captive audience, one is not only likely to lose his effectiveness, but the dead weight of the indifferent majority becomes overwhelming and is stultifying to the student as well as to the teacher. If we cleave to our purpose of developing an intellectual elite, anthropology should, insofar as possible, be discovered country and not a concentration camp.

It is high time for us to discard our outworn notion that the highest form of educational activity, and consequently the highest status among teachers, lies in the training of future anthropologists. We have a vast and necessary job to do and a very solid contribution to make to liberal arts education. It is essential that we survey our own subject matter, our teaching personnel, our students, the changing cultural compulsives upon us and upon our students, the needs of the times, our objectives, and our techniques—if we are to avoid a hackneyed, plodding, and stereotyped assault upon the students' time and deafened ears. We do have a vital part to play, and we should address ourselves to it with care and with intelligence.

REFERENCES CITED

EHRICH, ROBERT W.
 1947 The place of anthropology in a college education. Harvard Educational Review 17, No. 1.
 1954 Anthropology in a liberal arts curriculum. Journal of Higher Education 35, No. 7.
STURTEVANT, WILLIAM C.
 1958 Anthropology as a career. Smithsonian Publication 4343. Smithsonian Institution, Washington, D.C. (Rev. ed., 1960)

VERNE F. RAY

Objectives for
a Liberal
Education

I AM CONVINCED that the most significant and important concepts and objectives in the teaching of anthropology are precisely those which we share with sister disciplines in the social and biological sciences. Indeed, overriding even these considerations are the questions of procedures and goals in democratic and liberal education generally at the advanced levels. If as anthropologists we do not accept such an interpretation, we are surely denying the validity—or at least the significance—of a basic concept of our science, that of culture. Concepts of teaching are only valid as they relate to the character of our culture. Meaningful and defensible objectives cannot grow out of a subjective analysis of educaton in which one's own discipline is the sole or major point of reference.

Furthermore, anthropology has prided itself—rightfully so, I feel —in playing the modern-day role with respect to the behavioral sciences that philosophy formerly played for all of the sciences. If the integration of the findings of the more specialized sciences—the building of a picture of the whole man and man as a whole—is proper to anthropology and is successfully achieved, then certainly our concepts and objectives are primarily those of liberal educational training, not of anthropology *per se*.

We appropriately and properly utilize these fundamental concepts and strive for these objectives—we do not teach them. What we teach is anthropology; it is the only training we have to give. Anthropology cannot provide a student with a "general education" nor a "liberal education." Generality can only be achieved through a relatively exhaustive coverage of academic subject matter and methodologies, the criteria for "exhaustive" being practicality on the one hand and the educational philosophy on the other. No more, and for the same reasons, can anthropology provide a liberal education. But the subject matter can be liberalized, that is, treated from an educationally liberal point of view.

We may now consider the objectives which are said in one report to characterize a liberal education. First, the provision of the student with certain kinds of knowledge which every man is the better for possessing: self knowledge—his own biological and psychological nature; knowledge of others—the roots of human behavior; knowledge of the physical and biological world; knowledge of his own and other cultures; a historical view of man's achievements, social, intellectual, and artistic; and knowledge of his religious and philosophical heritage. The second objective involves competences—the ability to think clearly, rigorous thought, intellectual discipline. Finally, a liberal education must instill those attitudes, values, and habits of mind which characterize the educated man (Carnegie Foundation 1956).

Let us briefly examine these criteria from the point of view of anthropology; first, the kinds of knowledge which every man is the better for possessing. The entire content of anthropology is covered by one or another of the categories enumerated under this heading. Culture, and the historical view of man's achievements, are areas in which anthropology characteristically assumes priority and feels that it has the ability to make the most meaningful contributions. It seems quite clear, therefore, that in arena of content no valid or useful distinction can be drawn between anthropology under the banner of liberal education and anthropology flying the pennant of professional or specialized training. The only pertinent criterion is quality: good teaching or less good.

It is with respect to the second criterion, competence, that the identity of good liberal and professional training emerges most dramatically. What kind of a professional anthropologist can be turned out without "the ability to think clearly," the application of "rigorous thought" and "discipline" to the intellectual problems that he faces? These attributes may be important desiderata in the product of liberal education, but they are mandatory in the professional. I submit that there is no more efficient or effective way to achieve them than through good teaching of professional character.

With regard to the third goal, the development of attitudes, values, and habits of mind of the educated man, I observed earlier that anthropology can be presented from an educationally liberal point of view. The source of success in this effort certainly resides in the being of the professor, not in any program or pattern of presentation. Given the variety of attitudes and backgrounds which students bring to the university, the probability of success for any one professor, however talented, with the whole range of students is small. The attitudes and values of the educated man are much more apt to be found in the graduate who has received his training from a comparatively large number of professors—assuming that they, in turn, were educated men—than in those taught by but few. Hence, this objective of liberal education is better served by the large university than the small college, and by the program which allows a considerable number of electives in academic departments other than the major. This last is especially important for the small department or the small college.

The development of the attitudes, values, and habits of mind of the educated man is here accepted as a valid and significant objective of liberal education and one that is sometimes not achieved in professional programs of academic training. However, anthropology would seem to be in the most favored position of all the sciences, and better off than most of the humanities, in this respect. The character of our subject matter predisposes to success. If we have professionally competent teachers who are also educated men, we have little to fear.

Speaking of this subject matter, Kluckhohn observed that anthropology

. . . has explored the gamut of human variability and can best answer the questions: what common ground is there between human beings of all tribes and nations? What differences exist? What is their source? How deep-going are they? (1949:2)

As a broad subject, which is partly a natural science, partly a humanity, and partly a behavioral science and which ranges from statistics and measurements of the human body to the study of archaeological objects, languages, and values, anthropology appeals to undergraduates whose main objective is to obtain a liberal education. . . . At a time when educated men and women must recognize that the ways of other tribes and nations cannot remain matters of indifference or antiquarian curiosity, anthropology has a special place in general and liberal education. (1959:5)

The Unesco report on the *University Teaching of the Social Sciences* states that

the socio-cultural sciences provide an essential addition to human thought and experience. . . . These disciplines considerably broaden the horizons of the mind and, in an age remarkable for the complexity of its social organization, fulfil a function that philosophy alone cannot discharge. They provide a basis of facts and theories about human communities and social processes which enables the citizen to attain to a better understanding of the society in which he lives and of those around it. (1954:88)

Since it seems inescapable that anthropology's liberalizing role is a function of its subject matter and needs only good teaching to be realized, let us take another look at the relationships between the two and the concepts which may be appropriate to the ends sought. Dr. David French of Reed College, noted for its achievements in liberal education, expresses his convictions categorically:

Although undergraduate courses frequently have both anthropology majors and non-majors enrolled, it will be assumed here that the needs of the latter are not sufficiently different to require courses to be modified for their benefit. It can be argued that the functions of general education are best fulfilled when students take a wide range of courses, each taught in terms of the rationale of that discipline. (American Ethnological Society Symposium, Palo Alto, 1960.)

The solid base for views of this kind has already been mentioned—the intrinsic fact that it is the professional content of anthropology which gives it a quantitatively significant part in the large job of liberal education. This being the case, there seems to be no reason at all for attempting to train professional and general students differently. Under the circumstances how, indeed, could it be done? The fact is that we teach very few special skills, not many distinctive techniques. Our concern is largely with methods and, of course, content. Thus the criterion of technical versus general, which gives sharpness to the distinction between professional and liberal education, loses its edge in the case of anthropology.

Once the introductory course or sequence is behind the student he is ready for specialized training and specialized training in anthropology includes research. There is no logical reason why the initiation of the student into research should wait upon attainment of the baccalaureate degree. The distinction between advanced undergraduate and graduate levels of training in academic fields is highly artificial and is defensible only in terms of custom and administrative convenience. I state this with conviction, not only as a consequence of over twenty-five years in graduate and undergraduate teaching but also in the light of many years of graduate school administration. I concur fully with the Unesco recommendation that

Research techniques should be introduced into undergraduate courses by critical study of research work already carried out, or personal participation, on however modest a scale, in current research; individual experiment should be encouraged. (Unesco 1954:92)

A corollary to these conclusions is the proposition that teaching must not be divorced from research. It is hard to believe that any one would seriously question this assertion but there are nevertheless more and more college level anthropology courses being taught by nonresearchers. Most of these teachers are not only nonresearchers, they are also non-anthropologists. The Unesco report categorically states that "general courses unrelated to research are fruitless for teachers and students alike." (p. 92.) Lévi-Strauss declares that

> . . . no one should be entitled to teach anthropology unless he has carried out considerable field research. It is sheer illusion that anthropology can be taught purely theoretically. . . . The teaching of anthropology must be reserved for *"eye-witnesses."* There is nothing radical in this standpoint; it is adopted *de facto* (if not always *de jure*) in all countries where anthropology has attained some measures of development. (Unesco 1954:118)

Lévi-Strauss is speaking, primarily at least, of university teachers whereas most anthropology teaching by nonresearchers is in small colleges. However, the thesis here presented is that there are no valid bases for distinguishing between classes of students—college versus university or pre-professional versus general education—when the question is that of acceptable anthropological training. The certainty that anthropological courses will be offered by more and more colleges demands that consideration be given to the kinds of teachers that will stand before these classes.Many of them will undoubtedly hold only master's degress, some only bachelor's. Will they be anthropologists, or merely teachers? Certainly they can be anthropologists, if the universities in which they are studying will (1) start specialized training in the second year, (2) include research guidance and actual research activity—including field work—in the undergraduate program, and (3) offer a single program of training—anthropology—with no thought for distinguishing between pre-professional and general education aspects. A powerful argument for the adoption of these criteria is the circumstance that many of the students who will later find themselves teaching anthropology will have had general education, not pre-professional, objectives during much or all of their course of undergraduate studies. Equally important is the fact that avowedly pre-professional students will reach the graduate level far better prepared to complete the work for the doctorate, with distinction, within the nominal three years rather than five or more as is now the case. Nothing could be more wholesome for higher education and for the welfare of our country in these times of spiralling educational costs and fearful manpower shortage.

REFERENCES CITED

CARNEGIE FOUNDATION FOR THE ADVANCEMENT OF TEACHING
  1956   Liberal education. Annual Report 1955-1956.
  1959   Education of the academically talented. Annual Report 1958-1959.
KLUCKHOHN, CLYDE
  1949   Mirror for man. New York, McGraw-Hill.
  1959   Anthropology in Harvard College. Harvard Foundation Newsletter,
            December 31, 1959, pp. 4-6.
UNESCO
  1954   The university teaching of social sciences, sociology, social psychology
            and anthropology. (Including reports by Pierre de Bie, Claude Lévi-
            Strauss, Joseph Nuttin and Eugene Jacobsen; 252 pp.; Paris, France.)

MARGARET MEAD

Anthropology
and an Education
for the Future

Today, as we search for a new way of educating men and women who can both understand and cope with our intricate, just emerging universe with its tremendous contradictions, discrepancies, potentialities, and dangers, there is an urgent need for new alignments of subject matter in our undergraduate colleges. It is being increasingly recognized that before a man can become an engineer or a statesman, a production manager, an astronaut, or a poet, he must be made somehow into an educated man; that is, a whole man, to whom nothing in the world is alien, to whom no path of possible exploration is blocked or closed. Our experience since World War II has demonstrated with terrible vividness how few men there are—of any age or from any country—who have such an integrated relationship to all that man has been, is, and may become. The creation of a United Nations Educational Scientific and Cultural Organization was a bold venture in integration at the top, but only a handful of men in the world had the imagination to head it up. The tremendous vogue of C. P. Snow's "two cultures," the restless searching for new formulas—varying from new architecture on the old campus to proposals for floating universities that would visit landfall points in the underdeveloped countries—the plea for the scientist to become familiar with man as well as with the natural order of the universe, for the physician to learn about the heights of man's achievement as well as the failures of his body and mind, the scholar to come out of his library and watch the intricate new patterns which a microscope can reveal, or listen to a real nightingale against a real

595

sky—all of these are signs of the times we live in, and the task that lies before the colleges.

Anthropology is a uniquely situated discipline, related in diverse ways to many other disciplines, each of which, in specializing, has also inadvertently helped to fragment the mind of modern man. Anthropology is a humanity, represented in the American Council of Learned Societies, concerned with the arts of language and with the versions that human cultures have given of the definition of man and of man's relationship to the universe; anthropology is a science, concerned with discovering and ordering the behavior of man-in-culture; anthropology is a biological science, concerned with the physical nature of man, with man's place in evolution, with the way genetic and racial differences, ecological adaptations, growth and maturation, and constitutional differences are implicated in man's culture and achievements; anthropology is a historical discipline, concerned with reading the record of man's far past and establishing the links which unite the potsherd and the first inscription on stone, in tying together the threads between the preliterate and the literate world wherever the sequence occurs, in Egypt, in China, in Crete, or in a modern African state. Anthropology is a social science, although never only a social science, because in anthropology man, as part of the natural world, as a biological creature, is not separated from man as a consumer or producer, member of a group, or possessor of certain psychological faculties. Anthropology is an art. The research skills which go into good field work are as complex as the skills of a musican or a surgeon; a disciplined awareness of self is as essential.

Partly because anthropology is a late comer on the scene, including a curiously assembled set of subject matters—such as the preliterate past, the body of man, the behavior of preliterate surviving people, the formal study of spoken language—and partly because of the diversity of anthropological interests, it is an uncommitted discipline. Because it includes all of them, it does not fall, with relentless traditionalism, into any category of science or of humanities or of social science. It has sheltered under the wings of philosophy and anatomy, botany and history, aesthetics and geology. Wherever it has been placed it has been restive, not for the simple imperialistic reasons that all part-departments seek to be whole departments but because there was always, when anthropology was placed within any category, such a large part that did not fit. How did a course in primitive art fit into a sociology curriculum, a course in the diffusion of material culture into a psychology department, a course in child training into philosophy?

It is in this very anomalousness that I believe anthropology can make a unique contribution to a liberal education. As a part of liberal education, it is peculiarly fitted to fill a tremendous need.

I should like to review briefly some of the gaps in the knowledge and understanding of modern man, so fragmented, so myopically limited and specialized, even at this very moment when we are journeying into space. Then I will consider how anthropology can be taught not by professional anthropologists alone, but by those who have studied under anthropologists and, like all great teachers of the adolescent mind, are willing to immerse themselves in their material sufficiently to convey it to their students "with the dew still on it."

The gaps in men's minds and imagination which we need to bridge are appallingly conspicuous today: the gap between the understanding of the past, the grasp of the present, and an ability to deal with the future; the gap between the lively pursuit of natural science wherever it leads and the statesmanship which will be able to control the results of such pursuits; the gap between the mathematical and formal analyses of systems and the ability to analyze and predict the behavior of human beings; the gap between the scientist who "understands" a single approach to the natural world and the poet and painter who can find no foothold in modern man's response to changes which he does not understand; the gap between man's knowledge of things and his knowledge of people; between his awareness of the external world, which has never been so great, and his awareness of himself, which has seldom been so impoverished; the gap between our small ethnocentric, narrowly racial, class and time bound senses of identity and the grandeur of our membership in one human species, now bound together as denizens of one planet. On the verge of leaving that planet, we still fail to conceive our full place upon it, in time and in space.

The fully educated man, whether he was the young adult male member of a primitive tribe who had learned all that the elders had to tell him, the man of Greece or Rome, thinking about and understanding the known world, Renaissance man stirred to an aware excitement of the ancient world from which he had been cut off, and moved by the new discoveries—the great and the small seen for the first time through telescopes and microscopes—all of these had, in different measure, what we now seek to re-establish for our own time. In contrast, many members of great societies—the peasant, taught for centuries that his is a limited place in the world, the urban proletarian, starved and cynical in his slums near the palace, the bitter contentious member of one of the cults and sects that seek to narrow truth to the limits of their own impoverished emotions and intellects—these have never, no matter how great the civilization within which they resided, been men of a liberal education.

The essence of a liberal education is to share the full identity made possible by the state of civilization within which one lives: today that identity stretches back to the beginning of life on this planet, and soon perhaps in other parts of the universe; it comprises all members of the human species, all their work and marvels of hand and brain, heart and eye, the intricacy of their languages, the significance of their myriad experiments in human relationships, the cunningness with which their bodies are made, their relationships to all living creatures—to birds who are bipeds and build nests, and dolphins who, handless and lipless, devise ballets of their own in the sea; it reaches back into the past, out into the present, deeper beneath the sea and farther into the atmosphere than man has ever gone, and onward into a future for which each one of us, and each nation, holds today a terrible responsibility. Modern man is offered today an identity far greater than he has ever known. It is a task of a liberal education to help him develop it.

In order to appreciate fully how anthropology can contribute to this stupendous but rewarding task, something must be said of the way in which an anthropologist is educated, and what he does, when, as a research worker, he goes into the field. Every smallest research report, and every more generalized publication for the layman, bears the stamp of this education, of the presuppositions on which his work is based, and of the methods that, whatever his temperamental bent, he must pursue in the field. It is this experience of the field anthropologist, particularly of the field cultural anthropologist, which provides the possibility of integration. It is not that the anthropologist is widely read in the literature of the world, that he has an encyclopedic grasp of the history of science, that he has traveled and understood the ancient ruins of Angkor Wat or Crete, or undergone the rigorous disciplines of medicine, or one of the arts. His inclusiveness and universality are of quite another order. It is in his education and his research, based as they are in the whole of human history, embedded in the simplest and the most solemn moments of human life, that his integration lies.

In the United States anthropology has remained an inclusive and integrating discipline by successfully resisting the fragmentation which has occurred in most disciplines, which, as they became more specialized, with more workers, in more countries of the world, have progressively shattered into mutually noncommunicating parts. Anthropology has kept its own media of intradisciplinary communication. Just as the fragmented and over specialized biological sciences can still communicate through observation of scientific canons of presentation, argument, and experimental style, and the humanists in many tongues can still invoke the names of Plato and Aristotle, or physicians refer to a well-described case and lawyers to a carefully stated legal precedent, so too anthropologists have remained in communication with each other through the concrete materials with which they deal. They work not only with generalizations about culture, but also with the descriptions of particular cultures; not only with generalizations about language, but also with the auditory records of the speech of particular Indians or particular South Sea Island tribes; not only with tables of prehistoric time, but also with the actual artifacts and skeletal bits from which these tables are constructed. In their field work they go to various parts of the world, among living peoples who are different and speak different languages, or at a second remove, to the detailed accounts of those who did travel, and to the concrete specimens that they brought back.

Although it looked during the 1940's as if American anthropology, which had stood for such a unified approach to man in all his aspects, might fragment, it did not fragment. Graduate students in our universities today still learn about man's past, his place in evolution, the remains of his past civilization, the complexity of his languages, the nature of his culture and how to study it, and, increasingly, how to apply this knowledge, professionally, various contemporary social problems as practitioners. In such an education the student is not lectured about the various parts of the subject but is forced to experience some small part of each, to read monographs about the Chukchee and the Koryak, to learn the shape of a bone, to undergo the discipline of analyzing an unknown language straight from an informant's lips, to arrange an assemblage of potsherds and/or the contents of a single archaeological dig. Where this ideal is not fully realized, contact with those who have spent many years doing just these concrete things serves, to some extent, as a surrogate for the experience itself.

Along with this integrative, concrete, experiential training, there go certain basic assumptions: the psychic unity of mankind, as one species, with the expectation that because man is one species, all forms of his cultural behavior must have been invented or borrowed; and the recognition that all cultures, as systems of learned behavior within which groups have been able to reproduce and protect themselves over several generations, must be accorded a basic equal dignity, so that the cultural system of the smallest nomadic tribe must in these respects be treated as comparable to the civilization of Egypt or France; the insistence that no behavior, no item, no artifact, can be understood except in a complete ecological context; the expectation that in order to behave like an anthropologist one must be prepared to "go into the field."

There is also intense training in widening the student's expectancy, so that when he meets new forms—a hitherto unknown kinship form; or religious belief, that gods need not be parental figures, but can, as in

Bali, be children; or biological anomaly, like the strange, probably genetic disease of *kuru* in the highlands of New Guinea—he will not fail to note them because he is too ready to assimilate them to some older set of categories. This eager alertness to the unknown, the improbable, the unexpected, not only provides the necessary preparation for doing research where each piece of historically vanishing strange behavior is valuable just in proportion to its strangeness, but also provides an ideal state of mind for facing a world that is changing as rapidly as ours.

The young anthropologist, either during graduate training or in his first field experience, becomes aware of himself as a cultural being, each of whose categories for ordering experience bear the imprint of the culture in which he is reared, from such simple matters as the gesture he uses for assent, the way in which he groups colors, to the criteria of reality or illusion, and the position of the future—in front of an American, but behind a Balinese. His cultural ethnocentrism is transformed into a feeling of ability to move in and out of the categories of other peoples, past and present and future, as he expects also to learn to eat their food, sleep on their mats or wooden pillows, speak their language and respond quickly to signs that they are frightened or angry, delighted or bemused.

This attrition of an ethnocentrism which today keeps Americans and many other peoples of the world from learning the languages and responding sensitively and appropriately to the diplomatic maneuvers or technical deficiencies of other peoples is accomplished, not by admonition and preaching against prejudices or for the brotherhood of man, but by the experience of the value, in anthropology itself, of the diversity of human behavior which has been and will be recorded. The recognition of this is central to his becoming an anthropologist, to his professional identity. He is not a believer in the brotherhood of man, who *then* studies a social science to implement the accomplishment of his ideal—although such recruits to anthropology do, of course, exist—but rather, a deeply committed scientist-scholar, who as he works with the material about which he is delighted, curious, and eager learns his universal values as he works, tracing the pattern of a design on the edge of a pot, a myth of origin in its various forms, a wayward gene responsible for difference in blood type among peoples of an island world, or seven divergent spoken tongues back to their cradle land. As a result when the anthropologist teaches, he does not preach, he simply embodies the attitudes towards all human beings that are intrinsic to his work.

In the course of such a graduate training, the anthropologist also learns something about taking into account great wholes, how he must be aware of the context of the problem with which he himself will be immediately dealing. As he deals with the folklore, or the medical beliefs, or the ethnobotany—selected small detailed research elements—in two American Indian tribes, whose languages are related but who now live far apart, he must be aware of our accumulating knowledge of the age of man in North America, and behind that of the age of *Homo sapiens* and the appearance of the Old World of the tools and beliefs of which, under the pressure of a much later wave of historical contact with Europe, his Indians are just now losing the last memory. He must see the horses, which those Indians rode to war and to the buffalo hunt, not as a fixed attribute of the Plains Indians, who sit, immutable, with their feathered war bonnets outlined against the sky, but as they were, imported by the Spaniards and traded up to meet the guns which the French and English gave the Indians. Beneath the English within which he now communicates with his informants, he must be prepared to hear the syntax and the cadence and the categories of the Indian language that is not yet quite abandoned, and on the inhabited plains of the present time, criss-crossed by modern highways, he must be able to conjure up a period when in the loneliness of the Indian's vision quest, each encountered living creature became a supernatural messenger. At the same time he must be able, if his problem requires, to analyze the physical evidence for some connection between his two groups, as well as the linguistic, or to take into account the archaeological evidence which has been assembled about early man in North America.

So the context within which he works is not only the context of prehistory, of great migrations, of the overflow of Europeans, Africans, and Asians into the New World, of industrialization and change, which makes Indians today, as change has made so many people in the past, strangers in their own country. He also has to learn to live within an intellectual world of rapid change, of ideas that will come tomorrow from biochemistry or from microbiology, from brain physiology or studies of maturation, from a new method of esthetic analysis or a new vista in the relationship of man's old brain or his unconscious to dreaming and the arts. There will continually be new conceptual tools to work with, and new demands on his field work, to bring back droplets of blood, measurements of skin folds, records of perception, or moving pictures of a method of holding a child. However much of a scholar he is, he cannot be indifferent to science, however much a scientist he cannot ignore the demands for his materials, in all their entirety, undissected and clear; however little he knows of music, he can still collect the musical instruments, film their use, sound record the songs. He is part of a living enterprise, scientific, scholarly, and artistic. The music he brings back may stimulate the tired imagination of a composer, the carvings may set off a new mode in sculpture; and today, his work is also deeply political, as the new nations, so recently only of interest to anthropologists, administrators, missionaries, and traders, proudly plant their flags within the circle of the world's flags at the United Nations. He is forced to deal with the modern political realities, by the exigencies of planning field work, getting a visa, arranging to get his collections out, working with native labor, trying to find educated members of the people he studies, phrasing his results so that they will neither be impounded inside the country in which he has worked, nor forbidden entry to it. He cannot remain in any ivory tower of political unawareness. The record of his own personal vicissitudes becomes automatically part of the record of his work, of why the ethnobotanical specimens were lost or the publication of the second volume postponed.

Today, too, as anthropology is broadening its scope, from the study of primitive and near-primitive people to the study of peasant villages in Southeast Asia or Southern Europe, to mining towns in the British Isles or London neighborhoods, the anthropologist is brought ever more sharply into contact with the whole framework of modern life in all its complexities of technical change, political ferment, and changing bureaucratic structure.

The young anthropologist's growing appreciation of all of these things is gradual: some are learnt in the library, from the written regret of an ethnologist who arrived after the last old man who knew the tribal secrets was dead; some are learnt in the laboratory, working with fragments where wholes are needed and so must be reconstructed; some are learnt from the interpolated personal experience of his teachers in graduate schools, who have all been in the field themselves. But the focus is not on the learning so much as upon getting into the field. Here again the young anthropologist differs from the young scientist who wishes feverishly to find a spot where he can make a new discovery and win, if not fame, at least support for further work; he differs from the young scholar hopefully scouring the last pages of a famous text for new clues or using some new method of reconstructing a past with which many others have worked; he differs from the young artist or writer, wondering if he is, after all, an artist or a writer, or only one who enjoys the arts. He has very little of the preoccupation of the other social scientists—the sociologists, economists, and psychologists—anxiously watching problem and method not only for results but to be certain that their work looks and sounds like Science. His eyes are rather on the whole experience of doing field work or getting into the field. Depending upon the fashions current in different graduate schools or grant-giving institutions, he may set his work up with different kinds of problem orientation, but these are ways of organizing his research rather than ends in themselves. His end purpose is actually an account of some whole living part of man's experience, which will be good enough to generate new hypotheses in the years to come, long after his particular people have put on the blue jeans, the spectacles, the raincoats, and the sack suits of the industrial modern world.

For the anthropologist all of life is his subject matter, with the field the most vivid part of that life. A new costume on the street, a new word or phrase or cadence in the everyday speech, a change in posture, a new theme in popular songs, a new response in American life to some phase of Oriental or European philosophy, change in political stance in a social class, or an emerging architectural style borrowed from a Buddhist temple—all are grist to the anthropologist's mill. He may not be studying these particular things, but his disciplined awareness makes him conscious of them, interested in them, and as he walks the paths of his university campus or rides on a bus to a museum, his latent continuous codifying of human experience is enriched, or given tiny little jolts by the unexpected, that will in time become new questions, new hypotheses, new theories.

In the field itself, the anthropologist undergoes, simply because of his job, most of the experiences which the imagination of experimental educators or the well-filled purse of the traveled cosmopolitan provide for. He travels, and penetrates through several layers of culturally relevant groups of officials, planters, agency officials, police, learning by the need to get through these barriers, something about them. He goes almost always to a new terrain, and the closeness with which his "people" live to the natural world forces him, however abstract-minded he has been, to an awareness of it. His clock will give him scanty help in predicting when an informant will arrive; he must learn the meaning of "I will start when the second bird cries out." All the careful fussiness of oversterilized and fabricated world we live in is stripped off, not by artificial journeys by helicopter to experience the wilderness, or the costly delights of traveling for three days by canoe without a bath, but simply because these are the conditions of his work. The lamented softness of our young people who cannot imagine a world without porcelain latrines and orange juice simply disappears, because if it didn't, he couldn't survive. As he works his way into the community of strangers, very alert not to make some irrevocably false step which may end his work or even his life, his eye and ear become attuned to the significance of a whole new repertoire of sights and sounds, of lifted brows, or shifted betel basket. And, reflexively, he becomes aware of how he sits and stands, feels and thinks; increasing self-awareness goes hand in hand with his knowledge of the people he has come to study.

The world, whole, takes on a new meaning, as he selects a village small enough so that he can know everyone in it well enough to recognize by a change of companions or of pace that something is afoot. He builds his house by the most traveled road and takes events into account as they occur. He lives alone—almost all anthropologists have at least some experience of field work alone—and so comes face to face with himself, without the need to take a special pilgrimage to a Buddhist lamasery. He lives as a whole human being, aware of his body, which he must arrange to feed and shelter and compose into unfamiliar postures and gestures, of his mind, whose conceptualizing and analyzing and synthesizing abilities are invoked every instant, of himself as a human being among other human beings, both companions and counterpoints to his kind of self-realization and identity.

And the wholeness which he lives out is matched by the wholeness of the life he must record. Nothing can be wholly neglected; although some aspects of the culture may be treated sketchily, this very sketchiness must be handled systematically. If one does not map every taro patch in the bush, or count the catch of every canoe, list the gods of every clan, or explore the details of every ceremony, watch every birth, or sit at every death-bed, follow every artist and would-be artist as he works, and sit for hours at the feet of the only mystic or philosopher, one must always know the exact place in the whole of the part that is unexplored, the probable size of the unexplored area, and, most importantly, how it fits in with those things that one is studying in detail. Here the field work model becomes very easily the model for the educated man; it is not that he must know in detail all that there is to know, but he must know the shape of this knowledge and be able to make a reasoned judgment of what he does not know, how it fits in, how long it would take him to master any unknown piece. His mind must carry the imprint of the shape of the whole, however few details of any part of it his memory retains.

Within the culture of a people there is nothing that is alien, nothing that can be wholly ignored. When I went to Samoa to study adolescence, W. C. Handy was also considering a Samoan field trip to study religion. "Never mind, you won't overlap," said the director of the Bishop Museum, a geologist, "he won't be dealing with the mundane things that you are. He is interested in higher things." But, of course, he was wrong, as both Dr. Handy and I well knew, for the nature of the gods is expressed in the way a child is held, and the disposal of the umbilical cord may hold the key to past religious history. Within the web of a whole culture, just as each individual in the society is important and plays a part, be it philosopher or fool of god, so there is no part which can be ranked as "high" or "low." The historical snobberies of our European inheritance, with their distinctions between the aristocratic and the common people, between one race and another, between men and women, between adults and children, between fine art and popular art, epic and lyric, high architecture and domestic, all these inheritances from an earlier age are dissolved by a study of culture. The student who works with anthropological materials without being pushed into taking some new stance, and without the pendulum swings that accompany a snobbery transformed into aggressive egalitarianism, comes to feel the whole of human life as one, to see the shepherd's pipe and the great organ as part of the continuing human attempt to pattern sound and the shaped bit of clay, the David and the Nefertiti as related efforts.

If the emphasis is kept always upon the whole, however, it is possible to make a further and more exciting point—first made, I think, by Ruth Benedict—that rather than compare the simplest bits of primitive music and dance with the great developments of art in high civilizations, it is more fruitful to regard the culture of the simplest people as itself a work of art, its delicate complexity as aesthetically satisfying, as spiritually renewing, as philosophically moving, as any of the great achievements of individual artists.

But, it may be objected, the student on a liberal arts campus will not go into the field, he will not learn to eat dragon flies or translate the language of the drums, he will not be caught by the relationship between a pattern of a song and a pattern of a blanket. He will not have to make a whole from the inter-relationships of a carefully observed group of human beings, strange in form and speech. True, but if the anthropology is taught well, taught with a full recognition of the kind of original materials which anthropologists collect and produce, the student will experience something of this. Even if the teacher of undergraduates has never been the field, it should be a requirement that he should have studied in an anthropological graduate school and been taught by anthropologists. Undergraduate anthropology taught by someone trained in another discipline, with a very different ethos, will not, of course, communicate this to the students, even with the help of the original materials. Anhtropology is a discipline of the whole, the whole of man's history, the whole of man's culture, the whole of man's being, and this approach can only be communicated by someone who is himself, or herself, wholly involved, immersed, in it. But I believe the field experience, doubly embodied in the experience of the teacher who has studied under an original field worker, and in the materials which have been created by field work, will survive, *one generation.* The students of such teachers will not themselves be able to be anthropologists; for this they, too, need field experiences; they will not be able to train future anthropologists; for this, also, field experience is essential; but they will be able to communicate to undergraduates something of the world view, the integration of man's life on earth, which the practice of anthropology involves.

From the liberal arts colleges students emerge who wish to become various types of practitioners, physicians, lawyers, statesmen, architects, engineers, as well as those who will go on to become pure scientists or poets, bankers or builders, or those who will go to the graduate schools to learn to teach better what they themselves have been taught. Anthropology today offers not only a way of integrating the diversity of our existing knowledge and experience, but also a great variety of implications for the practitioners of the individual or socially healing arts. Applied anthropology is not suitable for undergraduate teaching, in most instances, particularly because those few who are adept at practicing it are too busy even to do their share of teaching in graduate school. But the student's mind can be opened to its possibilities.

And here we meet another contribution which anthropology can make, the full recognition of moral responsibility and the negation of an irresponsible scientism or the advocacy of sterile types of cultural relativity. Cultural relativity in the anthropological sense means that any act, or institution, must be understood as relative to the cultural system in which it occurs. Leaving the aged to die is murder in a society where it would be possible to save them, correct ethical behavior on the part of the aged and their children where saving them would compromise the survival of their grandchildren. And none understand better than anthropologists the unity of mankind, the significance of membership in one species, the levels of interdependence in the world, or the fragility and toughness of human culture, and the need for responsible cultural custodianship. These anthropology cannot escape. Again not because we hold them as dissociated high level values but because they are of the very essence of the work we do. Without them, we could not build the discipline we are so intent upon building. They show through our work, inform its every nook and cranny, and light up the empty spaces where work is still to be done. For characteristically the anthropologist does not say: "We do not know," but rather, "We do not know *yet*."

Finally, a close acquaintance with the cultures of the past can help us make workable models of the future. We have abundant materials on how one people have borrowed from another, house forms, tools, script and architecture, higher mathematics and electronic devices, but we have yet to devise a way in which aspiring men may safely build a model of an unknown future state which itself leaves the future open. Throughout history the attempt to construct desirable future states has been caught between the rock of insipidity and the rock of over-certainty. To build an image of heaven, compelling enough to make men want to go there, but still to interdict religious suicide, has challenged missionaries among peoples who take the vision too literally. Similarly, to build an image of a future culture which will compel men's allegiance without also authorizing a Gestapo to force their fellows to accept it, is equally difficult. A knowledge of many cultures, past and present, is one of the best sources of the cultural creativity which we need today.

From our college campuses must come the poets and builders of tomorrow, the artist's prefigurative vision, the scientific quest for the necessary knowledge, the scientist's experience of how to make the vision real—and not too real, but always open, always allowing for still another future, still a further vision. Today, as we move into new worlds of weightlessness, into space and under the sea, there will be new sources on which men's imagination can feed, as we seek to devise new cultures, which will never become prisons, never be static, but will remain launching platforms into a widening universe.

DATE DUE

DE 10 74			
MR22 '83			
GAYLORD			PRINTED IN U.S.A.